HOW IS IT
DONE?

HOW IS IT DONE? was edited and designed by
The Reader's Digest Association Limited, London

First Edition Copyright © 1990
The Reader's Digest Association Limited, Berkeley Square House, Berkeley Square, London W1X 6AB
Copyright © 1990, Reader's Digest Association Far East Limited
Philippines Copyright 1990, Reader's Digest Association Far East Ltd

Printed in West Germany

Reader's Digest

HOW IS IT DONE?

Published by The Reader's Digest Association Limited
LONDON · NEW YORK · SYDNEY · CAPE TOWN · MONTREAL

CONTENTS

EVERYDAY MIRACLES
PAGES 9–30

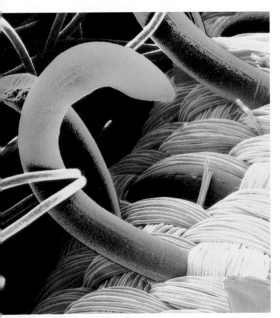
A close look at Velcro

MAJOR FEATS OF ORGANISATION
PAGES 31–72

Untangling city traffic

TECHNIQUES OF DECEPTION AND DETECTION
PAGES 73–100

Tall tales from the camera

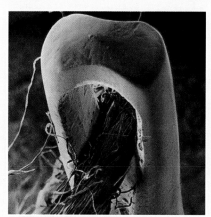

CONTENTS

CURIOSITIES OF FOOD AND DRINK
PAGES 373–394

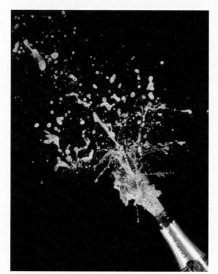

Where do the bubbles come from?

JUST FOR FUN
PAGES 395–437

Why don't they all fall out?

Contributors

THE PUBLISHERS WISH TO THANK THE FOLLOWING
WRITERS, ARTISTS AND PHOTOGRAPHERS FOR THEIR
VALUABLE CONTRIBUTIONS IN CREATING
HOW IS IT DONE?

Writers who contributed major sections of the book

Nigel Hawkes BA · Nigel Henbest BSc, MSc, FRAS
Graham Jones BSc (Hons) · Robin Kerrod · Terry Kirby
Theodore Rowland-Entwistle BA, FRGS, FZS
John H. Stephens ACGI, BSc, MICE, C.Eng · Nigel West

Other writers and specialist contributors

Neil Ardley · John Brosnan · Dr John R. Bullen
Professor Geoffrey Campbell-Platt · Mike Clifford BSc, PhD, MIFST
Jean Cooke BA · Mike Groushko · Ned Halley · Commander D.A. Hobbs, RN
Richard Holliss · W.F.A. Horner BSc · Dr Robert Ilson
Dominic Man BSc, MSc, AIFST · John Man · Dr J.R. Mitchell
Professor Frank Paine · Michael D. Ranken BSc Tech · Nigel Rodgers
Dr David A. Rosie · Andrew Wilbey FIFST

Artists

AMCS Microcomputer Services · Kuo Kang Chen · Mick Gillah
Gary Hincks · Inkwell Design and Art · Pavel Kostal · Ivan Lapper
Tony Lodge · Andrew Lucas · Malcolm McGregor · Maltings Partnership
Stanley Paine · Malcolm Porter · Precision Illustration

Photographers

Martin Cameron · Jonathan Green
Chris Morris · Titanic Photography

Everyday miracles

Without a second thought, we use the most amazing implements and materials every day of our lives – microwave ovens, striped toothpaste, non-stick pans, disposable razors. But how are these miracle ingredients of modern life actually made, how do they work and how were they conceived?

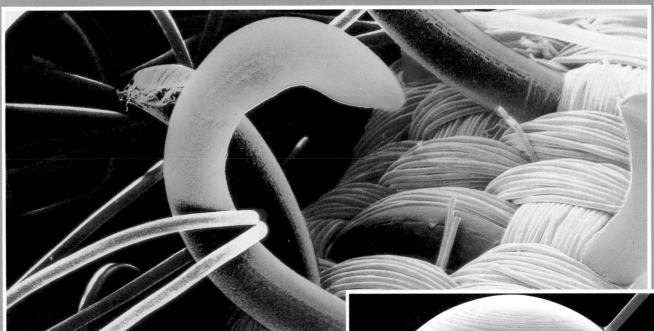

How Velcro clings, page 19.

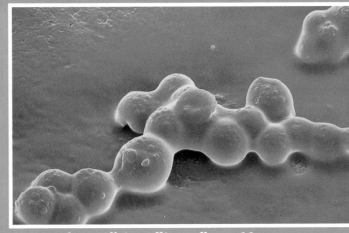

How scratch 'n' sniff gives off its smell, page 16.

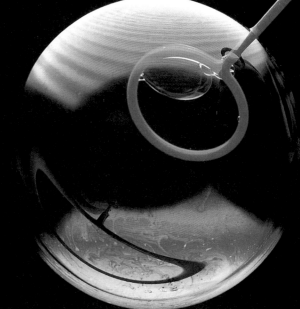

How a soap bubble is formed, page 27.

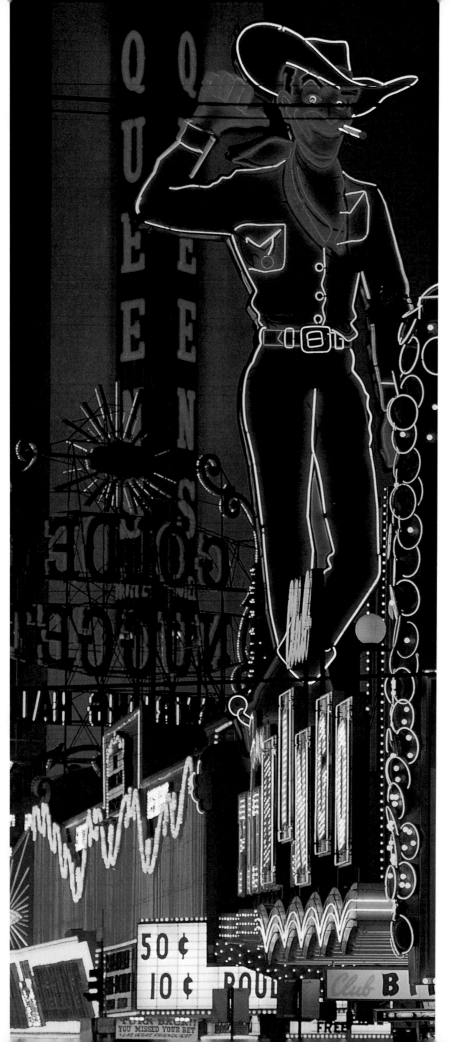

Neon: creating pictures and words with light

Neon lights create gaudy pictures and spell out brand names on advertisements the world over.

Unlike the traditional electric light bulb, neon lights in the form of thin tubes can easily be shaped into lettering and other intricate outlines.

To produce their distinctive light, they exploit what is called 'electric discharge through gases'. Ordinarily, gases do not easily conduct electricity – they are good insulators. They can, however, be made to conduct electricity if their pressure is lowered and a high voltage is applied.

In the late 19th and early 20th centuries, scientists investigating electric discharge through the rare gas neon at low pressures, first observed the striking red-orange glow the gas gives out.

To create neon light, electricity is applied to the ends of a glass tube filled with neon. Atomic particles called electrons stream from one end of the tube to the other, and on their way they collide with atoms of neon. As a result of the

Neon at night *Dominating the kaleidoscope of neon in Las Vegas is the Pioneer Club's neonised cowboy with his waggling cigarette (left). The figure was created in 1951. In Hong Kong, too, neon lights bustle in the air (above). Some of them, such as this dragon figure, are a glassbender's nightmare.*

collisions, electrons orbiting within the neon atoms are knocked out of orbit. They acquire extra energy from the impacts, just as a billiard ball acquires energy when struck by another. As they return to their original orbit, they give out their surplus energy as electromagnetic radiation.

This radiation has a frequency which lies in the visible light range and you see it as a brilliant red-orange glow.

When other gases are used in tubes, a similar process occurs. But the electrons give off radiation at different frequencies, which you see as different colours. Helium gives a golden-yellow light and krypton a pale violet. Other colours are produced by fluorescent materials in tubes containing mercury or argon, sometimes in combination with coloured glass.

How does the sun turn city lights on and off?

At dusk and dawn, millions of street lights are turned on and off throughout the world every day – many of them by the light of the sun itself.

Most lights are controlled by time switches, which operate a group of lights in nearby streets. The earliest time switches worked by clockwork and had to be wound up and adjusted every week.

Many modern time switches now have an electric clock with a rotating dial, containing levers or tappets, which turn the lights on or off at the chosen times. They are similar to many time switches on central-heating systems.

Since the sun rises and sets at different times throughout the year, street lights must also go on and off at different times, so these dials also alter the switching times according to the season of the year.

This is arranged in the time switch by a mechanical device which adjusts the 'On' and 'Off' tappets month by month to follow the changes in the hours of daylight.

Recently, street-lighting engineers have developed a photoelectric control unit called a 'pecu', which operates a switch in the electrical supply to the lights.

A photocell in the unit contains a light-sensitive compound such as cadmium sulphide or silicon. At dawn, light falling on the photocell causes electrons to flow from one atom to another, conducting electricity to the switch and turning it off. When darkness falls, the electrons in the compound become immobile, the current stops, and the lights are turned on. The exact time that the current is switched on and off depends on the weather conditions.

Why paper-thin bulbs are so strong

The glass of an electric light bulb is not much thicker than the paper of this page, yet it withstands a strong grip when you push it into a light fitting. The explanation for this lies mainly in the bulb's shape, which exploits the eggshell principle.

Aeons ago, Nature found a solution to the problem of preventing eggs from being crushed by the weight of the hen bird as she sat on the nest to incubate them. The solution was the characteristic egg shape, which provides structural strength, to withstand all-round pressure even with a thin shell. (If the shell were too thick, the chick inside would not be able to peck its way out.)

Light bulbs (and eggs) have a rounded profile over the whole surface. When you grip a bulb, the force you apply is transmitted in all directions away from the point of contact by the curve of the glass.

This results in the force being distributed over a wide area, and no excessive stress being set up at any one point.

Making bulbs from a ribbon of glass

Making light bulbs is an intricate and highly automated factory process in which the bulbs are blown into shape in moulds from a continuous ribbon of molten glass.

A vital component of the bulbs is the filament, a coil of tungsten wire one-hundredth of a millimetre thick. This is the part that becomes white-hot and produces the light when electricity flows through. It is mounted on a glass stem and clamped to the end of thicker wires that pass through the stem to the base of the bulb.

When the stem is inserted in the bulb, any oxygen in the bulb is eliminated (otherwise it would cause the coil to oxidise, greatly reducing its life). The bulb is then filled with an argon/nitrogen mixture. It is sealed and the metal cap is cemented in place.

A modern bulb-making machine can produce 30 bulbs in a few minutes, each able to pour out light for at least 1000 hours. Gradually, however, the metal filament evaporates. Eventually it will break and the light will fail.

Whistling bulbs

Why do some bulbs whistle before they fail? In fact, the filament breaks while the bulb is alight, but it stays alight because electricity arcs over the gap. It is the arc that emits the high-pitched whistle.

THE PRODUCTION-LINE PROCESS OF MAKING LIGHT BULBS

1 *Glass light bulbs are passed in front of a flame to heat and soften the neck, which is squeezed to the size of the metal fitting and then trimmed.*

2 *The still red-hot base of the bulb is then fused to the glass stem which holds the coiled-wire filament.*

3 *Finally, contacts at the base of the bulb are soldered to the wires leading from the filament.*

How batteries supply portable electricity

Experiments in anatomy in the 1780s led to the invention of the battery. Luigi Galvani, a professor of anatomy at Bologna University, noticed that the legs of dead frogs twitched when they were hung from hooks on a rail. He thought (wrongly) that it was because of some kind of animal electricity.

Another Italian professor, Allessandro Volta of Pavia University, realised that the electricity resulted from the contact between the copper hooks and iron rail the frogs were hung on – their legs were merely part of the circuit. As a result he produced a Voltaic cell in 1800, the forerunner of all modern batteries. It is called a battery because some types – such as a car battery – are in fact batteries of single cells. Although it is convenient, a battery wastes a lot of the Earth's energy: the amount of energy needed to make one is up to 50 times greater than the amount it produces.

Electric current is produced in a battery cell by the reactions of two electrodes (electrical conductors) with an electrolyte (a liquid or paste that conducts electricity). Each electrode is linked to one of the battery's metal terminals – the parts where it clips into a circuit. Once the battery is linked into the circuit, there will be a continual flow of electrons from one terminal (known as the negative) through the circuit to the other (known as the positive).

This is because the material of one of the electrodes starts to partly dissolve in the electrolyte – that is, its atoms start to break up and it releases positive ions (see box) into the electrolyte and electrons into the wire of the circuit at the negative terminal.

The other electrode is generally made of different material and does not dissolve in the electrolyte to the same extent. But it does lose electrons to positive ions in the electrolyte, and becomes deficient in them. So the continual flow of electrons from one electrode through the circuit to make up the deficiency at the other forms the current.

The cylindrical, single-cell battery of the type used in a torch is called a dry cell battery because the electrolyte is self-contained and needs no topping up. A common type is the acidic zinc-carbon battery.

The battery's metal casing is a zinc container that forms one electrode of the cell. It holds a mixture of ammonium chloride, which is the electrolyte, and manganese dioxide. The manganese is, in effect, the other electrode, because it loses electrons to the ammonium chloride. A

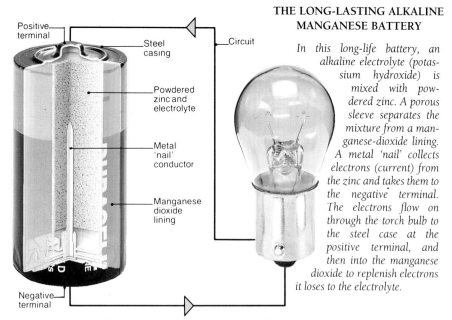

Positive terminal
Steel casing
Powdered zinc and electrolyte
Metal 'nail' conductor
Manganese dioxide lining
Circuit
Negative terminal

central carbon rod acts as a current collector, transferring electrons from the positive terminal to the manganese.

Such a dry cell battery has an output of

THE LONG-LASTING ALKALINE MANGANESE BATTERY

In this long-life battery, an alkaline electrolyte (potassium hydroxide) is mixed with powdered zinc. A porous sleeve separates the mixture from a manganese-dioxide lining. A metal 'nail' collects electrons (current) from the zinc and takes them to the negative terminal. The electrons flow on through the torch bulb to the steel case at the positive terminal, and then into the manganese dioxide to replenish electrons it loses to the electrolyte.

1.5 volts when new, but this decreases with use, as hydrogen bubbles form on the carbon rod, reducing the electrode surface area. The manganese dioxide partially re-

WHAT IS ELECTRICITY?

Electric current is a flow of electrons – minute particles far too small to see through any microscope – that are dislodged from atoms. The greater and faster the flow of electrons, the bigger the current. But it takes a flow of billions of electrons to make even a small current.

Atoms are the tiny particles that make up all matter. The much tinier electrons orbit round the atom's nucleus, or central core, in layers known as shells. Each shell may consist of a different number of electrons. The various chemical elements that make up matter – gases and metals for example – have different numbers of electrons in their atoms. Hydrogen gas, for instance, has only one in each atom, but copper has 29 of them, distributed among four shells.

An atom's nucleus is positively charged with electricity, and its electrons are negatively charged. So the atom is normally electrically neutral because the two charges cancel each other out. But electrons can be dislodged from the atom (usually from the outer layer) by heat, for example, or they can leave it to join another atom during a chemical reaction that involves a change in the nature of the substance, such as rust forming on metal. An atom (or group of atoms) that loses or gains electrons becomes electrically charged and is called an ion. The ion is positively charged if it loses electrons, or negatively charged if it gains them. Free electrons dislodged from an atom move

about at random. But a flow is set up if a number of them are attracted towards a source of positive ions.

An electric current will not flow through a circuit unless there is an excess of electrons at one end and a deficiency at the other. This is known as the potential difference, and it is measured in volts.

Metals are good electrical conductors because their atoms have lots of loosely bound electrons to speed the electron flow, which meets little resistance. Materials that do not generally conduct electricity, such as rubber, have atoms with electrons that are not easily displaced.

An electric circuit is a pathway of wire, usually copper, from a power source and back again. The power source can be a battery or an electromagnetic generator.

Mains electricity is transmitted from generators at power stations, with the outward and return wires in the same cable. As the electrons travel along their wire pathway, they are attracted first one way, then the other, according to the changing magnetic field of the generator's magnet. This gives alternating current, which has a wavelike motion.

Conventionally, electric current is considered to flow from positive to negative – as if the generated charge is pushing current to where there is none. This convention was established before scientists knew that electrons flow to a positive charge.

moves the bubbles, so minimises their effect.

Car batteries are storage batteries, also called accumulators, because they can be recharged – that is, the chemical reactions can be revived. Most have six linked cells, each with an output of about 2 volts.

Each cell has several electrodes, or plates, with negative and positive plates alternating. The plates are separated by insulating sheets to prevent short circuits, and are suspended in an electrolyte of sulphuric acid. All the plates are lead grids, the negative ones filled with spongy lead, the positive ones with lead dioxide.

The chemical reactions that create electricity result in both negative and positive plates turning gradually into lead sulphate, and the electrolyte into water. If this happens completely, the battery is flat. But once the car engine is running well, the current flow from its generator charges the battery by reversing the chemical reactions. So the lead plates are converted back to their original material and the strength of the sulphuric acid is restored.

While the car is running, its battery builds up a sufficient store of current to restart the engine next time it is used.

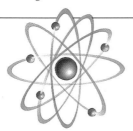

Neutral atom *The nucleus of an atom is positively charged. Its electrons are negative. So the whole atom is neutral.*

Positive ion *Loss of an electron results in the atom becoming positively charged. It is then called a positive ion.*

Negative ion *When an atom gains one or more electrons, it becomes negative and is called a negative ion.*

How the lead gets into a pencil

The 'lead' in a pencil has not been made of lead for centuries. The ancient Egyptians, Greeks and Romans all used small lead discs to rule lines on sheets of papyrus before writing on them with a brush and ink. By the 14th century, European artists were using rods of lead, zinc or silver to make pale grey drawings called silverpoint. And in the 15th century, Conrad Gesner of Zurich, in Switzerland, in his *Treatise on fossils*, described a writing rod held in a wooden case.

But lead ceased to be a writing implement when pure graphite was discovered at Borrowdale in the North of England in 1564 – and the modern pencil was born.

Graphite is a form of carbon, which is one of the softest minerals. When it is pressed against paper, thin layers flake off to leave a black mark.

Some of the best graphite for pencil-making comes from Sonora, in Mexico. It is powdery and extremely black.

The wooden outer case of the pencil has to be fairly soft, so that it can easily be sharpened as the graphite wears down. The most widely used pencil wood comes from the incense cedar of the Sierra Nevada mountains in northern California. The best wood is from trees between 150 and 200 years old.

The 'lead' is made by mixing together fine graphite and clay and then firing it in sticks in a kiln. Graphite cannot be ground in an ordinary mill because its flaky structure makes it a natural lubricant. So an 'attrition mill' is used. Jets of compressed air containing graphite particles are blasted at one another, and as the particles collide they break up.

The fine particles are mixed with pure china clay and water, producing a putty-like paste. The mix is fed into a cylinder and forced through a hole at one end, emerging as a continuous length the diameter of pencil lead.

The lengths are cut into pencil-sized sticks, and dried in an oven before being fired at a temperature of about 2200°F (1200°C). Finally, they are treated with wax to ensure smooth writing, and sealed to prevent them from slipping out of the wooden casing.

To make the casing, the wood is sawn into slats, each the length of a pencil, seven pencils wide, and half a pencil thick. Grooves are cut into the slats, the leads are inserted, and another grooved slat is glued on top. This 'sandwich' is then fed through machines that cut it into individual pencils of hexagonal or circular cross-section.

After shaping, the pencils are painted with non-poisonous lacquer.

Close-up of a pencil mark *The graphite used in pencils has a flaky layered structure. The layers are weakly bonded together and easily flake off, leaving a black mark when pressed against paper.*

HARD OR SOFT? THE ANSWER IS CHINA CLAY

To make pencil lead, graphite is mixed with fine clay – the sort that is used in the finest porcelain and bone china. The two ingredients are combined in different proportions to produce leads of different blackness and hardness.

The most widely used type of pencil is the HB (hard and black). Softer and blacker pencils (B and BB) have more graphite, and harder ones – graded from H (hard) to 10H – have progressively more clay.

The leads for coloured pencils or crayons contain no graphite at all. They are made from pure clay and wax, coloured with pigments.

How they put the ball in a ball-point pen

The heart of a ball-point pen is a precision-ground metal ball which transfers fast-drying, oil-based ink onto paper.

The ball is usually made of mild or stainless steel, about ⅟₃₂in (1mm) in diameter and ground to an accuracy of a few millionths of an inch. It may also be made of a compound of tungsten and carbon which is almost as hard as a diamond.

Sometimes the ball is textured, or roughened, so that it can achieve a better grip on the writing surface.

The ball is fitted into a steel or brass housing, designed so that it can rotate in all directions. The tip of the housing is then bent over so that the ball cannot drop out.

The ink is fed from a reservoir to the ball housing through a narrow tube. The ink reservoir must be open to the air, or have a hole in it. Otherwise, as the ink level falls a partial vacuum would be created preventing the ink from flowing.

Ridges in the metal housing distribute the ink evenly around the ball, so that when it is moved over a surface it rotates and draws a line.

The French company BiC sells more than 12 million ball-points a day worldwide. Each pen will produce more than 2 miles (3.5km) of writing if it has a fine point, or 1½ miles (2.5km) if it has a medium point.

Biro: ball-point inventor

A sharpened quill (the shaft of a feather) was the standard writing instrument for over 1000 years before the fountain pen was invented in 1884. Then in the 1930s, Ladislao Biro, a Hungarian artist and journalist, invented the ball-point pen in Budapest. He fled when the Second World War broke out, eventually reaching Argentina.

With the help of his brother Georg, a chemist, he perfected the pen and manufactured it in Buenos Aires during the war. In 1944 he sold his interests in the invention to one of his backers who produced the Biro pen for the Allied air forces, because it was not affected by changes in air pressure. Ladislao Biro disappeared into obscurity, although his name became a household word throughout the world.

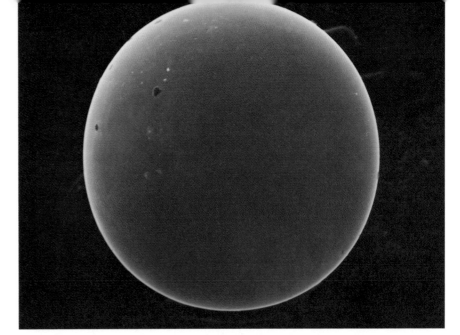

The ball *Usually made of steel, the ball (magnified 80 times) is ground to high accuracy.*

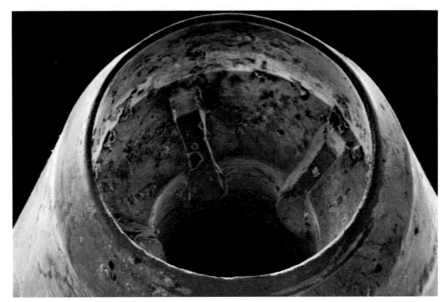

The socket *Ridges inside the socket in the pen's tip allow ink to spread around the ball.*

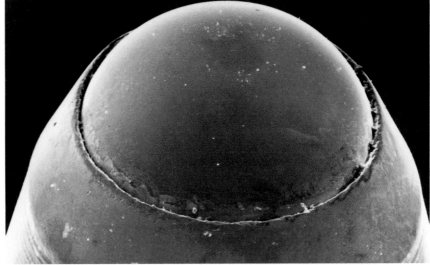

Ball in place *When the ball is inserted, the edge of the socket is bent over to hold it there.*

Pens and markers *Pen manufacturers have followed Ladislao Biro's lead in producing new pens. A variety of pens make different ink marks – fine or broad, permanent or temporary – and will mark different surfaces including metal, glass and plastic. With the exception of the ball-point, fine tubes in the pens' nibs carry the ink by capillary action to the tip.*

Felt tip *The nib is made from natural or synthetic wool.*

Fibre tip *Resin-bonded fibres last longer than a felt tip.*

Ball-point *The ink is drawn to the nib by the action of the rolling ball.*

Plastic tip *Free-flowing ink is fed through a hard-wearing plastic tip.*

Why modern glues stick so well

Until a century ago, glues were either gums from plants or boiled-down hides and bones of animals. These gums and glues took a long time to stick and they formed a joint that was not particularly strong. They were used mainly for woodworking. The liquid glue flowed into the pores of the wood and then dried, bonding the pieces of wood together.

Today, however, most glues are wholly synthetic. They dry quickly and form very strong bonds. The fastest-acting ones are called superglues or instant glues, and they set in seconds. There are also epoxy resins which are sold as two ingredients that have to be mixed together and then set in 10 to 30 minutes.

Superglue is an acrylic resin made from petroleum chemicals. When it is exposed to the slightest trace of moisture its small molecules join together to form longer ones – a chemical process called polymerisation.

In its tube, the glue is prevented from polymerising by an acidic stabiliser. When it is applied to a surface the most minute amount of moisture overcomes the action of the stabiliser, and the resin polymerises instantly. It is the presence of water ions – groups of atoms that have an electric charge – that triggers off the polymerisation process. The ions are present on practically any surface

that is exposed to the air, because the air always contains some moisture.

Superglues stick well to skin because it is moist. There have been many cases of people becoming stuck to all sorts of objects, from teacups to door handles. They can be freed by soaking the stuck part in warm water and gently prising it away.

This skin-bonding property is not always a bad thing. Superglues have been used in surgery as an aerosol spray to seal wounds and reduce bleeding.

Glue power *The yellow car on this advertising hoarding is attached to the wooden structure by epoxy resin glue. The red car rests on the roof of the first saloon – a powerful demonstration of the strength of the glue.*

15

THE PROCESS THAT MAKES SUPERGLUE STICK

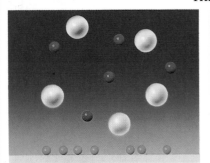

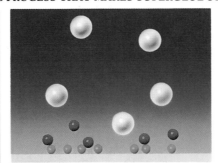

Superglue contains acidic stabiliser (red), which stops the adhesive molecules from linking and keeps the glue liquefied.

The acidic stabiliser is neutralised on coming into contact with moisture (blue) on the surface which is to be bonded.

Once the stabiliser has been neutralised, the adhesive molecules join together in long chains, forming a solid fixative.

A laboratory accident that made its mark on the world

Sticky little pieces of paper, coloured yellow, began to appear in offices around the world early in the 1980s. They were usually stuck to documents, and carried messages scribbled from one executive to another. Their great advantage was that they could easily be peeled off after being read, without leaving a mark.

As the decade advanced the sticky slips, called Post-it Notes, spread to colleges and finally into homes. Students and researchers began using them to mark relevant pages in books; and working husbands and wives left hurried messages to each other stuck to the refrigerator.

Post-it Notes were spawned by an accidental discovery in a laboratory in St Paul, Minnesota, where research was being conducted into superglue in 1968. An adhesive was produced that was so lacking in sticking power that the company, 3M, dismissed it as useless.

However, one of its employees, a chemist called Art Fry, was a choir singer and used the weak glue to make bookmarks for his hymn book. They could be removed when they were no longer needed, without damaging the page.

Fry tried to persuade the firm that they were throwing away an idea that could have worldwide uses. But it was not until 1980 that 3M began selling pads of notepaper with a strip of adhesive along one edge for use in offices. As well as being removable they could be re-stuck somewhere else.

Seen under a microscope, the sticky surface of a Post-it Note is covered with thousands of tiny bubbles of urea formaldehyde resin which contain adhesive. The bubbles break under finger pressure, but not all at once so the notes are reusable.

a microscope reveals the tiny drops of adhesive on the back of a Post-it.

Putting perfume on paper

Perfume manufacturers can advertise their products by actually enclosing the fragrance in a leaflet or a magazine page. Because the smell of the perfume is released by rubbing or scratching the paper surface, the method is known as microfragrance or 'scratch 'n' sniff'.

The scent is in minute capsules too small to see, laid on the paper in a resinous coating. The capsule shell is a plastic that breaks to release the essential oils of the perfume inside when it is scratched or rubbed. The technique, known as micro-encapsulisation, was pioneered by an American company, 3M, in the 1960s.

To fill the capsules, the oil is shaken up with water to break it up into tiny droplets

SMELLING BY NUMBERS

A spoof western called *Lust in the Dust* was made in America in 1984, using scratch 'n' sniff as an added attraction. The audience were each given a small card containing about half-a-dozen numbers.

At intervals during the film, a number was displayed in a corner of the screen – the signal for viewers to scratch 'n' sniff the appropriate number on their cards. This gave them whichever smell was appropriate to the action – the lure of perfume or the whiff of gunsmoke, for example.

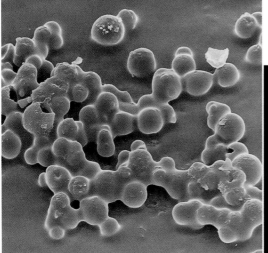

The aroma of apples *The microcapsules which contain the scent in a scratch 'n' sniff sticker are shown in this microscope photograph (above). When the capsules are scratched, the fragrance is released. The sticker of a sliced apple (right) is typical of those put in magazines. The area inside the dotted line would contain microcapsules to remind people how delicious apples smell.*

– rather like shaking a salad dressing of oil and vinegar. Then the droplets are scattered on a surface and covered with a layer of plastic resin.

They are left to set – or sometimes they are heated – before being coated to the paper with another resin. They are sometimes in an adhesive coating in the fold of a leaflet, and the fragrance is released as the coating breaks when the paper is unfolded.

Some cosmetics now contain microcapsules of skin-nourishing oils. They are not released until the preparation is applied to the skin, which ensures that they stay fresh in the container.

Newspaper photographs: dots before the eyes

A close look at a newspaper photograph reveals that the range of shades is made up of a combination of black dots. In dark areas, the dots are large and merge so that almost none of the white paper shows through. In lighter areas the dots are tiny and surrounded by large expanses of white.

The process of reproducing photographs as a dotted picture is called half-tone. The continuously varying shades in a photograph are converted into a pattern of different-sized dots by a method called screening. The photograph to be reproduced is itself photographed through a screen which is placed in contact with the film. It consists of a piece of transparent film carrying a diagonal pattern of lines.

Most newspapers use a fairly coarse screen to reproduce pictures on standard newsprint paper. The screen has about 50 to 85 lines per inch and, when printed, results in the same number of dots an inch.

Light reflected from the photograph passes through the screen and is broken up into areas of varying brightness. These are captured on high-contrast photographic film to produce a pattern of dots when the film is developed. The result is a negative image. Later processing produces a positive image in which the dark areas of the picture are represented by large dots and the light areas by small ones.

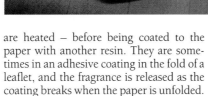

Sporting image *A half-tone black-and-white picture (above) as it appears in a newspaper. The enlargement (left) reveals that the picture is composed of a series of black dots interspersed with white spaces. The number of dots used determines how well the photograph is reproduced on the printed page.*

HOW PICTURES ARE PRINTED IN FULL COLOUR

Like black-and-white newspaper pictures, colour photographs are also reproduced as patterns of dots. The dots are of three different colours – yellow, magenta and cyan (greenish blue). Viewed from a distance, combinations of different-sized dots of these colours merge to simulate the whole spectrum.

Colour printing depends on the principle that all colours can be produced by combining in different proportions these three colours.

Filter photography

The first step in reproduction is to 'separate' the colours by photographing them through filters.

The three colour images are then screened, as in a black-and-white photograph, to produce a pattern of dots. From each colour a printing plate is made. A black plate is also made to add sharpness, and the method is known as the four-colour process. Nowadays, this is usually done by electronic scanners, rather than the traditional cameras.

All colours can be printed from combinations of these three basic colours: yellow, magenta and cyan.

Black is added to the three-colour printed image to provide depth, definition and contrast.

Finally, the naked eye is left to mix the coloured dots and turn them into other colours.

How a coin runs the gauntlet in a slot machine

A coin dropped into a slot buys you all sorts of goods and services from machines – railway tickets, telephone calls, drinks and snacks from a vending machine, copies from a photocopier and, occasionally, a jackpot from a fruit machine.

But before machines will deliver, they scrutinise each coin, subjecting it to a battery of tests. They reject coins of the wrong denomination, foreign coins, deliberate fakes and washers.

Every type of coin throughout the world has its own characteristics. Coins vary in diameter, thickness and weight. And they vary in chemical composition.

In slot machines all these properties are investigated, and only when a coin has taken the right path through a machine can it trigger off the operating mechanism.

A typical slot machine works as follows, although there are many variations. The checking system starts with the slot itself. Coins that are too wide, too thick or too bent will not go in.

Coins that do go through may be tested with a probe to discover if they have a hole in the middle (this detects washers). Genuine coins fall onto a precisely counter-balanced cradle. If the coin is heavy enough, it topples the cradle and is directed onto the runway. If it is too light, it fails to topple the cradle and falls into the reject channel.

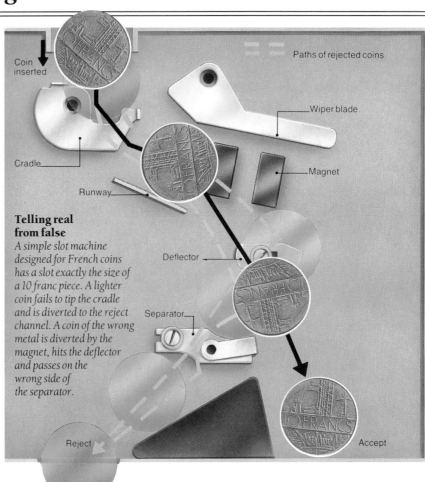

Telling real from false

A simple slot machine designed for French coins has a slot exactly the size of a 10 franc piece. A lighter coin fails to tip the cradle and is diverted to the reject channel. A coin of the wrong metal is diverted by the magnet, hits the deflector and passes on the wrong side of the separator.

An approved coin travels along the runway and past a magnet. Tiny electric currents are set up inside it as it passes through the magnet's field, causing it to slow down. The amount depends on its composition, since different metals respond to magnetic influence differently.

A coin with the correct composition slows just the right amount and falls off the runway in a trajectory that makes it miss the next obstacle, a deflector. Instead, it hits the separator below at just the right angle to be directed into the 'accept' channel. Overweight coins and those less affected by the magnet hit the deflector and rebound on the wrong side of the separator and into the reject channel.

Electronic slot machines

The latest generation of slot machines check coins electronically. As soon as a coin is inserted, its conductance – its ability to pass electric current – is tested.

Broadly acceptable coins then pass through a gate and are allowed to run down a ramp and between two magnets. Once again, the speed at which they leave the magnets depends upon their composition. Sets of light-emitting diodes and photosensors measure the coin's speed. If the values agree with those in the machine's memory, a gate opens to accept the coin. If not, the coin is rejected. Some machines can be programmed to cope with as many as eight different types of coin.

They can also be programmed to give change. As a coin passes through the checking system its value is identified. When it reaches the end of its journey a microchip releases the appropriate change from stacks of smaller-value coins that are kept in tubes inside the machine.

Velcro: like burrs sticking to socks

Velcro fasteners, those little pads of fuzzy plastic hooks and eyes, have found low and high-tech uses in and out of this world.

In the clothing industry they are used instead of press-studs and zips. In medicine, they are used to attach the chambers in the Jarvik 7 artificial heart. In the space shuttle, astronauts use Velcro tape to stick trays, food packages, scientific equipment, and occasionally themselves, to some convenient surface to prevent them floating away in the weightless environment.

Swiss engineer Georges de Mestral conceived the idea that evolved into Velcro after a walk in the woods one day in 1948. He came back home with burrs stuck to his socks and to his dog, and decided to investigate why burrs stick so well to wool.

Under the microscope he saw how tiny hooks on the ends of the burrs caught in loops in the wool.

De Mestral soon devised a method of reproducing the hook and loop arrangement in woven nylon. He called the product Velcro, a contraction of *velours* and *crochet*, the French word for 'hook'. The original patent on Velcro expired in 1978 and there are now many imitations, but Velcro remains a registered trade name.

Velcro is made by weaving nylon thread to produce a fabric containing densely packed little loops. This forms the looped part. To form the hooked part, loops in a separate piece of fabric are cut, so that half of each loop becomes a hook. The fabric is heated to set the loops and hooks permanently in shape. It is then dyed, bonded to a suitable backing and cut to size.

Velcro is particularly long-lasting. It can usually be fastened and unfastened many thousands of times and may well outlast the product to which it is attached.

Velcro is designed to be peelable – to be opened by hand with comparatively little effort. However, it has very high shear strength – resistance to sideways forces. Some Velcro is so strong in shear strength that a piece less than 5in (120mm) square can support a load of 1 ton. This property has prompted experiments in using Velcro to make aircraft bodies. The aim is to replace rivets with Velcro strips, saving weight and making assembly simpler.

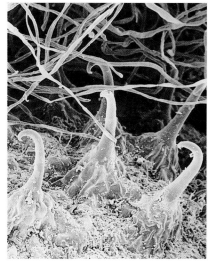

How burrs grip *The tiny seed pods (or burrs) of goosegrass have barbs which get caught in woollen clothing and animal fur.*

Copying nature *This microscope picture of Velcro shows how closely the fastener copies nature. The tiny nylon hooks on one piece of Velcro catch the loops on the facing piece, exactly as grass burrs catch onto woollen socks when you walk through woods. A thumbnail-size piece of Velcro contains about 750 hooks, with 12,500 loops on the other side. They can be fastened and unfastened thousands of times without wearing out, and are used on clothing instead of press-studs or zips.*

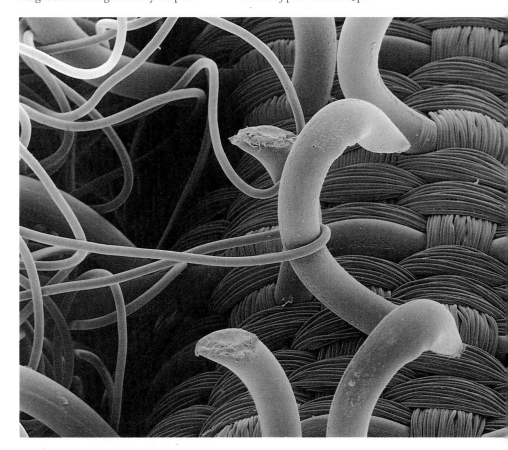

How the US Navy launched the zip fastener

The US Navy pioneered the use of zip fasteners in 1918 when it ordered 10,000 of them to do up 'wind-cheating' flying suits.

The first slide fastener – the ancestor of the zip – had been devised by an American engineer, Whitcomb Judson, in 1893.

He designed a 'clasp locker' as a quick method of doing up the men's high buttoned boots that were then fashionable. But his fastener, which used a slider to link hooks and rings, was cumbersome.

The breakthrough which resulted in the modern zip came 20 years later when a Swedish engineer, Gideon Sundback, was employed by Judson to improve the fastener. Sundback designed the so-called Hookless 2, almost the same as the modern zip, and developed machinery for making the teeth and fixing them to tape.

In 1918 the US Navy put in its order, and the zip was on its way to becoming one of the most common fastening devices.

The standard zip consists of two fabric strips with metal or plastic teeth along the edge. The teeth on each strip are staggered so that they can dovetail together. They have a projection on one side and a hollow on the other so that when they are meshed together the projections fit into the hollows.

When the zip is being closed, the two strips enter the metal slider at an angle, and are brought together so they interlock.

When the slider is moved to open the zip, the reverse occurs. The interlocked teeth enter the bottom of the slider and are angled away so they unlock.

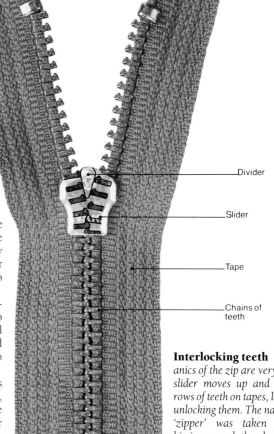

Divider

Slider

Tape

Chains of teeth

Interlocking teeth *The mechanics of the zip are very simple. A slider moves up and down two rows of teeth on tapes, locking and unlocking them. The name 'zip' or 'zipper' was taken from the hissing sound the device makes when the slider is pulled quickly up or down.*

How a plunging lift is brought to a safe halt

The world's tallest office building, the 1454ft (443m) Sears Tower in Chicago, has 103 lifts to whisk passengers between its 110 storeys at speeds up to 1800ft (550m) a minute.

But what would happen if the cable broke while a lift was high up such a tall building? A body falling from the top storey of Sears Tower would, in theory, smash into the ground at around 200mph (320km/h). To avoid disasters, lifts are designed with safety mechanisms.

The development of the modern passenger lift has its origins in 1854, when the American engineer Elisha Graves Otis introduced the first fail-safe mechanism for freight hoists at the Crystal Palace Exposition in New York. Previously, hoists had been notoriously unsafe. Ropes used to hoist goods on platforms frequently broke – sometimes killing people.

Something of a showman, Otis demonstrated his safety hoist in a dramatic way. The hoist was hauled up about 25-30ft (7.5-9m) with him standing on its platform, along with boxes, barrels and other freight. Then he ordered the rope to be cut. On earlier hoists it would have been disastrous. But Otis's fail-safe mechanism worked – and the hoist stopped dead after the rope was cut.

The secret of Otis's success was a bow-shaped spring attached to the top of the hoist platform. As the platform was hauled upwards, the spring arched and its ends did not make contact with notched guide rails on each side. But when the hoist rope was cut, the spring flexed back and its ends jammed in the guide rails, preventing the platform from plummeting down.

Otis installed the world's first passenger lift in New York City at the five-storey Broadway china store of V. Haughwout & Co, in 1857. The invention of the safety lift was a key factor in the development of the skyscraper. Previously buildings had been limited to six storeys, because people baulked at climbing too many stairs.

The passenger lift freed architects from height restrictions. And the development of iron-frame building techniques in the 1880s provided the means for high-rise construction.

A modern passenger lift is not fundamentally different from Otis's original. It is a boxed-in platform, hoisted by steel cables between two guide rails, and has a safety

Rapid ascent *The 110-storey Sears Tower in Chicago has high-speed lifts which travel at up to 20mph (32km/h). The lifts are fitted with safety devices in case the cables break.*

mechanism that jams into the guide rails if the cables break.

The cables lead from the lift car up and over a pulley device called a sheave, at the top of the lift shaft. The pulley is driven by an electric motor. The cables lead down to a counterweight, also on guide rails.

Overspeed governor

A key component in lift safety is an overspeed governor. A cable from the governor runs up and down the lift shaft and is attached to the safety gear mounted beneath the floor of the lift car.

The overspeed governor relies on centrifugal force, which causes a system of weights to swing outwards. Beyond a preset speed, their weight activates a safety switch, cutting off power to the drive motor. The pulley is then automatically braked, and the lift stops without having to activate the safety device.

However, if the car continues to accelerate, the overspeed governor will clutch the governor rope with sufficient force to trip the safety gear.

One type of safety gear wedges rollers or serrated-edged cams against the guide rails. They bite into the rails and bring the car to a halt. Another type of safety gear uses wedges in a similar way to the brake shoes on a car, reducing speed by friction.

Testing the smell in natural gas

In the high-tech natural gas industry, the final test of safety is the human nose. Natural gas, unlike old-style coal gas, has no smell, and a leaking pipe could easily go undetected and cause an explosion. But a smell can be added. And experts, employed for their sensitive smelling ability, make sure that in an emergency the gas has just the right smell to spark off the mental signal – 'gas leak'.

The experts, called rhino-analysts, sniff the gas to double-check that sophisticated testing equipment has done its job.

Natural gas is found under the ground or beneath the sea. The main ingredient is methane, also called marsh gas because it is found bubbling up from the organic ooze in marshes. The powerful smell that accompanies methane in a swamp is caused by rotting vegetable matter. The methane itself is odourless.

Natural gas was introduced in the USA in the 1920s and in Europe in the 1960s. As it had no smell, combinations of organic sulphur compounds were tested as odorants. The ideal odorant had to have a unique and powerful smell; it must not be absorbed by soil, or underground leaks might go undetected; and it had to be harmless to life and non-corrosive. The right formula was eventually devised.

This odorant, in liquid form, is sprayed into the gas as it leaves the processing plant. The technical term is 'stenched'. The quantity of odorant is precisely measured under computer control. It has such a powerful smell that only about 1lb is needed for every million cubic feet of gas (1.5kg for every 100,000 cubic metres).

Sophisticated instruments, such as a gas chromatograph, monitor the smell at various points in the distribution network. And humans check their accuracy.

Despite the addition of odorants, gas leaks in buried pipelines may still go undetected. So gas engineers frequently travel along pipeline routes with 'sniffing' equipment a thousand times more sensitive than the human nose. But the equipment looks for the gas rather than the smell. Sniffer probes close to the ground feed air to an instrument that can detect gas in concentrations of only a few parts per million.

The fibres that make tea bags remarkably tough

Every day in Britain alone, 150 million cups of tea are made from tea bags – small paper bags packed with enough tea to give one cup when steeped in boiling water. The net-like filter paper that forms the bag has holes big enough to let boiling water in, but small enough not to let any leaves escape. It is also strong enough not to break in a high-speed tea-packing machine, or during handling in use – when dry or wet.

No ordinary paper could meet these exacting demands. Tea-bag paper is made from two strong fibres – manila hemp, a long natural fibre (used to make rope) for strength, and thermoplastic fibres, to seal the bags. The two fibres are not woven together – they are laid down as a watery mixture in two separate layers. They form paper when the water drains away and the damp web remaining is squeezed dry through rollers. This gives the paper an irregular, web-like structure with pores varying in size.

The paper goes through the tea-packing machine in a sandwich of two strips and the machine measures out the amount of tea on the lower strip. The bags are formed by heat sealing the sandwich together round the edges. The thermoplastic fibres melt to form the bond which stays strong when it solidifies again on cooling. Its melting point is higher than 212°F (100°C) – so the bag will not come apart when boiling water is poured over it.

Filter holes *When a tea bag is magnified 60 times (left) the tiny filter holes show up clearly. The holes let water in but are too small for the tea to spill out.*

How matches are made by the million

If you strike a safety match anywhere but on the side of the box, it will not light. If you hit its head with a hammer, nothing happens. But a 'strike-anywhere' match will ignite if it is struck against any rough surface. Even the friction of a mouse gnawing the head can set it alight. Hit it with a hammer, and it will explode.

Safety matches work by a reaction that takes place between chemicals on the match and a chemical in the striking surface on the box. The reaction is triggered by the striking action, which generates heat by friction. If the head and the striking surface are not in contact, the match cannot light.

The forerunner of the modern match was produced by an English pharmacist,

John Walker, in 1827. Walker's matches were of the strike-anywhere variety, but they were not very reliable.

In 1830, Charles Suria in France hit on a much better match, using white phosphorus in the tip. Matches of this type, called lucifers ('light-bearers'), remained in use until the end of the 19th century.

Lucifers were reliable and kept well, but had a grave disadvantage. They could, and often did, kill. White phosphorus gives off poisonous fumes, prolonged exposure to which causes a disfiguring and eventually fatal disease called 'phossy jaw' because it causes the jawbones to rot.

Workers in matchmaking factories were affected most, and by the turn of this century, white phosphorus was banned. Its

Riots against the 'match tax'

In 1861 the firm of Bryant & May produced their first safety match at a factory at Bow, East London. By the end of its first year the factory was turning out 1,800,000 matches a week. They were so much in demand that in 1871 the Chancellor of the Exchequer proposed a 'match tax' of a penny a box. The proposal caused an outcry in

Parliament and the Press – and thousands of match workers protested at what they saw as a threat to their livelihood. Riots resulted, and so Parliament abolished the levy.

Throughout the world matchmaking techniques became more streamlined, until today more than 800 boxes of matches can be made every minute.

Mass production *In a match factory in the 19th century, foremen and craftsmen were identified by their bowler hats (top left). Matchsticks – double the final length – were rolled in coils and dipped at both ends, then cut in half (above). Rows of 'match girls' (left) finally packed them in boxes.*

Moving along *A steel conveyor belt takes wooden matchsticks – complete with red-dyed heads – down to meet matchboxes which move at right angles across the belt's path. The matches are automatically punched out of the belt so that they fall in the correct numbers into the boxes.*

place in strike-anywhere matches was taken by phosphorus sesquisulphide.

In the mid-1850s the Swedish manufacturer John Lundstrom pioneered the safety match by separating the phosphorus from the other combustible ingredients. He put red, non-poisonous phosphorus in the striking surface and the other ingredients in the head.

Matches today are made by automatic machines that produce up to 2 million matches an hour, boxed and ready for use. The standard wooden match starts as a log, which is cut into thin ribbons about ⅒in (2.5mm) thick.

The ribbons are chopped into matchsticks, which are soaked in a solution of ammonium phosphate. This is a fire-retardant, which ensures that the sticks do not continue to smoulder.

The sticks are then fed automatically into the holes of a long, perforated, moving steel belt. The belt dips the ends in a bath of hot paraffin wax. The wax soaks into the wood fibres, and will help transfer the flame from the head coating to the stick.

Next, the matches are dipped in the head mixture. For safety matches, the mixture contains sulphur and sometimes charcoal to create the flame and potassium chlorate to supply oxygen.

When the heads have dried, a punch knocks the sticks from the perforated belt into the inner parts of the matchboxes travelling on a moving conveyor.

The outer parts are travelling on a parallel conveyor. Every few seconds the conveyors stop, and the inners are pushed into the outers.

A strip coated with red phosphorus is applied to the sides to form the striking surface (glasspaper or a sanded resin strip is used for strike-anywhere matches).

Why does clingfilm cling?

Clingfilm clings for two reasons: when stretched, its elasticity makes it try to return to its original size; and it holds a static electrical charge, which creates a form of attraction to many other things.

The key to the film's elasticity lies in its molecular structure. Plastics consist of molecules which are 'long' – hundreds of thousands of repeated units of one carbon and two hydrogen atoms in a molecule of polythene, for example. Most common substances are made up of small molecules – a molecule of water has only two hydrogen atoms and one oxygen atom.

The long molecules of clingfilm are coiled and kinked, like the fibres in wool. When the film is stretched, the molecules straighten out. But, like wool fibres or an elastic band, the molecules try to return to their original state.

The stickiness of clingfilm occurs naturally in most thin plastic films. They stick because they acquire a static electric charge. The film can obtain, for example, a negative electric charge through friction displacing electrons from the surface of an adjacent piece of film or other material. This will result in a positive electric charge on the second surface, and the two will be bonded by the electrical attraction.

Clingfilm can be made from either of two plastics: PVC (polyvinyl chloride) and polythene. The chemical PVC is normally hard, but it is softened by the addition of a substance called a plasticiser. Polythene is naturally soft and requires no plasticiser.

PVC film is clearer than polythene film, but it suffers more from 'fatigue'. Within 24 hours of use it loses over two-thirds of its elasticity, while polythene loses only one-third.

The man-made material as slippery as ice

The non-stick interior of modern kitchenware is the most slippery material known to technology. It has approximately the same friction rating as ice, so if streets were coated with it they would be almost impossible to walk or drive on.

The non-stick finish, called PTFE, allows scrambled eggs or toffee to be cooked without leaving a sticky mess clinging to the pan. The same slippery quality also makes PTFE ideal for coating artificial hip joints, which must move with the least amount of friction.

PTFE is one of the most remarkable of

Spray-on surface *To make a non-stick frying pan, PTFE powder is mixed with water, sprayed on the pan and baked.*

Heart valve *A non-stick coating of PTFE lubricates a machine-made artificial heart valve (left).*

Sun and space *The plastic dome of this sports stadium in Japan (left) is coated with PTFE to reduce the heat of the sun's rays and keep the stadium cool. Astronauts' pressure suits (right) have several layers of material, including one of Teflon-coated, fireproof, abrasion-resistant cloth.*

man-made materials, and slipperiness is not its only unusual quality. It resists both very high and very low temperatures; it is quite impervious to attack from almost all chemicals; and it does not conduct electricity.

PTFE stands for polytetrafluoroethylene. It was discovered almost by accident in 1938 by an American engineer, Dr Roy Plunkett, when he was conducting experiments for the Du Pont company on a chemical used for refrigeration. The Du Pont trademark for the discovery was Teflon.

PTFE is a difficult substance to deal with, and no widespread consumer use was found for it until a French engineer, Mark Gregoire, became one of the first people to appreciate its domestic applications. He marketed the first non-stick pans under the name Tefal in the mid-1950s. Other manufacturers then produced a wide range of cookware, bakeware and appliances coated with PTFE.

However, from the early 1940s a wide variety of industrial uses had been developed. PTFE's slipperiness was put to use in bearings – machine components that support rotating shafts. PTFE bearings are known as self-lubricating because they need no lubrication other than their inherent slipperiness. To increase their strength, they are usually reinforced with other materials, such as glass fibre and graphite. They are used particularly in chemically testing environments in which metal bearings would corrode, such as for pumps in acid treatment plants.

Resisting acid attack

PTFE is not affected by any ordinary chemicals, including boiling alkalis and acids. Even that dissolver of gold and silver *aqua regia* (a mixture of concentrated hydrochloric and nitric acids) leaves it unscathed. The only substances that will attack it are molten sodium, molten calcium and very hot fluorine.

PTFE's chemical inertness means that it does not taint the food that is cooked on it. Indeed, it has no affect on any organic matter, including human tissue. This gives it applications in spare-part surgery. For artificial joints its slipperiness gives it a double advantage. It has also been used in the form of a fibre weave impregnated with carbon to reconstruct bones in the face.

Another major property of PTFE is its electrical resistance, which makes it excellent for sheathing wires. It has the great advantage that it retains its flexibility at temperatures ranging from $-454°F$ $(-270°C)$ (a few degrees above absolute zero) to $500°F$ $(260°C)$.

PTFE insulation is used on wiring in spacecraft, which undergo extremes of temperature. As they orbit the Earth, spacecraft are exposed to searing heat when they are in the sun, and temperatures well below zero when they enter the Earth's shadow.

PTFE's unique combination of properties results from its chemical make-up. The PTFE molecule consists of a long-chain 'backbone' of carbon atoms, each one attached to two fluorine atoms. The chemical bonds between the carbon and fluorine atoms are immensely strong, which is the reason that PTFE does not react with other chemicals.

Strong carbon-fluorine bonding also occurs between adjacent molecules, so that they attract one another more than they attract the molecules of other substances. This is why nothing sticks to it.

The strong intermolecular attraction also means that PTFE does not melt properly, even at high temperatures. Melting occurs when molecules get more energy from heat, and break away from other mole-

cules. In PTFE the intermolecular attraction is so strong that the molecules have great difficulty in breaking away.

How PTFE is made

PTFE is made from chlorodifluoromethane, a widely used refrigerant liquid known as Freon 22. The American engineer Dr Roy Plunkett discovered that heating Freon 22 produces the gas tetrafluoroethene.

Under a pressure of about 45-50 atmospheres and in the presence of a peroxide catalyst, this gas undergoes a chemical change, and the result is PTFE in the form of a powdery resin.

Because PTFE does not properly melt, it is mixed with a suitable binder and shaped in a mould. Then it is subjected to high pressure and high temperature, and the resin particles fuse together to form a solid mass. For non-stick cookware, the PTFE powder is suspended in water to form a non-stick finish which is then sprayed on the surface and baked.

How microwaves cook without heating the plate

Switch on a microwave oven, and you are switching on a powerful magnetic field which oscillates in the same frequency band that is used for radio broadcasts and radar. Microwaves in the field can be used to cook food rapidly by making the water molecules in the food vibrate at almost 2500 million times a second. This action absorbs energy from the magnetic field and heats the food.

As all the energy is absorbed by the food, and not wasted on heating the surrounding air or the oven itself, the process is far quicker and more economical than traditional cooking methods.

The microwave energy does not heat the utensils in the oven because the materials they are made of – such as china and glass – do not absorb energy from the magnetic field. However, the plates do not come out of the oven cold, because they are heated by the food.

Special cookware

Many other materials besides china and glass can be used in a microwave oven – such as plastic, paper and cardboard. And special cookware – which is transparent to microwaves – has been developed for use in microwave ovens.

Metal containers should not be used because metal does not transmit microwaves but reflects them. So foods should not be covered with aluminium foil.

Wooden utensils are also best avoided in microwave ovens because wood always contains some moisture, and this can cause it to split when it heats up.

Long-wave radio waves have a wavelength measured in thousands of metres. The microwaves used in microwave ovens have a wavelength of about 5in (120mm).

An electromagnetic wave is a vibration of electrical and magnetic fields, constantly going from negative to positive. Microwave ovens operate with waves that vibrate 2450 million times a second – a frequency of 2450 megaherz (MHz).

Water molecules have a positively charged end and a negatively charged end. The vibrating positive-negative microwaves interact with the positive-negative water molecules, attracting and repelling them and making them twist first one way, then the other. This also happens 2450 million times a second.

The most important part of the microwave oven is the electronic tube, or magnetron, that generates the microwaves. The magnetron was developed in 1940 by British researchers at Birmingham University, and was first applied usefully in radar. Its domestic potential was first realised by the Raytheon Company in the United States in the early 1950s.

Boiling over *When water is heated in a glass in a microwave oven, the temperature can rise to 230°F (110°C) without boiling. This is because the microwaves heat the water in the centre without heating the glass, so the water next to the glass is below boiling point. As the bubbles of boiling water mostly form on irregularities on the inside of the container, no boiling occurs. But put in some instant coffee and bubbles form around the grains, and the liquid boils over.*

How refrigerators make food cold

When you switch on an electric fire or cooker, you get heat. So how, when you switch on an electric refrigerator or freezer, does it make food cold?

It does so because the designers make use of two scientific principles. The first is that when a liquid evaporates it draws heat from its surroundings. It needs energy to maintain the change, so takes it in the form of heat. The second is that a liquid evaporates at a lower temperature when the pressure is low.

Any liquid that evaporates easily at low temperatures is a possible refrigerant, or cooling agent. It can be made to alternately vaporise and liquefy by being circulated through pipes in which the pressure varies. In most domestic refrigerators the refrigerant is one of the man-made substances called chlorofluorocarbons (CFCs).

The pipes on the inside of a refrigerator cabinet are wide, so the pressure is low and the refrigerant vaporises. This keeps the pipe cold, and heat is absorbed from the food.

An electric motor sucks the cold gas from the pipes in the cabinet, compresses it so that it heats up, and delivers it to the pipes on the outside of the refrigerator at the back. The air around the pipes takes away the heat and causes the gas to condense back again to liquid, still at high pressure.

Then a pipe with a very small bore, called the capillary tube, feeds the high-pressure liquid back into the cabinet where the pipe widens and it once again vaporises and starts the cycle again.

HOW FOOD IS PRESERVED

Chilling food in your refrigerator slows down the two main causes of decay – the growth of mould and bacteria, and chemical breakdown, as in the over-ripening of fruit.

In a domestic refrigerator the temperature is kept between about 34 and 41°F (1 and 5°C). This is low enough to keep most of the foods we use fresh for up to a week. Growth of decay-causing organisms is slowed down, but low temperatures do not destroy the organisms. Similarly, chemical breakdown is also slowed but not stopped completely – so the food will spoil if kept for too long.

The temperature in a home freezer is normally about 0°F (−18°C), which will preserve food for anything from a month to a year, depending on the quality and type of food frozen.

For thousands of years ice pits were the only means of keeping food fresh. They were used by the ancient Greeks and Romans, and the Incas of Peru.

Refrigeration developed in the 19th century, spurred by the need to get meat supplies from the vast grazing lands of Australia, New Zealand, South America and the American West to the main markets in Europe and the eastern United States.

One of the first to discover the principle of refrigeration and put it to use was a printer, James Harrison, who had emigrated to Australia from Scotland. While cleaning type with ether, he noticed its cooling effect on metal – ether is a liquid with a low boiling point that vaporises easily. He put his discovery to use by pumping ether through pipes to cool a brewery building in the gold-rush city of Bendigo, Victoria, in 1851.

Harrison's idea led to the first successful voyage from Australia with a refrigeration plant. The ship was the SS *Strathleven*, which carried a cargo of meat to London in 1880 – a two-month journey.

The first domestic refrigerator was developed in 1879 when the German engineer Karl von Linde modified an industrial model he had designed six years earlier. The refrigerant was ammonia and it was circulated by a small steam pump.

Electric refrigerators were pioneered by the Swedish engineers Balzer von Platen and Carl Munters in 1923 with their Electrolux model, which used an electric motor to drive the compressor.

HOW A REFRIGERATOR WORKS

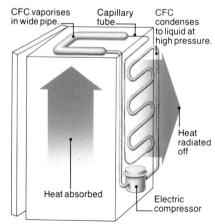

Warm air inside the refrigerator rises and is cooled as heat is drawn off by the refrigerant in the wide section of pipe. The refrigerant carries away the heat, which is dispersed by radiating from the narrower zigzag pipe at the back of the refrigerator.

How a pressure cooker cooks so fast

When you boil potatoes in a saucepan, they take 20-30 minutes to cook. But boil them in a pressure cooker, and they will be ready in 4-5 minutes. Why?

In a saucepan, water boils at 212°F (100°C). No matter how much you heat the water, the temperature can never go any higher. It just turns into steam.

But a pressure cooker has a sealed lid, so steam produced when the water boils builds up inside. As the pressure rises, so does the boiling point of the water. The cooking temperature is therefore increased, which reduces the time needed to cook the food.

The domestic pressure cooker evolved from a 'steam digester' patented in Britain by a French physicist, Denis Papin, in 1679. A typical modern cooker operates at an extra pressure of about 15lb per square inch (1kg per square cm), or at about twice normal air pressure. So the water boils at 252°F (122°C).

The pressure cooker has a saucepan-like base and a domed lid. A rubber gasket between the two ensures a pressure-tight seal. In the centre of the lid is a vent in which a weight is placed. The weight seals the vent, but lifts when the steam inside reaches the required pressure. Rings can be added or removed, giving the cook a range of temperatures. There is also a safety plug in the cover, which releases the pressure if the weight fails to rise.

WHY DO YOU GET A POOR CUP OF TEA ON MOUNT EVEREST?

Water boils when it begins to turn into steam. The bubbles are caused by the steam rising from the bottom of the saucepan to the surface.

The temperature of 212°F (100°C), which is normally given as the boiling point of water, is only correct if you are cooking at sea level. As you go higher the atmospheric pressure falls, causing the boiling point of water also to fall. Extra cooking time in both a saucepan and a pressure cooker is needed.

And that answers the old question: why can't you make a good cup of tea on the top of Mount Everest?

The summit of Everest is nearly 30,000ft (9000m) high, and the atmospheric pressure there is less than one-third of the sea-level pressure. Water boils at only 158°F (70°C).

This temperature is not nearly high enough to extract the best possible flavour from tea leaves, and the result is a poor cup of tea.

The cause and cure of kettle fur

People who live in parts of the country founded on chalky or limestone rock, and who have local water piped into their homes, end up with some of the rock in their kettles.

When rainwater percolates through a chalky landscape, it slowly dissolves away some of the mineral. When the water is boiled, the chalk comes out of the solution and sticks to the sides of the kettle as lime scale, or kettle 'fur'.

Water that is laden with chalk and lime (both of them forms of calcium) makes its presence felt in another way. You cannot get much of a lather when you wash in it with soap. Instead of lathering, the water reacts with the soap chemicals to form an insoluble scum. It is described as 'hard'.

Lime-scale stains also occur on baths and lavatories and around the outlets of taps.

The lime scale can be removed with proprietary descalers. A common type uses a concentrated solution of formic acid.

The acid dissolves the lime scale, making it fizz as carbon dioxide gas comes off.

The lack of a good lather in hard water is less of a problem than it used to be because modern detergents form no scum.

In some boilers and hot-water systems hardness can be more than a nuisance. The lime scale clogs up pipes and reduces the water flow. In boilers the scale forms a barrier that prevents the efficient transfer of the heat, leading to much higher heating bills. So, particularly in industrial plants, water needs to be softened before it enters hot-water systems.

Many waterworks remove hardness by chemical methods, such as treatment with slaked lime and soda ash, before pumping the water to houses and factories.

The beauty of lime scale *Flower-shaped crystals of calcium carbonate (above) lock their 'petals' together to form the lime scale which causes a hard deposit on the inside of a kettle or boiler. Stalactites (top), which hang from the ceilings of limestone caves, are massive lime-scale structures.*

The microscopic 'tadpoles' in your washing machine

The secret behind all washing powders is a chemical that makes water 'wetter'. Curiously enough, water left to itself does not 'wet' or spread over things very efficiently. This is because of surface tension, a phenomenon that causes water to have a kind of skin. On ponds, insects run on this skin, which is caused by an inward pull on the top layer of water molecules by the molecules underneath.

The addition of washing powder or liquid to the water weakens the forces between the molecules, and reduces the surface tension. This allows the water to spread more easily and wet things better. In the wash, the wetter water is able to penetrate the fibres of fabric more easily and help to lift off any dirt or grease.

The active ingredient of non-soap detergent is a petroleum derivative, alkyl benzene, treated with sulphuric acid and caustic soda.

The molecules of the detergent can be thought of as little tadpoles, with a head and a tail. The heads are attracted to water molecules – they are water-loving (hydrophilic) because water molecules are slightly electrically positive while the detergent heads are electrically negative. The tails, on the other hand, are water-hating (hydrophobic).

When dirty clothes are put in a detergent solution, the tails of the molecules attach themselves to greasy dirt in the fibres, because the tails are chemically similar to grease. They also work their way between the fibres and the dirt and loosen it. The dirt particles, having attracted the tails, effectively become coated all over with a layer of water-loving heads – like tiny balloons – and float away in the water. Agitation of the clothes by the washing machine helps to shake away the dirt.

Washing powder is a mixture of up to ten or more substances. It contains the basic detergent and other ingredients, including bleach.

Biological washing powders differ from other detergents by containing enzymes, which are types of proteins produced by plants and animals. The enzymes act as catalysts, or chemical triggers, to help in breaking down protein stains, such as blood, gravy and perspiration. The enzymes actually cause a chemical breakdown of proteins, whereas normal detergents work physically. Because protein stains are derived from living things, the washing powders are called biological.

WASHING CLOTHES IN WETTER WATER

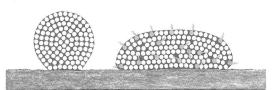

Water is not very efficient at getting things wet because water molecules join together and produce surface tension. This enables insects such as pond skaters to 'walk' on water (above). When detergent is added to a drop of water, the ball-shaped drop (left) collapses because surface tension is reduced.

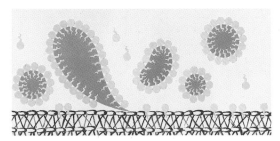

Detergents remove grease from fabric because the tails of the detergent molecules attach themselves to the grease particles. The heads of the molecules are attracted to water, so the grease particle is pulled away from the cloth as the washing is agitated. Mild electrical charges from the detergent prevent the grease particles from joining.

Cotton fabric before washing (left) has grease particles trapped among the fibres. During the wash, detergent molecules lift out the grease and leave the fabric clean (right).

THE WONDERFUL, RAINBOW-HUED SOAP BUBBLE

A soap bubble is created in the same way that detergents reduce the surface tension of water.

Pure water molecules attract each other strongly and will always pull together to form a droplet rather than a film. Detergent molecules reduce the attraction between them but the water molecules retain enough attractive force to create a film.

When a child blows a bubble, the film stretches and forms a sphere. As the water evaporates, the bubble bursts.

Rainbow colours *The 'rainbow' in a bubble is caused by light reflecting on the surface.*

Making toothpaste – with chalk and seaweed

People who cleaned their teeth in the 1840s probably used one of various brands of toothpowder which contained ground-up coral, cuttlefish bone, burnt eggshells or porcelain. The powder might have been coloured purple with cochineal, derived from the bodies of tropical scale insects.

Today's toothpastes – white, coloured or striped – contain ten or more ingredients. Some play a part in cleaning or protecting the teeth; some make the paste tastier; some bind the paste together; others help it to flow out of the tube.

The main ingredient in the white part of toothpaste is finely powdered chalk (calcium carbonate), or another mineral powder such as aluminium oxide, which is an ingredient of cement. These powders are slightly abrasive and help to remove the dulling film which is deposited by food and drink and contains decay-causing plaque.

Some titanium oxide, a white powder, is sometimes also added to whiten the toothpaste.

Clear gel toothpastes get their abrasive quality from transparent compounds of silica, often with a colouring added.

The cleaning and polishing ingredients are combined with water into a thick paste by the addition of a binding and thickening agent such as alginate, which is derived from seaweed.

A trace of detergent is added to create foam and help the cleaning process. To make the paste

Filling the tubes *Empty toothpaste tubes, called blanks, go through a machine for filling. A measured amount of toothpaste is packed in, then the ends are sealed.*

Striped toothpaste
The coloured stripes contain fluoride or mouthwash.

Putting in stripes *There are two methods of getting the stripes in toothpaste. In the tall container (left), the white and coloured pastes are put into the tube separately, and combine when they are squeezed out. In the traditional tube (right), the coloured paste is in a ring near the tip and goes through holes to give stripes to the white paste.*

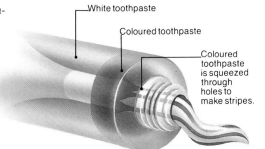

White toothpaste

Coloured toothpaste

Coloured toothpaste is squeezed through holes to make stripes.

palatable, it is usually sweetened with peppermint oil and menthol.

A moisturiser such as glycerine is also added to prevent the paste from drying out. In addition most toothpastes now contain fluoride which helps to strengthen tooth enamel. Disinfectant such as formalin may also be included to kill bacteria.

How they put in the stripes

Some toothpastes have the fluoride or mouthwash incorporated as a stripe.

The standard cleaning mixture is usually chalky white, while the fluoride or mouthwash is often a clear blue or red gel. The two pastes are mixed separately. As with all toothpastes, the empty tubes, called blanks, are filled from the wide end, which is then crimped and sealed. The two pastes contain colours that will not mix, so the pastes do not flow into one another. When the toothpaste is squeezed out of its tube, white and coloured stripes emerge.

How they make razor blades sharp

Every 24 hours, as many as 25,000 hairs grow up to half a millimetre on the face of the average adult male. The modern razor blade, honed to perfection, can cut its way through this stubble forest to give a close, smooth and safe shave.

Men began removing their fast-growing facial hair thousands of years ago, using slivers of flint and then bronze, and eventually iron blades. The world's first steel-edged 'cut-throat' razors were introduced in Sheffield in 1680. But the modern type of disposable safety razor blade did not appear until 1901, when a Wisconsin travelling salesman, King Camp Gillette, and an engineer, William Nickerson, were granted a patent.

A razor blade starts its life as a continuous coil of rolled steel strip about four thousandths of an inch (0.1 mm) thick – about the same thickness as the hair it is designed to cut.

The steel is an alloy containing about 13 per cent chromium, which gives it increased hardness and resistance to corrosion. The hardness is increased further by heating the steel and then plunging it into cool fluid.

The shaving edge is produced by grinding. The strip passes through three sets of grinding wheels, each grinding finer than the one before. The wheels are set at different angles to give what is called a gothic-arch (curved) cross-section. The shape is stronger than a straight-sided wedge. The sharpness of the blade is expressed as the radius of the curve

Gillette: inventor of the safety razor

Men would still be shaving every morning with old-fashioned cut-throat razors if not for the invention of an American, King Camp Gillette (1855-1932).

A travelling hardware salesman working in the mid-west of America, Gillette was shaving one morning in 1895 when he decided that his conventional long-bladed razor was neither efficient nor safe. He noticed that only a short length of the opened blade was used, and he considered how dangerous the razor was – it could, literally, cut a man's throat. And as a busy man, Gillette disliked wasting his time stropping the blade to sharpness.

Why not, reasoned Gillette, create a razor blade which never needed to be sharpened, was just the right size to shave a man's face, and was cheap enough to be thrown away when it wore out. Gillette recalled, also, the words of his former employer, William Painter, who invented the disposable crown cork. Painter was an inventor and businessman who believed that if you could make a product which people would use and then throw away, they would keep coming back to you for more.

Gillette and an engineer, William Nickerson, eventually perfected the double-edged safety razor blade, which fitted into a specially designed holder with a handle and an adjustable head. The carbon steel blades were guaranteed to stay sharp for 20 shaves, and were sold in packs of 12.

Gillette set up his Safety Razor Company and patented his razor in 1901. The first razors went on sale in the USA in 1904. Available from jewellery shops, chemists and ironmongers and also the new department stores, the razor and blades were sold together in boxed sets. The original razors had silver-plated handles, and even more expensive models were plated with gold.

The initial sales proved disappointing, however, and the company carried out an advertising campaign in newspapers and gentlemen's magazines in the USA and Europe to make the public aware of the new invention. By 1906, sales of razors had reached 90,000, and 12 million blades were sold.

Gillette's picture appeared on the packaging until recently, and he became world-famous and rich.

The safety razor and blade have changed very little in design from his original, although some razors are now made of plastic and are, themselves, disposable.

Wet and dry cut *A wet beard hair cut by a razor blade (left) shows a much cleaner cut than one done by an electric razor (right). Wetting the beard, necessary for shaving with a safety razor, makes it easier to cut. A dry whisker is as hard to cut as a copper wire of the same thickness.*

forming the extreme tip of the cutting edge: about five-hundred thousandths of a millimetre.

After grinding, the cutting edge is polished by rotating leather wheels. On a microscopic scale, however, the edge is still rough and because of friction, liable to snag the hairs and cause discomfort. To protect the cutting tip and reduce friction, the blade is given three successive coatings: chromium, ceramic and the plastic PTFE, more familiar as the slippery non-stick coating on pans. The chromium resists corrosion, the ceramic reduces wear and the PTFE produces lubrication.

The coatings are each less than one-hundred thousandths of a millimetre thick.

The razor blade fits into a holder with a handle which is comfortable to hold and has a head which may be adjustable and may screw open to take the blade.

How stainless steel was discovered by accident

Stainless steel was discovered by accident in 1913 by the British metallurgist Harry Brearley. He was experimenting with steel alloys – combinations of metals – that would be suitable for making gun barrels. A few months later he noticed that while most of his rejected specimens had rusted, one containing 14 per cent chromium had not. The discovery led to the development of stainless steel.

Ordinary steel rusts because it reacts easily with oxygen in the air to produce crumbly red iron oxides. Other metals, such as aluminium, nickel and chromium, also react in much the same way, but their oxides form an impermeable surface layer, stopping oxygen reacting with the metal underneath. With Brearley's steel, the chromium formed such a film, protecting the metal from further attack.

A variety of stainless steels are now made. One of the commonest alloys contains 18 per cent chromium and 8 per cent nickel – known as 18:8 – which is used for kitchen sinks. Kitchen knives are made of a steel containing about 13 per cent chromium. A more corrosion-resistant alloy is achieved by adding a small amount of the metal molybdenum – these steels are used as cladding for buildings.

Gateway to the West *The largest arch in the world is the monument to the westward spread of America, in St Louis, Missouri. It rises to a height of 630ft (192m), and the span is the same. A construction such as this could only be built with stainless steel.*

Major feats of organisation

*From controlling a city's traffic to putting on
the Olympic Games or building cars on a production line –
so many things that we take for granted sound simple . . .
until you discover what goes on behind the scenes.*

How the battle to control traffic is waged, page 50.

*How they run the world's
greatest sports festival, page 64.*

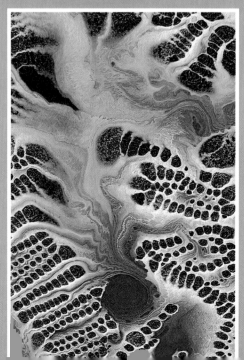

*How major cities get rid
of their waste, page 47.*

How do airports cope with millions of passengers?

An American couple once arrived at London's Heathrow Airport unable to recall the name of the family they were staying with near the airport or the name of the street. All they had was a street number, and 'Oh, yeah, the street's named after a tree, and it's close to some store called Sainsbury'.

To information officer Jan Hernando – one of 24 information staff – the problem was almost routine. She called the local post office, who gave her the answer: Beech Road. The Americans, two of the 100,000 people who arrive at Heathrow daily, went on their way, delighted.

An airport is a living organism with one prime function: to keep its life-blood – its passengers – flowing freely through its veins and arteries. The number of passengers is astronomical, and growing fast. In 1986, the world's 37 busiest airports each year processed a grand total of 740 million people between them. Worldwide, airports spend $5000 million a year in the quest to keep their passengers happy.

Jumbo jets

Take the world's busiest airport, Chicago's O'Hare, which is used by 50 commercial airlines. The airport handles 55 million people a year, which works out at 6700 passengers every hour. About 2200 aircraft pass through O'Hare each day. If several jumbo jets arrive within minutes of each other, thousands of people are disgorged at once, causing congestion that can undermine the plans and tempers of passengers, destroy confidence and cut into airport profits. Faulty machinery and strikes have the same effect.

When an air traffic controllers' strike in Spain coincided with the start of the annual French holiday at the end of June 1988, tens of thousands of passengers became stranded in airports all over Europe. At Manchester alone, 16,000 holidaymakers were delayed for up to seven hours – and a plane-load of people heading for Greece finally got away after a wait of 21 hours. Clowns and jugglers were brought in to entertain thousands of bored children.

Baggage is a major element of airport organisation. It is handled separately from the passengers, partly for security reasons and partly because it is stowed in a separate part of the aircraft. It is the baggage handlers' job to ensure that it ends up at the same destination as its owners. At the

Waiting for orders *Each jumbo jet that lands at New York's John F. Kennedy Airport disgorges up to 500 passengers. Then comes the wait for the next flight out.*

Ready for boarding *Passenger jets nose up to the terminal buildings at Frankfurt Airport. It is West Germany's main international airport – and one of the world's 37 busiest, which together handle a staggering 740 million passengers a year.*

United Airways terminal at O'Hare, computer-coded baggage tags are read by laser, and automatic baggage sorters process 480 pieces of luggage a minute, compared to the 75 that can be moved by hand. The baggage sorting area is the size of six football fields.

With increasing size and complexity of airports, problems multiply. As more people travel through an airport, more space is needed, everything takes longer and the passengers become more frustrated. For example, as car parks expand, passengers have to be given additional transport to take them from their cars to the airport terminal. More aircraft require more gates and terminals, and more miles of corridors.

The size of airports has become breathtaking. Whereas a large railway station covers about 9 acres (3.6 hectares), the largest US airport, Dallas-Fort Worth, covers about 27sq miles (71sq km). Its four terminal buildings handled more than 44 million passengers in 1988.

But even this huge airport looks small compared to the world's biggest, the King Khalid International Airport in Saudi Arabia, which covers 91sq miles (236sq km), over four times the size of Bermuda.

When they arrive at an airport, travellers are offered a bewildering range of services. And when they discover where one of them is, they may have to walk great distances to get there. At the world's largest airport terminal – Hartsfield Atlanta Airport, Georgia, USA – the floorspace covers more than 50 acres (24 hectares).

Each terminal comes to resemble a small city, with its own army of baggage handlers, cleaners, nursing staff, administrative personnel, stores, restaurant staff and maintenance men. London Heathrow's Terminal 3, which deals with most of the airport's long-haul flights, employs 3000.

Nor is this all. Eventually, to stay in business, all terminals need to be updated, as happened in Terminal 3 in 1987-90. The £73 million renovation had to be planned so that the staff and 6 million passengers each year could work and flow around the rebuilding.

New technologies, however, will allow more people to be handled by existing facilities. Travelators (moving pavements), computerised baggage handling, automated railways to bring people from remote car parks – all these innovations are designed to make mass air travel quicker and more pleasurable.

The constant vigil to prevent aircraft colliding

As the world's airspace becomes ever more crowded with airliners, the flying actually becomes safer.

In the United States, the number of air travellers rose from 315 million to 460 million between 1980 and 1987. Across the Western World, air traffic is growing at around 20 per cent every year.

So there would seem to be increasing chances of a midair collision – the catastrophe that pilots call 'the aluminium shower'. But each year, the accident rate goes down. In the USA, there were 1.72 deaths per 100,000 flying hours in 1978; in 1986 there were 0.92. In other words, an aircraft would have to fly 24 hours a day for nearly 12 years before anyone was killed.

Yet the system is showing signs of strain. In 1987, near-misses in the USA occurred at the rate of three a day – double the rate of 1984. On July 8, 1987, for example, two American jumbo jets – both flying towards the USA with a total of almost 600 people on board – missed each other by less than 100ft (30m) over the Atlantic.

The near-miss figures in Europe remain steady, but some experts fear that the American pattern will be repeated in Europe as traffic grows.

The responsibility for ensuring that aeroplanes do not collide in midair falls squarely on the shoulders of the air traffic controllers. And as the flow of aircraft increases, the volume of work becomes constantly greater. In the USA, the Federal Aviation Administration employs about 15,500 air traffic controllers – almost exactly the same number as in 1980.

The main danger points are the airports themselves, for 90 per cent of all collisions and near collisions involving airliners occur as the aircraft climb after takeoff, descend for landing, or circle while awaiting permission to land.

The rules of the air

The rules that control the flow of traffic are long established. Airspace is divided into control areas and air corridors. In the corridors across the Atlantic Ocean between New York and London, for example, aircraft are separated by 2000ft (610m) vertically and 60 nautical miles (110km) horizontally. Over land in Britain they are separated by 1000ft (300m) or more vertically and by 5 nautical miles (9km) horizontally.

Controllers must ensure that each air-

craft is handed over from one section to the next during its flight – even over the mid-Atlantic.

Before takeoff, each aircraft files a flight plan, which is updated on computer print-outs during the flight. The air traffic controllers monitor the journey from the print-outs. Each plane emits an identification signal that shows up on the airport's radar.

When an aircraft approaches a busy airport wishing to land, it is directed to a reporting point over a radio beacon, probably several miles away. It is then allotted its own flight path which takes it down to the runway. However, during busy periods more aircraft may wish to land at an airport than there is room for. In some countries they are instructed to form a stack, or holding pattern, by circling at different heights around the reporting point. In others they are not allowed to begin their flight until they have been guaranteed a landing space.

During heavy holiday congestion over Europe in July 1988, there were ten London-bound airliners circling one above the other at the same time over a beacon near Ostend in Belgium.

In the USA, some airports have commercialised the pressure, allowing those airlines that pay more to queue-jump.

In theory, air traffic control is a system of proven reliability. In Britain, for example, there has not been a midair collision between commercial flights in controlled airspace since air traffic control was introduced in the 1930s.

But as demand builds, problems multiply. Present computer systems are antiquated, and air traffic controllers, juggling dozens of flights, work under increasing pressure. A report on the crash of an airliner in a thunderstorm at Dallas/Fort Worth Airport, Texas, in 1985 revealed that air traffic controllers were dealing with one call every four seconds. They described the workload as moderate.

Across Europe, national computer systems are often not compatible with each other.

The chances grow that errors will be made, and not spotted. In April 1988, two flights bound for London – a Cyprus Airways Airbus and a Manx Airlines commuter jet carrying a total of more than 300 people – found themselves on a collision course at 8000ft, north of London. Both pilots took avoiding action and disaster was averted.

The way to preserve safety, and improve it still further, is with computerisation. The US Federal Aviation Administration is planning a revolution in air traffic control at a cost of nearly $20,000 million. The new system will quadruple capacity by using computers that have four times the capacity of the previous ones and are eight times faster. The system will suggest avoidance manoeuvres to the aircraft if it spots two planes heading towards each other. The radar screens will be in colour, and display weather information. Aircraft otherwise out of touch with air traffic control centres will be monitored by satellite. All flight plans and rescheduling will be updated automatically. It will warn of impending congestion.

Other improvements include microwave radio-guidance systems which will enable pilots to land even though they cannot see the runway because of bad weather.

A computer on board airliners will detect other aircraft in the vicinity and give avoidance instructions to the pilot in a synthesised voice. Another computer will cope with 'windshear', the sudden change of wind direction that can bring disaster to an aircraft as it comes in to land.

In this way, the skies may become more crowded. But they will be even safer – for a decade or two, at least.

How they choose air traffic controllers

Air traffic control is like playing chess in three dimensions – using potentially explosive pieces. If you are careful and keep a cool head, nothing will go wrong. The moves are all in the rule book, and there are computers to help plan each one and predict the consequences. Nothing should go wrong. Except, sometimes, it does.

On November 26, 1975, an air traffic controller at Cleveland, Ohio, had just taken over from a colleague. He had been looking at his radar screen for only 55 seconds when he realised he was watching a disaster about to happen.

An American Airlines DC-10, flying east from Chicago with 194 people on board, was climbing to its assigned position of 37,000ft. A TWA jumbo flying west with 114 people was cruising at 35,000ft. The controller realised that the two airliners were heading for a midair collision near Detroit, and it was only seconds away.

Reacting instantly, he made an urgent call to the DC-10: 'AA 182, Cleveland, what is your altitude?'

The reply came back from the airliner: 'Passing through 34.7 (34,700ft) at this time. We can see stars above us but we're still in the area of the clouds.'

Controller: 'AA 182, descend immediately to 33.0 (33,000ft).'

On the flight deck of the DC-10, Captain Guy Eby responded instinctively, pushing forward his control column. The plane pitched over with a stomach-churning heave, and unbelted passengers, air hostesses and food trolleys flew into the air as the floor plunged away beneath them.

For a brief moment, Captain Eby saw his windscreen fill with the TWA jumbo as it passed just overhead at a combined speed of 1000mph (1600km/h).

Flight data recorders later showed that the DC-10 had been within 47ft (14m) of the jumbo's altitude when it dived to safety.

The incident spotlighted the ideal qual-

Controlling the airways *Sitting before their complicated control panels, air traffic controllers at O'Hare Airport, Chicago, keep a painstaking check on the planes landing and taking off in the area – and maintain constant two-way communication with the pilots.*

ities of an air traffic controller: concentration, patience, swiftness of decision, and an authority that can be trusted instantly by pilots.

Trainee air traffic controllers need basic fitness, good eyesight, clear speech and school-leavers' qualifications that include English and a science. (English is the international language of the airways.) In their training, would-be controllers have to absorb technical information about aviation law, meteorology and radio theory, in addition to the formalities of communicating with pilots.

Trainees study in classrooms and on simulators, with practical sessions at control centres and airports. They are then posted to an airport or a control centre for supervised work and further training.

The intense training prepares them to analyse and act upon the mass of ever-changing information on their radar screens when they finally qualify as air traffic controllers. A major airport like Frankfurt handles an average of 805 flights a day – one every 60 seconds at peak hours – and a controller's radar screen may show two dozen images at any one time, all of them moving, all with pilots awaiting instructions.

But no amount of intellectual ability or

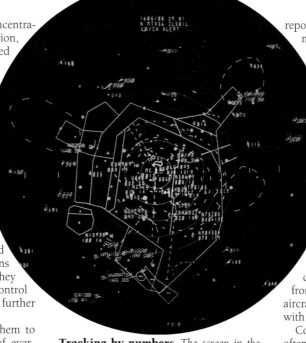

Tracking by numbers *The screen in the radar room at Washington's National Airport allocates a flight number to the planes in its airspace. So the movements of each plane can be seen and tracked by radar.*

technical knowledge can give a controller the essential personality skills needed to manage the task effectively. At some international airports, the pressure is so intense at times that controllers have

reportedly collapsed. Certainly, in every major airport, the level of concentration and the responsibility is highly stressful.

No wonder Britain's National Air Traffic Services, which take on more than 100 trainee air traffic controllers a year for 18 month courses, say that candidates must have 'a calm, even temperament, alertness and quick reactions'.

Dedication and self-discipline help, too. It is often a lonely occupation, involving shift-work through the night. Though in small airports controllers can watch the planes manoeuvring, in large airports many sit continuously in dimly lit rooms in front of radar screens. They never see the aircraft, and may have little direct contact with other people.

Conversation during working hours is often reduced to orders in the formal phrasing needed to ensure clarity and accuracy: 'Roger, seven-three-two. Descend to three thousand feet on QNH one-zero-two-four.'

It's not everyone's idea of fun. But the challenge of the job, the responsibility and the rewarding salaries ensure that there is no shortage of applicants to be air traffic controllers. But only one applicant in 20 is accepted as a trainee.

The never-ending hunt for airport terrorists

Ann Murphy, a 32-year-old Irish chambermaid, arrived at the El Al checkpoint at Heathrow Airport, London, on April 17, 1986. She was about to fly to Israel in the belief that she was to meet the mother of her Jordanian boyfriend and then get married. She was already five months pregnant. Her boyfriend, Nezar Hindawi, said he would follow in another plane because he had got a separate ticket through his work.

Ann Murphy queued up with the other passengers to board the Boeing jumbo jet

which was to carry 375 people to Tel Aviv.

A security officer asked her some routine questions and put her suitcase through an X-ray machine which showed nothing unusual.

He then emptied the case and found that it was 'quite heavy for an empty bag'. Alerted by the suspicious weight, he pulled at the bottom of the case and discovered a secret compartment containing 3lb (1.4kg) of plastic explosive. A pocket calculator among Ann's clothes contained a timer and detonator which would have exploded the

Calculated death-bid *Unknown to her, Irish maid Ann Murphy (above, left) had a time-bomb in her suitcase for a flight from London to Israel in 1986. It had been planted by her Jordanian boyfriend Nezar Hindawi (above, right), who was later sentenced to 45 years imprisonment for attempting to blow up the plane which carried 375 people. Among the evidence at his trial (left) were a gun, bullets, a bag, a passport, and a calculator for detonating the explosive.*

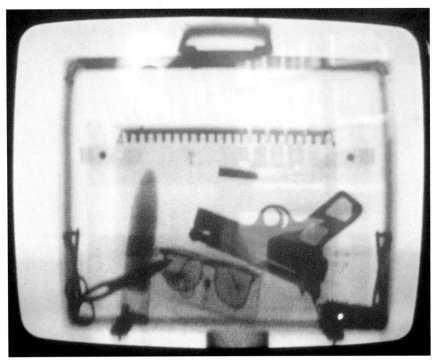

Seeing eye *Examinations of luggage by X-ray machines are carried out at airports throughout the world. Here an X-ray Rapide Monitor shows that the suitcase under inspection contains – as well as such things as sunglasses and scissors – a handgun.*

bomb at 1pm when the airliner was flying at 39,000ft over Austria.

Nezar Hindawi had given her the suitcase – already packed with explosive – because he said her own was too heavy, and had put in the calculator which he said was for a friend. On the way to the airport in a taxi, Hindawi had put a battery in the calculator which armed the bomb.

Hindawi, a Palestinian terrorist backed by Syrian intelligence, was caught and sentenced to 45 years in prison. Ann Murphy – who gave birth to his baby girl before the trial – was described in court as the victim of 'one of the most callous acts of all time!'

The airliner would have been destroyed in midair with all its passengers and crew – but for the alertness of the security man and the thoroughness of El Al's system of checking all passengers and their luggage.

El Al, the Israeli airline, has the reputation of being the most security-conscious in the world. Passengers have to check in about three hours before departure, and undergo a thorough body search. All their luggage is examined by hand.

The nightmare of terrorist action on a packed airliner hangs perpetually over everyone responsible for airline security. It is a nightmare that sometimes becomes hideously real, as when a Pan American jumbo was blown out of the sky over the Scottish town of Lockerbie on December 21, 1988, killing 259 passengers and crew and 11 residents of the little town.

Crime in the air, in particular hijacking and sabotage, goes back to 1930 when an airliner was hijacked for the first time – a Peruvian Airlines plane hijacked in Peru. Since then there have been more than 600 incidents, 90 per cent of them since 1968.

Hijackers usually demand either money, publicity or political action. And terrorists treat airlines as a symbol of a nation whose policies they oppose.

Each tragedy brings tighter security at airports, but security will always have its limitations. As new ideas and new technical advances succeed each other, security officials play a deadly game of leapfrog with terrorists. And there is always a conflict between the need for security and the need to process passengers quickly.

Though companies are wary of discussing details, there are half a dozen main forms of security at airports.

Checking the staff

Airports are huge areas employing thousands of people, and with many vulnerable points. Catering and cleaning staff, for instance, have smuggled weapons and explosives onto aircraft.

To tighten security, airlines may introduce 'covert tagging' – treating uniforms, vehicles and credentials with a chemical that can only be detected with special reading equipment.

X-raying luggage

Low-grade X-ray machines, commonplace in the 1970s, have been improved with solid-state circuitry to provide images sharp enough to spot electrical wire finer than a human hair.

But X-ray checks are only as efficient as the guards watching the images. Most people would spot a handgun in profile. But seen end-on it is harder to recognise.

Plastic explosive – like the Czech-made Semtex – is invisible to X-rays. The battery, detonators and wiring used to set off the explosion can easily be incorporated in a calculator, as in the El Al case, or a radio, as in the Pan-Am disaster.

Metal detectors

Machines which create magnetic fields have been widely used from the early 1970s to detect metal objects in luggage. Between 1973 and 1980, in the USA alone, they spotted 20,000 firearms.

To avoid setting off the alarms unnecessarily, however, operators often turn down the sensitivity, thereby increasing the risk that a small weapon will be missed.

And metal detectors may eventually become obsolete. Security experts fear that it will one day be possible to build a gun from plastic.

Tagging explosives

Some explosives manufacturers include in their products 'taggants', tiny colour-coded chips of plastic which reveal the place and time of origin, thus allowing the buyers to be traced. Though these only become useful after an explosion, their inclusion could deter terrorists by making detection more certain. International agreements may extend the use of taggants.

Searching passengers

Almost all airports now search some passengers and their baggage. El Al search them all. But airport authorities say it would be far too expensive and slow for every airline to search every single bag and person. Searches are usually random, unless there is reason to suspect a particular flight or passenger. Searches are now routinely backed by questionnaires to establish who has packed passengers' bags and whether anyone has given them something to take with them.

Remote sensing

Sniffer dogs are used to detect explosives and several types of vapour sampler are also used (page 97).

No machine or animal, however sensitive, can detect odourless or hermetically sealed explosives. Several techniques, however, are being developed. One is gamma-ray radiography, which passes mildly radioactive radiation through the baggage. Certain wavelengths are partly absorbed by the contents, giving the beam a 'signature' that identifies explosives.

Another device is the thermal neutron analysis machine. This bombards baggage with neutrons (subatomic particles), which react with the nitrogen used in most explosives, releasing a detectable gas. The machines are being introduced into some major airports specifically to detect plastic explosives.

Until new devices are developed, the best defence against terrorists is efficient and sensitive surveillance – sensitive, because thorough searches may alienate even the most patient passengers.

It was alertness that led officials to the bomb in Ann Murphy's bag and so probably saved the lives of hundreds of innocent people.

For the immediate future, the terrorist's best ally is a bored, slapdash security inspector.

How they provide meals on a jumbo

With up to 400 seats, a jumbo jet accommodates as many people as a medium-size hotel or hospital. On a typical intercontinental flight, passengers are given a meal of three courses (with a choice of main course), plus breakfast or afternoon tea.

Most major airlines prepare all the food in catering units at their home airports. British Airways' huge catering centre at London's Heathrow, the world's busiest international airport, has a staff of several hundred – including 80 chefs – who produce about 160,000 meals each week. On a typical day, they supply 30 jumbo flights, which could be carrying almost 12,000 people.

Menus for the flights are planned three months ahead, but there are constant requests for special-diet meals booked by passengers for health, religious or cultural reasons. Special meals can be ordered for children, too – from babies' bottles to sausages and mashed potatoes – right up to 24 hours before departure.

Working on information from the main reservations computer, the caterers start estimating requirements four days in advance. Flights may appear fully booked, but managers will 'undercater' according to computer predictions of how many seats will actually be occupied on the day. This is due to the perennial 'no show' problem of passengers who book but fail to turn up.

Early computer forecasts minimise waste of the fresh ingredients delivered daily. A typical weekly shopping list includes 30,000 chickens, 8000 lettuces and 175,000 tiny tomatoes.

In-flight catering

By departure day, the final meal requirements are in ASPIC, the centre's automated system for controlling the production of in-flight catering. This displays on screens the meals needed for each class – First, Club World, and Economy, each with separate menus – plus special meals, shown with the names of the passengers concerned.

About four and a half hours before departure time, the centre begins to assemble the trays. The components – including freshly prepared hors d'oeuvre

MENU

ECONOMY CLASS
Beef pastrami appetiser
∘
Chicken teriyaki
OR
Salmon fillet
∘
Pineapple and kiwi fruit mousse

——— ∘ ———

CLUB WORLD CLASS
Papaya and seafood salad in pastry
∘
Grilled breast of corn-fed chicken
OR
Salmon poached in white wine
OR
Cold roast fillet of beef and salad
∘
English summer pudding
OR
Cheeseboard

——— ∘ ———

FIRST CLASS
Caviar and smoked salmon with trout and salmon mousse
OR
Chilled mango with citrus fruits
OR
Hot croustade of wild mushrooms
∘
Chicken consommé with truffled galantine
OR
Poached baby lobster in Chablis and dry vermouth sauce
OR
Breast of duckling with truffled stuffing
OR
Vegetarian timbale of aubergines and hazelnuts
∘
Mirabelle flan with dairy cream
OR
Vanilla and mocca ice cream
∘
Fruit basket Cheeseboard selection

Food in flight *Airline food, particularly on long-distance routes, aspires to restaurant standards (above). Presided over by a chef (left), staff at British Airways' catering centre at London's Heathrow Airport lay out the food which will be served to the passengers travelling on a jumbo jet.*

and dessert, bread from the in-house bakery, cutlery and condiments – are delivered from their respective points in the 11½ acre (4.7 hectare) building.

Methods of preparing hot dishes vary between airlines. Some precook the food for reheating in ovens or by microwave on board. On BA flights, the meals are part-cooked and rapidly chillled so they can later be finished in the plane's fan-convector ovens (powered by the engines) and served freshly cooked.

When each tray has been assembled, 30 of them are loaded into the familiar aisle-wide trolleys. Along with the customs-documented drinks trolleys, serving equipment and other supplies, the meals are then wheeled to the marshalling area. The total 'catering uplift' for a single jumbo jet amounts to 35,000 items.

All must be checked and ready for loading two and a half hours before takeoff to give the fleet of trucks time to move the vast load to the aircraft.

It is now departure minus one hour. Any late items – a special meal for a last-minute passenger who happens to be diabetic, or perhaps an impulsively requested birthday cake – are supplied by a refrigerated van.

On board, the three sets of meals for the three different classes are stowed in their respective galleys – usually six in all. In the air, the meal is served according to the local time zone. The 15 cabin crew aim to pass out the trays as soon after the final cooking of the main 'hot insert' as possible.

With the trays collected and returned to their trolleys, all is ready to be unloaded at the destination by the catering vehicles which swarm to the aircraft as soon as it is

parked. Here, the airline's local contractor will sort and wash-up all the hardware.

The washing-up is a major operation. At BA's Heathrow centre, the wash-up employs 160 people, against 130 in the kitchen, in spite of intense automation. One device picks up all the cutlery – 90,000 pieces daily – by magnet.

Back at the aircraft's destination, the cycle is restarting. In the brief time the aircraft is on the ground, another 35,000-item uplift is loaded. Where the flight is of two or more legs – London-Abu Dhabi-Singapore-Sydney, for example – the airline will try to provide a different menu in each class for each leg.

At 5 miles (8km) above the ground, the change of fare represents the only distinction between one part of the journey and the next.

The privileged and risky world of the stock market

As the sound of gunfire subsided over the battlefield of Waterloo in 1815, news of the Allied victory over Napoleon was carried by relays of couriers to the banker Nathan Rothschild in London. The financier, one of the founders of the Rothschild dynasty, received the news more than 24 hours before it reached the British Prime Minister, Lord Liverpool.

Rothschild knew that the price of British government stocks would soar when the word came through. So he bought large amounts of stock. The price rose over the next four days, and Rothschild added to his already considerable fortune.

Today financial organisations around the globe are linked by electronic communications, and events are known everywhere almost as they happen. The world's stock markets act almost as one, each of them responding immediately to news from the others.

A dramatic example was the stock market crash of Monday, October 19, 1987, which rippled like a shock wave around the world as each exchange opened for business. The New York exchange had suffered a sharp fall the previous Friday, and a weekend of simmering financial panic followed. The Sydney exchange opened its doors on Monday morning while most of

the world was still sleeping. Stockbrokers were deluged with orders to sell, and millions of dollars were wiped off share values. Satellite communications carried

Black Monday *The worried faces of stock market dealers in London reflect the consternation caused by the worldwide stock market crash on 'Black Monday' in the autumn of 1987.*

the news immediately to the Tokyo exchange, where heavy selling occurred.

As the Earth rotated on its axis, bringing opening time to one stock exchange after

another, the wave swept around the globe – Hong Kong, Singapore, the exchanges of Europe, and back to New York. The value of American companies plunged by more than $500 billion before the end of the day.

'Black Monday' brought the stock market to the attention of people who normally are barely aware of its existence. How could such enormous losses happen, they asked. How do stock exchanges work?

For three centuries or more, exchanges have been the marketplace where companies – and some governments, too – have gone to raise part of the capital needed to finance their enterprises.

The traditional auction-room frenzy of buying and selling on the trading floors of the exchanges is now yielding to a high-technology hum as dealers become computerised. But basic principles remain unaltered. A stock exchange is the focus for the buying and selling of securities, a blanket term for stocks, shares, bonds and similar documents. They all represent an investment by the person who buys them and a source of funds for the organisation that issues them.

The stock exchange determines, through the free-market process of supply and demand, what any particular security is

On the double *Dealers on Tokyo's stock exchange rush frantically around the centre area in this time-exposure photograph (far left). The close-up picture shows dealers earnestly conferring.*

worth to the holder at any given moment.

Businesses needing extra money to finance their activities have, in free-market economies, two main ways of obtaining it. They can borrow it from a bank for a fixed period or they can raise it by selling a part of themselves in the form of securities to anyone willing to buy.

The second method has an advantage for the business, because the money raised does not necessarily have to be paid back if the company's ventures fail completely. The buyers of the securities, on the other hand, become entitled to some of the profit if the business thrives, and the securities should rise in value. They hope to receive a better return from that investment than they would by putting their money to other, less risky use.

Being listed on a stock exchange gives a company prestige, which in turn helps in its efforts to raise money. It also has, through the stock exchange, access to the most important pool of potential investors – and their money.

Stock exchanges do not admit a company automatically. They enforce rules to ensure that listed companies give investors full and accurate information about their business, and treat them fairly and lawfully.

It is both expensive and complicated for companies to obtain a listing in top markets such as the New York, Tokyo or London exchanges. In New York, for example, a quoted company must have assets worth at least $16 million.

Most countries have developed secondary markets for smaller companies which wish to offer their securities to the public. These markets apply less strict conditions than the main markets, but are still tightly controlled.

In America the function is fulfilled by the American Stock Exchange (Amex) – also known as 'The Kerb' from its street beginnings – and the more recent National Association of Security Dealers' Automatic Quotation System (NASDAQ). Britain has its Unlisted Securities Market and Third Market, and Tokyo has a two-tier system.

Who runs the exchanges?

As temples of free enterprise, the world's stock exchanges have traditionally been run by the people who set them up in the first place. They are much like private, very exclusive clubs. In many countries, membership can be bought, provided the current members agree to the admission and a vacancy, or 'seat', exists. The price is high – up to about $375,000 in New York and a staggering $6.6 million in Tokyo. In other countries, such as Britain, membership is not limited to a fixed number of 'seats', but open to any firm able to meet the entry requirements.

The members make the stock exchange rules, which must conform with the laws of the country. In some countries, an independent body, such as the Securities & Exchange Commission in the United States, has been created to watch over their day-to-day conduct on behalf of the public.

Market makers and brokers

The ultimate privilege safeguarded by stock exchanges for their members is the right to be a 'market maker' in securities – that is, to be the central point through which the securities are bought and sold.

The second, equally important privilege

Trading floor *Serried ranks of traders at the Hong Kong Stock Exchange sit by their screens and telephones buying and selling stocks, shares and bonds.*

Panic stations *Dealers stand around in dismay as the New York Stock Exchange plunges in October 1987 (above). There are tense moments (left) as dealers watch their screens for the latest market moves.*

Brokers generally work on commission which is linked to the value of the securities they buy or sell for their customers.

The price of securities

Publicly quoted securities are first issued with a nominal or face value – called 'par' for ordinary shares or common stock. For example, a company wanting to raise £10 million might put on sale through the stock exchange 10 million shares, each with a face value of £1. However, once the securities begin to be traded their market price may be higher or lower than the face value. When more people are buying a security than selling, the price goes up. When more are selling, it goes down.

In 'bull market' conditions, people buy

is to be a 'broker' – the person who has direct access to the market makers to buy or sell on behalf of investors. In London, the market maker is the key figure. On the New York Stock Exchange, a 'specialist' fulfils a similar role. Each specialist is allocated exclusive rights to deal in certain securities, which he can then buy or sell to brokers who approach him, or which he can buy or sell on his own account.

Trading is in the form of a loose auction on the stock exchange floor, in which brokers, with instructions from their clients, cluster round the specialist, shouting out the prices at which they are willing to buy a security ('the bid') or to sell it ('the ask'). The specialist matches buyers and sellers as best he can, using his personal holdings to correct any imbalances.

On the Tokyo exchange, the equivalents to New York's specialists are called *'saitori'*. They operate in a similar way, except that they are not allowed to buy or sell securities on their own account. They are strictly intermediaries in transactions on the exchange trading floor.

Market makers derive their income from the 'spread' in their transactions – the difference between bid and ask rates.

Computer know-how *Since the computerisation of the London Stock Exchange in 1987, brokers have been working from their offices. The screens show the market state.*

securities expecting them to rise in value, when they can be sold at a profit. In 'bear markets', security prices are falling; speculators can still make money by agreeing to sell, at a fixed price, securities they have not at that moment paid for. They hope that, when they do have to settle, the price will have fallen further. Then the amount they pay out will be less than they receive.

The price of securities is governed by the performance of the particular company, and also by national or world economic and political conditions.

National developments affecting security values are easy to identify, but their impact is difficult to predict. They could include a change of government, forecasts of economic downturns or uplifts, or sudden surges in the costs of key raw materials. Broking companies and big investors such as insurance companies are spending increasing sums on economic forecasting departments.

The value of securities is constantly changing as they are bought and sold. But it is convenient to 'freeze' them at regular intervals so that the performance of the market and of individual securities can be compared between one interval and the next. For each trading day, the closing price of each security is quoted in the newspapers. And the progress of the whole market is measured by an index consisting of selected key securities.

The best-known indexes include the Dow Jones Industrial Average (New York), the Financial Times/Stock Exchange 100 (London) and the Nikkei 225 Stock Average (Tokyo). Index 'fixes' are flashed around the world twice or more a day.

CURBING THE STOCK EXCHANGE CHEATS

Insider dealer *New York financier Ivan Boesky (centre) seen leaving the Federal Court in Manhattan in 1987. After admitting using inside information about company mergers for his own profit, he was fined $100 million and jailed for three years.*

From the earliest days of stock exchanges, people have attempted to perpetrate swindles. In the 1720s, Britain's Chancellor of the Exchequer, John Aislabie, was imprisoned in the Tower of London for 'infamous corruption'. He had lined his own pockets during the sale to the public of shares in the South Sea Company, a speculative enterprise which ruined many investors.

All countries have their own laws to prevent cheating, and some have agencies, such as the US Securities & Exchange Commission, to ensure the laws are being observed.

One of the most notorious offences, and one of the most difficult to stop, is insider dealing. This is the use of privileged, inside information about a company to make money from its securities. The 'insider' might buy shares just before the company announces an increase in profits. Or sell them before it announces a loss.

In 1986 an eminent New York financier, Ivan Boesky, was charged with investing in stocks using confidential information about company mergers. He had paid huge sums for the information, on one occasion giving $700,000 in used notes to a banker in a Wall Street alley.

Boesky made a detailed confession which resulted in the arrests of bankers and businessmen in both New York and London. He was sentenced to three years in prison.

Money to burn

Cynics have often claimed that governments seem to have money to burn. True enough: the world's governments incinerate hundreds of tons of worn-out notes every week.

Coins in circulation may last decades, until the image becomes worn or the denomination changes, but small-value notes change hands so rapidly that they perish in a few months. Even high-denomination notes last no more than two or three years.

Britain's method of destroying old notes is typical. The notes are withdrawn in two ways, under the supervision of the Bank of England's Banking Department.

At each of its five branches (Birmingham, Bristol, Leeds, Manchester and Newcastle) and its printing works in Essex, the Bank of England has note-sorting machines which decide whether notes are fit to be reissued. If they are not, it shreds them into ½sin (1mm) squares. Every week, the Bank's shredders destroy £50 million-worth of used notes.

The country's 13,000 High Street banks also sort out badly worn notes, and send them under guard to either the Bank of England's head office in London or to one of its main branches. Each bank is credited with the value of the delivery. The notes are then taken by armoured Bank of England truck to the Bank's printing works. There, an incinerator with a temperature of 3600°F (2000°C) burns £135 million-worth – 15 million notes weighing 12.5 tons – every week. The ash is then ground up in a mill and inspected to ensure that no trace of a note remains.

Every year, therefore, the Bank destroys almost 1000 tons of notes with a face value approaching £10 billion, an amount replaced by new notes from its printing works.

However secure the operation, there are always risks. In the Great Train Robbery of August 1963, a gang seized £2.6 million in used notes from a well-guarded train. The thieves were eventually caught and convicted, but the fact that the money was due to be destroyed, and thus in a sense had ceased to exist, added a bizarre touch to the crime.

The business of destroying used money may not always remain necessary. For its bicentenary in 1988, Australia issued a new $10 bill made of plastic, which is practically indestructible in everyday use. It will survive boiling, washing and burial in soil.

If the new money works, paper currency could well be replaced by plastic currency, with considerable savings in cost and substantial gains in security.

How all the parts come together to make a car

Cartoon films portray car factories with lumps of raw iron going in one end and gleaming automobiles purring away at the other. It is of course a false image. Cars are not made all in one place. But the reality is scarcely less remarkable, for the process can involve factories all over the world in the making of just one car.

At Saragossa, Spain, where the American company General Motors has a huge assembly line, the steel for the body may come from Spain, the engine from Britain, the suspension units, gearbox and fuel-injection system from Germany, the tyres from France or Italy, the radio from Holland or Japan, with contributions even from Australia and Korea.

Once things were a lot simpler. At the beginning of the century, the first cars were produced much the same way as horse-drawn coaches – with workers wandering around, slowly and expensively hammering metal panels individually onto wooden frames. Although the elements of mass production had long been established for products such as ship's pulleys and guns, it took an organisational genius to apply this to the motor industry – Henry Ford.

The first assembly line

In 1903, Ford started to make cars in Detroit. Within three years, he was the largest car producer in the USA. Within five years, he was concentrating on a single model – the Model T – in order to make the best use of his standardised parts.

Then in 1913 he introduced the concept that was to revolutionise car production – the assembly line. This reversed the relationship between worker and product, for now the product rolled past a line of stationary workers, each one of whom did one specific task. When first applied to the making of magnetos, the new process cut assembly time from 20 minutes to five.

Fired by this success, Ford extended the principle to chassis construction. A rope pulled a line of chassis along a track, at which stood 50 workers, each fixing their own allotted part to each chassis as it moved by. Assembly time for a chassis dropped from 12 to one and a half hours.

Manual assembly *In 1913, Henry Ford introduced assembly lines at his Detroit car factory. Moving belts carried the parts past flywheel mechanics (left), and the engines to assembly workers (above). By 1915 a ready-to-drive Model T Ford was rolling off the lines every one and a half minutes.*

Commercially, the results were astounding. In less than ten years, the price of a Model T dropped from $850 to $250. Ford sold 1.8 million of them. Profits and wages boomed. Ford Motors led the way again in 1951 by using automatic equipment to produce engine blocks. In 500 distinct operations, 40 machines transformed a rough metal casting into a finished block, reducing production time per engine from several hours to 15 minutes.

The world of robots

The urge to save labour has continued to inspire new developments, with robots replacing workers, cutting out tedious tasks and guaranteeing greater accuracy. On the Fiat Uno, just 30 of the 2700 welds are done by hand. Only specialised crafts, such as electrical wiring, now remain in human hands. In a typical car-assembly plant of the 1980s – such as the Fiat Uno works at Mirafiori or Rivalta, Italy, which produce a total of 3000 cars a day – the first stage involves sheet steel arriving at the press shop. Here, in areas as large as three football stadiums, robot cranes supply rolled sheets of steel to giant stamping machines which cut the pieces of metal to make up the car body.

Next, robots build the underbody or floorpan, making numerous welds and creating a complex shape with spaces for wheel arches, boot wells and spare wheels.

At the next stage, large jigs position the body sides and roof to be welded into place automatically. Meanwhile, the doors have been made on nearby assembly lines in a process that involves several different pressings to create an outer skin clinched over an inner frame.

Finally, on advanced assembly lines, lasers check every car body for the smallest distortion or irregularity.

The final touches

Painting a car is a major process – protecting against corrosion as well as providing an attractive glossy look. The car, now largely assembled, is cleaned in a degreasing tank, rinsed and coated with phosphate to make it more receptive to the paint. After further rinses, base primer coat is applied, in several layers. These primer coats are sprayed on electrostatically, using an electric field to attract the paint.

The last layers – usually three – are of

Automatic assembly *Computer-controlled robots perform the production work at the Fiat Tipo plant at Cassino, Italy. The robots paint, seal, polish, weld and assemble the cars with fine precision. On the right, a car receives one of its 2000 or so automatic welds.*

glossy acrylic paint. The paintwork on most mass-produced cars is 0.1mm thick. A Rolls-Royce has 22 layers of paint, giving a thickness of 0.2mm.

Special wax to protect against water, snow, grit and salt is then injected into hollow sections such as pillars and sills.

The next stage, the trim, fits out the interior. The car acquires its 'nerves' – the electrical system. Robots fit underfelt, carpets, seats and other fittings. Many factories use robot carriers to move components about, reducing possible damage as well as the need for human labour.

Windscreens and some other windows are often glued to the car, to make a better fit and reduce wind resistance and noise.

Robots apply the glue to the edge of the glass and then put it in place on the car with sucker grips.

In the final assembly, the car receives its heart. It is raised on a hoist, and a jacking system brings the engine, complete with clutch and gearbox, into position. The fuel tank is mounted at the rear end of the car. Next come suspension, steering, radiator and battery, and then the wheels and tyres.

With the addition of water, antifreeze, oil and petrol, the car is in full running order. Inspectors at the gate examine it, before it undergoes final tests – in particular a 'rolling road' test that assesses performance. When the car is given its final bill of health, it is ready for the dealer.

Weather forecasters: sentinels against natural disaster

On October 15, 1987, Britain's TV weather forecasts predicted strong winds, but nothing more. The BBC's TV weather forecaster, commenting on a viewer's report of a hurricane on the way, said: 'Don't worry, there isn't.'

That night, 'Black Friday', southern England was struck by the storm of the century. Winds gusting to 115mph (185km/h) tore down 15 million trees and caused 19 deaths and over £1000 million of damage. In the public outcry that followed, a major question recurred: Why was there no accurate warning?

The answer was simple: the evidence was not overwhelming, and the forecasters made the wrong judgment. Despite increasing accuracy, weather forecasting is an uncertain science, and always will be.

Growth of a science

For centuries, even local weather was often baffling in its unpredictability. People could only pray, or devise reassuring proverbs based on observation, like:

Red sky at night, shepherd's delight:
Red sky in the morning, shepherd's warning.

Local forecasting took a step forward in 1643 when the Italian physicist Evangelista Torricelli invented the barometer to measure the pressure of the air. It was soon noticed that rises and falls in air pressure corresponded to changes in weather, and that a fall often heralded a storm.

But it was only after the invention of the telegraph in the 1840s that it became possible to gather reports from widespread weather stations, so that imminent changes could be predicted with reasonable accuracy. Radio, in the early 20th century, provided another major step forward. In the 1960s, huge technical advances in gathering information and analysing data in computers suggested that meteorology might eventually become an exact science, capable of predicting weather weeks or months ahead.

The amount of information now available to forecasters is staggering. The World Meteorological Organisation receives reports from 9000 outposts and 7500 ships. Manned stations take measurements several times a day, sometimes hourly, under standard conditions (for instance, wind speed is measured at 33ft (10m) from the ground).

In addition, weather balloons released from 950 stations all around the world monitor the atmosphere up to a height of 18 miles (30km). Some 600 aircraft report every day from high over the oceans. Seven weather satellites scan the Earth from space, monitoring the atmosphere to a height of 50 miles (80km).

From all these points, a huge quantity of data – wind speed, wind direction, temperature, cloud cover, rainfall, humidity, air pressure – is amassed. Every day, observations produce 80 million binary digits of computer information – equivalent to the contents of several thousand books. This is fed into a network of 17 stations around the world that together form the Global Telecommunications System. Two centres – the USA's National Meteorological Center in Washington and Britain's Meteorological Office in Bracknell, Berkshire – are World Area Forecast Centres for civil aviation, duplicating each other's operations in case of breakdown. Computers able to perform up to 3500 million calculations a second process the measurements to produce predictions.

Knowing tomorrow's weather today is vital to life in the industrialised West. In air traffic control alone, global forecasts that allow airlines to take tail winds into account or re-schedule landings to avoid poor conditions save an estimated £50 million a year in fuel. Whole industries – like construction, shipping and agriculture – depend crucially on hourly and daily forecasts.

The most dramatic events to test the forecasters are tropical cyclones – huge circular storms that are born over tropical seas. Those that migrate westwards across the Atlantic are called hurricanes, those in the Pacific typhoons. They swing away from the Equator, and die out as they move over land. Hurricanes usually last about a week, and are powered by the warm, moist air above the tropical ocean. As it rises in the centre of the storm, the moisture in the air condenses into clouds, releasing heat and sucking more moist air into the system. Hurricanes usually die down when they reach land, because they become starved of moisture. During the hurricane season, June-November, more than 100 storms form off the African coast, of which about six become hurricanes.

When the typical swirling clouds of a tropical storm are spotted, usually by satellite, the USA's National Hurricane Center in Miami swings into action. Its staff sift a mass of data from satellites, radar systems, automated buoys and aircraft to predict its path – in particular where it will come ashore.

In early September, 1988, a trough of low pressure off the African coast grew steadily until, on Saturday, September 10, when it was over the eastern Caribbean, it

Airborne monitor *Weather balloons carry aloft radiosondes – packages of instruments that record humidity, atmospheric pressure and temperature. The balloons are released regularly by 950 stations throughout the world.*

Wind-lashed *Hurricanes are driven by warm moist air over the ocean. This one, Carol, struck near Narragansett Bay, Rhode Island, in 1954.*

was designated a hurricane, and named Gilbert. Two days later, Gilbert struck Jamaica with devastating force. Beneath slate-blue skies winds wrecked the island, making one-fifth of the 2.5 million inhabitants homeless, and destroying almost all the crops on which the economy depended – bananas, coconuts, coffee, sugar and vegetables. Prime Minister Edward Seaga called it 'the worst natural disaster in our modern history'.

Then, as Gilbert spun away from the stricken island, it nearly doubled in force, producing wind speeds of up to 175mph (280km/h) – the most powerful storm to hit the Western Hemisphere this century. Its course carefully predicted, Gilbert smashed into Mexico's Yucatan peninsula at dawn on Wednesday, leaving 30,000 homeless. It could have been far worse – in 1979, Hurricane David killed 1100 and Flora caused 7200 deaths in 1963. Gilbert's relatively low death-toll of about 300 people was a tribute to the benefits of good weather forecasting.

But the forecasters still could not say exactly what would happen. As Gilbert swung north, the coasts of Texas, Louisiana and Mississippi were put on the alert. People emptied supermarket shelves in a panic of buying and 100,000 of them clogged roads as they fled inland, leaving be-

hind them houses shuttered and boarded.

In the event, the warnings proved unnecessary. When Gilbert hit the US mainland, it was already dying. It brought strong winds, high tides and heavy rain, but little destruction. There were no further deaths.

Gilbert's unexpected demise highlights the major problem with weather forecasting: its lack of absolute certainty. Notwithstanding their expensive computers and worldwide resources, forecasters deal only in probabilities.

Weather systems are unpredictable in detail. The figures used to describe varying factors like wind speed and temperature are at best for one moment only. The next second, the same figure becomes an approximation. However small the deviations are from the true values, prediction and reality soon part company.

Scientists accept that tiny events can have huge consequences. They jokingly refer to this unpleasant fact as the Butterfly Effect – the notion that a butterfly flapping its wings in Peking, for example, can affect storm systems in New York. As a result, the current limit of useful forecasting is no more than a few days.

Often a forecaster's experience of the real world is a better guide to the immediate future than any computer model. For

instance, if air is moving from the cool North Sea to adjacent European countries, it can build cloud in a thin layer that may either bring rain inland the next day, or evaporate in the heat of the sun. The outcome may depend on a temperature difference of only a few tenths of a degree. But the effects can be dramatically different, producing either a cool, cloudy day or a hot, sunny one.

Even with the best computers and the most efficient information gathering, it is

Satellite view *Detecting instruments feed data to a computer that builds up cloud images in colour-code on a TV monitor. This image is of Hurricane Gilbert in 1988.*

unlikely that forecasts will ever be accurate more than two weeks ahead.

Medium-range forecasts have improved with technical innovations. Three-day forecasts for Europe, produced in the European Centre for Medium-range Weather Forecasts in Reading, Berkshire, are now as accurate as one-day forecasts a decade ago. But long-range forecasting (beyond ten days), on the other hand, has not proved reliable.

There is hope, of a sort. Scientists believe there is a relationship between changing sea temperatures and certain weather conditions. For instance, every three to seven years at Christmas time, a warm current known as El Niño, extends down through the chilly waters off the west coast of South America. Besides having serious consequences for the weather, wildlife and industries locally, El Niño also causes either milder or colder winters in the United States. No one yet knows why, but perhaps one day El Niño's effect will become predictable.

How a major city gets its water

Niagara Falls carries 19,000 million US gallons of water over its brink every day. It would take the thundering flow of Niagara 17 days to fill up the 21 main reservoirs that New York City relies upon: 320,000 million gallons. The largest city reservoir, Pepacton, alone holds enough water to flood the whole of Manhattan to a depth of 40ft (12m).

Each day New York consumes 1423 million gallons, including the water used by its factories and offices. That comes to about 200 gallons for every person in the city. New York's distribution system takes it to the consumers' taps via more than 5700 miles (9000km) of water pipes.

In Britain, the daily requirement – for domestic use only – of the Thames area, which includes London and Oxford, is 710 million Imperial gallons. The region's 12 million inhabitants each use an average of 35 gallons of fresh water a day. More than a third is flushed in lavatories and a further 12½ gallons is used for washing, showers and baths. The remaining 10 gallons are used for washing clothes, dishes and cars, drinking, cooking and – depending on the season – gardening.

City water supplies generally come from rivers – New York, for example, gets most from the Hudson and Delaware Basins. The New York-West Delaware supply tunnel, which runs for 106 miles (170km), is the world's longest tunnel of any kind.

More than half the tap water supplied in

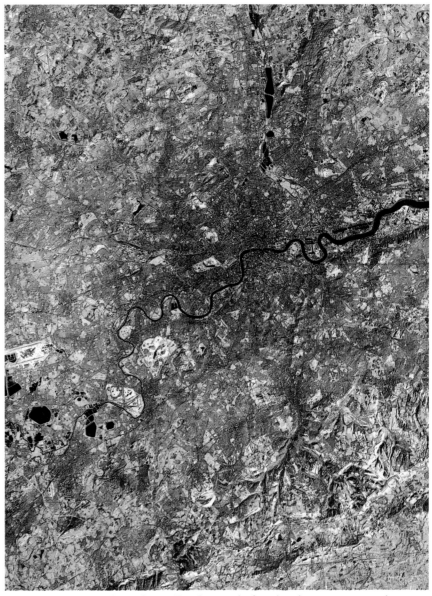

London's water supply In this satellite photograph of London, the city's reservoirs show up as black. The River Thames is the snaking black line cutting across the centre of the picture. Reservoirs are the black spots to the left and top; green areas are vegetation.

the Thames area is extracted from the River Thames itself, while the rest is raised from underground lakes and streams through boreholes or chalk wells. By 1996, London's water will be distributed via a 50 mile (80km) underground ring main consisting of pipes 8ft (2.5m) wide.

The water is channelled into screening and pumping stations, where coarse screens filter out the heavier debris and pumps raise the water to storage reservoirs.

Because water in reservoirs is still, solids sink to the bottom. At the same time, oxygen from the air neutralises other chemical or organic impurities.

A system of sluices takes water from the storage reservoirs to a treatment plant, where further purification takes place. The usual method involves filtering the water

twice through sand beds which are cleaned daily. In the first bed, the water sinks through coarse sand, which traps larger impurities. The process is repeated through finer sand.

The water is chemically treated with chlorine in a closed tank to kill bacteria, and then de-chlorinated to remove the chemical taste. It is then pumped under pressure into trunk mains – large underground or overground pipes – which carry it to the users' taps.

Treated water pumped into the mains may be used immediately – or diverted for temporary storage into service reservoirs or water towers. They are usually on high ground, although some service reservoirs are underground, beneath hills in public areas such as parks.

How a city gets rid of its waste

In June 1858, unusually hot and dry weather caused a sharp fall in the level of the River Thames in London. The stench that emanated from the depleted waters was so appalling that Londoners, who christened the phenomenon 'The Great Stink', could approach the banks or bridges only with handkerchiefs clamped firmly to their mouths and noses. River traffic was suspended. In the Houses of Parliament, beside the Thames at Westminster, sittings could not continue until the windows had been draped with curtains soaked in chloride of lime to counteract the smell.

The Great Stink was the final result of centuries of carelessness in waste disposal. Londoners, like the denizens of other crowded towns and cities throughout the world, had been accustomed to treat any handy waterway – often their sole source of drinking water – as a vast open sewer. Daily, urban rivers such as the Thames, the Seine and the Tiber received their loads of human and animal excrement, offal, household refuse, the unwanted by-products of crafts and trades and all other detritus of city dwelling. As populations grew and the flood of rubbish increased during 19th-century industrialisation, nature and man cried 'enough'.

Methods of treating raw sewage before discharging it were developed in Britain and copied and improved in western Europe and the United States.

Unfortunately, as methods of getting rid of excrement and other liquid waste have become more effective, the growth of modern cities has increased the output of solid waste – everything from discarded food packets to old light bulbs and batteries.

The average US household generates nearly 53lb (24kg) of solid waste every week; in France, the equivalent figure approaches 37lb (17kg) and in Britain it is 35lb (16kg). In a single year, the average inhabitant of New York City throws away eight or nine times his own body weight of solid waste.

Into the sewers

The basic treatment of liquid waste, or sewage, in cities such as London and Washington DC, has changed little from the methods developed in the middle of the 19th century, though the volume is constantly increasing.

In Washington, the original capacity of one sewage plant, at Blue Plains, was stepped up from 130 million gallons daily in the 1930s to 290 million gallons by the 1970s, and has been further enlarged since.

A network of sewers, usually underground, carries the waste, either under gravity or by pumping, from household and office lavatories, basins and baths to the sewage works. Originally, and in many cities still, the sewers were also storm drains, with the result that sudden downpours could flood them, bringing raw sewage to the surface. Now, where possible, civic engineers try to separate the two functions.

At the works, the sewage flows through screens which filter out large objects such as rags and wood. These are either torn by machines into small pieces and fed back into the treatment process, or taken for burning or burial elsewhere. Then the sewage is pumped through grit removal channels, where small stones and sand sink to the bottom. This detritus is dredged out and washed. It is widely used to fill holes in roads or on building sites.

The remaining sewage passes into preliminary sedimentation tanks, where the solid material settles to the bottom and is known as 'crude sludge'.

The sludge and the liquid separated from it then follow different routes. In London, the liquid goes to secondary treatment plants where microbes feed on and destroy the waste matter it contains in about eight hours. It then passes through final sedimentation, when the microbes themselves are separated out and re-used. The water that is left is clean enough to go into a river. Water from the River Thames is re-used several times before flowing into the North Sea.

In the USA, chlorine is added to the water at various stages to purify it.

Meanwhile, the crude sludge is pumped to digestion tanks. There, over three or four weeks, microbes convert part of the sludge into gas containing methane, which is piped off and used to create power to run the sewage works.

The rest of the sludge has more water removed before being sold to farmers as fertiliser. At Blue Mountain, Pennsylvania,

Treatment plant *Although this may appear like a picture of microbes, it is actually an aerial view of an industrial sewage-treatment plant north of Baton Rouge, on the Mississippi River.*

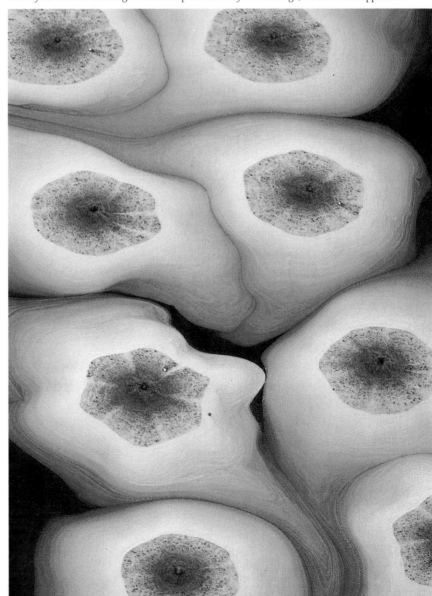

Filter beds *This aerial photograph shows rows of sewage filter beds at a treatment plant in Baltimore, Maryland. Once drained of water, dry sludge is sold to farmers as a fertiliser. Sludge not used on land is dumped in the sea.*

for example, sewage sludge has helped to reforest land destroyed by zinc extraction. Any sludge left over is dumped at sea.

Solid waste

Each day, New York City generates between 24,000 and 25,000 tons of solid waste – much of it household refuse carted away in twice-weekly, municipally organised collections. Virtually all of this mountain of rubbish is transferred to one site at Fresh Kills on Staten Island, where it is dumped into what began as a hole in the ground and is now the largest tip in the world, covering 3000 acres (1215 hectares).

Such waste disposal by controlled dumping is called a landfill. On a worldwide basis it is the most widely practised and cheapest way of ridding society of unwanted byproducts that cannot be flushed away through sewage systems.

But as the volume of waste continues to grow, landfills like Fresh Kills are less able to cope. Lack of space creates problems of pollution. Seepage from the rotting tips can contaminate surface and underground water supplies unless the tip is specially equipped to treat it.

When landfills are full or become a sufficiently serious hazard to public health, they have to be closed. Since the 1960s, New York has shut 14 and new sites are not easy to find. If they are too far away from the city they serve, the cost of transporting the rubbish to them becomes too high for municipal budgets.

In many countries, including Sweden, Germany and Japan, burning has long been used as an alternative to dumping. But in the United States incineration accounted, in the mid-1980s, for less than 5 per cent of solid waste disposal. The advantage of burning is that it reduces the volume of rubbish by two-thirds; the heat produced in the process can also be used to generate electricity or provide heating.

Against that, the ash residue may contain toxic chemicals which have been concentrated during incineration. The ash cannot therefore always be safely deposited in ordinary landfills. Other toxic chemicals, such as hydrogen chloride and dioxin, can be released into the atmosphere during burning if the proper gas-cleaning equipment is not used. In Los Angeles, citizens afraid of atmospheric pollution have stopped incinerators from being built.

Another reason against burning rubbish is expense. In the USA, the charge for burying it may be up to $60 a ton. To burn it can cost three times as much.

Health hazard *Uncontrolled dumping of waste on land can create hazards to health. But in most Western countries, new laws are tightening up on waste disposal.*

How they fight a bushland inferno

Trees explode into an inferno; balls of fire leap from tree top to tree top; the wind whips inwards to refuel the holocaust of fire and smoke. Close up, a forest fire is a terrifying spectacle.

But it is a scene repeated thousands of times a year in temperate forests around the world, most dramatically in the wilderness areas of California and the bushlands of southern Australia. These – as well as the scrubby *maquis* of the French Mediterranean and the evergreen *fynbos* of South Africa – fall easy prey to a dropped match, sunlight amplified through a discarded bottle, or a lightning-bolt. In Australia, the heat of a fire can vaporise eucalyptus oil, igniting whole trees in gaseous explosions.

The destruction can be massive. In 1949, France lost 385,000 acres of forest (156,000 hectares) in 350 fires. In 1971, fires in Wisconsin and Michigan burned 4.2 million acres (1,700,000 hectares) and killed 1500 people. In 1985, across the United States, 81,662 fires burned almost 3 million acres (1,200,000 hectares).

Flames can spread through tinder-dry bush at speeds of over 90mph (144km/h). Occasionally the combustion causes a fire whirlwind, a chimney of hot air supplied by inrushing winds that can uproot trees and shoot them into the air, starting new fires hundreds of yards away. To combat such destruction, major organisations like the US National Forest Service and Australia's State Bushfire Control Authorities assemble formidable forces. In Australia, most firefighters are volunteers.

In September 1987, when fires burned over a huge region in California, Oregon and Idaho, one night of firefighting in just one area – Stanislaus National Forest – involved 376 fire engines and water tankers, 94 bulldozers, 16 helicopters, 13 air tankers and 4500 firefighters.

Perhaps the greatest defensive weapon against forest fires is information.

Satellites, night-flying planes with infrared cameras, and computer coordination all allow fire conditions to be forecast and fires monitored when they break out. To combat a blaze, firefighters use a combination of two main strategies: cooling and containment.

Dousing a fire with water not only cools it: in large quantities it also breaks up burning material, and when turned into steam it reduces the amount of oxygen in the air to feed the fire.

But water by itself may not be enough. The fires can spread insidiously beneath mosses and lichens, and can survive inside

Firefighting with foam *Some forest fires – such as this one near Valencia, Spain – can best be fought with foaming agents. A firefighting amphibian (above) flies low over the blaze, ringing it with foam.*

Firefighting with water *A firefighting amphibian scoops water from a lake in Ontario, Canada (right). The planes can scoop up 1400 gallons (6400 litres) in ten seconds – and make more than 200 flights in a day.*

Mountain smoke-jumper *Descending by parachute, a smoke jumper goes into action against a lava fire on Mount Adams Wilderness in Washington, USA, in June 1987.*

hummocks and old stumps to break out again days later. To reduce these 'hot spots', chemicals called wetting agents are mixed with water to help it to penetrate. And dyes may be added to show which areas of forest have been treated.

Ground crews may create firebreaks to contain the blaze, while air tankers 'bomb' the fire with up to 4400 gallons (20,000 litres) of water and chemicals. One way of getting firefighters to the scene is by parachuting them in.

'Smoke-jumping', as the technique is called, is particularly useful in remote and rugged areas of the USA, where pine forests offer no great threat to parachutists.

American firefighters have been jumping into blazes since 1941. Now, the several hundred smoke-jumpers – there are 360 in the Pacific north-west alone – are the heroes of firefighting units in the mid-West and West.

Zooming down on their parachutes, they aim to isolate small fires before they spread. With fire raging below, air currents are chaotic, visibility is poor, and risks are high. In 1949, in Mann Gulch, near Helena, Montana, 13 smoke-jumpers died when a fire suddenly changed direction, driven by the change of wind.

Once safely down, smoke-jumpers clear a path around the fire and fell dead trees, aiming to contain the blaze until it burns out or ground crews arrive.

Increasingly, firefighters appreciate that fire is not always an enemy. Fires caused by lightning are natural events that are vital to forest ecology, providing space for new species or protection for established ones. Forest giants like sequoias depend on regular small-scale fires to preserve an open area around them. Preventing all fires only encourages easily combustible spruces and firs to grow up beneath the sequoias, guaranteeing their destruction when fire eventually strikes.

In 1968, the US Parks Service began controlled blazes, both to imitate nature and to avoid larger, uncontrolled fires later. Sometimes, they allow naturally occurring fires to take their course, fighting back only to preserve lives, stock and property. Firefighters recognise that there is a limit to what they can do, as shown by the fires that swept South Australia and Victoria on Ash Wednesday, February 16, 1983.

For days, temperatures had been 104°F (40°C), and the countryside was tinder-dry. That afternoon, fires broke out 45 miles (72km) north-west of Melbourne, and near Adelaide, 400 miles (660km) to the west. Within two hours, there were 20 major fires in a 600 mile (960km) arc, whipped by 70mph (112km) winds that tossed tussocks of burning grass through the air like tumbleweed and sucked the walls out of houses. Some 21,500 volunteers fought the blazes, with 800 fire trucks and some 200 bulldozers to clear firebreaks. Flames 120ft (36m) high swept

Bush firefighter *A volunteer fireman helps tackle a bushfire in the Grose Valley, New South Wales, in 1968. The heat is so intense that the water from the hose evaporates without having any effect on the flames.*

across the states, driven by oven-hot winds.

By the time the fires died down ten days later, they had destroyed almost 1 million acres (400,000 hectares) and 280,000 head of stock, caused $450 million worth of damage and killed 74 people. In these conditions, there is little anyone can do. Victoria's Fire Brigade captain, Graham Simpson, commented that a major bushfire is 'a cataclysm creating its own wind and weather, a demon with a mind of its own'.

Road traffic: how cities battle to keep control

After almost a century of improvement in the speed of cars, in roads and in traffic control, it takes as long to cross central London now as it did in 1900. Then, the average speed of horse-drawn carriages was 8mph (13km/h). In 1988, cars could move no faster.

London is not alone. The traffic in Lagos, Nigeria, was also travelling at 8mph in 1988; in Copenhagen it was 9mph; in New York and Brisbane 9.9mph; in Paris 10.5mph and Stockholm 11.2mph.

The problem is the weight of traffic, which locks cities into a vicious circle: more traffic inspires better roads and better control systems, which in turn encourage more traffic.

The result is anguish and wastage. London's stationary and slow-moving vehicles waste an estimated £1500 million a year. In Houston, Texas, traffic jams cost each resident $800 a year in time, fuel and other costs. In New York and other cities with streets built in grids, a rush-hour jam has on occasion produced 'gridlock', with traffic in whole areas totally unable to move for hours.

The beginnings of control

Throughout history, cities have tinkered with ideas to keep the traffic flowing. In the 1st century BC, Julius Caesar banned chariots from Rome during the daytime.

The greatest advance in modern times has been traffic lights, introduced in Cleveland, Ohio, in 1914. Soon after their introduction, groups of lights were synchronised to improve flow. The length of time they stayed green could also be controlled by the number of cars passing over control pads.

Computerised systems introduced in the 1960s could cope with traffic in a whole section of a city.

Most cities experiment with other ways of easing the flow, for instance by tightening up on no-parking penalties, encour-

Crush hour *Horse-drawn buses, brewers' drays, coaches, a hearse and a flock of sheep jam London's Fleet Street and Ludgate Hill in this illustration by the 19th-century engraver Gustave Doré.*

Traffic jam *Lacking any apparent order, traffic blocks a street in the commercial city of Medan, North Sumatra. In frustration, some drivers step out and take the air.*

Traffic flow *Keeping to their lanes, vehicles travel nose-to-tail in the rush hour over San Francisco's Oakland Bridge.*

aging vehicle sharing, and introducing bus lanes in streets.

All such measures, however, have proved to be mere stopgaps in the face of the steady growth of traffic. When Venezuela insisted in 1983 that cars in Caracas could only be driven on certain weekdays – according to the last digit on the number plate – thousands of people simply bought second cars. The jams remained, further hindered by masses of parked cars.

When drivers in Singapore were charged a high fee for entering the city at peak time unless they had two passengers, crowds of children offered themselves as 'passengers' for a few cents.

In 1987 the world contained more than 500 million working motor vehicles, and more than 40 million were being added to the total each year.

The only possible answer for cities, it seems, lies in ever more complex computerisation, which allows controllers to guide traffic as if it were water, using lights like sluice gates.

At the push of a button, lights can direct traffic away from an accident, roadworks, or a crowd pouring out of a football ground after a match.

Every city has its own problems. In Manhattan the complexities are forbidding. The time of day, the local business, the width of street, the weather, the time of year – all these variables affect each district,

and all districts affect all the others. The whole seething mass is additionally complicated by the need for traffic to cross the encircling rivers, squeezing over bridges and through tunnels.

In an attempt to cope, computers receive information from major intersections, where sensors beneath the surface monitor the speed and volume of traffic. Results can be dramatic – in New York's outer boroughs computerisation has reduced the number of stops made by each vehicle by 70 per cent.

In all of this, the individual driver, like a molecule of water, is passive. The real revolution in traffic control lies in in-vehicle navigation.

HOW DRIVERS AVOID THE JAMS WITH AN IN-CAR COMPUTER

1. *Testing an electronic guidance system in Berlin in 1988, drivers entered their destinations on a key pad at the start of a journey. Regular destinations could be entered with just one or two key strokes.*

2. *Each driver's destination was fed by an infrared transceiver in the car to the nearest beacon at one of 240 intersections in the city. From the beacon the information went to a computerised control centre.*

3. *Next, the control centre sent instructions for the quickest, jam-free route to the individual beacons. And the beacon beamed an electronic route map to the driver via the in-car transceiver.*

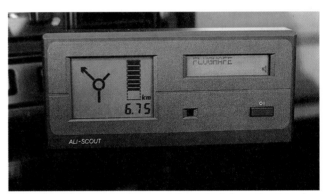

4. *Finally, the in-car computer translated the information into clear and simple advice on the car's display unit. Arrows showed the best route to take, plus the distance to the destination.*

The car would have its own computer, containing detailed maps and capable of receiving a steady stream of information about the state of the roads nationwide. The driver keys in the grid reference of a destination, and sets off. Almost at once, the car passes a roadside beacon, from which the computer links itself with a central bank of information on conditions ahead. It then begins to issue instructions, indicating by an arrow on a dashboard display which way the driver should turn for the fastest route to the destination. In experiments in Berlin and London, the computer also gives verbal instructions and warnings of fog, roadworks, lane changes and diversions in a synthesised voice.

The technology to introduce such a system already exists. In each car, the equipment would cost about the same as a car phone. A major problem, however, would be the installation of the thousands of beacons over an entire country.

Central control *An officer at the traffic control centre in Paris keeps a watchful eye on various streets and locations as snarl-ups start to occur. On average, vehicles can cross Paris at no more than 10.5mph (17km/h) – and the use of computer monitoring helps to pinpoint trouble spots.*

The case of Angela Jenkins: road accident victim

'Hello, ITU here. Can we help you?' Senior Sister Mary Reynolds is taking the first telephone call of the day in the Intensive Therapy Unit.

The answer is 'yes'. There has been a serious road accident on a highway near the hospital – the Luton and Dunstable, on the outskirts of Luton, in Bedfordshire – and medical help is urgently needed.

Three people – a taxi driver, his young woman passenger and a motorcyclist – have been injured in a pile-up with an articulated lorry on the M1, one of the busiest stretches of motorway in the world.

It is dawn on a grey, misty November morning and an ambulance, its siren blaring, is speeding the victims to the hospital – which is typical of any large general hospital throughout the world near such a highway.

If lives are to be saved, the first hour after the accident is all-important. And to those in the ambulance, it is clear that the girl – a 20-year-old secretary named Angela Jenkins, who had been on her way to Luton Airport – is the most seriously hurt. She is barely conscious, has extreme difficulty in breathing, is bleeding at the chest and appears to have grave internal injuries.

On arriving at the hospital Angela is hurried into the Accident and Emergency department, where dressings are applied to superficial cuts and X-rays show she has fractured ribs and a fractured pelvis. Her injuries have caused tissue fluid to leak from her circulatory system and gather in her lungs – and she is immediately taken up to the ITU on the second floor.

A wheeled, adjustable bed is ready for her in the open-plan ward with its soothing, pink walls. Once in bed, an equipment-bearing emergency trolley is brought in and she is surrounded by sisters and staff nurses in their 'theatre blues' – pale blue smocks and trouser suits – and white-coated doctors.

Because of her broken ribs, Angela finds it too painful to breathe. So a narrow plastic tube is passed through her mouth, down her windpipe, and attached to a ventilator. This, in effect, does her breathing for her, intermittently blowing a mixture of air and oxygen into her lungs.

24-hour supervision

Before long, a battery of life-supporting tubes and wires has been attached to the upper part of Angela's body. They include an electrocardiograph, which gives continuous information on her heart rate and rhythm; a drip-feed running into a vein in her neck, which replaces lost fluid – including blood – at a set rate; and a small tube inserted into an artery at her wrist, which monitors her blood pressure. As long as Angela remains in the ward, she will be closely observed and supervised every minute of the day and night.

Her breathing, blood pressure and pulse rate will be regularly monitored and the information recorded at the nursing bay – an L-shaped desk-cum-control-centre facing the ward's three main beds. The nurse assigned to Angela rarely leaves the bedside and notes any changes in her condition. If necessary, the nurse will call for advice and help – which will come immediately.

Like workers in a well-laid-out and highly organised kitchen, the nurses know exactly where each utensil and piece of equipment is kept. Nothing is more than a few steps away – from boxes of single-use body sponges to defibrillators, machines which give carefully measured electric shocks to the heart in order to restore it to a regular beat.

A closed and caring world *Once a gravely ill patient enters an Intensive Therapy Unit he will be closely monitored around the clock. The nurses assigned to him seldom leave his bedside – and constantly check the battery of wires and life-support tubes that are attached to him. A hospital's ITU is a closed world run by a multi-talented team of nurses, doctors, surgeons, biochemists and anaesthetists.*

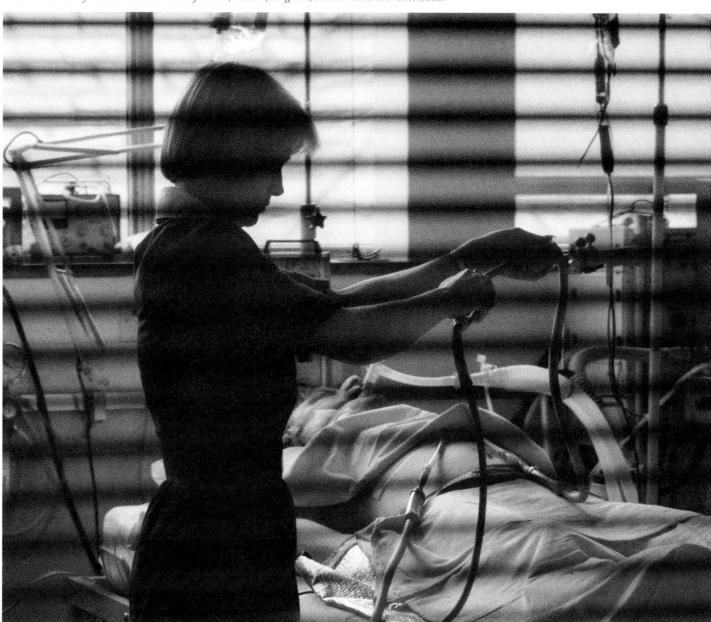

Now that Angela's breathing has been stabilised, the next stage in her treatment goes ahead. A fine tube is passed through her nose and down into her stomach to drain off the accumulated gastric fluids – the tube is left in place for as long as it is needed. A suction tube is then periodically inserted through her 'breathing tube' to draw off phlegm from the lungs.

Meanwhile, the ITU's morning routine gets under way. At a quarter to eight the doctors make a formal ward round, checking the condition of the patients. They leave, and there is constant bustle and noise: the hum of machinery, the bleeping of telephones and the high-spirited chatter of the nursing staff.

Although the patients there are on the brink – and have to be hauled back from it – the atmosphere is light and cheerful. It has to be, say the nurses, otherwise the work could gradually get them down. At half-past eight the physiotherapist arrives for the first of her two daily sessions with the other patients: Tom Patterson, a local government officer in his mid-forties with a ruptured spleen and other internal injuries, the result of a bad fall; and Muriel Barnes, a white-haired grandmother who is recovering from a major stomach operation the day before.

To remove phlegm from the chest, the physio encourages the patients to breathe deeply and cough. To prevent muscles wasting and joints stiffening, she helps the patients to move their limbs.

Tom – who so far has spent five days in intensive care – is turned onto his side.

'We're just rolling you over now, Tom, to treat your chest,' explains the physio. 'It won't take long – then we'll make you comfortable again.'

Birds and rainbows

Above the beds, turning lazily in the centrally heated air, are multicoloured mobiles of birds and rainbows. For much of the time, they are all that the wired-up, stretched-out patients can see.

At nine o'clock each patient's ventilator tubing is changed to prevent infection building up in the equipment; and at nine-thirty a surgeon comes in to speak to Muriel. 'Your operation went very well, dear,' he tells her genially. 'We're very pleased with you.'

Ten o'clock shows on the ward's electric wall clocks. A mobile X-ray machine is plugged in, and a radiographer takes X-rays of all three patients. Again, everything that is happening is explained.

'Just to see if there's been any change in your insides,' says the radiographer, moving smoothly from one bed to the other.

Half an hour goes by and the nurses take turns to have some tea and toast in the adjacent staff room, with its easy chairs and colour television – the gift of a grateful

former patient. Meals – coffee and sandwiches, mainly – are also taken there. The hospital canteen is one floor down, and the duty staff cannot afford to be that far away – in time and distance – from their charges.

At eleven o'clock the hospital chaplain looks in. He is one of three ministers – Church of England, Free Church and Roman Catholic – who are always on call. Although his main concern is with the patients, it is sometimes the nurses themselves who are most in need of his counselling.

'Whenever a patient dies, it's a terrible blow to us,' says Sister Reynolds. 'Especially if it's a child. We need to talk it over with someone who knows and understands our problems, but who isn't really one of us. That's where the chaplain comes in. He's sympathetic and gives us the kind of moral and spiritual support we need now and again.'

Shortly before noon, Angela's parents arrive from their home in London and are shown into the relatives' room. This faces the office of the consultant anaesthetist – an expert in resuscitation and life-support techniques – who is in overall charge.

The relatives' room has a warm, homely feel to it. It contains a pair of armchairs, two let-down beds in case a relative or close friend wants to spend the night, and some tea-making equipment.

Ruby – the unit's jovial domestic – suddenly puts her head through the swing doors leading to the ward. 'Sister,' she calls out. 'Angela's parents are here!'

Out of danger

Sister Reynolds hurries off to tell Mr and Mrs Jenkins that their daughter is now fully conscious and, as long as she remains stable, she will be out of danger. Angela's broken pelvis and ribs, adds the sister, will mend in time. But mainly she prepares them for the shock of seeing Angela festooned with pipes and wires that make her seem even more sick and helpless than she is.

Pale faced and apprehensive, Angela's parents are led into the ward and up to her bed. They spend the next hour sitting beside her and telling her about the family, the weather, their journey by car from London and how she is in the best of hands and receiving the very best of care.

Unable to speak because of the ventilator, Angela opens her eyes every now and again, letting them know she is conscious and taking in what they are saying. Finally there is nothing left to talk about, and Mr and Mrs Jenkins rise to leave. 'We'll come back and see you again tomorrow, darling,' Mrs Jenkins murmurs. 'You should be well on the road to recovery by then.'

At one o'clock Sister Reynolds and her team of nurses are relieved for lunch by the afternoon shift of a sister and three nurses.

For the next eight hours the patients are in their care.

Unless there are any further admissions – from another ward, another hospital, or operating theatre – the unit can expect to have an uneventful, but busy, afternoon. Only the clamorous alarm if a life-support system drops dangerously low may disturb the hours until the night shift arrives.

Potent cocktail

If all continues to go well, Angela Jenkins will be transferred to a general ward about a week after entering intensive care. Like nearly all ITU patients she will remember little, if anything, of her time there. Shock and the potent cocktail of painkilling drugs and sedatives that has been given to her, will see to that.

A few years ago – before ITUs were introduced throughout the world – Angela might well have died without the minute-by-minute observation, attention and treatment she has received.

It is nearing six o'clock and the consultant anaesthetist makes his last round of the day – seeing that all is well and that he can safely go home. Meanwhile, a radio by one of the patient's beds is softly playing pop music. The sisters and nurses hope it will be a quiet night and that they can concentrate on the patients already there. Then, abruptly, the desk phone bleeps again.

'Hello,' says the sister in charge, quickly picking it up. 'ITU here. Can we help you?'

How aerial photographs are used to make maps

Modern map-makers rely on a method that was used by some of the earliest cartographers. They go to a high place to get a picture of the terrain. In bygone centuries the cartographer would climb to the top of a hill, carrying instruments and drawing equipment with him, whereas today photographers go aloft in an aeroplane.

The first aerial photographs for mapping were taken in 1851 by a Frenchman, Aimé Laussedat, who floated across the French countryside in a hot-air balloon. Photographs taken from military aircraft were used to map the trenches during the First World War.

For aerial surveying, the aeroplane flies at a height dictated by the scale of photograph needed for the map. If the scale is to be 1:50,000 and the camera has a focal length of 6in (150mm), the flying height

would have to be 25,000ft (7500m).

The photographs are taken vertically downwards as the plane flies in strips back and forth across the land to be mapped. Each photograph overlaps the previous one by about 60 per cent, and the adjacent strips overlap by about 30 per cent. This ensures that all parts of the ground are photographed at least twice. An aeroplane flying at 25,000ft would need to take at least 12,700 photographs to cover an area the size of France.

Pairs of adjoining photographs are viewed through an instrument called a stereo-plotter which reveals a single three-dimensional image of the ground. This image is adjusted to fit a network of points whose exact position on the ground is known. The stereo-plotter can then be operated to measure, record and plot the position and height of all map details at the required scale.

The fixed points might have been established by surveyors for earlier surveys or created specially for the purpose. These points – like every other spot on Earth – have a latitude (the distance north or south of the Equator) and a longitude (the distance east or west of the Greenwich meridian).

To 'capture' the ground detail, the stereo-plotter operator guides a spot of light over each feature in the photograph, automatically recording the information as digital data on magnetic tape. The 'captured' map detail can be simultaneously displayed on a video screen or plotter for verification.

The taped information is then fed into a computer, together with other requirements such as the area to be covered by the map, the style of the map and its scale. Drawing machines run by the computer can produce both preliminary maps for checking and finished maps for printing.

All the information that has been gathered and analysed must eventually be turned into a map designed for a particular purpose, such as a road map for motorists or a land-use map showing urban areas, farmland, woodlands and marshes.

The area to be included in the map may be at a very large scale (covering only a small area of ground). The landscape will then be shown in great detail, including individual buildings and ponds. Maps like this are used by town planners to set out new roads, for example.

To produce a map at a smaller scale (and so show a greater area), the cartographer reduces several of the large-scale maps into one. But as the scale becomes smaller the amount of detail has to be reduced and

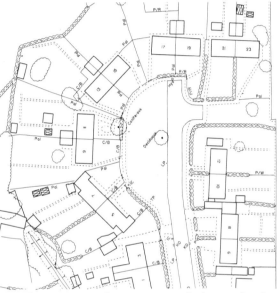

Aerial view, ground map *An aerial photograph taken vertically downwards (top) of a cul-de-sac of houses and gardens was used to produce a detailed map of the area (bottom).*

symbols have to be used. For example, a village or small town which started as a collection of individual buildings is amalgamated into a single shape.

As the scale gets smaller still, villages are omitted altogether and the towns are shown as dots or squares. Finally, on maps of whole continents or the world, only major cities can be included, marked by a spot.

The height of the land is usually shown by contour lines, which are lines joining points of equal heights. The closer together the lines (labelled in feet or metres) the steeper the slope. The contour lines may be combined with colours – called contour layer tinting – to illustrate the range from sea level (usually green) to high mountains (usually brown or purple). Hill-shading, which makes hills stand out from valleys, gives the map a 3-D effect. It may supplement layer tinting, or can be used alone.

A major problem which a cartographer must solve is how to represent the curved surface of the Earth on a map which is flat.

To do this without some distortion is impossible, like trying to flatten half a tennis ball without splitting it.

The answer is to use one of the many mathematically devised map projections. These arrange the latitude and longitude lines and other details to minimise the distortion for a particular purpose. This will always be at the expense of accuracy in some less important respects. For example, the familiar Mercator's Projection is used to plot straight navigation courses, but they distort scale so that countries far away from the Equator, such as Greenland, look much larger than they are.

A projection designed to show countries as close as possible to their correct relative sizes and positions will distort distances and be unusable for navigation.

The carefully designed map is then drawn, either by draughtsmen or, increasingly, by computers. Hand-drawn maps are done on layers of film, each one showing different features such as roads, rivers, contours and areas of colour. There may be 20 or more layers which are put together and combined photographically to produce a film for each of the four or six colours that are used to print most maps. Some computer-drawn maps eliminate the need for this complicated process, and produce the printing film directly.

Some computer-generated maps are never printed at all, but are sent electronically to computer screens in aeroplanes or ships for navigation.

Maps in the future may bypass the present system of aerial photography, ground surveys and conventional printing. Satellites, orbiting the planet, may beam images directly to computers, which would print out maps or send them as electronic signals to screens in planes, ships, or cars.

The scale of a map

One of the most important factors in map-making and map-reading is the scale. A motoring map might be at a scale of 1:250,000, meaning that every unit (inch, millimetre or centimetre) on the map represents 250,000 of those units on the ground. So the scale of the map could also be expressed as '1in represents 4 miles' or '1cm represents 2.5 kilometres'. A map of the world in an atlas might be at a scale of 1:60,000,000 (1in to 947 miles, or 1cm to 600 kilometres).

Maps at different scales are used for different purposes. It would be impossible to plan a motoring route from a world map scale, but a world map at 1:200,000 would be enormous – about 220yds (200m) wide.

How the mail travels across the world

The postal services of the world combine to make a planet-sized brain of stupendous complexity. Most of the world's 4000 million people could if they wished communicate with almost anyone else by post within a few days.

The quantity of mail handled by the world's 654,000 post offices is staggering. On any one day, almost 1000 million items pass through the international postal system.

To shift a letter physically (rather than communicating its contents electronically) is a slow-motion, labour-intensive operation that is a constant challenge to the millions who work for the 169 member-states of the World Postal Union.

From Peace River to Nice

Every item posted becomes part of this epic business. Imagine, for instance, that Pierre, a young French engineer newly assigned to Peace River, Alberta, in Canada, writes a letter to his grandmother who lives near Nice in the south of France.

In Peace River, a town of about 6300 people at the head of a broad valley rich in oil and natural gas, Pierre posts his letter on Monday morning, giving news of his safe arrival to do geological research.

After collection that afternoon, the letter joins a few thousand others in the local post office. The postal workers separate the local mail from letters going to other parts of Canada. They also sort international letters into two bundles, one for shipment west across the Pacific, the other for all points east, including Europe. By evening the bundles, minus Peace River's local mail, are travelling by truck 100 miles (160km) south-west to the larger town of Grande Prairie.

Here, the two international bundles join other similar bundles from nearby towns. Next morning, Tuesday, a second truck-ride carries the mail 300 miles (480km) south-east to the provincial capital, Edmonton. The size of the two international consignments increases again, before they are taken from Edmonton post office to the airport.

At this point, the two batches go separate ways – the transpacific bags flying west to Vancouver and the others east to Toronto, where they arrive late on Tuesday.

In Toronto, the letters are sorted by country, and in some cases by area within a country. The process takes most of Wednesday and Thursday, and Pierre's letter joins the 730lb (330kg) pile of mail destined for France.

On Thursday evening, an international flight leaves Toronto carrying the letter to Charles de Gaulle Airport in Paris, where it arrives early on Friday morning. The letter is now on the fifth day of its journey.

Letters from Canada are dispatched from the airport to Paris, where they merge with the 50 million objects handled daily by the country's highly mechanised system. The postcode for Pierre's grandmother's house is read by a coding machine which adds a bar code indicating where the letter will finally be distributed from. The machine deals with 40,000 letters an hour.

A second machine sorts the letters into bundles corresponding to the départements – the French equivalent of counties or states. A conveyor belt carries them from the machine to bags, which are carried by more conveyor belts to the trucks and trains which, along with planes, fan out across the country with their daily 3000 tons of mail. The post office uses an Airbus to carry mail to Marseilles and Nice, and Pierre's letter is aboard the Friday afternoon flight.

Overnight in Nice, the same collecting and sorting operation is carried out, but in reverse. The sorting depot divides the mail into sub-zones for local distribution. Early on Saturday morning, a van carries the mail from the sorting depot to the post office.

The post office puts Pierre's letter into one of the nation's 70,000 postal rounds, and his grandmother reads his news over her morning coffee on the sixth day of its journey from Peace River.

That, at least, is how it would work in an ideal world. Inevitably, there are complications. Like weekends and holidays. And ton upon ton of ungainly parcels and illegible envelopes. And strikes. And breakdowns. And Christmas rushes. Though such factors often combine to force delays, every delivery is a minor tribute to human ingenuity and cooperation.

How a worldwide courier service is organised

It is 5pm on Thursday afternoon in a busy engineering office in central Frankfurt, West Germany. Staff are frantically preparing specifications for a new diamond-cutting tool they have developed, a prototype of which is packed for delivery to Quito, Ecuador. The prototype must be delivered in time for a meeting with an Ecuadorian government minister early on Tuesday morning, while the 100-page specification document has to be with a manager in the New Orleans head office by Friday.

An international air courier service has been contracted to ensure delivery of both items. The call to their local office was made at 4.30, and the courier is at the engineers' office with a van to make the collection half an hour later. A computer link in the van indicates the best route for the driver.

The courier collects the large envelope containing the specifications and the parcel containing the diamond cutter. He sprints to his van, and drives to his company's sorting office near Frankfurt International Airport. There a laser scanner reads the envelope and the package, automatically logging their details into a central computer so that the progress can be monitored electronically. The same information is used to prepare export and import documentation, and an invoice for the engineering firm.

A conveyor belt guides the parcel into a bag marked 'South America' and the envelope into the US bag. Each bag will be placed on the first available flight out of Frankfurt, either on a scheduled airliner or on one of the courier's own aircraft. In this case, both bags are put on the evening flight to New York's Kennedy Airport, arriving early on Friday morning.

Someone in the courier's New York office puts the US bag on a flight to their main sorting office, where the envelope is placed in a bag for New Orleans and sent on the next connecting flight. It arrives and is delivered by hand on Friday afternoon.

Meanwhile, the South America bag is re-sorted in New York, and the parcel for Quito is placed on an afternoon flight that lands first in Bogota, Colombia, then in Guayaquil, a large port in Ecuador, and finally arrives in Quito on Friday night.

The customs office in Quito is closed until Monday, but the courier's representative there knows the customs' requirements and is able to prepare the correct documents and clear the parcel first thing on Monday morning. A van then delivers it to its destination by lunch time.

International courier services were started in the late 1960s because businesses everywhere were faced with a serious problem. It was possible to send a member of staff almost anywhere in the world by aeroplane within 24 hours, and businesses wanted to ensure the same efficiency when sending important letters and packages.

The post is not fast enough because postal systems are concerned with high-volume, low-speed deliveries – letters by the billion, delivered over a period of days or weeks, depending on the efficiency of the postal systems at each end. Air express services, on the other hand, can guarantee rapid delivery by offering a personalised postal system, using their own staff and the latest technology.

Air express companies spend millions of pounds a year on reserving space on scheduled freight and passenger airlines, allowing them to make use of the fastest routes. The large firms keep computerised information on all the world's airline schedules. Many firms now own their own planes and helicopters, and almost all firms own fleets of vans and motorcycles for door-to-door collections and deliveries.

Federal Express, the USA's largest domestic courier, owned 109 aircraft in 1988, and DHL, the largest international courier in terms of number of deliveries, handled 30,000 items every night of the week.

In Europe, most large courier services promise overnight deliveries to European destinations, and aim for deliveries within two days anywhere else in the world. All US air couriers offer same-day and next-day national services.

Many of the items delivered are envelopes or small packets of documents, but manufacturers are increasingly making use of courier services to deliver stock. Another area of competitive growth is 'remailing', in which international mail is air-expressed out of a country and then posted abroad, partially short-circuiting the postal services. This is faster than using the post at both ends, and is particularly valuable if there is a postal strike.

The market for express delivery, which doubled every two or three years in the 1970s, was worth about $4 billion in 1988. Even though the increased use of faxing has cut into the business, it seems likely that express couriers will continue to expand to meet the demands of businesses who must have things delivered in a hurry.

How a paper gets a news report from across the world

It is a red-letter day for South Africa's tennis fans – especially those living in and around Johannesburg. A local boy has reached the final of the Italian men's singles championship in Rome, and his success or failure will be headline news in both countries.

It will probably make the front page of the South African player's morning paper. The editor faces a choice on how to cover the match. He can rely on news-agency reports and pictures; or he can take the trouble to send his own sports reporter and a staff photographer to cover the game at first hand. In view of the keen local interest, he decides to fly out his own team.

The reporter and photographer arrive in Rome in time for a Press conference the day before the match. This enables the reporter to produce a colourful background article about the match and the build-up to it – complete with quotes from the two finalists.

The South African player is a teenager who has yet to win a major championship; his opponent is an older and far more experienced Scandinavian, the current title holder. It is, as the reporter puts it, a classic encounter between 'a young pretender and a reigning king'.

The match is due to start at 2pm Rome time, and could last the whole afternoon. So by South African time, the same as Rome's, the result should be known by about 6pm. The newsmen will have no problem sending their words and pictures within the deadline for their paper's morning edition.

In the Press Box, the reporter can type his copy into his portable word processor. This laptop machine, complete with screen and digital memory, is a remote terminal of the paper's main computer. When his story is complete, the reporter simply attaches the audio coupler, or adapter, to the nearest telephone, keys in the number of his newspaper, and the text is sent along

Two-handed technology *With a telephone in each hand, a journalist uses desktop technology to compile his news story.*

the wires directly into the computer 5500 miles (8850km) away. A 1000-word story is sent in about one minute.

Unexpectedly, the match ends in a brilliant and sensational victory for the young South African player. To add to the set-by-set account already keyed into his laptop machine, the reporter will now interview the winning and losing finalists.

Meanwhile, the photographer has a date with an international news agency whose picture-transmission equipment he needs. He processes his film, then feeds the best negatives into a transmitter. This sends the images along a telephone line – and they promptly emerge as high-quality duplicate negatives from the picture-editor's receiver back in Johannesburg.

After interviewing the tennis stars, the reporter returns to his hotel room and prepares his final copy, rearranging and correcting the text on the laptop-machine's VDU (Visual Display Unit) screen.

Press pack *No big sporting event is without its pack of Press photographers – whose pictures are sent by special transmitter.*

Making the page *Compositors (right) cut up bromides – type on photographic paper – and paste them onto newspaper-size cards.*

Filling and retouching *Any holes found in a newspaper negative after the page has been made up are filled in – or retouched – by using a special black pen (below).*

At 8pm he rings the hotel switchboard for an outside line, and transmits his follow-up story. This gives more background detail and 'colour' than is found in the news-breaking television and radio reports. It also contains speculation about the new champion's future prospects, plus an account of his lifestyle.

Front-page news

At about 9pm the South African sports editor calls up the tennis story on his desktop screen. As agreed earlier at an editorial planning meeting, the story will be the sports-page lead. The startling result ensures there will also be a front-page news item, adapted from the main story, which the news editor can call up on his own screen.

The big story is then checked and corrected by a sub-editor, who adjusts it to make it fit the space allocated on the page by the sports editor. The sub-editor can call up on his screen an image of the whole page as it stands so far, showing all the other stories, headlines and pictures – and advertisements, if any – that have already been processed.

Once the picture and sports editors have chosen the photograph that will illustrate the story, the sub-editor knows exactly what space there is. The copy is now finally edited, on screen, to fit the space, and a suitably dramatic headline written to fit the story and the space available. The sub-editor also keys in the picture caption. It is almost 10pm, by which time all copy for the first edition must be set in type.

The Rome story lines up with all the other copy for conversion into type by a high-speed phototypesetting machine. The 1000-word article is typeset in less than 30 seconds.

The typesetter produces a 'bromide' – a print of the type on photographic paper – for positioning on the page according to the approved layout.

Although pages can be made up by using the computer, most newspapers still prefer physically to cut up the bromides and paste them in position on a page-size card – a rapid process when carried out by a skilled compositor. The sub-editor checks that all the stories fit the allocated space, and that no errors have crept in before or during typesetting.

With all the text, headlines, pictures and between-column rules in position, the complete page is photographed to produce, in minutes, a film negative. This is a large black-and-white film, from which the printing plates for the presses are made.

First of all, photostatted 'proofs', or sample pages, are made for approval by the sports editor and the editor. Once the pages have been approved and checked by the proofreaders, they are taken to the printing department.

By midnight in South Africa, all the pages are ready to be photographically transferred to plastic-coated zinc or aluminium printing plates. In turn, the plates pick up the page images in ink and transfer them to the paper.

Speed, as at every stage of the process, is crucial, for the papers must be on time for the 80 or so lorries that will distribute them to sales points such as small general dealers and street corners throughout an area of some 100,000sq miles (259,000sq km).

The nearer the wholesalers are to the printing centre, the later are the editions they receive. Those later editions will often look radically different as fresh news stories break, claiming space on the front page. Some page-one stories are therefore relegated to relative obscurity on a revised inside page.

Satisfied reader

So, as he drinks his breakfast coffee, the Johannesburg sports fan avidly reads the account of the local boy's triumph. The sports reporter, meanwhile, is just waking up in Rome. For him, it is all just yesterday's news.

Writing a dictionary: a job that can last a lifetime

When Samuel Johnson wrote his influential English dictionary in the 18th century, the work took him seven years. In that time he had to write the meanings of 40,000 words.

The original *Oxford English Dictionary,* completed in 1928, took 50 years for its 12 volumes and 252,259 entries.

And in Germany, the 16-volume *Deutsches Wörterbuch,* begun by the Grimm brothers in 1838 and intended to cover the German language from the 15th century to the middle of the 19th, was not completed until 1961 – 123 years and two world wars later.

Most dictionaries require rather less time and effort, both because they are smaller and because their compilers can use earlier dictionaries as a source of information. A new edition of an already successful 'desk dictionary' can take about two years. And a small, specialised dictionary – perhaps a dictionary of abbreviations or a pocket crossword dictionary – could be written by only one person.

To write a dictionary, the lexicographer (dictionary writer) needs three things: an idea of what sort of dictionary he wants, a style guide to convert the idea into practice, and evidence about which items to include and what to say about them.

First the idea

The dictionary may contain words of all types, or only specialised words (as in a dictionary of chemistry). It may, or may not, include the names of real people and places. It may give many kinds of information about each of its entries (spelling, pronunciation, etymology, meaning, grammatical behaviour, synonyms and antonyms), or only some kinds of information (spelling and pronunciation only, as in a dictionary of pronunciation).

It may, or may not, have pictures and examples of how the words are used. It may be monolingual (with the meanings of English words given in English) or bilingual (with the meanings of English words given in French, say, and those of French words given in English).

It may be for adults or children. It may

be large or small, with its size depending on the number of entries and the amount of information given about them.

The style guide

Once the purpose of the dictionary has been decided, rules for writing it have to be drawn up. When is a word to be a main entry or a sub-entry? Will *blackbird,* for example, be a main entry (like *black* and *bird*), or a sub-entry under *black,* or a sub-entry under *bird*?

Kick the bucket will probably be a sub-entry – but will it go under *kick* or under *bucket*? Will *limp* (*verb* 'to walk lamely'), *limp* (*noun* 'a lame walk') and *limp* (*adjective* 'not stiff') all be in one entry (because they all have the same spelling)? Will there be two entries (because two of them have the same basic meaning but the third a different meaning and perhaps a different etymological origin)? Or will there be three entries (because one is a verb, one a noun and one an adjective)?

And if a word appears more than once as a main entry, which order will the entries come in: older before newer, more frequent before less frequent or even adjective before noun before verb?

Or, if a word has more than one meaning, which order will the meanings come in: older before newer, more frequent before less frequent, literal before figurative or general before technical?

The evidence

The starting point for deciding what to include is the lexicographer's own knowledge of, and feeling for, the language. Ideally, too, he will have a large collection of examples of how words and phrases are actually used, culled from published writing and perhaps from manuscripts or even from recorded speech. This 'corpus' should represent as wide a range of language as the lexicographer wants to describe. Both humorous magazines and scholarly works might be examined. *Webster's Third New International Dictionary* of 1961 had a corpus of more than 10 million examples; the original *Oxford English Dictionary* had 5 million.

A computer concordance may be made of every example of every word in the texts chosen for investigation. This would help to ensure that important uses of words are not missed simply because they are too commonplace to attract the lexicographer's attention.

The lexicographer will refer to other dictionaries and books, and articles about language. He may also consult experts for information about specialist words, and ordinary people about their preferences and reactions to how words are used.

But he will have to interpret all this evidence carefully. If someone writes about 'wearing what we used to call a "frock"', that suggests that *frock* is an old-fashioned word. But before labelling it *old-fashioned* or *obsolescent* in the dictionary, the lexicographer must check the evidence for how widely *frock* is still used – and by whom. Is it used unselfconsciously by people under 50? Is it used about modern fashions?

Organising the project

Although it is possible for one person to write a dictionary, most are team efforts.

Members of the team assemble the evidence. Samuel Johnson employed six people to collect quotations for his dictionary. The *Oxford English Dictionary* needed scores, many of whom gave their services free of charge out of love for the work they were doing – and for the English language.

Lexicographers lucky enough to have quotations will use the quotations in writing the entries. And they must coordinate their work so that, for instance, the entries for *anabolism, catabolism* and *metabolism* will relate to one another even though they begin with different letters of the alphabet.

A single entry may be the work of a single lexicographer, but it is more likely to be the work of several specialists: one or more for meaning, another for pronunciation, a third for etymology (the origin and evolution of the word or phrase).

Supplementary material, such as pictures or charts, may be prepared by other specialists. Everything must be checked for accuracy, clarity and consistency.

Today much of the drudgery can be handled by computers. They can process great quantities of evidence, ease revision (as by printing out lists of items previously flagged for potential deletion to make room for new words and meanings), and ensure consistency of treatment (but not accuracy or clarity).

Writing the dictionary

In a normal alphabetical dictionary, related words like *at, in* and *on,* or *disinterested* and *uninterested* may be widely separated. But the entries can be written at the same time to ensure that the meanings have been correctly contrasted and that they cross-refer to each other.

A general-purpose dictionary will include new words (like *AIDS*) and new meanings of older words (like *alien* meaning 'extraterrestrial'). But it should not overlook older words (like *parlourmaid*) that other dictionaries may have missed.

Some technical terms may be easier to explain than many everyday words. It is easier, for example, to distinguish a *stalactite* (which points down) from a *stalagmite* (which points up) than a *cup* from a *mug.* And having done his best with *cup* and *mug,* the lexicographer may then wonder why a certain drinking vessel is called a *paper cup* rather than a *paper mug,* and be forced to the conclusion that *paper cup* should be a dictionary entry, too.

In writing definitions the lexicographer will try to strike a balance between clarity and informativeness. If a *shrimp* is called 'a ten-legged creature', everyone will understand. If it is called 'a decapod', many readers will have to look up *decapod*. But if they do so, they will find more useful information, including the fact that shrimps are related to lobsters and crabs, which are decapods, too.

One compromise is to call a shrimp 'a decapod (ten-legged) creature'. But that requires extra space, which can add up over the whole dictionary, and may reduce the number of entries that can be included.

Considerations of space as well as of the users of the dictionary will also have to be balanced in deciding how much information to include. Should the definition of *water* include its chemical formula (H_2O) and its sea-level freezing and boiling points?

Importance of dictionaries

Despite all the problems, the lexicographer can be comforted by the knowledge that dictionaries are among the most important tools of self-education. They are a kind of embodied memory of the culture in which they are produced, and also a means of gaining access to that culture – even without an official teacher.

Some years ago in Britain, a woman who had been injured by a surgical operation decided to sue for compensation. Before doing so, she prepared herself by spending six months reading medical dictionaries so as not to be mystified by the medical terminology that would be used in court.

She won her case.

How they feed and supply an army at war

From January to May 1942, 5500 German troops were isolated near the town of Kholm, between Moscow and Leningrad, cut off by the Russian Army. It was the worst winter for a century. At −22°F (−30°C), the German soldiers, frost-bitten and lice-ridden, huddled in their foxholes in the frozen ground, praying for relief.

Suddenly they heard the distant murmur of engines, which rose to a roar as 20 Junkers Ju-52 transports, escorted by two squadrons of Messerschmitt fighters, swept overhead. The sky filled with scores of parachutes falling with crates of food, ammunition and medical supplies.

For more than three months the air-

Airborne force *On a training exercise, US Army Rangers practise parachuting behind enemy lines, carrying basic supplies.*

drops continued, enabling the beleaguered Germans to hold off the Red Army's repeated assaults. On May 5, German tanks managed to batter their way through to the besieged troops from the west. The Kholm Pocket had survived, thanks to good logistic support.

Logistics – the ability to supply a fighting force with food, ammunition and equipment – has always been an essential element in the art of war. And in modern warfare, successful attack or defence depends more than ever on continuous and rapid re-supply.

A modern heavy division of about 16,000 men and 1000 armoured vehicles engaged in combat will use at least 5000 tons of ammunition and 2700 tons of fuel every day. In Vietnam, by late 1968, the Americans were supplying more than 1,300,000 men, including South Vietnamese and troops of other nations. An average of 760,000 tons of supplies arrived, mainly by sea, each month.

Without this logistic lifeblood, an army dies. Napoleon's adage that 'an army marches on its stomach' is as true now as it ever was. The inability of the Red Army to withstand Hitler's invasion in 1941 was partly due to its inadequate supply system. Front-line troops had to fetch their own supplies from depots in the rear. Stalin ended that system in June 1943.

The Japanese failed to take Imphal and Kohima, on the Indo-Burmese border, in 1944 partly because they did not have the supplies. When the British and Indians advanced, they found starved Japanese corpses with grass in their mouths.

Massive US troop movement

The problems of arranging for new supplies are formidable, as a US military exercise, Reforger 87, showed in September 1987.

The exercise involved the largest movement overseas of US Army forces in peacetime. The 35,000 men of III Armored Corps based at Fort Hood, Texas, were to

be sent to West Germany, as if they were reinforcing their Allied colleagues at the outbreak of a Soviet invasion of Western Europe.

The troops and all their equipment were scattered over 30 American states in active and reserve units. The troops were flown or driven to the US airfields, and then all 35,000 men were flown to airfields in Europe. They were then taken by road and

Combat meals *Honduran infantrymen collect combat meal packs during a joint military exercise with US troops in 1985.*

Tank drop *An 18 ton Sheridan tank is pulled from an American Hercules transport aircraft by giant parachutes. This technique, known as low-altitude parachute extraction, allows heavy loads to be delivered to a battle zone without the aeroplane having to land.*

rail either to depots where they were supplied with NATO equipment, or to ports where they received heavy equipment that had been brought by ship across the Atlantic.

It takes four days longer to carry equipment across the Atlantic by sea in fast merchantmen than by air, so pre-positioned NATO equipment was essential for the first troops.

The Corps then moved to its staging area near Münster and Osnabruck. From there, two days later, each of the two divisions and supporting brigades moved to a tactical assembly area nearby for refuelling and reprovisioning (in war, this would also include new supplies of ammunition). From the time they were called up to the time they were in their fighting positions took no more than a week.

Today's armies are ever more complex, and the need for speed ever increasing. Computers can pass on requests instantaneously. Urgent supplies can be flown in by helicopter or STOL (short-take-off-and-landing) transports. In a future war, supertankers, nuclear-powered merchantmen, cargo submarines and even airships could augment conventional air and sea supplies.

Strategically, though, nothing has changed. However powerful the cutting edge of infantry, armour, artillery and air power may be, once the food, ammunition and fuel runs low, the forward forces are useless. As Marshal Rokossovsky, the famed Soviet tank commander in the Second World War, said: 'It's not the troops' job to think of the rear, but the rear's job to think of the troops.'

Around the clock at a luxury hotel

As 1am nears on a sultry Hong Kong morning, most of the 1000 or so guests of the Hilton hotel have retired. The hotel's seven restaurants and two bars are closed. Shopping arcade, sauna, gymnasium, tennis courts and swimming pool are deserted. Staff in the administrative departments – buying, sales, accounts, personnel – have long since gone off duty.

In the front office, where a staff of up to 75 are busy during the day, only night clerks and a handful of receptionists remain. Lights in public rooms and corridors are dimmed. Yet great hotels never sleep. And the organised frenzy of yesterday merely yields to a brief night of preparation for tomorrow.

So it is at the Hilton, a 25-storey, glass-and-concrete tower perched beneath Victoria Peak. While most of the 1250 staff – from the general manager downwards – take their rest, the 50-odd night workers prepare the hotel for the coming day.

This is the side of hotel life that the guests do not see.

1am-7am: kitchens and cleaners

In the kitchens, where some 3750 meals must be prepared in the next 24 hours, the baking of bread and pastry for breakfast has been under way since midnight. Altogether, almost 550 people work at preparing and serving the hotel's food and drink.

The overnight cleaning team is washing and scouring kitchen equipment and polishing the breakfast silver. Room-service employees are preparing overnight orders, and standing by for the occasional insomniac's call for a headache pill, a glass of Bourbon, or a full, five-course dinner for him and his friends.

In the basement, the engineering team which maintains the hotel's life-support systems – air-conditioning, refrigeration, light and power, hot water – is well into its night shift. Altogether about 180,000 gallons (819,000 litres) of water are used on a peak day. And some 4½ tons of rubbish awaits daily collection.

In the housekeeper's department the last supply baskets containing changes of bed linen and towels for the guest rooms are being filled.

Bell service – the 43-strong network of porters and bellhops – has checked its records of departures and arrivals. Morning newspapers are put out for room deliveries, and notices of the day's events in the hotel are posted in the main lobby.

The floor staff clean the public areas and arrange the rooms needed for early morning functions, such as working breakfasts and business meetings.

7am-9am: action stations

The hotel is wide awake – and so are many of the guests, eager for breakfast and a new day. The kitchen is in full swing. Pastry baked overnight has been set out, and room orders are fulfilled.

In the front office, the tired night clerks give way to the day staff. Check-ins and check-outs are organised, rooms assigned, mail distributed. Bookings are taken, arrival and departure times verified.

Stewards make certain that public rooms have been cleaned properly. Night attendants on the housekeeping staff hand over to their daytime counterparts, and the cleaning and replenishment of the 750 bedrooms begins.

The night engineering shift gives way to the morning shift, with a list of maintenance work to be tackled. The change is marked by adjusting the public-address system from its soft, night-time volume to the level needed to be heard above the noise of the day.

9am-noon: the administrators arrive

As the bustle of early morning departures begins to ebb, and the last leisurely breakfasts are being eaten and cleared, the hotel's backroom administrators start work.

In the buying department, staff start to run a last-minute stock check to ensure they have all the food and drink needed for that day. This includes 3250 eggs, 700lb (316kg) of meat, 145lb (68kg) of fish, 200 bottles of wine, 70 bottles of spirits, 790 bottles and cans of beer, and various other items – including almost 1200 flower arrangements for the various rooms. But for most of their time the staff are planning at least 24 hours ahead.

Accounts clerks take their places behind calculators and computers to scrutinise and control the hotel's finances. Personnel staff prepare for a day that may include hiring or firing, or simply looking after the job welfare of employees.

Sales executives meet to develop strategy and tactics for marketing the hotel and its facilities – not only the overnight accommodation, but its resources for exhibitions, conferences, receptions and banquets. Complementing their work, the five-strong public-relations team develops its themes for keeping the hotel in the public eye.

Meanwhile, the 62 engineers make their daily full inspection of the hotel, carrying out routine maintenance and repair, as well as checking the swimming pool and the equipment in the health club – where a staff of eight looks after the sauna, steam bath and massage facilities. The chief steward puts the final touches to arrangements for the day's special functions – for example, a local firm's lunch.

In the shopping arcade, the 60 or so shops, drugstore and beauty parlour – with its staff of six – are open for business.

Just off the ground-floor lobby the Business Centre has also opened its doors. It can provide secretarial help, cable, facsimile, 24 hour telex, photocopying, worldwide courier services and a business reference library.

Noon-3pm: time for lunch

In the kitchens, the last breakfast remains have been cleared away. Preparations for lunch for some 1500 people are well-advanced, though replenishments for the buffets will be needed at 1pm. In the restaurants, tables are laid and reservations checked. In all, about 200 cooks, waiters and dishwashers will be involved in preparing, serving and clearing-up the meal. Meanwhile, room service prepares trolleys and trays for guests who prefer to eat in their rooms, and organises fresh supplies for fruit baskets in the bedrooms.

At the front office, new guests are being checked in. The 30 bellboys deliver incoming luggage and usher guests to their rooms, opening the doors with computerised security cards rather than the traditional keys, which can be stolen and copied.

3pm-6pm: afternoon tea
As the restaurants and bars empty, guests on the Executive Floors take afternoon tea, housekeepers replenish ice-buckets in the bedrooms, waiters and barmen prepare for evening opening time, and in the kitchen, dinner is well under way.

Once a week, around 3pm, the afternoon shift of engineers tests the fire alarm, the guests' lifts and the public-address system. And by 4pm the 72 bedroom attendants and 14 public-area cleaners will have completed their tidying up.

Meanwhile, front-office clerks check the daily reports from the housekeepers' department – after food and beverages, the second biggest in the hotel, with 217 employees. So any irregularities in the guest rooms are quickly dealt with by the floor staff. The hotel laundry, which washes, among other things, 10,000 towels and 500 shirts a day, gets ready to close.

6pm-8pm: cocktail hour
For most of the administrative staff, the working day ends around six, just as most guests begin to think about cocktails and dinner.

In the bars, the Hilton's 17 security guards discreetly step up their floor patrols. They are on the lookout for bar girls, known or suspected criminals, pickpockets, conmen and crooks who impersonate members of hotel staff.

8pm-midnight: dinner is served
Most of the 1500 guests and visitors dining in the hotel are eating their meals. In the Eagle's Nest restaurant, on the 25th floor, the orchestra is starting its four-hour stint. In the kitchen, food for the next day is already being ordered amid the bustle.

In the front office, clerks prepare registration cards for the next day. By 11pm, they will have drawn up and printed tomorrow's arrivals list.

Midnight: the working night begins
The wind-down from the day has started. It is signalled almost surreptitiously by the engineers, who switch the background music and radios to their quieter night-time level. In the early closing restaurants, tables are being laid for tomorrow's breakfast, as they are in the kitchens.

The hotel gradually adjusts to its small-hours mode as the guests go to bed. Room-service staff collect door-order menus for breakfast. A group of the hotel's 90 accounts staff tots up the previous day's takings of some HK$1.2 million (US$ 154,000). Another night of preparation is under way.

A day in the life of an ocean queen

The early afternoon sun streams down on the port of Southampton as gangs of dockers start to load fresh food and supplies aboard the *Queen Elizabeth 2* – the flagship of the Cunard Line and the only passenger ship to regularly cross the Atlantic. The liner docked at 1pm – and she will set out on the return voyage to New York seven hours later.

There is no time to be lost, and most of the supplies – including fruit and vegetables, tinned and frozen foods, and deep-frozen meat and fish – are carried on conveyor belts up four narrow gangways.

Meanwhile, most of the wines, spirits and soft drinks, packed into metal containers, are lifted gently aboard by crane. And 6000 gallons (27,300 litres) of draught beer are pumped straight from tankers parked at the quayside into huge stainless-steel tanks – which are linked by pipe to the QE2's seven duty-free bars.

The food and drink will suffice for the five-day transatlantic crossing. By 7pm the supplies have been loaded; the cleaners have vacuumed the equivalent of 142 tennis courts of carpeting; the 1000 crew members are at their stations; and most of the 1800 or so passengers have arrived. They are greeted by a jazz band playing popular tunes from the latest hit shows, and are directed to their cabins by almost 80 stewards and stewardesses.

Everything has been arranged for the passengers' enjoyment and comfort – from saunas and Jacuzzis to feature films and a computer centre where they can learn 'new skills', such as how to operate word processors.

Each of the ten passenger decks has its own pantries (combinations of kitchens and storerooms), and these allow the stewards and stewardesses to prepare and serve anything from early morning cups of tea and coffee to elaborate late-night suppers.

Once at sea, the 14 bakers start their long working day in the three main kitchens at 5am and begin to prepare the 3000 or more rolls, croissants and Danish pastries served at breakfast. At the same time, the ship's confectioners make the 6000 pieces of cake needed for afternoon tea and the 5000 petits fours for the evening buffet.

At 7am the first chefs arrive to prepare the ingredients for the day's soups and

stews – amounting to almost 3500 pints (2000 litres). The 75 all-male chefs – including a special kosher cook in his own kitchen – start work on the 2800 lunches and dinners as most of the passengers are finishing breakfast.

The 60 or so young cooks regularly work for up to 12 hours a day in the hot, windowless kitchens. They frequently feel homesick and tired – and occasionally some of them quit on docking at Southampton or New York. For most of them, however, it is a valuable way of gaining work experience and of seeing the world.

Hundreds of food items are kept in the storerooms, and vast meat safes stretch almost the width of the ship – 105ft (32m). Inside, the temperature of 14°F (−10°C) could kill anyone trapped there for more than 12 hours. To avoid any such accident, there is an alarm bell inside each meat safe in case the doors are shut by mistake.

Farther along from the storerooms, the QE2's giant machinery is housed in the engine room – actually several enormous high-ceilinged areas, two decks deep. The nine engines themselves are each the size of a double-decker bus. They generate 130,000hp and can slow the ship down

Ruling the fiords *As well as sailing the Atlantic – the* QE2 *sometimes cruises in the Norwegian fiords.*

Stirring work *In the kitchens, soup-making begins at 7am . . . well in time for lunch.*

Cold plate *In the buffet a chef – flanked by a decorative ice eagle – serves up.*

Curtain call *In their dressing room the cabaret dancers get ready for a show.*

Repair job *In the workshop a carpenter makes a start on repairing a broken bed.*

Planning ahead *On the bridge a navigator charts one of the ship's future cruises.*

from a top speed of 32½ knots (37mph) to standstill in 3 minutes and 39 seconds – over a distance of about 1¼ miles (2km).

The engine room also contains a water-purification plant which takes sea water on board and purifies it for drinking. The plant processes about 480 tons of water a day – enough to fill seven swimming pools the size of those on the ship. In addition, four vacuum evaporators produce 250 tons of water each day. Checking the various water tanks – which are at the very bottom of the vessel – is the responsibility of the ship's carpenters. Some of the tanks are there to help keep the ship properly balanced; others hold the drinking water and water used for washing the laundry.

If, for any reason, more water is used from a tank on one side of the ship than on the other, the vessel will begin to list. To correct this, extra water is quickly pumped into the depleted tank.

In a small room above the engines another team of professionals – the printers – play their role in the daily life of the liner. Late each night a printed programme of the following day's events – ranging from children's parties to clay-pigeon shooting – is delivered to each passenger cabin. Early each morning newsletters are delivered to the cabins containing news from around the world, which is transmitted by satellite to the ship each day.

Nerve centre

The QE2's nerve centre is the bridge, high up on Signal Deck. For security reasons, there is only one staircase leading up to the bridge – and only one entrance door, which can be opened only from the inside. The bridge bristles with the latest navigational equipment, including automatic steering. However, the wheel is still regularly used when there is heavy traffic, or whenever the liner is leaving or entering port. In addition, there is a collision avoidance system, which can show the course, speed and direction of up to 20 ships at a time. There is also a satellite navigator, the first to be fitted to a passenger ship, which is linked to various satellites orbiting the Earth. It plots the QE2's position at intervals of from 35 to 100 minutes. The readings are accurate to within 110yds (100m).

As the ship's control headquarters, the bridge is in close communication with the engine room – by direct-link telephone – and other key areas. To cut errors and misunderstandings to a minimum, important orders are given to the engine room by means of a panel of labelled buttons. So when one of the buttons is pressed on the bridge, the equivalent button in the engine room's main control section lights up – and the engineer knows exactly what is required of him. Even so, the engines can also be controlled directly from the bridge.

The crew includes six girl dancers, and everyone, from the captain downwards, receives a regular check-up. Anyone who is overweight is sent ashore until the excess weight has been shed.

The liner's hospital is situated midships near the water line, where the movement of the 963ft (292m) long ship is hardly noticeable. The hospital is staffed by two doctors, three sisters and three medical attendants, who can deal with anything from dental work to removing an appendix in the fully equipped operating theatre.

As night begins to fall over Southampton the passengers have all boarded the liner – and everything is ready for yet another crossing. So at 8pm the *Queen Elizabeth 2* steams majestically out of port and heads for the Atlantic.

Wining and dining

For the crew, there are busy hours ahead. The waiters – at least two to every nine passengers – get ready to serve dinner in the ship's four restaurants.

The à la carte menu is crammed with delicacies such as smoked salmon, caviar, lobsters and oysters – as well as cordon bleu creations of beef, lamb and poultry. By the time they reach New York the waiters will have served up some 12,500lb (5650kg) of beef, 11,000lb (5000kg) of fresh fruit, 750lb (340kg) of lobster, 50lb (22kg) of pâté de foie gras – and brought in about 4800 jars of jam and marmalade and 100 bottles of sauces and pickles.

In addition, they and the barmen will have uncorked 600 bottles of assorted wines and 500 bottles of champagne – and opened 500 bottles of whisky, 300 bottles of gin and 120 bottles of brandy. In the bars themselves, the staff will have poured 6000 bottles of beer and 3000 gallons (13,650 litres) of draught beer.

Altogether, some 25,000 items of glassware will have been used and washed, as well as 32,000 items of crockery, 18,000 items of cutlery, and almost 3000 tablecloths will have been laundered and laid.

After dinner, the ship's 60 entertainers – musicians, croupiers, dancers and singers – provide the passengers with a wide-ranging choice of amusements.

The night life does not end until dawn – shortly before the first sitting for breakfast, when the waiters are back on duty and the stewards and stewardesses offer the luxury of breakfast served in bed.

Whatever the hour, in whichever part of the ship, there is always work for the crew to perform.

From the bridge – manned around the clock – to the darkroom – where overnight the photographer develops pictures taken at functions such as the Captain's Cocktail Party – the bustle builds up again as another day aboard the world's most regal liner gets under way.

How they put on the world's greatest sporting festival

On the morning of September 6, 1972, Avery Brundage, president of the International Olympic Committee, addressed 75,000 mourners gathered in the Olympic Stadium in Munich. Early the previous day eight Palestinian terrorists had broken into the Olympic Village, taking hostage nine Israeli athletes and killing two others. German sharpshooters moved in to rescue the hostages, but all nine were killed in a gunfight in which five of the terrorists were shot dead.

For the next 34 hours the Games were suspended and their fate hung in the balance. Then, at an open-air memorial ceremony watched on television by an estimated 1000 million people throughout the world, 84-year-old Avery Brundage, a former American track star and sports administrator, stated: 'The Games must go on – and we must continue our efforts to make them clean, pure and honest and try to extend the sportsmanship of the athletic field into other areas.'

If it had not been for Avery Brundage's determination, the 1972 Olympic Games might have been abandoned – and the future of the Olympics jeopardised. It takes a full six years to plan and organise the Games – and preparations were already underway for the next Olympics – in Montreal, Canada, in 1976.

By then the Irish peer Lord Killanin was the president of the International Olympic Committee, and he later recorded: 'The horror of the assassinations in the Olympic Village in Munich changed the whole concept of security, which, as a result, took a very high priority in the Montreal Games . . .'

The number of armed troops and policemen outnumbered the 6189 athletes and set the pattern for future Games – such as those in Seoul, South Korea, in 1988, when in the weeks leading up to the Games the 100,000-strong security and anti-terrorist forces had to deal with bands of rioting students demanding political freedoms.

In terms of competitors, the Seoul Games were the biggest so far – with more than 9400 men and women representing 160 countries, competing in 237 events covering 23 different sports. Like all the modern Olympics, the event was run by the International Olympic Committee (the IOC) based in Lausanne, Switzerland. The IOC, the guardian of the Olympic ideals, chooses where the Games will be held and decides which sports will be included.

Choosing the city

Only cities – and not countries – can be candidates to host the Games. This is intended to eliminate, as much as possible, governmental influence.

Before the city is chosen, a National Olympic Committee (NOC) makes sure that the city is able to provide all the staff and facilities to stage the Games. And an

Sporting scene *Rice fields near Seoul were transformed into a 135 acre (55 hectare) sports complex for the 1988 Olympics. As well as the Olympic Stadium (in the foreground) there were a baseball stadium (behind it) and boxing and basketball arenas (to the right).*

Showing the flags *At the opening ceremony of the Seoul Olympics in 1988, thousands of South Korean volunteers created the 160 flags of the competing nations. As each national anthem was played, the participants held up differently coloured cards, which together formed the appropriate flag. The 'flag-holders' were carefully rehearsed in advance – and their movements were timed to the beat of the music.*

Organising Committee is appointed to plan and oversee the entire operation – and to report regularly to the IOC.

The staging of the Games inevitably involves improving, modernising, and sometimes changing the face of the city concerned.

For the Tokyo Games in 1964, the world's longest stretch of monorail was built from the city's Haneda Airport to the specially built National Stadium. Super-highways, subways and miles of new sewers were rapidly built – and 22 dilapidated main arteries were designated 'Olympic Roads', and were widened.

There was a similar situation in Seoul, where in 19 months thousands of acres of rice fields were turned into a concrete mini-metropolis containing the Olympic Park and Village. The work included a new air terminal, an access road, the Olympic Drive, and flats and temporary homes for 35,000 athletes, journalists – Press, radio and television – and officials. In addition, 200,000 visitors had to be housed in hotels or apartments. Private developers seized the opportunity to build 178 luxury high-rise apartment blocks near the two main Olympic centres. The apartments were put on sale for up to the equivalent of £90,000 each and were snapped up by their new owners – who rented them out for the Games and moved in afterwards.

Living space was at a premium during the 1960 Rome Olympics, when the Olympic Village was built on a 74 acre (30 hectare) site near a bend of the Tiber. It included a 4500-room apartment development designed to house 8000 athletes.

However, many of the 100,000 visitors to the Rome Games – who arrived at the newly built airport of Fiumincino at the rate of 6000 a day – were not as fortunate. They had to sleep in convents, monasteries and school dormitories, and camp out in the city parks and green spots. One camping place was even set up in the grounds of the Emperor Hadrian's villa in the nearby hill town of Tivoli.

But the Olympic villages consist of more than just sleeping quarters and training facilities. There are also beauty parlours, cinemas, discothèques, boutiques, post offices, churches and cobblers' shops – which do a brisk trade in repairing the athletes' running shoes.

5200 calories a day

Feeding the athletes is another major responsibility of the Organising Commit-tees. At Montreal in 1976, for example, a staff of 1400 served over the 16 day Olympic period a total of 1135 tons of meat, fish and vegetables. It worked out as a daily average of 8lb (3.5kg) and 5200 calories per athlete – served in a 24 hour cafeteria larger than two football fields.

And at the Los Angeles Olympics in 1984, a team of 135 chefs prepared some 60,000 meals each day. The fresh food was delivered daily from more than 100 suppliers, and included an order for 45,000lb (20,400kg) of meat every day. Kosher food is prepared for Jewish contes-tants (in Rome in 1960 this was supervised by the city's chief rabbi) – and Muslims look after the kitchens providing food for their fellow Muslims.

But the number of cooks (300 at the 1964 Tokyo Games, for instance, recruited from Japan's top hotels) is greatly exceeded by the number of interpreter-guides need-ed for each Games. Almost 1000 in-terpreters, well-versed in sporting terms, attended the athletes in Tokyo. And by the time of the Seoul Olympics, 5000 in-terpreters were on hand. Their duties included acting as translators for the National Olympic Committees, the hun-dreds of assorted diplomats, and more than 1000 journalists. Over 30 languages were spoken – including the IOC's two official languages: French and English.

In addition to this in 1988 almost 30,000 South Koreans volunteered to serve with-out pay as guides, ushers and ticket sellers. A thousand English-speaking inhabitants met foreign visitors at Seoul's modern airport – many of whom became guests in the volunteers' homes during the Games.

In whichever country the Games are held, the weather frequently plays a key role. In Los Angeles in 1984, for example, smog occasionally threatened to blot out one event or another; and in Helsinki, Finland, in 1952 – when the Soviet Union took part in the Olympics for the first time – the threat of cold and snow had to be taken into account. So at each Games an international team of meteorologists issues up to 20 bulletins a day. As a result of the forecasts, some of the events have to be hastily re-scheduled – usually to avoid gales, hail or rainstorms.

Equally important are the 'sports bul-letins', or computerised results services, which flash out the Olympic results and times. In Tokyo's vast National Stadium, for example, the electronic scoreboard was big enough to display up to 500 letters or numbers at once. And the timing device for the track events was timed to one-thousandth of a second.

But no matter how carefully the Games are planned, there is always something that goes wrong.

Montreal was a prime example. The main Olympic Stadium – in 1976 the world's largest prefabricated structure – proved a major problem. First of all political quarrels, and the complexity of the design, delayed the start of fitting together the stadium's 11,770 concrete pieces. Then three months of union strikes, slowdowns and walkouts – staged to gain substantial pay rises for the construction workers – brought work almost to a halt.

Blizzards and plunging temperatures – the wind-chill factor hit a low of −63°F (−53°C) – intensified the holdups. Some of the 3550 workers had to fight wind gusts of up to 60mph (96km/h) and accidents cost the lives of at least 12 men. Because of all this, turf was still being laid in the stadium on the morning of the opening ceremony.

Once the various Games are over, the task of dismantling the villages, or converting them to other and profitable uses, begins. In Munich, for instance, the Olympic Village was originally divided into two sections: one for men and the other for women. Today the men's section has been sold or rented out as living accommodation – and the women's section is used as a students' residential hall.

Mounting the Olympics is a highly expensive business – it cost $8000 million to put on the Moscow Games in 1980 and a 'mere' $850 million to stage the Seoul Games eight years later. Much of the money comes from the governments concerned, as well as from private sponsorship, donations from local businesses, and contributions from the cities' residents.

Television rights
However, the rewards can be equally impressive. The Seoul Games made a record profit of almost $500 million – more than twice the profit made in Los Angeles in 1984. The bulk of the Seoul profit came from the sale of television rights – the USA alone paid $325 million.

The modern Olympics were inaugurated in Athens in 1896, when their founder, the French scholar and educator Baron Pierre de Coubertin, coined the slogan, 'Not to win, but to take part' – which is quoted at the opening ceremony of each Games.

The words of the late Avery Brundage are also recalled: 'The Olympic Movement is a 20th-century religion. A religion with universal appeal which incorporates all the basic values of other religions. A modern, exciting, virile, dynamic religion!'

Ingredients of a Hollywood movie: money, power, expertise and magic

Hollywood feature films originate in the chaos of creative egos and live or die by public whim. Only in production, when a film falls into the hands of technicians, are there firm rules.

The whole process breaks down into major stages: conception, pre-production, production, post-production.

The concept
The basic idea, or concept, for a film sometimes comes from a novel, but may simply be an idea, often expressed as little more than a title, sometimes in conjunction with a star's name.

In the words of the director-writer Steven Spielberg: 'If a person can tell me the idea in 25 words or less, it's going to make a pretty good movie.'

Usually the concept is written up in the form of a brief presentation, which evokes the plot, characters and appeal in a few pages.

Some ideas move with astonishing ease. When, in 1976, Dino de Laurentis decided to remake the 1933 version of *King Kong*, he gave screenwriter Lorenzo Semple Jr the go-ahead in a ten-minute meeting. On the other hand, the writer William Goldman researched *Butch Cassidy and the Sundance Kid* (1969) for eight years on and off before he even started the screenplay.

Pre-production
The pre-production period may take years, during which deals are discussed and stars and directors approached. This is followed by months of rewriting, location finding, budgeting, designing sets, rehearsing and scheduling transport and shooting.

The first essential is 'the deal'. Decades ago, major film studios such as Paramount, MGM and Twentieth Century-Fox controlled ideas, production, stars and budgets. Now the studios concentrate on financing and distribution, and all the other elements must be pulled together by 'the deal'.

As an investment, a film is a gamble. Those who control access to film finance – like agents and managers – have assumed huge influence. Agents often become independent producers, who are the forces behind some Hollywood deals. With his 'elements' – the idea (or sometimes a script), a star or two and a director – the producer sells the package to a major studio for development money (which would be around $100,000). By getting the deal off the ground, the producer can at least cover his expenses – the major one being the creation or purchase of the script.

At this stage, most projects are either shelved, or are rejected by the studio and go back into the marketplace. However, if the studio approves the script, it goes into production. Only then does the producer – who receives much of his fee when the cameras start to roll – start to make money.

The basic script remains the skeleton of the film. As a piece of writing, it is sparse – around 135 pages is considered a rough standard – containing little but the dialogue and simple directions to suggest character and atmosphere.

The images presented by the script can only live when fleshed out by the director – the person who chooses the camera angles, commands the actors, and gives the film its artistic shape. The script is usually heavily rewritten once the cast, director, budget and location are known. It frequently evolves further during shooting, into the final shooting script.

The stars used to be controlled by studios, who could use a contract to enforce whatever they wanted, including extensions to the contract. As David Niven wrote: 'Some of us gave 12 or 14 sulphurous years of our short actor's lives working off a seven-year contract.' Now major stars, the keys to success, wield enormous power. At any one time, there are about 15 important stars whom everybody wants. Since they can make huge sums for the film, they are paid accordingly. Robert Redford, who received $500 for his first film, *War Hunt*, in 1961, earned $100,000 a day for *A Bridge Too Far* (1977).

Negotiations may last for months, with offers and demands in the millions. Many stars depend on their images, and refuse to be bought unless the part is right. Robert Redford, Steve McQueen, Paul Newman, James Caan and Warren Beatty all refused $4 million to play *Superman* (1978).

The Missouri Breaks (1976) teamed Marlon Brando (who was to receive $1.25 million plus 11.3 per cent gross receipts over $8,850,000) with Jack Nicholson ($1.25 million, plus 10 per cent of gross receipts over $12,500,000). The deal took almost a year to set up and the film was a box-office failure.

Directors, too, are a part of the star system. Success breeds success; but equally important in Hollywood is 'word of mouth'. When George Lucas made *American Graffiti* (1973) his studio, Universal, described it as a 'disgrace', and almost did not release it.

Lucas had at this point received just $20,000 in three years, and was in debt.

On location with Lord Jim *The 1964 feature film* Lord Jim *was shot on outdoor sets in the Far East. Here the star of the film, Peter O'Toole – wearing a black cap – stands beneath the sound boom as the action unfolds and the camera rolls. Perched on the ladder above him is one of the lighting crew – while a team of cameramen and sound technicians is gathered behind him.*

But *Graffiti* was a hit, and he used his new-found status to work a deal with Twentieth Century-Fox. The film was *Star Wars* (1977). It made him a millionaire.

Budgets of feature films are a constant source of fascination to both film makers and the public. No two are the same. 'Below the line' costs – those directly related to the craft of movie-making, such as sets and technicians – are estimated from the script. 'Above the line' costs of producer, director, stars and writer are open to negotiation. Both run into millions. One of the most expensive films ever was *Cleopatra* (1963), which cost $44 million in 1962, and lost money at the box office. Average budgets for American films in the 1980s were around $10 million, of which $7-8 million might be 'below the line' and the remaining $2-3 million 'above the line'.

After the elements are in place and the deal agreed in principle, contracts are drawn up, an epic operation in itself. The negotiations are so tortuous that they themselves may become books and films.

Even relatively straightforward films may take years to evolve. *The Dogs of War*, the film of Frederick Forsyth's 1974 best seller, was six years in pre-production. Developed with money from United Artists, it had two writers and two producers before John Irvin was contracted as director. A third script acted as a basis for location research. The producer, Larry de Waay, contracted to shoot in the Seychelles in cooperation with the country's president, James Mancham. But Mancham was ousted in a coup before work started. De Waay finally settled on Belize, in Central America. This time, shooting went ahead. The film was released in 1980.

Production

A major feature demands a small army of specialist departments. The main ones are sound, camera, lighting, art, make-up, hair and wardrobe, publicity and script.

On different films, different specialities acquire particular significance. Stanley Kubrick's design department for *2001: A Space Odyssey* (1968) had three production designers and an art director to oversee the sets. *Close Encounters of a Third Kind* (1977) needed 60 arc lights strung 80ft (24m) above the ground. Franklin Schaffner's *Sphinx* (1981) needed dozens of live bats.

Direction has been compared to war –

hours of mind-numbing boredom occasionally interrupted by moments of pure terror. One shot of a battle scene in a war movie may cost millions. Possibly the budget will not allow for a reshoot. Perhaps the director is contractually liable to repay costs that are over budget.

A major source of stress for the director is that many of the people under him, or her, can make or break the film. This is particularly true of the cameraman. Francis Ford Coppola's *Apocalypse Now* (1979) was crucially dependent on Vittorio Storaro's ability to control anything up to ten cameras at once.

Since camera work is so important and so expensive, sound has come to take second place on the set. The sacrifice must be redeemed later, and dialogue is dubbed on after shooting.

The art department may have to solve demands like Franklin Schaffner's for *Sphinx*: produce an Egyptian tomb with 800-900 jewellery artefacts. *Jaws* (1975) required a 25ft (7.6m) automatic shark.

Location managers have an equally vital role. For *Apocalypse Now*, Vietnam was re-created in the Philippines; but the difficulties drove an original budget of $13 million up to $31 million. Location managers can save costs by doing deals in North Africa or Eastern Europe, where studio and location costs may be under half those in America or Britain.

After shooting, the immense amount of film must all be carefully processed. The loss of any one of the hundreds of reels can be fatal for the movie. The potential for disaster is huge – in August 1978, masked men robbed a Boston studio of 15 unedited reels from *The Brinks Job* (1978), and demanded a ransom of $600,000 (the money was not paid; the film was edited without the reels; and it lost $9 million).

Creating special effects and stunts

Special effects are a particularly demanding area, in whichever country a film is made. Back in 1966, in *One Million Years BC*, the British special-effects man Les Bowie created the world in six days for £1200, using porridge for lava. But today's special effects demand high technology (page 406). In 1988 a sequence showing asteroids in *The Empire Strikes Back* included 40 shots, some of them with up to 28 separate optical effects, involving 100 pieces of film.

Stunts have always been important to film makers (page 414). Stunting is a dangerous and highly paid occupation. In *Highpoint* (1984), Dar Robinson was paid $100,000 to leap off the 1815ft (553m) CN Tower in Toronto, breaking his fall with a 'decelerated cable'. For *Steel* (1979), A.J. Bakunas jumped off a 350ft (107m) building into a huge air pad; his fall split the bag, and he was killed. Car crashes,

fires, fights, explosions – all demand their own skills, and have their own dangers. One particularly controversial area is stunting with animals. In the first version of *Ben Hur* (1925), 100 horses were killed. As a result of this and other similar abuses, controls were tightened.

Post-production

Editing – in which a film is cut and then assembled ready for release – can also make or break a movie. Scenes will have been shot in many different ways to provide a wide choice. Stanley Kubrick shot over 200 miles (320km) of film for *The Shining* (1980), of which only about 1 per cent was used. A typical shooting ratio is between 10 and 20 to 1.

One vital element remains to be added: music. The American composer Bernard Herrmann once said: 'Music is the connecting link between Celluloid and audience,' completing the film's psychological effect. It can only be written when editing is almost complete.

Because of the pressure of time, the composer usually works with assistants who fill out his musical sketches by writing the dozens of orchestral parts required. John Williams' 90 minute score for *Star Wars* ran to 900 pages, written by himself and four orchestrators.

After editing, another huge machine – promotion – swings into action: this involves advertising, printing and distribution. For *Alien* (1979), for instance, Fox spent over $18 million on so-called 'overheads' – $15 million on advertising and $3 million on prints for distribution to over 2000 cinemas.

Only then is a film ready for its audience. Only then will the army of people involved in its creation know whether they have made a disaster or something magical.

One reason why up-front money is so huge and the negotiations so demanding is that studios are notoriously slow to pay any share of profits to the stars, writers, producers and directors. They refuse to declare a profit, setting income against 'overheads'. *Alien*, which cost Twentieth Century-Fox $10.8 million, brought in almost $50 million in its first year (1979), and still Fox did not declare a profit.

A major reason for the 'no-profit' mentality is that films not only cost hugely and earn hugely – they lose hugely, and do so more frequently than they earn. In the 1980s only three out of seven major features made money – a reminder that the public's taste in subject and stars is notoriously fickle.

No one dares predict success. *Whose Life Is It Anyway?* (1981), the story of a dying cripple, was highly successful as a play. As a film, it flopped. *Raiders of the Lost Ark* (1982), one of the most successful films ever, was turned down by every major

studio except Paramount. Columbia researched *ET* (1982), concluded there would be no audience, and turned it down.

Why? Because as scriptwriter William Goldman writes emphatically in his book *Adventures in the Screentrade*, the 'single most important fact of the entire movie industry' is:

'NOBODY KNOWS ANYTHING'

– anything, that is, about what the audience will want next year. Despite the millions of dollars, the tons of scripts, the heart-stopping negotiations, the scrupulous technicalities, movie people do not really know how to make a movie work; they only know how particular movies *have* worked, and hope against hope that the future will be like the past.

The risks and rewards of staging a musical

The lights dim, the hubbub dies down and the audience settle back in their seats. Then the curtain goes up for an evening of music, lights, dancing and hit songs. But how does a stage musical ever come to be presented?

No other form of entertainment requires the delivery to a live audience of such a complex blend of creative and performing skills, nightly for sometimes years on end.

The skills needed to put on a straight play – from financing the production to rehearsing the cast – are all present in a musical, but it has many more complications uniquely its own. There is the music itself, which must be composed, arranged for an orchestra and dovetailed into the plot. There is dancing, which needs to be choreographed. There are the costumes and sets, often more lavish than in a conventional play. There is the need to find players who can sing and dance. Finally, the theatre itself must be big enough and suitable to accommodate the show – with good acoustics and room for an orchestra.

All this makes big musicals the most expensive form of theatrical production. Andrew Lloyd Webber's *The Phantom of the Opera* cost about £2 million to mount in London's West End, and *Ziegfeld*, which opened there in 1988, cost an initial £3.2 million. On Broadway in New York, the starting price is around $7 million.

Just to break even, a big musical needs to play to full houses for a year, compared with about three months for a play.

The rewards of success with a musical can be phenomenal. Another Lloyd Webber hit, *Cats*, generated £250 million in three years in the mid-1980s. The show played at the same time in Britain, America and eight other countries around the globe. The record album sold millions, and souvenir items such as T-shirts added to the takings.

Failure can be equally spectacular, particularly on Broadway, where the fate of a show can be determined by the critics virtually from the opening night. The Royal Shakespeare Company's *Carrie* closed there after a week, losing $7 million. Even lyricist Alan J. Lerner, whose *My Fair Lady* is among the most successful musicals ever, suffered the ignominy of seeing his *Dance a Little Closer* taken off before its third night.

Man in the middle
The risk and responsibility of putting on a musical rests with the producer. He selects the show, organises the money, and superintends everything to do with the production. There are two types of producer – the impresario and the manager.

Impresarios operate independently, with their own production organisations. They are largely free to stage what they wish, when and where they choose. The real restrictions are financial. Impresarios must be able to raise the money to pay the bills, and their ventures must show the promise of a useful profit if financiers are going to back them.

Managers, most commonly, are employees appointed by the board of trustees of a particular theatre to mount their own productions. The theatre itself may be privately or publicly owned.

Because of the money involved, large-scale musicals have usually been the province of impresarios. And forms of co-production have evolved. Both *Cats* and *The Phantom of the Opera* were presented jointly by the London-based impresario Cameron Mackintosh and Andrew Lloyd Webber's group, The Really Useful Theatre Company.

Choosing the show
Original musicals involve three separate strands – the lyrics, the dialogue and the music. They are rarely all ready together when the producer is beginning his deliberations, because it usually takes at least three people to create them.

To simplify the problem, many of the best-known musicals take their plots or story lines from works that already exist in another form. *Kiss Me Kate* and *West Side Story* raided Shakespeare; *My Fair Lady* came from George Bernard Shaw's stage play *Pygmalion*, itself built on an ancient Greek legend. *Cats* originated from light-hearted poems by T.S. Eliot. *Oliver*, *Les Misérables* and *Man from La Mancha* were adapted from novels by Dickens, Victor Hugo and Cervantes.

By borrowing a ready-made story line, authors and composers have a concept that can be easily grasped by a producer. Additionally, they may assume that the plot has already proved its attraction.

The genesis of *The Phantom of the Opera* illustrates how the various strands of a musical can come together. The original novel was written by a French journalist, Gaston Leroux, in 1911. It was made into a film three times. A stage version was put on at the Theatre Royal in Stratford, London, in 1984, using the music of operatic composers such as Verdi and Offenbach.

The composer Andrew Lloyd Webber became interested in the Stratford show, and considered putting a version of it on in the West End. At that point, he too planned to borrow the music; only later did he decide to write his own.

The project was still at the idea stage when Lloyd Webber approached Cameron Mackintosh to co-produce it. So the producers were involved with the show from the start.

The creative team
In any stage production, a key figure is the director. He is responsible to the producer for the casting and for all artistic and technical aspects of the production. He is responsible, too, for rehearsing the performers and the technicians in charge of sound, lighting and scenery.

Lloyd Webber chose Hal Prince, whose musical successes included *Fiddler on the Roof* and *Evita*. Even before Prince was in place, Lloyd Webber had decided on the set and costume designer – Maria Björnson, who had previously worked for the English National Opera and the Royal Shakespeare Company.

To write the lyrics for the songs, they appointed a young unknown, Charles Hart, after hearing his work in a competition. And the dialogue, or 'book', was by Lloyd Webber and Richard Stilgoe – who also wrote additional lyrics.

Casting the parts
In major productions, the star parts are normally cast a year or even longer in advance. Early casting ensures the widest choice of top names – leading actors usually stay in one role for six months to a year. But, equally important, the commitment of a star performer helps to raise the vital money.

For that reason, the producer has the final say about who plays the leading roles, though he will take the director's advice. The other parts are left to the director to fill.

Christine, the female lead in *The Phantom of the Opera*, was written by Lloyd Webber specifically with his wife, the soprano Sarah Brightman, in mind. At that time, she was not a front-rank star, and others were auditioned before the role was finally given to her.

The male lead, Michael Crawford, was personally chosen by Lloyd Webber. Crawford was a household name in Britain, from the television series *Some Mothers Do*

Model man *Maria Björnson's set models for* The Phantom *included one of its most dramatic effects – the murder of a stagehand, whose body suddenly dangles over the stage.*

Off to see the Wizard *For the Royal Shakespeare Company's version of* The Wizard of Oz, *the Scarecrow, the Lion, the Tin Man and Dorothy rehearse a scene. Then at the dress rehearsal (below), they march down the yellow brick road to meet the Wizard.*

'*Ave 'Em*. He had also had a huge hit in the musical *Barnum* which had had a long run in the West End.

Raising the money

While the director is assembling all the components of a production, the producer is putting the final touches to the finances. His budget itemises all the main costs.

Some costs are fixed from the start – for example, the sets and costumes, which will be needed however long the show runs. For *The Phantom*, they cost £900,000. Others, such as theatre rental and wages to the less senior members of the company, are partly fixed – they no longer represent a cost if the show closes.

Some costs are tied to the income from the production, as fixed percentages. The star may receive a flat fee in rehearsal, plus perhaps 20 per cent of the ticket income until the show recovers its investment, and then 12.5 per cent after that.

Other key personnel, such as the designer and the musical director, are on smaller percentages – say, 2 per cent. So are the writers and the composer.

The less money a producer needs to raise from outside sources, the more profit he can keep for himself. However, few impresarios wish to take all the risk themselves. Their proportion varies from 10 per cent to 70 per cent, either directly in cash or in personal guarantees to secure a loan.

The usual sources for the rest are companies or individual investors, who put money into a show as they might buy shares on the stock exchange. Most producers have their own lists of companies and individuals – known as 'angels' –

who are potential investors, but sometimes the opportunities are publicly advertised. Angels do not begin to see a return until the initial expenses have been met in full.

Producers of musicals have other opportunities to raise money – for example, by interesting a record company in advance in the album rights for the show, and by licensing merchandise associated with it. Andrew Lloyd Webber and the lyricist Tim Rice – collaborators in *Jesus Christ, Superstar* and *Evita* – pioneered the techniques of releasing single records, albums and pop

Production coordinator *In the prompt box at* The Phantom of the Opera, *the deputy stage manager, Anni Partridge, coordinates lighting, sound, curtains and special effects on her electronic console.*

videos before the show opened – in effect testing the response, creating public awareness, and raising money.

Once the finances have been worked out and the company begins to assemble, work on the show can begin in earnest. One early priority for the producer is to book a theatre and set a date for the opening night.

Depending on the type of show, the official first night may be a year or more ahead. Some productions are given a provincial tryout before they are brought to a major centre such as the West End or Broadway – to identify and correct any flaws before the grand opening. Others may have previews before invited audiences. In either case, these dates must be built into the timetable.

Those associated with the production divide, loosely, into two groups. The producer and his associates concentrate on the business matters, including publicity and advertising. Much of their effort is directed towards advance ticket sales. *The Phantom of the Opera*, for example, opened in New York with a guaranteed box office advance of $19 million – assuring it financial success. Few producers can count on anything like that.

All the other aspects of the production are under the overall control of the director. First, he will want to make sure that the script is nearing its final form. He may call on the writers to make changes, sometimes right up to opening night and even after that.

The musical score is the responsibility of the musical director, who may edit it with the help of the composer, supervise its arrangement for the orchestra and prepare it for the show.

Simultaneously, the designer will be working on the sets and costumes. The sets may begin as detailed models or drawings, and they must be approved at each stage by the producer and director.

A number of specialists may work alongside the designer – creating the lighting or working out special make-up, for example. A master carpenter and his assistants eventually collaborate with the designer in building the sets. A wardrobe mistress supervises preparation of the costumes. A property master assists in obtaining such items as furniture needed to dress the sets.

Meanwhile, the director is beginning his work with the cast. He must also make sure he has suitable understudies – reserves for the leading players – and 'swing' or utility players available for minor roles in an emergency.

Rehearsing the cast

From the time they are hired, the actors begin familiarising themselves with the script. Before proper rehearsals start, the director sometimes conducts readings involving the entire company, indicating how he wishes each part to be played.

These 'read-throughs' can be held anywhere. But in the next phase, where the actors move according to stage directions, a rehearsal room or stage is needed. As there are usually no sets, their positions are indicated by coloured tapes on the floor.

The early rehearsals are conducted both with the whole company together, and also with only certain individuals or groups who require special instructions for their parts. The musical director takes the singers and musicians through their paces. The choreographer or dance master instructs the dancers. An arranger may be brought in for flying stunts or fights.

Gradually, under the director's eye, the separate elements come together, and a move into the theatre becomes essential. As the sets are built, the stagehands may be given practice in scene-shifting. Lighting and effects are rehearsed. Singing, dancing and other special stage routines are integrated into the rehearsals.

The final stage – perhaps a week before the first performance to an audience – is the full-scale dress rehearsal. The actors are in costume and make-up, the sets and lighting are in place. The full orchestra is assembled. Only minor changes remain before the theatre opens its doors and the audience and the critics deliver their judgment.

The perilous job of a mountain rescue team

Stung by freezing rain, buffeted by high winds, and with snow crashing down on them every few minutes, two young mountaineers – Philippe Berclaz and Philippe Héritier – had spent four days trapped on a tiny ledge more than 10,000ft (3000m) up in the Swiss Alps.

The two Philippes, both in their early 20s and training to be professional mountain guides, had set out in August 1975 to climb the almost vertical, north-east face of Piz Badile. The mountain rises 10,850ft (3300m) like a gigantic knife blade on the borders of Switzerland and Italy. The climbers had got to within some 500ft (150m) of the summit when dark clouds rolled down and they found themselves in the middle of a blizzard.

Unable to go on to the top, or back to the bottom, they abseiled 130ft (40m) down to a narrow ledge, with a sheer drop of 2200ft (670m) beneath them. They attached themselves by ropes and pitons, or iron pegs, to the granite face and spent their first two days there in agonies of cold. Repeatedly they shouted for help, but each time the wind mocked them and carried their cries away.

On the afternoon of the third day there was a break in the clouds, the storm eased, and their desperate yells and whistles were heard by two German tourists, far below in the Bergell Valley.

News of their plight was telephoned to Swiss Air-Rescue in Zurich, the volunteer organisation that deals with mountain rescues in Switzerland. By then dusk was

Stretcher rescue *A rescue team on Ben Nevis – Britain's highest peak – lowers an injured mountaineer to safety by stretcher.*

falling, and fog had blotted out Piz Badile. No rescue attempt could be considered that night.

At dawn the next morning, however, the air-rescue service went into action. They rang Beat Perren, head of Air Zermatt, a commercial helicopter service, and commissioned him to undertake the rescue. Within minutes he and his chief pilot, German-born Siegfried Stangier, were flying the 100 miles (160km) to Piz Badile in a powerful Lama helicopter, equipped with a winch.

They reached the mountain in an hour and saw the two stranded mountaineers clinging like flies to the white wall of the north-east face. Strong gusts of wind threatened to send the chopper – with its whirling rotor blades – crashing into the mountain. Siegfried Stangier was unable to get as close to the two men as he would have liked.

So a cable was later lowered 150ft (45m) to the ledge. On the end of the cable was a sack containing a walkie-talkie, warm clothing, flasks of hot tea, dried beef and vitamin sweets. The mountaineers were soon in radio contact with their rescuers, and reported that they still had the strength to lock their rope harnesses into the safety catch which was fitted to the cable.

But cloud and wind delayed the rescue bid until six that evening, when the conditions suddenly cleared. Only one man at a time could be winched to safety, and it was agreed that Philippe Berclaz would be the first off.

Cautiously, Stangier

Avalanche rescue *Mountain rescuers are trained to search with avalanche probes to locate victims who are buried in the snow.*

Dog rescue *Specially trained dogs such as German shepherds can be lowered by helicopter to locate people lost in the snow.*

manoeuvred the chopper until the tip of the rotor was about 25ft (7.5m) from the mountain face. Berclaz unhooked himself from the wall and held Héritier – who was still anchored to the granite – tightly around the waist. Héritier grabbed the cable with numbed, frost-bitten fingers and snapped the cable's safety catch onto his friend's harness.

Suddenly, Berclaz was whisked into the air, dragging his friend off the ledge. Helplessly, Héritier dangled there by his rope and piton. Then, using every last ounce of determination and strength, he managed to scramble back onto the ledge. Meanwhile, Berclaz – suspended from the end of the helicopter cable – was flown to a stone shelter on the plateau above the village of Bondo, between St Moritz and the Italian border. There, helpers guided him gently to the ground.

Later that night Héritier – in the face of freezing wind – succeeded in fastening himself to the rescue cable at the fourth attempt. Soon he, too, was swinging through the air to safety.

Land based

Since the early 1970s, helicopters have proved the most effective way to locate victims of mountaineering accidents and take them and their rescuers to safety. The choppers' manoeuvrability and speed are essential in getting badly injured people to hospital.

But they are not the perfect answer. They are expensive and cannot operate in fierce winds, heavy snow and thick cloud. The noise of their rotor can also trigger off an avalanche. They are best suited for hazar-dous alpine rescues – and are not suitable for prolonged and remote rescues, where refuelling can be a problem.

So the traditional land-based means of rescuing people trapped on mountains, or buried by avalanches, are still employed.

On Mont Blanc, for instance, overland rescue teams are involved in more than 400 rescues a year.

The highest peak in Western Europe, Mont Blanc towers almost 15,800ft (4800m) above the borders of France and Italy. It attracts more than a million visitors a year – many of whom want to climb to the top (in summer, some 200 people a day do so). In 1987 the mountain claimed 44 lives, and almost 300 people were injured.

Almost every mountain region has some kind of rescue service, but the more popular resorts – the Alps, the Scottish Highlands, the Rocky Mountains in North America – have highly trained teams of professionals, with sophisticated networks to coordinate their operations.

Everywhere, mountain rescue organisations work closely with the armed forces, local police, the Red Cross and other medical services, and various rescue specialists such as the coastguard and dog handlers.

A basic mountain rescue team consists of a team leader or controller, who directs the operation from a base off the mountain; the party leader, who directs the team during the search and rescue; and as many people as necessary, depending on the scale of the accident or disaster.

Team members are almost always local expert climbers familiar with the terrain and weather conditions. They are all trained to work in snow, ice, bare rock and atrocious weather. They also receive first-aid training, even though larger teams have doctors or paramedical staff. Communication is by radio or portable telephones.

Depending on the terrain and weather, the team may climb on foot, or with snowshoes or skis; they may travel by horse or motor vehicle; they may use sledges or snowmobiles; or they may arrive by helicopter.

Rescue teams usually use specially trained dogs to locate victims who are lost, and to help dig out people buried in an avalanche. A dog, with its acute sense of smell, can search an area in the time that it would take 20 men to cover the same ground. Dogs – usually German shepherds, labradors and border collies – are trained to locate any person lost in the area. (St Bernards, traditionally associated with alpine rescue, are considered too cumbersome to work in difficult terrain.)

In March 1985, for instance, a group of Royal Navy sailors – nine ratings, two officers and a member of the Women's Royal Naval Service – were mountain walking in Wales. They became stuck on a slippery ledge 500ft (150m) from the summit of Glyder Fawr – a 3280ft (1000m) sister peak of Snowdon. The party was reported missing when it failed to return home by 9.30 that evening.

'A good hot-water bottle'

Two local mountain rescue teams set off for Glyder Fawr, as did Philip Benbow – a builders' merchant and member of SARDA, the Search and Rescue Dog Association. With his black labrador, Jet, he scrambled through the icy darkness with Jet sniffing the winds for any human smell.

Suddenly, Jet shot off up a steep slope followed by his master – who was guided by a small green light on the dog's jacket.

'Jet was far ahead when I knew by his bark he had found the group,' Benbow said later. 'The coldest was the young Wren, so I put Jet in a sleeping-bag with her to thaw her out. A dog has a higher-than-human body temperature and makes a good hot-water bottle.'

Benbow contacted the mountain rescue base on his radio, and before long team members arrived with casualty bags to warm the rest of the frozen walkers. Daylight broke and an RAF helicopter arrived and winched the party – Jet and Benbow included – from the ledge and back to safety. 'Jet didn't look too cheerful as we dangled from the aircraft,' commented Benbow, 'but it's all in the job!'

Rope rescue *A mountaineer in the Swiss Alps makes his way down by rope to reach someone trapped in an ice-bound crevasse.*

Techniques of deception and detection

In war and in peace, a never-ending struggle goes on to gain advantage by deception and to discover the truth that lies below the surface.

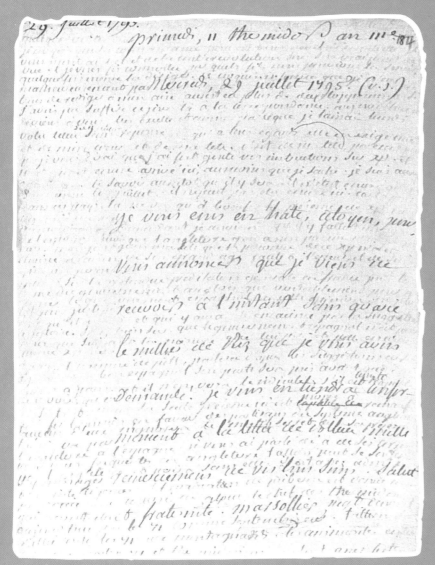

How they write letters with invisible ink, page 81.

How photographs are made to lie, page 82.

How camouflage works, page 76.

The warplane that is 'invisible' to radar

In the late 1950s the American Central Intelligence Agency began sending Lockheed U2 'spy-planes' over the Soviet Union to take intelligence photographs. The U2s flew at 80,000ft (24,000m) to be out of range of anti-aircraft fire, but it became clear that radar was not detecting them.

Stealth bomber *Radar-absorbent paint on the leading edge of the high-altitude American B-2 Stealth bomber helps to make it virtually invisible to enemy radar. Its fan-shaped wings show a low radar echo.*

These extraordinary planes were little more than jet-powered gliders built of plastic and plywood. On takeoff they jettisoned their small outrigger wheels from the ends of their wings – and they landed on their main, retractable wheels in the centre.

It was not until May 1960, after more than four years of overflights, that the Russians shot one down using new radar equipment belonging to SA-2 surface-to-air missiles. And even then the U-2 did not receive a direct hit. A missile exploded

close enough to put the fragile aircraft into an uncontrolled dive, and the pilot, Gary Powers, had to eject.

The success of the U-2s led to highly classified research work in the United States, known as 'Stealth', to create a military aircraft that was invisible to radar.

The U-2 had gone undetected for so long because it was made of non-metallic materials which absorbed radar waves rather than reflecting them back to the radar ground station as normally happens.

The Stealth programme aimed at design-

ing high-performance military aircraft incorporating, among other features, a minimum of metal and with the exterior clad in highly absorbent tiles. The aircraft would be almost invisible to radar and could make most radar-controlled anti-aircraft systems obsolete.

Key targets

After being developed under a blanket of secrecy, the high-tech B-2 Stealth bomber was unveiled at the Northrop company's manufacturing plant in Palmdale, California, in November 1988.

An audience of invited guests and journalists was kept well away from the plane – which is designed to slip through enemy radar defences without being de-

tected and then drop up to 16 nuclear bombs on key targets.

To help achieve radar invisibility, the bomber is coated with radar-absorbent paint on its leading edge.

A similar technology of radar invisibility is used underwater to foil sonar detection. Modern submarines are coated in a thick layer of a top-secret resin which is highly absorbent acoustically, and reflects only a minute amount of the energy transmitted by sonar detectors.

Ground clutter

Another technique used by aircraft to avoid radar is to fly at very low levels where there is a great deal of 'ground clutter' – radar reflections given off by buildings and other

objects. Low-level aircraft can go undetected by most radar systems. But the latest, most sophisticated ground-defence systems are designed to discriminate between ground clutter and hostile planes. In addition, ground clutter is partly avoided by using 'look-down' radar systems, which track aircraft from other aircraft flying above.

Blackbird *The shape of the USA's high-speed spy plane, the SR71 Blackbird employed in the 1960s, was later developed by Stealth.*

Camouflage: how do you hide a warship?

During the American War of Independence in the late 18th century some British units took to wearing buckskins in place of their traditional red coats. The men found that red made a good target for the American riflemen, whereas the dun-coloured buckskin was not so readily visible.

The use of such camouflage was taken further during the Afghan War in 1880. A colour known as *khaki* (the Urdu word for 'dust') was generally adopted to make the soldiers' movements less obvious to the natives. Veterans who had served in India – and who had stained their white helmets brown with tea – knew that lack of visibility was the key to their survival in wartime.

During the Boer War of 1899-1902, however, British troops were still wearing bright scarlet uniforms. They had been traditional since the English Civil War, 250 years earlier, when Parliamentarian soldiers were provided with red coats simply because a large amount of red cloth was available. These conspicuous uniforms made the British soldiers easy targets for the Boer riflemen.

When the First World War broke out in 1914, dull colours such as khaki and grey had become the standard colour for uniforms, enabling soldiers from both sides to blend in with their combat surroundings.

Even so, the use of spotter planes left troops dangerously exposed on the ground. Camouflage netting and the 'dazzle painting' of weapons in zebra stripes was gradually introduced.

Desert deceit *Painted to blend in with the wartime terrain – and not be seen from above – a German Messerschmitt Bf 109E flies low over the Libyan desert in 1941.*

Operation dazzle *The dazzling zebra stripes on this US Navy torpedo boat give the illusion of the vessel having several bows. This was designed to confuse the enemy in the Second World War as to the boat's true course. Here the torpedo boat sails gently on a practice mission.*

During some military manoeuvres on Salisbury Plain, the commander of a British army division – a survivor of the Boer War – told his men to attach pieces of foliage to their helmets, conceal their vehicles with drab netting and take advantage of the natural cover to hide themselves from aircraft.

The ruse was so successful that the division became indistinguishable from the surrounding countryside. The idea of an entire unit losing itself in the landscape grew so attractive to the military command that camouflage gradually became accepted as an important weapon in the modern arsenal.

During the Second World War, camouflage was widely used as a technique of deception. As in the First World War, vulnerable installations such as fuel depots and munition stores were covered with netting so, from the air at least, they merged with the background. Decoys were deliberately displayed close by to draw enemy fire. Conspicuous areas of water like the canals, used by bomber navigators as landmarks at night, were sprayed with coal dust to prevent them reflecting moonlight.

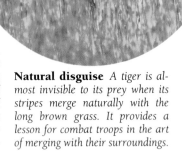

Natural disguise *A tiger is almost invisible to its prey when its stripes merge naturally with the long brown grass. It provides a lesson for combat troops in the art of merging with their surroundings.*

During the North African campaign of 1940-3 a dummy railway line was constructed to resemble a new supply spur to a tank assembly point. It even carried a fake train, complete with freight wagons and flat cars, and an impressive-looking locomotive with a disused camp stove billowing smoke from a cardboard funnel.

The hoax diverted attention away from the genuine railhead which was used to support General Auchinleck's offensive against Tobruk in November 1941. His main forces and fuel dumps were so well hidden that the enemy never found them.

Camouflage has also been used to reduce the visibility of aircraft and ships.

When the underside of a bomber is painted light blue, it merges with the daytime sky, and when painted black, with the night sky. Some planes are painted on top so that – when seen from above – they merge with the ground below. Similarly, the familiar outline of a warship can be distorted by skilful paintwork designed to reduce the silhouette and even give the impression of a less threatening outline,

Camouflaged killer *His helmet and machine gun draped with artificial foliage, a US Marine Corps sniper crawls through undergrowth to his 'kill' and then escapes virtually undetected. At the Corps' Sniper School at Quantico, Virginia, trainees are taught to vanish into their background in the way that many moths and spiders do.*

perhaps that of an unarmed merchantman.

A false bow wave painted onto the hull of a warship can mislead a submarine captain about the speed of his target, and a false water line can confuse the range.

Camouflage techniques have been used to deceive air reconnaissance. During the Falklands campaign in 1982, British commanders were advised that the beleaguered Argentine forces could not be resupplied because Port Stanley's only airfield was unserviceable, having been damaged by the RAF's bombs. Reconnaissance pictures showed what appeared to be a deep crater across the main runway.

In reality, heavily laden Argentine planes flew in every night, under cover of darkness, right up to the day before the surrender. It was only discovered much later that each morning a group of raw conscripts – equipped with nothing more than buckets, spades and wheelbarrows – left a circular pile of earth on the runway. When viewed from a height, their handiwork resembled a bomb crater.

Voice scramblers: sending gibberish over a public telephone line

When a government official wants to make a confidential telephone call to, say, an embassy abroad he uses a voice scrambler. As the conversation travels between the two telephones it is nothing but incomprehensible noise to anyone 'tapping' into the line.

Most scramblers are electronic ciphering machines that invert the high and low tones of a human voice to make it unintelligible. Other scramblers conceal the voice in a background of continuous noise.

At one time scramblers were issued only to senior military commanders who had to exchange sensitive information over telephone lines that might be listened into by the enemy. Now scramblers have become more easily available, and are often used by international businessmen anxious to protect trade secrets from unscrupulous competitors. Modern technology has reduced their size so they fit into a briefcase.

Double unit

Scrambling requires two units, the transmitter and the receiver. The transmitter converts the caller's speech into the unintelligible form and sends it down a normal telephone line. The receiver reverses the process so that the voice can be understood at the other end. Eavesdroppers tapping into the line will hear a highly distorted, synthetic noise that is hardly recognisable as human speech.

Most scramblers work by splitting the

sound of the voice into five frequency bands which are then mixed through a complicated electronic process which moves and inverts them. In theory there are about 3840 possible combinations, but standard scramblers use 512 permutations.

Voice scramblers are not a complete safeguard against skilled eavesdroppers, as conversations can eventually be unscrambled. But the process is extremely time-consuming, requiring the use of specially programmed data processors and highly trained operators, so scramblers do give short-term protection.

In the early 1960s, the US Embassy in Moscow managed to pick up the scrambled conversations passing between the Politburo's fleet of limousines. Although there was a long delay before the signals could be unscrambled, the exchanges contained some extremely useful political information – and quite a bit of Kremlin gossip. The operation eventually ended when new security measures were introduced.

How secrets are sent by codes and ciphers

On the eve of the Japanese attack on Pearl Harbor in December 1941, an apparently innocent weather forecast, 'East wind rain, north wind cloudy, west wind clear', alerted Japanese diplomats around the world that war was imminent.

The message was one of the simplest forms of code – a prearranged message which had a special meaning to those who received it.

Similar messages were broadcast by the BBC during the Second World War to the French Resistance. A sentence such as 'Romeo embraces Juliet' or 'Benedictine is a sweet liqueur' might convey prearranged information about the dropping of agents or supplies. The first line of a poem by the French writer Paul Verlaine ('The long sobs of the violins of autumn') told the Resistance that the D-Day landings were about to begin.

More complex codes replace words or whole phrases with other words or phrases. Alternatively, groups of unconnected letters may be used to create a whole dictionary of words and phrases. For example, the order 'Provide supporting fire' might be conveyed by the letters GYPHC. Long military reports can be transmitted in these five-letter groups – only intelligible to someone who can look them up in the correct codebook.

If a codebook falls into enemy hands, however, vital information can be intercepted without the sender's knowledge. In the First World War the German naval codebook was recovered from the wreck of the light cruiser *Magdeburg*. Consequently many of the German High Seas Fleet's most sensitive orders were read by the British. Even when the German Admiralty discovered its loss, it took weeks before it could supply every German ship with a new codebook.

The other major method of sending secret information is with ciphers. A cipher substitutes letters, numbers or symbols for the real letters of the alphabet. The Morse code is actually a cipher, conveying each letter by combinations of short and long signals which can be sent by radio bleeps, telegraph or signal lamps. The letter E, for example, is a single dot, while Q is dash, dash, dot, dash (– – . –).

One-time pad
Tiny cipher pads are used by spies for decoding secret messages from their spymasters. Coded instructions sent by radio relate to groups of five-figure numbers on a specific page in the pad. Once the message has been received and decoded, the receiver and the sender tear the relevant page from their pads. For this reason, they are known as 'one-time pads'.

Another common, and simple, form of cipher is worked out on a grid called a cipher box. The message 'Enemy troops embark December first' could be written in a grid of, say, six columns, alternately writing left to right and right to left. The letters are then written out again in groups of five following a diagonal course through the grid:

```
E N E M Y T   E N E M Y T
E S P O O R   E S P O O R
M B A R K D   M B A R K D
E B M E C E   E B M E C E
R F I R S T   R F I R S T
```

So the cipher that is transmitted reads:
TYRDO MEOKE TCRPN ESAES RMBEM BIFER.

The person who receives the message uses a similar grid to decipher it.

A weakness of the system is that the frequency of letters and combinations of letters remains the same as in normal language. E, for example, is the most commonly used letter in the English language, and Z is one of the least common. The combinations EE and OO occur frequently. Someone trying to break the cipher can assume the most-often occurring letter represents E, and so on.

So immensely complicated ciphers, involving numbers as well as letters, have been developed by mathematicians.

During the Second World War the German government used a cipher machine called Enigma. However often a particular letter was keyed, it would never repeat the same cipher letter. Each day a new basic setting was made, according to a schedule known only to the Germans.

A team of university mathematicians and linguists in Britain eventually unravelled Enigma's ciphers in 1940. Their work played a major part in winning the war by giving Allied Headquarters an up-to-the-minute picture of the German plans in the North African campaign and the air war.

With the advent of computers, codes have become far more complicated and difficult to break. Complex programs use thousands of calculations, and without knowing the sequence of key commands, they could take thousands of years to decode.

The underground world of 'moles'

In November 1979, the British Prime Minister Margaret Thatcher announced to the House of Commons that one of the most respected men in the British art world, Sir Anthony Blunt, Surveyor of the Queen's Pictures, had been working as a spy for the Russians.

Blunt had become a Communist in the 1930s and had worked for the British Security Service (MI5) during the Second World War, passing secrets to Moscow. In 1951 he helped two other British spies, Guy Burgess and Donald Maclean, to flee to Russia when they came under suspicion.

Blunt was an example of the type of spy known as a 'mole' – agents who are prepared to wait for years, building up their cover, until they get access to vital information.

Unlike more conventional spies who are recruited by their own country to undertake a mission in another, the mole is often someone who, usually for ideological reasons, has chosen to work for an alien cause. Having taken that decision, he deliberately manoeuvres himself into a position where he can inflict the most harm. And all the while he plays the part of a patriot.

Some moles are recruited by intelligence specialists known as case officers. Others recruit themselves by volunteering their services.

Probably the most renowned case since the Second World War was that of the four British spies Blunt, Burgess, Maclean and Kim Philby. All decided, while still at Cambridge University in the 1930s, to work secretly for the Soviet Union.

They were initially recommended by 'talent-spotters' who passed each onto a Soviet case officer who taught them the rudiments of espionage, and told them to give up their memberships of radical political groups. They were to make themselves as attractive as possible to official organisations.

Each man deliberately cultivated people in positions of influence whom he believed might assist him to find a useful job. Eventually Burgess and Maclean joined the Foreign Office, Philby the Secret Intelligence Service (MI6), and Blunt the counter-espionage service, MI5.

Once they were in their target organisations, the four men progressed to the most sensitive levels of government, gaining

False image Sir Anthony Blunt – Surveyor of the Queen's Pictures and long-time spy – fooled people with his social pedigree.

access to the most damaging information.

Maclean, Burgess and Philby all fled to Moscow and eventually died there. Blunt made a full confession to the British Security Service and was not prosecuted. He died in 1983.

A mole who spied against his own country purely for the money was Heinz Felfe, a former officer in the German SS who rose to an eminent position in the West German Federal Intelligence Agency in the 1950s.

In 1951, while looking for a job, he agreed to work for the Soviet secret service (later the KGB), for a salary of 1500 marks a month. At the same time he joined the Federal Intelligence Agency. For the next decade he worked as a double agent,

Family spy ring For 17 years, former US Navy chief warrant officer John Walker (bearded) of Norfolk, Virginia, was a Russian spy. In 1986 he was jailed for life for running a family spy ring that included his son Michael.

feeding 'disinformation' about the KGB to the Germans and in return sending the KGB highly damaging information about the German spy network behind the Iron Curtain.

Suspicions about him finally arose when he bought a house which was too expensive for a man on one salary. When he was arrested in 1961 it was discovered that his activities had lost the West Germans 94 contacts behind the Iron Curtain, including 46 active agents. In 1963 Felfe was sent to prison for 14 years.

Another turncoat spy – who operated in the USA from the late 1960s to the mid-1980s – was John Walker, a former naval officer. His Russian spymasters paid him $1000 a week to run a family espionage ring, consisting of his brother Arthur, a retired Navy lieutenant commander, and son Michael, a seaman aboard the aircraft carrier USS *Nimitz*. Their activities enabled the Soviets to decipher countless top-secret communications and receive more than 1500 secret documents.

Traitor While working as First Secretary at the British Embassy in Washington, Donald Maclean (bow-tied) gave American atomic secrets to Russia.

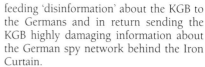

Free to smile *The German secretary-spy Renate Lutze smiles happily in the days before her arrest and imprisonment. She was released after serving 27 months.*

A quite different type of mole is the 'sleeper' who enters a foreign country on false documentation and burrows deep into the fabric of his adopted society.

Peter and Helen Kroger, US citizens of Polish extraction, were just such a couple. Outwardly he was an antiquarian bookseller who, with his wife, led a comfortable suburban life at Ruislip in west London in 1961. In reality, the Krogers operated an illicit KGB wireless link with Moscow until they were arrested.

When their bungalow was searched, even the most innocent-looking household item was revealed to be part of the paraphernalia of espionage. An apparently ordinary tin of talcum powder contained compartments for storing microfilms and a microfilm reader like a tiny telescope.

Renate and Lothar Lutze were deep-cover East German moles operating in West Germany before being arrested.

Born in Brandenburg, East Germany, in 1940, Renate Ubelacker, as she then was, got a job as a secretary in the West German Ministry of Defence in Bonn. Her work involved handling top-secret documents – including those dealing with NATO plans. In September 1972 she married Lothar Lutze, then a spy for the Ministry for State Security in East Germany. She succeeded in getting him a clerical job in the Defence Ministry.

For the next four years the couple gave vital information to the Russian-controlled East Germans. They were unmasked and arrested in June 1976. After spending three years on remand, Renate Lutze received a six-year sentence for spying and her husband was jailed for 12 years. She was released from prison in September 1981.

The most effective moles are those who are the very last to fall under suspicion. Burgess had been educated at Eton; Maclean's father had been a Cabinet minister; Philby had joined SIS from *The Times*, and at the time of his exposure Anthony Blunt had been appointed Sur-

veyor of the Queen's Pictures at Buckingham Palace and had been knighted.

Some moles can be given a period of training before going into the field. For their own security it is vital for the moles to learn about secret methods of communicating with their own side and ways of spotting whether they are being watched.

The CIA operates a large base disguised as a military establishment at Camp Peary, in Virginia, USA; the French maintain a remote school high in the Alpes Maritimes in south-eastern France; while the Russian KGB have training centres near Leningrad.

However, it is occasionally impossible for a mole to undergo training, and he may have to be taught basic techniques while actually operating.

Oleg Penkovsky, a Russian lieutenant colonel, volunteered his services as a spy to the British in 1960. When he made a rare visit to the West in a Soviet trade delegation the following year, he was shown how to use a miniature camera and briefed on cipher systems. Instead of slipping away from his group, he simply pretended to go to bed early at his London hotel. In fact the British and Americans had hired the entire floor of the hotel directly above his room, and installed all the equipment necessary for the training sessions. The arrangement worked perfectly, and by the time he was due to return to Moscow Penkovsky was a fully fledged agent.

But his spying career was short-lived. Penkovsky was arrested by the KGB the following year and sentenced to death.

Bugging: the art of the modern eavesdropper

In the modern era of bugging, no conversation in office or home is safe from eavesdroppers. The bugging is usually done by smuggling a small but sensitive microphone into the room.

One type of bug uses a low-powered radio transmitter attached to the microphone to send its signals to a receiver a few yards away. Another type has the microphone connected to a receiver by a cable.

Although a wired-in system requires careful concealment of the cable, it has the advantage of not broadcasting a radio signal, which is easy to detect. And most rooms or offices have so much cable already installed that the extra wire goes unnoticed. The microphone can be designed to resemble a household appliance, like a light bulb, television or telephone.

Provided a listening post can be found within a reasonable radius of up to a mile, every word spoken in the target room will be relayed over the wire. An existing cable, such as a spare telephone line, is usually used to carry the voices.

One of the reasons why diplomatic buildings are so closely guarded when under construction is the fear that a foreign intelligence agency might try to incorporate cable conduits into the fabric of the building. This occurred in Moscow in 1987, where all the steel beams delivered to the site of the US Embassy were discovered to be hollow.

If an eavesdropper cannot gain access to a room, he can put a bug called a stethoscope to one of the walls from the outside. It is a simple microphone pressed to the wall, and rigged to an amplifier. Alternatively, a hole can be drilled through the wall from the outside, ending as a tiny pinhole on the inside of the room. A microphone in a tube is placed in the hole and connected to a tape recorder outside. A variation is the 'spike' which only penetrates part of the wall, but nevertheless picks up all the sounds in a room.

Inserting a device into a target room can be difficult if the room's occupants know they may be spied on. So the laser has been

exploited to help the eavesdroppers. A laser beam is focused on the window of the room. When a conversation takes place inside the room the glass in the window vibrates to the voice waves, and the microscopic movements of the glass can be detected by measuring the tiny variations in the length of the fixed laser beam. This information can then be converted back electronically into an intelligible form.

The cavity microphone is probably the ideal cordless device, requiring neither batteries nor maintenance. It consists of a capsule, about 1in (25mm) wide, containing a sensitive aerial and a diaphragm (a thin disc). When a radio beam is directed at the room from outside, the capsule is transformed into a radio transmitter that picks up sounds in the room, allowing any conversations to be overheard.

One of these bugs was found in a model of the American Great Seal that had been presented to the US Ambassador by the Mayor of Moscow in 1952 and had hung over his desk for years.

Invisible inks for secret messages

A special form of carbon paper is used as a modern form of invisible ink. A spy lays the carbon paper on another piece of paper and writes his message. His handwriting is transferred invisibly onto the paper underneath, and can only be revealed when treated with a chemical. So it is possible to send messages by post 'written' on the pages of, say, women's magazines.

This method was used by the Czechoslovakian spy Erwin van Haarlem, who in 1989 was jailed for ten years for his

Heated words *A secret message written in lemon juice was revealed when this receipt for a consignment of rice was heated. The message, in small writing, reports on the activities of Royalists in Paris in 1795, during the French Revolution.*

espionage activities in Britain. Since 1975 he had sent some 200 secret messages to his spymasters in Prague – many of them in invisible ink. The information included facts about British firms working on America's Star Wars defence system.

Most chemical invisible inks need a second liquid – known as the reagent – to make them visible. One of the most popular inks is copper sulphate diluted with water. When the paper is later immersed in a weak solution of sodium carbonate (washing soda) and water, or ammonia and water, the writing appears blue.

A particularly sensitive chemical ink used by German spies during the Second World War involved chemicals used in photography. The ink was a solution of lead nitrate and water. The reagent was a

small amount of sodium sulphide in water. It produces a shiny black print.

It was a crystal of concentrated invisible ink chemical, concealed in a hollow key, that led a Second World War German spy, Oswald Job, to the scaffold. The ingenious hiding place was discovered when Job was searched, and it led to his confession and execution in 1944.

The search for the perfect truth drug

The objective of a truth drug is to relax a person's mind so that he gives completely open and truthful responses to whatever he is asked – even if it means betraying his country.

Research into so-called truth drugs began in earnest during the Korean War in the early 1950s, following reports about 'brainwashing' interrogation methods carried out by the North Koreans and Chinese on prisoners of war. The US Air Force began a project to find a 'truth serum' so that American pilots could be given it and trained in how to resist brainwashing.

Experiments began with barbiturates, amphetamines, alcohol and heroin, but most of the drugs just helped the subjects to tell lies more skilfully.

Purge trials
Fear of mind-control techniques had been raised during Joseph Stalin's notorious purge trials in the Soviet Union and the Eastern Bloc countries in the 1930s and 1940s. Defendants appeared in court in an apparently befuddled state, with glazed eyes, admitting to crimes that they could not possibly have committed.

Sodium pentothal, a barbiturate used by anaesthetists to relax hospital patients before surgery, is often described as a truth drug. Its use in this context is to help create a disorientated state in which the subject's awareness of his surroundings can be manipulated.

The subject is given a strong dose of the drug which makes him unconscious. He is then injected with the stimulant Benzedrine to revive him, but only partially. With the subject in a state of semi-consciousness, a psychiatrist can use hypnotic techniques to change his perception of what is going on around him.

When this method was used on a suspected Soviet spy in West Germany in 1955, his mind was taken back to a stage where he believed he was talking to his wife at home, and he freely gave a detailed account of his undercover activities.

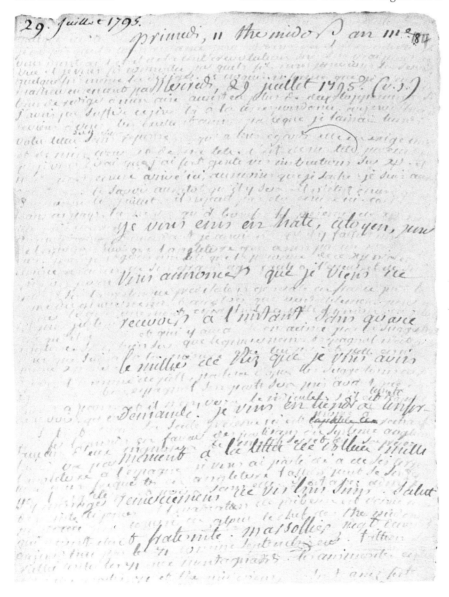

How they make the camera deceive the eye

For almost as long as they have known how to take photographs and develop them, photographers have also known how to fake them. When the first unrecorded and no doubt accidental double exposure occurred on a photographic plate, it revealed the possibilities of adding extra images to a picture.

Photographs of alleged spirits of the dead, the levitation of objects and people, faked 'Unidentified Flying Objects' – even photographs of fairies – have fooled, if only temporarily, both laymen and experts.

Photographers realised they could take one picture of an image – then add another by re-exposing the same plate. In times when people were less informed about how photography actually works, it was easier to hoodwink them into thinking that seeing was believing.

And as photography has moved into the computer age, ever more sophisticated techniques have been devised to make the camera 'lie'.

Sky picture

Model aircraft

Landscape scene

Foreground fence

Six pictures in one

This rural scene, interrupted by menacing images of modern man – jet fighters and barbed-wire fencing – does not exist as it appears. The photograph is a multiple image, a combination of several photographs. They were assembled by a London photographer, Chris Morris, as a record sleeve design for the Quaker Peace Foundation.

The two aircraft are in fact one model photographed in a studio from slightly different angles. They were superimposed on a photograph of the sky, by sandwiching the transparencies between glass and copying them.

Another photograph of sky was added to provide the lighter section close to the horizon.

The main image, a woman and child in a meadow, was a straightforward colour photograph.

The foreground images – one of trees and a gate, another of a fence – were sandwiched together and copied on a large black-and-white film.

In the final stage, the sky and jets, figures and field, and trees and fence were sandwiched and copied as one picture.

Record cover *By combining pictures (opposite page) and copying them, Chris Morris, a London photographer, created a scene implying military menace. 'But it never existed as you see it', he says. The picture was composed as a record sleeve design for the Quaker Peace Foundation.*

Perfect fit

'Super-reality' is how the creator of this photograph describes his picture of Westminster Abbey, in London. For although the vividly coloured stained-glass window is authentic, it only appears in such shining glory when seen illuminated by daylight shining *into* the abbey.

The photographer Chris Morris first captured the front of the abbey from the outside. He paced out the distance between the building and the camera, and measured the same number of paces on the inside. Then he took a photograph of the sunlight streaming through its west window's stained-glass panels.

'I made only one slight tripod adjustment,' he says, 'to compensate for the slightly lower level of the abbey floor.'

Because of the careful pacing out, the interior shot of the window fitted precisely when he superimposed it – by rephotographing the two images.

'Any slight flaws in matching up were masked by the aurora of light around the window,' he said, 'an effect I created during the superimposition.'

All aglow *This striking picture of Westminster Abbey suggests that a powerful inner light radiates from the abbey, illuminating its window. In fact this effect is visible only inside the church, where the image was photographed. It was then superimposed onto a shot of the church's façade.*

Flight simulation

This 'photographic record', of the aviator Alberto Santos-Dumont's first aeroplane flight in Europe of more than 80ft (25m), is a fake. Yet the pioneer did make a flight of 200ft (61m) – in Paris on October 23, 1906.

A photograph of Santos-Dumont's aircraft was taken when the aviator suspended it on a cable to check its balance. Then a print was cut out and mounted over a photograph of people watching a balloon. The montage was then copied.

Record flight *The trees (left) would have prevented takeoff.*

Phantom flower girl

For some 60 years, various books and journals published this picture of a little girl, with a posy of flowers and an envelope, standing in front of a man seated at a desk. It was offered as proof that 'spirit photography' was genuine. The photograph first appeared in 1919 and was taken by a faith healer and spiritual medium, Dr T. d'Aute Hooper of Birmingham. He claimed that one of his patients, staying as a guest, asked him to take a photograph because he felt an unseen presence.

'I got the camera and before I exposed the plate,' wrote Dr Hooper, 'I told him I saw a beautiful child with him ... The gentleman himself took the plate to the dark room and developed it; and there appeared the beautiful spirit form of a little girl ... The exclamation of the gentleman was "Good heavens! It's my daughter, who died thirty years ago".'

It was not until the revival of interest in spirit photography in the 1980s that several researchers 'recognised' the girl in the photograph. She appeared in a picture entitled *For You* painted in 1879 by Charles T. Garland and used to advertise Pears' soap around the turn of the century.

Double exposure *A late 19th-century advertisement (left) was used in an alleged 'spirit photograph' (right).*

Hooper had prepared in advance a plate on which he had copied the girl's image – with its background erased. When his patient developed the picture that Hooper had taken of him on the same plate, the second exposure had added the background. It was a technique common to so-called 'spirit photographers'.

But why should Hooper's patient have immediately expressed the thought that the girl was his late daughter?

'Perhaps,' commented the astronomer and investigator of unexplained phenomena, Arthur C. Clarke, 'in his grief, he had been clutching at straws, a victim of understandable self-delusion.'

UFO hoax picture

Photographic experts were at first convinced that this photograph (right), of an alleged Unidentified Flying Object, was genuine. It was taken by an airline pilot over Venezuela in 1965.

But when Dr B. Roy Frieden, of the University of Arizona, examined the print in 1971, he pointed out that the 'flying saucer' was too sharply defined to be a distant object – and suspected that the shadow beneath it had been drawn in.

Then an engineer in Caracas admitted to being the hoaxer. He confessed that the UFO was a photograph of a button, placed over the aerial shot and re-photographed. The shadow was chemically 'burned in' during processing.

'Flying' button *This clever fake 'UFO' fooled experts for six years.*

Fantasy *Cut-outs copied from a book became 'fairies'.*

A midsummer day's dream

For nearly 70 years, two cousins kept their secret of the fairies they claimed to have photographed in a leafy dell at Cottingley, in West Yorkshire. During that time, their controversial pictures became internationally famous and baffled photographic experts and psychic researchers the world over – including Sir Arthur Conan Doyle, the creator of fiction's best-known detective, Sherlock Holmes.

It was in July 1917 that Elsie Wright, then 15, and her ten-year-old cousin Frances Griffiths, borrowed a box camera from Elsie's father, Arthur Wright – and went to play by a stream in the dell. When the photographs they took on that and subsequent days were developed, they showed one or other of the two girls, along with images of what appeared to be fairies dancing, leaping and perching on branches. One showed Elsie with a winged, capering gnome. The photographs came to the notice of Conan Doyle through the Theosophical Society, when Elsie's mother Doris mentioned them at a meeting in 1919.

Conan Doyle, an ardent Spiritualist, engaged a photographer and leading Theosophist, Edward Gardner, to investigate the photographs. He ultimately became convinced of their genuineness – and of the honesty of the girls, who swore that the fairies were real. In November 1920, Conan Doyle published the photographs in *The Strand* magazine and wrote: 'When our fairies are admitted, other psychic phenomena will find a more ready acceptance.'

Over the years, the two girls stuck to their story. But there were some who doubted. And in 1978 the American conjuror James Randi drew attention to the similarity between the figures in one of the photographs and a drawing of fairies in *Princess Mary's Gift Book*, published two years before the pictures were taken.

Yet it was not until 1983 that Elsie and Frances, by then elderly widows, confessed. Elsie had drawn and painted the fairies on art board and they had been pinned to branches or supported by hatpins. The girls' prank, Elsie revealed, had originally been planned to get Frances out of trouble for falling in the brook.

Frances died in 1986, aged 79. Elsie, who died two years later at 87, told the London *Times*: 'The joke was to last two hours, and it has lasted 70 years.'

Juggling with reality – by rearranging picture images on a computer

Photographic wizardry has reached almost magical dimensions by being introduced to computer technology. Thanks to a technique called computerised image processing, any image in a photograph – a building, a mountain, a ship, even people – can be electronically made to disappear. And the space can be filled in so naturally you see no trace of where it has been. In the same way images can be added. The technique involves recording every tiny element of a picture and rearranging them.

In a glossy magazine advertisement, for example, a new car parked on the edge of the Grand Canyon may never have moved out of the showroom where it was photographed. Computer processing can transplant its image onto a transparency of the canyon. And, by electronic juggling with the picture elements (pixels), the car can be transformed from a four-door into a two-door model with different hub caps. The shadow effects on its paintwork can be made to match that of the canyon.

The process can delete a boat from a cobbled quayside (below).

The electronic scanner traverses an illustration and records each pixel. They are broken down into their basic elements: red, green, blue and black. Each pixel is stored in a computer in digital form. The illustration can then be reprinted with its pixels rearranged in any order.

In the case of the disappearing boat, the pixels were removed and then replaced by others duplicating the cobblestones.

Disappearing boat *Computer image processing can remove or add any photographic element, and replace it with natural-looking background.*

Detecting lies with a machine

In the early 1980s at least a million people every year in the USA were subjected to lie-detector tests – most of them applicants for jobs. However, the tests resulted in some people being falsely accused of dishonesty. One such victim was a college student, Shama Holleman, who was dismissed by a New York department store after a test indicated that she might be a drug dealer and might have served a prison sentence. Both were untrue.

Since then, US companies have been

HOW TO BEAT THE LIE DETECTOR

Medical experts in the USA and Britain say that it is quite possible for a suspected person to beat the lie detector. The trick is to make the responses to the control questions appear as similar as possible to the responses to the real questions. For an answer to be classified as 'deceptive', it must register much more strongly than the control answers.

Dr David Thoreson Lykken, professor of psychology and psychiatry at the University of Minnesota Medical School, writes in his book *A Tremor in the Blood* that the interviewee could identify the control questions during the pre-test interview. He could then do something to increase his response to control questions during the test – something different each time so as not to arouse suspicion.

'After the first control question, I might suspend breathing for a few seconds, then inhale deeply and sigh. While the second control is being asked, I might bite my tongue hard, breathing rapidly through my nose. During the third control question, I might press my right forearm against the arm of the chair or tighten the gluteus muscles on which I sit. A thumbtack in one's sock can be used covertly to produce a good reaction on the polygraph.'

Dr Archibald Levey, of Britain's Medical Research Council, who wrote a report on lie detectors for the British Government in 1988, says that meditation techniques can be used to achieve the opposite effect – by lowering the responses to all questions.

The interviewee could think himself into a relaxed state, concentrating on a different subject or imagining himself to be somewhere else.

prohibited from using lie-detector tests to screen employees. However, government agencies and some security services and drugs firms are still allowed to use them.

Other major users of lie detectors are police forces, who test suspects and witnesses in criminal cases. More than 60 years after the invention of the lie detector its use remains controversial.

The lie detector works on the assumptions that people who tell a lie become stressed emotionally, and that the stress speeds up their pulse and breathing rate, and makes them sweat. These effects can be detected by sensitive instruments.

The first person to use instruments to detect stress through bodily changes was an Italian criminologist, Cesare Lombroso, in the 1890s. His apparatus measured variations in a person's pulse rate and blood pressure.

In 1921 the first modern lie detector using continuous monitoring was developed, in conjunction with the local police, by a medical student, John A. Larson, at the University of California, Berkeley.

Larson's machine recorded simultaneously a person's blood pressure, pulse rate and rate of breathing. The results were recorded by three pens making ink traces on a continuous roll of paper. The machine, called a polygraph, was soon dubbed a lie detector.

Later the polygraph evolved into the modern instrument with the addition of a fourth measurement – that of the skin's ability to conduct electricity, which varies according to the amount of perspiration.

Ideally, lie-detector tests are conducted under strictly controlled conditions. The person to be tested is wired to the machine and asked a series of innocent questions (called control questions), such as: 'Is your name John Smith?' (which it may or may not be). This is to elicit a response from the subject that will provide reference traces on the polygraph.

Then if the person lies, the polygraph should be able to detect the changes caused by the stress of lying, and record them.

One drawback is that some people are so nervous that they may appear to lie even though they are telling the truth.

Other people may be so much in control of their emotions that they will be able to lie without affecting their polygraph traces. But this is exceptional.

HOW A LIE DETECTOR PRINTS OUT ITS VERDICT

The lie detector is an assembly of three different instruments. Their outputs are fed separately to the lie detector and recorded as separate traces on a graph.

One instrument, the pneumogram, records breathing patterns. A rubber tube is strapped across the chest, and instruments measure fluctuations in the volume of air inside the tube, which are brought about by variations in breathing.

The second instrument, the cardio-

sphygmometer, detects variations in the blood pressure and pulse rate. The information is picked up by a bladder and cuff placed over the upper arm, in the way that doctors check blood pressure.

The third instrument is the galvanometer, which monitors the flow of a tiny electric current through the skin. The skin conducts electricity better when it is moist with perspiration. Electrodes are usually taped to the hand.

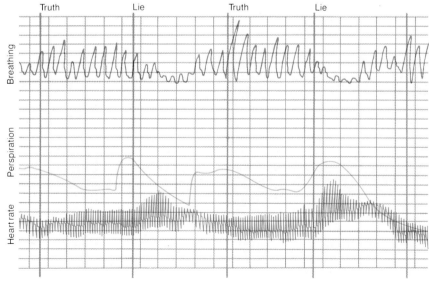

Truth gauge? *Truth and lies are recorded as graph variations of a person's heartbeat, breathing and perspiration during lie-detector tests. But the method is questionable.*

Tracing the cause of a fire disaster

On New Year's Eve, 1986, one of the most disastrous fires since the Second World War killed 97 people in a hotel in Puerto Rico. Workers at the hotel, the Dupont Plaza in San Juan, had become angry over the lack of a pay settlement, and two of them used methylated spirit to set fire to cardboard boxes and other rubbish in an empty ballroom.

Within 15 minutes the flames had engulfed the entire ground floor and trapped hotel guests on the top floor of the 21-storey building. Many of the 1400 occupants had to be rescued by helicopter. As well as the 97 dead, there were 140 people injured.

Investigators from the US Bureau of Alcohol, Tobacco and Firearms were on the scene while the fire was still raging. When they examined the charred remains of the furniture in the ballroom later, they discovered traces of the methylated spirit and decided that the fire had been caused by arsonists. The FBI was then brought in to interview hotel staff.

Eventually, three employees were arrested – one charged with lighting the fire, one with assisting him, and the third with supplying the spirit. All three were convicted and given prison terms ranging from 75 to 99 years.

Fire investigators are among the first on the scene after a fire has been put out. Their first task is to preserve and record the remains. Sometimes it is clear that an arsonist has been at work: fires may have been started at several points, or someone might have been spotted running from the scene just before flames were noticed.

The next task is to locate the place or places where the fire began, and where it was most intense. The spread of the fire must also be tracked. Much can be learned by looking at smoke patterns and damage to surfaces. Metals and glass can be useful guides. A metal rail will distort or melt according to its proximity to the hottest part of the fire. The density of cracks in glass usually corresponds to the intensity of heat.

Expansion of metals can also be revealing – a steel joist 33ft (10m) long and heated to 932°F (500°C) will expand by 2¾in (70mm). The depth of charring in wood or in layers of carpet also gives an in-

UNDERGROUND-STATION FIRE
After the fire at King's Cross Underground Station, London, in 1987, trials showed how a lighted match could ignite an escalator. Seven minutes, 54 seconds after a match ignited grease and fluff beneath the treads (above), fire broke out on the wooden stairs (right) – the white arrow shows where the match entered. Flames then raged through the escalator tunnel (below). A computer mock-up (bottom right) traced the flow of hot gases on the escalator and into the upstairs ticket hall.

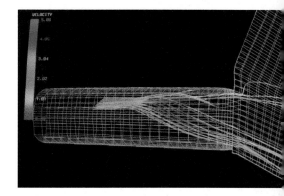

dication of the heat or duration of a fire.

Against this must be balanced factors which help to spread fire. Lift shafts, air vents and stairwells give a chimney effect, raising hot gases to other parts of a building and creating secondary seats of fire. The investigator can be confused by localised fires caused by broken gas pipes or stored fuel. Exploding aerosol cans can create fireballs several feet across.

Having found the seat of the fire, the investigator will look for signs of the cause – an empty petrol can left by an arsonist,

charred wiring that indicates a faulty electrical connection, even a fragment of carelessly discarded match.

Forensic scientists are skilled at examining fragments of burnt materials. After one of Italy's worst fire disasters, the burning of the Statuto Cinema in Turin on February 13, 1983, in which 64 young people died, the projectionist was able to point to the

Towering inferno *Fire gutted four floors of the 62-storey First Interstate Tower, Los Angeles, in May 1988. One person died and 40 people were injured in the late-night blaze.*

site where the flames first appeared. Fire inspectors discovered the remains of old wiring which had started the blaze.

When remains of the wallpaper, carpeting and upholstery were sent for forensic examination in Rome, scientists found that contrary to Italian fire safety regulations none of these had been fireproofed. After a lengthy trial, the cinema owner, the supervisor of the redecoration work and two local fire officers, who had declared the cinema to be safe, were all sent to prison for between four and eight years.

If no cause of a fire is apparent the investigator might find that a dead body was a murder victim, suggesting the fire was started to cover up the crime. A human body is extremely difficult to burn away completely and the remains can tell investigators a great deal. There could be more intense burning of the body than its surroundings, suggesting that it had been set alight first; or evidence of asphyxiation in the remaining lung tissue, indicating that the person had been strangled.

The fire which killed 31 people at King's Cross Underground Station in London in November 1987 was first believed by some to be arson. It began on an escalator and was fanned by the draught of air coming from the train tunnels below ground. Investigators finally concluded that it began in accumulated fluff and grease under the escalator, almost certainly ignited by a discarded match. Smoking had been banned on underground trains in July 1984, but many people lit cigarettes on the escalator as they were making their way out of the station.

The art of discovering old paintings under newer ones

When Jean François Millet's dramatic picture *The Captivity of the Jews in Babylon* was unveiled in the late 1840s it was vilified by public and critics alike.

The Paris critics thought the picture's surface was too heavily encrusted with paint, and at least one of them complained about the undue savagery of the scene. 'The soldiers are pressing the Jewish women . . . with more violence than is necessary,' he wrote. 'They behave as if they were attacking or sacking a city.'

The picture then vanished from sight and art experts assumed that Millet had destroyed it. In the winter of 1983, however, art restorers at the Museum of Fine Arts in Boston, Massachusetts, used X-ray radiography to reveal the presence of another picture under the surface of Millet's portrait *The Young Shepherdess*.

The X-ray picture showed the image of Millet's 'long lost' and controversial *Captivity*. It is now assumed that, far from destroying the picture, Millet reused the canvas more than 20 years later when art materials were in short supply during the Franco-Prussian War of 1870-1.

How paintings are X-rayed

An X-ray – as used on the Millet picture – is the most common method of uncovering hidden paintings. Long wavelength X-rays are used because they are easily absorbed by paint. The degree of absorption depends on the type of paint. For instance, lead and cadmium-based paints are more absorbent than those containing chromium or cobalt. Thicker layers of paint will absorb more than thinner ones.

Photographic film is placed behind a suspect painting, and X-rays are passed through it from the front. When the film is developed, the ghostly outlines of earlier pictures may be seen.

In the early 1980s, for instance, two art restorers in Glasgow – both of them superintendent radiographers in a local hospital – X-rayed Rembrandt's *Man in Armour*. They discovered what appeared to

be a white plume blowing in the wrong direction from the top of the helmet. However, on turning the X-ray picture around, the 'plume' was seen to be part of an abandoned work by Rembrandt: a lady in a flowing white dress and headdress. *Man in Armour* is in the Glasgow Art Gallery and Museum.

Similarly, a painting by the 16th-century Italian painter Paris Bordone – *Saints Jerome and Antony Abbot commending a Donor* – was found after X-ray to have two donors, one of them by an unknown artist. The painting is also in the Glasgow gallery.

X-rays are also used to study *pentimento*, the changes an artist makes while producing a painting. Alterations to the composition, changes in the angle of an arm or a head, will all show up under X-ray, and are useful to art historians and restorers. (The word *pentimento* comes from the Italian word *pentersi*, 'to repent', suggesting a change of mind by the artist.)

Charcoal outlines

Infrared light is also used to discover paintings beneath paintings. When infrared light is shone on the picture it penetrates the surface paint and is reflected. The reflection is recorded on a camera. The effect is to make the thin, upper paint levels transparent, so revealing the charcoal outlines of the artist's preliminary drawing. The technique has been used by New York's Metropolitan Museum to study Flemish Renaissance paintings.

In some cases it reveals details not apparent on the final painting, and helps in understanding the artist's technique.

Triple image *Three heads – including that of a young woman – have been revealed by X-ray photography of* Portrait of a Young Man *by the 17th-century Dutch artist Karel du Jardin. Scientists at London's National Gallery took samples of the paint and photographed them edge-on through microscopes. This showed that the cross-section of jawline marked 'a' contained seven layers of paint. 1 Red-brown ochre ground. 2 First grey priming. 3 Pale female flesh of first portrait. 4 Second grey priming. 5 Flesh of second portrait. 6 Third grey priming. 7 Shadow of man's jaw.*

The lost portrait *When Goya's early 19th-century portrait* Dona Isabel de Porcel *(right) was studied with X-rays at the National Gallery, London, an unknown man was found painted beneath (left). The use of another technique, infrared photography, shows the man's right eye (above).*

Using fingerprints to track down criminals

The police might want to take your fingerprints for two reasons. They might suspect you of committing a crime, or they might want to identify 'innocent' prints while they are investigating a burglary in your house.

As everyone in the world has a unique set of fingerprints, the technique of fingerprinting is a major aid in fighting crime.

The police will take your prints by pressing the ends of your fingers and thumbs onto an inked pad, and then pressing the finger onto a piece of paper to create an impression of the patterns in the skin. These can then be compared to the traces left on surfaces at the scene of the crime.

Plastics and paint

The traces, actually called fingermarks, consist of tiny amounts of moisture which form patterns corresponding to the ridges and lines on the fingers and other parts of the hand. Non-absorbent materials such as plastics and painted surfaces produce better marks than absorbent ones like fabrics. Marks are normally invisible unless they have been left by paint or blood. So a police fingerprint expert coats likely surfaces with very fine dust, often powdered aluminium. The particles stick to the moisture traces, making them visible. Sticky tape is then placed on the mark to lift away an impression of the pattern, which can be taken away and photographed. Some fingermarks are now photographed on site.

Modern technology is now helping the police to obtain marks from some previously unproductive surfaces, such as polythene bags and smooth leather.

One method called vacuum metallisation involves putting the surface into a container from which the air is expelled,

Telltale patterns *The large blue photograph shows the fingerprint of a male thumb, displaying its unique pattern of skin ridges. The small photographs show four standard patterns (left to right) of arches, loops, whorls and composites. Taken together, the pattern can help police and courts to determine a suspect's innocence or guilt.*

creating a vacuum. A layer of gold, then a layer of zinc, is evaporated onto the surface. The gold is deposited uniformly over the area, but it is absorbed by the ridges of moisture which make up the fingermark pattern. Zinc will only condense onto another metal, so it adheres to the gold-coated areas, enhancing them to provide a contrast with the uncoated fingermarks. The pattern of marks is then photographed.

Once the photograph is obtained, it is compared with fingerprints of known criminals held on police files. There are four main types of fingerprint pattern. The patterns are divided up into such features as 'forks', 'lakes', 'spurs' and 'islands'.

For an identification to be presented in court, a number of recognisable features of the mark of a single finger or thumb must correspond with the same number of features on the print. The number varies between countries, but can be as high as 17. If the mark shows more than one finger the court will usually accept fewer features per finger. Most fingerprint officers and detectives regard more than eight features as enough to confirm identity. Although this

would not be presented in court, it would be enough to concentrate investigation on a suspect.

Glove prints

Gloves yield distinct prints in much the same way as human flesh because of the grease which accumulates on the surface. Glove prints can also be revealed by a layer of powder and if they can be matched with a glove found in the possession of a suspect, it becomes powerful evidence.

The prints can distinguish the type of leather or fabric, its age, and the type of stitching used.

The first case of its type in the world was in 1971 at the Inner London Quarter Sessions. Police had obtained a print from a left-hand glove a burglar was believed to have worn while breaking a window. The print matched that of a pair of sheepskin leather gloves found in the possession of the suspect. He pleaded guilty.

Matching up the prints

The matching of fingerprints requires good eyesight and intense concentration.

The process is similar to one of those

puzzles where you have to spot the differences between two apparently identical pictures. With fingerprint identification, the reverse applies – the fingerprint expert has to look for the similarities.

Fingerprints are normally stored by name on card-index systems at a control fingerprint bureau. In most countries, only the prints of convicted criminals together with unidentified marks in unsolved cases are kept.

Some countries keep a national archive of fingerprints but because of the time it can take to search, it is usually considered as only a back-up, for use if a mark is not matched locally.

Files of criminals with known specialities, such as car thieves or handbag snatchers, are also kept. Secret police forces and intelligence organisations also keep their own files of people they consider to be revolutionaries or enemy agents.

A fingerprint officer will begin by examining the marks taken from the scene and memorising their characteristics. He will then compare them against prints taken from innocent people who might have left marks at the scene – members of the family or policemen, for example. Any marks that match the innocent prints are rejected. The fingerprint officer then takes from the file all prints of possible suspects, whose names have been supplied by the investigating detective.

If these do not match, the officer has to make a wider and more painstaking search. If he is searching for a burglar, he will begin looking through all burglary cases in the locality and then all those from the adjoining town or area.

Depending on how much time was ordered to be spent on the search, he might pursue it through neighbouring fingerprint bureaus in other police forces. The search for a house burglar can be widened to other potential types of criminals, such as safe-crackers, but the officer might not feel it worth while to extend the search to criminals who only pass bogus cheques.

Fingerprint officers also check the fingerprints of newly arrested criminals against unidentified marks from other crimes in the hope of clearing up unsolved cases. They will also compare unidentified marks against new marks to see if a series of crimes can be established. Officers can make dozens of comparisons a day, but many work for days without ever having a positive identification.

Most of this work is manual and can be very laborious. In the early 1980s electronic systems were developed to speed up the work. Prints and marks can now be stored and retrieved on electronic indexing systems, so that the press of a button calls up all the prints of, say, known car thieves living in a certain area and aged under 30. Systems can now be linked up between neighbouring forces, or with national collections, to widen the potential search. However, the actual comparison still has to be carried out by the fingerprint officer.

Scientists around the world are developing computer systems which store, retrieve and, most importantly, match prints and marks. Some matching methods, which can make 60,000 comparisons a second, are already being used by local police forces. But a fully automated, national fingerprint system is still in the future.

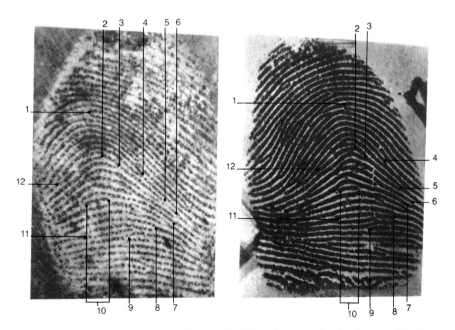

Fingermarks and fingerprints *A fingermark (left) at the scene of a crime has been lifted by a police scientist using fine dust which sticks to the moist marks. The fingermark is compared to a suspect's inked fingerprint (right) and shows 12 corresponding features.*

THE ASTOUNDING CASE OF FOUR BROTHERS

Fingerprint evidence led to probably the only case in which two brothers, jointly convicted of murder, were executed by two other brothers.

In 1905, Alfred and Albert Stratton were accused of murdering an elderly couple who were battered to death above their shop in London.

Lying on the floor next to the bodies was an emptied cashbox in which the couple had kept their takings. On the box's metal tray, fingerprint officers found the impression of a sweaty or oily thumbprint which did not match those of the dead couple – or that of the first police officer at the scene.

Suspicion fell upon the Strattons, both known housebreakers. They were arrested and tried at the Old Bailey. The thumbprint was the main piece of evidence.

Both men were found guilty and sentenced to death. They were hanged together by the brothers John and William Billington, the public executioners, on May 23, 1905.

'Mr Fingertips'

The comparison of fingerprints for catching criminals was first developed in the 1890s by Edward Henry, the British inspector-general of the Indian police in Bengal.

Previously, the usual method of registering the characteristics of criminals was the anthropometric system, developed by Alphonse Bertillon, a French criminologist. It involved measuring the criminal's arms and legs, and taking photographs from the front and sides.

Edward Henry became interested in fingerprints which had previously been used to study racial characteristics and evolution. He instructed his police officers to take impressions of criminals' left thumbs in the belief that as most people were right-handed the ridges on the left thumb would be less worn. He then went on to devise a system based on the patterns of prints which was adopted in India.

His revolutionary ideas attracted interest in England, and in 1901 he was put in charge of the Criminal Investigation Department at Scotland Yard. He set up the first Fingerprint Branch which made more than 100 successful identifications within six months.

Henry later became Commissioner of the Metropolitan Police. He retired and was made a baronet in 1918, but was always known as 'Mr Fingertips'.

Genetic fingerprinting: the sure-fire identity parade

Genetic fingerprinting has changed the course of crime detection. It is the most accurate method yet developed of identifying individuals. The probability against any two genetic fingerprints being the same by pure chance is greater than the number of people on Earth. The technique can also prove paternity of children and is being used to control the breeding of rare animals.

Professor Alec Jeffreys, a British geneticist at Leicester University, discovered genetic fingerprinting in 1984. He was conducting research into DNA – the chemical substance in the nucleus of every living cell which determines a person's individual characteristics, such as the colour of hair and eyes. The structure of DNA is different in everybody, with the exception of identical twins.

Professor Jeffreys discovered that within the DNA molecule there is a sequence of genetic information which is repeated many times along the structure of the DNA, which looks like an endless twisting ladder.

The length of the sequence, the number of times it is repeated and its precise location within the DNA chain are unique to each individual. A process was developed to translate these sequences into a visual record. The finished picture, the genetic fingerprint, is a series of bars on an X-ray film, rather like the bar codes printed on food packets.

To obtain a DNA specimen, a scientist only needs a biological sample containing some human cells. This is usually blood, semen or hair, and only very small amounts are necessary.

Genetic fingerprinting is as important in establishing innocence as guilt. For example, a burglar who breaks a window may leave a blood sample behind on the glass. This can be used to create a genetic fingerprint. When police arrest a suspect, a blood sample can be taken from him and compared. If it matches, he is the burglar. If it does not, he is innocent.

When the police have a genetic fingerprint, but no suspect, they can fingerprint groups of people by taking samples of their blood. The first mass genetic fingerprinting happened in Leicestershire in 1987 when samples were taken from 5500 men living around a village where two young girls had been raped and murdered.

The killer was eventually found when a

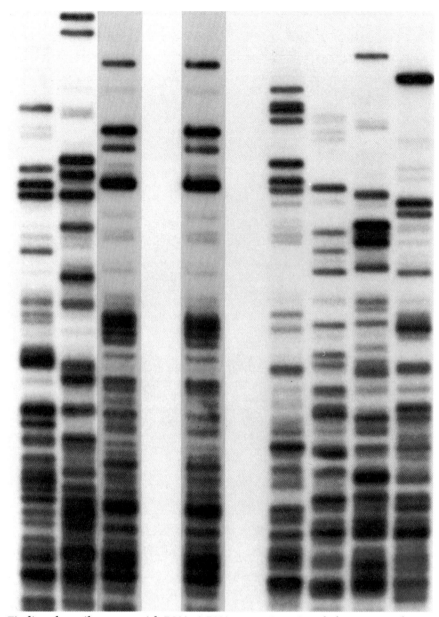

Finding the guilty party with DNA *A DNA pattern (centre) made from a scene-of-crime bloodstain is compared with those of seven suspects. Only the pattern on the immediate left is an exact match. The others are in some ways similar, but not identical. So the guilt of one person – and the innocence of six others – can be quickly established.*

man was heard to say that a workmate had asked him to take his place when the samples were being taken. Another man who had previously been accused of one of the murders was freed because his genetic fingerprint did not match those made from the scene-of-crime evidence.

Genetic fingerprinting can also determine who is the father of a child and resolve paternity disputes. A DNA strand is made up equally of the characteristics of each parent. By comparing the genetic fingerprints of mother and child, a scientist can say with certainty that the parts of the child's fingerprint which do not match those of the mother must have come from its true father.

Another use is in bone-marrow transplants which are given to people suffering from leukaemia. Doctors can check whether the genetic fingerprint extracted from a patient after a transplant matches that of the donor. If it does, the transplant has been successful and is producing healthy white blood cells. If it does not, the transplant has failed to take. This allows the possibility of another transplant.

Zoologists can use genetic fingerprinting to control the breeding of rare animals and preserve species. They can compare genetic fingerprints taken from animals to ensure that inbreeding among endangered species, which is known to lead to weaker animals, is avoided.

How do police create an Identikit of a wanted man?

In February 1959 an armed robber held up a liquor store in southern California and made off with the takings. It was a typical small-time crime, but for one thing: the store owner gave Sheriff Peter Pitchess of Los Angeles County Police a detailed description of the robber. This enabled the police to create a lifelike portrait of the wanted man.

Pictures of the robber were circulated in the area and, as a result of them, he was identified and arrested. He confessed to the crime and was duly punished – so becoming the first criminal in the world to be caught by means of Identikit.

The system had been conceived in the mid-1940s principally by Hugh C. McDonald, a detective with the Los Angeles Identification Bureau. Taking some 50,000 photographs of people's faces, he cut them into some 12 main sections – and used them as the basis of what he called Identikit.

This consisted of almost 400 different and contrasting pairs of eyes, lips, noses, chins, hairlines, eyebrows, beards, moustaches and so on. To build up a likeness, the various features were drawn on transparent plastic sheets, which were changed and overlaid until a composite portrait was created that matched eyewitness descriptions of the wanted person.

The use of photographs or artists' impressions to identify and apprehend criminals dates back to the 1880s in France. Then a French criminologist named Alphonse Bertillon introduced a system which he called *portrait parlé*, or 'speaking portrait'.

It involved the use of front and side photographs of captured criminals, cut into sections and mounted so that particular features – a hooked nose, a pointed chin, protruding ears and so forth – could be studied. This helped police officers to recognise wanted criminals in the street.

In the mid-1970s a second and now more commonly used Identikit system was introduced in North America. It was developed by Pat Dunleavy, an officer in the Royal Canadian Mounted Police, and it uses plastic sheets which contain actual photographs of facial features.

In the United Kingdom a system called Photo-FIT (Facial Identification Technique) has been used by the police since 1970. Photo-FIT also uses real photographs of 'ordinary' people mounted on thin plastic sheets. The basic five-section kit consists of 195 hairlines, 99 eyes and eyebrows, 89 noses, 105 mouths, and 74 chins and cheeks, which enable billions of possible combinations to be assembled.

Gendarme murderer *Following the construction of an Identikit picture in France, a killer was recognised as a gendarme involved in the same investigation.*

Features such as facial hair and spectacles are available as overlays. The pieces are cut so that the length and width of the composite face can be fitted into a frame which holds them in place.

The basic kit relates to Caucasian (white) faces and there are supplementary kits to give North American Indian, Indian subcontinent and Afro-Caribbean features. A kit has not yet been developed for Oriental faces, which are usually drawn by artists.

Witnesses of crimes are interviewed by the police as soon after the events as possible – as most people's ability to recall starts to diminish after about a week.

For both Photo-FIT and Identikit, detectives begin by asking witnesses to recall details of the crime itself. They then move on to general descriptions of the suspect or suspects. For instance, were they short and burly, or lean and tall? What sort of clothes were they wearing? And what did the suspects actually do at the scene of the crime? Only then are the witnesses asked about facial details.

They leaf through books, or 'feature atlases' containing the various Photo-FIT or Identikit sheets, from which they make their selections. Faces are put together sheet by sheet, or strip by strip.

Often, a police artist is then called in to heighten the picture. A clear plastic sheet is laid over it and fine details such as hair shade, skin blemishes, scars or shaped eyebrows are added. The picture is then covered with an artist's fixative spray and is signed by the witness.

Recently, computer technology has been introduced to enhance the pictures. This enables extremely lifelike faces to be drawn on computer screens according to eyewitness descriptions, and fine alterations can be made to the image. From this, a photograph-like print can be obtained.

In addition, police mugshots (photographs of arrested criminals) can be stored on computer. They are coded according to physical characteristics and the computer can choose a selection which most closely matches witness descriptions.

Machine-made man *In the latest computer-aided identification system, E-FIT, the initial description of a person (1) can be altered, say by adding facial hair (2), then the shape of the face can be modified (3), and features such as scars added (4).*

How handwriting experts catch criminals

On the afternoon of July 4, 1956, Mrs Beatrice Weinberger brought her month-old baby, Peter, back from an outing near their home in Westbury, Long Island, USA. She left the pram on the patio of her house and hurried inside to get the baby a clean nappy. When she returned a few moments later, the pram was empty – and a scrawled note was lying where Peter had been.

The note said: 'Attention. I'm sorry this had to happen, but I'm in bad need of money, and couldn't get it any other way. Don't tell anyone or go to the police about this because I am watching you closely. I'm scared stiff, and will kill the baby at your first wrong move.

'Just put $2000 (two thousand) in small bills in a brown envelope, and place it next to the signpost at the corner of Albemarle Rd. and Park Ave. at *exactly* 10 o'clock tomorrow (Thursday) morning.

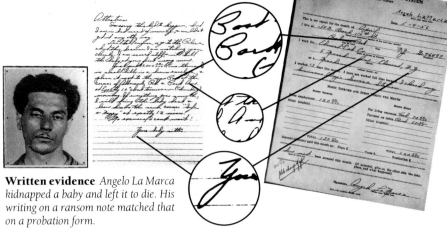

Written evidence *Angelo La Marca kidnapped a baby and left it to die. His writing on a ransom note matched that on a probation form.*

'If everything goes smooth, I will bring the baby back and leave him on the same corner "Safe and Happy" at exactly 12 noon. No excuse, I can't wait! Your baby-sitter.'

Despite the kidnapper's warning, Mr and Mrs Weinberger, frantic with worry, contacted the police.

A dummy parcel containing cut-up pieces of newspaper was placed on the corner the following morning. But the kidnapper did not show up. He failed to keep two other 'appointments' with the Weinbergers, and left a second note signed 'Your baby-sitter'. By then, police felt that the baby was no longer alive.

The FBI was called in and the Bureau's handwriting experts set to work to try to track down the kidnapper. In both the ransom notes an unusual z-shaped stroke was placed at the front of the y in words such as 'money' and 'baby'.

Starting with the New York State Motor Vehicle Bureau, the analysts spent the next six weeks combing through local records and at probation offices, work places, factories, aircraft plants, clubs and schools.

Altogether, more than 2 million signatures and handwriting samples were examined by eye and compared to the writing on the ransom notes.

Then, in the middle of August, the experts' painstaking efforts paid off. The handwriting of Angelo John La Marca, of Plainview, Long Island, matched that of the kidnapper's – especially in the peculiar formation of the y's.

Some time previously La Marca had been put on probation for making illegal alcohol. On being shown the handwriting samples, he broke down and confessed to the kidnapping of baby Peter.

It had been a spur-of-the-moment crime, he stated, committed to ease his financial problems. He told the police he had left Peter alive and well in a nearby park on the day after the kidnapping. But when officers hurried to the spot, all they found was the infant's dead body. La Marca was later executed in New York's Sing Sing Prison.

Even if La Marca had tried to disguise his handwriting he probably would still have been caught.

No matter how hard someone may try to disguise handwriting quirks and characteristics – or adopt those of somebody else – the 'individuality' of the writer shows through. The very angle at which he or she holds a pen; the way a *t* is crossed and an *i* is dotted; the height and size of capital and small letters; the amount of space between words; the use (or misuse) of punctuation marks. All these can identify a person as surely as fingerprints.

In 1983 Gary Herbertson, the head of the

WHEN A NEW JOB DEPENDS UPON YOUR HANDWRITING

Applicants for the job of deputy personnel manager of a computer company had been whittled down to two young men of equal experience, skill and qualifications. Outwardly, there seemed little to choose between them – so the interviewing board called in a graphologist, or handwriting analyst, to assess character and potential.

The handwriting of the first applicant was large, fluid and rounded; that of the second was small, sharp and angular. According to the graphologist, the first handwriting showed someone who was self-confident, flexible and who got on well with people. The second handwriting, however, portrayed someone who – despite his social and professional 'front' – was self-doubting and rigid. So the job went to the first applicant.

Graphologists maintain that handwriting is a form of 'brain-writing', in which the unconscious mind is conveyed to the fingers and reveals itself on paper (see below).

In the United States more than 3000 businesses – from public relations companies to banks – use expert handwriting analysts for sifting through job applications, requests for promotion, and business ideas that come through the post. In West Germany 80 per cent of major companies employ graphologists for personnel selection – and the practice is growing around the world.

Its adherents claim that it is an effective way of deciding whether a person can be trusted. In the USA – where firms lose up to $40,000 million each year to dishonest employees – graphology has taken the place of polygraph, or lie-detector tests, which are no longer legal.

Polygraph screening was found to have no firm validity. And critics of graphology level the same accusation against the handwriting experts – many of whom are self-trained and whose evaluations often contradict each other.

However, most graphologists agree on certain basic concepts – such as the importance of assessing character on a

---

SIZE

Large writing *Denotes ambition or 'thinking big'. It is often found in the writing of people in show business.*

Small writing *Modesty and feelings of inferiority can be indicated by small writing, although the writer may be objective and scientific.*

SLANT

Left slant *Writing with a left-hand slant can indicate people who are retiring and shy. They tend to stay in their shell, hide their emotions and set up a passive attitude.*

Right slant *Writing that slants to the right suggests an outgoing personality. The writers like to mix with other people.*

WIDTH

Narrow *People with narrow writing are usually disciplined, but inhibited. They may also be mean and restricted in view.*

Broad *Those whose writing is broad are normally uninhibited and like travel. They may also be rash and uncontrolled.*

FBI laboratory's document department, stated: 'Any time you try to change your handwriting, you do things that look unnatural. A forger's writing doesn't have the speed, fluidity, the smoothness of natural writing.

'You can see blunt beginnings and ends of strokes, rough curves, inappropriate breaks, little tremors. Two letters may be the same shape, but you can tell if one's written quickly and the other is carefully drawn.'

In addition to their knowledge, handwriting experts use sophisticated instruments and machines in their work. These include infrared and ultraviolet scanning devices with which they look beneath erasures and changes; split-screen equipment for comparing dubious documents with genuine ones; and tools for greatly magnifying handwriting and comparing different ways of joining up letters.

The most notorious handwriting case in recent times involved the forging in the early 1980s of the 'diaries' of Adolf Hitler – in which the Nazi leader supposedly committed his innermost thoughts in an antiquated German script. They included an entry on the Russian attack on Berlin in April 1945, when – in his bunker hide-out – Hitler allegedly wrote: 'The long-awaited

offensive has begun. May the Lord God stand by us.'

The 60 diaries were bought by the German weekly news magazine *Stern* for a reputed 6 million marks. *Stern* then sold subsidiary rights in France, Spain, Belgium, Holland, Italy, Norway and England – where extracts were published in the *Sunday Times*.

Publication in Germany began in the spring of 1983. And two of the diaries – from 1932, the year before Hitler became dictator, and 1945, the year of his suicide – were sent to the American magazine *Newsweek*, which was also interested in publishing them.

The magazine called in a leading handwriting expert, Kenneth Rendell, of Boston, Mass – who was immediately suspicious. 'Even at first glance,' he stated, 'everything looked wrong.'

Using a powerful microscope and samples of Hitler's genuine handwriting, he compared the two sets of writing – particularly the capital letters E, H and K – and found major discrepancies and dissimilarities between the two. These convinced Rendell that the diaries were fakes. In addition, the ink proved to be modern; and Hitler, when he had made notes and records in the early 1930s, had used only the finest quality, gold-embossed paper. He would not have resorted to the sort of cheap, lined notepaper on which the fake diaries were written.

As a result of the exposé, a German criminal with a string of convictions – Konrad Paul Kujau – was later arrested along with two accomplices and tried for forging the diaries. In July 1985 he was found guilty by a Hamburg court and sentenced to four and a half years imprisonment. Once again, the handwriting expert had exposed the handwriting cheat.

combination of several main factors, and not any one 'peculiar' characteristic.

They divide handwriting into three 'zones': the upper and lower zones, formed by the tops and bottoms of capital letters and other letters such as b, d and g; and the middle zone, containing the remaining small letters. The relative forms and sizes of the zones are said to reveal people's true selves.

For example, a large upper zone indicates someone who is outgoing and cheerful; a small lower zone suggests someone shallow and emotionally stunted; and an average-sized middle zone may point to someone who is well-organised and practical.

SPACING

Convinced   at   his

Wide spacing *People who write with wide spaces between the words do not mix easily in company. They can be stand-offish and solitary.*

Your Children are not your

Narrow spacing *Small spaces between words denote a gregarious personality. But they also suggest that the writer chooses friends indiscriminately.*

How dogs and machines sniff out drugs and explosives

After five women from Bogota, Colombia, aroused suspicion at London's Heathrow Airport in 1988, sniffer dogs were brought in to examine their luggage. The dogs led customs men to 20 LP records in each of the women's suitcases. When the vinyl layers of the records were split open, cocaine was discovered sandwiched between the halves. A total of 16 kilos of the drug was found in the records and in the jackets of books. The women were all jailed for 14 years.

Sniffer dogs are used by police and customs throughout the world to detect drugs and explosives.

Dogs that are trained for the job include natural retrievers used in field sports, such as labradors, collies and spaniels. Dogs have a far better sense of smell than people because the smell receptors at the top of a dog's nose are 100 times longer than in humans.

The training course for a sniffer dog normally lasts about 12 weeks. The dog is first taught to recognise a particular drug or explosive.

Its handler conceals a sample of the substance inside something the dog can grip in its mouth – a rolled-up newspaper, a piece of pipe or a rag – which is known as a training aid.

The dog is commanded to bring the aid back to the handler, and then receives a reward. The reward will be whatever that particular dog enjoys doing – usually a friendly fight with the handler or a game of hide-and-seek.

Bag check
This vapour-sensitive portable explosives detector is now in use at many of the world's major airports.

The dog learns to recognise the smell of the training aid, which is in fact the smell of the drug or explosive. The type of training aid is changed regularly, but the smell always remains the same. At first the aid is placed within sight of the dog, but is then hidden out of sight.

Smells such as perfumes, which some

Sniffer dog *A customs dog-handler at Miami International Airport gives directions to her dog in the constant hunt for drugs.*

smugglers spread to disguise the scent of drugs, are also used so that the dog becomes familiar with them.

A dog can eventually be trained to respond to up to 12 different types of explosives and four different types of drugs, usually cannabis, cocaine, heroin and amphetamine.

When a dog is sent out to search for drugs, perhaps in a lorry or warehouse, it is put into a special harness – a signal that it should start working. When it locates a smell which it knows will lead to a reward, it will become agitated and excited.

Other customs or police officers then take over.

The handler drops a training aid where the dog will see it and return it, and the dog then gets its reward.

Air samples

Machines that are used to detect drugs and explosives suck in air through a tube that can be inserted into concealed spaces such as petrol tanks, panelling in vehicles or gaps between walls.

They also take air samples from containers and lorries where drugs and explosives might be hidden.

The samples are analysed by a machine called a mass spectrometer which breaks them down into their chemical parts and indentifies minute traces of individual substances used in explosives or drugs.

It is claimed that traces as small as one-trillionth of a gram can be detected.

Electron movement

'Sniffer' machines large enough for people to walk through have been installed at the Houses of Parliament in London and at some international airports, including Seoul before the 1988 Olympic Games. They can detect dynamite or nitroglycerine, which gives off a vapour that attracts electrons. A current running through the sniffer machine detects the movement of the electrons.

Old and new ways of outsmarting smugglers

Customs officers at Southampton were highly suspicious of part of a cargo on its way from Colombia – a major drug-producing country – to the Netherlands. The padlocks on a container filled with ceramic tiles seemed to have been tampered with. So, with nothing more than this and intuition to go on, the officers decided to investigate.

The cargo had been unloaded from a container ship for routine re-stowage and the officers had to act swiftly and secretively.

They removed the container for examination and came across a hidden steel compartment 4in (100mm) deep running the length of its top. The compartment was cut open with oxyacetylene torches and inside was found 460lb (208kg) of cocaine, in 263 small packages, with a street value of some £51 million.

The container was sealed up again – with bags of grain substituted for the drugs – and put back on the ship without anyone being the wiser. The ship continued its voyage and the container was unloaded at the Dutch port of Rotterdam. Together with its load of tiles it was taken to a caravan site. There a gang of eight men began cutting into the roof. As they did so, Dutch police moved in and arrested the smugglers – who were later tried and imprisoned for up to six years for importing and dealing in cocaine.

The incident took place in the autumn of 1987 and was typical of the way in which modern customs officers work. Despite the introduction of electronic surveillance techniques, the tried-and-true methods of experience and intuition – plus underworld tip-offs and international co-operation – have a large part to play.

Dark glasses

Any incoming foot or vehicle passenger who behaves nervously will attract the customs men's attention. The officers are on the lookout for anyone who is unduly agitated – who blinks more than the usual 20-30 times a minute; who wears dark glasses to hide such telltale signs; who perspires unduly (particularly, with men,

on the backs of the hands); or whose breathing is fast and noisy.

Once their suspicions are aroused, customs officers may use special equipment to probe further. With a spectroscope – a long thin tube with a lens on the end – they can look into petrol tanks or behind door panelling. Optical fibres in the tube carry a picture back to a small eyepiece. The device is like a telescope that sees around corners.

Special X-ray machines give a colour picture and are 'tuned' to detect anything concealed inside a container. For instance, they show the size and relative positions of objects inside a bag, even if a large number of bags are stacked together.

One of the most useful machines used by the officers is also one of the simplest: the weighing machine. Officers know what an average luggage bag weighs when full. So bags belonging to suspect people are weighed, and if they are found to be overweight they are searched. Or a bag might be emptied and then weighed. If it weighs more than the weight given by the manufacturers it could be searched for drugs, diamonds, gold or other contraband

Sweet subterfuge *Heroin hidden in sweet and toffee papers was seized by customs men at London's Heathrow airport in 1988.*

Seeing eye *A customs man at Dover car hall uses a spectroscope – an internal viewing instrument – to look into a petrol tank to see if any cannabis is concealed inside.*

THE STRANGE CASE OF THE DRUG-CARRYING SNAILS

In July 1988 a customs officer at Hanover airport in West Germany became suspicious of a passenger carrying a battered holdall who had just flown in from Lagos, the capital of Nigeria in West Africa.

The holdall was opened and found to contain a plastic bag full of live edible snails – agate snails, or *Achatina fulica*, whose shells are as big as a fist. Breaking open one of the shells, the officer discovered beneath it several small packages, each containing just under 1oz (28g) of heroin.

Similar packages were found hidden in the other snails, making a total of some 21oz (595g) of the drug.

The smuggler was arrested – and the Hanover customs men reported the case of the 16 drug-carrying snails to their colleagues throughout Germany. From then on a keen eye was kept on passengers from Nigeria.

Two weeks later another Nigerian was caught at Hanover airport trying to smuggle in a slightly larger cache of heroin also under the shells of agate snails. Thanks to an officer's alertness, an ingenious new means of smuggling had been thwarted.

Piecing together an airliner's last disastrous moments

Travel by aircraft is normally an extremely safe method of transport. Statistics show that each year some 1100 people are killed in air accidents throughout the world – compared to 40,000 people killed in road accidents in the USA alone.

Yet accidents have occurred since the earliest days of flight. The first to be recorded was in 1908. Lieut Thomas C. Selfridge of the US Army, a distant cousin of the founder of the famous London store, was killed when Orville Wright's aircraft crashed at Fort Myer, Virginia, after a wooden propeller splintered. Wright, one of the pioneers of manned flight, escaped with a broken leg. Selfridge, his passenger, died almost instantly.

When a modern aircraft crashes there is always an intensive investigation to establish the cause so that lessons can be learned to prevent future tragedies. This applies whether it is a light aircraft with only a couple of passengers or a jumbo jet

hidden in compartments in the lining.

Sometimes, a bag is singled out after it leaves an aircraft by an X-ray machine or a sniffer dog. Customs men wait until the bag has been reclaimed by its owner – and they stop him as he passes the checkpoint.

Customs officers pay close attention to passengers arriving from countries with a reputation for exporting drugs. In particular, they are on the lookout for 'swallowers' and 'stuffers'.

These are poorly paid couriers who put the drugs, mainly cocaine or heroin – into condoms. They then either swallow the condoms – and retrieve them later by

defecating or vomiting – or stuff them into bodily orifices.

At ferry ports and frontier crossings, drivers or passengers who cannot give an adequate explanation for their trip, those that appear tense or hesitant, or a scruffy person driving an expensive car, might be subjected to a check.

Many seizures are the result of chance suspicions; but many more are due to hours of painstaking detective work on the part of the customs men. This involves surveillance, undercover work and informers – in many countries and often over long periods of time.

Airshow tragedy *Three people died in a French Airbus which crashed while taking part in an airshow near Mulhouse in eastern France in June 1988. The crash happened when the aircraft ploughed into a 40ft (12m) high line of trees. Miraculously 133 other people on the Airbus survived the crash, although the aircraft itself was almost totally destroyed. The plane's descent was apparently cushioned by the trees it landed on. The pilot was dismissed by Air France after the 'black box' flight recorders indicated he had not responded to audible warnings from the controls to increase height.*

airliner carrying more than 500 people.

Whether the suspected cause is a terrorist bomb or a faulty component, the principles of the inquiry are the same.

The first steps include recovering the wreckage, which may be on a mountain or under the ocean. Air accident investigators, who are usually employed by the transport department or air travel authority of the country concerned, go to the scene of the crash. They map out the area across which wreckage is scattered, since this may reveal the sequence in which the plane broke up. Samples of all parts of the wreckage are taken in case they might indicate some reason for the crash. Metals crack or melt differently according to types of heat, pressure or blast.

Recovery and examination of the bodies will be conducted by medical experts, who can determine the time and cause of death which may contribute to establishing the cause of the crash.

The worst single year for aircraft accidents was 1985 when more than 800 people died in two crashes involving Boeing 747 jumbo jets. At first, it was thought that the two crashes were caused by a mechanical fault in 747s. The investigations, however, succeeded in disproving the theory.

The first crash was an Air India 747 bound for Delhi from Vancouver via London. At about 31,000ft above the North Atlantic, west of Shannon in Ireland, the aircraft disintegrated and plunged into the ocean with the loss of all 329 people.

Although more than 130 bodies and some pieces of wreckage were recovered quickly, it took three months to locate and map out the rest of the aircraft. Most of it was on the seabed, 6500ft (2000m) below. It was located using sonar equipment and mini-submarines working from surface recovery vessels.

The first and most important pieces of wreckage to be recovered were the flight data recorder and cockpit voice recorder. The recorders are often called 'black boxes'. In fact, they are usually bright orange or red, so they can easily be spotted.

Terrorist bomb

When the cockpit voice recorder, which captures on tape the sounds inside the aircraft's cockpit, was replayed, investigators believed they heard the sound of an explosion. It was recorded on the last millisecond of tape before the aircraft disintegrated. Although there was no direct evidence of a terrorist bomb, there were enough signs from the wreckage to make it a strong possibility. The seats were scorched underneath and the front cargo door appeared to have been blown out, while others remained intact.

Scientists also pinpointed where the recovered bodies had been sitting in the

---

THE MACHINES THAT REPLAY THE TRAGEDY

Investigators (left) examine the flight recorder of an Air Florida plane which crashed into the Potomac River, Washington DC, in February 1982. A cockpit voice recorder (right) has a tape which records the crew's conversations while they are flying the plane.

The most important pieces of wreckage to be recovered are usually the two recorders carried on all civil airliners.

The flight data recorder provides a record of the movements of key instruments, such as airspeed and altitude indicators, and the positions of rudders and spoilers. The information is recorded as electronic pulses on a tape. When the tape is played back, it will give a computer printout of the aircraft's movements. A computer screen can also be programmed to look like the main instruments, giving a more realistic playback.

In the future it may be possible to increase the items recorded and to play them back through a flight simulator, which is normally used for training pilots, to re-create the cockpit of the aircraft in the hours before it crashed. Flight data recorders can record up to 200 hours of flying time.

Cockpit voice recorders pick up conversations and sounds of the crew. They work on a continuous tape lasting 30 minutes, so at any time only the last 30 minutes is recorded. A weakness of the system is that if a crash does not stop the recorder working, it can remain switched on and erase the vital section.

The recorders are installed in the rear of aircraft – the area most likely to survive a crash. They are housed in a case made of two shells of stainless steel with heat protective material between. They must be able to survive a temperature of 2000°F (1100°C) for 30 minutes.

---

airliner and established patterns of different injuries, which supported the theory that the aircraft exploded in midair.

Another clue came when Canadian investigators discovered that the aircraft had been loaded with the bag of an Indian passenger who had not boarded the plane.

A similar set of circumstances surrounded an explosion of a bag at Narita Airport in Tokyo, which killed two baggage handlers, at about the same time as the Air India crash. Both bags were later traced back to one man in Vancouver and the explosions were believed to be the work of Sikh terrorists.

Two months after the Air India crash, a Japan Airlines 747, on a flight between Tokyo and Osaka, crashed into Mount Osutaka, 70 miles (113km) north of Tokyo. All but four of the 528 passengers died, making it then the worst disaster involving a single aircraft.

A few minutes after takeoff, a loud bang was heard from the rear of the cabin, followed by the complete failure of all instruments. The crew fought for 32

minutes to keep the plane airborne until it crashed in a spot so remote it took 14 hours before the first rescuers and investigators arrived. The aircraft had almost completely disintegrated, with wreckage covering a wide area. The four survivors had been sitting together in seats in the centre.

Although there was a tape of the conversations between the crew and the air-traffic control, it revealed little of value. However, the history of the plane showed it had been repaired by its makers, Boeing, after landing badly at Osaka in 1978, scraping the rear on the tarmac.

Examination of the wreckage showed that the repairing engineers had left a very small gap between reinforcement plates on a riveted join in a bulkhead. This gap had exposed the join to pressure and it had eventually ruptured, allowing air from the cabin into the tail section. This had snapped hydraulic control lines, ripping off the rudder and the vertical stabiliser fin, which made the aircraft impossible to control, despite the crew's desperate half-hour struggle.

Ingenious solutions and artful ideas

Capturing a speeding bullet on film, converting the wind into electric power and transforming single fibres into thread – human inventiveness devises the answers to a host of fascinating questions.

How they take high-speed pictures, page 128.

How cotton is turned into thread and cloth, page 110.

How electricity is generated by the wind, page 124.

How pure metals are won from the earth

Iron *Haematite, an*
iron ore, gets its name because it looks like
dried blood (haima is Greek for 'blood').

Very few metals emerge glittering and perfect from the earth. Nuggets of gold are sometimes found; in fact in 1869 a nugget of pure gold weighing 154lb (69.92kg) was found in Victoria, Australia. And in 1856 a 500 ton lump of pure copper was dug up from a mine in Michigan, USA.

Some other metals, however, appear in drab disguises, combined with oxygen, sulphur, carbon and other elements to form ores that look little different from rocks or earth.

The first step towards obtaining the pure metal is to separate the ore from the dirt and stones dug up with it. Different methods are needed for different metals.

One way is said to have been discovered by the wife of a lead miner who found that particles of lead stuck to the froth when she washed his dirty clothes.

Lead and copper-mining companies now add ore to aerated, frothing liquid containing a chemical called a collector that enables the mineral particles to cling to the surface of air bubbles, while the waste is wetted and sinks. The valuable material is carried away on the froth to be skimmed off and dried.

Heat is often used to extract the pure metal from the ore, in a process called smelting. Early man discovered that when ores were heated in a fire with charcoal, a spongy mass of metal was left which could be beaten into weapons, tools or ornaments.

Copper was smelted in this way in ancient Egypt, and later the same method was used to produce an even more useful metal, iron. In medieval England it was found that the use of furnaces, with bellows to produce a forced draught of air, would increase the temperature of the fire and produce not a lump of metal, but a stream of liquid iron that could be cast in moulds.

Iron ore is known chemically as iron oxide because the metal is combined with oxygen in its natural state. In the smelting process, the iron oxide reacts with charcoal, made by converting wood into carbon. The oxygen atoms are detached

Gold *Deposits of gold, called lodes, are found in veins of quartz. Nuggets are broken-off pieces.*

from the iron, and attach themselves to the carbon, forming carbon oxide gas. This escapes, leaving behind the iron.

The modern version of the same process uses coke as a source of carbon rather than charcoal, and takes place in huge blast furnaces capable of producing thousands of tons of iron a day.

The iron produced is called pig iron. This contains too much carbon to be useful, so must be converted into steel, by removing the carbon, or into cast iron by blending. Steel is the most important form of iron.

Aluminium occurs in combination with oxygen in bauxite ore. Though it is the most plentiful metal of all, making up 8 per cent of the Earth's crust, it was not produced in any quantity until the end of the 19th century, because it requires a large amount of energy to separate it from oxygen.

The method used is electrolysis. An electric current is passed through a molten bath of aluminium oxide, which removes the oxygen, leaving behind liquid aluminium. The major difficulty is the very high melting point of aluminium oxide – over 3600°F (2000°C), compared to about 2900°F (1600°C) for iron.

The problem is solved by mixing the aluminium oxide with a mineral called cryolite (sodium aluminium fluoride) which lowers the melting point to a more manageable and cheaper 1800°F (1000°C).

Gold is one of the metals produced by chemical means. It often occurs as fine grains in the beds of streams. The problem is to separate the very small amounts of gold from the mass of useless material.

In ancient times the fleece of a sheep, immersed in a stream, was used to collect grains of gold – perhaps the origin of the Golden Fleece sought by the Argonauts. And prospectors 'panned' for gold – swirling the dirt from a stream in a pan of water until the lighter gravel was washed away, leaving the denser gold in the pan.

Today a chemical is used. The crushed

Ore into iron *Iron ore is turned into iron in a blast furnace, where the ore reacts with coke and limestone at a temperature of 2900°F (1600°C). The molten iron is then cast into bars of pig iron (above).*

Gold graining
Molten droplets of gold are poured into a cold-water bath (above). The resulting gold grains, shown actual size (right), can be precisely weighed when bought by a jeweller.

ore is mixed with a solution of potassium cyanide, which dissolves the gold. The solution containing the gold is then filtered, to remove undissolved impurities, and the gold is finally precipitated out. A ton of ore will produce just over one-third of an ounce (10 grams) of gold.

How they turn sand into glass

Five thousand years ago, on some beach in the Middle East, someone probably lit a fire and later found shiny, transparent globules like jewels among the sand. How were these new curiosities transformed into one of the major household and building materials of the 20th century – glass?

The raw material from which glass is made is silica, the most abundant of all the earth's minerals. Milky white in colour, it is found in many forms of rock, including granite. And as every beach in the world has been formed by water pounding rocks into tiny particles, sand is the major source of silica.

When you are next at the seaside, examine a handful of sand. Any grain which is semitransparent – rather than black, red, yellow or some other definite colour – is a grain of silica. Sand also contains other minerals, but silica is the main component because it is hard, insoluble and does not decompose, so it outlasts the others.

Pure silica has such a high melting point that no ordinary fire would convert it into glass. So the first Middle Eastern glassmakers must have lit their fire on sand which was impregnated with soda (compounds of sodium) left behind by evaporated water from a lake or sea. The soda reduces silica's melting point.

Today, lime and soda are combined with silica to produce soda-lime glass, used for making bottles, window panes and cheap drinking glasses. When glass cools, its structure does not return to the crystalline structure of silica, which is opaque. Instead, it forms a disordered structure rather like a frozen liquid, which is transparent.

Ovenware and lead crystal

Other materials may be added to provide colour, or to improve the quality of the finished glass. Glass containing 10-15 per cent of boric oxide, for example, is resistant to sudden heating or cooling and is used for ovenware. Adding lead oxide, a technique discovered in the 17th century, produces a heavy glass with a brillant glitter – lead crystal.

Modern sheet glass is made by heating the mixed ingredients in long tanks. The mixture always contains broken glass, known as cullet, which melts at a lower temperature than the other materials and helps them to combine thoroughly.

As newly made glass is taken out from one end of the tank, in a sheet up to 10ft

Bullet-resistant glass *The windows of a diplomat's car are made from glass strengthened with layers of toughened plastic. The window absorbs the energy of the bullet, and the plastic prevents any glass splinters.*

MAKING PERFECT GLASS ON A BATH OF MOLTEN TIN

Cullet hopper — Frit hopper — MELTING FURNACE — Glass floating on tin — Flames in furnace

Float glass *Enormous furnaces are used to melt the raw ingredients for making float glass.*

The ingredients *A mixture of sand, soda and lime, called frit, is combined with cullet (waste glass) and salt cake, ready for heating in the furnace.*

Melting furnaces *Jets of flame pour from the sides of the furnace, which reaches a temperature of 2890°F (1590°C) to melt the ingredients.*

(3m) wide, raw materials are poured in at the other, so that the level in the tank always remains constant.

The tanks are lined with heat-proof bricks and remain in continuous production for as long as their linings last, which may be several years.

Stronger than steel

Glass is thought of as a fragile material, but actually it is very strong. If it is pulled lengthways, a flawless fibre of glass is five times stronger than the best steel. Glass fibres set in plastic produce a tough and resilient material suitable for boats or car bodies called glass-fibre reinforced plastic, or GRP.

Extra-strong glass is produced by heat toughening or by lamination. In toughening, the glass is heated to just below its melting point, then suddenly chilled with jets of air. This makes the surface of the glass cool and shrink before the inner part. As a result, the surface is compressed inwards. This built-in compression has to be overcome before the toughened glass will break. So toughened glass can be bent more, or struck harder, before it breaks. When it does, it disintegrates into tiny fragments, rather than the dangerous shards of ordinary glass.

Laminated glass is a sandwich of two layers of glass and one of plastic. Although the plastic layer may be very thin, it is tough. Impacts may shatter the glass, but it will remain sticking to the plastic and does not form splinters, which makes it parti-

Making window panes, the old way

The technique for making thin, flat window glass was perfected in Normandy, France, in the 14th century. Known as crown glass, each piece was blown by a craftsman. An accomplished glass-blower could make only about a dozen windows in a day, making medieval window glass an expensive luxury.

For each pane, the molten glass is blown into a large bubble using a blowpipe. The bubble is then flattened and attached to the end of an iron rod, called a punty, which is rotated as fast as possible by the craftsman.

The flattened bubble of glass fans out to form a circle 3ft to 6ft (1m to 2m) wide, depending on the size of the original bubble and the skill and strength of the craftsman.

The round, flat glass sheets were then cut for use as small window panes, particularly in churches. The 'bullseye' at the centre of the disc was the least transparent section, but because glass was so expensive, it would have been used anyway.

Crown glass *A glass-blower spins a sheet of crown glass on a punty.*

cularly suitable for the windscreens of cars.

Aircraft windscreens must be able to withstand high pressure, extreme temperatures and impacts from flying birds. Three or four layers of glass are interleaved with layers of vinyl, then bonded together. This produces a windscreen which is able to withstand the impact of a large bird while the aeroplane is flying at up to 400mph (650km/h). The same glass also gives the pilots of military aircraft protection against bullets.

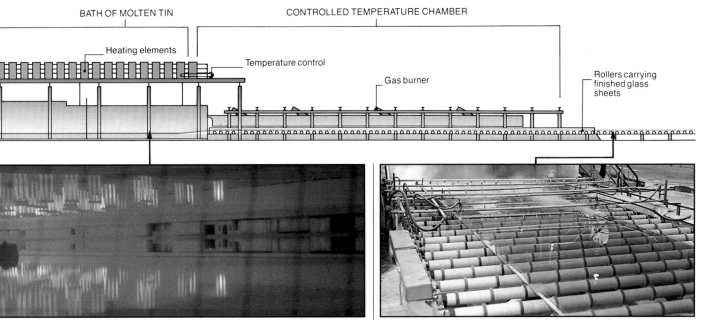

BATH OF MOLTEN TIN   CONTROLLED TEMPERATURE CHAMBER

Heating elements

Temperature control

Gas burner

Rollers carrying finished glass sheets

Molten tin *The melted glass is poured in a stream on the surface of a bath of molten tin. As it floats, the glass cools to 1100°F (600°C) and solidifies, smoothing out irregularities in the surface.*

Glass sheets *When cooled, the glass emerges from the bath onto rollers. It is cut into sheets and washed with jets of water. Float glass has a uniform thickness and is absolutely smooth on both sides.*

The glories of medieval stained glass

The structure of glass, though strong, contains a lot of empty space, because its molecules are packed randomly together like a pile of bricks, rather than lined up in neat columns as they would be if the bricks were made into a wall.

These cavities can be occupied by metal atoms which affect the way light is transmitted through the glass. Different metals absorb light of different frequencies, giving the glass that contains them a characteristic colour.

It was this principle that gave rise to one of the glories of the medieval cathedral, the stained-glass window.

When added to the molten glass, copper turned it ruby red, cobalt blue, iron green, antimony yellow, and manganese purple. Sheets about the size of this book were manufactured in different colours and then cut to the required shapes. They were then assembled into complete windows.

Variations in the thickness of the glass, inevitable with medieval technology, enhanced the beauty of the windows by providing a subtle variation of tone. When the techniques of glass-making improved, a lot of this subtlety was lost.

Intense colours *This window portrays the Coronation of the Virgin in the church of Notre Dame at Châlons-sur-Marne, France. The variation in the blues is due to the difference in thickness of the pieces of glass.*

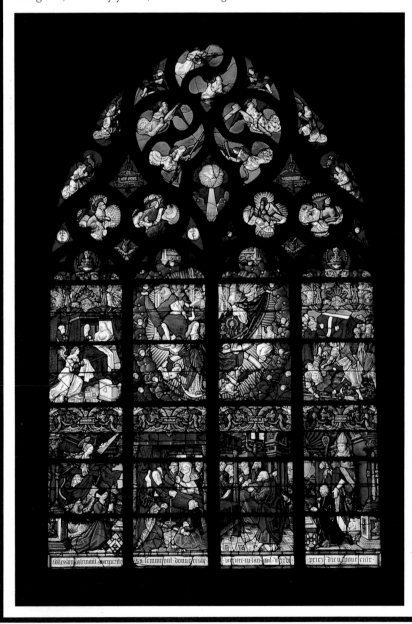

How do they make paper from trees?

It was a Chinese official attached to the Imperial court, Ts'ai Lun, who discovered how to make paper in about AD 105. Until then most documents had been written on parchment, made from the skin of sheep or goats, or vellum, which is made from the skin of a calf. The ancient Egyptians had used papyrus, made from reeds beaten flat, but this was not a true paper, which is made from fibres that have been pulped, then reconstituted.

Though serviceable and very long lasting, parchment and vellum could never have coped with the growing demand for a material on which to store man's unending accumulation of information. It has been estimated that a single book 200 pages long would have needed the skins of 12 sheep.

Ts'ai Lun made his paper from mulberry fibres, fish nets, old rags and waste hemp.

MAKING WATERMARKS IN PAPER AND BANKNOTES

The first watermark happened by accident at the Fabriano paper mill in Italy, where paper has been made since AD 1260. The mould that was being used to press the water from the wet paper had a small piece of wire projecting from it. The paper was thinner where the wire dug into it, causing a line that could be seen by holding the paper up to the light.

It was realised that if a complete design was made of wire, a decorative watermark would be created. In 1282 the first deliberate watermark was made – it was just a simple cross.

Much the same method is used today. The wet paper is squeezed by a roller known as the dandy roll. Soldered or sewn onto the dandy roll is the raised pattern that creates the watermark.

Watermarks have been used for centuries to identify the makers of fine stationery. More elaborate watermarks are used to make forgery of banknotes difficult, by impressing the portraits of heads of state or national heroes on the notes.

Foolscap got its name at the beginning of the 18th century from a watermark of a fool's cap used on paper that was 13½in (340mm) wide, and 17in (430mm) long.

Bond paper *High-quality bond paper, used for stationery and documents, usually has some rag pulp. It is often sized with casein, which comes from milk.*

Newsprint *Chemically treated low-grade wood pulp is used for newsprint, which has a rough texture. It yellows in a few days if exposed to sunlight.*

Tissue paper *Flat, loosely woven fibres give tissues and toilet rolls their soft texture. The paper is made from wood pulp treated with plant resins to make it absorbent.*

Almost any fibrous material can be used for making paper. It is mashed to a pulp with water, bleached, sealed with a sizing agent to prevent too much ink absorption, then pressed into sheets.

Until 1850 the basic raw material was linen and cotton rags, which made excellent paper. But by then demand was growing so rapidly that a new raw material was needed. Wood pulp – usually from softwood trees such as conifers – was the answer.

Wood – indeed all plants – consists of cellulose, an organic material which forms strong fibres about $\frac{1}{10}$in (2.5mm) long. After felling, trees are turned into wood chips and fed into huge digesters where they are mixed with chemicals (usually sodium sulphate) and subjected to high temperatures and pressures to separate out the fibres and produce pulp.

Impurities, such as resin and pitch, are removed, the pulp is bleached, and mixed with chemicals to give it the right colour, or to make it whiter. The mixture then flows from a large tank with a narrow slit onto a moving screen which allows the water to drain away but retains most of the fibres. The sheet is pressed to remove more water and dried by passing around a series of steam-heated cylinders.

The paper may finally be coated with pigments such as clay, chalk, or titanium dioxide to improve its surface.

Paper mill *This 17th-century German engraving shows a paper mill of the time. A wooden water wheel powers the pulverising rods, which mix together the rags and water in the large tank. This is measured out, then pressed into sheets, which are then hung up to dry on wooden poles. The dried sheets are tied into bales, and finally delivered by donkey to the printers.*

WHY DO OLD BOOKS AND DOCUMENTS LAST LONGER THAN MODERN ONES?

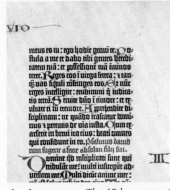

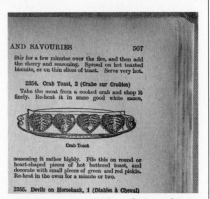

Ageing paper *The 15th-century Gutenberg Bible (left) was printed on fine parchment paper, which is still in excellent condition. Wood-pulp paper containing acids survives much less well. The 1914 cookery book (right) is already turning brown.*

The discovery that paper could be made from wood was the key that made the mass market in books and newspapers possible. But unlike parchment, vellum or rag-based papers, paper made from wood pulp has a limited life. Librarians have begun to realise that modern books are deteriorating rapidly.

The problem is that they contain chemicals, including acids from the bleaching process, that eat them away. For most readers, it hardly matters, because they have read the books long before the decay becomes evident. But for archivists and librarians it is a disaster. It means that potentially all the books that have been published since 1850 could be slowly self-destructing.

'The irony is that the paper of older books published since the beginning of printing in 1475 can be in much better condition than something printed only 40 years ago, which is collapsing', says Mr Mike Weston of the British Library.

Librarians are now trying to find some inexpensive way of treating their vast stock of books. At present, the only way is to strip off the bindings and treat the pages one by one to remove acid. While this might be justified for some valuable first editions, it is impractical for the bulk of books. However, some manufacturers are now producing paper which has a neutral sizing, to prolong its life.

How plants are turned into petrol

One of man's oldest pastimes has been making alcoholic drinks from fermented plants. But today, as oil is running out and its price is high, alcohol from plants is being put to another use – providing an alternative fuel for vehicles.

The world's largest producer of fuel alcohol from plants is Brazil. Two years after the oil crisis of 1973, Brazil launched its alcohol programme, in response to the increasing costs of importing fuel. The Brazilians use a raw material with a low market value and which they grow in abundance – sugar cane.

Initially the process is the same whether the end product is to be an expensive brandy, or fuel alcohol which can drive a car. The raw sugar is mixed with water and yeast and fermented in large tanks, until it turns into an alcoholic liquid, rather like wine or beer.

One hundred per cent (200 proof) alcohol is needed for fuel, so to concentrate the mixture it is distilled. This is done by heating the liquid to vaporise the alcohol, then condensing the vapour to extract the alcohol and leave the water behind. This last stage, to produce anhydrous alcohol, needs a lot of energy, and has led to criticisms that producing fuel in this way can actually consume more energy than it provides.

The US Department of Energy found that when corn is used to produce alcohol, every 100 British Thermal Units (Btus) of fuel require 109Btus to produce them – 44 Btus to grow the corn (in the form of fuel for agricultural machines, and the energy used to create fertilisers and weedkillers), and 65Btus to produce the alcohol from it.

Despite this, alcohol production in Brazil has boomed. More than 80 per cent of the cars sold in Brazil now run on pure alcohol, or a mix of alcohol and petrol, and the bill for imported oil is down by about $2 billion a year. Annual production is over 11 billion litres and will need to increase by another 2 billion litres to keep up with demand.

In the USA, corn-based alcohol is also produced commercially, thanks to generous tax credits. US alcohol is usually mixed with ordinary petrol to improve its performance and replace lead.

Is coal the answer to an oil crisis?

In South Africa, where coal is plentiful and cheap, a process has been pioneered by the Sasol company to convert coal into oil.

Coal is loaded into large containers, set alight, and blasted for several minutes with a mixture of steam and oxygen under high pressure. The coal burns and produces large amounts of gas which is rich in hydrogen and carbon – the basic building blocks from which oil can be made.

As oil contains about twice as many hydrogen atoms as coal, extra hydrogen has to be added to the coal gas. It is provided by the steam. The burning coal generates enough energy to separate the water molecules in the steam into hydrogen and oxygen atoms. The hydrogen produced gives the gas the right balance of hydrogen and carbon.

This gas must be 'washed' with methanol to remove sulphur and cyanides. Then it is transferred to reactors where further chemical treatment determines the final product. The reactors can produce petrol, oil, waxes, liquefied petroleum gas and chemicals such as alcohols, aldehydes and ketones.

It is an expensive process, justified in South Africa by the very low price of coal and the fear of an oil embargo.

Capturing the fragrance of flowers

The fresh scents of a garden in summer or the tropical fragrances of an equatorial rain forest are caused by minute droplets of oily liquid produced by plants. These essential oils, together with synthetically produced scents, form the basis of the perfume industry.

Why plants produce essential oils is uncertain. Some may attract insects, and therefore increase the chance of pollination; others may be designed to ward off parasites or marauding animals. Of the many thousands of plants in the world, only about 200 produce the range of essential oils from which perfumeries create their fragrances.

Some perfumes contain as many as 100 different oils, others have only a few. But they all share three elements: a 'top note', consisting of the more volatile ingredients which create the immediate effect; a 'middle note', which modifies the initial impression and is intended to give the perfume body; and a 'base note', which persists longest and leaves a lingering impression.

The ancient Greeks and Romans produced fragrant ointments by immersing flowers, leaves and roots in fatty oils, usually animal fat or olive oil, which drew out their scents. Both men and women wore these ointments, but even then they were expensive and only the rich could afford them. When Cleopatra went to greet Mark Antony she drenched the purple sails of her barge with perfume, seeking to impress him.

St Luke tells the story of a woman, identified by some scholars as Mary Magdalene, who poured ointment onto the feet of Jesus in the house of a Pharisee. The ointment would almost certainly have contained spikenard, an aromatic oil obtained from the Indian valerian tree.

It was the Arabs who first used the technique of distillation to extract essential oils, and a similar process is still used today. Flowers or leaves of the scented plant are chopped or crushed, then heated with steam to force the volatile oils to vaporise. The vapour passes through a chilled glass tube which causes the oils to condense. The amount produced from most plants is very low, usually less than one-thousandth of the total material collected. But its fragrance is so intense that even diluted a hundredfold it is still overpowering.

Distillation cannot always be used because there are some fragrances that spoil if they are heated. In Grasse, the perfume centre of Provence in southern France, a technique known as enfleurage is still used for these delicate oils. Flowers are laid out in frames on layers of highly purified tallow and lard. Left in a cool dark room for between one and three days, the fat absorbs the oils from the flowers, producing a material called pomade. The unwanted fat is removed by adding alcohol, leaving just the oils in the alcohol solution, ready to be blended.

Perfume oils are often produced in remote areas by family businesses whose methods have not changed for hundreds of years. Bulgaria still produces 70 per cent of the world's rose oil. In the valleys under the Balkan mountains the rose-pickers gather when it is still dark. The petals have to be picked before dawn to ensure that they keep their fragrance. It takes more than 2000 petals to make every gram of the precious oil.

In many places oils are often produced at the rate of only a few tons a year. The oils are bought by brokers who sell them to exporters, and finally to the perfumeries who compose their own fragrances, a technique which is a difficult and delicate art.

Some perfumes are floral in character, dominated by scents such as rose or gardenia. Others are oriental, herbal or spicy, containing oils of cinnamon from China, Burma and Sri Lanka, or nutmeg from Indonesia or the West Indies. Men's aftershave often contains spicy, woody or leathery accents.

To increase the lasting power of the perfumes, fixatives are used. Formerly these came from exotic animal products – ambergris, from the intestines of the sperm whale; musk, from a gland of the male musk deer; civet, a secretion of the civet cat; and castoreum (or castor) from the gland of a beaver. However, fixatives are now chemically synthesised.

Once a fragrance has been composed, from as little as 20-30 oils or as many as 300, it is sold in a variety of forms. Toilet water or cologne generally contains from 2 to 6 per cent perfume, dissolved in alcohol. Perfumes are much stronger, containing 10 to 25 per cent, again in alcohol solution.

Not all perfumes are made in traditional ways. Chemists, having analysed the substances that produce the scents, can re-create them synthetically. The results are used in millions of applications where conventional perfumes would be too expensive – for things like polishes, air fresheners, disinfectants and shampoos.

Fragrant fields *Lavender flowers ready for harvesting. The oil distilled from them is used as an ingredient in floral-based perfumes.*

How natural fibres are made into cloth

Wool was probably the first fibre to be made successfully into fabric, during the New Stone Age around 7000 years ago. It gave man his first alternative to wearing animal skins. Flax and cotton fibres were also well known in the ancient world.

In Egypt – where wool was thought to be 'unclean' – mummies from 3400 BC have been found wrapped in linen shrouds, made from flax, 1000yds (900m) long. Cotton was used in India in 3000 BC; and cotton fabrics from around 2000 BC have been found in Peru.

Two processes are needed to turn fibres like wool, flax and cotton into cloth. The first is spinning, in which the fibres are twisted together to form a yarn; the second is weaving, in which two sets of yarn are interwoven at right angles to form a fabric.

Spinning was traditionally a woman's task, hence the term spinster for an unmarried woman. Weaving was done by men. Before the Industrial Revolution, when spinning was all done by hand, it took the combined output of five to eight spinsters to keep one weaver employed. Fabric was expensive, and clothes had to last a long time. In one day, a woman could spin about 550yds (500m) of wool.

The most important of the animal fibres is sheep's wool. Most wool fibres are from 1in to 8in (25mm to 200mm) long.

Flax is a fibre found in the stem of the flax plant, from which it is extracted by splitting the stalk and soaking the fibres in water for several weeks to separate them from the resinous material that glues them together. The fibres are from 6in to 3ft 3in (150mm to 1m) long.

Cotton fibres grow in the seedpod of the cotton plant. They are much shorter than flax, forming flat, twisted ribbons from ⅛in to 2½in (3mm to 65mm) long. The fibres have to be teased out of the seedpod, and disentangled from the seeds, a process done by a cotton gin.

Other plant fibres include jute, used for making sacks, bags and carpet backings; and hemp, which is made from the cannabis plant and is used in sailcloth, canvas and tarpaulins. One of the most unusual plant fibres was made from stinging nettles. Mary, Queen of Scots slept in sheets made from the fine linen they produced.

How the fibres are turned into yarn

None of these fibres – animal or vegetable – is long enough to be woven into cloth without further treatment. In order to make a usable thread, the fibres have to be laid out parallel to one another and twisted together, the process known as spinning.

Originally the tool for doing this was the spindle, a weighted stick which hung free and to which the fibres were attached. When spun between finger and thumb, the spindle imparted a twist to the fibres, which would then be drawn out from fibres stored on a second stick, the distaff.

Spinning machines achieve the same result mechanically. The first spinning wheel – which simply turned the spindle – was introduced to Europe, probably from India, in the early 14th century. But it was not until 1767 that a British weaver, James Hargreaves, built an eight-spindle spinning jenny, and introduced the possibility of mass production to the industry. Throughout the Industrial Revolution spinning machines were improved and refined, and in 1828 the forerunner of many modern spinning machines – the ring-spinning frame – was devised in America. A modern ring-spinner may have as many as 500 spindles, each carrying up to 4 miles (6400m) of yarn.

How a spinning machine works

The principles of spinning are exactly the same now as when the task was performed by hand. The fibres are first 'carded' – arranged parallel to one another – by working them between two parallel moving surfaces faced with sharp points. Next they may be combed to remove short fibres, then fed into machines with rollers

Cotton bales *Cotton awaits shipment in Arizona, USA. After picking, the cotton is compressed into 400lb (180kg) bales*

which draw out the fibres, making the yarn finer, and introducing a twist which holds the fibres together.

A very intense twist induces a kink in the yarn, as in crepe materials. Yarns may also be twisted together to produce a stronger, thicker thread – as in two-ply or three-ply knitting wool. Blended-fibre yarns may be made by spinning together fibres from different sources, mixing wool with polyester fibre, for example, to produce a better combination of warmth, strength and ease of washing.

Finally, the finished yarn is wound onto a bobbin, ready for dispatch.

How the yarn is turned into cloth

Primitive peoples wove fabric in just the same way as we do today. By the time of the death of the young Pharaoh Tutankhamun in the 14th century BC, immensely complex fabrics were being made, with delicate patterns in several colours. No items of ancient Greek fabrics survive, but the decoration on a vase of the 6th century BC shows both spinners and weavers. The loom, about 5ft (1.5m) high, is the same type as that used by Penelope as she waited for the return of her husband Odysseus in Homer's epic poem *The Odyssey*.

Weaving uses two sets of yarn, the warp and the weft. The warp threads run parallel along the length of the cloth, and the weft is threaded through them, over and under successive warp threads.

The yarn is woven on a loom, a framework of wood or metal which makes the repetitive process of threading the weft through the warp easier and quicker.

In a simple mechanical loom, the warp threads run off a roller as wide as the finished bolt of cloth will be. The threads pass through a set of wires running vertically, which can be moved up and down. Each wire has a small eye, or ring, in the middle through which the warp yarn runs. By simple mechanical arrangements it is possible to raise every alternate ring, making a space through which the weft can pass. In traditional looms, the weft is carried in a boat-shaped device called a shuttle, but many modern looms are shuttleless and use a rapier-like rod, or jets of air or water to carry the weft.

When the weft has passed through the warp, it is pushed down tightly against the previous thread with a comb-like frame. The rings carrying the warp threads are now depressed, the shuttle is turned round, and a second pass between a different set of threads is made. The fastest industrial looms of today can make well over 200 passes a minute.

The result of this process is plain weaving, in which each weft yarn passes over and under each warp yarn. It makes a tough, hard-wearing material.

Many other possibilities exist. Satin

Wool thread *A microscope photograph of spun wool shows the spaces between the fibres which help to hold air.*

WHY DOES A WOOLLY VEST KEEP YOU WARM ON A COLD DAY?

To keep warm in a cold climate needs effective insulation to stop the body heat escaping. Mammals have hair or blubber to insulate their bodies, but man has no blubber and relatively little body hair, so he has to rely on clothes.

In the wild, mammals have two kinds of hair on their bodies. The longer, guard hairs are stiff and can stand erect when the animal is frightened or angry, like the hackles of a dog. Below them lies a dense layer of softer underhairs, which trap air next to the skin. Air is a poor conductor of heat, so a layer of air, trapped in the underhairs, retains the body's heat and keeps the animal warm in cold weather.

When it rains, or the animal goes into water, the guard hairs mat together to form a waterproof layer which prevents the skin and soft underhairs from getting wet and losing their insulating properties. When the rain stops or the mammal gets back to dry land, a single shake clears the water from the guard hairs.

By using the natural qualities of wool, man can mimic the behaviour of wild mammals. Clothes worn next to the skin trap air which is kept warm by the body's heat, creating a warming layer all over the body. A waterproof coat prevents the clothes from getting wet and losing their insulating properties.

FIBRES UNDER THE MICROSCOPE

ANIMAL FIBRES

Clothes made of cashmere are soft because the fibres are rounded and smooth.

Fibres of merino wool are thicker and less rounded, making more durable fabric.

Mohair has a rough texture because the fibres are thick and coarse.

PLANT FIBRES

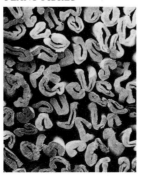

Cotton has fine fibres, but they are irregular in shape like most plant fibres.

Linen's rough texture is produced by the thick, coarse fibres of flax.

Jute fibres, used to make sacking, are hard and thick, with a very open texture.

the warp lie on the surface of the fabric, it has a lustrous appearance, but may not wear well as it is easy for these exposed lengths to become snagged.

A variation on satin weave is damask, used for tablecloths, furnishing and silk fabrics. Subtle colour variations are achieved by alternating areas in which the warp lies on the surface with areas where the weft does. Minute differences in the reflection of light create the pattern.

Other weaves include twill, with characteristic diagonal lines – used in gabardine, serge and whipcord – and pile weaves, used for producing corduroy, plush, velour and velvet. The thick 'pile' of a velvet is created by cutting some of the surface threads after weaving.

Woven linen *Flax is spun into thread, then woven into linen. This sample is the most basic weave, called plain, or tabby, weave.*

weave, for example, results when the warp is interwoven with only every fourth or fifth weft thread. Because long lengths of

Silk: the precious fibre made by moths

For thousands of years silk has been traded from East to West, and it is still the most precious fabric by weight.

Silk is a fibre spun by the domestic silkworm, *Bombyx mori*, to create a cocoon in which it turns into a moth. Each cocoon consists of a single filament up to 1 mile (1.6km) long. It takes 110 cocoons to make a tie, 630 for a blouse and 3000 for a kimono.

Chinese legend dates the discovery of silk to the year 2640 BC, in the garden of Emperor Huang Ti. According to the story, Huang Ti asked his wife, Xi Lingshi, to find out what was eating his mulberry trees. She

discovered it was white worms that spun shiny cocoons. Dropping one by accident into warm water, she found that she could draw out a fine filament, and wind it onto reels. She had discovered how to make silk, and it remained a Chinese secret for the next 2000 years. Imperial law decreed that anybody revealing the secret would be tortured to death.

Manufacturing silk has four stages: the cultivation of mulberry trees, the raising of silkworms, the reeling of the silk fibre from the cocoons, and the weaving of fabric.

Silkworms will eat the leaves of a variety of trees – one type of silkworm feeds on oak

leaves – but mulberry leaves produce the finest silk. In 1608 King James I ordered 10,000 black mulberry trees to be planted across England to create a domestic silk industry, but the project failed. He had unfortunately chosen the wrong variety – silkworms prefer the white mulberry.

In China the mulberries are cultivated as low bushes, so their leaves can be easily harvested and fed to the silkworms.

Silkworms are raised in the spring, in two months of intensive activity. The eggs, stored in a cool place from the previous season, are incubated as soon as the mulberry bushes come into leaf. They take

FROM COCOON TO EMBROIDERY, THE TRADITIONAL CHINESE WAY

Sorting cocoons *Women sort through the cocoons, removing any that are damaged. Each cocoon produces about 1 mile (1.6km) of thread.*

Reeling strands *The traditional method of reeling silk involves heating the cocoons after washing, then pulling out the thread in a single long strand. Threads of different colours, caused by chemicals excreted by the worms, are boiled until white.*

Silk cocoons *Silkworm cocoons, shown life-size. These will produce about 11 miles (18km) of thread, which will make a woven silk square a little smaller than this picture.*

Silk fibres *A microscope picture shows the triangular shape and closeness of the fibres.*

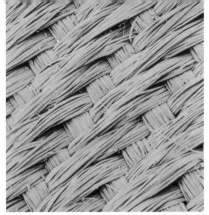

Catching the light *The thick, multi-thread weave of silk makes the fabric shine.*

about eight days to hatch, then the worms feed continuously on the mulberry leaves for almost a month. They increase their body weight 10,000 times in this four-week period. Even breathing does not interfere with their eating, because they breathe through holes in their bodies.

To be productive, silkworms must be cosseted. In China it was said that the worms liked warmth and hated cold, liked dryness and hated damp, liked cleanliness and hated dirt. But they were also said to dislike noise, the odour of frying fish, tears, shouting and women who were pregnant

or had just given birth. Even today, in the Chinese province of Hangzhou, the women who look after the silkworms are forbidden to smoke, wear make-up, or eat garlic.

After their fourth moulting the silkworms set about making their cocoons. They begin to exude a semiliquid mixture from the two silk glands that run the length of their bodies. The single thread which emerges is made up of the two threads joined together.

First they anchor themselves by making a fine net. Then tossing their heads in a figure-of-eight motion, they slowly build up a waterproof cocoon that completely surrounds them. It takes a worm about three days to spin the entire cocoon, during which it will have shaken its head about 300,000 times.

Left to its own devices the worm will turn into a moth in about two weeks, exude an enzyme to weaken the cocoon and emerge to begin the life cycle once more. In practice only a few are allowed to do this, to provide for the following year. The rest are

killed. By preventing the cocoon being damaged by the emerging moth, an unbroken thread can be recovered.

The process of obtaining the thread is called reeling. It is done by soaking the cocoons in warm water, finding the end of each silk thread and winding it onto a reel. Fibres from several cocoons, usually between five and eight, are wound on to the same reel to make a thread of sufficient thickness. Today automatic reeling machines do much of the work.

If two silkworms are placed together they create a twin cocoon. The silk that emerges is known as dupion. It has 'slubs' or lumpy places along the thread and is used to make fabrics with variations in texture.

World production of silk is small, around 50,000 tons a year, only a fifth of 1 per cent of total textile fibres. Its shimmering texture is created by fibres that are not round but triangular, and therefore reflect the light. It still makes the best ties and the most luxurious underwear.

Making thread *The unbroken strands from between five and eight cocoons are twisted together to make silk thread, which is then twisted into skeins. Traditional wooden frames like this one have largely been replaced by machines.*

Silk embroidery *The skeins of silk are dyed and used either to make fabrics, or for embroidery. This woman is making a floral design with silk threads.*

◼ *How the secrets of silk were carried from China to the West* ◼

The two monks were most insistent – they had to see the emperor. They had, they said, a valuable secret to impart, and had travelled all the way from China to Constantinople (modern Istanbul) to reveal it to the court.

The year was about AD 550 and the emperor, Justinian I, was the ruler of the Eastern Roman (Byzantine) Empire. The monks' secret was well worth Justinian's attention. They offered to bring him the means of making silk as the Chinese made it.

Some of the soft, luxurious fabric was made on the little Greek island of Kos, from local wild silkworms which fed on oak leaves. But it did not compare with the Chinese silk, made from cultivated silkworms which fed on the leaves of the white mulberry. The Eastern Romans bought Chinese silk from traders who carried it more than 3000 miles (4800km) along the dangerous Silk Road through central Asia, from Luoyang on the Huang river to the eastern Mediterranean. The journey took eight months.

By the time the silk reached Europe it was worth, literally, its weight in gold. And it was getting more expensive and difficult to obtain because the Silk Road ran through war-ravaged lands.

Justinian had been trying to import it through Ethiopian merchants who traded with China by sea.

The monks were Persians who had been preaching Christianity in China for many years, and had learned the secrets of silk cultivation. Now they put a proposition to Justinian: it was obviously impossible to keep silkworms alive on such a long journey, but the tiny eggs were another matter. Just 1oz (28g) of those eggs is enough to produce 36,000 silkworms.

Justinian loaded the monks with gifts and promised them rich rewards. The two men returned to China and acquired a supply of silkworm eggs. Then, leaning on stout bamboo canes, they made the long walk back to the West, with the precious eggs hidden in the canes.

On their return the two monks taught the Eastern Romans how to incubate the eggs and hatch the silkworms that were used to make Europe's first fine silk. Some silkworms were kept to mature into moths for breeding and a silk industry was born. But despite the monks' efforts, the silkworms still prefer the Chinese white mulberry, and Europe still imports some of its raw silk from China.

How chemicals are turned into clothes

Chemists had been trying to create a cheap man-made fibre for several years when the American Wallace Carothers invented nylon in 1935. Nylon stockings were introduced in 1938, and they were soon in enormous demand. The manufacturers said the new fibre was as 'strong as steel and as delicate as a spider's web'.

Carothers was an organic chemist, and in 1927 he was invited to lead a research team at E.I. du Pont Nemours and Company in Wilmington, Delaware. His goal was to invent a new synthetic material. It took him and his team nearly 11 years, while du Pont had to invest $27 million in the project.

Carothers was sure that a new material could be made by polymerisation (combining small molecules into larger ones, so forming new compounds). He was trying to create a polymer with the same structure as silk that could be made in bulk.

In 1931, after four years of frustration, Carothers discovered a fibre finer and stronger than silk. By mixing adipic acid with hexamethylenediamine he produced a sticky compound which could be easily drawn out into a thin fibre. The first fibres he produced either melted at low temperatures or were too weak, and it took another four years to perfect 'polymer 66'. He found that the polymerisation process was inhibited by water droplets that the compound contained. By evaporating the water Carothers produced a very strong and elastic fibre.

Carothers had suffered from depression for many years, and on April 29, 1937, 20 days after applying for a patent for his invention, he committed suicide. He never knew that his discovery was to be called 'nylon', and he probably never dreamed that he had started a 'materials revolution'. Today man-made fibres like nylon, acrylic and polyester far outsell natural fibres like wool and cotton.

The technique for producing synthetic fibres has remained largely unchanged. Polymers in a liquid form are blown through very thin nozzles, called spinnerets. The fine jet solidifies almost immediately, and forms a fibre about a quarter the thickness of a human hair.

Next, the fibres are stretched, which aligns the long molecules along the length of the fibre, and gives nylon its shine and transparency. Nylon can be stretched up to five times its original length, before the molecules become aligned and bond tightly together to resist further stretching. The strong threads are then made into cloth.

Man-made fibre fabrics can already re-create most properties that natural fibres possess. Acrylic can be used to make fluffy fabrics or synthetic fur, with its very fine, downy fibres. Because of its strong but elastic molecular structure polyester has a wonderful

ability to spring back into shape, which prevents garments from creasing.

Man-made fibres can also be combined with natural ones, so drip-dry material that needs no ironing can be made to feel natural.

Man-made fabric is easier to mass produce than either wool or cotton, which is just as well – each pair of nylon stockings is made from a single filament of nylon 4 miles (6.4km) long and knitted into 3 million loops.

Nylons *US film star Betty Grable sold her nylon stockings to raise $40,000 for war bonds. The interlocking loops (inset) make nylon stockings smooth and stretchy.*

Liquid to fabric *Nylon fibres are made by forcing liquid polymers through thin nozzles called spinnerets. Each stream solidifies into a thread.*

Putting the patterns into cloth

The Chinese have been exchanging gifts of richly patterned fabrics for thousands of years. At about the time of Christ's birth the wife of a Chinese nobleman, Ho Kuang, gave another, Shunyu Yen, 'twenty-four rolls of a silk brocade with a grape design, and twenty-five rolls of thin silk woven with a pattern of scattered flowers'.

The Chinese mastered the art of weaving, using silk threads of many colours and complex weaves to produce brocades and tapestries. With primitive looms, weaving patterns into cloth was a job that needed a great deal of skill and patience.

Even with the inventions of the 18th century, a weaver had to know which of the warp threads (running down the length of the loom) to lift and which to leave to make a pattern. Only the threads that were lifted would be woven into the design when the shuttle carrying the weft (the threads running across the loom) was 'thrown' across the loom.

It was not until the beginning of the 19th century that a French silk weaver, Joseph Jacquard, found a way to make detailed patterns without skilled weavers. A chain of cards punched with holes was attached to a rotating block above the loom. Only where there were holes could threads be picked up by small hooks and become

woven into the pattern. After each card had been used to make a small part of a pattern, the block was given a quarter-turn, bringing the next card into place.

It took 24,000 cards to weave a silk portrait of Jacquard, so accurate that it could hardly be distinguished from a portrait in oils. The cards were tied together in a long strip which slowly passed over the loom. Jacquard looms are still used to make luxury fabrics.

Many patterned fabrics can be woven on simpler machines. The timeless patterns of tweed are still woven on hand looms.

The direct printing of patterns onto woven fabrics originated in India, and the first printed calicos were brought to

Printed fabric *This modern Liberty-print cotton fabric was screen-printed following a late 19th-century design for block printing. The enlargement shows the small spaces between the different colours, which the block printer needed to prevent the colours running into each other.*

Europe in the 16th century. From the Hindi word 'tchint' comes 'chintz', which we still use to describe printed fabrics that are glazed to give them a slight sheen.

Modern textile printing uses metal rollers on which the design is engraved, with each colour applied by a different roller. The rollers pass through a colour trough as they rotate and then transfer the dye to the fabric. As many as 16 rollers may be used to produce a fabric.

Electronic control ensures that each successive roller matches its pattern perfectly with the one before. As the fabric comes off the final roller it passes through an oven where it is dried. Modern machines can print in 16 colours at speeds of 200yds (180m) of fabric a minute.

How they make clothes to fit almost everyone

The traditional tailor can take account of long arms or a spreading waistline and achieve a perfect fit. But made-to-measure clothes get more expensive every year, and the modern clothing industry has to make off-the-peg clothes that fit most people with no alteration.

One of the first proper surveys into people's measurements was carried out by the US Government, who measured 1000 recruits during the First World War to determine the best sizes for uniforms.

In Britain, 5000 women were measured in the early 1950s, with some unexpected results. Existing size charts were based on an average height for women of 5ft 6in (168cm) – but the survey found that the real average was 5ft 3in (160cm).

Today, in large companies, from a basic pattern produced by a designer, a computer produces a range of sizes to cover the normal variations of the population. Unusually small or large people complain that they can never find anything to fit them, and they are right; it does not make economic sense for manufacturers to produce the limited number of garments that would be sold.

The next step is to use the patterns to cut out the material for the garment. Rolls of material, which can be more than 100ft (30m) long, are laid out perfectly flat by machine. Hundreds of layers are spread on top of one another so that a large number of garments can be cut out at once. Computers are used to arrange the patterns on the material so that the minimum of cloth is wasted. A paper computer printout, called a marker, is laid on the layers of fabric ready for cutting.

Jacquard weaving *Intricately patterned furnishing fabric is still made on a Jacquard loom, invented in France in the 19th century. One of the earliest automated machines, the Jacquard loom uses punched cards to guide the shuttle-drawn weft (horizontal) threads through the warp (vertical) threads stretched on the loom frame. About 10,000 cards would have been used to weave this floral pattern. The enlargement (left) shows the variation in the texture and thickness of the yarns. This fabric is made from cotton threads, but any fibre, or combination of fibres, can be woven. Some Jacquard looms are now controlled by electronics rather than cards.*

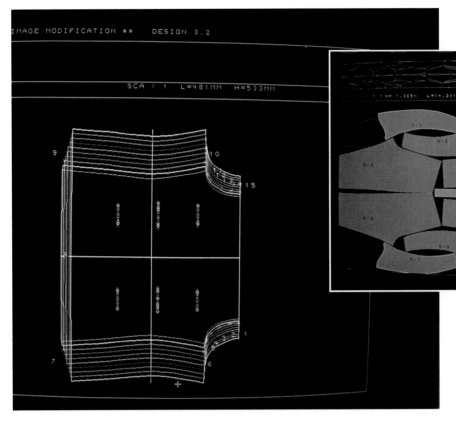

IMAGE MODIFICATION ** DESIGN 3.2

SCA < 1 L=481MM H=533MM

Patterns by computer *Computers are used to scale a single design of garment to all standard sizes. Each coloured outline (left) represents a different-sized trouser leg. Computers also help to plan the best use of fabric (above). Pattern pieces of a suit are arranged on the computer screen before being placed on the cloth as a cutting guide. This avoids wasting fabric.*

The actual cutting of the material is done by knives guided from above, or in some modern factories, by laser beams controlled by computers. The laser, an intense beam of light, burns a clean cut through the material, far sharper than the cut of any knife.

Next, the pieces of material have to be sewn together. Many operations, such as buttonholing, can be done automatically. A hand-sewer averages 20 stitches a minute; modern machinery can sew up to 7000 stitches a minute. Some clothes are not stitched in the traditional way at all, but fused together.

Finally clothes are pressed, to mould them into the right shape and to make sharp creases or pleats. Special presses, called buck presses, are designed for each part of a garment.

Winning fresh water from the sea

The world faces a growing water shortage. In some areas of low rainfall, such as the Middle East, the natural water supply is inadequate. One answer is desalination – removing the salt from sea water.

One method of desalination has been known since the 4th century BC, when the Greek philosopher Aristotle noted that when salty water is boiled the steam that rises leaves the salt behind. Condensed into water again, it is pure.

The simplest desalination plant is a still in which water is boiled and the steam condensed. A simple solar still can be made with a glass dome over a pool of salt water. The water is heated by the sun, vaporises, and then condenses on the glass and runs down it to gather in channels around the edge. A still one yard square in area should produce a gallon (4·5 litres) of fresh water a day.

To produce really useful amounts of water a much larger still is needed. The water is first heated to above its atmospheric boiling point, but in a vessel that is under pressure so that it does not boil. It then flows into a separate chamber at a lower pressure, where some of it instantly 'flashes' into vapour. The vapour is then

TWO WAYS OF CUTTING LAYERS OF FABRIC

Cutting with a knife *A high-speed electric knife cuts through layers of fabric, in three colours, to make sleeves for blouses.*

Cutting by laser *Computer-controlled laser cutters are used to burn through the fabric, making clean, unfrayed cuts.*

HOW FLASH DISTILLATION MAKES SEA WATER FRESH

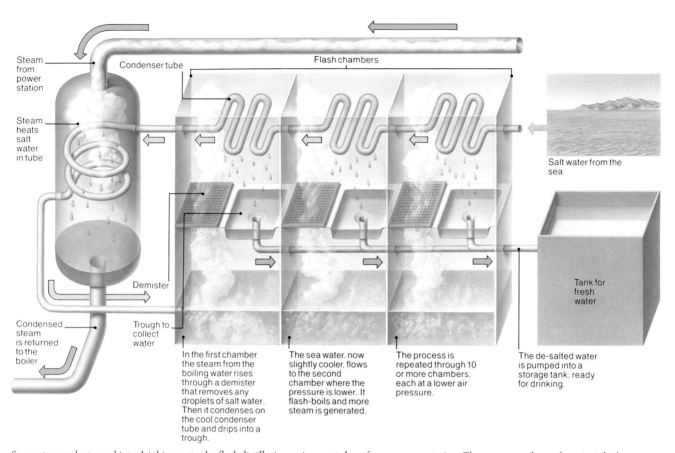

Steam from power station

Condenser tube

Flash chambers

Steam heats salt water in tube

Salt water from the sea

Demister

Condensed steam is returned to the boiler

Trough to collect water

Tank for fresh water

In the first chamber the steam from the boiling water rises through a demister that removes any droplets of salt water. Then it condenses on the cool condenser tube and drips into a trough.

The sea water, now slightly cooler, flows to the second chamber where the pressure is lower. It flash-boils and more steam is generated.

The process is repeated through 10 or more chambers, each at a lower air pressure.

The de-salted water is pumped into a storage tank, ready for drinking.

Sea water can be turned into drinking water by flash distillation, using waste heat from a power station. The system works on the principle that water boils at a lower temperature than normal if the air pressure is also lower. Heated water passes through a series of chambers, each with a lower air pressure. The water boils in each chamber and the steam condenses into pure water.

condensed by contact with tubes carrying the incoming supply of cool sea water. The hot salt water that did not boil in the first chamber moves on to a second, at slightly lower pressure again, where more of it flashes into vapour and is condensed.

A more modern desalination system, called reverse osmosis, is more cost-effective than flash distillation. It uses

membranes made of plastic which have tiny holes in them big enough for water molecules to pass through, but too small for salt molecules. The membranes are formed into a tube and salt water is pumped into them under pressure. Pure water drips from the outside of the tube.

One of the world's largest reverse osmosis plants has been built in Bahrain.

The plant produces over 12 million gallons (54 million litres) of fresh water every day.

As more arid areas are opened up for habitation and cultivation, the demand for desalination increases. By 1988 there were more than 2200 plants operating. But the cost of the water is high, which means it can only be justified for drinking, industry, or high-value crops.

Turning rubbish into electricity and heat

Every year Americans throw away 250 million tons of rubbish. New York alone generates almost 10 million tons a year. It has been estimated that America's garbage could provide as much energy as 100 million tons of coal. However, most of it is buried, and never used.

About half of the world's domestic waste is paper, while kitchen waste makes up a quarter and plastics less than a tenth. Only a fifth will not burn and most of that can be recycled.

Western Europe has more than 200 plants which burn rubbish to produce

electricity. A large plant at Edmonton in London, which opened in 1974, burns about 400,000 tons of refuse a year. The burning refuse heats water to create steam which powers the electric generators. Within ten years the plant has saved a million tons of coal.

In Dusseldorf, West Germany, six similar plants supply steam to generate electricity for district heating schemes.

In Peekskill, New York, a plant has been built to handle 2250 tons of refuse a day, generating 60 megawatts of electricity – enough to supply 70,000 people.

Rubbish can also be burned by factories instead of coal or oil, but it must be treated first. The rubbish is separated by feeding it through a vibrating screen which sifts out the fine organic particles to be turned into compost for treating land. In Sweden a quarter of all solid waste is turned into compost and recycled.

Next the heavy part of the rubbish, mainly metals, must be sorted out and removed, leaving mainly paper and textile waste. These are pressed into cylindrical pellets and sold as fuel.

Even rubbish dumped in the ground can

be used as a source of fuel. As it begins to rot, it produces methane gas – identical to the natural gas found in pockets under the Earth's crust. Each ton of refuse can produce over 8000 cubic feet (227 cubic metres) of methane. Left alone, the gas will find its way to the surface and escape, sometimes causing explosions. But it can be tapped very cheaply and used to generate heat or electricity. There are more than 140 such schemes in operation in 15 countries, saving a total of at least 825,000 tons of coal a year. In England, for example, a large tip has been drilled with wells to extract the gas, which is piped to a brickworks where it replaces coal.

Other plants use the gas on site to generate electricity by burning it in simple gas engines. This allows all the gas to be used, rather than trying to match output to the fluctuating demands of a factory.

In the future, production of gas in rubbish tips may be improved by 'seeding' the tips with bacteria. Some strains of bacteria break down refuse faster than others. By introducing the best mix of bacteria for the particular waste in a tip, the maximum amount could be produced.

Rubbish for burning *Domestic rubbish is lifted from huge bunkers in London to be burned in a power plant. The heat is used to create steam to power electric generators.*

MAKING BIO-GAS FOR COOKING IN INDIA

In third-world countries, gas can be made from manure and water stored in tanks.

Ceramic gas rings, made from local clay, are fitted to a pipe leading from the tank.

The methane gas – called bio-gas – is used for cooking in village huts. Bio-gas is the main source of cooking fuel in parts of rural India, making use of the manure from farm animals.

Making new goods from rubbish

Recycling rubbish not only makes economic sense – it also helps the environment. Pollution created by burning rubbish is reduced and valuable resources are saved. Some 75,000 trees would be spared every week just by recycling the Sunday edition of the *New York Times*.

Many countries encourage recycling and new technology allows more and more waste to be reprocessed. Most of the world's rubbish can be reused – paper, metals, glass, even some plastics.

Plastic is one of the most difficult substances to recycle, because it comes in so many varieties. A plastic tomato-ketchup bottle, for example, consists of six layers of different plastics, each designed to give the bottle certain qualities – shape, strength, flexibility. And as yet there is no simple way to turn an old plastic bottle into a new one.

Plastic can only be turned into a product of lower quality – a plastic lemonade bottle might be cleaned, shredded and used to stuff seat cushions or insulate sleeping bags. A mixture of plastic waste can be recycled into plastic 'timber' and used to

RECYCLING COMPUTER GOLD

Printed circuit boards from obsolete computers contain a small amount of gold, interwoven in complex patterns with other metals and plastic (above). The old circuit boards and other electronic scrap materials are shredded by machine (right).

The shredded metals are sorted and any recovered gold is melted down and poured into ingot moulds (left), producing bars of impure gold (above).

Impure gold bars are chemically refined to produce pure gold, then recast into ingots.

Recycling cans *Used tin cans are crushed into bales in the first step towards recycling. In the US, about half the drink cans, which are made of aluminium, are melted down. They then return to the supermarket shelves, refilled with drink and relabelled, within six weeks.*

make durable fencing. But a lot of plastic waste still has to be thrown away because its value as scrap is so low.

Metals are different. Any car on the road today will consist, in part, of earlier cars that have been scrapped and recycled into new steel and other metals.

The more valuable the metal, like gold and silver, the more it pays to recycle it. Aluminium is worth recycling because extracting it from bauxite consumes a huge amount of electricity. Largely thanks to recycling programmes the energy used to make aluminium has fallen by a quarter since the early 1970s.

More than 70 billion canned drinks are bought in America every year, and all the cans are made of aluminium. About half are remelted after use and within six weeks they have been made into new tins and are back on the supermarket shelves.

Glass is also worth recovering. The most sensible method is to use glass bottles as often as possible. The average British milk bottle makes about 30 trips to and from the dairy.

Many countries now have compulsory deposit schemes to make people return bottles to shops. When such a law was passed in the state of New York in 1983, it was estimated that within two years it had saved $50 million on rubbish collection, $19 million on waste disposal costs, and about $75 million in energy costs.

Some supermarkets now have machines that accept glass bottles and aluminium cans and give cash or redeemable vouchers to the customer. They read the computer codes on the containers to work out how much to pay.

Broken glass, known as 'cullet', can also be recycled, and many countries have bottle banks into which used bottles can be thrown. Usually there are no payments – bottle banks depend on people's goodwill. The success of bottle banks varies widely from country to country. The Swiss and Dutch recover 50 per cent of their glass, while in Britain only 12 per cent is recovered.

Glass is best separated by colour, since cullet of mixed colours can be used only to make green glass. Broken glass can be remelted in furnaces and then it can easily be shaped into new bottles or other objects.

Half the world's waste consists of paper. Many countries import waste paper rather than new pulp for their paper mills. The waste is pulped, cleaned and bleached to remove most of the ink and dirt, before it is turned into new paper in the same way as wood pulp or rags. Japan now makes half its paper by recycling.

How uranium is turned into electricity

A small handful of uranium provides as much electrical energy as 70 tons of coal or 390 barrels of oil. A power station big enough to supply a city of a million people consumes just 6.6lb (3kg) of uranium a day, so it is by far the most concentrated source of energy used by man.

Uranium is one of the densest naturally occurring elements and each of its atoms teeters on the edge of instability. The heart of the atom, called the nucleus, needs only a tiny 'push' to cause it to divide. And when a nucleus splits it releases huge amounts of energy, in a process called nuclear fission.

The 'push' can be provided by neutrons, tiny particles much smaller than atoms, which strike the nucleus and cause it to split. In the process of splitting, at least two extra neutrons are produced, which fly off and cause further fissions – so that once the process has started it can continue almost indefinitely.

The energy of fission can be released slowly, bit by bit, and used to heat water. The steam from the water is then used to drive a generator, which produces electricity. This is the principle of the nuclear reactor.

Fuel assemblies

Inside most reactors, the fuel assemblies are made from small pellets of uranium dioxide, loaded into thin tubes. The tubes are usually put into vertical bundles with 'spacers' to separate them.

Once inside, a fuel assembly may stay there for as long as three years, but even after that length of time, all the uranium has not been consumed. But by-products begin to accumulate; some are gases like krypton, others are solids like caesium, strontium and plutonium. Before these by-products have built up too much, and water corrodes the fuel tubes, the assemblies are removed. To recover the unburned uranium, the spent fuel may be taken to a special plant where it is reprocessed to separate out uranium, plutonium and waste products.

The plutonium is a useful by-product of the nuclear power industry. It can be used

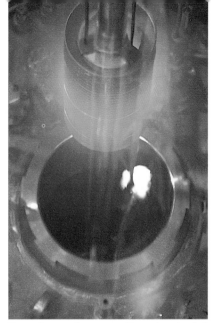

Experimental reactor *Removing the fuel element from water in a High Flux Isotope Reactor at Oak Ridge, Tennessee, USA. It is used for research on man-made substances which may give more power than uranium.*

as a fuel in power stations, because plutonium, like uranium, has nuclei that can split and release energy.

Uranium occurs in several different forms, identical chemically but with different-sized nuclei in their atoms. Of these different forms, called isotopes, one is uranium-235, which gets it name from the 235 particles making up its nucleus. Only seven atoms out of every 1000 in naturally occurring uranium are U-235. The rest consist almost entirely of uranium-238.

When U-238 is struck by neutrons it does not split as readily as U-235. It may be converted into a completely new element, plutonium-239. So if a reactor is made

Nuclear power station *This pressurised water reactor at Biblis, West Germany, supplies electricity for industry in the Rhine valley.*

GENERATING POWER WITH A PRESSURISED WATER REACTOR

Unpressurised water

Concrete shield

Steam drives turbo generator, producing electricity

Steam generator

Uranium fuel rods in the reactor produce heat

Pressurised water is heated by the reactor, and boils unpressurised water in the steam generator

The pressurised water reactor is the most successful reactor in terms of the numbers of them in use around the world. The reactor is cooled with water under high pressure which does not boil even when heated above boiling point. The water is passed through a heat exchanger, where it gives heat to a second water circuit. This circuit is not pressurised, so the water boils and produces steam to drive generators which produce electricity.

using natural uranium as fuel, the danger is that too many neutrons will be absorbed by U-238 before they can hit U-235 atoms and cause further fissions. If this happens the reactor will never get going.

There are two ways around this problem. One is to increase the amount of U-235 in the reactor fuel, by a process called enrichment, from seven atoms to between 30 and 40 in every thousand. This is done before the fuel is manufactured, usually in a centrifuge – a machine that whirls round, separating U-235 from U-238 by the outward pushing forces of high-speed rotation. The second way is to make the very best use of the available neutrons inside the reactor by slowing them down, which increases their chances of causing further fissions.

The way to slow them down is to make them ricochet to and fro off light atoms of an element such as hydrogen or carbon, like balls in a pin-ball machine. The light elements act as a 'moderator', because their job is to moderate the speed of the neutrons. Most modern reactors use both enriched fuel and moderators. Some are moderated by water (which, of course, contains hydrogen), while others are moderated by carbon in the form of graphite, which is the hard dark material

known as the 'lead' in an ordinary pencil.

Obviously, a nuclear reactor produces a great amount of heat, and to stop the reactors from overheating, coolants have to be used. Pressurised water reactors use water as a coolant, so these plants need to be built near rivers or oceans. Advanced gas-cooled reactors, first built in Great Britain, are cooled by carbon-dioxide gas. In Canada, heavy water – in which hydrogen atoms are replaced with an isotope of hydrogen called deuterium – cools fast breeder reactors. France has pioneered the use of liquid sodium as a coolant for their fast breeders.

How they store deadly nuclear waste

High-level radioactive waste is lethal and it remains dangerous for thousands of years. If someone were to stand 30ft (9m) away from a small amount of fresh waste from a nuclear reactor for ten minutes, he would have only a 50 per cent chance of living. A

nuclear reactor's spent fuel contains a deadly cocktail of radioactive products, like plutonium, strontium and caesium.

Fortunately the volume of high-level nuclear waste is small. A typical plant, generating 1000 megawatts of electricity, produces about two and a half cubic yards (two cubic metres) of waste a year.

Storage methods vary. In the USA, some processed waste is stored in double-walled stainless-steel tanks surrounded by 3ft (1m) thick concrete cladding. But most is immersed in special pools near the nuclear plants, in the form of spent fuel rods still inside the original cladding. Unfortunately this is not a long-term solution.

In Britain the waste is stored as a liquid, the colour of strong tea, in steel tanks encased in concrete, similar to those used in America. The waste generates heat as the radioactive atoms decay, so the tanks have to be cooled to prevent the liquid boiling dry, which could eventually cause a radioactive leak. Cold water is pumped through coils inside the tanks.

However, although they have already been used for 40 years, tanks are also only a temporary storage solution.

Possibly the best answer at the moment is to fuse the waste into glass cylinders to be stored deep underground. A demonstration plant in Marcoule, France, has been carrying out this process since 1978.

The waste is dried and reduced to a solid residue by heating it inside a rotating drum. It is then mixed with silica and boron, and other glass-making materials, poured through a vertical chamber and heated to 2100°F (1500°C). A stream of molten glass emerges from the bottom, to be cast into stainless-steel containers about twice the size of an old-fashioned milk churn. A year's output from a 1000 megawatt plant fills 15 of these canisters. After the glass has solidified, the lids are welded on.

The canisters are stored in special 'pits' in a neighbouring building at Marcoule. Each canister produces 1.5 kilowatts of

Vitrified waste *The high-level radioactive waste can be made into glass – and stored in containers about twice as big as a milk churn.*

Pouring the waste *Molten glass containing nuclear waste is poured from a platinum crucible into a stainless-steel mould, at a temperature of about 1100°F (590°C). When it has hardened, the glass is put in a container.*

heat and is cooled by air. The British and the Americans are also beginning to adopt this process. The waste is safe so long as it is monitored, but ultimately it should be put where it can remain without further human intervention.

One proposal is to surround the canisters with a jacket of cast iron or copper, and then store them in underground caverns. The canisters would be placed in holes or trenches, then covered with concrete or a clay called bentonite, which absorbs escaping radioactive material.

The canisters should last up to 1000 years before they become corroded and let any radioactivity escape. After 500 years the radioactivity will have dropped to about the level of the original uranium ore. Experts believe that as long as the caverns are well sited and sufficiently deep – several hundred yards – it would take a million years before any material could seep to the surface, and by that time all but the tiniest traces of the radioactive waste would have decayed. The areas chosen for the 'dumps' should contain no valuable minerals, in case some future civilisation should stumble across the waste while mining. Eventually the caverns could be sealed off and forgotten. The waste would be sealed behind so many barriers that escape in any imaginable time scale would be impossible.

The difficulty is finding sites where local people agree to have nuclear waste stored. Nobody relishes the idea of a nuclear dump close to their home. In the end, the nuclear waste authorities may well be forced to drill caverns beneath existing reprocessing facilities, or under the sea, rather than try to find new sites on land.

Using the tides to produce electricity

The tides have been used to provide power for hundreds of years. In the 18th century, the coast of Europe was dotted with tidal mills, which let the incoming tide into a reservoir through open sluices. At high tide the sluices were closed and the only way the water could escape as the tide fell was by passing through and propelling a waterwheel, so providing turning power.

The same principle was used in a power station built in France in the 1960s. A dam was built across the estuary of the River Rance at St Malo in Brittany, with 24 machines that could be used as turbines in either direction.

As the tide comes in, it is allowed to build up against the dam until there is a difference of 5ft (1.5m) between one side and the other. Then it is allowed to pass through the turbines, driving them and generating electricity. When the tide begins to fall, the turbine blades are reversed, and the water generates electricity again.

The amount of electricity generated depends on the 'head' of water – the difference in the level of the water between one side of the dam and the other. The larger the head, the greater the amount of electricity that will be generated, because the water is under greater pressure and so turns the turbines with more force.

At high tide the sluices are shut and extra water is pumped from the sea into the estuary. The water level in the estuary is raised above high tide, so when the sea falls back to low tide the difference in levels has been accentuated.

Once all the water has been allowed to flow into the sea – driving the turbines as it does so – extra water is pumped out to make the level in the estuary artificially low.

When it is high tide again, the turbines are reversed, water flows back into the estuary, and the cycle starts once more. Of course, pumping consumes electricity, but the additional heads produce considerably more electricity than the pumps use.

The scheme at La Rance generates 240 megawatts at peak output – sufficient for a medium-sized city such as Rennes or Caen, but it has had few followers. The immense cost of building the dams and the lack of suitable sites have discouraged everybody except the Russians and Canadians.

The Bay of Fundy in Nova Scotia has the biggest tidal range in the world, with up to 59ft (18m) height difference between tides. A successful pilot plant was opened across an inlet of the bay at Annapolis Royal in 1984. If the power of the tides across the whole bay could be harnessed it would produce ten times more energy than could be used locally. The surplus electricity could be used in New England and New York. Experts believe that it is just a matter of time before the project goes ahead.

Getting electricity from the wind

The potential for using the wind to generate electricity is huge. A recent study for the European Community estimated that there were sufficient sites in Europe for about 400,000 big machines – enough to provide three times Europe's present needs.

Modern wind generators are very different from the old windmills. They are more like giant propellers with two or three blades, called rotors, mounted on top of tall towers of steel or concrete. The rotors turn a shaft which drives an electric generator.

The size of the blades and the height of the tower determine how much electricity the machine can generate. Wind generally gets stronger as you go higher, and the power of the wind you capture depends on the swept area of the blades. Double the length of the blades and the power increases four-fold. More important still is the speed of the wind, for the power that can be extracted goes up as the cube of

wind speed – if it blows twice as hard, there is eight times as much power to be had.

However, wind generators do not need, or want, stormy weather. Most machines are designed to operate at wind speeds between Force 3 and Force 10 on the Beaufort Scale – 13 to 60mph (21 to 97km/h). Above Force 10 the machines automatically shut down to save themselves from flying apart.

Most machines are designed to produce much the same power throughout their working range, the blades automatically 'feathering' as the wind increases so that the machine does not accelerate too much. It is better to have a steady output over a wide range of wind speeds than to be able to take advantage of the few really strong gusts.

Wind generators must point in the right direction, either directly towards the wind or directly away from it. For this reason the rotor is mounted on a turntable and controlled by an electric motor connected

Darreius Turbine *These machines, which look like giant egg-beaters, have bow-shaped blades attached to a rod. The wind causes the whole assembly to rotate.*

to sensors which tell it which way to face.

This problem of wind direction can be avoided completely if the blades are mounted on a vertical rather than horizontal axis. Then it does not matter where the wind is blowing from.

These vertical machines, called Darreius Turbines, have other advantages. The

Wind farm *In 1988 California had 16,000 wind turbines. One wind farm is at Altamont Pass, near San Francisco.*

HOW TURBINES AND GENERATORS CREATE ELECTRICITY

Turbogenerator *An engineer inspects the fans on one of the 660mW turbogenerator units at a coal-fired power station in Yorkshire.*

Turbines consist of a series of fans, one in front of the other, which drive a shaft when they rotate. The shaft in turn drives a generator. Alternate fans always remain stationary. The position and shape of these fans direct the pressurised steam, or water, onto the rotating fans with the maximum possible force.

At the end of the shaft is a large magnet, which is surrounded by a coil of wire, inside the generator. As the magnetic core rotates, it causes an electric current to flow through the wire coil.

Recreation spin-off from geothermal power *Bathers enjoy the heated Blue Lagoon, filled with waste geothermal water produced by the Svartsengi Power Station in Iceland.*

heavy generating machinery that converts the power into electricity can be placed on the ground, rather than at the top of a tower. The rotor is, therefore, subjected to less stress than in the horizontal-axis generators. A disadvantage is that they often need a push to get started, either by hand or by an electric motor.

One of the main problems of using wind turbines is environmental. While people like the idea of wind power, they are less keen on having every hill crowned with a whirling turbine.

Serious examination has been given to placing the turbines out at sea. But there would be problems anchoring them and in transmitting the power back to land. The British Department of Energy has estimated that clusters of wind turbines built in shallow water around the coast could produce one and a half times Britain's present electricity demand, but engineers first want to study the performance of land-based machines.

The people of Fair Isle, off the north coast of Scotland, have already been making use of wind power. They installed a small wind generator in the early 1980s and have cut electricity bills by more than three-quarters from the old diesel engines.

Hot rocks: a natural source of electricity

The nearer you get to the Earth's centre the hotter it becomes. Nuclear reactions, caused by the decay of radioactive materials, constantly heat the molten core to 7200°F (4000°C). Because of this geothermal energy it is several degrees warmer at the bottom of a mine than it is at the top.

In some places hot rocks lie quite near the surface, causing hot springs, geysers or steam to rise out of the ground. These can be used to produce electricity.

The first geothermal power station was built in 1904, at Larderello in northern Italy, where steam was coming out of the ground at temperatures between 280°F and 500°F (140°C and 260°C). The steam was piped to turbines which powered generators.

In New Zealand, the Philippines, California and Mexico, power stations have been built where the Earth's heat reaches the surface naturally. But in most places geothermal energy has to be tapped by drilling. In some cases there may be no water present at all, just dry hot rocks, whose heat can only be used if water is pumped down to them and then recovered as steam. The steam is then used to drive turbines and generate electricity.

The granites of Cornwall are a source of geothermal energy that has recently been tested. Some 6500ft (1980m) beneath Camborne in Cornwall, the rocks reach temperatures of about 158°F (70°C).

To extract energy two boreholes would have to be drilled, cold water pumped down one and pressurised hot water returned up the other. The water would flow from one borehole to the other through fissures in the rock created by blasting it with explosives. Although the water is at 390°F (200°C), the pressure it is under prevents it from boiling. But when it is returned to normal atmospheric pressure at the surface, it instantly 'flashes' into steam – ready to drive the turbines.

Like other sites where geothermal energy could be tapped, Camborne has several problems. Minerals will have to be removed from the hot water, otherwise they could fur up pipes and corrode turbines. Tests have also shown that only one-third of the water pumped down finds its way back to the surface – the rest is lost. The third problem will be drilling deep enough.

If all these problems can be solved, the potential is enormous. It has been calculated that the Cornish granites alone contain as much energy as the whole of Britain's coal reserves.

More and more countries are looking into geothermal energy as an alternative to fossil fuels. A major power station has been started in New Mexico, and a joint French and German project is being carried out near Strasbourg.

How scientists trace the sources of acid rain

When a rainstorm hit Pitlochry, in Scotland, on April 10, 1974, it beat the world record – not for volume, but for acidity. The rain that fell that day was roughly equivalent to lemon juice, and more acidic than vinegar. It was several hundred times more acid than normal rain should be.

While the Pitlochry figures were exceptional, many places in Europe and North America have rainfall that is tens or hundreds of times more acidic than it ought to be. Acid rain rots buildings, damages soil, kills fish in lakes and helps to destroy trees, which are dying in a wide swathe across Europe.

Acid rain is an environmental problem that knows no boundaries. The atmospheric pollution that causes it is carried by the prevailing winds from major industrial areas to the mountains, lakes and forests that lie to the east.

Not even the Arctic is free of the air pollution that causes acid rain.

Where does the acid come from? There is now no doubt that most comes from man's activities – from cars, homes, factories and power stations. There has always been some acid in rain, coming from volcanoes, swamps and plankton in the oceans, but scientists know that it has increased very sharply over the past 200 years. Ice formed before the Industrial Revolution and trapped in glaciers has been measured, and found to be just mildly acid, consistent with natural sources.

Rain is made acid mainly by two

ONE OF THE CAUSES OF ACID RAIN, AND TWO OF THE EFFECTS

Tall chimneys send fossil-fuel pollution high into the air, where it drifts for thousands of miles.

Stunted growth in a fir tree from the Black Forest in Germany is shown by the change in the thickness of the growth rings. Thin outer rings at the top, grown over the last 20 years, contrast with the thick, even, centre rings before heavy acid rain.

Ornamental stonework on a church in Bristol is eroded by acid in the air. Old masonry is particularly vulnerable to acid created by the sulphur dioxide given off by fossil fuels such as oil and coal. The gas mixes with water to make sulphuric acid.

Lime spraying *Forests in Europe are sometimes sprayed with lime to neutralise the acidity of the soil and to assist the growth of the trees.*

Capturing the heat of the Sun

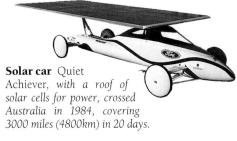

Solar car *Quiet Achiever, with a roof of solar cells for power, crossed Australia in 1984, covering 3000 miles (4800km) in 20 days.*

elements, sulphur and nitrogen. Sulphur is found in coal and oil. When burned, it turns to sulphur dioxide, which mixes with the water droplets in clouds and is converted into sulphuric acid. Nitrogen, from the air and also in the fuel itself, is turned into oxides of nitrogen by burning, and then reacts with water molecules to form nitric acid. Some of the sulphuric and nitric acid falls locally, while the rest can be carried thousands of miles.

Since the 1950s, chimneys 500ft (150m) high have been built to carry pollution away from urban areas, but their effect has been to spread it more thinly and more widely. This, coupled with the big increase in the amount of pollution, especially from power stations in recent decades, has resulted in places like Scandinavia being affected by pollution from factories in countries thousands of miles away. Swedish scientists have estimated that 70 per cent of the sulphur in the air over Sweden comes from fuel burning, and that most of it comes from outside Sweden, particularly from eastern Europe.

To discover if any of the acid rain was coming from Britain, samples of air were collected by aircraft and tested by British scientists. On one flight it was found that air reaching the west coast of Britain across the Atlantic on the prevailing wind contained less than half as much sulphur and a quarter as much nitrate as air along the east coast. As it blew across Britain it had picked up the pollutants that it then carried to Scandinavia.

It was even possible to trace the 'plumes' of pollution from a particular power station by releasing a chemical, sulphur hexafluoride, from its chimneys. Instruments on the aircraft could tell when it was flying through that particular plume, and take measurements.

The energy that reaches the Earth in the form of sunlight is immense – more than 12,000 times greater than the world's fuel consumption. The sunshine falling each year on the surface of America's roads alone contains twice as much energy as all the coal and oil used every year in the entire world.

But collecting and storing this abundant supply of free energy is difficult and expensive. The Sun sheds its rays thinly over a vast area and its heat must be

Concentrator cells *Photovoltaic cells, when stacked in huge modules, will be able to concentrate a vast amount of energy from the Sun to create electricity. This working model was built at the Solar Test Facility in Albuquerque, USA.*

HOW ACIDITY IS MEASURED

Acids can gradually wear away and destroy almost everything they touch. All are soluble in water, and their strength is measured by their pH (potential of Hydrogen).

The pH scale runs from 1 to 14. One is extremely acid, 7 is neutral, and 14 is very alkaline (the opposite of acid).

The pH content of a liquid is measured with a pH metre or with Universal Indicator paper, such as litmus. A strong acid turns the indicator paper red, while a neutral liquid turns it green. Strong alkaline liquids turn the indicator purple.

LIQUID	COLOUR OF INDICATOR	pH NUMBER
Concentrated sulphuric acid	red	1.0
Lemon juice	red	2.3
Pitlochry storm	pink	3.0
Vinegar	pink	3.3
Rain in industrial regions	pink	4.3
Normal rain	orange	5.0 to 5.6
Distilled water	green	7.0

Mirrors produce power for 20,000 people *A vast circle of mirrors collects the Sun's rays and reflects them onto a 20-storey power tower at the centre of the circle (right). The heat produces steam to generate electricity. This Californian installation creates enough power to supply the needs of the population of a small town.*

collected and concentrated before it can be used in homes or power plants.

In domestic hot-water systems that use the Sun's energy, solar collectors (panels) are mounted on roofs facing the Sun. They have glass or plastic panels behind which water circulates in pipes painted black to absorb maximum heat. The heated water is then pumped into the hot-water tank.

Japan has 3 million solar panels on its roofs, and half the houses in Israel have them. They are popular in California, but cloudier Europe, which gets only half the sunshine of Israel or California, has far fewer. Only a fraction of energy collected in direct sunlight can be trapped on an overcast day.

Solar energy is also used to generate electricity. For direct uses of the Sun high temperatures are needed, and to achieve them, sunlight must be concentrated by focusing.

Mirrors, rather than lenses, are arranged in a semicircle, reflecting the sunlight towards a concrete 'power tower'. The concentrated sunlight shines on a receiver at the top of the tower and heats a fluid which circulates through pipes. If the fluid is water, the high-pressure steam that is produced is used to drive electricity generators.

The largest power tower in the world is near Barstow, California, in the Mojave Desert, which has 300 days of sunshine a year. Its reflector covers 100 acres (40 hectares) and consists of 1818 mirrors in concentric circles focused on a boiler at the top of a tower that is 255ft (78m) high.

Europe's biggest solar energy plant is in France, at Themis in the western Pyrenees. Built in June 1981, it has a generating capacity of 2.5mW.

Virtually every spacecraft and satellite has depended on solar cells for its electricity since the US Satellite *Vanguard* in 1958. Solar cells exploit the discovery, made in 1887 by the German physicist Heinrich Hertz, that certain substances generate electricity when exposed to light – the photo-voltaic effect.

Cells are made from a thin layer of silicon placed next to an even thinner layer of silicon impregnated with boron, which alters the electrical behaviour of the silicon. Light falling on the outer layer causes electrons to migrate into the silicon backing, creating a voltage between the two layers. A series of cells must be connected together so their output adds up to a usable amount. Although silicon is cheap – it is the basic constituent of sand and rock – converting it into the single crystals necessary for solar cells is expensive. And huge numbers of cells are usually needed.

The *Solar Challenger*, an aeroplane powered by 16,128 solar cells generating 2.5kW, crossed the English Channel in 1981. Solar cars carry batteries, but only to store solar energy for use when it is cloudy or when the car is climbing hills.

Everyday applications of solar energy, like solar-powered watches and calculators, are widespread. Solar-heated swimming pools are also becoming popular.

The first solar-cell power station of significant size – with an output of 1mW – was completed near Victorville, California, in 1982. One of the largest solar-cell projects in Europe is on the island of Pellworm, off the West German coast, where 17,500 solar cells covering an area as big as two football pitches provide the electricity for the island's health spa.

How high-speed photographs are taken

To freeze the beating of an insect's wing needs a far shorter exposure than an ordinary camera can manage. Even at 1/1000th of a second the wings are a blur. Exposures ten or twenty times shorter are needed.

The British photographic pioneer W.H. Fox Talbot also pioneered high-speed photography as long ago as 1851. He attached a copy of *The Times* newspaper to a wheel, rotated it rapidly, and succeeded in taking a clear picture by illuminating the wheel very briefly with an intense spark of light which lasted only 1/100,000 of a second. If this technique is used in a blacked-out room, the camera shutter can be left open, and the film is exposed for an instant when the spark goes off.

The amazing art of filming nature

Nature photographers can catch the lightning tongue of the chameleon as it snatches an insect, or follow the growth of a plant through an entire season.

Time-lapse photography can make a plant appear to spring from the ground, flower and die in just a few seconds. A camera is fixed in position and programmed to take a series of pictures at intervals of minutes or hours. The film is then projected at the normal cine speed of 24 frames per second, speeding up the action thousands of times faster than reality.

It can take weeks to get a final minute's worth of film, and the whole sequence can be ruined if the camera moves, or if anything obscures the object being photographed. Time-lapse photography needs scrupulously careful setting up and very reliable equipment.

At the other extreme is high-speed filming, which slows down action that is

Nature under the microscope *Camera bodies are attached to special microscopes to photograph minute plants and animals, such as this plankton, which floats on water.*

too fast for the human eye to see. The fastest modern cinecameras can take 11,000 frames a second, compared with the normal cine speed of 24 frames a second. The film moves past the lens at almost 200mph (320km/h), and the film spool is turning 33,000 times per minute. If anything goes wrong the camera is jammed with useless film in a split second.

Usually much slower speeds suffice: birds, bats and insects need 500 frames a second to show their wing beats and frogs leaping about the same, but it takes 1000

'FREEZING' A DROP OF WATER
High-speed photography captures the progress of drops of water falling into a bowl of liquid. A series of short, rapid flashes have pictured a drop falling, touching the surface, then sinking and forcing a column of water to rise.

The greatest difficulty is to arrange for the flash to go off when the subject is in exactly the right position. Often the best way is to make the subject – such as a bullet speeding through an apple – trigger the shutter or flash (or both) itself, by breaking a fine infrared beam or light beam that is focused on a reactive cell, for example.

A series of flashes may be used, with the film moving between each one. This technique was pioneered by an American, Harold Edgerton, in the 1930s. By using ten flashes a second and superimposing all the images on the same frame, he was able to show a drop of milk splashing into a bowl.

CREATING A NATURAL SETTING IN A STUDIO

This photograph of a leopard frog leaping out of the water took less than a second to snap, but the studio setting took hours to construct. Because it is difficult to photograph animals in the wild, elaborate natural-looking sets are built (right). The frog is placed on the rock (inset), and its behaviour captured on film. In this case, the camera was triggered by a photoelectric cell, activated by the frog when it jumped, momentarily blocking the beam of light shone on the camera. The result appears so natural that it is impossible to tell it was filmed indoors.

Underwater photography
A photographer wading in shallow water uses a type of upside-down periscope to take a picture of a Portuguese man-of-war (right) from underneath. These creatures, which are found in warm water, have stinging tentacles that can be as long as 30ft (9m).

frames a second to capture the jump of the athletic flea. The highest speeds are needed for filming a drop of water splashing on a surface, a bullet penetrating glass, or a golfer hitting a drive.

Filming animals in the wild is fraught with problems. Even with a zoom lens, just getting near enough to most animals is difficult. Before filming, photographers often watch the animals for some time, so they know their habits and can position themselves in a good vantage point downwind.

Photographers sometimes have to use tricks to fool their audience. Films showing animals such as foxes prowling at night are in fact often taken at dawn or dusk, when there is sufficient natural light. Then the film is doctored using filters to make it look as though it was much darker. Occasionally animals really are filmed at night, but even with image intensifiers that make them easier to see, the pictures are still not very clear.

Many films of 'wild' animals rely on using half-tame animals or even trained ones. Several photographers have looked after birds from the moment they hatch, so the birds instinctively follow them everywhere. By mounting a camera on a truck or on a fast boat, the photographers can take close-up film of the birds as they fly behind them.

Many animals are filmed in studios. Some animals cannot be trained, and it is not practical to film them in the wild. The surroundings of a trout spawning in a mountain stream, for example, can be convincingly imitated in a glass tank. Many of the most intimate scenes of small

mammals giving birth and bringing up their young are achieved by building nests in the studio with clear windows which enable the animals' private lives to be filmed. These nests are shallow, so that the animals remain within focusing range of the camera. When the film is edited and combined with other film taken outside, the viewer never suspects that some of the film has been shot in the studio.

Some of the toughest problems come in filming forms of life too small to see with the naked eye, like tiny bugs or insects. They have to be filmed through a microscope, but that reduces the light reaching the film. Extra lighting is needed but care has to be taken that the heat of the lights does not damage the tiny creatures being filmed.

Another problem with filming such small creatures is vibration. Even the tiniest movement between camera and object destroys the focus. This difficulty is overcome by an 'optical bench' which is a platform with the camera rigidly fixed at one end and the creature at the other. If a passing lorry causes vibrations, the camera and object vibrate as one, so the film remains perfectly in focus.

Some of the most dramatic film can be taken with an arrangement rather like an upside-down periscope. A typical project might be to film an insect, at its own eye level, as it wanders over the forest floor. It can be followed as it disappears beneath a leaf, or dives underwater. The periscope is suspended from a camera running on rails on an overhead gantry, so that it can be focused while it is rotated, tilted or moved backwards and forwards.

Making plastic self-destruct

One of the advantages of plastic is that it does not rust or rot. But this can also be a problem – plastic cups, bags, wrappers and containers litter the countryside and beaches all over the world. Unless they are picked up, they go on accumulating year after year.

To deal with this problem, various forms of degradable plastic have been developed. The secret is to incorporate into the plastic a chemical that can be attacked by light, bacteria or other chemicals.

Biodegradable plastics can be made by adding starch. If the plastics are buried, bacteria that feed on starch will gradually break them up into tiny pieces that disappear harmlessly into the soil.

Chemically degradable plastics can be broken up by spraying them with a solution that causes them to dissolve. They can be used, for example, as a protective waxy covering for new cars, and washed off at the dealer's garage by a specially formulated spray. This reacts with one of the components in the plastic and causes it to dissolve into harmless materials which can be flushed down the drain.

One of the most successful uses of degradable plastics is in surgery, where stitches are now often made using plastics which dissolve slowly in body fluids, saving the patient the anxiety of having the stitches removed. Drugs are often prescribed in plastic capsules which dissolve slowly, releasing the drug into the bloodstream at a controlled rate.

Photodegradable plastics contain chemicals that slowly disintegrate when exposed to light. In France, strips of photodegradable plastic about 3ft (1m) wide are used in the fields to retain heat in the soil and produce early crops. They last for between one and three years before rotting into the soil. But they have to be used in a country with a consistent amount of sunshine so they decay at a predictable speed.

In the USA, about one-quarter of the plastic 'yokes' that link beer cans in a six-pack are made of a plastic called Ecolyte, which is photodegradable. But to stop them decaying too early they must be stored away from direct sunlight, which can be an inconvenience for the retailer.

Degradable plastic has other problems. For example, it cannot be recycled because there is no easy way to measure its remaining life span. The biggest drawback has been the cost of producing it, but Japanese scientists believe they will soon be able to produce a much cheaper multipurpose biodegradable plastic.

How did oil bring about the 'plastic revolution'?

PLASTICS: THE MOST VERSATILE MATERIALS

Since plastics were invented at the end of the 19th century there has been a materials revolution throughout the world. Today, most toys, sporting goods and many household articles contain at least some plastic material. Even synthetic feather dusters are made from it. Because plastics are water-resistant and do not rot, they are ideal for things used outside, like drainpipes and flowerpots. Plastics can be moulded to almost any shape quickly and cheaply – the yellow guitar case, the chairs, the ice-tray and the tough safety helmet are just a few examples.

If you removed everything from your home that contained plastic, how much would be left? Many kitchens would be almost bare. Most carpets and rugs would go, many clothes and perhaps the curtains would vanish. There would certainly be no telephone, hi-fi or television.

And think of all the other things made of plastic, such as riot shields, credit cards,

artificial snow and hip joints. Now Australians are even buying their plastic goods with plastic banknotes.

The term 'plastics' covers a wide range of materials man-made from two basic ingredients: carbon and hydrogen. By adding extra chemicals, plastics can be given special properties like extra strength, heat-resistance, slipperiness and flexibility.

There is almost no end to the number of plastics that can be created by combining chemicals in different ratios and patterns. Scientists are already trying to develop a plastic as tough as steel, as clear and waterproof as glass and as cheap as paper.

Plastics are made up of large molecules called polymers, which are formed by smaller molecules joining together in long chains. These chains become tangled, giving plastic its strength – considerable force is needed to pull the chains apart.

When most plastics – called thermoplastics – are heated to about 390°F (200°C) the chains stay intact but move apart enough to slide over one another. This allows thermoplastics to be repeatedly heated and moulded into new shapes. Once the plastic has cooled it holds its new shape and maintains its strength.

However, there are other plastics which,

THE BIRTH OF A BILLION-DOLLAR INDUSTRY

The modern plastics industry began in the 1860s with a competition in America to find a better billiard ball. A prize of $10,000 was put up for anyone who could find a cheap replacement for ivory balls. The winner was John Wesley Hyatt, an American inventor, who made a ball from a substance he called Celluloid.

Other uses for Celluloid were quickly found – among them spectacle frames, knife handles, windscreens for early automobiles and photographic film. Without Celluloid the film industry could never have started.

Celluloid is not completely man-made because its raw material is cellulose, which is found in plants. Nevertheless, Celluloid gave Leo Baekeland, an American industrial chemist, the idea to create the first completely synthetic material. He achieved success in 1907 by mixing phenol (carbolic acid) and the gas formaldehyde – producing a plastic which he called Bakelite.

Many other plastics were invented in the wake of Baekeland's momentous discovery. But even he would be amazed at the growth of the plastics industry, which now has an annual turnover of more than $100 billion in the United States alone.

together. Hydrocarbons range from simple molecules like methane (a gas made up of one hydrogen atom combined with four carbon atoms) to tars and asphalts, which may have hundreds of atoms.

In the process of refining crude oil many different hydrocarbons are produced. One of them is the gas ethane (two carbon and six hydrogen atoms) which can be converted to another gas, ethylene, and then polymerised to make polyethylene (polythene). Similarly, propane gas becomes polypropylene. These two plastics are used to make bottles, pipes and plastic bags.

PVC – polyvinyl chloride – is chemically similar to polythene, but its hydrogen atom is replaced by a chlorine atom. This slight change makes PVC 'flame retardant', making it safer to use in the home. If four fluorine atoms are used rather than the chlorine atom, polytetrafluoroethylene, PTFE, is made. This, known as Teflon, is used for nonstick frying pans and bearings.

Many polymers have been made in the laboratory, but only those with the most useful qualities, like polystyrene, PTFE and nylon, are produced industrially.

once moulded, remain hard and keep their shape even when reheated. These are thermosetting plastics.

The process of getting small molecules to join up and form larger ones, called polymerisation, differs from one plastic to another. But it often involves high pressures and the use of special agents, called catalysts, to encourage the small molecules to link up.

The carbon and hydrogen atoms that form the base of all plastics come from crude oil. Oil consists of hydrocarbons – hydrogen and carbon molecules bonded

How oil is extracted from the ground

When oil was struck for the first time in the Forties Field under the North Sea in 1969, it led to the discovery of at least 350 million tons of oil. But how is oil actually won from beneath the sea or the land?

Oil wells are drilled with special cutting tools, known as drill bits, which spin round to chip away at the rock. The steel, or diamond-studded steel drill bit is at the end of a strong steel pipe called the drill string, which is rotated either by a motor at the surface or by a turbine down the hole.

The rock chippings are carried upwards and out of the hole by pumping a material known as 'mud' down through the drill string. It is not real mud, but a combination of chemicals and water which brings up the chippings and prevents the drill bit from becoming too hot from friction.

As the hole gets deeper, fresh sections of drill string have to be added – usually in 30ft (9m) lengths. At the top of the drill string is the kelly, which fits into a rotating table on the floor of the drilling derrick, like a nut fits a spanner. To fit a new section, the drill string is lifted up enough to remove the kelly, then the new section is attached to the top of the drill string before the kelly is replaced – allowing drilling to continue.

Twin sources *Two oil-rig drilling derricks (centre) are flanked by cranes. At each side, flare stacks burn off excess gas from the oil reservoir beneath the sea.*

From time to time – every few hours, or every few days, depending on the rock – the bit itself has to be replaced. Then the entire drill string has to be pulled up, separated into 90ft (27m) 'stands', each consisting of three lengths, and stacked

vertically on the derrick. When the bit finally emerges and is replaced with a new one, the whole string has to be reassembled and lowered down the hole again. The process, known as a 'round trip', can take up to ten hours if the well is already deep.

To prevent the hole caving in, it is lined with casing – heavy steel pipes are lowered in as drilling proceeds and cement is pumped around them to fix them in place. The casing gets progressively narrower as the well deepens. A 15,000ft (4500m) well may have 30in (760mm) diameter casing at the surface, decreasing in steps to 7in (180mm) at the bottom.

If the drill strikes oil, the weight of the mud ensures that the oil cannot escape, but there is an additional safeguard – a special valve called a blow-out preventer is fixed to the top of the casing.

The rate at which a well is drilled depends entirely on the type of rock. It can be as slow as 12in (300mm) an hour in the impervious cap rock, or as fast as 200ft (60m) in soft, sandy rock.

When oil is found, a whole series of production wells has to be drilled to bring it to the surface.

Offshore and in difficult terrain, the first step is to drill a number of wells designed to reach all corners of the oil-bearing rock. This can be done from a single derrick by angling the holes to different parts of the oil field. In a large field, several derricks or drilling platforms may be used, each drilling directionally according to a plan so that the whole area is exploited.

When the production wells have been drilled and lined with casing, a perforating gun is lowered down them to drive explosive charges through the casing and cement and into the rock beyond – allowing the oil to get into the wells. As the oil is extracted, pressure may be maintained by injecting water or gas into the reservoir rock to displace the oil towards the production wells.

Later, electrical or mechanical pumps may be used. But even with the help of such techniques it is seldom possible to extract more than about 30 to 50 per cent of the oil in a field.

Computer drillings *Computers can create outlines of alternative drilling pathways (shown as the coloured lines passing through different rock layers) after seismic tests have been carried out.*

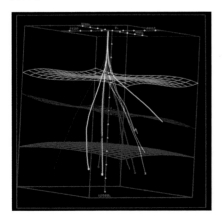

How they know where to drill for oil

By the year 2020 the world's known oil reserves are due to run out. By then, new oil fields will need to be found, probably in more and more inaccessible places.

Three things are needed for an oil field to form in nature: the right kind of sedimentary rock to create the oil; a layer of porous rock to store it; and a 'cap' of impermeable rock to trap it. Sedimentary rock is formed over millions of years from sediment that contains fish, shellfish, plankton and plants. As these organic materials break down with heat and time, they produce oil and gas. If there is a layer of porous rock, it will soak up the oil like a sponge. An impermeable bed of rock above the oil will contain it, so long as the 'cap' is the right shape – ideally a dome.

Prospectors searching for oil look for all three types of rock. To find sedimentary basins which could be oil-bearing, magnetic surveys and gravity surveys are often used. All rocks are magnetic, but the magnetism varies slightly from one rock to another, giving geologists clues to the structure and type of rocks that lie underground. Other clues lie in the varying densities of rocks.

In magnetic surveys, magnetometers – instruments which measure magnetism – are usually towed over the region by an aircraft. From readings of the variations in magnetism, a picture of the structure of the ground below can be built up.

Gravitational surveys rely upon the measurement and comparison of the densities of sub-surface rocks. A device called a gravimeter can measure changes in

Seismic tests *In the vast Arabian desert, prospectors search for oil. They set off explosions and measure the shock waves to build up a picture of the underground rock formation. This tells them whether oil is likely to be present or not.*

gravity of one part in 100 million of the Earth's gravitational field. There is even a gyroscopically established version of the instrument to take readings at sea.

The information gathered is processed by a computer and interpreted by geologists. If the results are promising, more detailed information is obtained by seismic surveying.

This starts by sending shock waves into the ground by causing explosions or vibrations on the surface. The shock waves travel at different speeds depending on the type of rock they are travelling through.

When the waves hit an interface between two different types of rock they are reflected and return to the surface. Microphones and recording instruments pick up the returning shock waves. Computers can then be used to calculate the positions of the rock layers from the time the waves take to return to the surface. A detailed cross-section of the area can then be produced.

This method has proved very successful, but geologists can never be certain that oil will be found even if all the indications are there. Sometimes even the best prospects from seismic surveys have no oil at all, while less promising sites turn up trumps. One of the main reasons for this is the difficulty in telling whether oil has been trapped in its original position or not.

Oil pools can seep upwards or sideways through porous rocks.

Cleaning up a major oil spill

Oil is the greatest pollutant of the Earth's oceans and river estuaries – and the giant tankers that transport it are the world's worst culprits.

Nearly ten years after the Libyan-owned tanker *Amoco Cadiz* was wrecked off Brittany in March 1978, scientists reported that fish were still not breeding properly along that section of coast.

Plaice had abnormal and defective reproductive organs and local oysters were contaminated.

In 1989, a giant oil slick in Prince William Sound, Alaska, contaminated the breeding grounds of seals, sea lions and birds. Ten million gallons (45 million litres) of oil was spilt when the 216,000 ton tanker *Exxon Valdez* hit a reef.

No one knows precisely how much oil is accidentally spilt or deliberately jettisoned in routine ballast-dumping into the world's waters.

Contamination is often caused when tankers wash out their empty tanks with sea water after a delivery.

The residue, which is pumped into the sea, can be considerable.

Left to itself, an oil spill will eventually disperse, breaking down to harmless residues – but not before it wreaks havoc on marine wildlife. The breakdown can be speeded up by spraying the oil with chemical dispersal agents, which are basically detergents.

But these too, can have undesirable effects. They destroy the natural oils on seabirds' feathers, which give the birds their buoyancy.

After the supertanker *Torrey Canyon* went aground off the Scilly Isles in 1967, releasing about 21,000 gallons (95,000 litres) of oil, scientists believed the chemicals used to disperse the oil did more damage to shellfish than did the oil itself. Other, less damaging, chemicals have been developed for dispersing oil, but even they have to be used with great care.

Contaminated coastline *The black beaches of Brittany (above) after the Libyan-owned tanker the* Amoco Cadiz *was wrecked in 1978. A giant inflatable floating boom (left) was used to try to trap the offshore oil slick. Onshore cleanup operations are frequently carried out by volunteer workers using just shovels and pails, as was done in 1988 when an Italian tanker sprang a leak off Brittany.*

If possible, it is better to trap an oil slick before it spreads, and then pump it from the surface of the sea.

To do this, the slick is surrounded by a long, floating boom of inflatable tubes. Because oil floats on water, the boom stops it from spreading. One of the largest boom systems developed in the 1980s was British Petroleum's weir boom. The ends of the boom are attached to supply ships. These move it slowly through the water, trapping the oil. One of the ships pumps the oil through a floating pipeline to a nearby tanker. The system can collect 15,000 tons of oil-and-water mixture a day.

Several other devices have been developed to suck up the oil slick once it has been trapped. These include sorption skimmers and weir skimmers.

Sorption skimmers use rollers, belts or mops, whose surfaces are treated with synthetic chemical materials to which oil sticks but water does not. A drum or belt rotates in the slick, picking up the oil and carrying it to a container, where it is scraped off with a blade that resembles a windscreen wiper.

Weir skimmers work by placing a weir just below the surface so that the oil flows over it. The level on the other side is kept lower by pump, and as the oil flows over the weir, it is pumped into a reservoir.

The simplest form of this manoeuvre uses open-topped oil drums weighted with stones, placed in water so shallow that their rims are just beneath the surface. The floating oil flows into the drums and can then be pumped out.

Spills on land or oil washed ashore can be difficult to clean up. Sometimes earth-moving equipment is used, or drainage trenches are dug. Straw, sawdust or peat can be used for a final clean up.

How they put out an oil-well fire

The Devil's Cigarette Lighter – as the oil-well fire was dubbed – had been burning for almost six months far out in the sands of the Sahara.

Turning and twisting, the orange-red flame plumed 450ft (137m) into the air and was blown into fantastic shapes by the desert wind. It was visible for 100 miles (160km) in the central Algerian sky, and had been seen by the American astronaut John Glenn as he orbited the globe in February 1962.

Gas was surging from a 13in (330mm) wide pipe faster than the speed of sound, so fast in fact that there was no flame until the gas was 30ft (9m) in the air. The noise was a non-stop, thunderous roar. The desert floor trembled, and the sand sizzled like something frying in a pan. According to an eyewitness, 'It was the nearest you could get to a living hell-on-earth!'

Trouble had started early in November 1961, when gas in the well had erupted, hurling out the steel drill pipe. Gas poured into the sky at a rate that would have supplied the needs of a city the size of Paris. There were no flames yet, just a high-powered jet of gas. But the threat that filled the minds of everyone watching was that a single spark would ignite an inferno.

The French owners of the well called on the world's number one oil-well and gas-field trouble-shooter, the stocky Texan Red Adair, to deal with the emergency. Already occupied with a major fire in Mexico, Adair immediately sent two top assistants to the Gassi Touil oil and gas field, in the desert south-east of the Algerian capital, Algiers.

For seven days the Adair team pumped mud into the well to try to block the gas that was gushing out. Then, at noon on November 13, there was a violent explosion and the almost invisible column of gas caught fire. The cause was probably a spark of static electricity created by the constantly blowing sand.

It was now a job for Red Adair himself. At the age of 47, he had been fighting such fires for the past 24 years. His job was one of the most dangerous on Earth. Once on the scene, he realised that the fire, if left unchecked, could burn ceaselessly for up to 100 years.

To put out the fire – or 'kill' it in oil-field parlance – he had to deprive it of oxygen. To do this he would detonate a powerful explosive charge close to the flame. In effect, he planned to blow out the fire, just like blowing out the candles on a gigantic birthday cake.

It took five months to assemble all the equipment he needed, and have it flown to Algeria and then transported out into the desert. It was not until April 1962 that he and his team were ready to start work. By then the 30-man strong oil camp had grown into a settlement of some 500 as helpers and observers crowded in from all over the world. Bulldozers, pumps and lengths of iron pipe arrived daily by truck.

At the time Algeria was waging a bitter war for its independence from France. As well as hiring a French interpreter, Adair employed guards armed with machine guns to defend him and his men in case they got caught up in the fighting between the controlling French army and Algerian nationalists. But the task in hand was his overriding concern.

First of all he needed water, which he and his assistants drilled for – creating a reservoir which could be used to pump water onto the blaze when it was needed. Then the seven-storey oil derrick – which the fire had reduced to 600 tons of charred, tangled steel – was dragged away by a vast water-cooled hook and a gigantic 'rake'.

The next stage – setting and detonating

the explosive – was far more tricky and dangerous. The only way Adair and his gang could work in any degree of safety was under tons of water falling constantly from eight huge nozzles – which were lined up like a battery of guns.

Shortly after eight o'clock on a Saturday morning, Adair – wearing high-necked red cotton overalls, a red safety helmet, red rubber boots and red flannel long johns, was ready. He had prepared a caterpillar tractor with a 50ft (15m) boom, welded to the end of which was a black iron drum wrapped in aluminium and asbestos.

Watched by scores of oilmen, firemen, policemen and nurses – and with two helicopters standing by to rush people to hospital if anything went wrong – he began to pack the drum with 550lb (250kg) of dynamite.

He next threaded detonator caps and wire into the drum. The wire led to a trench 200yds (180m) from the fire, in which a blaster would set off the explosion.

The sun was blazing down when, at about nine o'clock, Adair and his assistant climbed into the tractor. Adair took the controls and the machine lumbered forward like some long-necked prehistoric monster into the downpour of water from the eight pumps.

The Devil's Cigarette Lighter

As the tractor neared the fire, the assistant jumped out into the deluge of water and guided Adair with hand signals. Slowly, the boom brought the drum of explosives to within a few inches of the spot where the grey pillar of gas became flame.

He then dashed for the shelter of the trench. Adair leaped down from the tractor and set off after him, as fast as he could run. Once both men were in the trench the assistant pushed down the blaster, and the fire's roar was drowned by the sound of a mighty 'crrrr-ump'.

Thick black smoke covered the scene. The fire's thunder was replaced by a shrill, whining noise of escaping gas. The Devil's Cigarette Lighter had finally been put out.

Next came the equally hazardous task of capping the well with a 10ft (3m) high steel block weighing 8 tons called a control head. But Adair decided to wait until the following Monday before tackling that. First of all there was an outcrop of small fires around the well head to be snuffed out; then he had to make sure that the pipe itself was intact. With all the fires killed, and the well cooled by a constant barrage of water, Adair was relieved to find that the pipe was still sound. So, early on the Monday morning, he prepared to cut through the pipe and fit the control head over it, against the immensely powerful upward gas pressure.

For the next two days Adair and his team worked in a cloud of highly explosive gas

RED ADAIR: THE MAN BEHIND THE LEGEND

Called 'Red' because of his flame-coloured hair, Paul Neal Adair's first job was stoking the smithy fire for his blacksmith father in his home town of Houston, Texas.

In 1938, aged 23, he was working as a labourer on an oil rig when a valve blew and he was thrown 50ft (15m) into the air. While everyone else ran for cover, he – although bruised and badly shaken – calmly replaced the valve.

His courage was noted by the pioneer American oil fire-fighter Myron Kinley, who asked young Adair to help him deal with a blow out in Alice, Texas. The two men worked together until the United States entered the Second World War in 1941. Adair became a bomb-disposal expert in the Pacific, but was reunited with Kinley after the war. He stayed with him until 1959 when he formed the Red Adair Oil Well Fires and Blow-outs Control, with the motto: 'Around the Clock, Around the World.'

Three years later, his success at Gassi Touil made world headlines. His fame quickly grew and in 1968 his dare-devil exploits inspired a Hollywood film, *Hellfighters*, starring John Wayne as an intrepid oil-well fireman. But some of Adair's most dramatic feats were still to come. These have ranged from snuffing oil fires in the Gulf of Mexico to the North Sea – including the Piper Alpha oil-platform disaster off the north-east coast of Scotland in the summer of 1988.

A multimillionaire and grandfather, Red Adair works out of an office in Houston which – like his automobile and his powerboat – is coloured fire-engine red. In his 50-odd years of fire-fighting he has dealt with more than 1000 oil-well flare-ups and blow outs.

'There are two things I really like about my job,' he once told an interviewer. 'When the phone rings I never know where I'm heading to next – and I'm never bothered by life-insurance salesmen!'

Texan trouble shooter *Red Adair, photographed in 1968. He has never failed to put out a fire. Some have taken six months, some only 30 seconds.*

which could ignite at any moment and burn them alive. Using a separated steel cable 10,000ft (3000m) long, they sawed through the pipe sticking out of the ground and cut it off. To combat any sparks, the work area was drenched with water. Then the massive control head – a complicated arrangement of valves, flanges, cocks and outlets – was wheeled in.

Once in place, the huge head would divert the rush of gas away from the danger area to a horizontal, 1200ft (365m) long crosspiece known as flow lines. The flow lines would then be lit at the ends and the well would finally be under control – just as the gas in a kitchen stove is a hazard only when the burners are open and unlit.

Because of the potential danger, a crane – which could give off sparks while being operated – was not used to swing the control head into position. Instead, a gang of 20 workmen hauled the head by ropes and swung it over the well.

As the head was eased into place over the cut-off pipe, the workers were soaked in a rain of gasoline condensed from gas – which sprayed out in a wide circle around the well. Adair and his team moved in, and for the next three hours they knocked home the bolts with brass hammers (less likely to give off sparks than steel ones). Fires were then lit at the ends of both flow lines; the biggest oil-field fire thus far in history had been capped.

Piper Alpha: deadly fireball

On July 6, 1988, the world's worst oil disaster struck the Piper Alpha oil platform in the North Sea, 120 miles (190km) off the Scottish coast. Two massive explosions engulfed the platform in a fireball, killing 167 men. After the 63 survivors had been rescued, the problem was to extinguish five blazing wells.

The twisted platform was covered with slippery oil and smouldering wreckage, some pieces weighing more than 20 tons. Before any of the fires could be put out, the debris had to be cleared. But the platform's temperature had reached well over 1000°C and it was tilting at 45 degrees. It was in danger of collapsing completely and the burning wells could have exploded.

Red Adair flew in from America. Fortunately, *Tharos* – a 30,000 ton emergency vessel, was near the platform, packed with fire-fighting equipment. Designed by Adair, it had a 135-man crew, three cranes, a diving bell and a decompression chamber, a 'fire-boom' and 16 water cannons.

Some of the water cannons were used to throw up a blanket of water to protect *Tharos* from the intense heat as it came within 85ft (26m) of the platform. The rest were directed at the fires.

The fire-boom is a telescopic mechanical arm that can move up and down, or from side to side. It can extend 62ft (19m) beyond the deck. The main crane lifted the debris from the platform.

While the deck was being cleared the cannons sprayed millions of gallons of sea water on the deck, and eventually the fires were extinguished. But oil was still pouring from the well heads over the platform.

Once the deck had cooled sufficiently, sea water was pumped into the wells under very high pressure, stemming the flood of oil. As soon as the oil stopped flowing out, cement was pumped into each well to seal it permanently. Red Adair and his crew cleared all the debris and controlled the wells in just 36 days.

Every oil-well fire has its own particular problems, but the same basic methods are used to extinguish them. The simplest is to stop the flow of oil or gas by closing the pipeline valves. But after a blow out these valves are often damaged, or impossible to reach because of the heat.

After an explosion on the Ekofisk platform in 1977, oil was pouring out of a well at great pressure and at temperatures of nearly 100°C. The force of the escaping oil was too strong to be countered by pumping in sea water. Red Adair tried using hydraulic rams to push two semi-circular discs together to shut off the top of the well head. But fitting the rams in such conditions was not easy. One spark and the oil would have ignited. After five attempts, more powerful hydraulic rams were used and succeeded.

Relief wells may be drilled to divert some of the oil from a ruptured pipe or well and reduce the pressure and volume.

In case the initial plan of using water and cement to control the Piper Alpha blow out had failed, the semi-submersible drilling rig *Kingsnorth* had already begun to drill another well to a depth of 8500ft (2600m) beneath the seabed. The idea was to seal the well with cement from the bottom and block the oil flow, but this was never necessary. The Red Adair team were able to cap all the wells.

Action man *Red Adair (centre), at 73 in 1988, said he had no intention of retiring. Here he directs the capping of methane gas near Franenthal, West Germany, in 1980.*

North Sea inferno *The 1988 Piper Alpha oil-platform disaster was the world's worst, with 167 men killed. Water cannons (inset) doused the fires that raged after two explosions rocked the platform. Red Adair's operation, including plugging five wells, took 36 days.*

How do they measure a mountain?

In 1749 the British 'Survey of India' identified a lofty peak in the distant ranges of the Himalayas. It was called Peak XV, but it was not until 1849 that another survey set out to measure its height. When the survey was completed in 1852 it was confirmed that Peak XV was the highest mountain in the world.

Various names were suggested for it, including Devadhunga (Throne of Gods) and Guarishankar (Gleaming White Bride of Shiva). The Tibetans call it Chomolungma (Goddess Mother of the World). But the name approved by the Royal Geographical Society in London was suggested by Andrew Waugh, then Surveyor General of India. He thought it should be named after his predecessor – Sir George Everest.

Classical surveying techniques were used to calculate Everest's height. First of all a baseline several miles long was measured along the ground at a known elevation above sea level. The top of the mountain could be seen from both ends of the line, and bearings were taken to the peak with theodolites – instruments which accurately measure angles.

From a knowledge of two angles and the length of one side of a triangle, the lengths of the other sides can be worked out – giving the distance of the peak from the baseline. Further calculations can then give the height (see diagram). The surveyors measured Everest from six different sites – producing six figures ranging between 28,990 and 29,026ft (8836 and 8847m). The average came to exactly 29,000ft (8839m) – but because it sounded like an approximation they added 2ft (0.6m), and

produced their authoritative answer – 29,002ft (8840m).

Everest's position as the world's highest mountain went unquestioned until 1986, when George Wallerstein, from the University of Washington, using a different method, claimed that another Himalayan mountain, K-2, might be 36ft (11m) higher.

Wallerstein's claim was so startling that an Italian expedition visiting the Himalayas in 1987 decided to check it. They placed receivers part-way up Everest and K-2, and used Navstar signals to establish their exact height and position. This was critical because discrepancies in the heights of mountains are usually due to errors in the height of the baseline on which calculations are based.

The team, led by geologist Ardito Desio, then calculated the heights of the two mountains using theodolites set up on the receivers' positions. Their conclusion was that Wallerstein was wrong: Everest was measured at 29,108ft (8872m), a full 840ft (256m) higher than K-2.

Making the sea yield its sunken secrets

On the bed of the Atlantic, 2½ miles (4km) down, Dr Robert Ballard saw the bulk of the liner *Titanic* looming in front of him. He and the crew of the miniature submarine *Alvin* were the first men to set eyes on the ocean giant since she was sunk by an iceberg nearly 75 years earlier. 'Directly in front of us was an apparently endless slab of black steel rising out of the bottom – the massive hull of the *Titanic*,' he wrote.

Of a second dive – one of nine he made in the *Alvin* during July 1986 – Dr Ballard recalled: 'Here I was on the bottom of the ocean, peering at recognisable, man-made artefacts designed and built for another world. I was looking through windows out of which people had once looked, [at] decks along which they had walked, rooms where they

Tudor treasures *Among perfectly preserved artefacts recovered from the* Mary Rose *are blocks and tackle from the rigging.*

Square gun *A unique square-mouthed gun fired several bullets at once. Surrounding it are gunpowder dispensers and gun shot.*

Archery tackle *Five out of 4000 arrows recovered from the* Mary Rose *are contained in a leather spacer beside an archer's wrist guard and a leather sword cover or scabbard.*

had slept, joked, made love. It was like landing on the surface of Mars only to find the remains of an ancient civilisation similar to our own.'

The *Titanic* sank about 450 miles (720km) south of Newfoundland, in the early hours of Monday, April 15, 1912. Of the 2200 people on board, only 705 were saved. It was the liner's maiden voyage.

But it was not until September 1, 1985 – thanks to modern technological aids – that the wreck was located by a joint French-American expedition, headed by Dr Ballard.

The first step in finding a lost wreck – if it is not found by accident – involves meticulous research in historical archives

What the surveyor does *A baseline is measured between two points (A and B), both at the same altitude. The surveyor stands at A and points a theodolite at the summit C and then at B. This tells him the angle x. He does the same at B to get the angle y. He can then calculate the distance to the point D which is directly below the summit at the same altitude as the baseline. Still at B, he establishes the angle z with a levelling instrument. Knowing that BCD is a right-angled triangle, and the length of BD, he can calculate the length of h, which he adds to the altitude of the baseline to give the total height of the mountain.*

Mary Rose An artist's impression shows the Mary Rose *before she capsized in 1545. The pride of Henry VIII's naval fleet was 130ft (40m) long and carried 91 guns and 415 men.*

Personal items *A manicure set, a shoe, wooden combs and case, a pomander and a bronze purse mount indicate a lady's presence.*

Barber-surgeon's kit *In a chest that was retrieved there was a bleeding bowl and syringe, a metal mortar, a drug flask and canisters – obviously for a surgeon's use.*

Leisure time *Displayed on a wooden gaming board are a book cover, a leather purse, a wind instrument, trading and gaming tokens, two dice and the spur of a gaming cock.*

which should establish as accurately as possible where the vessel went down. Sometimes, this can be quite straightforward.

The *Mary Rose*, King Henry VIII's flagship, sank in 1545 in relatively calm waters in the Solent – within sight and hearing of hundreds of people ashore, including the king.

As she set sail with a fleet of 60 other warships to confront a French invasion fleet, she heeled in the wind and water poured through her starboard gunports. Her cannons broke their moorings and rolled across the decks, adding their weight to the starboard side. The *Mary Rose* capsized, drowning 650 men. Her position

Bronze cannon *This cannon was among additional artillery on board the* Mary Rose *as she set off to fight the French. The extra weight may have caused her to capsize.*

was known, then lost or forgotten. And it was more than 400 years before she could be raised.

The location of ships that went down in sight of land is usually well documented. The Scilly Isles and Britain's western approaches harbour at least 400 recorded wrecks and hundreds of unrecorded ones. And an estimated $1 billion worth of gold, silver, jewellery and porcelain lie around the coasts of Florida, the West Indies and Central America.

One of the richest finds was a flotilla of

Spanish treasure *A chest containing silver coins was part of the booty discovered near the wreck of a Spanish galleon off the Florida coast. The ship was wrecked in 1622.*

ten Spanish treasure ships off Florida. They set sail for home from Havana, Cuba, in July 1715, laden with gold, emeralds, pearls and 2300 chests of newly minted coins from Mexico City – treasure worth at least $50 million in modern currency. The ships were caught in a hurricane and went down south of Cape Canaveral.

During the 1950s, local hotelier Kip Wagner, an avid beachcomber, found a few blackened silver coins in Sebastian Inlet, 40 miles (64km) south of Cape Canaveral. Researching their origin, he read about the fleet – and became convinced he had found some of its treasure. He sent a coin to the Smithsonian Institution in Washington, which told him that it could not be from the fleet, because it had sunk 150 miles (240km) farther south.

Undeterred, Wagner and a friend, Dr Kip Kelso, continued their own research and found that Bernard Romans, an English mapmaker, in 1775 had described

the place where the fleet went down and had even drawn a map. Armed with a secondhand mine detector, Wagner searched the beaches near the area described – and found a huge hoard of valuables, including a gold chain and pendant, auctioned for $50,000, and a diamond ring worth $20,000.

Wagner put to sea and began to dive to find the wrecks. The treasure he ultimately recovered was worth more than $5 million.

Wagner's use of a mine detector triggered the use of modern technology in the search for wrecks. In 1970, Rex Cowan, a London solicitor, decided to search for a Dutch East Indiaman, the *Hollandia*, lost off the Scilly Isles in 1743. He knew from contemporary accounts roughly where the wreck might be, but divers could find no trace. Cowan used a magnetometer – an instrument towed behind a ship which detects anomalies in the magnetic field caused by iron objects such as cannons.

After months of crisscrossing the likely area in a grid pattern, Cowan and his team finally got a reading only a few days before the end of the diving season in September, after which weather conditions tend to be unfavourable. They went below, found nothing, but returned the next day – and discovered cannons bearing the monograph of the Amsterdam chapter of the Dutch East India Company. Next they discovered a silver spoon bearing the crest of a Dutch family, the Imhoff-Bentincks, one of whose members was known to have been aboard the *Hollandia*, confirming the source. Ultimately, more than 35,000 silver coins, worth around £1 million, were found.

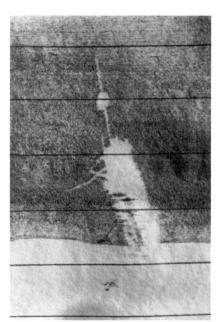

Sonar images of an Arctic wreck *The* Breadalbane, *a British ship, was lost in 1853 in Canada's Northwest Passage while searching for survivors of the ill-fated Franklin expedition. The wreck was detected in 1980 using sonar scanning equipment. The ghostly images revealed the ship with the sails still hanging from her masts, entombed at 340ft (104m) beneath the ice.*

Magnetometers proved unsuccessful, however, in rediscovering the *Mary Rose*. Although she had sunk only a few hundred yards from the shore, she was covered by mud and sand when the search for the wreck began. A magnetometer found a buried cable not recorded on Admiralty charts – but no wreck.

The breakthrough came from another modern invention – sonar. Developed for underwater warfare, sonar sends out sound signals and records the echoes as they are reflected off solid objects.

A type of sonar called a sub-bottom profiler, which can detect objects embedded in mud or sand, produced signals suggesting the presence of a mound on the seabed – and something solid beneath. Three years later, tides had removed some of the silt from the port side of the wreck and timbers could be seen. Then began the historic recovery and the painstaking recording of its contents – a unique time capsule of life aboard a medieval man-of-war.

But the rediscovery of the *Titanic* must rank as the most remarkable deep-sea find. It lies too deep for divers and finding it in the immensity of the North Atlantic with only a rough idea of where it lay called for special skill. The joint French-US team used a deep-sea sonar device to search the ocean floor and find the wreck – then a remote-control underwater camera to take the first pictures. A year later, Dr Ballard, a marine geologist from the Woods Hole Oceanographic Institute, Massachusetts, saw the wreck for himself, from the three-man submarine *Alvin*.

The submarine landed on the bow and the bridge. A remote-control underwater robot camera, *Jason Junior*, descended the Grand Staircase, photographing still-hanging chandeliers, clocks, silverware, and the interiors of staterooms.

With such techniques, few wrecks anywhere beneath the Earth's oceans are beyond man's reach. If they are worth investigating, mankind now possesses the technology.

How does an aqualung work?

Ever since the 19th century, scientists had tried to invent an effective self-contained breathing device for divers. But if their inventions worked at all, they involved cumbersome diving suits or restricting safety lines. Then in 1943 a French naval captain, Jacques-Yves Cousteau, and his colleague Emile Gagnan, invented the aqualung. Cousteau used the invention to dive to depths of 200ft (60m).

A person's lungs are not powerful enough to expand against the pressure of water below about 18in (450mm). Water pressure increases rapidly with depth, and at 33ft (10m) it exerts a pressure equal to 2 atmospheres – nearly 30lb per square inch (2 kilos per square centimetre).

To breathe underwater, a diver has to receive air at the same pressure as the surrounding water. This is what the aqualung – or scuba (self-contained underwater breathing apparatus) – provides. Air is stored at high pressure – up to 3000lb per square inch (200 atmospheres) – in cylinders on the diver's back with a tube to a mouthpiece.

Air reaches the diver through a two-stage regulator. The first stage reduces the pressure to about 150lb per square inch (10 atmospheres) above the surrounding water.

The second stage, in the mouthpiece, supplies the diver with air at the same pressure as the surrounding water. A flexible diaphragm in the mouthpiece is open to the water on one side and to an air chamber on the other. As the diver inhales, the diaphragm is drawn inwards and presses against a lever in the chamber. This opens a valve to let in air from the tube, which drops in pressure as it enters.

When the diver finishes inhaling, the air coming into the chamber pushes against the diaphragm, shutting the valve and cutting off the airflow.

Even when the diver is not inhaling, an increase in water pressure as he dives pushes the diaphragm forward to open the valve and let in air from the tube. So the air in the mouthpiece chamber is always at the same pressure as the surrounding water.

Breathing underwater
The air this diver breathes from her aqualung cylinder is regulated to match the pressure of the water on her body. When she inhales (bottom left), a diaphragm in the mouthpiece is drawn forward to open a valve and let in air. This drops in pressure to match that of the water bearing on the diaphragm's outer side. When inhalation finishes, incoming air pushes the diaphragm back to close the valve. This stops the airflow (bottom right). Exhaled air escapes through exhaust valves to leave a trail of bubbles in the water. The purge button at the front of the mouthpiece can be depressed by hand to let in air or to clear water from a flooded mouthpiece.

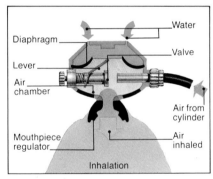

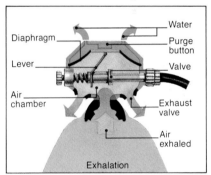

How are undersea telephone cables repaired?

Most of the world's international telephone conversations are carried by cables laid along the seabed, linking the continents. Communications satellites have not yet removed the need for submarine cables – even the 'hotline' between Washington and Moscow uses them. But what happens when a cable fails?

The first transatlantic telegraph cable, laid in 1858, failed within a few weeks. Today the risk of failure has been much reduced by using polythene insulation, and by choosing safer routes that avoid volcanic activity, strong currents and fishing grounds where trawlers may snag their nets on the cables. In shallow seas, cables are often buried.

Despite these precautions, failures still happen. Large telecommunications companies, such as Cable and Wireless, have maintenance ships standing by round-the-clock to carry out repairs.

The job is done by remote-controlled submersibles, as big as a medium-sized van, which are lowered into the water from the maintenance ship, dive to the seabed, locate the fault and attach lines to the damaged cable. The cable is then pulled to the surface and repaired on board the ship.

CIRRUS (Cable Installation, Recovery and Repair Underwater Submersible) and its even more sophisticated successor ROV128 are controlled through an 'umbilical' cable from the ship and powered by hydraulic thrusters.

A submersible's first job is to find the fault. It follows the line of the cable on the seabed, picking up faint low-frequency signals sent along the cable from the terminal station ashore. If a cable is broken, the water will form a short circuit that will link the individual wires together. When the signal disappears, the submersible settles on the ocean floor and

exposes the damaged cable with a powerful jet of water which blows away the layer of sand and silt.

CIRRUS is equipped with powerful lights and television cameras, both colour and black and white, which enable operators on board the ship to see every detail of the seabed. Using the pictures as guidance, the operators extend powerful manipulator arms and grip the cable. CIRRUS uses a special blade to cut the damaged cable, and leaves an acoustic 'pinger' on the seabed to mark the spot.

It then rises to the surface, picks up a strong steel line, takes it down to the seabed and clamps it to one end of the cable. The cable is then winched up to the surface. The same process is used to retrieve the other end of the cable.

Once the cable has been repaired and joined together on board the ship, it is lowered carefully back to the seabed.

Making diamonds in the laboratory

Two types of graphite *The brilliance of diamonds is emphasised by the dull lead used for pencils. Both are made from graphite, which is a form of carbon.*

Natural diamonds are created in the bowels of the Earth from graphite – the same substance that is used for the 'lead' in pencils. Both pencil lead and diamonds are forms of carbon. The only difference is that a diamond has been subjected to such tremendous temperatures and pressures beneath the Earth's crust that its molecules have been forced together, and its crystal structure has changed. Diamond, the world's hardest naturally occurring substance, is 55 per cent denser than graphite.

The notion of man-made diamonds has an obvious appeal, not just for their value and glamour as precious stones, but also because they have many industrial uses – in drilling, mining and cutting through concrete, for instance. Inventors have long tried to reproduce the conditions that create diamonds within the Earth.

Among the leaders in research were the General Electric Company who, in the early 1950s, set up a team of scientists, working in a laboratory in Schenectady, New York. The breakthrough came in 1954. Working with graphite as the base material, the researchers used two pistons housed in hard metal cylinders to exert

pressures, of up to 100,000 atmospheres (103,500 kilograms per square centimetre). An electric furnace was built inside the pressure cell capable of generating a temperature of 4500°F (2500°C), but after consistent test runs no diamond was produced.

It was clear that a catalyst was needed to help the reaction (in the same way that bread needs yeast to make it rise). For three years the scientists experimented with many different catalysts, but with no success. Then, on December 15, 1954, a laboratory technician noticed that during a routine examination, samples produced by physicist Herbert Strong had damaged his polishing wheel. He rang Strong up to complain. Strong and his team rushed over to the laboratory, and began examining the sample. Tracy Hall, one of the chemists, pronounced that the sample that had cut into the wheel contained two diamonds.

The next problem facing the team was how to duplicate the process to produce more diamonds. Strong had been using ferrous metals and alloys as catalysts in his tests, but for several days and nights the scientists failed to make any more.

Almost in desperation, Tracy Hall used his apparatus at maximum pressure, which gave a reading of about 100,000 atmospheres – and at last he succeeded. Previous experiments had probably failed because there had been the wrong combination of pressure, temperature and other chemical conditions.

The team were now concerned whether their diamonds would be as good as natural ones for industrial cutting and drilling. General Electric's carboloy department, which produced cutting tools made from one of the strongest metals, tungsten carbide, asked for a sample of 25 carats to test. The diamond team could only supply 22 carats, but that was just enough to make a grinding wheel.

The carboloy department used the grinding wheel to cut and sharpen their tools. They were delighted – if anything, the artificial diamonds cut better than natural diamonds and were just as durable. They asked when they could have more.

Eventually the most effective catalyst was devised, and in 1957 General Electric began selling synthesised diamonds commercially.

Today, more synthesised diamonds have been made than all the natural ones dug up over thousands of years – over 1000 tons. Man-made diamonds can be grown to order, which makes them ideal for industrial use.

The price of man-made diamonds has come down as the process of making them has been perfected; in 1957 it was $6 a carat, now it is only about 50 cents for the same kind of diamond, compared to thousands of dollars a carat for a good gem-quality natural diamond.

The biggest challenge for scientists now is to find a cheap way to make synthesised gem diamonds. Although blue, white and canary-yellow gem diamonds have been made by General Electric, they are as expensive as the real thing. A crystal takes more than two weeks to grow 1 carat of gem quality. It takes an expert to distinguish

---

WHY DIAMONDS SPARKLE

Brilliant cut *The true brilliance and colours of a well-cut diamond.*

At the end of the 17th century an Italian jeweller, Vincenti Peruzziot, invented the 'brilliant cut', which is still used for most diamonds. A brilliant-cut diamond is round, with 33 separate facets on its

upper surface and 25 on the lower, hidden face. The angles are precisely calculated so that light entering the diamond is reflected internally and emerges again from the top. Poor cutting can spoil this effect.

When Queen Victoria was presented with the 186.5 carat Koh-i-Nor diamond in 1850 she was disappointed by its lack of brilliance and had it re-cut to a final weight of 108.93 carats. The result was better, though still not perfect.

The high refractive index of diamond – the extent to which it 'bends' light entering it – means that with proper cutting all the light can be reflected.

A diamond's brilliance is also caused by the light that enters it being broken up into the separate colours of the spectrum, making its reflections multi-coloured. Because of its extreme hardness, the facets which give diamond its sparkle never wear off.

a natural diamond from a man-made one.

A new method of making synthetic diamonds developed by Soviet scientists at the chemical research institute at Kharkov, avoids using extreme heat and pressure. A fast-moving beam of carbon ions is produced and sprayed on a surface. Ions are atoms that have gained or lost electrons. Because electrons have a small electric charge the ions are no longer neutrally charged, and they can be accelerated to high speeds by magnetic fields. The energy with which they hit the surface is sufficient to bond them together and form diamond.

The result is not a single crystal of diamond but a material that looks rather like glass. It has already been used to make the hard edges of machine tools and hi-fi speaker diaphragms, and it has even been suggested that it could be used for making everlasting razor blades.

How diamonds are cut by hand and machine

An uncut diamond, no matter how large, looks as unimpressive as a rough lump of cloudy glass. To show its fire and brilliance it must be cut and faceted with pinpoint accuracy. A great deal of skill and patience is needed, since diamond is the hardest natural substance in the world.

The first step with a big stone is to cleave it along the natural planes of weakness in the crystal's structure. For diamonds of crown-jewel size it is the most risky part of the whole operation. Before Joseph Asscher successfully cleaved the massive Cullinan diamond in Amsterdam in 1908 (page 144), he studied the stone for several weeks. One slip could have turned it into a mass of fragments.

The cleaver has to calculate from the shape of the uncut stone the right direction for the cut. The sequence of photographs on the right, taken at the factory of the British diamond cutters A. Monnickendam, shows how the cleaver first marks the position of the cut on the stone in Indian ink. Then a smaller diamond is used to score along the line. A heavy steel blade is placed in the groove and struck a sharp blow. If all is well, the diamond will divide in two. If not, it can shatter into splinters.

Once the stone has been cleaved, a saw has to be used for the rest of the cutting process, which is usually carried out by another man. The stone is clamped in padded claws, called a 'dop', or in a mount of plaster of Paris. Then it is lowered onto the edge of a paper-thin disc of phosphor bronze, which is a very hard and strong

MARKING AND CLEAVING A DIAMOND

The rough stone resembles a lump of glass before cutting. First, a diamond designer marks the stone along the grain.

The cleaver fixes the stone to a stick with pliable adhesive, and scores along the line with a diamond chip.

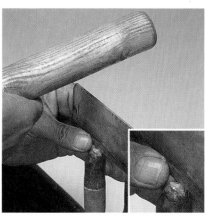

A steel blade is placed in the score line. The cleaver taps it, and the diamond splits along the grain.

metal alloy. The disc rotates between 4000 and 6000 times per minute. The edge is coated with a mixture of diamond dust and oil, which saws slowly through the diamond. A diamond weighing 1 carat (one-fifth of a gram) will take between four and eight hours to cut.

Next the stone must be roughly shaped by rubbing it against another diamond in a process called 'bruting'. One diamond is rotated by a lathe while the other is held against it. The tiny fragments of diamond dust chipped off are carefully collected for sawing and polishing the stone later on. The final shape of the gem depends on the

USING A DIAMOND SAW

A brilliant-cut diamond is usually sawn into two pieces with a thin metal disc that has diamond powder around the edge.

To make the stone circular, it is fixed in a bruting lathe and rotated at high speed against another diamond.

To grind and polish the facets, the diamond is clamped at the required angle against a rotating disc.

form of the original stone, but because it has to be cut in certain ways a lot of diamond is lost. The final gem usually weighs just under half the uncut stone.

The last stage is to cut and polish the facets that give diamonds their brilliance. The stone is mounted in a 'dop' and then held against an iron wheel coated with diamond dust and oil. The wheel spins at about 2500 revolutions per minute, grinding and polishing each facet in turn. The diamond is finally plunged into boiling sulphuric acid to clean off all traces of grease and dirt – a process which does no damage to the diamond at all.

Joseph Asscher: cutting the Cullinan diamond

On the afternoon of February 10, 1908, master gem cutter Joseph Asscher prepared to cut the world's largest and most celebrated rough diamond, the Cullinan. The blue-white stone belonged to Edward VII of England – and on the vital afternoon Asscher was watched by representatives of the king, members of the Press, and a group from his own company. The diamond was fixed in a holder shaped like an outsize egg cup. In turn, this was carefully placed in a hole in the front of the cleaving box. Joseph Asscher inserted a blunt steel blade in the groove, raised the metal rod and brought it crashing down.

The onlookers gasped as the steel blade snapped and the diamond remained intact. Wiping his brow, Asscher called for another blade. The stone split in two and – according to rumour – Joseph Asscher fainted with relief. He later hotly denied this, stating that far from collapsing he

Life-size The uncut diamond – almost 4in (100mm) long and 2½in (64mm) high – was about the size of a woman's fist. When he first saw it, the mine superintendent, Frederick Wells, thought he was the victim of a practical joke – and that the huge stone was made of glass. But it turned out to be real.

celebrated by drinking champagne with his four brothers and co-directors of Joseph Asscher and Company of Amsterdam (now the Royal Asscher Diamond Company).

The Asschers' next job was to recut and

polish the two pieces so that individual diamonds made from them could eventually form part of the Crown Jewels of England. Meanwhile, newspapers throughout the world told their readers the full story of the jewel so far.

The stone had first been sighted in January 1905 when a miner working in the Premier Mine, near Pretoria, the capital of the Transvaal, noticed something 'big and bright' glittering in one of the side walls. He called the mine's superintendent, Frederick Wells, and Wells dug the object out of the wall with his penknife.

It was soon established that the stone was genuine. It weighed about 24oz (680g) and was some 4in (100mm) long, 2½in (64mm) high and 5in (127mm) across. It was placed in the mine's safe and later taken 50 miles (80km) by mule cart to the company's headquarters in Johannesburg, with the rest of the week's diamond haul.

There it was named after the company chairman, Thomas Cullinan, a former bricklayer who had made his fortune out of building and had bought the Premier Mine some years before. However, he was not entirely happy about his ownership of the gem. With an uncut weight of 3106 carats,

THE BUILD-UP TO THE 'BIG BLOW'

Amsterdam jewel-cutter Joseph Asscher and his associates carefully studied the Cullinan diamond – considering whether to cleave it or saw it in two. Either way, there was the risk that the stone would shatter into a comparatively worthless pile of fragments. After six months' deliberation, taking into account the stone's odd shape and internal structure, Asscher decided to cleave it. He spent two weeks at his work-table making a groove in the stone with sharp pieces of diamond – as a diamond can only be cut by another diamond. Then, on the day of the 'big blow', he made diamond-cutting history.

The first cuts *The stone was split into three uneven pieces.*

The largest pieces *This life-size picture shows the seven largest pieces into which the stone was next cut. Despite its size, the diamond was thought to be only part of a much bigger stone. Marks on one of its faces suggested that it had been 'split by nature'. The Asscher family still believe this – and hope that one day the 'missing half' of the wonderful gem will be found in a South African diamond mine.*

Two giant gems *Gradually, the two main stones were cut and polished until they assumed their final shape.*

the Cullinan was potentially more than three times as valuable as the world's previous largest diamond, the Excelsior – discovered in another South African mine, the Jagersfontein, in 1893. Because of the risk involved in cutting it, the London syndicate which owned the Excelsior had been unable to sell it in its rough form. Thomas Cullinan feared that, because of its unprecedented size, his diamond would be even more difficult to sell.

Eventually it was bought by the Transvaal government for £150,000, at the suggestion of the premier, General Louis Botha – who presented it to Edward VII on the monarch's 66th birthday on November 9, 1907. It was regarded as a gesture of final conciliation following the Dutch settlers' defeat by the British in the Boer War of 1899-1902 and the establishment of the Transvaal as a British crown colony.

The diamond was shipped to England amid great publicity, including stories that a decoy was being sent to foil any would-be thieves and that the real stone would be sent on later. The following year King Edward invited the Asscher brothers – who in 1903 had successfully cut and polished the Excelsior diamond for resale – to

London to examine the Cullinan with a view to polishing it as one large stone.

After a brief inspection the Asschers told King Edward that this was impossible. The diamond was flawed by a big black inclusion, or spot, which would reflect through all the gem's sides. The Cullinan would have to go to Amsterdam for cleaving and removal of the spot. The king agreed to this, and the Press were told that the diamond would be taken to Holland aboard a heavily guarded destroyer.

In fact, one of the brothers – Abraham Asscher – simply slipped the diamond into his pocket at Buckingham Palace and went home with it by train and ferry.

Regal glory *In 1908 the smaller of the two stones, Cullinan II, was set in the British Imperial State Crown, immediately below the Black Prince's ruby. Two years later, the larger diamond, Cullinan I, was mounted in the Sceptre with the Cross.*

Once it was safely at the company's headquarters, the Asschers set about studying the mighty stone. It was judged to be in the highest of nine colour categories ranging from blue-white at the top, to yellow at the bottom. Apart from the black spot it was absolutely pure.

When the historic split had been made, the two pieces of diamond were cleaved again and further divided into seven major gems and 98 small, brilliant-cut stones. Next came the delicate job of polishing the diamonds.

The largest of the finished gems – the pear-shaped Cullinan I, or First Star of Africa, weighing 530.2 carats and with 74 facets – was placed in the Sceptre with the Cross. The stone is still the biggest cut diamond in the world. The second largest gem – Cullinan II, or Second Star of Africa, oval-shaped, weighing 317.4 carats and with 66 facets – was set in the Imperial State Crown. The diamonds are among the Crown Jewels in the Tower of London.

Eventually, the rest of the Cullinan diamonds were acquired for Queen Mary, the wife of Edward VII's son George V. Two of the jewels were set in Queen Mary's own crown. The others became heirlooms of the Royal Family, and are fondly called 'Granny's Chips' by Elizabeth II, Queen Mary's granddaughter.

How does a dowser find underground water or minerals, using only a rod?

An 8000-year-old cave painting in the Atlas Mountains of North Africa shows someone using what appears to be a dowsing, or water-divining, rod. But the first recorded dowsers were medieval German miners in the coalfields of Saxony. The German mineralogist Agricola (George Bauer), writing in the 16th century, describes how the miners used forked twigs to locate underground mineral seams.

The Baroness de Beausoleil, of Nice in France, was the first person known to have used dowsing for water-divining. In the 17th century, she wrote about it in a survey.

Traditionally, a dowser uses a forked stick – typically a Y-shaped hazel or willow twig. The stick's purpose is to magnify the involuntary movement of the hand muscles when the dowser makes a find, and it is held under tension with a branch of the Y in each upturned hand and the stem pointing forwards. Many modern dowsers prefer to use two L-shaped metal rods, one in each hand, held like pistols pointing forwards. The rods will swing and cross each other when the 'target' is reached.

The dowser walks slowly forwards until the stick or rods start twitching, bending, pulling downwards, or even jumping out of his grasp. This signals a spot where digging should uncover a supply of water, for example.

A good dowser will estimate the depth of the water by marking the spot where there was a strong signal, then dowsing from it in several directions, marking points where there is another signal. On level ground, the distance from each outer spot to the centre equals the depth where water should be found.

Dowsing is used by some civil engineering companies to locate existing pipelines or cables when making site surveys. They often find that dowsing rods are more reliable than modern detecting instruments. David Baker, of the British Pipeline Agency at Norwich, personally used dowsing rods to locate underground obstacles before supervising site drainage to an oil installation near Norwich in 1987. The rods showed him 21 potential obstacles, and digging to the required depth for the drainage pipes revealed 19 of them.

Scientists in the Soviet Union have been using dowsing to find ore and oil deposits as well as underground streams for years. They call it the Biophysical Effects Method.

No one is sure how dowsing works, and many are sceptical of its claims. Yet some dowsers do make finds that cannot be attributed just to chance.

The physicist Albert Einstein thought the answer probably lay in electromagnetism. Research by a number of scientists suggests that this may be so. Just as migrating birds are believed to navigate by the pattern of the Earth's magnetic field, so a dowser's muscles may react when he unconsciously tunes in to minute fluctuations caused by underground water or minerals.

A French researcher, Professor Yves Rocard of the Ecole Normale, Paris, claims that a good dowser has less electrical resistance between the palms of the hands than a poor dowser. Robert Ashford, a British dowser employed by Dorset County Council, described in 1977 how he felt electric shocks all over his body when he was near underground water.

How do rainmakers make it rain?

The Hopi Indians of south-west America still try to make rain by sacrificing golden eagles and dancing with live rattlesnakes in their teeth. But while they perform their traditional rain dances to please their gods and get rain for their crops, others have adopted a more scientific approach.

In 1946 Vincent Schaefer and Irving Longmuir started their work at the General Electric Research Laboratories in Schenectady, New York, which proved that rain clouds could be artificially encouraged to produce showers.

Clouds are made up of billions of particles of water too small to fall as rain.

Only when the droplets grow to a quarter of a millimetre or more will they fall as a fine drizzle. Smaller droplets evaporate before reaching the ground.

One way the droplets grow is by freezing to form particles of ice. In a cloud containing some ice particles and some water droplets, the ice particles grow rapidly as the droplets evaporate and the vapour is transferred to the ice. Since the temperature of clouds is often below freezing it might be expected that the droplets would freeze easily. But the water can be 10 or 20 degrees below freezing (supercooled) without actually freezing.

The reason for this is that the water in clouds is absolutely pure, without any dust or other contaminants which can form the centre of an ice crystal. If tiny particles are provided, the droplets freeze, grow quickly until they are large enough to fall, and then melt as the temperature rises, reaching the ground as rain.

Schaefer and Longmuir proved that small particles, usually of silver iodide, added to supercooled clouds could create rapidly growing ice crystals. These particles have been dropped from aircraft, carried by rockets or even released at ground level for air currents to carry them aloft.

In the Soviet Union, 70mm artillery guns have been used to fire silver iodide particles into clouds, exploding at the right height to disperse the chemical.

As long as the clouds are supercooled the technique may work – increasing rainfall by up to a fifth. But since it is impossible to know how much rain would have fallen anyway there are still question marks over the method's economic effectiveness.

How will they build the wonder planes of tomorrow?

At Kittyhawk, North Carolina, in 1903, the world's first aeroplane flew only a few feet above the ground at barely the speed of a racehorse. Less than 100 years later, today's aircraft commonly travel more than 10 miles (16km) high, and can fly at the speed of a rifle bullet.

Modern aircraft designers aim to produce planes that are ever faster, more reliable, and more economical. So they look for designs that reduce drag (air resistance while moving), materials that make the aircraft lighter without loss of strength or increase in costs, and engines that are reliable and easily maintained but that give more thrust through the air for a smaller amount of fuel.

Design for speed

As speeds increase, shape becomes a more crucial design feature. Aircraft designers test an idea for a shape on a computer that simulates the airflow round the plane; then they use a scale model in a wind tunnel, where air is sucked over the model to simulate flight.

Such tests give a fairly accurate idea of the behaviour of a full-sized plane. All parts of the prototype are tested on the ground for reactions to heat, noise and stress. The tests are carried out in ovens, acoustic chambers, and load-test frames where pressures are applied hydraulically. Then the plane is put through its paces in the air.

Wind-tunnel testing has led designers to develop new shapes for high-speed planes. Swept-back wings were devised to delay the onset of the shock waves suffered by straight-winged planes when approaching the speed of sound. The shock results from the faster air moving over the top of the wings reaching the speed of sound – about 760mph (1200km/h) at sea level.

Super streamlining

Jets of the future are likely to have tiny triangular ridges, or riblets, lengthways along their bodies, an idea borrowed from nature. Such ridges help sharks to swim swiftly through the water because they reduce friction between the water and their skin by breaking up small eddies that

increase the drag on their movement. The American yacht that won the America's Cup in 1987, the *Stars and Stripes*, had similar riblets along its keel.

In aircraft, drag is caused by tiny whirlwinds formed as air flows over the body surfaces, so the American National Aeronautics and Space Administration (NASA) used wind tunnels to test the idea of riblets on aircraft. They found the riblets reduced drag by 8 per cent provided they were kept within crucial limits of size, angle and spacing. Every 1 per cent of drag

decreased means nearly 1 per cent of fuel saved. The European company Airbus Industrie is testing the riblets under flight conditions on its A340/330 series of long-range jets planned for service in 1992.

These new long-range jets will also have wings with small triangular fences at the ends, above and below the tip. The fences have been designed by British Aerospace. At the wing tip, high-pressure air from under the wing creates turbulence as it rushes over to the top. The fences slow down the flow and reduce drag.

Up and away

Its swing-wing design gives the Panavia Tornado a fuel-efficient conventional shape at low speeds (left), and the outline of a paper dart (above) with swept-back wings for flying at speeds faster than the speed of sound.

Lightening the load

For every kilogram saved in the weight of a large commercial aircraft, about 33 gallons (150 litres) of fuel are saved in a year's flying. If a Boeing 747 jumbo jet weighed 10 per cent less, its operating costs during its 20 year life could be cut by about $4 million.

Lighter materials such as carbon fibre – threads of pure carbon produced from heat-treated organic fibres – are therefore finding their way into aircraft design. Such materials have been developed so that they are light and strong, yet stiff enough not to bend under the stress of flight, or to buckle under compression.

A West German research aircraft, the *Egrett*, was designed by the Berlin Space Institute for flying in the stratosphere – about 9-30 miles (15-50km) high. Because long narrow wings are more subject to stress than short wide ones, its wings are made from carbon and glass fibre, a combination that allows them to be 20 times longer than they are wide. The wings of a conventional plane made with aluminium alloy can be only about eight times longer than their width.

Lightweight but stiff materials such as fibreglass have made possible the development of the tilt-rotor craft or convertiplane – the machine that may replace the helicopter. This has its engines and propellers at the end of short, stubby wings, so the wings need to be very stiff.

The American Bell-Boeing V22 *Osprey*, a

tilt-rotor craft that made its debut in 1988, takes off with its 38ft (12m) long three-bladed propellers turning horizontally, like a helicopter's rotors. Once the craft has enough lift, the propellers are gradually tilted forward 90 degrees to give the forward thrust of a conventional aeroplane. This gives the *Osprey* a cruising speed of around 360mph (576km/h), almost twice that of a helicopter.

Lithium is the lightest metal known. Mixed with aluminium it produces an alloy which is 8 per cent lighter than other aluminium alloys.

The new lightweight alloy is being used by British Aerospace in the prototype for the next generation of European fighter aircraft. A new airliner being developed by Boeing for the 1990s, the 7J7, will save weight by the use of aluminium-lithium alloy and a carbon-fibre material in the construction.

Flying by wire

Another design development that has saved weight and space is computer-controlled 'fly-by-wire' technology, which also ensures that the plane controls are not asked to operate beyond the limits of their ability. The pipework and tanks that once fed the aircraft's hydraulic control system have been eliminated. Instead, control surfaces such as flaps and ailerons have small on-the-spot hydraulic activators electrically linked to a computer and controlled by electronic signals. This type of

transmitter system was introduced in the European A300 airbus series of airliners. The Boeing 7J7 airliner will have an even more advanced control system that needs about 44 miles (70km) less wiring.

Power and propellers

Engines make up 20-30 per cent of an aircraft's cost. Although jet engines have been developed to be more reliable and much quieter than they were ten years ago, propellers are now making a comeback. American manufacturers such as General Electric and McDonnell Douglas have tested the use of short, stubby propellers attached to the back of a jet engine. The propeller blades accelerate the air passing round the engine, so increasing the aircraft's forward thrust. These 'propfan' engines have been found to produce more power and at the same time use up to 40 per cent less fuel than conventional jet engines.

Speed, sound and space

The needle nose, wasp waist, and sharply swept-back triangular wings of the Anglo-

Return of the prop *A team of NASA scientists at Cleveland, Ohio, has used propellers of an unusual shape to boost the power of a jet engine. A computer diagram tracked gas-flow, and showed low-pressure areas in blue and high in maroon. Propellers could return to commercial jets in the 1990s.*

French airliner Concorde make it effective for flying at speeds faster than sound. But to avoid unacceptable noise from sonic booms, it has to fly overland at less than the speed of sound, and at slow speeds it is uneconomical. At 500mph (800km/h), Concorde uses eight times as much fuel as some conventional airliners.

One answer to the problem of a shape suitable for both high and low speeds is the swing-wing plane such as the Panavia Tornado interceptor/strike aircraft developed jointly by German, Italian and British companies. Its wings can be swept forward for low-speed flying and back for high speeds, so it can loiter at less than 200mph (320km/h) but accelerate to Mach 2 – about 1400mph (2250km/h), twice the speed of sound.

Aircraft planned for the 1990s will escape the problem of sonic boom altogether by climbing through the atmosphere and going into orbit for part of their journey – flying at 25 times the speed of sound. Such a craft, known as the space plane or X30, is being developed by the United States.

In 1986, President Reagan described the space plane as an 'Orient Express', able to take off and land at an ordinary airport but whisk passengers from New York to Tokyo in two hours rather than 14. The X30 is expected to cost more than $3 billion to

Wings of fame *The American-designed Voyager on its historic nonstop flight round the world without refuelling in December 1986. The carbon-fibre construction meant it could carry nearly five times its own weight in fuel. The journey took nine days.*

develop. It will probably have jet engines that use hydrogen as fuel, and will be propelled in space by rockets.

Encircling the globe without refuelling

A nine-day, nonstop, round-the-world flight by two American aviators in 1986 was made possible by the lightness of their carbon-fibre aircraft. The spindly, three-bodied plane – named *Voyager* – had a wingspan longer than a Boeing 727 airliner but weighed less than a ton, so was able to carry nearly five times its own weight in fuel – some 1240 gallons (about 5600 litres).

The pilots who made the flight – the first round the world without refuelling – were Dick Rutan, brother of the plane's designer Burt Rutan, and Jeana Yeager. Their cockpit in the central fuselage was roughly the size of a phone box. Most of the plane's space was taken up by its 17 fuel tanks. Weight was such a crucial factor that before the flight Jeana Yeager had her long hair cut short, thus saving 1lb (0.5kg).

Voyager set off from an air force base in California's Mojave Desert, and flew westwards to take advantage of the trade winds. The speed for the 24,986 mile (40,212km) flight averaged about 116mph (186km/h), and on landing there was still a little fuel left in the tanks.

The plane had two engines, one at each end of the central fuselage. The front, air-cooled engine was shut down after three days; it had served its purpose of providing extra power for takeoff and while the plane was still heavy with fuel. The rear liquid-cooled engine ran for nearly 250 hours – about ten times as long as a conventional engine without servicing.

How does a man-powered aircraft fly?

Myths and fairy tales have told of man-powered flight for thousands of years, but the idea only became a reality in 1977. Earlier flight attempts failed because materials were too heavy for a man to power.

With the help of modern technology, a Californian engineer and former gliding champion called Paul MacCready built an

Muscle behind the myth *Kanellos Kanellopoulos pedals his plane a record-breaking 74 miles (120km) from Crete to Santorini, re-creating the myth of Daedalus, who escaped from Crete on wings.*

aircraft that was 30ft (9m) long, had a wingspan of 96ft (29m) and weighed just 70lb (32kg). It was called *Gossamer Condor*. MacCready was determined to win the Kremer Prize, established in 1949 by a British industrialist, Henry Kremer, for the first man-powered aircraft to fly round a special course. To win, *Gossamer Condor* had to take off and fly in a figure of eight around two pylons ½ mile (800m) apart, passing over a 10ft (3m) barrier at the start and finish.

MacCready gave his aircraft huge wings to get maximum lift at very slow speeds – about 10mph (16km/h). *Gossamer Condor* was built with aluminium tubes braced with piano wire. Other materials were balsa wood, corrugated cardboard (which formed the leading edges of the wings), plastic foam, and plastic sheeting to enclose the cockpit and flying surfaces.

The craft was driven by a bicycle chain connected to a large propeller behind the cockpit, and it was steered by pulling a lever that twisted the wings.

MacCready calculated that to fly in a straight line required about one-third of a horsepower – close to the limit a man can deliver for even a few minutes. The plane was to be piloted by a 24-year-old cycling and hang-gliding enthusiast, Bryan Allen, also from California.

On August 23, 1977, *Gossamer Condor* accelerated down the runway at Kern

County Airport in Shafter, California. After it had covered 30ft (9m) the nose lifted and the flight began. The aircraft cleared the 10ft (3m) barrier and flew round the 1¼ mile (2km) course in 7 minutes 22.5 seconds to win the £50,000 prize.

MacCready went on to design a more sophisticated plane, the *Gossamer Albatross*, to fly 23 miles (37km) across the English Channel. The plane was about the same size as its predecessor, but was built from tougher materials. The wings and fuselage were made of plastic, reinforced with carbon fibre, and covered in a polyester film. It also had improved steering mechanism and was manoeuvred by a pair of small wings, with adjustable flaps, mounted ahead of the main wings.

Once more the pilot was Bryan Allen. On June 12, 1979, he made a successful crossing of the Channel, at an average height of only 2½ft (760mm) above the sea. It took him just under three hours.

In April 1988 an even more astonishing flight took place, when the 14 times Greek cycling champion Kanellos Kanellopoulos retraced the flight of Daedalus. In ancient Greek legend, Daedalus and his son Icarus escaped from King Minos's Labyrinth on the island of Crete by flying with wings made from feathers and wax. Icarus flew too close to the sun, his wings melted and he plunged to his death. Daedalus made it to the small island of Santorini, 74 miles

Landing at sea *An F-4 Phantom jet lands on board HMS* Ark Royal. *The jet comes to a halt in 100-150yds (90-135m) when its tail hook catches on wires stretched across the deck.*

(120km) to the north of Crete. Kanellos Kanellopoulos's aircraft, *Daedalus*, was designed by the Massachusetts Institute of Technology and the National Air and Space Museum in Washington DC, and Kanellopoulos was supported by a team of 36 scientists, engineers and meteorologists. The total cost was $1 million

Daedalus had a 112ft (34m) wingspan (considerably larger than Concorde's), and weighed only 70lb (32kg), being made from carbon fibre and Kevlar – a new man-made material five times stronger than steel and lighter than fibreglass.

Thirty-year-old Kanellopoulos had been training for months for the flight, which physiologists described as the equivalent of running two marathons.

Weather delayed the attempt for 25 days, but on April 23 conditions were right. Kanellopoulos flew about 20ft (6m) above the sea and averaged 18.5mph (30km/h) with a tail wind. The flight went without a hitch until he turned the craft against the wind to land at Santorini. The wings and tail broke up and it crashed into the sea a few yards from the shore. Even after nearly four hours of exertion, Kanellopoulos was strong enough to break through the fragile cockpit and swim ashore. He had flown 74 miles (120km), smashing the distance record for man-powered flight.

How aircraft land on a carrier in rough weather

Picture an aircraft carrier pitching up and down in a heavy sea. The dark clouds and the rain reduce visibility. A single-seat fighter is flying 200 miles (320km) away and getting low on fuel. It needs to return to 'mother', the name that the pilot uses for the carrier.

The fighter climbs high to make the most efficient use of its fuel and sets a heading for the briefed position of mother. The heading is refined by radar signals sent either from the carrier or from an airborne early warning aircraft, on patrol from the carrier.

When the pilot gets to within 120 miles (190km) of mother he will get an accurate 'fix' on her using the aircraft radar or a radio navigation aid, such as TACAN – short for tactical air navigation.

The pilot descends and begins an orbit, known as a 'wait', at a distance of about 15 miles (24km) from the carrier.

Several aircraft may be entering other 'waits' at the same time, but all of them are at different heights and distances from mother.

The first aircraft is taken under radar control and is directed into the Carrier Controlled Approach pattern. It will be directed to descend to 1500ft (460m), still hampered by cloud, rain and turbulence.

The pilot is told to carry out his pre-landing checks by the talkdown controller on the carrier and is given the latest weather conditions on the surface. He is warned about the excessive amount of deck movement.

Recovery

Mother then turns into the wind and the 'recovery' begins. The aircraft is controlled by radar down a three degree glide slope.

This is the ideal approach path and the controller will warn the pilot if he strays from it. Half a mile (800m) from the ship, the pilot is told 'look up for sight' and he takes over visually for the rest of the flight.

Now the pilot flies by reference to mother's deck lights and the projector sight – a bank of lights on the carrier that indicates the aircraft's position relative to the glide slope with the use of green, red and amber lights. Positioned next to the projector sight is a Landing Safety Officer who monitors the approach and transmits corrections to the pilot: 'Slightly high, a little left. More power. Keep it coming.' These corrections provide the aircraft pilot with vital information and also reassure him.

Safely home to mother

As long as the pilot follows the sight and verbal corrections, the tail hook of his aircraft will catch one of four wires ranged across the deck. The wires are well forward of the stern, so the effects of deck pitch are less severe. They bring the aircraft to a halt in a remarkably short distance: aircraft land at a speed of about 135 knots (250km/h) and come to a halt in between 100 and 150yds (90 and 135m).

Now the deck crew moves swiftly into action – the controller will already be starting to bring down the next aircraft. He aims to land one aircraft every minute. It would be dangerous to taxi on a wet, rolling deck, so a special tractor is attached to the aircraft which is towed safely to the deck park where its wheels are chocked and it can be lashed to the deck. Sortie completed.

Steam catapults: launching aircraft from a ship

Without steam catapults most modern, heavy aircraft would be unable to take off from their carriers. Today, every aircraft carrier has them.

In operation, the aircraft taxis into position and a wire loop called a holdback is connected between the rear of the aircraft and a strong point on the deck; it has a weak link in its centre.

A towbar near the aircraft's front wheel is lowered into a 'shuttle' that attaches the aircraft to the catapult with a hook mechanism. It is the only part of the catapult visible on the flight deck.

Two parallel cylinders, at least 150ft (45m) long, run under the deck ahead of the aircraft. The cylinders house two pistons which are both fixed to the shuttle. Steam is supplied to the cylinders from the ship's boilers via an accumulator where pressure is built up. Pressure is varied for launching aircraft of differing weights.

At launch, the aircraft selects full power, but is restrained by the holdback. When

Catapult takeoff *An F-4 Phantom jet prepares for takeoff from the deck of a carrier. A towbar attaches the front of the fighter to a steam-catapult mechanism.*

the catapult is fired the combined force of the engines and steam pressure break the weak link and the aircraft hurtles forward, reaching about 135 knots (250km/h) in 50yds (45m).

At the end of the launch the aircraft flies out of the shuttle. Probes on the front of the pistons ram into a water reservoir, bringing them to rest in a few feet. The shuttle is then repositioned for the next launch –

carriers can launch an aircraft every 2 minutes per catapult. American carriers have up to four catapults, so a plane can be launched every 30 seconds.

The steam catapult was invented by Commander C.C. Mitchell, of Britain's Royal Navy, and in 1949 it was installed for trials in HMS *Perseus*. Steam catapults were installed on carriers worldwide after the US Navy adopted the equipment in 1954.

Locate and destroy: tactics of modern fighter pilots

A First World War pilot flying a Sopwith Camel at about 100mph (160km/h) could turn in only 80yds (73m) to evade the machine guns of a German Fokker Triplane. By 1953, an American F-86 Sabre fighter flying at 600mph (960km/h) in the Korean War needed more than 1½ miles (2.4km) to make a similar turn.

Today's jet fighters fly at over 1500mph (2400km/h) and their turning circles are so large – about 15 miles (24km) – that it is difficult for the opposing pilots to see each other at all. Four out of five pilots who are

shot down never even see their attackers.

The problem for every fighter pilot remains the same as it was in the early days of aerial combat – to find and destroy the enemy and remain alive. Spotting the enemy first, usually by detecting him with radar, is the top priority. So modern fighters are part of a complex defence system that uses radar (page 154) to give an early warning of an attack – either ground-based radar or 'look-down' radar on board other aircraft.

One type of early warning aircraft is the

American subsonic E-2C Hawkeye. In the Israeli invasion of Lebanon in 1982, it was so effective in spotting the enemy (sometimes even before he had taken off) that the Israelis destroyed over 80 Syrian aircraft with only one loss, even though both sides flew supersonic jet aircraft with similar top speeds.

NATO's AWACS (Airborne Warning And Control System) can fly nonstop for ten hours, sending radar signals back to their ground base, up to 240 miles (385km) away. Each plane's radar has a scanning limit of over 400 miles (640km), depending on how high the plane flies. The plane's computers can track 500 enemy aircraft at once and instantly transmit information to command bases in Britain.

To avoid ground-based radar detection, pilots fly at ground-hugging altitudes. At this level, the Earth's curvature – together with mountains and buildings – hide the plane from radar beams. Trainee pilots learn tactics at 250ft (76m) in peacetime to reduce noise nuisance, but have to be prepared to fly 'on the deck' (as low as possible) in a war. Once they are engaged in combat, they climb to provide space to manoeuvre.

Computerised warfare *A screen displays computer images directly in the pilot's line of vision. The images enable him to lock on to an enemy fighter and shoot it down.*

Rocket fire *Flames glow under the wings of a Harrier vertical takeoff jet as it fires SNEB rockets to strafe an enemy target on the ground. Harriers can carry 9000lb (4080kg) of missiles including bombs, rockets and shells, so are not only extremely versatile in aerial combat, but can destroy enemy aircraft while they are still on the ground and also give support to friendly ground forces.*

Flying in close formation – sometimes only a matter of feet apart – also confuses enemy radar, which cannot distinguish how many aircraft are in the pack.

The technique taught by air forces today is to attack the enemy as quickly as possible. As soon as the 'bogey' (an enemy plane) is spotted, the attacker tries to draw close enough to get the vulnerable part of the aircraft – the cockpit area – in his sights for just half a second, all it takes to achieve a kill.

Combat tactics developed by Russians and Americans in the Korean War in the early 1950s are still taught in some air

forces. One of these is the high speed yo-yo. The attacking pilot climbs steeply above his adversary and swoops down out of the sun. He then goes into a roll – corkscrewing through the air to slow down. This saves him from flying past the enemy fighter at the end of the dive. This manoeuvre is often executed in pairs, with a 'wingman' protecting his 'leader' by positioning himself to attack in case the enemy survives and turns to do battle.

If two combatants are following each other in a circle at about the same speed, the aggressor may use low yo-yo tactics to get closer. He swoops downwards into the

centre of the circle and then up under his quarry as it continues turning. By slicing off a section of the flight circle he is able to draw close enough to fire a cannon or heat-seeking missile. Most enemy aircraft are destroyed in combat by heat-seeking missiles such as the Sidewinder, which pursue the heat from the enemy's exhaust, and can be fired from as far away as 11 miles (18km). When a pilot realises that a missile has been launched at him, he will start a violent zigzag course, or release flares to attract and set off the missile.

The pilot's quick reactions, experience and judgment are even more vital than the

Defensive break by a Harrier
Using a unique manoeuvre, a Harrier (the blue flight path) shoots down a faster enemy fighter (orange flight path). **1** *The Harrier detects the enemy aircraft astern.* **2** *The enemy comes within firing range.* **3** *The Harrier rotates its jet outlets downwards, suddenly losing speed and forcing the enemy to overshoot.* **4** *The other fighter, now in front, becomes an easy target.*

plane's electronics. Unpredictable 'seat-of-the-pants' tactics are just as crucial today as they were in the First World War. Usually victory goes to the faster aeroplane, but in the Falklands War the subsonic British Harriers successfully fought the supersonic Argentine Mirages.

One major reason for the Harriers' success was the astonishing manoeuvrability. They can land and take off vertically, and a Harrier pilot can alter the angle of thrust of his engines during flight by swivelling the jets' discharge nozzles. This enables him to reduce speed by 200mph (320km/h) in a few seconds while at full throttle. A Mirage pilot who had been on the Harrier's tail would find that he was now in front, and vulnerable.

Because they had closer supporting radar than the Mirages, and the latest Sidewinder missiles, the Harriers shot down 38 Argentine aircraft without loss.

The latest jet warplanes, such as the

American F-16 Fighting Falcon, a multi-role fighter with a top speed of 1333mph (2145km/h), are built for great manoeuvrability. The Falcon's revolutionary design gives it a centre of gravity so far back that it is permanently tail-heavy, and on the ground it looks as if it is begging to fly upwards.

It can be put into a steep climb very quickly, but needs an onboard computer to control its flying surfaces – its wing flaps, ailerons, rudder and elevator. The computer continuously adjusts the surfaces in movements so small and rapid that no human pilot could accomplish unaided.

There are in fact four computers, each monitoring the performance of the others. And if one breaks down, the other three take over without the pilot even noticing the difference.

The computers, each the size of a shoe box, help the pilot to control the plane. The joystick, sensitive to minute changes of pressure from the pilot's fingers, sends electronic messages to the computers which in turn pass them on to the hydraulics controlling the plane's flying surfaces. This system is known as fly-by-wire, and the pilots who fly the F-16 have nicknamed it The Electric Jet. Without its computers, it could not get off the ground.

A similar principle is used in the US

Navy's F/A-18 Hornet – top speed 1190mph (1915km/h) – a $20 million aircraft whose computers will override the pilot if he makes a mistake, like trying to climb too steeply at low speed and so risking a stall, or attempting to turn so tightly that the aircraft's wings would be torn off.

The computers are also the key to effective fighting at supersonic speeds. The pilot uses them to call up details of his target's altitude, direction and closing speed. The details are displayed in his line of vision in a head-up display (HUD), a transparent screen between his head and the front of the cockpit. He can monitor the information without moving his eyes. The latest versions project the information onto the visor of the pilot's helmet, which also acts as a sight. The pilot looks at the target through the helmet-mounted sight, then locks onto it by pressing a button. This directs radar and other sensors to find the target, and a weapon can then be fired either automatically or by the pilot.

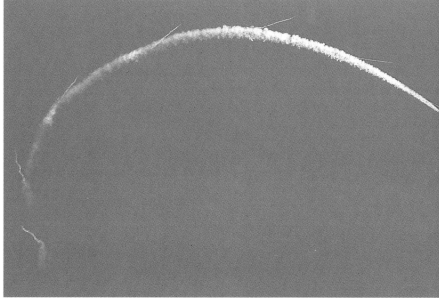

Attack and defence *The pilot of a Tornado F-3 (left) demonstrates an aircraft fighter tactic employed since the First World War. He climbs swiftly above the enemy plane, then swoops down out of the sun so that the enemy fighter pilot is blinded by the glare. Threatened with attack (above), the pilot of a US F-16 Fighting Falcon fires flares to distract heat-seeking missiles. The enemy missiles are attracted to the heat of the flares rather than to the aircraft's exhaust.*

How aircraft and ships 'see' with radar – just like bats

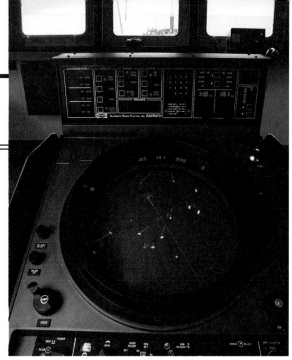

Bats navigate by emitting shrill squeaks that are reflected back to their ears from insect prey or obstacles in their path. Radar works in a similar way, but uses reflected radio signals to detect objects up to 2000 miles (over 3200km) away. Without radar, complex air-traffic control and missile early warning systems would be impossible to operate, and ships at sea would risk collision in the dark or in fog.

Radar derives its name from the term 'Radio detection and ranging'. It was first developed in Europe and America in the 1930s, after the Italian engineer Guglielmo Marconi (the pioneer of radio) suggested the idea in 1922.

The French liner *Normandie* – which in 1935 set the Atlantic crossing record at just over four days – was fitted with radar in 1936, for detecting icebergs. By 1939 Britain, thanks to the work of the physicist Sir Robert Watson-Watt, had a radar network on its south and south-east coasts for detecting aircraft. The system proved invaluable to the country's defences during the Battle of Britain in 1940. It had a range of about 40 miles (64km), and operated day and night, passing the range, bearing and height of German planes to the RAF defence network.

Modern radar is sensitive enough to locate all the aircraft coming into a busy airport and allow air-traffic controllers to stack them at different heights in the sky while they organise a landing rota. Airliners are fitted with a radar beacon or transponder (transmitter-responder) on the underside. This sends their radar signals to the ground and back to give the pilot his altitude, and reflects signals from the airport's two radar systems. The primary system gives warning of the aircraft's approach and distance, and the secondary system sends coded signals to the transponder, which gives back the aircraft's identity and height.

Radar signals can also be reflected from raindrops. Weather forecasters use radar networks to locate rain and snow clouds. Airliners have nose-mounted radar scanners that give the pilot a map of the weather up to 200 miles (320km) ahead, so that he can avoid storms. In case of necessity, the pilot can tilt the scanner to get a rough map of the ground below.

Spacecraft and satellites orbiting the Earth use radar beams to gather information about the Earth's surface for map-makers, geologists and oceanographers. Radar is also used to find out about the surfaces of other planets.

How radar works

Basic radar equipment consists of a transmitter to generate the radio signals, a revolving scanner – the aerial or antenna that sends out and receives the signals – and a video screen on which the returning signals are displayed. The radio signals are transmitted as pulses (short bursts) at microwave frequencies, which are between 1000 and 35,000 million cycles per second. By comparison, the sound waves from a bat's signals have frequencies of 30-120 thousand cycles per second.

Radar pulses are timed to allow one signal to hit its target and bounce back before the next one is emitted. Because radio waves travel at the speed of light, about 186,300 miles (300,000km) a second, pulse timing is measured in micro-seconds – millionths of a second. By measuring the time a signal takes to return, the distance to the target can be calculated.

If the object is moving, the returning signal has a slightly different frequency from the outgoing one. This is known as the Doppler shift, and is caused by the radio waves bunching up if the object is approaching, or stretching out if it is going away. From this shift, radar operators can distinguish a moving object from a stationary one (such as a mountain) and can work out the direction in which it is travelling. From the size of the shift, they can also calculate the speed. Radar microwave beams from orbiting spacecraft or satellites respond differently to the conditions they encounter – dense forests or cultivated fields, for example. Computers analyse the differing strengths of the return signals and build up a picture of the surface.

Ships ahead *On the bridge of an oil tanker, an anti-collision radar screen shows other ships as dots, with their direction of travel as short lines. The long line is the tanker's own course.*

Defending ships from missiles and torpedoes

In May 1987 two Exocet missiles hit the American frigate USS *Stark* in the Persian Gulf, killing 38 men. It showed how vulnerable modern warships can be. The Iraqi pilot who fired the missiles never saw the target, except on a radar screen. He was more than 30 miles (48km) away when he launched them. And the crew of USS *Stark* became aware of the missiles only a few seconds before they were hit.

SEEING THROUGH WATER BY SOUND ECHOES

The sinking of the British liner *Titanic* in 1912, after it collided with an iceberg, spurred scientists to find a means of detecting underwater obstacles. An early form of sound detection was used by British and American forces for submarine detection during the First World War. Modern sonar (sound detection and ranging), which uses the echoes from emitted sounds, was developed by the French scientist Paul Langevin.

Today, echo sounding is used in ship navigation to determine water depth and by fishing vessels to spot shoals of fish, as well as for marine research and mapping the seabed. Sound pulses, generated electronically, are beamed through the water and echoed back to the ship by any obstacle up to about 6 miles (10km) away. The returning signals are displayed on a video screen.

Sound travels through water at about 1600yds (1500m) a second – around four times faster than in air. As with radar, the distance to the obstacle is calculated from the time the echo takes to return, and the Doppler shift of the sound waves shows if the object is moving.

The first form of defence against such attacks is dominance in the air, provided by carrier-based aircraft which patrol constantly and try to prevent enemy aircraft getting close enough to launch their missiles. But this can be difficult against the Soviet SS-N-3 'Shaddock' missile, which can be launched more than 250 miles (400km) from its target. Defending aircraft may carry antimissile missiles such as the American Phoenix, but cannot guarantee to destroy a missile in flight.

If a fleet's supporting aircraft fail to prevent an attack, ships have to rely on their own defences. Britain's navy uses the Sea Wolf missile, which is guided by radar and is quick enough to destroy a shell or missile travelling at up to twice the speed of sound. Sea Wolf operates automatically. Once the command to fire is given, its radar and TV trackers pick up the target. The missile then aims, launches and homes in without any human intervention.

Other countries' navies have similar antimissile missiles: the Aegis missile defends US ships; Canadian 'City' class helicopter destroyers have Sea Sparrows; and Soviet ships have the SA-N-3 (Goblet) and SA-N-4 systems.

Waves often cause interference on a ship's radar, enabling sea-skimming missiles to get quite close to their target before they are detected. During the Falklands War of 1982, for example, the British destroyer HMS *Sheffield* was hit by an Exocet missile on May 4, and sank six days later. The attacking Argentinian Super Etendard aircraft escaped the ship's radar by flying low over the water and firing from a range of about 20 miles (32km).

When attacking missiles evade all other defences, the ship's short-range, 'last ditch' protection is provided by its guns, which can throw out a curtain of fire so dense that some shells are almost certain to hit the oncoming missile. The American Phalanx guns pour out 20mm shells at the rate of 3000 a minute. The lead shells have a core of uranium, and are heavy enough to stop any missile they hit.

Other nations use bigger shells – the German/Dutch Goalkeeper system uses 30mm Mauser cannons each capable of firing 300 rounds a minute. All gun-aiming is radar controlled, so is very accurate.

Even if weaponry fails, the missile's (or the launching aircraft's) radar system can be disrupted by firing Chaff guns, which create clouds of aluminium strips that produce hundreds of images (snow) making it impossible to distinguish the target.

The target is hit *The American frigate USS* Stark *flounders in the waters of the Persian Gulf after being struck by two Iraqi Exocet missiles fired from a Mirage F1-EQS aircraft.*

Antimissile missiles *An aircraft carrier launches missile-bearing aircraft to defend itself from enemy attack. Here F18 combat/strike aircraft wait on deck at the ready.*

Sub hunts sub *Warships get some protection from submarines such as USS* Sturgeon, *which track and destroy enemy submarines.*

No similar systems exist for stopping underwater torpedoes. Sometimes a ship can dodge or even outrun a torpedo, but the only effective defences are either hunter-killer submarines that track and torpedo enemy submarines, or sonar-equipped helicopters working with surface ships. The helicopters tow sonar detectors in the sea to spot the position of enemy submarines, which are then attacked with air-to-surface missiles or depth charges.

Aircraft carriers are a prime target for torpedoes. The only way to protect them is with a ring of accompanying warships that detect and destroy enemy submarines.

The last resort *If enemy missiles manage to penetrate a warship's defences, they can be destroyed with guns such as the Phalanx.*

155

How missiles are guided to their target

Testing a cruise missile *Launched from a submarine 400 miles (640km) away, and guided by a computer which monitors the terrain it flies over, a US Tomahawk cruise missile homes in on a building on San Clemente Island, California, with devastating accuracy.*

The German V2 rockets used at the end of the Second World War had a fairly primitive guidance system and the missiles were inaccurate. It was only because London was a large target that they did so much damage. Since the 1940s many precise guidance systems have been developed for all kinds of missiles. Scientists are continually devising new ones.

The simplest guidance system is the human eye. Antitank missiles like the Franco-German Milan, the Soviet AT-3 Sagger, or the British Swingfire, trail a thin wire connecting them to the operator's miniature joystick which is used to steer them. The wire link is simple and, unlike a radio signal, it cannot be 'jammed'. But the need for the wire restricts the missile's range and, to some extent its speed, since there is a limit to how quickly the wire can unwind. Wire-guided missiles are effective only against tanks or other fairly slow-moving targets that can be kept in view throughout the missile's flight.

For attacking aircraft a different sort of guidance system is needed. The answer is a self-guiding missile fitted with a computer that replaces the human operator. These missiles have a range of about 30 miles (50km). Their actual form of guidance may be active or passive.

An example of an active guidance system

Wire-guided missiles *Connected by wire to a launcher, and guided by a human operator, an antitank Milan missile seeks its target.*

is the British Sea Wolf missile that sends out a radar beam to its target and homes in by using the returning echoes.

Other weapons using active guidance include surface-to-air missiles (SAMs) like the British Rapier, or the Franco-German Roland, which use ground-based radar or optical systems to track the target and follow the missile once it has been launched. Computers then send instructions by radio to the missile, directing it to the target. The Rapier has a range of about 4 miles (6.5km) while the Roland has a range of 3.7 miles (6km).

In passive guidance, the missile is guided by signals from the target itself – usually radar or heat. The American air-to-air Sidewinder and the surface-to-air Stinger missiles both detect infrared radiation from an aircraft's exhaust. An on-board computer steers them by operating very small wings set at the front of the missile. Once the missile has been launched, the operator need do no more. They are 'fire-and-forget' missiles.

Antiship missiles such as the French-designed Exocet are aimed automatically by feeding the position of the target into a launch computer. The missiles themselves are fitted with inertial navigation systems, which continually work out the exact position of the missile by detecting any change in its direction or speed from the moment it is launched. All these changes

Antiship missiles *An Exocet missile launched from an aircraft skims about 8ft (2.4m) above the water to its target. A radio altimeter in the missile measures and controls its clearance of the waves.*

are monitored by a computer in the missile, and if it thinks the missile is straying from its target, because of high wind or some other reason, it adjusts small fins to steer it back on course. When the on-board computer calculates the missile is within 9 miles (15km) of its target, it switches on a radar scanner that picks up the ship. The computer then works out how far the target has moved since the Exocet was launched, and adjusts the missile's direction.

Long-range cruise missiles use the most sophisticated guidance system of all – TERCOM (terrain contour-matching). Computers on board the missiles store a three-dimensional model of the terrain they will fly over. Every point on the ground is recorded by a set of figures indicating the position and the missile's height above it. They fly at heights between 50 and 300ft (15 to 91m). As the missile flies along, accurate altimeters on board measure the contours of the ground below, matching them with information in the computer to keep the missile on course. The instruments also locate the target and lock onto it. After travelling up to 1600 miles (2570km), missiles can strike within 50ft (15m) of the target.

By comparison, intercontinental ballistic missiles are relatively inaccurate. As they are launched they use their inertial navigation system to establish their course, but then they fly free like a javelin – falling to earth at a position determined by their initial speed, direction and elevation. The most accurate American Minuteman III missiles are expected to land within 720ft (220m) of their targets, which – given the enormous power of their nuclear warheads – is close enough.

How a soldier can 'see' in the dark

The nightsight can turn night into day for a soldier, which means that darkness no longer provides cover for enemy troops. With a nightsight their movements can easily be detected, exposing them to accurate fire.

A nightsight looks like an oversized telescopic sight. It enables a soldier to see clearly on all but the darkest nights by amplifying moonlight or starlight. First a highly sensitive photoelectric cell converts the image into an electrical signal, just as it would in a TV camera. Then the electrical signal is amplified by circuits similar to those of a hi-fi amplifier. It is finally turned back into an image and displayed on a small TV screen.

Even on a night that most people would describe as pitch black, there is usually some light, if only from the stars. In such conditions a soldier can accurately aim at a target up to 400yds (365m) away. More powerful versions, with a range of 1100yds (1km), are used by artillery, tanks, helicopters and aircraft.

If there is not even a glimmer of starlight, a different instrument can be used – an infrared camera, which detects heat rather than light. Objects that generate heat – for example aircraft, missile outlets, or army camp fires – can be detected at a range of several miles. These sights are used routinely in surveillance operations. During the Falklands War, they were used by British troops to detect the position of Argentine defences. Infrared cameras can also detect the body heat of an enemy soldier.

When all soldiers, tanks and aircraft are regularly equipped with nightsights, battle will be possible 24 hours a day.

Sight in the night
Using street light and general urban 'sky' light, a soldier's nightsight picks out a terrorist 90yds (80m) away (top). Even on a moonless night in woods (above) starlight illuminates this target 32yds (30m) away.

What makes a rifle bullet fly in a straight line?

Early muskets and rifles were hopelessly inaccurate. They fired lead balls, which were loaded by pushing them down the barrel from the muzzle end. Even if a ball was heading straight for its target when it left the barrel, it would often veer away.

Today people take it for granted that a bullet will travel in a straight line, but how has this been achieved?

Early musket balls fitted loosely inside a smooth barrel. As they were fired, the balls bounced from side to side along the barrel and left the muzzle in unpredictable directions. Also, any slight unevenness in shape made a ball swing in flight.

A solution to these problems was devised as early as 1500. First the balls were made to fit the barrels tightly, to reduce the bouncing effect. And secondly, the inside of the barrel was engraved with spiral grooves, known as rifling, which would grip the ball and make it spin as it went down the barrel. A spinning ball of uneven shape does not swerve in the air, since any tendency to veer in one direction is cancelled out as the ball rotates and tries to veer the opposite way.

Although these changes improved a rifle's accuracy, there were also disadvantages. It was difficult and expensive to make the rifling until as late as the 19th century, when machine tools became accurate enough to cut the rifling and make the balls exactly the right size. Even then, it still took time to ram the tight-fitting balls into muzzle-loading rifles, which reduced the firing rate. Also, the soft lead balls would become misshapen during loading, impairing their accuracy. And the explosive powder used to fire them could clog up the rifling, making loading difficult.

By the 1840s, balls had become the familiar bullet shape – elongated with a conical tip. The better aerodynamics increased their range and improved their accuracy, but they were still hard to load.

Then in 1847 Captain Claude-Etienne Minié of the French army devised a lead bullet with a slightly hollow base. When the bullet was fired, the soft lead base expanded to grip the rifling. These bullets could be dropped into the barrel quickly and easily, making rifled weapons practical in warfare.

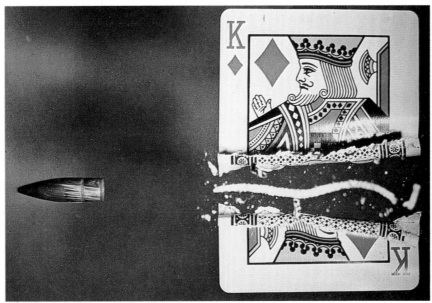

Dead centre *Flying at 2102.4mph (3383km/h), a .30in calibre bullet slices through a card. Its rifling marks, made by the grooves on the inside of the gun barrel, are clearly visible.*

Minié's bullets were quickly adopted in Europe and America. They were first used on a large scale in the Crimean War (1853-6) and the American Civil War (1861-5).

By the 1870s, the development of self-contained metal cartridges to hold the charge led to breech-loading rather than muzzle-loading guns. Jacketed or solid bronze bullets were being produced for breech-loaders by 1886. They had much greater penetration than soft lead bullets, going right through trees or fences that would have stopped the lead bullets.

At about the same time 'smokeless' charges replaced black-powder charges. These were more powerful, and also reduced fouling in the barrel. A black-powder charge could send a bullet at just under 1000mph (1600km/h), a smokeless charge at up to 1600mph (2600km/h). The extra speed gave the bullet a flatter trajectory, allowing a rifleman to aim at targets at close range and up to 400yds (366m) without having to adjust his sights.

During the 20th century, bullets became much more pointed at the nose. And although modern bullets are still basically cylindrical, their tails now taper slightly to reduce drag.

Bullets also tend to be smaller than before. A small, light bullet will travel faster and farther than a large one, if fired by the same-size charge. And a smaller charge will cause less recoil. This helps to improve a marksman's accuracy.

Modern army rifles fire bullets at about 2250mph (3600km/h) and can repeatedly hit a 4in (100mm) target at a range of 100 yds (91m) — adequate for most military purposes. Over the same range the best target rifles can hit a ¼in (6mm) target.

How do they build nuclear weapons?

Nuclear weapons have kept the world in an uneasy balance of peace and terror since the only two ever used forced Japan to surrender on September 2, 1945, ending the Second World War. The awesome power of these weapons comes from the release of huge amounts of energy from the hearts (nuclei) of atoms by the reactions of fission and fusion.

Fission is the process by which an atom divides; it is the basis of the atomic bomb. Fusion is the opposite – the combination of atoms to form a larger one. It releases even larger amounts of energy than fission, and provides hydrogen bombs with their power. It is also believed to be the source of the Sun's energy. Most modern nuclear weapons make use of both processes.

Fission bombs must have one of two ingredients – uranium or plutonium. The bomb dropped on Hiroshima on August 6, 1945, used uranium, and Nagasaki was destroyed on August 9 by a plutonium bomb. Both uranium and plutonium are fissile materials – with nuclei that can be split by subatomic particles called neutrons.

Every time a nucleus is split it produces at least two new neutrons. With a small lump of a fissile material these neutrons will fly off into the air harmlessly. But if the lump of plutonium or uranium is large enough (about the size of a grapefruit, and known as the critical mass), the neutrons collide with other nuclei before they can

escape into the air. This results in two new fissions, which create four new neutrons, and four fissions, which in turn produce eight neutrons and so on.

Each stage happens in about one-hundred millionth of a second. In well under a millionth of a second, the chain reaction has multiplied so rapidly that there is an explosive release of energy.

The source of the energy comes from the fact that the light atoms produced weigh less than the heavy atom that is split. So matter appears to be destroyed. Instead, the matter is converted to energy when the mass combines with light going at its maximum speed. This sets off a chain reaction, which stops when the original matter is used up or when it blows apart, so the neutrons can no longer cause fission.

About half the energy is taken up by a blast – a bomb equal to 20,000 tons of TNT can destroy buildings up to half a mile (800m) away. Just over a third of the energy is in the form of heat, so intense that it sets light to anything combustible within a range of 4 miles (6.4km). The rest is released as radiation – gamma rays and X-rays. After a nuclear explosion, millions of small radioactive particles, known as fallout, float to the ground.

Although the chain reaction only needs a split second to take place, the bomb

Hiroshima A-bomb *'Little Boy', the nuclear bomb that devastated Hiroshima in 1945, weighed 9000lb (4100kg) but had the force of 12-13,000 tons of TNT.*

A deadly load *The five nuclear warheads of the American MX 'Peacekeeper' intercontinental missile are programmed to strike different targets at the same time.*

designer still has to make sure that a critical mass of uranium or plutonium stays together long enough before it blows itself apart. The Hiroshima bomb used a conventional explosive charge to drive one piece of uranium down a tube into the other piece. On its own, neither piece was large enough to explode; but thrown together they exceeded the critical mass and exploded with a force of 12-13,000 tons of TNT.

The Nagasaki bomb took advantage of the fact that the critical mass is reduced if the fissile material (plutonium in this case) is compressed to increase its density. A subcritical mass of plutonium was surrounded by conventional explosive charges. When they were detonated they compressed the plutonium so that it became supercritical and produced a blast equal to 22,000 tons of TNT.

Thermonuclear weapons

To make even more powerful bombs it is necessary to use nuclear fusion. The first thermonuclear bomb (the hydrogen bomb) was built by the USA. It had a yield equivalent to about 10 million tons of TNT, and was detonated in Eniwetok Atoll in the Pacific in November 1952.

In fusion bombs two forms of hydrogen are used – deuterium and tritium. When the nuclei of these elements combine there is a massive release of energy. But to get them to fuse requires temperatures comparable to the temperature at the heart of the Sun – 14 million degrees centigrade. The only way to achieve these temperatures is with a nuclear fission bomb. So hydrogen bombs rely on both fusion and fission.

The most powerful bomb ever exploded was detonated on Novaya Zemlya, a large island off the north coast of Russia, on October 30, 1961. Estimates of the bomb's yield range from 57-90 million tons of TNT. The shock wave circled the Earth three times.

However, practical weapons are much less powerful. The smallest nuclear bomb in the US armoury is the W-54, which has a yield of 250 tons, and the largest bomb is 2 million tons.

Apart from the fission and fusion materials, a typical bomb or warhead for a missile contains a neutron gun to start the fission process, an arming or disarming device, a microprocessor which controls the sequence of operations when it is fired, a fuse that sets off the detonation, and safety devices which make the weapon safe to transport. The precise details of how the components are arranged is secret.

The first nuclear weapons were bulky. 'Fat Man', the Nagasaki bomb, was 12ft (3.6m) long and weighed 10,800lb (4900kg). Today, bombs the same weight are more than 600 times as powerful. And the smallest nuclear bomb, the W-54, designed for blowing up bridges and other

The invisible destroyer *In a test programme, a Titan I missile (left) was the target for a chemical laser. Seconds after the laser was activated, it destroyed the missile (right).*

Star Wars research *Two converging chemical laser beams are directed at a gold target the size of a full stop, to evaluate their accuracy and destructive capacity.*

structures, can be carried on a soldier's back.

Every American weapon (less is known about Soviet ones) contains safety devices to prevent unauthorised or accidental detonation.

In early weapons the safety measures were comparatively simple, amounting to a wire seal, a switch and a lock. Modern weapons have code-controlled arming and fusing devices, which make it impossible to detonate the weapon or set its fuse without knowing complex codes which are changed daily. If the wrong numbers are keyed in several times, the weapon locks and disables itself so completely that it cannot be fired until it has been repaired.

If an aircraft carrying a nuclear bomb crashed and caught fire, there would be no danger of a nuclear explosion – the bomb would not be armed. But the chemical explosives used to trigger the nuclear bomb might explode. To avoid this possibility, the most recent warheads use very stable chemical explosives to prevent their detonation in an accident.

How lasers could be used in space

If a nuclear attack were launched on America, it could involve hundreds of missiles carrying thousands of warheads, each travelling at up to 4 miles (6.4km) a second towards targets they would reach within 30 minutes of launch. To protect themselves, the Americans have therefore developed their Strategic Defense Initiative (SDI) or 'Star Wars' programme.

A major part of this programme is to develop lasers (p.229) that will shoot down enemy missiles within five minutes of their launch. Any later, and the defence system becomes much more difficult because the missile releases up to ten separate warheads and many decoys, greatly increasing the number of targets that have to be hit.

Lasers destroy their targets by directing

onto them an intense beam of energy which travels at the speed of light – 186,000 miles (300,000km) a second.

The simplest method of destruction is to focus a beam of infrared radiation on a missile so that it burns a hole in the rocket casing, causing fuel to escape so stopping the missile from reaching orbit. Or the beam could disrupt the rocket's electronic guidance system.

The Americans are developing a chemical laser in which hydrogen and fluorine react together to form hydrogen fluoride, a corrosive gas or liquid which can be made to release a powerful burst of infrared radiation. The laser is focused and aimed by prisms and mirrors.

A chemical laser of sufficient power (at least 25 megawatts) could destroy a missile almost 2000 miles (3200km) away.

The lasers would attack their targets from battle stations in space – a few hundred miles above the Earth. However, a total of 100 such battle stations would be needed to give America the possibility of complete protection, and getting so many into orbit would be a task that would dwarf any previous space project. Just the hydrogen fluoride needed to fuel the lasers would weigh about 2000 tons.

An alternative might be to base the lasers on land. The difficulty then is that the atmosphere would disperse the laser beam, making it impossible to focus it on the missile's skin.

Putting the lasers on the top of high mountains would reduce the distortion – because there would be less atmosphere to penetrate. Advanced optical techniques designed to counteract the dispersive effect of the atmosphere might also help.

Even so, no more than a tenth of the power of the laser could be expected to reach the target, which means that the lasers fired from Earth would need to be very powerful indeed. They would need to have the power of around 400 megawatts each – the same as the electricity consumption of a medium-sized city, and 1000 times more powerful than any laser known to exist today.

Mirrors would have to keep the laser locked onto the missile for several seconds before it was destroyed. Even if this were achieved the enemy could still defeat the laser by putting a heat shield around the missile or by making it spin so that the beam could not be focused on the same spot long enough to burn a hole.

The Star Wars programme has also been developing lasers which produce X-rays rather than a beam of light. These rays are produced in a single pulse rather than a continuous beam. The source of the X-rays is a small nuclear explosion. When the pulse of X-rays hits the enemy missile they are absorbed by its skin, vaporising it and blowing the missile apart. Because X-rays

are rapidly absorbed by the atmosphere they would also have to be fired from space, when both the laser and the missile it was attacking had risen above the atmosphere – at least 50 miles (80km) above the Earth.

The idea is not to station the lasers permanently in space, but to launch them only when satellite observations show that an enemy attack is already under way. The X-ray lasers would be launched from submarines, and would then be quickly boosted into orbit where they would be fired and aimed automatically.

How do they put out a deadly nuclear fire?

Since the beginnings of the nuclear power industry, in the mid-1950s, there have been three major accidents. The reactor that overheated on Three Mile Island in Philadelphia, in March 1979, never caught fire, but there were serious fires at Windscale in north-west England in 1957, and at Chernobyl in the Ukraine in April 1986. Both of the fires were extinguished, but in different ways.

When a nuclear reactor catches fire it cannot explode like a nuclear bomb, but a series of smaller explosions, or the fire itself, can destroy the reactor and release vast amounts of harmful radioactivity into the atmosphere. All the time that the

The entombment of Unit 4 *A thick concrete wall, started in 1986 (top), was built to entomb the radiation of the destroyed reactor at Chernobyl (above).*

Chernobyl and Windscale fires were being tackled, radioactivity was escaping, making the fire-fighting work critical and extremely dangerous.

The reactor at Windscale was designed for producing plutonium for British nuclear weapons. It burst into flames after an

The heart of the heat *A photograph of the Chernobyl accident, taken by an American Landsat satellite, revealed two heat sources (the small blue patches), which suggested to some American observers that a second nuclear reactor was about to melt. In fact it did not.*

operator made an error, which allowed the temperature of the core to rise too high. The result was a fire which burned for almost two days before it was brought under control.

First the engineers, wearing protective clothing against the radioactivity, sprayed the fire with carbon dioxide, hoping to douse it by starving it of oxygen, but that failed. They were reluctant to use water on the conflagration because they feared that it would react with burning graphite to form hydrogen which would explode, blowing the reactor to bits.

Eventually they decided they had to take the risk and flooded the reactor with a huge volume of water through fire hoses. It worked, and the fire went out, though not before substantial amounts of radioactivity had escaped. The ruined reactor was later filled with concrete and abandoned.

The fire at Chernobyl was much worse. It started after operators overrode a series of safety systems to discover how long the turbines would go on generating electricity after the steam supply was turned off. The reactor went out of control, and after two violent explosions it started burning fiercely. The top of the reactor was blown off, exposing it to open air. White-hot particles of radioactive fuel sprayed out, setting light to the power station building and threatening a neighbouring reactor.

First on the scene were local firemen, who with immense courage, and without protective clothing, went into the inferno and put out as much of the fire as they could using ordinary fire hoses. Although many of these men died, this action almost certainly saved the nearby reactor and prevented an even worse disaster.

But the Russians were still faced with a terrible problem – a wrecked reactor with its top blown off, glowing like a red-hot furnace and spewing out huge amounts of radioactive material into the sky.

Helicopter bombardment

A completely untried method was used to tackle the fire. Using a fleet of helicopters, they bombarded the reactor from the air with more than 5000 tons of dry clay and sand, to try to smother the fire. Boron carbide was added to absorb neutrons which would prevent the reactor from exploding again. Lead was also dropped to absorb heat by melting and to seal the reactor as it eventually cooled and solidified. Powdered limestone was also dropped to generate carbon-dioxide gas, which would blanket the reactor's core and prevent the fire from starting again.

It took two weeks of almost continual flying but it worked – the deadly fire at Chernobyl was put out and the release of radiation was stopped.

Ironically the method of extinguishing the fire was only possible because the

accident had been serious enough to blow the top off the reactor. When radiation levels finally fell, a concrete sarcophagus over 3ft (1m) thick was built around the reactor, entombing it for ever.

Chernobyl was the nuclear industry's worst ever accident, killing 31 people, including six firemen. Many others may die of cancer in years to come from exposure to high levels of radiation. Four years after the accident many local people could not return to their homes because radiation levels were still too high.

How can a boat sail into the wind?

The wind is the only thing that propels a sailing boat, so how can a boat sail against it? Amazingly, the most important force that drives a boat into the wind is suction.

A boat's sail is like an aircraft's wing on its side. On the outwardly curved, leeward side the wind has to flow around the sail, creating a powerful suction effect – pulling the sail towards it. The same principle applies to an aircraft, which gets lift from the suction on the top of its wings.

The suction effect is produced by the laws of aerodynamics. The air that is diverted around a curved sail becomes compressed so that it can squeeze past. When a moving stream of air is compressed its speed increases – a draught under a door can be surprisingly strong for this reason. And when the wind's speed increases, a loss of pressure occurs. This is because the faster the air is moving, the fewer molecules there are in any given space.

The area of low pressure on the leeward side sucks the sail towards it with twice the force that the same strength of wind can push into it from the windward side.

So the wind forces the boat sideways. However, the keel – or centreboard – of the boat resists the sideways movement. The wind's force is then converted partly into a forward movement of the boat and partly into a tilt to leeward which the yachtsman has to counteract by leaning out from the other side of the boat. A boat sailing close to the wind is bound to move substantially sideways – an effect called leeway. But the helmsman can compensate when plotting his course.

No boat can sail directly into the wind, but a 12 metre yacht can sail only 12-15 degrees off the wind. To go in the direction the wind is coming from, the boat has to zigzag, or make a series of tacks. The closer a boat sails to the wind, the slower its speed will be. The helmsman can go faster by making wider zigzags at a bigger angle to the wind, but then he has to travel farther.

Racing into the wind *Sidewinder yachts tack (zigzag) against a stiff wind.*

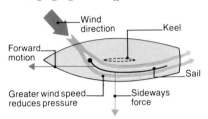

Wind force *As the wind travels faster around the curved side of the sail, it creates suction, forcing the boat sideways. But the keel resists the movement and converts part of the suction into forward motion.*

Restoring a masterpiece

Leonardo da Vinci's *Last Supper*, one of the greatest achievements of Western art, has probably suffered more damage than any other great work. The 12ft (3.6m) high mural, or wall painting, was finished in the late 1490s and within 20 years paint was already flaking off. By 1587 the painting was described as 'half-ruined'.

In 1652 the Dominican friars of Santa Maria delle Grazie, Milan, in whose dining hall Leonardo had painted the masterpiece, decided to enlarge a door – which involved cutting off Christ's feet in the painting.

In the 18th century they put up a curtain in front of the mural, trapping moisture which ran down the painting in rivulets. Every time the curtain was drawn back, for visitors to see the painting, it scraped the surface.

More damage was caused in 1796 when Napoleon's troops used the refectory as an armoury. They threw stones at the Apostles in the painting, and even climbed ladders to scratch out their eyes. And in 1943 an Allied bomb came within a yard or two of completing the destruction.

Now the mural is being restored, and not for the first time. This is the seventh major attempt since 1726, when a painter called Michelangelo Bellotti was hired to repaint the entire work. He was so incompetent

Continued on page 164

Michelangelo: painting the Sistine Chapel

Sitting on the highest part of the wooden scaffolding, his head and shoulders flung back, his neck aching, his face running with paint, his eyes smarting, Michelangelo worked daily from dawn till dusk on his monumental frescoes for the Sistine Chapel ceiling in the Vatican, Rome.

At times, he laboured for up to 30 days at a stretch. He felt sick with pain, his head reeled and he feared that he was going blind. In 1510, midway through his marathon task, he wrote a poem in which, loosely translated, he stated:

'I'm in the wrong place – and I'm not a painter!'

Indeed, Michelangelo Buonarroti regarded himself first and foremost as a sculptor in marble – and had a low opinion of his own painting skills. Born in 1475 – the son of the mayor of Caprese (now Caprese Michelangelo), south-east of Florence – he was aged 33 when Pope Julius II summoned him to Rome and commissioned him to repaint the ceiling of the Sistine Chapel.

The ceremonial chapel was named after Julius's uncle, Pope Sixtus IV, for whom it was built between 1473 and 1481. Its walls were filled with magnificent paintings by such masters as Botticelli and Perugino; but on its ceiling there was only a comparatively ordinary representation of a starry sky by Piermatteo d'Amelia.

At first, Pope Julius had wanted Michelangelo – who accepted the commission with reluctance – to decorate the vaulted ceiling with portraits of the 12 Apostles. But the artist thought them to be 'poor things', and decided to cover the surface with his vision of the creation of the universe.

To reach the lofty ceiling, he designed movable wooden scaffolding. This enabled him to paint standing up, if he wished, and allowed him to walk about. Even so, over a period of four-and-a-half years he found it painfully restricting – especially after he had a sloping ramp added to the highest platform so he could work on fine detail with his eyes just inches from the ceiling.

He started work in the summer of 1508 with the aid of six assistants – who mixed his paint, ground the plaster, and sometimes helped with the actual painting. His master plan was to fill the vault from the windows upwards with frescoes – watercolours painted into freshly applied wet plaster (from the Italian *fresco* – 'fresh'). This had to be done very quickly while the plaster was still damp.

A mistake meant chipping away the plaster and starting again. Michelangelo had to do this only once.

First of all, he drew his designs on a sheet of paper and perforated the outlines with a pin. Next he held the paper against the ceiling, and blew powdered charcoal through the perforations to stencil the design onto the wet plaster. Then he painted along the stencil marks, sometimes improvising and elaborating as his confidence grew.

His nine scenes ran in a straight line directly overhead. They ranged from the 'Separation of Light from Darkness' (the Creation) above the altar, to the 'Drunkenness of Noah' (showing man at his farthest from God) above the entrance. Surrounding and interspersed with the large frescoes was an animated array of prophets, sibyls (ancient prophetesses), the ancestors of Christ, Ignudi, or male nudes (portraying perfect human beauty), and scenes representing the Salvation of mankind.

Altogether, he created some 300 figures from the Old and New Testaments – each with his or her own features, facial expression and pose – over 11,000sq ft (1022sq m) of painted surface.

Gradually, as the work progressed, he dismissed most of his assistants, claiming they lacked inspiration. A sinewy, broad-shouldered man of medium height, he resolutely withstood the rigours of the Roman winter – when a chill north wind whistled through the chapel, and rain leaking through the roof caused mould on parts of the paintings.

He ate as he worked – mostly chunks of bread – and at night slept fitfully in his nearby studio in his clothes and boots. He suffered mentally as well as physically, and in January 1509 he wrote to his father, stating: 'I do not ask anything of the Pope as my work does not seem to me to go ahead in a way to merit it. This is because of the difficulty of the work and also because it is not my profession. In consequence, I lose my time fruitlessly. May God help me.'

The Pope shared Michelangelo's misgivings and periodically visited the chapel, climbing up the ladder to the top of the scaffolding to inspect the paintings. This led to some bitter exchanges between them. In the summer of 1510, for instance, when the work was half completed, Pope Julius wanted to know when the rest of the ceiling would be finished. 'When it satisfies me as an artist,' replied Michelangelo. The Pope frowned and said tartly: 'And we want you to satisfy us and finish it soon!'

On another occasion, the 66-year-old Pope threatened to have the artist physically thrown down from the scaffolding if he did not work faster. 'When will it be ready?' demanded Julius. 'When it is ready,' replied Michelangelo shortly. The

Lonely genius *Made in 1565, this bronze bust of Michelangelo by his friend Daniele da Volterra shows the loneliness of a man whose entire life was devoted to his work.*

Pope flushed with anger and mimicked: 'When it is ready! When it is ready!' He then raised his walking stick in rage and struck Michelangelo on the shoulder.

The two men later made their peace and Michelangelo resumed work until the autumn when, not for the first time, he ran out of money. Not until February 1511 was there enough money for work to continue.

By now, people working in the Vatican had become used to Michelangelo's weird appearance as he strode to and from the chapel. His hair and beard were streaked with colour; his clothes were ragged and matted with plaster; and his head was held low as the outside light hurt his eyes. In the streets outside, many thought him a 'madman' and jeered at him as he went by.

Working alone and without distraction, he finally completed his vast work in the autumn of 1512 – almost four-and-a-half years after he had signed the contract with the Pope. The scaffolding and covers were removed, and Julius and his court saw the finished ceiling on All Saints' Eve (October 31). The next day the chapel was ceremonially reopened for the Pope's dedication. Michelangelo did not attend the service. He was anxious to get back to his sculpting, and wrote to his father: 'I have finished the chapel which I was painting. . . The Pope is very satisfied. . .'

The works of God and man *The creation of the universe by God is shown by Michelangelo in a series of nine panels on the ceiling of the Sistine Chapel in the Vatican. Some modern scaffolding (bottom left of picture) shows the scale of the chapel, whose ceiling rises to 69ft (21m) high and has a surface 131ft (40m) long and 43ft (13m) wide.*

Retrieving the _Last Supper_ _The restoration of Leonardo da Vinci's 500-year-old mural in Milan has been a long process. It takes a week to clean an area the size of a postage stamp, and took six years to restore the right-hand quarter of the work._

that another painter, Giuseppe Mazza, was paid to go over the wall with a scalpel to remove what Bellotti had done. But Mazza's scraping did more harm than good.

The most recent restoration began in 1977 and is still going on. The restorer, Dr Pinin Brambilla Barcilon, spent three years examining the mural and the wall it is painted on, to build up a detailed knowledge of the problems. Dr Brambilla studied a tiny area at a time, examining it through a microscope which enlarges the surface by 40 times.

The first task was to clean off the dirt of 500 years, and the varnishes and overpainting of earlier restorers. She applied a specially developed solvent, then blotted it quickly before it could reach and damage Leonardo's original colours. This process had to be repeated several times to prise off the layers of grime and varnish.

Gradually delicate details returned – a once obscured image became a lemon slice reflected in a pewter plate. The bright colours that Leonardo used are slowly being revealed as the dark overpainting is painstakingly removed.

Some of the restorers altered the original work quite dramatically. For example, experts believe that Judas has been made to look much more sinister than Leonardo intended. One of the 'restorers' even signed his name. In fact very little of the _Last Supper_ bore much resemblance to Leonardo's original before Dr Brambilla began her work.

Much of the painting is irretrievably lost, and Dr Brambilla fills these empty areas with a neutral, easily removable, watercolour that helps to make the best of what

is left. She will leave it to future generations to repaint these areas and try to recapture Leonardo's original vision.

Another equally important restoration has been going on in Rome – that of Michelangelo's ceiling in the Sistine Chapel in the Vatican, which was painted between 1508 and 1512.

The ceiling is in far better condition than the _Last Supper_, and the main task is to clean it. For nearly 500 years the fresco has been gradually blackened by burning candles and charcoal braziers, used by the priests to illuminate and heat the chapel.

The Italian chemical company Montedison has invented a kind of poultice to clean frescoes. A thick, foul-smelling paste is applied to strips of porous paper which are pressed against the fresco, left for about ten minutes and then removed like a sticking plaster, taking the dirt with them.

At the Sistine Chapel a similar technique has been used, though the cleaning agent stays on the wall for only three minutes before being washed off. The process is repeated after 24 hours.

In spite of the immense care being taken, the restoration of the ceiling is bitterly controversial. The brilliant colours emerging from beneath the grime are not what Michelangelo intended, the critics say. They believe that the restoration will remove the small parts of the painting that the artist added _a secco_ (after the plaster had dried) and that the cleaned part of the ceiling looks unsubtle and brash.

Many other experts dismiss such criticism. The uncleaned ceiling needed 30,000 watts of halogen lamps to make it visible, so dark had it become. The restored

ceiling is easily visible in normal light – 'as Michelangelo intended it to be: spacious, harmonious, sunlit', in the words of British art critic William Feaver.

More and more sophisticated techniques are being used in picture restoration. Some restorers use infrared reflectography to peer beneath the surface of paintings and reveal the artist's initial charcoal drawings before he painted over them.

Other methods use image-enhancers – the same machines that are used by NASA to improve pictures of outer space.

Computers are used to calculate how much a painting's pigments have altered and produce a colour-corrected image of the picture. The computer must take many things into account because some colours change much faster than others and certain pigments may have been affected by the varnish.

Queen's tomb _A conservator (art preserver) injects acrylic resin emulsion behind flaking plaster to bind it, in the 3200-year-old tomb of Queen Nefertiti, at Thebes._

Exploring the Universe

*As astronauts take their first tentative steps into
the immensity of space, astronomers are developing powerful tools
that allow them to seek the very edge of the Universe.*

How astronauts steer in space, page 168.

The force that drives a space rocket

On April 12, 1981, the first space shuttle, *Columbia*, lifted off from Cape Canaveral on its maiden flight into space. *Columbia* was powered by three liquid-fuelled engines and a pair of giant strap-on, solid-fuel boosters, and was controlled by five sophisticated, interlinked computers. But despite the space shuttle's apparent complexity, the basic principle that makes it work is exactly the same as that behind a simple firework rocket or a balloon that zooms across the room when you let go of its neck. It is the principle of action and reaction.

In the 17th century, the English physicist Sir Isaac Newton summed up one of the basic rules of the Universe in the statement: 'Action and reaction are equal and opposite.' For example, when the neck of an inflated balloon is released, and air rushes out through the aperture, the equal and opposite reaction to the escaping rush of air pushes the balloon forward.

Unlike a balloon, a rocket does not contain compressed gas. Instead, it manufactures gas by burning solid or liquid fuels. But once the gas has been produced, the principle is the same. As the hot exhaust gases escape from its rear, the rocket is pushed forward in an equal and opposite reaction to the rush of escaping gases. But, unlike a balloon, which darts in all directions, the rocket is designed to keep a stable course.

Columbia's three liquid-fuelled engines, which together burn 100 tons of fuel a minute, produce a downward stream of gases that cause an opposite, upward force or reaction of 640 tons. The gases from the two solid-fuel boosters produce a reaction of 2400 tons. The total upward reaction on the shuttle is therefore more than 3000 tons. But the fully fuelled shuttle weighs only 2000 tons, so the reaction is sufficient to lift it off the ground and accelerate it towards space. Once in space, the shuttle goes into its regulated orbit around the Earth.

The first reusable spacecraft *Spewing flames and clouds of smoke, the space shuttle* Columbia *blasts into space on one of its many voyages. Its twin rocket boosters strapped to the large fuel tank fall away after two minutes and parachute back to Earth, to be used again. The large tank is jettisoned six minutes later, and breaks up on its way down through the atmosphere. The shuttle itself eventually returns to Earth, intact.*

How astronauts navigate in space

In January 1986, the unmanned spacecraft *Voyager* 2 swung past distant Uranus, photographing this giant planet and its many moons at close quarters. To get the best pictures, the mission controllers on Earth had to know precisely where *Voyager* was – and they were able to pin down its position to within an accuracy of 60 miles (100km), even after the spacecraft had travelled 3078 million miles (4954 million km). This accuracy is equivalent to a golfer achieving a hole-in-one on a fairway 1560 miles (2520km) long!

Space engineers have a number of ways of achieving such amazing feats of navigation. For example, rockets launched into space carry an inertial-guidance system, which operates independently of signals from outside the craft. This system contains two devices. One is a set of gyroscopes, which enables the direction that the rocket is heading in to be monitored. The other is a set of accelerometers, to measure the rocket's acceleration or deceleration. A computer on board keeps track continuously of all the changes in the rocket's direction and speed, and so can work out at any instant just how far the rocket has gone, in what direction, and how fast it is travelling.

During the *Apollo* flights to the Moon, the ground controllers also kept track of the craft by using the astronauts' radio communications links. From the radio signals they picked up, the radio telescopes on Earth could pinpoint the direction of the craft. In addition, these signals enabled the mission controllers to find out the distance from Earth to *Apollo*. They measured the time it took for the radio signals to reach *Apollo* and return to Earth, and divided it by the speed of the signal (which is the same as the speed of light – 186,000 miles per second). Knowing the craft's direction and distance, the controllers could calculate where it was.

A careful study of the signals also revealed the speed of the *Apollo* craft. If a source of radio waves is moving, then the frequencies and wavelengths of the radio waves are altered by an amount that depends on the speed of the source. This is an example of the Doppler effect. The frequency of the waves rises or falls depending on whether the spacecraft is moving towards Earth or away from it. The faster the spacecraft is moving, the greater the change in the wavelengths. The change in *Apollo*'s frequency was about 0.01 per cent of the speed of light.

Before each flight, the planners had

Maintenance men in the skies *To rescue the stranded communications satellite* Westar VI, *American astronaut Dale Gardner (left) flew into space from the shuttle* Discovery *by means of a jet-powered backpack, or manned manoeuvring unit (MMU). Locking onto the satellite, he then fired the MMU jets to stop the satellite rotating. Meanwhile, his companion, Joseph Allen, rode out to the satellite on an extending robot arm. The arm retracted to bring the satellite and astronauts safely back to the shuttle.*

calculated the exact path and speed that the *Apollo* astronauts should be taking. If the radio signals and inertial guidance showed that they were straying slightly, the ground controllers instructed the astronauts to fire small rocket motors which would make a 'mid-course correction' to change the spacecraft's speed and put them back on the correct route.

The latest American-manned craft, the shuttles, follow orbits closer to the Earth than *Apollo*. If their direction needs to be altered, computers on the ground instruct the shuttle's own computer to fire the thrusters needed to change the craft's orbit.

Unmanned space probes have inbuilt navigational aids. For a spacecraft to prevent itself from tumbling haphazardly through space it needs to fix its position on three different axes. In the case of the far-flying *Voyagers*, one axis is provided by the direction of our planet: the craft always travel with their radio communications dish pointing towards the Earth. The other two 'fixes' are made by light-sensors. One picks out the direction of the Sun, and the other 'locks' onto a bright star – Regulus, in the case of *Voyager 1*, and Canopus for *Voyager 2*.

Another space probe that required a

a distance of 5000 miles (8000km) they took the first, rather distant, pictures of its nucleus. These showed where the nucleus was, relative to the two *Vega* spacecraft.

Using radio telescopes set up all over the world, American scientists tuned into the Soviet radio transmissions to work out exactly where the *Vega* spacecraft were. Armed with these positions and the *Vega* photographs, the Soviets could pin down the position of the comet's nucleus. This information allowed the Europeans to guide *Giotto* to the correct distance from the nucleus. As the nucleus hurtled past, 380 miles (605km) away, *Giotto* was able to take close-up photographs that astounded astronomers. The nucleus of Halley's Comet (the dense core of ice and rock particles) turned out to be a jet-black, potato-shaped object about 10 miles (16km) long and 5 miles (8km) wide, which erupted enormous geysers of brilliant white gas and steam more than 1000 miles (1600km) into space.

Weightless meals on a spacecraft

During the pioneering space flights of the 1960s, the astronauts had to live on appetite-depressing food pastes which they squeezed into their mouths from toothpaste-type tubes.

In the age of the space shuttle, however, they enjoy appetising meals that include scrambled eggs, steaks, asparagus and butterscotch pudding – all eaten with knife, fork and spoon and served on a tray.

Before Yuri Gagarin blazed the astronaut trail on April 12, 1961, no one knew how well a human being could endure the rigours of space flight. Could the human body withstand the crushing forces unleashed by the launching rocket – forces that made the body up to six times heavier? Could the body cope immediately afterwards with the state of weightlessness? Would the astronauts still be able to eat and drink, with no gravity to draw food and liquids into the gullet?

After more than a quarter of a century of manned space flight, the answer to all these questions, with certain reservations, is 'Yes'.

In space, astronauts live cocooned in an atmosphere of nitrogen and oxygen at ordinary sea-level atmospheric pressure, and in a pleasant 'shirt-sleeve' temperature provided by their spacecraft's life-support system. Stale air and odours are eliminated by circulating the air through carbon dioxide absorbers and charcoal filters, and the humidity is carefully controlled. The nitrogen for the air pressurisation system is supplied from pressurised tanks. The oxygen is obtained from supplies of liquid oxygen carried on board.

The mechanics of eating and drinking in space differ from those on Earth. In space you cannot, for example, toss a peanut into the air and catch it in your mouth. The nut will carry on upwards until it bounces off the roof of the cabin.

You must carefully place food in the mouth. Once it is there, weightlessness is of no importance. The body's swallowing reflex takes over to force the food down the gullet – though 'down' is not an appropriate word because in space there is no 'down' or 'up'.

Drinking, however, presents a problem. You cannot pour out a glass of orange juice because the juice remains inside its container. You could shake it out into the glass, but it would only bounce out and shower globules of juice everywhere.

So drinks must be squirted into the mouth from a gun-like device, or be sucked up from a container through a straw. Sucking works just as well in space as it does on Earth, because it relies on air pressure to force the liquid up the straw.

3000 calories a day

The range of foods available to shuttle astronauts is vast, and great care is taken to ensure it looks and smells appetising.

Meals are organised to provide the astronauts with an average of 3000 calories a day, which seems high for living in an enclosed environment in which there is no gravity. But astronauts can expend a great deal of energy in doing the simplest things. For example, if they try to turn a handle, they turn themselves as well. If they bend down to do up a shoelace, they start turning somersaults. Finding unusual ways of doing such ordinary things uses up the surplus calories.

The space diet is balanced rather differently from a terrestrial diet. This is to try and compensate for changes that take place in the body during space flight. Bodily changes begin as soon as astronauts go into space and are quite noticeable after even a week. The longer the flight, the more the body is affected.

Among the most serious changes is calcium loss, which causes a marked reduction in the mass and strength of the bones. There is also a progressive loss of red blood cells. What causes these effects is not known, and the question must be answered before long-duration space flight is really safe.

The heart muscles, with no gravity to battle against, start to waste away. The leg muscles waste away too, since walking, as

precise path was the European Space Agency's *Giotto* probe. It was programmed to fly through Halley's Comet in March 1986, and send back detailed pictures of the solid nucleus at the comet's centre. *Giotto* had sensors to keep track of the Earth and the Sun but could not lock onto a particular star for its third fix because it was designed to spin continuously. Instead, *Giotto* had a star mapper which kept track of all the brighter stars.

If a star's apparent path was incorrect, the ground controllers instructed thrusters on board to correct *Giotto*'s orientation.

Navigating *Giotto* accurately was relatively simple; establishing its object – the position of the comet's nucleus – was more difficult. Here a remarkable international collaboration helped. Two Soviet probes called *Vega* reached the comet about a week before *Giotto*. Flying past the comet at

Chasing a ball of orange juice *Weightlessness can make for entertaining meals. Normally in space, the surface tension of a liquid keeps it in its container and it can be drunk through a straw. But if liquid like this orange juice is jolted, it floats into the air like a ball.*

done on Earth, is impossible in orbit where there is nothing to keep the feet down.

A mineral-rich diet can help to reduce the extent of the changes, but not as much as space doctors would like. Exercise also helps to reduce muscle wastage and is vital on very long flights like the 6-12 month missions endured by Russian cosmonauts in their Salyut and Mir space stations.

Growing food on a flight to Mars?

No one yet knows the limit of human endurance in space. If astronauts can withstand two years or more of continuous weightlessness, then mankind's dream of visiting other planets could become reality in the early decades of next century.

Both the Americans and the Russians are making provisional plans for a manned mission to Mars which would take about two years for the return journey.

Providing food for the crew on such a mission would be a formidable problem. One solution would be for them to grow their own food in on-board greenhouses, an activity that would help to relieve the boredom of the long flight.

A day's menu for a shuttle crew

A typical day's menu for shuttle astronauts would be:
Breakfast: peaches, bran flakes, scrambled eggs and cocoa. Lunch: corned beef with asparagus, strawberries and an almond crunch bar. Dinner: shrimp cocktail, steak, broccoli au gratin, butterscotch pudding and tropical punch (alcohol-free). There are enough alternative foods on board to provide a totally different menu for six successive days.

The latest preservation techniques have

been used to retain the appeal of the foods. Like many foods, the scrambled egg is dehydrated. Dehydration helps to reduce weight, which is at a premium on any spacecraft. Dehydrated foods have to be mixed with water before eating. Curiously, there is no shortage of water on the shuttle since it is a plentiful by-product of the fuel cells that supply the craft with electricity.

The steak is precooked and comes in sealed packs. The butterscotch pudding, which is also precooked, comes in a can. The strawberries are freeze-dried, which preserves their shape and texture. They can be rehydrated with water or in the mouth with saliva. Bread is sliced in natural form, preserved by irradiation.

Shuttle meals are individually packed for each astronaut, and are prepared by the astronaut 'chef of the day' in the galley which has an oven, pantry and water dispenser. The chef rehydrates foods that require it, puts in the oven foods that have to be heated, and inserts straws into the drinks containers. He then assembles the food on individual trays, using magnets, Velcro fasteners or sticky tape to hold them in place.

The astronauts attach their tray to the portable dining table or anywhere else suitable, even the cabin walls. They usually eat standing up, with their feet in foot restraints to prevent them drifting away.

When they open their food packages, the food does not float away, as some people thought it might. Much of it is moist and covered in sauce or gravy, and surface tension helps to keep it inside its container.

Eating with a knife, fork and spoon presents few difficulties, since the food clings to them as well. But the astronauts

must eat slowly and gracefully, avoiding jerky movements, which would dislodge the food, which would then float off around the cabin.

Disposing of bodily wastes

During the first few days of a space flight nearly 50 per cent of astronauts succumb to space sickness. They experience nausea, headaches, sweating and vomiting. It is a severe form of the travel sickness that some people suffer on Earth, and is caused by weightlessness, which confuses the balance organs in the inner ear.

Disposal of bags of vomit must be done hygienically, since germs could breed rapidly in the confined living space.

The other vital aspect of waste disposal is delicately referred to by the National Aeronautics and Space Administration as 'digestive elimination'. Excreting body wastes in weightless conditions is a problem. Since there is no gravity, they remain hovering where they leave the body.

In early spacecraft, astronauts taped bags over the appropriate part of the body. But it was an unpleasant operation.

On the space shuttle, however, astronauts have a flushing toilet, which is flushed by air, not water, and has a separate tube for removing the urine. It is also fitted with foot restraints and a seat belt.

The urinal tube is flexible and has a cup at the top contoured so as to be suitable for both male and female users. The urine is drawn through the tube by air flow and is stored temporarily in a tank with other waste water. Periodically the contents are dumped overboard where they evaporate.

Solid wastes are flushed away into a container by an airstream that enters just beneath the seat. They are dried when the container is later exposed to the vacuum of space and are taken back to Earth for disposal.

How satellites orbit the Earth

On October 4, 1957, a Soviet rocket blasted a metal sphere, Sputnik 1, into space. Sputnik did not fall back to the ground, nor did it head off into the depths of space. Apparently defying gravity, it stayed near the Earth, going round and round only a few hundred miles above the ground. Three months later it burnt up.

Despite appearances, satellites do not really defy gravity. They are in fact falling towards the Earth all the time, just like the apple Sir Isaac Newton watched fall and which led him to discover the laws of gravity. The key difference between the apple and the satellite is that the satellite is

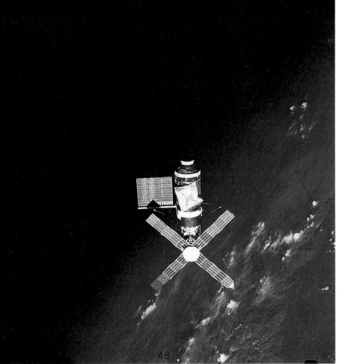

48

A giant space laboratory *Orbiting 270 miles (435km) above the Earth, the Skylab space station conducted experiments in physiology and physics. The drag of the atmosphere slowed it down, and in its 34,981st orbit it fell to Earth, burning up over Western Australia.*

Launching satellites from space *While in orbit, the space shuttle Discovery launched a communications satellite from its cargo bay in August 1985. This is a geostationary satellite, remaining at the same point above the Earth during its orbit.*

moving very fast – around 18,000mph (30,000km/h) – and at a much higher altitude. This means that as the satellite falls towards the Earth, the Earth's surface curves away from it, so that it never actually gets closer.

Imagine that you are on top of a mountain which rises 100 miles (160km) above the Earth's surface. If you take an apple, and just let go of it, the apple drops down vertically. Now suppose you throw it towards the horizon. The apple will still fall, but it follows a curving path. If the apple is hurled at a great enough speed, the downward curve of its path as it falls will

match the curve of the Earth's surface. Although the apple is falling all the time, the Earth's surface is curving away underneath it at the same rate. As a result, the apple never gets any closer to the surface of the Earth. It is in orbit.

When a rocket launches a satellite, it must therefore give the satellite sufficient horizontal velocity that its falling trajectory will always miss the Earth.

By choosing a suitable combination of upward and horizontal thrust, mission controllers can put a satellite into an orbit of any size and any shape from circular to highly elliptical (egg-shaped). The greater

the thrust, the larger the orbit. The greater the horizontal thrust, the more elliptical the orbit will be.

To send a satellite on an elliptical orbit, it is boosted fast enough from Earth to counteract the Earth's downward pull. It therefore moves away from the curvature of the Earth. But the Earth's gravity is always exerting a pull on the satellite, and it eventually slows down and begins to fall back to Earth. The sideways momentum of the satellite means that it misses the Earth. But as it falls it speeds up again, so that by the time it has completed an orbit, the satellite is travelling fast enough once again to pull away from the Earth and begin a second elliptical orbit.

Almost all the world's communications satellites, which relay television and telephone messages, are in circular orbits above the Earth's equator, at a height of 22,300 miles (35,800km). A satellite in such an orbit circles the Earth at the same speed as the Earth's rotation, so it always lies above the same point on the Earth's surface.

Communications companies prefer such 'geostationary' satellites because they can employ fixed aerials to send signals to and from the satellites, rather than having to follow a moving target across the sky.

Although a satellite in orbit should stay in space forever, this is often not the case. If a satellite's orbit brings it within a few hundred miles of the Earth's surface, the atmosphere that still exists at this height causes friction, or a 'drag' on the satellite. Eventually this drag slows the satellite down and it falls into the atmosphere and burns up.

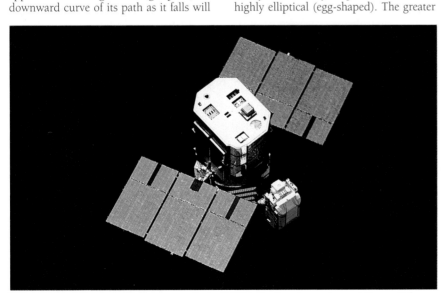

The Ace Satellite Repair Company *In April 1984, the American astronaut George Nelson – in his Manned Manoeuvring Unit (lower right) – jetted from the shuttle* Challenger *to recover Solar Max, a satellite launched in 1980 to observe the Sun. The astronauts who repaired the satellite 290 miles (460km) above the Earth, jokingly named themselves the Ace Satellite Repair Company.*

171

How they control space probes to other planets

Astronomers know a lot about the planets of the Solar System. They have detailed maps of Mercury, Venus, Mars and dozens of the moons of the outer planets. They have cinematic film of the weather on Jupiter and of the rotation of Saturn's rings. They even have photographs taken on the very surface of Venus and Mars. All this information has been gathered by unmanned spacecraft, controlled from Earth.

In many ways, operating a spacecraft is similar to directing a robot by remote control. The only way to send signals across space is by radio, but over such distances radio signals become very weak.

So, to send commands to the space probes, enormous saucer-shaped dishes and antennae have been built around the world. Among them are three constructed by the American space agency NASA. Each dish of its Deep Space Network (DSN) is 210ft (64m) across. They are sited in California, Spain and Australia, so that at least one antenna can always be in touch with a space probe.

The control room for American space probes is at the Jet Propulsion Laboratory

Voyager 2 visits the planets *Since its launch on August 20, 1977, Voyager 2 has flown past Jupiter, Saturn, Uranus and Neptune collecting scientific data and photographs which it transmitted to Earth. The first inner ring in the picture represents Earth, the second Jupiter, the third Saturn and the last Uranus. The next planet was Neptune.*

in Pasadena, California. From here, the controllers send out commands by radio links to the appropriate DSN dish. A powerful transmitter then sends the message up to the space probe, which picks it up by means of its dish aerial.

These dishes on the space probes are very large in order to receive signals from Earth clearly. As a result, some space probes are virtually built onto the back of the dishes. The *Pioneer* dishes are 9ft (2.7m) across, and the *Voyager* dishes are 12ft (3.7m) across.

The dish sends the signal to a computer on board the spacecraft, where it is decoded. The computer then instructs the appropriate part of the craft to take action.

Saturn seen in false colours *By enhancing Voyager's photographs of Saturn with false colours, scientists can view the bands of atmosphere around the planet more easily. Voyager also photographed the cratered and grooved surface of Enceladus (right), one of Saturn's many moons, from a distance of 74,000 miles (118,400km).*

VOYAGER'S NUCLEAR POWER GENERATORS

Each of the two *Voyager* craft gets its electrical power from a miniature nuclear generator, which consists of three metal cylinders, each 17in (430mm) long and 13in (330mm) wide, connected end to end. The cylinders are packed with plutonium dioxide, a radioactive substance.

Surrounding the core of each cylinder are hundreds of thermocouples. These are miniature electric circuits, consisting of a piece of silicon and a piece of germanium. One end of each thermocouple is heated by the decaying plutonium; the other faces outwards into the cold of space.

The difference in temperature between the two ends of the thermocouple causes an electrical current to flow through it. When electrons in the silicon are disturbed by heating, free electrons will tend to move to the germanium, creating a current.

When each *Voyager* was launched, in 1977, the three cylinders together produced 475 watts of electric power. But the power decreases by 7 watts per year, as the plutonium decays.

Mercury in mosaic Mariner 10 *took a sequence of more than 200 photographs of Mercury in 1975, which were then assembled into a mosaic, or composite, image. This photograph revealed that the surface of Mercury, the smallest planet in the Solar System, strongly resembles the Moon's surface, which suggests that it is probably about the same age – at least 4000 million years old.*

For example, the computer may command a thruster to fire in order to change the space probe's course, or tell the camera to start a sequence of photographs.

The spacecraft also sends signals back to Earth. Some are just routine 'housekeeping' messages which tell the controllers that all the systems on the craft are working correctly. Other signals carry scientific data, such as photographs of the planet.

However, a spacecraft has a limited amount of power to send its signals. If it is destined to fly near the Sun, it will be equipped with solar panels which convert sunlight into electricity. But a spacecraft flying far from the Sun must rely on small nuclear generators (see box).

As the space probe travels billions of miles farther into space, its signal becomes even weaker. At the moment, the spacecraft *Voyager 1* is farther away than the planet Pluto, some 3000 million miles (4800 million km) from the Earth. Despite the huge size of a DSN antenna, the total power it picks up from *Voyager* is only a few million-millionths of the power that operates an electronic wristwatch. But by amplifying the signals, it can boost them so that they are received clearly at the Jet Propulsion Laboratory.

Another problem of communicating with distant spacecraft is the amount of time it takes for the radio signals to reach them from Earth. When *Voyager 2* passed Uranus in January 1986, for example, it was about 3000 million miles (4800 million km) away. Even travelling at the speed of light, the television signals from *Voyager* took two and a half hours to reach Earth and the same time was required for a signal to travel back to the spacecraft from Earth.

This five-hour delay meant that all the commands had to be worked out months ahead of the encounter, and then sent to *Voyager* in advance, to be stored in its two computers. During the encounter itself, mission controllers could only wait and keep their fingers crossed. Fortunately, all the systems worked as planned and *Voyager* sent back 700 detailed photographs of Uranus and its moons.

Jupiter and its moons *In 1979,* Voyager 2 *photographed the planet Jupiter and some of its moons. The small disc above the planet's surface is Europa, and the inset (below) shows the moon Io. This moon's yellow-orange colour comes from sulphur emitted by its active volcanoes.*

Mars, the red planet *In 1976 a small landing craft from the spacecraft* Viking 1 *was directed from Earth to dig up some of the red rocky soil of Mars and test it for signs of living organisms. None was found.*

173

How satellite photographs help to predict drought and discover oil

In the mid-1970s, a team of scientists in America identified 25 crops growing in almost 9000 fields in California's Imperial Valley, without ever having been near the valley. What made it possible for them to name the crops, which included maize, lettuce and tomatoes, were pictures taken by a satellite that had passed over the valley at an altitude of 570 miles (920km).

Several satellites, including the American Landsat series and the French SPOT satellite, have been launched for the sole purpose of taking pictures of the Earth. These 'Earth resources satellites' can pick out particular crops and monitor their health. They can detect pollution, such as oil slicks at sea. And they can help geologists to find oil and minerals.

Photography using ordinary light is good enough for some purposes – for example, in helping cartographers to make maps more accurate. The first Landsats found that charts of the Pacific had marked some small islands up to 10 miles (16km) away from their correct positions.

But scientists can often obtain much more information when they take pictures at a wide range of wavelengths. Landsat takes photographs of the ground at seven different wavelengths. Three are visible: blue, green and red. The other four are infrared or near-infrared wavelengths, which are invisible to the human eye.

These different colour bands allow scientists to tell one kind of terrain or vegetation from another. In a limited way, it is possible to do this by eye. The leaves of a conifer, for example, are a bluer green than those of a deciduous tree. But this comparison involves only blue and green wavelengths. When Landsat scientists look at all the colour bands, they can detect a distinctive 'fingerprint' for each type of plant, which is brighter when viewed at some wavelengths and darker at others.

The contrasts between different types of vegetation show up more clearly in the infrared than at visible wavelengths. The colours in photographs are therefore changed, so that the normally invisible infrared radiation is depicted as a visible colour. The usual scheme is to colour the infrared image red, the normally red image green, and the green image blue.

Once a picture has been false-coloured in this way, vegetation appears red, because plant leaves are good at reflecting infrared. The shades of red in each field or plantation correspond to the different ways that various plants reflect infrared radiation, and they allow scientists to identify plant species accurately.

Satellites using infrared photography can also help to establish the dryness of a region, monitoring areas that are not normally accessible or that are not cultivated. The amount of water in a plant's leaves determines the amount of infrared radiation that it reflects. By taking pictures at the appropriate wavelength, scientists can find out whether plants are suffering from a lack of water, and hence allow farmers to control irrigation and to predict droughts.

Geologists also use Landsat images to predict where oil and minerals can be found. In a real colour photograph, the

Colour-coding cotton crops *To establish the distribution of fields of cotton in California's San Joaquin Valley (above) in 1975, a Landsat satellite photographed the valley using a range of wavelengths of light. Red represents cotton, yellow is safflower, green is stubble and blue is fallow ground.*

Retreating rain forest *This Landsat image (right), taken in 1981, records the deforestation (blue) that has occurred over a period of five years in the Amazon jungle, in the Rondonia region of Brazil. The clearing has resulted from farmers cultivating deeper and deeper into the jungle (red).*

colour of exposed rocks can give a clue to their composition: chalk and limestone are white, granites are generally pale, and basalts dark. But, as with vegetation, different rock types have distinctive 'finger-prints' when observed at infrared wave-lengths. These make it possible to pick out the type of rocks that contain, for example, manganese and chromium. Even where the rock is covered by a thin layer of soil, it is possible to tell something of the rock type by identifying the vegetation growing on it.

The bird's eye view of satellite pictures reveals faults in rocks, and domes and dips in the rock strata, which may not be evident to someone on the ground. By mapping these features, geologists can work out where there are likely to be seams of minerals or oil deposits.

Soviet geologists have obtained a vast amount of information from cameras on board their manned space stations, the Salyut series and Mir. These cameras take six simultaneous pictures at visible and infrared wavelengths. The results have led to the discovery of new gas and oil fields in the Volga region and between the Caspian and Aral Seas.

Future satellites will take these possi-bilities further. Scientists at NASA's Jet Propulsion Laboratory in Pasadena, Cali-fornia, have developed instruments that can scan the ground at many more wavelengths than the Soviet cameras, simultaneously. The Airborne Imaging Spectrometer measures 128 bands in the infrared, and its successor will cover 224. With this amount of information, the 'fingerprints' of specific minerals which are exposed will be unmistakable. These new instruments will even be able to distinguish plants that have absorbed unusual ele-ments from the underlying soil. In this way, detailed satellite studies of plants will be indispensable to mineral prospectors.

How do satellite pictures get back to Earth?

Circling around the Earth far out in space are giant cameras which can see details on the ground only 12in (300mm) across. The cameras are fixed to satellites as big as a single-decker bus 50ft (15m) long, and take up half the area of the satellites. Military commanders use these satellites as 'spies in the sky' to check the extent of other countries' arsenals.

But satellite photography has other purposes. Every day, TV weather forecasts show pictures of the Earth photographed by cameras on board satellites. Geologists

Spy in the sky *In 1984 a US satellite took this detailed image of the Nikolaiev shipyard in the Soviet Union, where Russia's first nuclear-powered aircraft carrier was being built. The ship is in two parts – the bow under the gantry cranes, the stern alongside.*

and economists study photographs taken from space that reveal rocks and crops on Earth. And astronomers look at distant stars and galaxies, unhindered by the Earth's atmosphere. But how do these images reach Earth?

The most common way to send photo-graphs from space is to use radio waves and beam the pictures down in the same way that TV pictures are sent. The amount of detail that you can see depends on the spacing between the lines that make up the picture: the more lines, the more detail you can make out.

The world's most advanced commercial satellite for surveying the ground, the French SPOT satellite, transmits 6000 lines per picture – nearly ten times as many as the 625 lines used on most of the world's TV sets. This means that in a picture which covers an area of 40sq miles (100sq km) and taken from a height of 570 miles (920km), details as small as 30ft (10m) across are visible. In a photograph of the whole of Paris, for example, you could pick out the Arc de Triomphe.

Military intelligence experts generally want to be able to make out even finer

detail. When monitoring a war, they need detailed photographs that will enable them to count the number of troops on a battlefield, or reveal different types of aircraft or ship.

The most modern American 'spy satel-lites', the KH-11 series, relay their pictures by television techniques. But, in general, television images cannot show as much detail as a fine-grained 16mm or 35mm film. When film is used, it has to be returned to Earth physically. If the photo-graphs are being taken in manned space-craft, the cosmonauts can bring the film back with them, but this is obviously impossible with unmanned spacecraft. So the Americans and the Russians – and more recently the Chinese – have developed satellites that return a film to Earth automatically.

The American 'Big Bird' satellites have perfected this technique. The exposed film is put into one of six re-entry capsules, which is then jettisoned and drops back into the Earth's atmosphere. As it para-chutes down, the capsule is captured, or lassooed, in a wire loop which trails behind a C-130 Hercules transport plane.

Albert Einstein: 'God does not play dice with the Universe.'

Genius in old age *Einstein lived to be 76, and in old age he showed he was no respecter of persons – especially those who photographed him on his birthdays.*

On August 2, 1939, the physicist Albert Einstein signed what he called 'a letter of conscience' to the President of the United States, Franklin D. Roosevelt. Alarmed by the rise of Nazi Germany – and fearful that Hitler could soon possess the atomic bomb – Einstein renounced his lifelong pacifism.

'Certain aspects of the situation [which has arisen] seem to call for watchfulness and, if necessary, quick action on the part of the Administration,' he, and a group of other scientists, wrote. 'In the course of the last four months it has been made probable . . . to set up a nuclear chain reaction in a large mass of uranium, by which vast amounts of power and large quantities of new radium-like elements would be generated.'

He warned that new and 'extremely powerful' bombs could soon be built by German physicists. 'A single bomb of this type, carried by boat and exploded in a port, might very well destroy the whole port together with some of the surrounding territory,' he stated.

On receiving the letter, Roosevelt immediately set up an Advisory Committee on Uranium. But the decision to make an American atomic bomb was not taken until December 1941, shortly after Japan attacked the US naval base at Pearl Harbor, in Hawaii, bringing America into the Second World War. After his initial warning, Einstein played no further part in the development of the bomb, which was successfully tested in July 1945. The following month atomic bombs were dropped with devastating effect on the Japanese cities of Hiroshima and Nagasaki. The bombings forced Japan to surrender. But when Einstein learned of the mass death and destruction, he put his head in his hands and cried despairingly in Hebrew, *'Oh weh!'*

In 1905 – when he was aged 26 – Einstein published the simple-sounding equation $E=mc^2$ (where E is energy, m is mass, and c is the speed of light), which showed that a small mass can be converted into a huge amount of energy. Among other things, this led to the invention of the atomic bomb: a fact which preyed upon Einstein's conscience for the last two decades of his life.

Einstein in Berlin *In 1916, aged 37, Einstein worked at the Prussian Academy of Sciences in Berlin. In that year, he suggested that gravity was not a direct force but a curved field in space – a theory that was later proved.*

He was born in the industrial city of Ulm, now in West Germany, on March 14, 1879. The following year he and his family moved to Munich, where his father and an uncle opened a small engineering works and electrical plant. Albert's interest in the workings of the physical world began when he was about four, and was ill in bed. His father gave him a magnetic compass to play with, and the youngster was fascinated by the fact that no matter which way he turned the compass, the needle always pointed to the north. He was aged six when his mother introduced him to music and he later became an enthusiastic violinist, with a special love of Mozart. He excelled at mathematics and by the age of 11 was taking physics at university level. He also studied Latin, Greek and French, but was surprisingly weak at French – which later gave rise to the myth that he had been a dunce at school.

In 1895 – when he was 16 – his poor French caused him to fail the entrance exam for the renowned Federal Technical Institute in Zurich. However, as the normal entrance age was 18, he was advised to continue his studies elsewhere and apply again in about a year's time. Armed with a general diploma, he was then given automatic entrance to the Institute, and spent the next four years there studying mathematics and physics.

After a short spell as a mathematics teacher in Zurich, he became a Swiss citizen and in 1902 he was employed by the Swiss Patent Office in Berne, the capital, as a 'Probationary Technical Expert, Third Class'. In 1905, while working there, he published four momentous research papers – including the first part of his revolutionary Theory of Relativity, the Special Theory (see box).

He also mathematically deduced that mass and energy are interchangeable, and expressed this in his equation: $E=mc^2$. As well as paving the way for the atom bomb, this theory unlocked the secret of how the Sun shines. Both processes are nuclear reactions, in which a minute amount of nuclear mass is liberated as light and heat (energy). In 1909 Einstein resigned from the Patent Office and spent the next few years teaching theoretical physics at universities in Berne, Zurich, Prague, and finally in 1914, Berlin. Two years later, midway through the First World War, he published the second part of his Theory of Relativity: the General Theory.

In 1921, Einstein was awarded the Nobel prize for Physics – chiefly for his work on the photoelectric effect, which showed that light travels not in a continuous flow, but in separate 'wave packets' called photons.

His Theory of Relativity had proved too controversial for the Nobel prize committee, and he determined to popularise his work. He spent the next few years touring the world and, as he put it, 'whistling my relativity tune'. He made headlines with his saying, 'God does not play dice with the Universe' – a fanciful way of stating that there are patterns in the Universe, if only we could discover them.

In 1933, while he was in the USA, Hitler came to power in Germany. The Führer did not believe that a 'mere Jew' could have constructed the Theory of Relativity. He even claimed that Einstein had stolen the idea from some papers found on the body of a German officer who had been killed in the First World War. The Nazis also detested Einstein for his much-publicised support of Zionism, which sought to establish a self-governing Jewish state in Palestine.

In Einstein's absence, storm troopers burned his books, ransacked his riverside home near Berlin (where he indulged his love of sailing), and seized his bank account and the contents of his wife Elsa's safe-deposit box.

Later that year Einstein decided to settle in the United States. He became an American citizen in 1941, and 11 years later he refused the Presidency of Israel, declaring that he was 'too naive' to be a politician. He died in Princeton, New Jersey, in April 1955, and to the end he abhorred the terrifying means of annihilation which the nuclear physicists had set loose on the world.

'If I had known that my theories would lead to such destruction,' he once stated, 'I would rather have been a watchmaker.'

EINSTEIN'S PARADOXES OF TIME AND SPACE

Even in his teens, Albert Einstein had been curious about the speed at which light travels. 'What would the world look like if I rode on a beam of light?' he wrote.

In his Special Theory of Relativity, he maintained that all motion in the Universe was relative because far out in space there is nothing to measure it against. He also maintained that the speed of light – about 186,000 miles (300,000km) per second – is always the same relative to an observer, regardless of the observer's motion. He was saying that light from a star ahead of the Earth's line of travel would reach Earth at the same time as light from a star behind, even though the Earth was travelling towards one star and away from the other at 18,000mph (29,000km/h).

He concluded that the speed of light was the only constant physical property in the Universe. And if it was always the same, regardless of the movement of the observer, other physical properties must be different for people travelling in different directions and at different speeds.

He calculated that time would pass more slowly in a space ship travelling at near the speed of light, compared to the time as measured by a person who was stationary in relation to the craft. The space ship would also appear shorter to the stationary person. And it would increase in mass. At the speed of light, its mass would be infinite, so no object could reach that speed because to do so would require an infinite force. The Special Theory leads to the 'paradox of the twins'. If one twin travels in space at close to the speed of light, he will not feel any different from his twin on Earth. However, time aboard the spacecraft will pass about half as quickly as it does on Earth. So, if the astronaut is away from Earth for, say, ten years, he will return only five years older – while his twin will have aged ten years.

Einstein's time theory was proved in July 1977, when extremely accurate atomic clocks were placed aboard a United States satellite and sent into orbit. On their return, the clocks were com-pared with a similar clock at the Naval Research Laboratory in Washington, DC – and it was seen that the satellite's clocks had slowed down by a tiny amount. Time had therefore passed more slowly aboard the satellite.

Einstein's formula $E=mc^2$ means that the mass of an object can actually be converted into energy. He arrived at the equation from his statement that the mass of an object increases with its speed. It follows that its energy must also increase – as a heavier object has more energy than a lighter object travelling at the same speed. The extra energy equals the increase in mass multiplied by the square of the speed of light.

In his General Theory, he maintained that a beam of light would be bent by gravity as it passed a star. The gravitational field of the star would cause the light beam to curve inwards – and in a sense cause space itself to be curved. So the shortest distance between two points was a curved line.

In 1919, Einstein became famous when the theory was verified by a British team of astronomers who photographed a total eclipse of the Sun – when it is possible to take pictures of stars shining near the Sun. The photographs were compared with photographs of the same stars when the Sun was not near them. The different positions of the stars on the two photographs showed how the starlight was deflected by the Sun.

Lecture notes *These calculations were written on a blackboard by Einstein during a lecture at Oxford University when he was a visiting professor in 1931. Two years later he renounced his German citizenship when Hitler became Chancellor, and left Germany for the USA.*

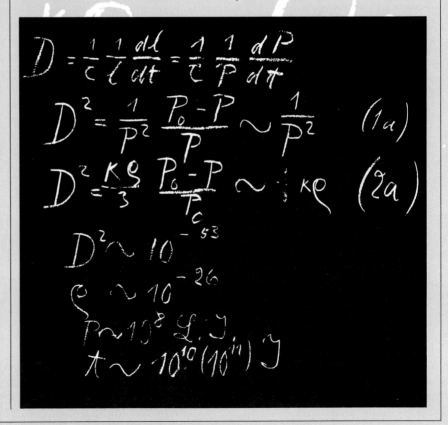

Running a tape measure over the Universe

Seeing into the great void *The Andromeda Galaxy, a spiral galaxy like our own Milky Way, can be seen with the naked eye as a faint patch in the sky, yet it is 2.2 million light years away. This distance is about one twenty-thousandth the diameter of the visible Universe.*

If you look at the night sky during the last few months of the year in the Northern Hemisphere, you can spot a dim patch of light in the constellation Andromeda. This faint blur is, in fact, a giant collection of stars, the Andromeda Galaxy. It is the most distant object you can see with the unaided eye. Its light takes 2.2 million years to reach you.

Scientists express distances in space in terms of the fastest thing in the Universe – the speed of light. A beam of light travels at 5878 million million miles (9460 million million km) in a year. So we can describe a distance as the time it takes light from a star or some other body in space to reach us. This distance is expressed in light years.

It may seem impossible that anyone could measure distances as vast as this. But for astronomers, finding the distances to stars, and even galaxies a thousand times farther away than Andromeda, is now a routine process.

The Moon

The Moon is the nearest object to Earth in the Universe – an average of 238,900 miles (384,400km) away. Its distance varies slightly because it follows an egg-shaped (elliptical) orbit around the Earth.

When the Apollo astronauts visited the Moon, from 1969 to 1972, they left behind small 'retro-reflectors', rather like the reflectors on the back of a car. Astronomers on Earth shoot a powerful pulse of laser light at these retro-reflectors, and about two and a half seconds later their telescopes pick up a faint flash as the pulse of light returns to Earth. They then multiply the time it takes for the pulse to leave Earth and return, by the speed of light, and divide the result by two to arrive at the Moon's distance from Earth.

The measurements of the Moon's distance are accurate to within a couple of inches. By monitoring them constantly, scientists discovered that the Moon is now about a foot farther away from the Earth than it was when the Apollo astronauts went there.

The Moon and the Earth are drawing apart because the friction between the Earth's ocean floor and the water heaped up in the tides is gradually slowing its rotation. This is making it lose energy. In return, the bulges of the Earth's ocean tides pull the Moon forward in its orbit, making it gain energy. The Moon is therefore gradually moving away from the Earth as it is pulled into a larger orbit.

The planets

When it comes to the planets in the Solar System, astronomers do not have reflectors to return pulses of light. Instead, they use radar. Before radar was available they used the speed of light and the parallax method

(see right) to calculate the distance of planets. Today, however, they send a pulse of radio waves towards a planet, and wait for the faint echo to return after the waves have bounced off the planet's rocky surface. Radio waves travel at the speed of light, so the calculation is the same as for measuring the distance to the Moon.

Radio astronomers have picked up radar reflections from all the planets with rocky surfaces – Mercury, Venus and Mars – and even from the rings of Saturn, which are made of billions of tiny lumps of ice. They cannot detect a radar echo from Saturn itself, or Jupiter, because both consist of gases and do not reflect radar.

The Sun

Radar cannot be used to work out the distance of the Sun because it is not solid. Instead, astronomers base their calculations on the law of planetary motion. This is the third law discovered by the astronomer Johannes Kepler (1571-1630) in 1618. It states that the square of the time it takes for a planet to complete a journey around the Sun (the orbital period) is equal to the cube of the planet's mean distance from the Sun.

Using Kepler's law, astronomers could calculate the average distance of the Earth from the Sun. This value is now known to be 92,955,630 miles (149,597,870km). The Earth-Sun distance is defined as one unit, called an astronomical unit, or AU. Astronomers use this unit to calculate how far the other planets are from the Sun. First they must find the distance from the Earth to the planet. To do so they can use either parallax or radar.

Using radar, it is possible to tell, for example, that the distance of Venus from Earth, when the two are at their closest, is 26 million miles (42 million km). But astronomers also know that it takes Venus 224.7 days (or .615 of a year) to orbit the Sun. According to Kepler's law, then, Venus's distance from the Sun is .72AU (since .615 of a year equals .72AU cubed).

The near stars

The stars lie millions of times farther away than the Sun, so astronomers have to use different techniques to establish their distance. The most important is the method of parallax, which involves measuring the angle of the movement of a star between two points, and relating it to the Earth's orbit.

A simple experiment illustrates the method. Hold a finger in front of your face; close one eye and notice where the finger is in relation to the background. Now close that eye and open the other. The finger seems to have moved. The nearer the finger is to your face, the greater the distance it seems to move.

In astronomy, the finger is the nearby

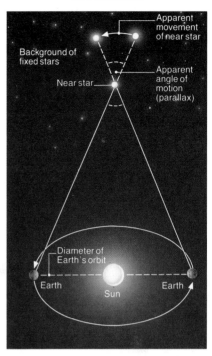

Since astronomers cannot use radar to work out the distance of a star, they use the parallax method. Photographs are taken of the sky from the same position on Earth all through the year, and these reveal that some stars remain 'fixed', whereas others seem to 'move'. Those stars that show visible movement are closer to the Earth than those which do not. To find the distance of a star which 'moves', astronomers look at two photographs taken six months apart, from the same observatory. (It takes six months for the Earth to reach the far points in its orbit.) Using the diameter of the Earth's orbit as a baseline, two lines are drawn from each end of the baseline to the star, one to each shifted position. Where the two lines intersect, they form the apparent angle of motion, which is measured in arc seconds. Knowing the diameter of the Earth's orbit and the size of the angle of motion, astronomers can calculate the distance to the star using trigonometry.

star whose distance is being measured. Astronomers observe its position relative to very distant stars, looking at it from two different positions in the Earth's orbit. By measuring the angle of the star's apparent movement between these two positions, also known as the parallax angle, and knowing the diameter of the Earth's orbit, astronomers can calculate the distance.

The parallax angle is measured in arc seconds. One arc second is 1/3600 of a degree in the sky, or roughly 1/2000 the apparent size of the Moon. The distance to a star, in light years, is 3.26 divided by the parallax angle. The result is given in parsecs, which is a unit of distance that corresponds to a parallax of one second of arc, or 3.26 light years. Using this method, astronomers have found the distance to hundreds of the nearest stars. For example, the nearest star to the Sun is a faint one called Proxima Centauri, which lies 4.22 light years away, or 1.2 parsecs. The brightest star in the sky, Sirius, is 8.6 light years away, or 2.64 parsecs.

Distant stars

For stars more distant than 300 light years, astronomers need a different technique. One method involves finding out the direction a star is moving in, and its actual speed.

To establish the direction, it is much easier to work with a cluster of stars than with a single star. Many stars belong to clusters that consist of hundreds, or even thousands, of stars moving through space. Perspective makes the stars in each cluster appear to converge. The angle of their converging lines reveals the direction the cluster is heading in space – towards Earth, away from Earth, at a 45 degree angle, and so on.

A star's speed can be deduced from its light. The star's motion towards or away from Earth changes the wavelengths of the light that it emits – so that it becomes blue if it is coming towards Earth and red if it is moving away (a phenomenon called the Doppler effect).

By combining the rate of change in the star's spectrum with the direction of movement of the cluster, astronomers can work out its real speed through space, and hence calculate the distance to the cluster.

The farthest stars in the galaxy

To establish the distance of stars that are even farther away, astronomers use the star's temperature and brightness. They can measure a star's temperature surprisingly easily: a bluish star is hot, around 20,000°C; a white or yellow star has a medium temperature; and orange or red stars are cool – about 3000°C.

The hotter a star, the brighter it is. A star with a temperature of 10,000°C, for example, is 40 times brighter than the Sun (which has a temperature of 5500°C). So, if a star of 10,000°C is found which appears very dim, then it must be a long way off in space, its brightness diminished by its great distance. Before astronomers can use this relatively simple method they need to know the relationship between brightness and temperature, and distance from Earth. This is why they first use methods such as parallax, on nearby stars. After measuring the brightness of those stars they can then use what they know as a guide to ascertain the relative brightness of more distant stars.

The measurement of star brightness allows astronomers to measure distances to any star in the Milky Way, some lying as much as 100,000 light years away.

Near galaxies

A particularly bright kind of star acts as a beacon for measuring the distance to the near galaxies. These stars are called 'Cepheid variables', which change in brightness in a regular way.

Astronomers can measure the time it takes a Cepheid to 'flash' from maximum brightness, down to minimum, and back to maximum. This time is called its period. Brighter Cepheids 'flash' more slowly than fainter ones, so once a Cepheid's period has been established, its brightness can be deduced. If a Cepheid is found with a period of two weeks, for example, astronomers can say that it is 4000 times brighter than the Sun. By investigating the apparent dimness of Cepheids in distant galaxies they can tell how far away the galaxies lie.

The outer reaches of the Universe

In the 1920s the American astronomer Edwin Hubble made an astounding discovery about galaxies: they are all moving away from the Earth at speeds that depend on their distances – the farther away they are, the faster they are receding. This is known as 'Hubble's law', and it occurs because the Universe itself is expanding, which means that all the galaxies are rushing apart from one another.

It is quite easy to measure a galaxy's speed, by looking at its light and seeing how the wavelengths change according to the Doppler effect. Hubble's law tells astronomers how to calculate the distance from the speed. So if a distant galaxy is found to be receding at, say, 2 million miles per hour, by multiplying Hubble's Constant (about 20, when calculating in mph and light years) by the galaxy's speed in miles per hour, they can work out that it is 40 million light years away. In this way, astronomers have measured distances to galaxies that lie a staggering 12,000 million light years away.

Giant mirror to explore the heavens

In a workshop in Tucson, Arizona, a huge oven spins round and round, once every seven seconds. Inside it, the temperature is 2138°F (1170°C).

In this intense heat, molten glass flows in a circular honeycomb mould to form a

disc, more than 11ft (3.5m) across, with a slightly concave surface. After months of cooling, shaping and polishing, this disc will become the mirror at the heart of one of the world's largest telescopes.

To produce a well-focused image of a star or planet, telescope mirrors must be exactly the right shape – and stay that shape. A major problem is the change in temperature during the night. All the materials in common use, including ordinary glass, expand or contract as the temperature changes. Because a telescope mirror is thinner in the centre, this part cools quicker, and contracts more, than the outer part. This distorts the mirror's shape and also the image it reflects.

Until well into this century, telescope mirrors were made from ordinary glass. But astronomers were demanding increasingly larger mirrors, which meant a greater degree of distortion. They were saved by the invention of Pyrex glass, which expands and contracts only a third as much as ordinary glass. It enabled them, in 1948, to complete the largest telescope at that time: it has a 200in (5m) mirror made of Pyrex, and is sited on Palomar Mountain in southern California.

Today, most telescope mirrors are made of a glass-ceramic mixture, which hardly expands at all. The surface is coated with a layer of reflective aluminium.

When making an ordinary telescope mirror, a mirror-maker melts the raw glass-ceramic material in a shallow circular mould which is the correct diameter for the

An eye opens on the universe *The William Herschel telescope on La Palma, in the Canaries, is one of the world's biggest telescopes. With its 164in (4.2m) mirror it could detect a single candle burning 100,000 miles (160,000km) away, or quasars millions of light years away.*

telescope. Once it has melted into shape, the mirror 'blank' is cooled extremely slowly, over several weeks or months. This ensures that no strains form in the blank which may distort the mirror later. The blank is then ground to shape in a process which is monitored by a computer that gauges the correct shallow curve.

The mirror's face is then coated with its reflective surface. To do this, the whole mirror is put into a vacuum chamber, a heater vaporises a coil of aluminium wire, and the metal condenses in a thin layer on the front of the mirror.

These techniques have been satisfactory for telescopes built so far. But designers are now planning much larger telescopes, and the mirrors would be extremely heavy if made in the traditional way. This means that the rest of the telescope would have to be scaled up too, making the engineering more difficult and the whole project much more expensive. For example, the mirror of a 315in (8m) telescope made to the same pattern as the Palomar 200in would weigh four times as much.

The team at Tucson have created their revolving furnace with large but light-weight mirrors in mind. Before the glass chunks are added to the mould, hexagonal cement blocks are placed inside it. When the glass melts, it flows between the blocks to form a network of thin walls, very like the wax structure of a honeycomb. The resulting glass structure consists of hexagonal 'cells' closed off at the top and bottom with a plate of glass. The lower plate is perforated, so that when the whole assembly has cooled, the mirror-makers can wash out the brittle cement (the 'honey') with water jets to leave an empty glass honeycomb. This honeycomb mirror is only a quarter as heavy as a solid mirror of the same size.

But how can a honeycomb structure be ground to make it curved? It isn't. If you spin a bucket of liquid fast on a vertical axis, the liquid will be forced outwards and up the sides of the containers. As a result, the surface becomes concave.

Multiple-mirror telescopes

Astronomers building the 396in (10m) Keck Telescope, due to be sited on a mountain in Hawaii, believe that it is too difficult to make a single mirror that size. Instead, they are making a large reflective surface consisting of 36 smaller six-sided mirrors which will fit together like bathroom tiles to make the complete surface.

To ensure that the surface remains the correct shape, the builders are mounting the individual mirrors on a complicated framework. Between the mirror segments are 168 sensors, which can tell when adjacent parts of the mirror move out of line – when the telescope is tilted, for example. Nine computers check the signals

---

In the 17th century, the English physicist Sir Isaac Newton recognised that there were problems with the traditional refracting telescope, which used glass lenses to focus light from a star.

The lenses produced a fringe of false colours around the star. This happened because when a beam of light coming through glass is bent, its waves, being of different lengths, are bent at different angles. Blue light, for example, which has short waves, is bent (or refracted) more sharply than red light, which has longer waves.

So Newton designed a reflecting telescope which collected and focused light by means of two mirrors. (These mirrors were made from an alloy of tin and copper, known as speculum metal.) The front of the mirror which collected the light was curved, rather like a shaving mirror. As a result, it could focus light just like a lens.

Large modern telescopes all use mirrors to collect light, although they have grown in size from Newton's 1in (25mm) mirror to a Soviet monster 236in (6m) in diameter.

---

from these sensors and send commands to 108 precision screws attached to the rear of the segments. The screws turn in response to the command to realign the mirror sequence.

Another approach is being taken by European astronomers embarking on the world's biggest telescope, the Very Large Telescope. To be sited in Chile, for the best views of the southern skies, it will consist of four adjacent telescopes, each with a mirror 315in (8m) in diameter. Small mirrors will take the light from the four telescopes to the same focus, so that they work together as a single eye. When complete, in the mid-1990s, the Very Large Telescope will be ten times more powerful than any telescope that exists today.

How do astronomers count the stars?

Glance at the sky on a clear night, and it looks as though you can see millions of stars. In fact, your eye shows you no more than about 6000 stars in all. By taking photographs with large telescopes, however, astronomers can now literally count stars by the million.

Astronomers do not just count the stars – they also want to know exactly where each star lies in the sky so that they can record it in a star catalogue. Even before the telescope was invented, in about 1600, astronomers had measured the positions of all the stars that the eye can see, using simple sights like those on a rifle.

A telescope not only magnifies what you see in the sky, it also collects more light than the unaided eye can, and so shows up many more, much fainter, stars. Even a pair of low-powered binoculars will show you ten times as many stars as you can see with the naked eye.

In the 1860s, the Prussian astronomer Friedrich Argelander measured the positions of all the stars he could see from Bonn, with a telescope that had a lens 3in (75mm) across. The final catalogue he produced contained some 458,000 stars. Astronomers in Argentina later measured stars too far south to be seen from Germany, and extended the total by almost three times as much, to 1,072,000 stars.

The largest telescopes in the world today can reveal a thousand fainter stars for every one that appears in these catalogues. Instead of counting them by looking through a telescope, astronomers take long-exposure photographs through telescopes and measure the positions of the stars on the photographic plates.

Even so, it is not an easy task. A single photograph of this kind is crammed with more than a million images. It would take months for an astronomer to measure all the stars on just one photograph.

Here lasers and computers can help to speed up the process considerably. The British astronomer Edward Kibblewhite has built an automated photographic measuring system at Cambridge which measures a photograph in one hour.

Kibblewhite's machine focuses a helium-neon laser beam onto the plate, narrowing it down to a very small spot which scans back and forth across the plate.

Because the plate is a photographic negative, a star appears on it as a dark spot against a bright background. As the laser beam passes through the dark image of a star, its brightness is dimmed. The computer keeps track of the laser's changing brightness to record the exact position of each star and its brightness. All this information is stored on magnetic tape. By the mid-1990s, when the machine has analysed photographs of the whole sky, it will have accumulated information on more than a thousand million stars.

How the Universe began – and how it is likely to end

Fifteen thousand million years ago the Universe suddenly came into existence in a tremendous explosion – the Big Bang. The gases rushing outwards from this explosion eventually turned into galaxies, stars and planets, including the Sun and the planet Earth. But how can astronomers confidently calculate the time at which all this happened?

In the 1920s, the American astronomer Edwin Hubble discovered that galaxies are rushing away from each other and that the more distant galaxies are moving away faster than the near ones, as if they were the shrapnel from a gigantic cosmic explosion. By dividing the galaxies' distances by their speeds, Hubble could calculate when this explosion took place. The answer (using the most modern and accurate observations) is 15,000 million years ago.

To check on this result, astronomers have measured the ages of clusters of stars. Stars change in colour and size as they get older, turning into red giants and then into white dwarfs. Stars of different masses (weights) change at different rates, so even though all the stars in a particular cluster were born at the same time, some have 'aged' faster than others.

Within each cluster, astronomers look for the most massive ordinary stars that are about to turn into red giants. They know, in theory, how long a star lives before becoming a red giant: for example the Sun will live for 10,000 million years, whereas a star 20 times heavier will turn into a red giant after only 20 million years. From the mass of stars about to become red giants, astronomers can calculate the age of the whole cluster.

Some star clusters are quite young on the cosmic scale – around 70 million years old. (The Sun, for comparison, is around 5000 million years old.) Many are very much older, in particular the globular clusters. This type of cluster is a giant swarm of about a million stars. Astronomers have found that the stars in these clusters are very old – around 12,000 million to 14,000 million years old. They were probably the first stars to form from the gases of a Big Bang, and suggest that it occurred about 15,000 million years ago.

There is a final, and extremely persuasive, piece of evidence that there was a Big Bang, even though it does not reveal when it occurred. Radio telescopes can pick up a faint background noise that permeates the entire Universe. The most likely explanation is that this is caused by electromagnetic waves which emanated from the hot gases of the Big Bang and are still pulsating through the Universe.

Although astronomers agree on the birth of the Universe, they do not yet agree on the way in which it will end. There are two possibilities. The momentum from the Big Bang may be sufficient to keep the galaxies moving apart for ever. The stars in each galaxy will reach the end of their lives, as black holes or dark solid objects called black dwarfs or neutron stars. Eventually, about a million million years in the future, the Universe will just die.

On the other hand, the pull of gravity between the galaxies may slow down the impetus of the Big Bang and start to draw the galaxies together again. The Universe will then begin to contract. This theory is less popular at the moment, but some astronomers have calculated the consequences if it is true. In around a hundred thousand million years' time, the galaxies will rush together to a single point, in the Big Crunch. What happens after that is even less certain. The concentration of matter may explode again, as another Big Bang, giving birth to another Universe.

Searching for the edge of the Universe

Astronomers from Europe are at the moment considering building a telescope ten times more powerful than any that exists – the Very Large Telescope. With it, they hope to look farther into the Universe than ever before. Even so, no one really expects to see to the edge of the Universe.

Modern studies of the Universe are based on Einstein's General Theory of Relativity. This theory states that matter has a gravitational field which distorts space and time so that space becomes curved and time runs fast or slow. The gravity of matter also bends light.

In testing the effects of the General Theory, scientists have found that it accounts for the motion of planets circling the Sun and stars orbiting other stars.

Accepting that the theory can be applied to the Universe as a whole, cosmologists also accept one final prediction of Einstein's theory – that the Universe has no edge. The theory in fact says that there are two possibilities for the Universe. One is that it curves round on itself, like the surface of a planet. Although it has no edge, it is finite. A space traveller setting off in one direction and never changing course would eventually arrive at his starting point. This is a 'closed' Universe.

The other possibility is that the Universe is infinite, that space goes on for ever in all directions. In this 'open' Universe, however far you travelled you would always come across new regions of space.

Whichever possibility is correct depends on the amount of matter in the Universe. If there is enough matter, its gravity will bend space around so that the Universe is closed. In this case, the gravity is strong enough eventually to halt the expansion of the Universe, and draw galaxies together into a Big Crunch.

The most recent estimates of the amount of matter indicate that there is not enough matter to 'close' the Universe. The Universe is thus likely to be infinite in size, with no end. This also means that the Universe will keep on expanding for ever.

Seeing the invisible – a black hole

When a massive star dies, it may leave behind the darkest and most destructive thing in the Universe – a black hole. This object emits no light, or any other radiation, so it cannot be seen with any kind of telescope. Yet astronomers are confident that they have discovered at least half-a-dozen black holes.

A black hole is the collapsed remains of an old star. Some of the matter that previously made up the star becomes compressed under its own gravity into a tiny volume, smaller than the nucleus of a single atom, called a singularity. Because this material is so compressed, its gravity is immensely strong. In the immediate area around the singularity, its gravity is absolutely irresistible. This region, a few miles across, is the black hole.

Once something approaches too close to a black hole, it is drawn inwards inexorably to be crushed into the singularity. No force can prevent this, and even light cannot escape.

If black holes cannot be seen, how do we know they exist? One method relies on detecting their effect on nearby stars. Most stars do not exist alone; they have a companion star (the Sun is among the minority) and the two stars orbit each other. If one star dies and collapses, the resulting black hole and its companion star continue to orbit each other.

As the companion star gets older, it swells to become a giant or super-giant star, hundreds of times bigger than the Sun. The

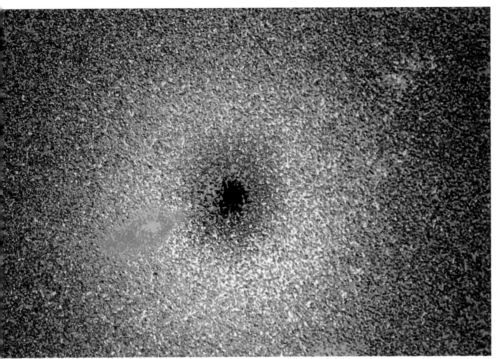

Virgo's little black heart *The Virgo cluster of galaxies contains the radio galaxy M87. The stars around the centre of the galaxy are so tightly packed and moving so fast into the centre that it is thought to contain a massive black hole. The blue jet streaming from the galaxy's black core is a beam of electrons resulting from the energy produced by the black hole. This photograph has been given colour values to indicate the increased packing of stars towards the core.*

outer parts of this swollen star draw uncomfortably near the black hole, which begins to tear off the outer gases. This gas ultimately ends up inside the black hole, but it does not fall straight in: the gas first swirls around the upper surface, like water going down a plug hole. In the process, it becomes extremely hot, with its temperature rising to a thousand million degrees centigrade. Gas at this temperature produces copious amounts of X-rays.

So astronomers who are looking for black holes first scan the sky with X-ray telescopes to detect X-rays coming from the depths of space. They then use ordinary telescopes to examine the X-ray sources in more detail.

In 1971, the American X-ray satellite Uhuru managed to pin down the position of a powerful X-ray source in the constellation Cygnus. Astronomers then found that the source, Cygnus X-1, was a star called HDE 226868, which lies 6000 light years away from Earth. But an ordinary star like this does not produce X-rays. When the astronomers investigated HDE 226868 with ordinary telescopes, they found it orbited an invisible companion every six days. The X-rays had to be coming from gas that was spiralling down towards the invisible companion.

The companion was immediately suspected of being a black hole. However, astronomers first had to investigate the possibility that it was a very small and dense kind of star called a neutron star. This type is so faint that it cannot be seen when it is close to a star like HDE 226868.

One way of eliminating the possibility of a neutron star is to test its weight (see box). Astronomers weigh in terms of the Sun. They found that Cygnus X-1 weighed as much as ten Suns, which is too heavy for a neutron star. If a neutron star gets heavier than three Suns, it collapses to become a black hole. The conclusion, then, is that Cygnus X-1 must be a black hole.

The return of the serpent from outer space

On October 16, 1982, astronomers in California swung the world's most powerful telescope to focus on a particular point in the constellation Canis Minor. They were on the track of something that had not been seen for more than 70 years and which was due for another visit to the inner Solar System – Halley's Comet. As the astronomers watched the television screen which relayed the view through the great Palomar telescope, they suddenly saw the tiny spot of light they were looking for. Halley's Comet was on its predicted path.

Sightings of the comet have been recorded since 240 BC, after which there have been 29 appearances. It is named after Edmond Halley, a British scientist in the 17th century who established that comets have orbits which can be calculated. He saw the comet in 1682 and predicted that it would return in 1758. The vision of comets in the past has given rise to a multitude of fears. They were believed to be horrific visitors to Earth, bloodthirsty serpents sent to devour human beings, and messengers of sickness.

A comet's appearance depends on the fact that comets move around the Sun, in orbits that are governed by gravity. While

---

HOW ASTRONOMERS WEIGH STARS

The stars in any double-star system, such as Cygnus X-1 and HDE 226868, swing around their common centre of gravity. If the stars are equally massive, their centre of gravity lies halfway between them. If not, it lies closer to the heavier star. So a double-star system forms a natural balance which allows astronomers to 'weigh' stars. By studying the motion of the star HDE 226868, astronomers found that the centre of gravity lay so close to the star that it suggested its companion must be half the weight, or mass, of the star itself.

HDE 226868 is a type of star called a blue super giant. It is 20 million miles (32 million km) across and shines 50,000 times more brilliantly than the Sun. A blue super giant is about 20 times heavier than the Sun. That is, it has 20 times the mass of the Sun. So if its invisible companion, the black hole Cygnus X-1, is half this weight, it must weigh as much as ten Suns.

The Sun itself weighs as much as 300,000 Earths, or 1989 million million million million million tons. Astronomers calculate this figure by using the theory of gravity. Careful experiments in the laboratory have revealed the gravitational pull between two large lead spheres of known masses. This force depends partly on the masses of the spheres and partly on the distance between them. This experiment can be 'scaled up' so that the distance between the spheres becomes the distance of the Earth from the Sun. It can then be deduced how massive the Sun must be in order to exert the gravitational pull needed to keep the Earth and the other planets in orbit around it.

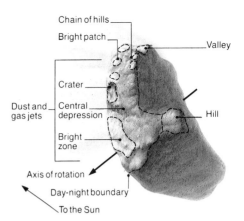

Chain of hills
Bright patch
Valley
Crater
Dust and gas jets
Central depression
Hill
Bright zone
Axis of rotation
Day-night boundary
To the Sun

The comet's core *The nucleus of Halley's Comet is shaped like a peanut 10 × 5 × 5 miles (16 × 8 × 8km) in size. It is hilly, pitted and spurts out jets of gas and dust.*

Close-up of a comet *Braving a fierce dust storm which threatened to tear it apart, the space-probe Giotto passed within a few hundred miles of Halley's Comet and photographed the nucleus itself. The nucleus is composed of ice, rocks and stones, and an unknown heat-resistant organic compound. Most of the surface is covered with a thick dark crust of unknown composition. The whole comet has been referred to as a 'dirty snowball'. The comet came within 94 million miles (150 million km) of the Earth on March 15, 1986 (inset). It was most clearly visible in Australia, where this photograph was taken.*

the orbit of a planet around the Sun is fairly circular, comets follow an elongated path. When Halley's Comet is at the far end of its orbit, it is 35 times farther away from the Sun than the Earth is. It is then invisible, even to the world's largest telescope. But at its closest to the Sun, the comet passes within the Earth's orbit. As the Sun heats it up, and the icy core is surrounded by a huge cloud of gas and dust, it can become – for a few months – a brilliant sight in our skies.

Just as the Earth goes around its orbit once in a year, so Halley's Comet has an orbital period of 76 years. You would therefore expect to see the comet reappear at regular intervals, tracing the same path around the Sun. This would be the case if the comet felt the gravitational influence of the Sun alone. However, comets are also tugged by the planets of the Solar System, especially by massive Jupiter and Saturn. If a planet is roughly in front of a comet, its gravity will pull the comet forward and speed it up. If the comet is moving away from a planet, the planet's gravity will tend to pull the comet back and so reduce its speed.

The fastest orbit of Halley's Comet was only 74.5 years. After passing the Sun in

November 1835, the planets hastened its motion so that it returned in April 1910. But observations of its orbit between AD 451 and 530, recorded by Chinese and Japanese astronomers, show that it took 79 years to complete one orbit, which suggests that the planets slowed it down.

Because astronomers know the positions and the gravitational pull of each planet, they can calculate the precise effect that the planets will have on comets. But the calculations are very long and tedious. When three French mathematicians predicted the return of Halley's Comet in 1759, they had to calculate it by hand, using long division and multiplication. It took them six months to complete the work. Now the whole thing can be done by a computer in just a few minutes.

In the 1970s, Donald Yeomans, of the Jet Propulsion Laboratory in California, began to collect all the observations that have ever been made of Halley's Comet. These told him how the comet had moved, up to the time that the most recent photograph was taken, on June 15, 1911. He then used a computer to calculate the effects of all the planets on the comet, from 1911 to the mid-1980s. It was his prediction that proved so astoundingly accurate when the astronom-

ers at Palomar picked up the comet in their telescope in 1982. Halley's Comet eventually passed the Sun within a few hours of the time that Yeomans had predicted – after having spent seven decades out of sight.

How astronomers discover unknown planets

Five of the planets in the Solar System – Mercury, Venus, Mars, Jupiter and Saturn – are so bright that astronomers have known about them for thousands of years. But in the past couple of centuries, astronomers have found three more distant and fainter planets: Uranus, Neptune and Pluto. There are also indications of a tenth planet beyond Pluto. The discovery of these and new planets requires both mathematical calculations and luck.

Until 1781, no one suspected that there were planets beyond Saturn, so no one was actually looking for them. Then on March 13, the amateur astronomer William Herschel found Uranus, while looking for pairs of stars. He knew it was not a star because it had a visible disc, just like the Moon shows when it is full. As astronomers tracked its motions, they decided it had to be a planet.

After this largely accidental discovery, astronomers began to wonder if there might be another planet, even farther out. This suspicion was reinforced when they discovered that Uranus did not orbit the Sun at a constant rate. It seemed that the planet was feeling the gravitational pull of a more distant – and unknown – planet.

Two brilliant mathematicians – John Couch Adams, in Cambridge, and Urbain Leverrier, in France – calculated independently where this new planet would be. On August 31, 1846, Leverrier sent his predictions to the Berlin Observatory and the astronomers there identified a 'star' as the new planet, now called Neptune.

By the end of the last century, it was suspected that both Uranus and Neptune were being pulled by the gravity of a planet farther out still. This time it was an American astronomer, Percival Lowell, who calculated where this 'Planet X' should be. In 1930, Clyde Tombaugh, working at the observatory founded by Lowell, detected a faint speck of light that moved from night to night. It was indeed a new planet, close to Lowell's calculated position, but much fainter than Lowell had predicted. This planet was called Pluto.

But many astronomers believe that Pluto is too small to affect the giant planets Uranus and Neptune. In 1978, astronomers at the US Naval Observatory found a moon orbiting Pluto. The motion of this moon revealed Pluto's gravity, and it is far too weak to pull on Uranus and Neptune.

Is there a Planet 10?

So it was only pure luck that Lowell's calculations on the motions of Uranus and Neptune had led to the discovery of Pluto! Astronomers are now asking what else could be pulling on Uranus and Neptune. The answer seems to be a massive planet lying much farther out in the Solar System.

Bob Harrington, of the US Naval Observatory, has calculated that this planet is currently in the southern part of the sky, where few people have looked for planets so far. Every few weeks, a telescope in New Zealand takes photographs of Harrington's suspect part of the sky.

Harrington has allies in his research that no previous planet-hunter could call on – space probes. If Planet 10 is pulling on Uranus and Neptune, it should also disturb the paths of the three spacecraft – Pioneer 10, Pioneer 11 and Voyager 1 – that are currently leaving the Solar System. Scientists are measuring their motions carefully, to see if Planet 10 is pulling them off-course. So far, the results are negative.

Other astronomers are not convinced by the calculations made so far. They believe that Planet 10 could be anywhere in the sky, and so they are taking a different approach. Planets produce copious amounts of infrared radiation. In 1983, the Infrared Astronomical Satellite scanned the whole sky, looking for objects in the Universe that produce infrared radiation. If Planet 10 exists, then the satellite will probably have picked it up. The results from this survey were recorded on 60 miles (100km) of computer tape, and astronomers are wading through this vast amount of data. They have found many interesting objects – comets, asteroids, new-born stars and dust-filled galaxies – but Planet 10 has still to come to light.

Searching for life in space

Throughout history, many people have believed there is intelligent life on other worlds in space. Until recently, some scientists thought that the 'canals' on Mars, first mapped in 1877, were the work of intelligent beings. It was not until 1965, when the first photographs of Mars were taken by spacecraft, that they recognised them to be the result of wishful thinking. Mars is just another lifeless planet.

Astronomers today know that there is no life in the rest of the Solar System, but many think that if conditions were right for advanced life to evolve on Earth, the same thing should have occurred on millions of other planets with similar conditions, throughout the Universe.

How might we on Earth make contact with other beings who may live somewhere in the vastness of space? In fact, several messages from Earth are now on their way to any creatures who may be 'out there'.

In 1972 and 1973, the Americans launched two space probes, Pioneer 10 and Pioneer 11, which were programmed to fly past Jupiter (and Saturn, in the case of Pioneer 11) and take photographs. They will continue their journey beyond the Solar System, heading out towards the stars. Each Pioneer has a 'visiting card' from mankind fixed to its side, in case it is eventually found by an alien civilisation.

The messages consist of a gold plaque, 6×9in (150×230mm) in size. Engraved on the plaque is a map showing the location of the Solar System, relative to nearby pulsars. (These are natural radio beacons which future space travellers could use as cosmic lighthouses.) There is also a line drawing of the spacecraft, and of a man and a woman. The man has his hand raised in greeting.

Five years later, American scientists launched two more spacecraft that will eventually leave the Solar System – Voyager 1 and Voyager 2. Instead of a plaque, each craft carries a long-playing record, complete with stylus and symbols indicating how the record is played. This 'Sounds of Earth' LP includes music, which ranges from Bach to Chuck Berry, greetings in dozens of languages, and whale song. Some of the tracks are pictures coded in sound waves, showing images of the Earth which range from a beautiful sunset to a supermarket.

It is very unlikely that one of these tiny spacecraft will ever be found in the immensity of space. Even if it were, the 'visiting card' could be answered only by unravelling the star maps and seeking out

the Earth. To establish a conversation with another civilisation, a different method of communication is needed.

The answer is surprisingly simple – radio. Ordinary radio waves travel freely through space, and any creature 'out there' with a sensitive receiving set could pick up radio and TV programmes from Earth.

On November 16, 1974, astronomers sent the first deliberate radio message, from the Arecibo Radio Observatory in Puerto Rico to a cluster of stars called Messier 13. This cluster contains 300,000 stars, so it is likely to have many planets too.

The message from Arecibo consists of a series of 1679 radio pulses, rather like Morse code. If an alien arranged the signals in a rectangle of 23 pulses by 73, a pattern would emerge among the dots and dashes. This pattern will reveal the chemicals of which life is made, the shape and size of an average human being, the population of the Earth, and the place of the Earth within the Solar System.

Unfortunately, the odds are against the reception of even a sophisticated message like this. If there are intelligent beings in Messier 13 with a sensitive radio receiver, they would have to have it pointed towards the Earth at the critical moment. They would also have to be tuned in to exactly the right wavelength.

There is another problem with interstellar dialogue. Messier 13 is so far away that 25,000 years will pass before the message arrives there. If an alien does pick it up and send an answer, the response will take as long to reach the Earth. So we will have to wait 50,000 years for a reply.

The quest for messages from outer space

Rather than waiting, several astronomers are already searching the sky to see if any civilisation is sending messages towards the Earth. The first search started in 1960, and since then many searches have been conducted for intelligent signals from the sky. Two radio telescopes in the United States, in Ohio and Massachusetts, now spend every hour of every day scanning the sky for radio messages.

With funding from Steven Spielberg, the director of the film E.T., researchers of the Search for Extraterrestrial Intelligence (SETI), at the Oak Ridge Observatory in Massachusetts, have built a device that can tune in to 8 million different frequencies simultaneously. Computers monitor all these frequencies to check for signals that seem unnatural.

Despite all this effort, no message has been picked up. But as more astronomers become involved in SETI, the efforts are increasing all the time. It is unlikely that they will discover another intelligent race in the Universe, but if they do, it will rate as one of the most important events in the history of mankind.

Marvels of science

When scientists first split the atom, the world took a step into the unknown. Now we look ahead to an age when it may be possible to re-create extinct creatures and produce machines that think.

How they know the continents are drifting, page 207.

How they photograph subatomic particles, page 199.

How scientists try to predict earthquakes, page 204.

Making clones of plants and animals

Gardeners have been making clones of plants for centuries. Every time they take a cutting of a geranium, a rose or any other plant, they are producing a genetically identical copy – a clone. Cuttings may be taken from roots or shoots, and inserted into soil or compost where they develop into a new plant.

Modern scientific techniques have greatly extended the range of cloning. Today, copies can be made of varieties of plants that refuse to grow from cuttings, and even animals can be cloned, so that the offspring is an exact replica of a single parent. Ultimately, there seems no biological reason why human beings should not be cloned too.

When plants are cloned, the object is to choose the most productive or decorative plant and copy it thousands of times. The technique starts with a small cutting. It can be taken from any part of the plant, since all the plant's cells contain the genetic information from which an entire plant can be reconstructed.

The cutting is placed in a culture medium, a soup of nutritious chemicals that supplies all its needs. The medium includes a growth hormone which stimulates the cells in the cutting to divide, producing a mass of plant cells that doubles in size every six weeks or so.

Eventually this mass of cells begins to produce small white globular points known as embryoids. In due course the embryoids develop roots, or throw up shoots, and begin to look like tiny plants. Transplanted carefully into compost, the plants will grow into exact copies of the parent plant from which the original cutting was taken. It takes up to 18 months to reach this stage.

This process, called tissue culture, has been used for some time to make clones of the oil palm, a valuable and widely grown tropical species which produces a thick oil used in cosmetics, margarine and cooking oil.

When planted together, all the clones will sprout and grow at the same rate and produce oil of the same quality and

Test-tube plants *Tissue culture involves growing disease-free plants from a single cell, like this grapevine seedling.*

quantity, at the same time. Their productivity is 30 per cent higher than plants produced from seed, which show a wide variation in character.

Similar methods are being used for asparagus, pineapples, strawberries, brussels sprouts, cauliflowers, bananas, carnations, ferns and other plants.

As well as producing thousands of identical copies of the best plant available, tissue culture helps to control viral diseases of plants, which are usually passed on from generation to generation through their seeds. A disease-free plant can be used to produce thousands of disease-free clones.

For animals, the technique is more difficult, and not yet in general use. But its feasibility has been proved on mice at the University of Geneva, on sheep at the Institute of Animal Physiology at Cambridge, and on calves at the University of Calgary. It could soon be used to produce herds of cows in which all achieve champion milking standards, or produce beef of uniform taste and texture.

A technique called nuclear transfer enables up to 32 clones to be produced at a time. Using tiny surgical tools, an embryo that has developed to the 32-cell stage is split up into 32 separate cells.

To make them develop successfully they must be combined with single-celled embryos of the same species from which the nucleus has been removed. The nucleus of a cell contains the genetic information from which the organism develops. When it is removed, the embryo has no blueprint from which to operate. But a fresh blueprint can be provided by fusing the empty cell with one of the 32 cells taken from the developing embryo. If all 32 are used in the same way, the result is 32 embryos with identical genetic information. Each one can be transplanted into the womb of a surrogate mother to produce 32 identical individuals.

To produce really large numbers, however, the embryos produced in this way would themselves have to be cloned again, and then again. They could then be stored by freezing, and finally transplanted into the wombs of surrogates.

The technique could be particularly valuable to developing countries, since embryos created in another country can be frozen and then flown out to be inserted into the mothers. This would short-circuit the lengthy process of livestock improvement by selective breeding.

Breeding super-cows *Coloured test tubes each contain a single cow embryo (right, top). A micro-manipulator will be used to manipulate the embryos, splitting them at an early stage of development (right, bottom). The divided embryos are then implanted in a surrogate cow mother to produce identical twin calves (below).*

Discovering the secrets of cells

All living things consist of microscopically small units called cells. They vary greatly in size, but one-hundredth of a millimetre is fairly typical. The simplest forms, such as bacteria, consist of a single cell. A human being has more than 50 million million.

Cells were discovered in 1665 by the English scientist Robert Hooke, who looked at slices of cork through a microscope and saw a series of tiny compartments which looked like the rooms, or cells, occupied by monks in a monastery.

Later, biologists found that cells were the universal building blocks of life. In plants and animals, the cells each have specialist functions and cooperate to make the whole organism work. Each cell is a miniature living unit. It can feed, 'breathe' and reproduce itself. It can respond to messages from other cells, and send messages out.

How do we know what goes on inside cells? First, by looking at them through microscopes. Stains such as carmine and crystal violet can be used to colour the various parts of the cell. Cells of many different kinds all have features in common. A nucleus at the centre is surrounded by a fluid called cytoplasm, which contains other structures. The whole cell is held together by a membrane.

Even more detail can be seen using an electron microscope, which uses a beam of electrons rather than light. It can magnify more than 500,000 times, compared with a limit of 1500 times for optical microscopes. Electron microscopes have revealed tiny structures in the cell.

The function of some of the components of the cell can be surmised by their appearance, but detailed investigation involves breaking up cells into their component parts. One way of doing this is by mixing them in a blender like those used in a kitchen. Then the components are separated by spinning the mixture in a centrifuge. The heaviest components are thrown to the bottom of a test tube as it is whirled around at high speed, forming a sediment with a clear liquid above it. The sediment can then be studied.

By spinning the remaining liquid at even higher speeds, components of decreasing weight can be separated out.

Gradually, using techniques like these, the activities of all the cell's components have been identified. One of the most important is the nucleus, which carries the genetic information enabling the cell to function properly and to reproduce.

The chemical nature of the nucleus was first investigated in 1869 by the Swiss biochemist Friedrich Miescher, who was dissolving cells in pepsin (a digestive enzyme) and found that the nucleus contained phosphorus as well as more usual elements such as carbon and oxygen. Later scientists found that a major constituent of the nucleus is nucleic acid. Later, nucleic acid was found in fact to be two acids, ribonucleic acid (RNA) and deoxyribonucleic acid (DNA). DNA stores the genetic code which passes hereditary characteristics from parent to offspring.

INSIDE A PLANT CELL

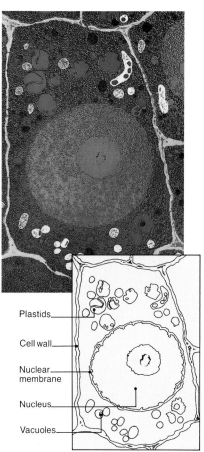

Plastids

Cell wall

Nuclear membrane

Nucleus

Vacuoles

This electron microscope photograph shows the inside of a single maize cell. Both plant and animal cells have a nucleus in a fluid (cytoplasm). A plant cell has a distinct cell wall, shown above in yellow.

AN ANIMAL CELL DIVIDES IN TWO

All plant cells and many animal cells have the ability to reproduce themselves by a process called mitosis, or cell division. These electron microscope photographs show a whitefish cell dividing into two cells. In prophase (right) all the chromosomes clump together in the centre. Anaphase (below, left) sees the two groups of chromosomes begin to pull apart, or polarise. By metaphase (below, centre), the chromosomes have formed two distinct groups, each of which becomes the nucleus of the two new cells that become apparent at the interphase stage (below, right).

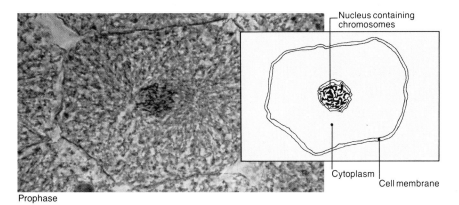

Prophase

Nucleus containing chromosomes

Cytoplasm

Cell membrane

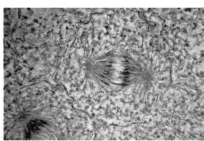

Anaphase

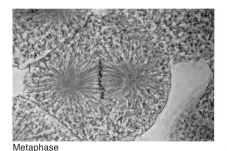

Metaphase

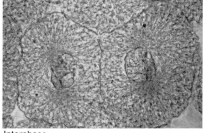

Interphase

Creating 'geeps' and other new animals and plants

Every breed of dog in the world – from the miniature Yorkshire terrier to the Dobermann Pinscher – derived originally from the wolf.

By selecting desirable characteristics and breeding to achieve them, man has produced hundreds of breeds of dogs so different that it is hard to believe they are members of the same species.

Plants have been manipulated equally successfully to produce high-yielding cereals, fruit and vegetables, as well as decorative plants that flower more brilliantly than any in the natural world.

Traditional techniques of breeding both plants and animals involve mating a male and a female of different varieties in the hope of combining the best of both – high productivity from one parent, high disease resistance from another, for example. But these breeding programmes take several generations. And they can only be used between varieties of the same species. You cannot create a new super-vegetable by crossing the carrot and the cabbage using conventional means.

Modern science has devised revolutionary breeding techniques. One of them, called cell fusion, has produced the 'geep', born in Cambridge in 1982, a cross between the sheep and the goat.

In cell fusion, the tough outer membrane around sperm and egg cells of an animal is stripped off, using chemicals called enzymes. This leaves the cells protected only by a delicate inner membrane. Cells in this fragile condition are called protoplasts. Mixed together, they can be persuaded to combine, usually with the aid of chemicals or viruses.

The result may be the creation of a new life form taking characteristics from both of the parents. In the case of the geep, the combined cells were replaced in the womb of a sheep and born as a combination of the two species – a creature which has horns and has both sheep's wool and goat's hair in its coat.

Interestingly, although the geeps can breed normally with each other, any offspring would be either pure sheep or pure goat, depending on which cells formed the reproductive organs. The young would never look like the parents.

Genetic engineering

Another approach is to reprogramme the genetic material, which dictates how some part of a plant or animal will behave. The species will then produce better fruit, richer milk, or even some product quite foreign to its normal nature. This is done by the techniques of genetic engineering.

The character of any species is carried in the form of a code in long sinuous molecules of DNA (deoxyribonucleic acid) found in the nucleus of every living cell. The chains of DNA are built up of just four building blocks, called nucleotides. It is the order of these nucleotides along the chain that stores the information needed by cells to function and reproduce themselves.

With gene splicing, small sections of the chain responsible for a particular process are cut out and then re-inserted into the DNA of another species – plant, animal or even bacterium.

One of the first examples was the removal of the section of DNA responsible for making insulin in the human pancreas and its re-insertion into a bacterium. The gene was cut out using an enzyme, a biological material which breaks the DNA chain at certain points. The same enzyme was then used to cut the DNA of a

Stronger plants *A microscope picture shows the joined nuclei of two tobacco leaf cells. The cells have been treated with a chemical to break down the cell wall, promoting fusion, to create a hybrid plant.*

bacterium, *Escherichia coli*, in the same places, and the fragment of human gene was inserted into the bacterium. Then, as the bacterium was allowed to grow, it produced human insulin as well as its normal products. The insulin was extracted and since 1982 has been used to treat diabetics, who lack the ability to produce sufficient insulin for themselves.

Applied to plants and animals, the technique is already producing extraordinary results. At the Institute for Animal Physiology and Genetics Research near Edinburgh in Scotland, a flock of normal-looking sheep graze on a hillside. Yet they

have been turned into walking drug factories, by reprogramming their genetic code so that, in addition to milk, they produce a clotting agent previously found only in normal human blood. It is called Factor IX, and its absence from the genetic code of some people causes haemophilia, the condition in which the blood does not clot when the skin has been cut.

The scientists isolated the gene responsible for the production of Factor IX in normal humans, removed it, and re-inserted it into the right place among the genes of a sheep embryo. The sheep grow up to produce milk containing Factor IX, which can be extracted and used to treat haemophiliacs.

Improving food plants and animals

Applied to plants, the technique has enormous possibilities. The greatest prize would be to insert into cereal crops like wheat, barley and rice the ability to make use of nitrogen from the air. Some plants, including beans and clover, possess this ability, which means that they can grow successfully without needing large quantities of nitrogen fertilisers. If genetic engineering could give the same ability to the important cereal crops, large amounts of money could be saved every year, and nitrate pollution of streams and rivers could be reduced.

A technique already exists to make plants resistant to some diseases. Scientists working for Monsanto took a bacterium called *Agrobacterium tumefaciens*, which normally causes plant tumours. They cut out the tumour-producing genes and replaced them with useful ones. Then they infected plants with the bacterium to get the useful genes into the plant's own DNA.

In 1983 they produced tomatoes with a gene that enabled them to withstand the tobacco hookworm, a common pest, and tobacco mosaic virus, a disease which reduces yields. In trials, tomato yields went up by 20-30 per cent.

Next they inserted another gene that made the plants resistant to one of Monsanto's own weedkillers, Roundup. This means that weeds growing around the plants can be killed by spraying them with Roundup, without damaging the tomatoes.

Similar work has been done to improve the characteristics of animals. In 1982 scientists at the universities of Washington

WHEAT THAT GROWS IN SALT

Genetic engineering is being used to develop wheat that will grow in salty soil. Large areas of the world's irrigated land have become salty because the river water used for irrigation leaves traces of salt, which build up year by year.

In the Indus Valley of Pakistan, for example, some of the farmland has become so salty that it is now useless for wheat growing.

Scientists at the Institute of Plant Science Research at Cambridge are developing a salt-resistant strain by transferring cells from sand couch grass to wheat. This produces a hybrid wheat that will grow on salty land.

The sand couch grass tolerates salt because it discriminates between different chemicals, and takes up less sodium from salt than other plants do. This characteristic is passed on to the hybrid wheat by the transfer of genes.

and Pennsylvania inserted into mice the gene that produces growth hormone in rats. The result was a breed called 'mighty mouse' – mice that grew far bigger than normal. In 1986 the US Department of Agriculture's experimental station at Beltsville, Maryland, adapted the technique for agriculture. They produced pigs with human growth hormone, to make them grow bigger and leaner. The pigs were big, and their meat contained 5 per cent fat instead of the usual 25 per cent, but they were lame from arthritis. The foreign gene had done more than simply increase their size.

Future experiments will have to get around this difficulty, for it would be unethical – and in some circumstances illegal – to engineer in this way a species that was forced to live in discomfort simply to produce more meat.

In the future, genes for a whole range of useful characteristics, from disease resistance to litter size, will be inserted into farm animals.

How do scientists create new drugs?

Many of the triumphs of modern medicine are the result not of better medical techniques, but of better drugs. The success of drugs like antibiotics (page 288), which have saved millions of lives since they were introduced during the Second World War, has inspired drug companies to invest heavily in research in the hope of finding something else just as effective.

There are four main approaches. The first is to isolate or imitate natural compounds which are known to have medicinal properties. For example, the bark of the willow was used for centuries to relieve pain because it contains the compound salicin. Salicylic acid, a closely related compound first produced artificially in 1874, forms the basis of aspirin.

The second is to copy an existing drug, modifying it slightly in the hope of making it more effective. This can sometimes produce drugs with quite unexpected properties. A whole class of diuretic drugs, used to treat illnesses where fluid accumulates in the tissues (such as kidney failure), was produced by modifying the chemical structure of the antimicrobial drug sulphanilamide.

The third is to pick at random among the millions of organic compounds – those containing carbon – that have been produced by chemists, and try them on animals in the hope of finding one with useful properties.

The fourth is to try to understand the functioning of the human body, and to design drugs from scientific principles. For example, a precise understanding of how acid is produced in the stomach led to the development of drugs that 'block' the process and have transformed ulcer treatment.

All these methods have produced success. The first synthetic drug was produced by the German bacteriologist Paul Ehrlich in 1910. Ehrlich wanted a 'magic bullet' that could destroy the bacteria responsible for diseases such as tuberculosis, cholera and diphtheria, but leave the rest of the patient's own cells undamaged.

He started by looking at dyes that would stain bacteria but not other cells, reasoning that a chemical that reacted more strongly with bacteria than with other cells might kill them, too.

He discovered a dye, which was later given the name trypan red, which would kill trypanosomes, the organism responsible for sleeping sickness.

However, it was not clinically satisfactory mainly because the margin between a curative dose and a dangerous one was too small. He turned instead to the possibilities of compounds containing arsenic.

Ehrlich produced a large number of arsenical variations of trypan red, and started testing them one by one. In 1909 a Japanese student of Ehrlich's, Sahachiro Hata, found that compound 606, which was useless against trypanosomes, was deadly against the bacterium that caused syphilis. Compound 606, which was later given the name Salvarsan, was the first effective drug against a disease that until then had no cure.

Ehrlich's success was based on guessing

roughly where to look; on having the sense to modify the compound to increase its effectiveness; and on painstakingly checking every compound not only against the disease he was really interested in, but against others as well. The modern chemist works more or less along the same lines.

Testing drugs for safety

Chemists can produce organic compounds in huge numbers. Tested in animals, most either have no effect at all, or are so toxic that they cannot be considered as drugs.

At least two different groups of animals are used. Usually small rodents – like rats, mice or guinea pigs – are tested first, then larger animals like dogs or monkeys.

More refined tests with smaller doses are carried out on young animals, to make sure that the drug does not prevent growth, and on pregnant animals to check that the drug does not harm their young. Other animals are watched for rashes, or unusually active or inactive behaviour.

Despite all these tests the results may still be misleading. Drugs do not always affect animals in the same way as humans. Penicillin, which has saved millions of human lives, might never have been marketed if it had first been tested on guinea pigs, because a very small dose will kill them. Toxicity testing is highly complex and can often take more than two years to complete.

The next stage is to test drugs for side effects in healthy human volunteers. Very small doses are given in strictly controlled circumstances.

If the drug appears to have no harmful side effects the volunteer group is expanded. In America between 5000 and 15,000 people are usually monitored before the results of the tests are sent to the licensing authority (the US Food and Drug Administration).

The drug company reports all its findings in a document that often runs to many thousands of pages. If the report is approved, the drug undergoes clinical trials on patients to see how effective it is.

Most new drugs are 'double blind' tested. Half the patients are given an identical-looking placebo (something that has no effect). Neither doctors nor patients know which patient is given which.

The results of the tests must be sufficiently convincing for the drug to pass the clinical trials. There must be no doubt that it was the drug that relieved the patients' illnesses – not their own natural resistance. During all tests, doctors continue to search for any side effects that were not picked up in earlier tests.

Even after a drug has passed clinical testing and is marketed, testing still goes on. Doctors prescribing the drug are expected to report to the authorities any adverse reactions suffered by their patients.

How animals are taught to communicate with humans

The understanding that can develop between people and animals is often almost uncanny. Dogs are good at interpreting their owner's wishes so that at times they appear to possess a sixth sense. Horses, too, can respond to the subtlest of cues, as the complex movements of dressage demonstrate. But will it ever be possible for people to communicate with animals using ordinary language?

Some years ago intensive efforts were made to communicate with dolphins. These mammals have brains which are similar in size to that of a human being, and they seem to be very intelligent. Dolphins are also capable of making a wide range of sounds, including squeaks, groans, clicks, barks and whistles, to indicate alarm, threat and recognition.

Attempts to interpret this language have not been successful. But scientists have proved that these creatures, and sea lions, can recognise hand gestures – a form of language – and can respond correctly.

Rocky, a 13-year-old sea lion at the Long Marine Laboratory in Santa Cruz, California, has been trained to identify objects, by being rewarded when he gets it right, and he can now collect from his pool only the toy that he is asked for. His trainer, Ron Schusterman of the University of California, scatters up to a dozen different toys in the pool – balls, discs, bottles and so on. An assistant who sits on the edge of the pool makes signs to the sea lion asking him to collect a particular toy, and Rocky picks up the right item 95 per cent of the time.

More significantly, he has also been taught the meaning of much more complex commands such as 'take the ball to the disc', or 'take the small black disc to the bottle'. The success rate of his responses on such tasks is only 40 per cent. However, it would be impossible for him to do even that well by chance. To some extent at least, he appears to understand simple sentences.

Sign language for chimps

Similar experiments have been done with chimpanzees, orang-utans and other apes. Because they do not have the same vocal cords as humans, apes cannot be expected to speak. So the pioneers of this research, Allen and Beatrice Gardner of the University of Nevada, had the idea of teaching one of them sign language. In 1967 they obtained a one-year-old female chimpanzee named Washoe, and by 1971 had taught her to use American Sign Language, the method used by the deaf in the United States. She was repeatedly shown the signs and then was rewarded with a tickle or with food when she responded correctly. Washoe learned fast and soon knew a large number of words. She was eventually able to use 150 hand gestures.

Walking by a lake one day, her trainer pointed at a duck. 'What's that?', he asked in sign language. 'Water bird', said Washoe, apparently inventing her own word for ducks. Encouraged by this, other American scientists started training their own chimpanzees, using a range of different methods of communication. Some involved the identification of plastic shapes which symbolised, among other things, objects such as apples, or the trainer's name. Others meant pressing different keys on a computer to communicate words or phrases. The result seemed to show that the chimps could indeed master 'language': they could respond to simple commands and use the language to ask for things.

Later, cold water was poured on the whole idea by another American psychologist, Professor Herbert Terrace of Columbia University, New York. When Terrace analysed all Washoe's two-word phrases, he found that the word order was in fact random. Washoe might just as easily have said 'bird water'. Terrace also found that, unlike human babies learning language,

Doleful look *With downcast eyes, Lucy makes the fingers-to-mouth sign Dr Fouts taught her to indicate a concept – 'Hurt'.*

How Lucy learns *A psychologist, Dr Roger Fouts, teaches sign language to Lucy, a six-year-old chimpanzee, one of several at the University of Oklahoma primate colony. Lucy watches intently as Dr Fouts makes the gesture for 'What do you want?'*

Name-dropping *When Lucy wants to say her teacher's name, the right-hand-on-left-ear gesture is her method of expressing 'Roger'.*

the chimps did not gradually increase the complexity of their 'sentences'.

More recently, a pygmy chimpanzee called Kanzi has rekindled interest. Kanzi lives at the Language Research Center near Atlanta, Georgia. His success in picking up the elements of language appears to show that pygmy chimpanzees have greater intellectual potential than gorillas, orangutans and common chimpanzees.

Kanzi has been provided with a keyboard, linked to a computer. Each key is marked with a geometrical symbol which represents a word. As a baby, Kanzi played in the laboratory while his mother was taught to use the keyboard, and apparently picked up the skill by watching her. To the surprise of the scientists, Kanzi began using the symbols correctly at the age of two and a half, and by the age of three had acquired skills which common chimpanzees could not manage at the age of seven.

Communicating loneliness

Kanzi's trainers do not claim that he can create grammatical sentences, but he does produce two-word and three-word statements that appear spontaneous, he comments on his actions and describes to his trainers those he intends to carry out. He uses the keyboard to communicate with other pygmy chimpanzees undergoing the same training, such as telling one to tickle the other. His sentences also represent his own response to a situation. For example, when deprived of the company of another chimpanzee called Austin, Kanzi apparently felt lonely without the normal bedtime visit from his friend. After several nights, he punched the symbols for 'Austin' and 'TV' on his keyboard, and was shown a videotape of Austin, after which he went happily to sleep.

There is no evidence yet that animals are capable of abstract ideas, or of active conversations. Even if we do improve our understanding of how they communicate, they may not have anything of enormous interest to say to us.

Word power *Hands together in a prayer-like fashion indicate the word 'book'. Some apes have acquired large vocabularies.*

Will mammoths walk the Earth again?

The woolly mammoth, the flightless dodo bird and the quagga, a type of zebra, are all extinct. But the modern techniques of genetic engineering have made it possible to study their genetic make-up – or even to think of giving them life again.

To do so, scientists would have to obtain a sample of the genetic blueprint needed to re-create an entire creature. This blueprint is contained in the deoxyribonucleic acid (DNA) of the creature's cells. It can be obtained only from flesh that has somehow been preserved since the creature became extinct.

Since most extinct species survive only as fossils, they have left no traces of tissue preserved in its original condition. But some creatures, such as the mammoth, a hairy relative of the elephant, which became extinct about 12,000 years ago, have been frozen solid in the ground in Siberia, Alaska and northern Canada. When dug up, their flesh still contained traces of the DNA. The first step in reproducing a living specimen would be to extract the DNA and copy it. This has already been done for a number of extinct species, including the mammoth and the quagga. The object of the experiments was not to reconstruct the creatures, but to study the DNA and try to learn from it.

Half zebra, half horse

For example, pieces of quagga skin kept at the Natural History Museum in Mainz, West Germany, provided DNA for cloning by two scientists in California, Dr Oliver Ryder of San Diego Zoo, and Dr Russell Huguchi of the University of California at Berkeley. The quagga, described by early travellers in the Cape Province of South Africa as 'half zebra, half horse', went into decline when settlers began to fence its territory and introduce their own grazing stock. Uncontrolled hunting killed the last ones in the wild, though the quagga lingered on in zoos until the last specimen died of natural causes in Amsterdam Zoo in 1893. The taxidermists who stuffed the Mainz specimen had left fragments of muscle and fat on the skin, from which parts of the quagga's DNA could be extracted and put into the DNA of a bacterium. By allowing this bacterium to grow, the extinct DNA could be copied.

The DNA showed that the quagga was indeed a subspecies of the zebra, and suggested that its characteristics may still be contained in modern wild populations of Plains zebra. This has inspired an attempt to bring back the quagga by selective breeding. Reinhold Rau of the South African Museum in Cape Town established a group of interested conservationists who went into the Etosha Game Reserve in South West Africa and captured eight zebra with reduced striping on their hindquarters – like the quagga. For the next ten years the scientists will breed the zebra selectively, to try to match the patterns found on the hides of preserved quagga. 'The bone structure of the two animals as far as is known from the skeletons is identical, to quite a minute detail,' says Quintus Hahndiek, a member of the team. 'Some of the zebra only have to lose a few stripes to resemble a quagga.'

DNA samples have also been studied from an Egyptian mummy preserved for more than 2400 years, and from an ancient Briton, whose body, dating from about 2000 years ago, was found well preserved in a Cheshire peat bog in 1984.

Mummy of a baby boy

The mummy – a baby boy less than one year old when he died – is part of the collection of the Egyptian Museum in Berlin, East Germany. A Swedish scientist, Svante Paabo, of the Wallenberg Laboratory, University of Uppsala, took a small sample from the lower part of the left leg and successfully cloned it in 1985. But the DNA fragment he extracted was only about one-twentieth of the total DNA a living person possesses. Reconstructing any creature from such a small sample would be impossible – it would be like trying to rebuild a motor car when you had no more than a diagram of the headlights. But it may make it possible to answer some questions about the ancient Egyptians. Whether, for example, they suffered from genetic diseases, or had any evidence of inbreeding.

Might it one day be possible to go further and reconstruct an entire animal? Suppose the complete genetic blueprint of a mammoth could be recovered from a specimen preserved in the permafrost, cloned, and then inserted into the embryo of an elephant. If the embryo was replaced in the elephant's womb, then the elephant would give birth to a mammoth. Again – at least in theory – the same might be done with quagga genes, or those of the dodo, or even the ancient Egyptians.

So far, it is only a theoretical possibility. Fragments of DNA recovered have provided an insufficient fraction of the complete blueprint, and reconstructing the remainder appears impossible. And even this slight possibility does not exist for creatures that survive only as fossils – so the prospect of dinosaurs once more walking the Earth appears likely to remain science fiction.

How they build up a prehistoric animal from a few bones

When the first example of Neanderthal man was found in the valley of the Neander river, West Germany, in 1856, his fossilised skeleton suggested that he walked stooped over, with his knees permanently bent and his knuckles practically scraping the ground. Soon this shambling, beetle-browed figure became generally accepted as the prototype of primitive man.

It was based, however, on a total misconception. By an extraordinary mis-chance, the first complete Neanderthal skeleton found was that of a man who had suffered from severe osteoarthritis, which had twisted his back and given him his stoop.

In fact, as later finds revealed, Neander-thals stood as upright as modern man, and possessed a brain a fraction larger than ours. Nevertheless, the false image stuck.

Reconstructing an extinct species is an uncertain business. Occasionally, prehis-toric creatures are found intact. Whole mammoths have been preserved deep-frozen in the Siberian permafrost. Insects extinct for millions of years have remained untouched by decay inside drops of fossilised tree sap.

But often palaeontologists are confront-ed with a confusion of bones, splintered, scattered and incomplete. Mistakes in reconstruction are common. In 1822 in England, the first remains of what was called an iguanodon by her husband, Dr Gideon Mantell, were found by Mrs Mary Ann Mantell in a pile of stones beside a lane in Sussex. One of the giant creature's teeth seemed to resemble that of a modern lizard, so it was named iguanodon ('igua-na-tooth'). But what did it look like? Presumably, it walked about on four legs like modern iguanas.

One bone seemed to offer more of an insight. It looked like a rhino-ceros horn, and was duly placed on the iguanodon's nose. In-

deed, a life-size model of the lumbering quadruped was made in 1854, for the grounds of the Crystal Palace, which had opened in London in 1851. It was not until more than 20 years later that iguanodons were recognised as giant two-legged herbi-vores. This came to light when the skeletons of a whole herd of the 16ft (5m) tall creatures were found down a coal mine at Bernissart, in Belgium. There were 20 or so skeletons, many of which were com-plete. What had been mistaken for a horn, turned out to be a thumb-like spike on the forepaw with which it may have defended itself – or used to tear down the plants on which it fed. The giant creatures are believed to have roamed the countryside about 120 million years ago.

The more bones there are in a find, and the more finds, the greater the certainty with which the animal can be reconstruct-ed. The several examples of diplodocus skeletons, for instance, have enabled scien-tists to know precisely where each bone of the 30ft (9m) long giant goes. Any missing bits can, if necessary, be modelled in glass fibre and resin from other similar finds.

The key to successful reconstruction is to make meticulous records of the position of bones as they are uncovered. Each fragment is numbered and labelled. The remains are then carefully packed, often encased in plaster of Paris or polyurethane foam. Once unwrapped, the bones can be mounted on a metal framework.

It is intricate and expert work. Scientists must be able to spot minute irregularities where muscles and ligaments were origi-nally attached, and then compare the structure with the skeletons of present-day creatures – reptiles in the case of dinosaurs – to ensure that the bones are placed in the right position.

Once the skeleton is complete, an even more intractable problem remains: how to clothe the skeleton in flesh. Again, a detailed knowledge of the anatomy of present-day creatures helps. And the surface of the skin can be guessed from the fossilised skin patterns formed when dinosaurs died in mud.

One thing must remain forever un-certain: the colour of a dinosaur's skin. The best that can be done is to make compari-sons with modern reptiles, which may be drab to provide camouflage, bright to attract partners or scare predators, vari-egated, or even variable, like a chameleon.

One of the most contentious areas of reconstruction is that of early man – largely because the fossil remains are few, and different scientists interpret them in differ-ent ways.

Mistaken image *The mid-19th-century assumption that iguanodons were horned quadrupeds – as in the models in the grounds of Crystal Palace (above) – proved wrong. A Belgian discovery of skeletons in 1877 produced a more accurate reconstruction (left).*

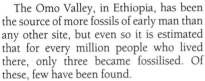

The Omo Valley, in Ethiopia, has been the source of more fossils of early man than any other site, but even so it is estimated that for every million people who lived there, only three became fossilised. Of these, few have been found.

Among the finds, a complete or even partial skeleton is a rarity. Those who study early man often propose sweeping theories on the basis of half a jawbone – with consequent disputes about the precise course of human evolution.

Chinese dinosaur *A reassembled skeleton of a tuojiangosaurus, is held in a metal and plastic framework. Some 23ft (7m) long, it lived in China 150 million years ago.*

MAKING A DINOSAUR MODEL

The first step in reconstructing a dinosaur in miniature is measuring the bones (top left). A scale drawing of the skeleton is made (centre), showing how the creature stood. Then a wire and clay model is built from which a mould is made. From it, a laminated glass-fibre model is cast, ready for painting. But skin texture and colouring are mainly guesswork. Though fossil impressions in hardened mud have been found, giving some guide to texture, colouring could have been drab, bright, variegated or even changeable, like a chameleon. The creature modelled here, a gallimimus, roamed Mongolia in central Asia 70 million years ago.

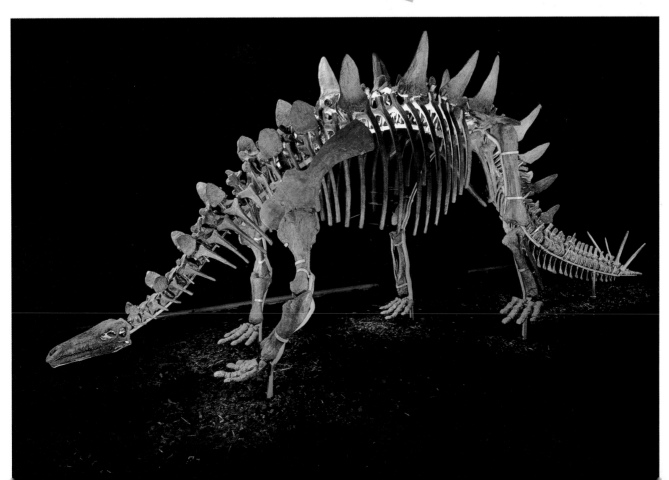

The search for the thinking machine

Computers can already play chess, produce new proofs for mathematical problems, read and translate languages. But no machine, however complex, has yet come close to mimicking the full range of human thought.

Nobody has yet built a machine that can learn to speak a language. Yet this is something that children master in their first few years. It took a good deal of effort at Edinburgh University in the 1970s to produce a computer that could 'recognise' simple items like a cup or a saucer, another thing human beings regard as trivially easy.

Scientists who work in the field believe that one day the workings of the brain will be completely understood and then it will be duplicated electronically.

One of the difficulties is that computers and brains are organised differently. The brain is a network of cells called neurons. It contains between ten and 100 billion neurons, each of which is connected to about 10,000 others, and all of which function at the same time.

Computers, by contrast, contain millions of individual logic circuits, each linked to only one other circuit, and each working one after the other. The information flowing through the computer goes along a single path, rather than being distributed widely, as in the brain.

Computer circuits work much more quickly than the neurons, and at some tasks the computer is better – long, complex mathematical calculations, for example. Yet the brain with its relatively sluggish neurons is far better at recognising patterns, and at learning – a process which may have something to do with increasing the density of connections between the neurons as learning takes place.

Today an increasing number of scientists in Japan, the USA and Europe are working with computers that attempt to copy the architecture of the brain. These computers are known as neural networks. The basic elements are electronic circuits just like those in ordinary computers, but they are wired up differently, with many connections between them like those between the neurons in the brain.

The computers are not programmed in the normal way by feeding in a set of instructions. They undergo a learning process in which information is fed in, together with examples of the conclusions the computer should reach, or feedback about how well it is doing. The process is similar to teaching a child.

Professor Igor Aleksander of Imperial College, London, devised a neural network called Wisard in 1981 which could recognise a human smile – one of the very first things a baby learns. It was taught by being shown a series of pictures, some smiling, some not. From this it was able to look at faces it had not been shown before, and display on screen or printer whether they were smiling.

At Johns Hopkins University in Baltimore, in the 1980s, Dr Terrence Sejnowski produced a neural network that could pronounce correctly words in English that were typed into its keyboard. The network learned just as a child does, its efforts corrected until it got them right.

The Japanese broadcasting organisation NHK has a neural network that can recognise handwritten Japanese characters with 95 per cent accuracy, regardless of size, position and changes in scale.

Neural networks are still at a very early stage of development. But if ever a computer is to be truly intelligent, most scientists believe this is how to achieve it.

How does a computer translate?

It is easy for a computer to translate single words and short phrases, but not so easy to translate entire documents. Translation is much more than a word-for-word substitution. Most languages are full of ambiguities and words that can be understood only from their context.

Dozens of words have two or three meanings, and the grammar of a sentence can also be ambiguous. The sign 'No electric passenger carrying vehicles beyond this point' can easily confuse a computer. It cannot tell whether the vehicle or the passenger is electric, or whether the vehicle is carrying the passenger or the passenger carrying the vehicle.

Colloquial or technical words make the computer's job even harder. One early translation program that was used to translate a technical text baffled engineers by constantly referring to 'water-sheep'. What it really meant was hydraulic rams.

In 1954 IBM developed the first translating program. It converted simple Russian sentences into English, like 'Gasoline is prepared by chemical methods from crude oil'. But it made many mistakes and made no sense at all of some everyday sentences.

Despite these difficulties, computer translation programs have now been used by companies for some time. In their memories they have extensive dictionaries of the languages they translate – up to 100,000 words and phrases in the most advanced systems. They use them to find and substitute the nearest appropriate word in the other language. But simple word substitution leads to many mistakes, and the text needs careful editing by professional translators. They argue that this editing process takes almost as long as translating the document from scratch.

However, by 1988, systems had been developed with an accuracy rate of 96 per cent. This was achieved by making the computer better able to cross-reference words with one another and by translating whole phrases as well as individual words. Technical terms are programmed in when needed, and the computer would check ambiguous meanings and choose the correct terms. The speed of translation has also been increased.

Computers can already translate fast – that is their main advantage. If a company wants to bid for a tender, it has to act quickly, but the tender may run for hundreds of pages. However inelegant the language may be, a computer could translate it faster than a human. It could take a person up to half a day to translate 1000 words from one European language to another. A computer could print out a basic translation in about 20 minutes.

The US Air Force, wanting to monitor Russian broadcasts concerning the space programme, developed the Systran translator in 1970. It has since been adapted to pairs of European languages, including French, Dutch, German and Italian.

Systran can translate 360,000 words an hour with 80 per cent accuracy. A human translator does the final polishing. Systran is used by General Motors and Aerospatiale to translate service manuals. And Canada's meteorological office uses it to translate weather reports into French.

The most advanced machine translation system in the world is Eurotra, designed to help the European Community in Luxembourg and Brussels to translate nearly a million pages of text each year.

British Telecom is developing a system for automatic translation over the phone in five languages: English, French, Swedish, German and Spanish. The computer can match what the caller is saying with appropriate words in the other language. Then a voice synthesiser passes the message on to the listener in his native tongue. At the moment the system is relatively slow and can only cope with a limited vocabulary. But similar systems are already in use in Japanese hotels, where computers are used to take reservations.

Computers that can hear and talk back to you

Talking to a computer – asking it questions and having it answer you back – is not science-fiction fantasy: it is already happening. The user-friendly computer which can 'hear' your voice, interpret your words, and answer in spoken language is used in telephone systems and home banking, for example.

The first step in making a computer speak is to store common speech sounds – called phonemes – in the computer memory. They are stored digitally as combinations of 0 and 1, and each combination represents a different sound. The computer is programmed to assemble the sounds into words or sentences, then uses a microphone to 'tell' you what you want to know.

Computers which 'hear' have been programmed with a similar system to enable a receiver to recognise the phonemes. Most computers can interpret only certain words, spoken in a pre-scribed order, or by a previously introduced voice, but advanced systems can now recognise and respond to any human voice, and some even understand more than one language. However, a computer cannot think, so does not hold a real conversation. A computer-generated voice does not sound like a human voice. Talking computers sound jerky and mechanical because they pronounce each speech sound in an identical, neutral way, without the varying stresses of the human voice. Researchers in the Netherlands have tried to solve this problem by combin-ing the speech sounds in smaller chunks, and assembling them to produce more human-sounding words.

Most computer-speaking sys-tems are used with telephones. In the USA, telephone companies use a computerised voice if they need to tell callers that the number they have dialled has been changed. The voice then speaks the new number. This computer cannot 'hear' a question, and is merely responding to the incorrectly dialled number.

Research in the USA and France aims at creating a computerised telephone directo-ry which will respond to your request with the correct number. Such a system would also be useful as a talking timetable for trains, buses and airlines.

The talking computer in a home banking system developed by British Telecom went on trial at the beginning of 1988. The customer telephones a special number, answered by the computer, and gives his name, personal code number and a password. The computer makes a 'voice-print' of the speech patterns, which plays the same role as a signature, preventing anyone else from dialling the number and using the account.

When the computer has accepted the call and identified the caller, it will then recognise a number of spoken commands and respond to them in English. For example, the computer can give details of the last transaction, supply the account's balance, pay bills, and confirm orders for cheque books and statements.

Computer speech synthesisers have been produced – at a high cost – to provide a voice for some children in the United States who have no voice of their own. The synthesiser is programmed with a realistic voice – possibly based on the voice of the child's brother or sister.

A synthesiser for a child as young as four would have an appropriately small vocab-ulary, and the child selects the words he wants to say by moving a joystick to appropriate pictures.

An older child or adult types statements on a keyboard, and the statements are then spoken by the synthesiser. For someone who is paralysed, a sensor attached to the eyebrow can act as a computer joystick. Another technique is to use an electronic sensor that detects movements of the eye itself to enter the commands.

The potential for talking computers is great, and work is going on to develop fast systems with large vocabularies. Talking computers are already used for translation work; information services, such as stock market trading figures; airline reservations; and security to prevent access to buildings and to computer files.

In years to come, portable voice syn-thesisers will probably allow an English-speaking person to ask simple questions that will be translated in, say, Japanese on a screen. To reply, a Japanese person would use a similar machine programmed from Japanese to English.

SYNTHESISERS – COMPUTERS THAT RECORD AND DISPLAY SPEECH

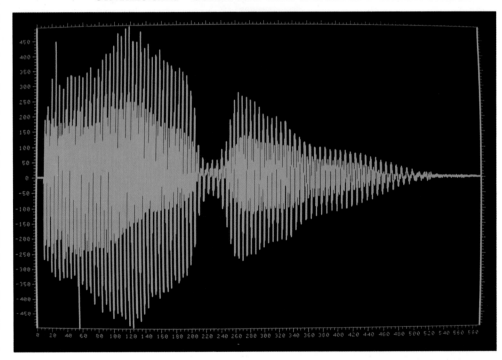

The voice-print of a woman's voice saying the word 'baby' is reproduced by a synthesiser and displayed on a screen. The keyboard and display unit of a speech synthesiser (right) is linked to a computer which can recognise and interpret human speech. The system is used to study speech and to make computers 'talk'. Similar systems are also used as security devices for office buildings.

How do they split atoms?

As long ago as the 5th century BC, the Greek philosophers Leucippus and Democritus put forward the theory that all matter was made up of indivisible particles. Their concept of the atom – from *atomos*, Greek for 'indivisible' – as nature's tiniest component, endured for more than 2000 years. Then in 1919, the atom was split for the first time. It happened at Manchester University, in a gloomy cellar laboratory.

This momentous achievement, which ushered in the nuclear age, was the culmination of experiments by the New Zealand-born physicist Ernest Rutherford. He had been investigating fast-moving alpha particles, given off by the radioactive element radium.

In the end of a hollow tube about 8in (200mm) long, Rutherford inserted a rod, on the end of which was a brass disc coated with radium. The other end of the tube was sealed with a thin metal disc and beyond this was a screen coated in zinc sulphide. The tube could be filled with different gases.

The metal disc stopped most of the alpha particles given off by the radium. But any high energy (long range) particles, formed by the action of the alpha particles on atoms of gas in the tube, passed through. As they hit the zinc screen they caused tiny sparks as their energy was released.

When the tube was filled with oxygen or carbon dioxide, the frequency of the sparks diminished because of the ability of these gases to stop alpha particles. But when air was used the flashes increased and this was attributed to its nitrogen content.

This was confirmed by using pure nitrogen. Rutherford concluded that the alpha particles had disintegrated the nitrogen atoms, resulting in the formation of charged hydrogen atoms. These high energy particles passed through the metal disc. Rutherford eventually called them *protons*, from the Greek for 'first'.

'We must conclude,' Rutherford wrote in a specialist paper, 'that the nitrogen atom is disintegrated.' The Press put it more dramatically: 'Rutherford smashes the atom.'

Later experiments confirmed Rutherford's conclusions. The dense alpha particles struck a nitrogen nucleus and combined with it, before disintegrating to produce the protons Rutherford saw on his screen, as well as atoms of a completely different element, oxygen. In effect, he had achieved what the medieval alchemists had tried vainly to do – he had transmuted one element, nitrogen, into another, oxygen.

More efficient ways of splitting atoms were soon discovered. In 1928, John Cockcroft and Ernest Walton, working in Cambridge, substituted protons for alpha particles. Using a device called a voltage multiplier, which boosts electrical energy enormously and can be used to accelerate particles, they made the protons hit their targets with greater force. In 1932, when they fired protons at atoms of the metal lithium, the result was two atoms of helium for every one of lithium.

Their success led to a flurry of experiments in which various particles were tested, bombarding a variety of 'targets'.

By January 1939, it was concluded by Otto Hahn and Lise Meitner at McGill University, Toronto, that when the heavy element uranium was bombarded with neutrons, which along with protons form the nuclei of atoms, the uranium atoms split almost in two, producing lighter elements and a huge release of energy. Each time an atom was split it produced at least two fresh neutrons, which could go on to split further atoms. This formed the principle of the chain reaction required for the atom bomb and nuclear power.

Experimental 'gun' *Rutherford's atom smasher – a sealed tube into which he introduced gases and radioactive material. The original is now in the Cavendish Museum, Cambridge.*

RUTHERFORD SPLITS THE ATOM

Some radium at the end of a rod was put into Rutherford's 'gun' which contains air. The radium emitted alpha particles, whose energy caused sparks on a zinc sulphide screen.

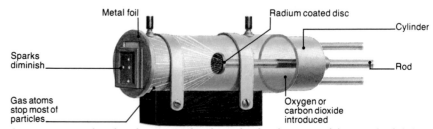

When oxygen or carbon dioxide was introduced into the chamber, most of the particles failed to reach the screen, reducing the number of sparks.

When nitrogen gas was introduced, the sparks resumed. Rutherford concluded that the alpha particles had collided with the nitrogen atoms, creating charged hydrogen atoms (protons), which were causing the sparks. He had disintegrated the nitrogen atom.

Probing the inner world of the atom

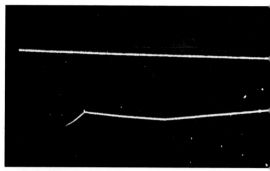

Early evidence *An alpha-particle track, as it collided with atoms, was recorded in a cloud chamber by its inventor, the English physicist C.T.R. Wilson.*

Scientists exploring the structure of the atom face an immediate problem: atoms are too small to see with any microscope. Typically they are only about 20 millionths of a millimetre across – and most of that is empty space.

The dense nucleus at the heart of an atom takes up less than 100,000th of its total volume.

Around it whirl electrons – virtually weightless subatomic particles that carry negative electric charges, balancing the positive charge of the nucleus.

More extraordinary still, these basic atomic particles have been proved to consist of even smaller particles.

But how can scientists know all this if they cannot actually see the particles? The facts have emerged from a long series of experiments in which generations of physicists have taken atoms apart with the help of complex devices called particle accelerators.

Early concepts of an atom envisaged it as a hard, solid, uniform particle like a miniature billiard ball. But in England in 1897 – at the Cavendish Laboratory, Cambridge – the Manchester-born physicist Joseph John Thomson discovered the tiny electron.

Pinhead-sized

Thomson envisaged the atom as resembling a plum pudding – a positively charged sphere in which the negatively charged electrons were embedded, like currants. But his simple model did not survive experiments begun in 1906 by the New Zealand-born physicist Ernest Rutherford, which culminated in the atom being split (facing page).

Rutherford deduced that the nucleus, although containing almost all the mass of the atom, must be extremely tiny indeed. If the atom were, say, the size of an average house, the nucleus would only be the size of a pinhead.

Initially, all of this had to be accepted in theory only, as there was no way of seeing the individual particles. But before long the British physicist Patrick Maynard Stuart Blackett, who began his research around 1919, was the first to take pictures of particle collisions resulting in transmutation. He used an apparatus called a cloud chamber – a glass vessel containing moist air. If the pressure inside the vessel were suddenly reduced, the water vapour would

condense into mist. The process of condensation could be triggered by the passage of charged subatomic particles. Just as aircraft high in the atmosphere leave vapour trails, so the particles left trails in the cloud chamber.

Blackett actually recorded the smashing of the nucleus in a cloud chamber. To do so he painstakingly took 23,000 photographs showing 400,000 alpha-particle tracks. It took him until 1925, six years after his work began, to record eight branched

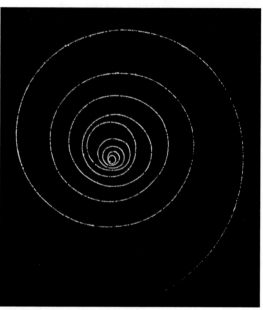

Whirling electron *The spiral path of an electron in a magnetic field in a bubble chamber, photographed at the Lawrence Berkeley Laboratory, California.*

tracks, showing the nucleus of an atom actually being smashed.

The cloud chamber, and later the bubble chamber in which the particles leave a trail of bubbles in a liquid, have been basic tools of particle physicists ever since.

Super colliders

As the speeds of the colliding particles were increased by ever more powerful machines, further subatomic particles were discovered.

The simple atoms envisaged by J.J. Thomson and Ernest Rutherford were in reality found to be extremely complex. By 1950, at least 14 elementary particles were known, and by 1964 the total had risen to more than 80.

Every increase in the energy of the atom smashers produces new data which has to be explained by theoretical physicists. But to attain these higher energies, increasingly bigger accelerators, with names like

Collision course *The streaks are the paths of particles colliding in liquid hydrogen inside a bubble chamber.*

cyclotron and synchrotron, have been developed.

The largest of all is due to be built at the town of Waxahachie, south of Dallas, Texas. It will be a giant tubular ring, 53 miles (85km) around. Two beams of protons will whirl around in opposite directions. Super powerful electromagnets will guide the proton beams round the rings as they are accelerated by electric fields to speeds approaching that of light – until they collide. The results are expected to provide confirmation of a range of hypothetical particles, with names like Higg's boson, or the top quark, which is believed to have existed only momentarily at the birth of the Universe.

The Super Collider, as the accelerator is called, will be built in underground tunnels.

It will occupy 1000 acres (405 hectares) and will cost $4.4 billion. It should be ready by 1996.

Photographing the building blocks of the Universe

The first images of atoms, the building blocks of all matter, were produced in 1956 by the German-born physicist Erwin Wilhelm Mueller, of Pennsylvania State University. His breakthrough came after 20 years of experiments with specialised types of microscopes.

In the 1950s, he injected helium gas into a vacuum chamber containing an extremely fine needle tip. Those atoms of helium which chanced to strike the tip, to which a high positive electrical voltage was applied, lost some of their outer 'cloud' of electrons. In the process, the atoms were modified into helium ions. (An ion is an electrically charged atom.) The positively charged ions shot away in straight lines – attracted by a fluorescent screen of negative voltage. On the screen, they produced an accurate

Atom array *The first visual image of how atoms are arranged in the benzene molecule was achieved by researchers in Zurich.*

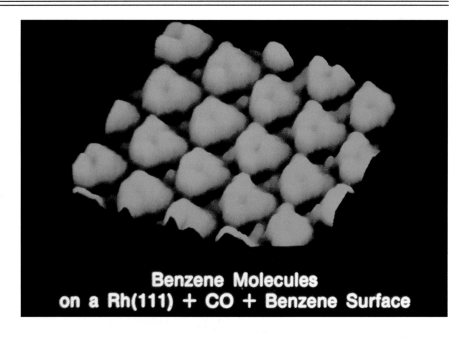

**Benzene Molecules
on a Rh(111) + CO + Benzene Surface**

BRINGING THINGS DOWN TO MICROSCOPIC SIZE

Miniaturised information storage will be a boon to such establishments as libraries who have to store great numbers of bulky books, newspapers and reports. At present, the British Museum adds an estimated 8 miles (13km) of books to its library shelves every year.

Scientists at the Cavendish Laboratory, Cambridge, used an electron beam (see *Electron microscope*, page 245) to generate patterns of dots to form both microscopic pictures and lettering in aluminium fluoride. In this way they can reduce printed words to a density of 10 million words a square millimetre.

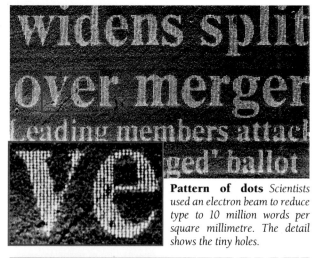

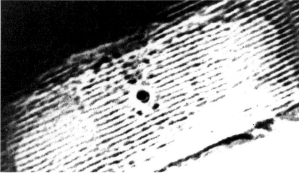

Pattern of dots *Scientists used an electron beam to reduce type to 10 million words per square millimetre. The detail shows the tiny holes.*

Smallest card *A Christmas card, with a picture of a robin, was produced by a scanning electronic beam making patterns of holes. It is about 1 billionth the normal size.*

Near-atomic size *The hole drilled by an electron beam is close in size to the actual distance between atoms. The ridges represent the atomic planes of the aluminium fluoride in which the hole is made.*

image of the needle tip, magnified 5 million times. The positions of individual atoms showed up as bright little dots. Although Mueller's invention – the field ion microscope – is used to study atomic reactions on surfaces, its applications are limited.

During the 1980s, much more dramatic images of atoms have been produced using the scanning tunnelling microscope (STM). It was invented in 1981 at the Zurich laboratories of IBM. It produces the image of the surface of a specimen as a contour map showing the positions of the individual atoms.

A needle, sharpened by chemical etching to a single atom at its point, is held a few atoms' distance from the specimen. A potential difference between the tip and the specimen causes a current to flow. As the tip is scanned across the specimen, resistance to the flow of the current varies as it passes over successive atoms. Measurements of the variation in resistance can be used to plot a contour map of the surface, detailed enough to record individual atoms, as well as spaces where atoms are missing (vacancies) and any disorder in the atomic structure. It can even record the layer of atoms beneath, showing how they relate to the top layer.

The result is an extraordinary image, showing the atoms fitting together like a laboratory model. The STM has the advantage that, unlike an electron microscope (page 245), it does not damage the specimen. It will prove immensely valuable in developing new electronic microchips, whose behaviour is determined by the accurate placing of layers of different atoms.

How the speed of light was measured

A French physicist, Jean Foucault, measured the speed of light remarkably accurately in the mid-19th century, using two mirrors set 66ft (20m) apart.

One mirror was fixed and another rotated at 800 revolutions a second. Beams of light were directed at the rotating mirror. When a light beam hit the mirror while it was at just the right angle, it was reflected to the fixed mirror, bounced back to the rotating mirror and then reflected back to the source (see diagram).

In the time it took to make the return trip between the mirrors, the rotating mirror had turned through a small angle so the beam that returned to the source deviated slightly from the original path.

By using the deviation of the beam to measure the angle through which the mirror had moved, and knowing the speed of rotation, Foucault could work out how long the light had taken for its trip, and its speed. Foucault's final result, reported in 1862, worked out at 187,000 miles a second (300,939km a second).

Foucault's method was refined in the 1920s by Albert Michelson, an American physicist, who sent light through a vacuum tube a mile (1.6km) long to remove the effect of air on its speed. Modern measurements have refined the figure to 186,282 miles (299,793km) a second.

A physicist at the Paris observatory, Jean Foucault (1819-68) spent 12 years on his speed-of-light experiments.

FOUCAULT'S EXPERIMENT WITH MIRRORS

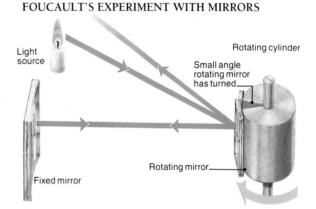

Light source

Rotating cylinder

Small angle rotating mirror has turned

Rotating mirror

Fixed mirror

The speed of a rotating mirror and its angular movement between reflections were vital to Foucault's calculations.

How did they measure the speed of sound?

As anyone who has watched a distant building site knows, the sound of a pile-driver at work lags behind its image. The sight of the hammer falling reaches you almost immediately. The sound is slow by comparison.

A thunderclap may be heard several seconds after the flash of lightning which caused it. For a storm a mile away, the gap is about five seconds. Just how fast sound travels was a problem that baffled scientists until a century ago.

An obvious way of measuring the speed of sound is to make a loud noise and measure how long it takes to travel a known distance – for example, by setting off an explosion on a distant hill, starting a stopwatch when the flash is seen, and stopping it when the sound is heard.

But the result would be only an approximation, dependent on the speed of human reaction. And a century ago no clock was precise enough to measure hundredths of a second.

To get around these problems, a French chemist and physicist, Henri Victor Regnault, devised an apparatus in 1864 to carry out the measurement automatically.

His device was a rotating paper-coated cylinder, on which a pen drew a line. The pen, which was electrically wired, had two possible positions against the cylinder – one when the current flowed, another when it was broken.

The pen was controlled by two circuits, one in front of a gun muzzle a considerable distance away, the other through a sound-sensitive diaphragm close to the cylinder.

At the start of the experiment, the current was switched on. The cylinder turned, and the pen traced a line. When the gun fired, it broke the first circuit, causing the pen to jump to its second position. A second or two later, the sound of the gun triggered the diaphragm, which closed the circuit again, causing the pen to flick back into its initial position.

The result was an irregular trace on the cylinder. As the cylinder's rotation speed was known, the jump on the trace recorded the time taken for the sound to travel from the gun to the diaphragm. The result: the sound of the gunshot travelled at about 750mph (1200km/h).

Since Regnault's day, scientists have shown that sound travels about four times faster in water than in air, and more than ten times faster through a solid. A simple experiment can sometimes be carried out to prove this. Find a long, straight iron railing. Put one ear to it, and get somebody some distance away to strike the railing with a hammer. You will hear two separate sounds. The noise will reach the ear against the railing a fraction of a second before it reaches the other ear.

Chuck Yeager: the man who broke the sound barrier

Two days before his attempt to break the sound barrier, Captain Charles 'Chuck' Yeager of the United States Air Force was knocked almost senseless in a riding accident and broke two ribs. The next morning his cracked ribs were taped up by a local doctor. Even so, he was unable to move his right arm because of the pain. He knew that if news of his injuries got out, the air force authorities would postpone the top-secret attempt scheduled for October 14, 1947.

The orange painted Bell X-1 rocket plane would be dropped from the bomb bay of a Boeing B-29 Superfortress, and after a short powerless glide, it would start to climb when Yeager fired the four rocket chambers in quick succession.

To get from the belly of the B-29 into the tiny cockpit of the X-1 (also known as the XS-1), Yeager had to scramble down a short ladder. The cockpit door then had to be lowered by a detachable length of cable from the bomb bay.

Once the door was in place, Yeager had to close it from the right-hand side – a simple enough matter providing you did not have two broken ribs and an immobilised right arm. Then his flight engineer Jack Ridley had a brainwave. The pilot could use some kind of stick in his left hand to raise the door handle and lock it.

'We looked around the hangar and found a broom,' Yeager recorded afterwards. 'Jack sawed off a ten-inch piece of broomstick, and it fit right into the door handle. Then I crawled into the X-1 and we tried it out. He held the door against the frame, and by using that broomstick to raise the door handle, I found I could manage to lock it.'

At around 8am on October 14, the B-29 took off from Muroc Air Base (now Edwards Air Force Base) in the Mojave Desert in southern California. To begin with, Yeager travelled in the bomber – which had the X-1 cradled in its belly.

Despite the pain he was in, 24-year-old Yeager – a much-decorated Second World War pilot – was quietly optimistic. He had already made a series of test flights in the rocket plane and aimed to be the first man to exceed the speed of sound – about 760mph (1220km/h) at sea level. The higher the altitude, the slower sound travels. For his attempt, Yeager planned to fly at about 700mph (1126km/h) at around 40,000ft (12,200m) above sea level.

The speed of an aircraft compared with the speed of sound in the vicinity is known as the Mach number, after the Austrian

physicist Ernst Mach (1838-1916). An aircraft flying at the speed of sound is said to be travelling at Mach 1.

Unless an aircraft is specially designed for supersonic flight, strong shock waves hit the wings and body when it approaches Mach 1. Airflow around the plane becomes unstable; and there is usually severe buffeting, causing instability and loss of flight control. Theoretically, the X-1 – with its streamlined nose and smooth lines – would not be affected by this.

Nevertheless, it had a nasty habit of hurling the pilot about the cramped cockpit so roughly that he risked being knocked unconscious. To protect himself, Yeager wore a large leather football helmet over his flying helmet.

As the B-29 neared 7000ft (2100m), Yeager made his way forward to the bomb bay. From there, rails ran down to the side of the X-1. He pushed the aluminium ladder down the rails and slid feet-first into the cockpit of the X-1.

'Going down that damned ladder hurt,' he recorded. '...I picked up the broom handle and it raised up into lock position. It worked perfectly.'

He next had to contend with the icy conditions in the cockpit. 'Shivering,' he described, 'you bang your gloved hands together and strap on your oxygen mask inside the coldest airplane ever flown. You're being cold-soaked from the hun-

dreds of gallons of liquid oxygen (LOX) fuel stored in the compartment directly behind you at minus 296 degrees. No heater, no defroster; you'll just have to grit your teeth for the next 15 minutes ... it's like trying to work and concentrate inside a frozen food locker.'

During the test flights, Yeager's perspira-

Good-luck charm *'Chuck' Yeager (left) named his plane after his wife Glennis (right). 'You're my good-luck charm, hon. Any airplane I name after you always brings me home.'*

Breaking the barrier *Only 31ft (9.5m) long, and with a wingspan of 28ft (8.5m), the stubby Bell X-1 was no beauty to look at. Piloted by Captain 'Chuck' Yeager, the rocket plane blasted through the sound barrier at a speed of 700mph (1126km/h).*

The baby in the bomb bay *To conserve its fuel load of 600 gallons (2700 litres) of liquid oxygen and alcohol, the X-1 was cradled like a baby in the bomb bay of a B-29 Superfortress. To start its flight, the X-1 was dropped from the mother plane just like a bomb.*

plan and the aircraft started, as he put it, to 'chug-a-lug a ton of fuel a minute'.

The X-1 climbed at a speed of Mach .88; as it did so, it began to buffet. Yeager immediately threw the stabiliser switch and the plane levelled off at 36,000ft (11,000m). He turned off two of the rocket chambers – and at 40,000ft (12,200m) was climbing at Mach .92. Again he levelled off – this time at 42,000ft (12,800m). He switched rocket chamber three back on – and instantly hit Mach .96 and rising.

'We were flying supersonic!' he stated. 'And it was as smooth as a baby's bottom: Grandma could be sitting up there sipping lemonade. I ... then raised the nose to slow down. I was thunderstruck. After all the anxiety, breaking the sound barrier turned out to be a perfectly paved speedway.'

To eliminate the risk of an explosion when the X-1 landed, Yeager jettisoned the remainder of the fuel and seven minutes later the plane touched down safely. Yeager had opened the way for man's exploration of space.

'And so I was a hero this day,' he stated matter-of-factly. 'As usual, the fire trucks raced out to where the ship had rolled to a stop on the lake bed. As usual, I hitched a ride back to the hangar with the fire chief. That warm desert sun really felt wonderful. My ribs ached.'

tion had added an extra layer of frost on the windshield. To counter this, his chief mechanic had put a coating of hair shampoo on the shield. 'For some unknown reason,' stated Yeager, 'it worked as an effective antifrost device, and we continued using it even after the government purchased a special chemical that cost 18 bucks a bottle.'

The two planes, still shackled together, were flying at about 15,000ft (4570m) and climbing. At 20,000ft (6100m) the B-29's

pilot, Major Bob Cardenas, began the countdown. '... five ... four ... three ... two ... one ... DROP!' He pressed the release button, and with a jolt the X-1 was on its own and falling nose-up through space. The fall lasted for about 500ft (150m), while Yeager wrestled desperately with the controls. Finally, he got the plane's nose down and then fired the four rocket chambers. He knew that the fuel could 'blow up at the flick of an igniter switch and scatter your pieces over several counties'. But all went to

How scientists try to predict earthquakes

On February 4, 1975, officials in the Chinese province of Liaoning, Manchuria, issued an urgent warning that an earthquake was on the way. A series of small shocks in the morning seemed to warn of something catastrophic. People were urged to remain outdoors, even though it was winter, and bitterly cold.

The same day, just after 7.30 in the evening, a strong earthquake struck. Hundreds of houses collapsed, but – because they had stayed outside – very few people were injured.

This was one of the first-known cases in which an earthquake had been successfully predicted, and it resulted from a programme started by the Chinese government in 1965 to try to reduce the terrible toll of earthquakes.

The success of the prediction, though, was something of a fluke. The methods used have since failed to predict worse earthquakes – like the catastrophic one the following year that killed more than 240,000 people in Tangshan, eastern China. And some predictions have given rise to false alarms. It did, nevertheless, make clear just how valuable an accurate earthquake forecast would be.

In the past the Chinese, like many other people, believed that earthquakes could be predicted astrologically or by observing natural portents such as unusual behaviour by animals. However, the evidence is all anecdotal and there is really nothing to support it.

Modern scientific attempts to predict earthquakes focus on a number of changes that occur in the Earth's crust in the build-up to a major one. Many quakes, for instance, are preceded by a series of small shocks, as in Liaoning. But foreshocks alone do not offer an infallible means of prediction. Sometimes big quakes occur without them. Sometimes the foreshocks merely die away.

There is no single reliable indicator of a coming earthquake. At present, seismologists can only hope to refine predictions based on four main indicators.

The first is the speed at which shock waves travel through the ground. As subterranean stresses build up, pressures in the rock alter the way in which shock waves travel. Their speed seems to decline and then increase again just before a quake. Small explosions and foreshocks can be analysed to reveal the changes.

The second indicator involves changes

in the level of the surface of the ground, which rises fractionally as pressure below ground increases. An area in the region of California's San Andreas Fault has risen 16in (400mm) in 20 years.

The third is the emission of greater quantities of radon, an inert, radioactive gas that seeps out of the earth all the time, but which appears to increase in concentration before an earthquake.

And the fourth is any change in the electrical or magnetic behaviour of rocks in the moments when they come close to their breaking point before an earthquake.

Such measurements have already allowed prediction – of a sort. In November 1974, American scientists detected magnetic changes, tilts in the ground and changes in the speed of shock waves near Hollister in central California. One scientist, John Healy, of the US Geological Survey, argued that the signs were clear enough to issue a warning, but his

Fault line *The San Andreas Fault – a major fracture in the Earth's crust – travels north-westwards through southern California and along the San Francisco Peninsula.*

colleagues disagreed, so no warning was given. The very next day, a magnitude-5 earthquake hit Hollister – too small, fortunately, to do much damage.

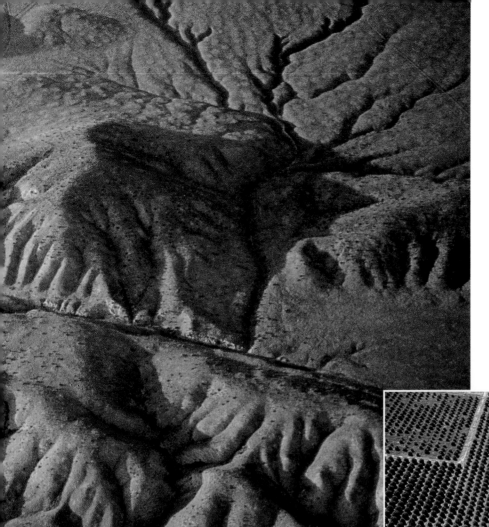

Change of course *The San Andreas Fault is the result of movement of two major plates of the Earth's crust – the eastern Pacific and the North American. The movement has changed the course of a river (top right of picture) that once ran straight across the fault. The river now runs along part of the fault, and resumes its journey on the other side in its original bed (lower left).*

At present, however, scientists can make predictions only in long-range statistical terms, stating for example that Los Angeles is due for a major earthquake by the year 2020, killing up to 20,000 people.

Businesses and people can be insured against earthquakes, but not against the consequences of a false alarm that might cause the panic-stricken evacuation of whole cities. Crying wolf just once might lead to a genuine prediction being ignored, thus guaranteeing precisely the catastrophe that the prediction was supposed to avoid.

Out of line *In 1940, earthquake activity in California's Imperial Valley moved rows of trees in this orange grove out of line. The grove lies along the track of a fault.*

FATAL EARTHQUAKES IN THE 20TH CENTURY

DATE	PLACE	MAGNITUDE	DEATHS	DATE	PLACE	MAGNITUDE	DEATHS
1906	San Francisco, USA	8.3	700	1970	Peru	7.7	50-70,000
1908	Italy	7.5	83,000	1976	China	7.8	242,000
1920	China	8.6	180,000	1978	Iran	7.7	15,000
1923	Japan	8.3	99,000	1979	Ecuador	7.9	600
1927	China	8.3	200,000	1980	Algeria	7.7	3500
1931	New Zealand	7.9	255	1980	Italy	7.2	3000
1932	China	Unknown	70,000	1981	Iran	7.3	2500
1935	Pakistan	7.5	20-60,000	1983	Japan	7.7	58
1952	California, USA	7.7	11	1983	Turkey	7.1	1300
1962	Chile	8.5	4-5000	1985	Chile	7.4	177
1964	Alaska	8.5	178	1985	Mexico	8.1	4287
1968	Iran	7.4	12,000	1988	USSR (Armenia)	7.0	25,000

By measuring the intensity of an earthquake's shock waves, scientists can determine its magnitude – the amount of energy released at its focus. This is measured on the Richter scale – from 1 to 10 – devised by Californian seismologist Charles Richter in 1935. The scale is logarithmic; a shock of magnitude 8 is 10 times greater than 7, 100 times greater than 6, and so on.

THREE WAYS OF DETECTING EARTHQUAKES

A laser house, with electronic instruments which record every quiver of the San Andreas Fault, stands at Parkfield, California.

A strainmeter – an instrument for recording the expansion and contraction of rock – is checked by a scientist at Parkfield.

A creepmeter consists of a wire strung across a fault, and a measuring device. This one is set up on the San Andreas Fault.

A hole deep enough to pierce the Earth's crust

Geologists know more about the rocks on the Moon than they do about those that lie 10 miles (16km) beneath their feet. Astronauts have recovered samples from the Moon, but the rock below the Earth's crust remains beyond reach.

The crust, a hard, rough skin that lies over the entire surface of the Earth, is relatively no thicker than the skin of an apple, ranging from about 6 miles to 40 miles deep (10-64km). It is thinnest at the bottom of the deepest oceans, and thickest on land.

The first attempt to drill through the Earth's crust was launched in the late 1950s, with Project Mohole, an American attempt to penetrate beyond the point where the crust meets the mantle, a boundary known as the Mohorovičić discontinuity (page 210). However, after some preliminary holes had been drilled from a drill ship off the California coast in 1960, the scheme was cancelled because of the cost.

In 1970, the Russians began drilling the world's deepest hole to explore the geology of the Earth's crust. It goes down through the barren rocks of the Kola Peninsula, which lies inside the Arctic Circle, just east of Finland. By the late 1980s, it was more than 8 miles (13km) deep, and was the first hole to reach the lower crust. But its ultimate target of 9.3 miles (15km) is only halfway to the mantle, which lies about 19 miles (30km) down at this point.

The Kola well used special techniques developed for the oil industry to reach its record depth. Conventional drilling uses an engine at the surface to rotate the drill string, a length of pipe with a bit on the end. But below 5 miles (8km) the stresses on the upper part of the drill string become too great, because it has to bear the weight of the drilling pipes and also turn them rapidly.

So at the Kola well the bit is turned by a turbine (a series of fan blades) fixed to the drill string near the bottom of the hole. Mud pumped down the hole at great pressure drives the turbine, which rotates the bit through a gearbox.

Because the drill string does not have to transmit rotary forces, it can be made of light aluminium alloys instead of steel, halving the weight which has to be supported by the derrick – a building 30 storeys high.

When the bit is lifted for replacement, samples of the rock can be removed for study. The Russian scientists have found veins of gold, iron, cobalt and zinc, probably formed from minerals that had been carried by water through the cracks in the rock.

They also found an unexpectedly rapid rise in temperature as they drilled down. At a depth of 6 miles (10km), the rock was at a temperature of 356°F (180°C), not the 212°F (100°C) that had been predicted.

The Russian methods might make it possible to penetrate through the Earth's crust for the first time. But the temperatures would create a problem; the alloys used for the drill string become weakened at temperatures of more than 450°F (230°C), so an expensive material like titanium might be needed.

And to find the thinnest area of crust, the drilling would have to be done in the deep ocean, which would increase the difficulties.

How do they know the continents are drifting?

As long ago as 1620, the English philosopher Francis Bacon pointed out the close fit between the coastlines of South America and Africa. The shapes suggested that they had once been joined but had drifted apart.

In 1912 the German meteorologist Alfred Wegener put forward detailed arguments in support of the theory. But it was not proved to the satisfaction of most geologists until the 1960s.

The fit between the two continents is good, particularly the continental edge rather than the shorelines. Their shape has been altered by the eroding effects of tides. But the continental outlines where the ocean is 3000ft (900m) deep show the average 'misfit' when joined to be only about 50 miles (80km).

Other evidence that the continents were once linked includes common geological features, such as similar types of rock of a similar age. And many plants and creatures appear to share a common origin. For example, many freshwater fish in South America are closely related to African species, and it is difficult to accept that they could have swum the Atlantic Ocean.

The guinea pig is found in the wild in both Africa and South America, but nowhere else. Also, monkeys are indigenous only in those continents and it is unlikely they would have evolved independently in each place.

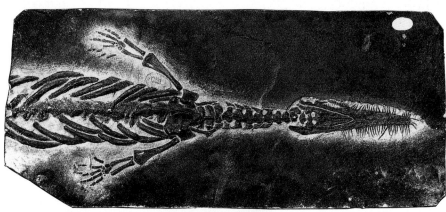

Earth's changing face *Our planet's seven continents were connected some 250 million years ago (top). The supercontinent was called Pangaea (all lands) in 1912 by the German meteorologist Alfred Wegener. By 100 million years ago they had drifted apart.*

Giant 'jigsaw' *The landmasses as they are now (left). If they could be joined, Africa's west coast would fit neatly into the east coast of South America. More evidence for continental drift is provided by fossils such as Mesosaurus (above), found on both continents. A freshwater creature that lived some 280 million years ago, it could not have crossed the ocean. Some freshwater fish still living on both continents are closely related.*

OUR RESTLESS PLANET

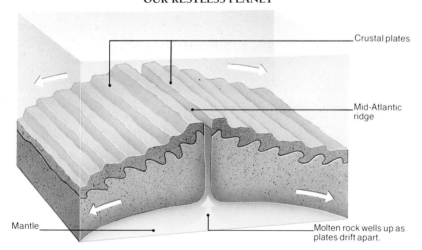

Crustal plates

Mid-Atlantic ridge

Mantle

Molten rock wells up as plates drift apart.

Shifting seabed *Ocean ridges are formed at places where molten rock wells up then cools to form new crust, as continental plates move apart. The Mid-Atlantic Ridge is an example.*

But it was a more practical kind of evidence that convinced the doubters. Samples of the Earth's crust taken from the seabed by an American research ship, the *Glomar Challenger*, during the late 1960s showed a curious pattern. The geologists gathered samples by drilling cores up to 3½ miles (5½km) deep in the ocean floor.

As molten rocks solidify, they take up the magnetic field of the Earth. The tiny iron particles in the molten rock swing to face the North Pole and are then fixed for ever as the rock hardens.

The samples taken from the rocks at the bottom of the Atlantic showed that at many times in the past the magnetic field had reversed itself, so that North became South, and vice versa.

On both sides of a ridge that runs down the centre of the Atlantic, the same pattern of reversals was identified, which suggested that the sea floor was spreading

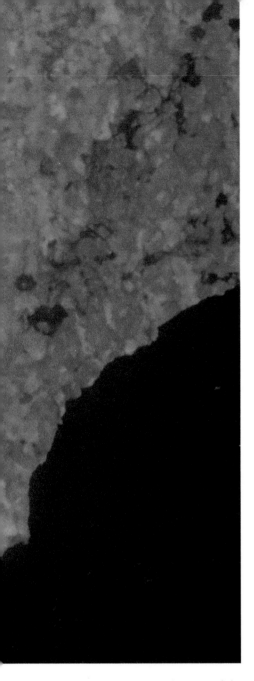

Earth in upheaval *Iceland is part of the Mid-Atlantic Ridge where it rises out of the ocean. A volcanologist studies an eruption of Krafla, one of its volcanoes.*

outwards from the centre. As new rock was formed, it adopted the magnetism of the Earth at that time, recording like a geological tape recorder the process of regular reversals. The pattern of reversals to the east of the Mid-Atlantic Ridge was the mirror image of the pattern on the west.

The ridge runs right through the middle of the North and South Atlantic Oceans, dividing Europe from North America and Africa from South America.

Only one explanation fitted the facts. New rock was being continuously produced under the centre of the ocean and was forcing its way up, driving the old rock apart. As the ocean floor spread outwards in both directions, it carried the four

MEASURING THE SPEED OF DRIFTING CONTINENTS

Once the idea of continental drift was accepted in the 1960s, scientists began to wonder how fast the plates carrying the continents were travelling.

In one sense the sums are simple. Knowing the width of the Atlantic, for instance, and the time it has taken to form, it is easy to calculate the speed of its formation. It turns out that Europe and America have moved apart at an average of 12 miles (19km) every 1 million years. That's an average of ¾in (19mm) a year. But how fast are the plates moving now?

Measuring such imperceptible movements was impossible until the 1980s, when scientists developed a sophisticated technique based on strange objects many millions of light years from Earth. These objects – quasars, or quasi-stellar radio sources – seem to be star-like, but radiate more energy than galaxies.

They are so far away that they can be treated as fixed points.

Quasars can therefore be used for a refined sort of triangulation, the system by which surveyors take sightings of one point from two others to work out distances. In this case, the 'surveyors' use radio telescopes on different continents, two (or more) of which take a fix on a quasar, and record its signals on magnetic tape.

Though the telescopes receive the same signal, they do not record it in the same way because of the distance

Bouncing beams *Lasers aimed from two different continents and reflected back by a satellite provide coordinates to measure the distance between them. Regular checks will reveal any change in their positions as the continents move.*

between them. When the recorded signals are compared, the distance between the telescopes can be measured. Later comparisons can detect any slight change in the positions of the telescopes. The method of triangulation is so sensitive that it can detect a change of only ½in (13mm).

Another monitoring method with a high degree of accuracy is laser ranging. Two observatories on different continents aim lasers at the same reflector satellite.

The reflected beams can be used to calculate, by triangulation, the distance between the observatories. Repeating the process at intervals reveals any relative movement of the landmasses on which the observatories are sited.

continents with it, at the rate of about 1in (25mm) a year. That may seem slow, but it is quick enough to have created the whole of the Atlantic Ocean in comparatively recent geological time. The Atlantic started to form 165 million years ago, and within 40 million years the North Atlantic was 12,000ft (3600m) deep and 600 miles (965km) wide. Then the South Atlantic started to form as South America eased away from Africa, widening slowly to form the ocean that exists today.

Cause of earthquakes

Scientists have deduced that oil deposits in Alaska and coal sources in northern Europe were formed in the tropics and that continental drift has moved them to their present northern locations.

Mountain ranges are formed when the plates on which continents 'float' grind against each other, which is also a cause of earthquakes. The Himalayan massif, for example, is thought to have been created when India collided with the Asian continent at the geologically high speed of 15 miles (24km) in 1 million years.

How do they calculate the age of the Earth?

The Creation, according to Archbishop James Ussher, took place at 8pm on October 22 in 4004 BC. The Irish cleric made his calculation in the mid-17th century after study of the ages of the Old Testament patriarchs, long genealogies and other Biblical details.

His view was challenged in 1785 when a Scottish naturalist, James Hutton, declared that the formation of mountains and the erosion of riverbeds must have taken millions, not thousands, of years.

But it was not until the discovery of radioactivity by the French physicist Antoine Henri Becquerel in 1896 that an accurate idea of the Earth's age was made possible.

Scientists now accept that the Earth's

crust solidified around 4700 million years ago. This calculation has been made possible by a study of the decay of various radioactive minerals.

When rocks are formed by the cooling and solidification of volcanic lava, radioactive elements are trapped inside. These elements decay at a precise rate, defined as 'half-life' – the time it takes for half the radioactivity to decay.

Careful study has determined the half-lives of individual elements. By measuring the amount of any radioactive element in a sample of rock, the process of decay can be used as if it were a clock which started ticking when the rock was formed.

It is not the precise quantity of the radioactive element left that matters, because that depends on how much there was originally. What is important is the ratio between the quantity of radioactive material and the substance into which it changes. The older the rock, the lower the radioactive material it will contain and the greater will be the proportion of its decay products.

In examining rock samples, several different dating systems can be used. A common one is the decay of the radioactive element potassium-40, a process with a half-life of 11,900 million years. The decay of uranium into lead (half-life 4500 million years) is also used. In the case of the Earth, about half its original uranium has decayed into lead. So the age of the Earth is about the half-life of uranium.

How scientists picture the centre of the Earth

The deepest man-made hole in the world penetrates more than 8 miles (13km) down through the frozen Kola Peninsula of Lapland, in the north-west corner of the USSR (see page 206).

Deep as it is, it is only a pinprick in the Earth's surface. To reach the centre of the Earth it would have to continue for nearly 4000 miles (6440km).

Geologists are nevertheless able to paint a picture of what the inside of the planet is like. They believe that the Earth's inner core, which is 1700 miles (2700km) across, consists mostly of iron heated to 7000°F (3800°C). At the very centre the iron is kept solid by the pressure of the Earth around it. This picture is partly based on the Earth's apparent weight compared to its size.

The first estimates of the weight of the Earth were made by the English scientist Henry Cavendish in 1798. He had discovered the value of the gravitational constant, the amount by which heavenly bodies attract each other. By studying the orbit of the Moon, he was able to use this figure to calculate the Earth's weight. To his surprise he found it was twice what would have been expected from the density of the rocks on the surface.

The weight of the Earth is 6595 million million million tons, and its density is 5.522 times that of water. But the density of surface rocks is only 2.8 times that of water. The discrepancy can be explained by assuming that a large part of the centre consists of iron, which is dense enough to make up the difference and which is also found in meteorites.

Serious study of the inner parts of the Earth did not start until the discovery that vibrations caused by earthquakes can travel thousands of miles through the Earth's interior. These vibrations, or seismic waves, are of two types: compression waves which are similar to sound and cause the rock to vibrate back and forth, and shear waves which cause the rock to move from side to side and up and down. It is the shear waves which do the greatest amount

OUR MULTI-LAYERED PLANET

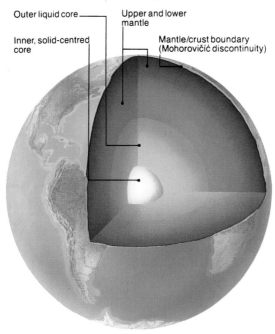

Outer liquid core

Inner, solid-centred core

Upper and lower mantle

Mantle/crust boundary (Mohorovičić discontinuity)

The Earth has many layers, rather like an onion. Beneath the crust lie the upper and lower mantles, and beyond that the outer and inner cores, consisting mostly of iron.

of damage to buildings in an earthquake.

Compression waves (called P waves) can travel through liquids as well as solids, while shear waves (called S waves) can travel through solids only. The speed of the waves depends on the density of the material they are travelling through.

Geologists have used the seismic waves rather as a doctor uses X-rays. In 1906 the British geologist R.D. Oldham found that P waves slow down at a certain depth, and that at the same depth S waves either disappear or are reflected back to the surface. He suggested that this depth marked the boundary between a solid mantle (outer region) and a liquid core.

Three years later the Yugoslavian seismologist Andrija Mohorovičić discovered a second boundary, about 20 miles (32km) below the surface, where the density and perhaps the type of rock changed abruptly. He concluded that this boundary, now called the Mohorovičić discontinuity, marked the dividing line between the mantle and the Earth's crust.

Further work suggested that the very centre of the Earth was solid. So geologists concluded that the Earth has a small solid region at the centre, surrounded by a liquid core, a dense mantle and finally the lighter rocks of the crust.

More sophisticated seismology added detail to this picture, dividing the crust into at least two layers, and the mantle into three.

But in the 1980s computers analysed the seismic waves to produce a much clearer picture. They established, for example, that the mantle and even the core vary in thickness from place to place, just as the crust does. They also showed that the continents have deep cold 'roots' that penetrate 125 miles (200km) into the mantle.

Much remains unknown about the Earth, however. The centre is known to be hot because of the heat that constantly flows out of it. Molten lava erupts from volcanoes and a mine is hotter at the bottom than at the surface. The temperature of the inner core is estimated to be about 7000°F (3850°C), but the source of the heat is not known.

One source of heat could be the decay of radioactive materials like uranium and thorium, and the much more plentiful but more weakly radioactive potassium and rubidium. Alternatively, the heat might have been generated at the time of the formation of the Earth, by the collapse of the atoms which formed it.

How does it work?

*How does a laser beam make music? How does a 'smart card'
pay your bills? Why is an atomic clock so accurate?
The last years of the 20th century are filled with astonishing
examples of technology at work.*

How chips are running the world, page 238.

How robots are replacing humans, page 246.

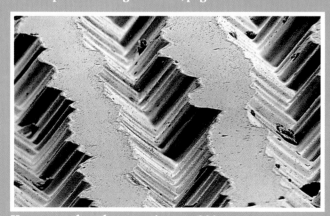

How a record produces music, page 222.

How an electron
microscope sees into
inner space, page 245.

How people can talk together across the world by telephone

Over 500 million telephones are now in use throughout the world. In just over 100 years – since the Scottish-born inventor Alexander Graham Bell patented the first telephone in 1876 – telephones have revolutionised world communications.

Today, telephone networks relay not only voices but pictures and written information as well, by land and sea cables and through the air on microwaves, which are super-high-frequency radio waves (page 216). Calls can be made across half the world with less than a second's delay in connection, and no difficulty in hearing. Multinational companies can even hold cross-world video conferences, with executives speaking to each other from one screen to another.

Satellites, microchips and lasers

The modern inventions that have made this revolution possible include space satellites, microchips and laser beams. *Early Bird*, the world's first commercial satellite, was launched in 1965 by the International Telecommunications Satellite Organisation (INTELSAT).

Now there are about 130 satellites orbiting in space, relaying messages on microwaves from Earth station to Earth station. They orbit the Earth at heights of about 22,500 miles (36,000km) above the Equator once every 24 hours, so appear to remain in the same place.

From the Earth stations, microwaves carrying messages are beamed up to the satellites from huge dish aerials, some of which are 98ft (30m) across. They are computer controlled so that they always point directly at the satellite. Microwaves are not only used for satellite links – dish aerials beam messages across land too, in straight lines from towers located to ensure a clear path.

Microchips on the satellites amplify the relayed signals. Microchips have also brought about clearer, speedier communication by providing the fast switching needed for sending telephone messages by digital transmission. And lasers have

Linking the world *Silhouetted against a German sunset, these huge dish aerials at Raisting, in Bavaria, make up one of the many Earth stations in the international satellite link. They link all parts of the world in seconds, at any time of day or night.*

MOUTHPIECE

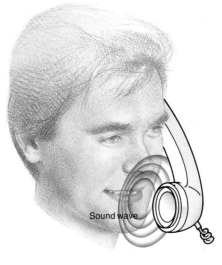

HOW A TELEPHONE WORKS

A telephone handset has a transmitter (traditionally a carbon microphone) in the mouthpiece and a receiver in the earpiece. The handset rests on a cradle switch linked to the exchange. As you lift the handset, electric current passes through carbon granules or electromagnets in the microphone. Modern telephones no longer use carbon microphones, but operate in a similar way.

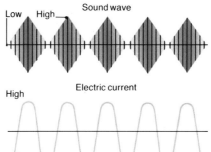

As the diaphragm vibrates, the current through the microphone fluctuates because the tighter the granules are pressed, the more current they pass. So the current copies the pattern of the sound waves.

EARPIECE

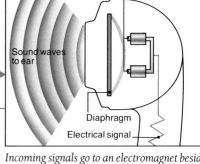

MICROPHONE

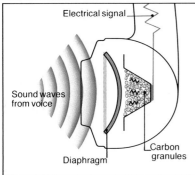

The sound waves of your voice vibrate a thin metal diaphragm in the microphone. This vibration makes the diaphragm press more or less against the carbon granules, according to the strengths of the sounds.

TELEPHONE EXCHANGE

Each telephone is connected to a local telephone exchange by a pair of wires, and exchanges are linked by cables. The circuits are separate from the national electricity supply, and the current through the circuits is much weaker.

RECEIVER

Incoming signals go to an electromagnet beside a diaphragm. The fluctuating current makes the magnet draw and release the diaphragm irregularly. Its vibrations make sound waves like those entering the microphone.

enabled the use of fibre optic cables – glass threads that carry digital messages at the speed of light, so fast that they could go seven times round the Earth in a second.

Telecommunications services now available include fax, radiopaging (bleepers), cordless telephones, car telephones and even aircraft telephones, allowing passengers to make calls while flying.

Dialling – how you get a crossed line

When you lift the receiver and complete the circuit to the exchange, dialling a number sends a series of electrical pulses down the line. Older telephone exchanges have automatic electromechanical switchgear, named after the American, Almon Strowger, who conceived it in 1888. This has banks of fixed contacts, each in a half circle round a mobile selector arm.

The number is selected step by step. The first dialled digit sends the arm up to a bank corresponding to the digit. The arm then rotates to find a free contact – one that will

connect it to the next bank ready for the next digit dialled. If no contact is free, the engaged tone is sounded. If contact is made, the next selector arm searches for the second digit, and so on. The final selector makes contact with the line of the number being called.

If the selector accidentally touches and sticks on an incorrect contact for the digit dialled, you get a crossed line.

The latest telephone exchanges work electronically. Dialling sets up audible tones, and connections are made by circuits incorporating microchips that interpret the tones. Because there are no moving parts, electronic switching is silent and more reliable than electromechanical gear, and crossed lines are rare.

Carrying the current

Two wires, or conductors, are needed to complete the circuit between a telephone transmitter and receiver. Some exchange cables carry thousands of pairs of wires.

If every call needed a separate pair of conductors for transmission throughout the telephone network, the simultaneous transmission of thousands of calls from one exchange to another would be unmanageable. A pair of ordinary copper wires can be made to handle only a limited number of calls at once because they are designed for low-frequency current. Higher frequencies would allow more simultaneous calls, but unless a different design of cable is used, the signal radiates away and loses strength.

Most trunk lines between telephone exchanges are now coaxial cables, in which the signal is confined to prevent loss of strength and interference. Instead of a pair of wires, each coaxial cable has a central copper wire with an outer copper conductor that surrounds it like a sleeve. They can handle high frequencies and carry thousands of calls. Built-in amplifiers boost signals about every 1¼ miles (2km).

Using a technique known as frequency multiplexing, the electric signals corresponding to the voice sound waves are modulated – that is, combined with an electromagnetic carrier wave in the same way as radio waves. A number of carrier waves of different frequencies are then sent along the same pair of conductors.

At the receiving exchange, the signals are separated from the carrier wave by a process called demodulation. They are then filtered to the correct receiver.

Sending voices by number

Until the 1970s, most telephone calls were transmitted as electric signals corresponding to the vibrations of the voice. These are known as analogue signals because they are analogous – similar in structure – to the sound. Electrical interference in the transmitting circuits can distort voices.

After the 1970s, the analogue system began to be replaced by a digital system which cuts out most interference and distortion. The analogue electrical signals from the microphone are changed to binary numbers (page 241) in electronic circuits at the exchange and transmitted in coded form.

To do this, the wave heights of the electric current are measured thousands of times every second. The measurement is expressed as a sequence of the digits 1 and 0. Current is then converted to a series of pulses – a flow for 1 and a break in flow for 0 – representing the wave measurements. This is known as pulse-code modulation (PCM). As each pulse is very short, the pulses of one telephone message can be interleaved between the pulses of others.

This technique of time multiplexing allows 32 simultaneous calls to be sent along a single pair of wires, or thousands of messages to be sent at once along the same coaxial cable.

Telephoning on the move

Mobile telephones fitted into cars are really radios linked to the ordinary telephone system. The radio-telephone network is operated on a cellular system – the territory covered is split into small areas, or cells, about 3 miles (5km) across. Each cell has a central low-powered transmitter connected to the telephone network.

Several cells form a group, and each cell in a group operates on a different frequency. The same set of frequencies can be used in an adjacent group without causing interference, because the range of each transmitter is limited.

The cell transmitters are linked by cable to a central computer, which transfers a note of the car's position from one cell to another as it travels. When a telephone call is made to a car, the computer switches the telephone link to the closest cell transmitter for the best reception. When a call is made from the car, the nearest cell aerial picks up its signals and routes the call.

Radio: sending sounds at the speed of light

When you listen to a live concert on the radio, you hear the music sooner than someone listening in the concert hall. This astonishing fact is because radio waves carry the sound to your home at the speed of light. Sound waves (the vibrations of voices or instruments) take longer to travel through the hall on their own.

From sounds to electrical signals

When sound enters a microphone, sound waves cause a thin diaphragm in the microphone to vibrate. The vibrations are converted into corresponding electrical signals, which are amplified then fed into a modulator – a device that combines them with an electrically generated radio wave that can then carry them through the air. The carrier wave is vibrated at the same

frequency as a natural wave by a device called an oscillator. After modulation, the carrier wave is amplified and fed by cable to the aerial for transmission.

Sending the signals through the air

Broadcasting takes place in wave bands – ranges of radio waves of certain wavelengths or frequencies. Programmes being broadcast simultaneously are each transmitted at a different frequency.

The aerials (or antennae) that send out the signals are usually on a tower or mast some 500-600ft (150-180m) high. Each is basically a loop of wire or a metal rod, and varies in length according to the frequency to be transmitted. Current surges through the aerial, which radiates electromagnetic waves in much the same way that a lamp

From crystal set to transistor

A German physicist named Heinrich Hertz first demonstrated in 1888 that it was possible to transmit electrical energy through the air.

Between 1894 and 1896, the Italian scientist Guglielmo Marconi developed a method of using Hertzian waves to send signals in Morse code – a method that became known as wireless telegraphy. By 1901 Marconi had improved his system so much that he was able to send wireless telegraph signals across the Atlantic from Cornwall to St John's, Newfoundland.

A Canadian engineer made the world's first public radio broadcast – from Massachusetts, USA, heard by ships around 100 miles (160km) away – on Christmas Eve, 1906. He was Reginald Aubrey Fessenden, who had found a way of combining the signals from a microphone with an electromagnetic wave. The name 'radio' was given to the method.

At first, listeners had earphones linked to receivers that used crystals to pick up the radio waves. These eventually gave way to sets with loudspeakers, diode

Historic broadcast
Edward VIII of England abdicates in 1936, to marry 'the woman I love' – the American divorcee Wallis Simpson.

valves (invented by an Englishman, John Ambrose Fleming, in 1904), and more powerful electronic circuits following the American Lee de Forest's invention of the triode valve in 1907. With the earliest valves (used to amplify signals), sets had to be switched on to warm up for five minutes before the programme began.

Regular public broadcasting did not begin until 1920, from radio stations in Pittsburgh and Detroit. Edwin H. Armstrong, an American engineer, improved the receiver in 1924, and by the late 1950s, compact transistors were replacing bulky valves.

Early wireless
Many would have heard the king's words from a receiver of this type.

filament radiates electric light. These waves, carrying the signals, spread out from the aerial tower in all directions.

Picking up the signals

When they have been broadcast, radio waves can be picked up by an aerial tuned to the right band of frequencies. By turning your radio to the programme you want, you alter the electronic characteristics of a tuning circuit until it allows through only the waves of the desired frequency.

The incoming carrier wave is then mixed with a wave of a lower frequency, generated in the radio receiver, to produce a signal at a fixed, intermediate frequency. The fixed frequency makes it easier to amplify the signals and reject unwanted ones, so you can receive the programme with the minimum distortion.

After amplification, the electrical signals are separated from the carrier wave by a demodulator and are amplified again, then fed to a loudspeaker. The loudspeaker works like a microphone in reverse, and changes the signals into exact replicas of the sounds that entered the microphone.

AM and FM signals

There are two ways in which the electrical signals can be made to modulate, or alter, the carrier radio wave – either amplitude modulation (AM) or frequency modulation (FM). Amplitude modulation alters the amount by which the carrier wave loops up and down. Frequency-modulated signals

---

MODULATING A RADIO CARRIER WAVE

Carrier *A wave produced electrically, with loop size and spacing uniform.*

Sound signals *Electric current from the microphone, with a varying form.*

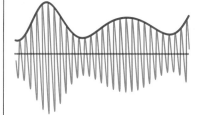

Amplitude modulation *The loop sizes of the carrier wave have been varied to match those of the sound signals.*

Frequency modulation *The spacing of the carrier-wave loops has been varied to match the sound signals, and is widest at sound wave troughs.*

---

are made to alter the number of times that the carrier wave loops every second.

AM signals are more subject to electrical interference, which produces noise in radio sets known as static. FM signals are free from static but they can be transmitted in a straight line only – as far as the horizon – so are used for short-range broadcasts.

AM and FM wavebands

Amplitude modulation is normally used for long-range broadcasts on wavelengths between 1000 and 2000 metres. These waves can travel for thousands of miles from their starting point because they are reflected by electrified layers, known as the ionosphere, in the upper atmosphere about 80-100 miles (130-160km) above the Earth. The waves are also reflected from the ground, and travel great distances by multiple reflections from ground and sky.

AM signals are broadcast on three wavebands: long (1000-2000 metres), medium (187-577 metres), and short (10-100 metres). Short waves are reflected best at night, so are used for very long distances.

FM wavebands include very-high frequency (VHF) broadcasts on frequencies 87MHz-108MHz (see right). VHF is also used by police, taxis, and citizen band (CB) radios. Ultra-high (UHF) frequencies of 450MHz-855MHz are used for television. Radio wavelengths below 12in (300mm) are known as microwaves. Radar and satellite communications use microwaves, at super-high frequencies of 3-30GHz.

THE WAVES OF THE ELECTROMAGNETIC SPECTRUM

The natural invisible waves of radiant energy, such as light, come from the Sun or from other bodies in space. The waves range from about 62 miles (100km) long to infinitesimally short. For uses such as radio or X-rays, artificial waves are generated electrically, with matching wavelengths. The shorter a wave, the higher its frequency, or hertz number, per second.

FREQUENCIES

| One hundred million cycles per second | Ten thousand million cycles per second | One million million cycles per second | One hundred million million cycles per second |

Remote control *Radio waves carry signals for long-range control – as for powered model cars or planes.*

Radio *Many sound programmes go out on long and medium waves. Orson Welles broadcasts H.G. Wells's* War of the Worlds *in news style in the USA in 1938.*

Television *Ultra high-frequency radio waves carry TV signals. The American spacemen on the Moon in 1969 were viewed by millions.*

Radar *Ships navigate by emitting microwave radio signals. Objects in their path bounce back the signals, which show up on a screen.*

Infrared radiation *This shows heat as colours on special film. Doctors use a print (thermogram) to spot cancer or arthritis.*

THE INVISIBLE WAVES AROUND US THAT ARRIVE FROM SPACE

When you see a rainbow, you are actually looking at light waves. Normally, light is invisible, but when it passes through raindrops it is bent (refracted) because a raindrop is denser than air and slows the light wave down. The light is separated into seven different colours because each of the colour waves that make up white light is bent at a different angle.

Each colour wave is vibrating (looping up and down) and each has a different wavelength – the distance from the crest of one wave to the crest of the next. The shorter the wavelength, the more the wave is bent. Violet has the shortest wavelength and red the longest.

Light waves are only a small part of the electromagnetic waves – including radio waves – that exist all around us. They are the radiant energy that is emitted from the Sun or other bodies in space. Sound waves are pressure waves – not electromagnetic waves. The radio waves generated electrically to carry sounds as signals are similar in structure to naturally occurring radio waves.

How wavelength is measured

All electromagnetic waves travel at the speed of light – about 186,000 miles (300,000km) per second. They are called electromagnetic because they consist of both electric and magnetic fields acting at right angles to each other. The fields leap-frog each other, giving the wave its motion – like the snaking of a length of rope when it is jerked.

The height of a loop – half the distance between the crest and the trough – is called the amplitude. Waves can also be measured by their frequency, that is, the number passing a given point each second. The longer the wavelength, the lower the frequency.

Frequencies are measured in units called hertz, named after the German, Heinrich Hertz, who in 1888 demonstrated that electric signals could be sent through the air.

He passed a high-voltage current through a loop of wire that had a metal sphere at each end, causing a spark to jump the short space between them. At the same time, another spark jumped between the spheres of a separate, similar wire loop placed on the other side of the room.

Hertz proved that the energy transmitted from one loop to another was electromagnetic radiation, which had been predicted theoretically by a British scientist, James Clerk Maxwell, in 1864.

The hertz measurement of a frequency gives the number of complete waves, or cycles, per second. Frequencies are usually expressed as kilohertz (thousands of hertz), megahertz (millions of hertz) or gigahertz (thousand millions of hertz). Light waves are extremely short. The longest, the red, measure about 36,000 to an inch (14,000 to a centimetre) and have a frequency of around one hundred million megahertz. Radio waves used for communication, however, range in length from about one twenty-fifth of an inch (1mm) to about 18-20 miles (30km), and have frequencies ranging from 10,000 hertz to about 30,000 megahertz.

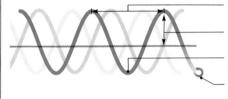

Wavelength The distance between the crests of adjoining waves.

Amplitude Half the height between a wave crest and trough.

Frequency The number of waves passing a given point each second.

Speed As they vibrate, waves also travel forward vast distances per second.

Ten thousand million million cycles per second

One million million million cycles per second

One hundred million million million cycles per second

Ten thousand million million million cycles per second

Sunlight *Seven waves of different frequencies make up light. They show up separately in a rainbow.*

Ultraviolet light *Sunlight that is not visible in a rainbow. It is a source of vitamin D, but too much exposure to it causes skin cancer.*

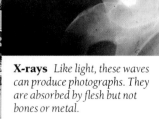

X-rays *Like light, these waves can produce photographs. They are absorbed by flesh but not bones or metal.*

Gamma rays *Radioactive atoms emit gamma rays during decay. The rays are part of the fallout of a nuclear explosion.*

Cosmic rays *These waves are from outer space, perhaps from exploded stars such as the Crab Nebula.*

217

Television: live pictures sent on radio waves

When you switch on your television set, the picture you see is created from a pattern of light formed by electrical signals. The television camera converts the picture it takes into electrical signals, and they are broadcast on radio waves at the speed of light. A football match, for example, can appear on your screen at virtually the same moment that the action occurs.

The colour on a television screen is produced by mixing together different proportions of coloured light. Light colours do not mix in the same way as paint colours. For television, the three primary colours used – the colours that generate all other colours – are red, green and blue. Almost all colour shades can be produced by mixing one or two of them with varying proportions of white.

The television camera splits the light from the scene into the three primary colours and directs each colour to a different camera tube through a glass plate known as the signal plate. Behind the signal plate there is a photoconductive layer (called the target), which conducts electric-ity when light strikes it. The brighter the light through the photoconductive layer, the greater the amount of electricity. So it forms a pattern of electrical charges, the areas with the most charge corresponding to the areas of brightest light.

In each colour tube of the camera, a beam of electrons (cathode rays) is fired at the target from behind. The beam moves from left to right and scans the target from top to bottom in a series of horizontal lines. As it scans, it first strengthens the electrical charges, then continually tops them up as they lose strength between scans. The brightest areas need the most topping up. It is this topping up, which mirrors the charge pattern, that creates the electrical signals that pass to the signal plate, which is connected to a circuit. Current flows through the circuit at varying voltages corresponding to the brightness levels.

The electron beams scan at a given rate, producing either 625 or 525 lines accord-ing to the system being used; 625 lines gives better definition, and is used in Europe, much of Asia and Australia. The 525 system is used in most of North and South America and Japan.

The scanning takes place half a 'field' at a time – that is, first the odd-numbered lines then the even-numbered lines. This pro-duces a complete picture every twenty-fifth of a second. The human eye retains an image for a twenty-fifth of a second, so a series of pictures run at that speed appears to be one continual picture. If they were run more slowly, the picture on the screen would flicker more and the action would be jerky. The scanning is done in two steps because there are technical difficulties in scanning the whole field in one step at the required speed.

Before the signals can be broadcast, they have to be modulated (combined with a radio wave) at the transmitting station. The modulated wave is broadcast by the TV transmitter at the same time as the sound signals are broadcast on another trans-mitter close by.

In most countries, television signals are beamed from ground-based transmitting aerials, which, at the ultra high frequencies

HOW A TELEVISION PICTURE TRAVELS FROM CAMERA TO SCREEN

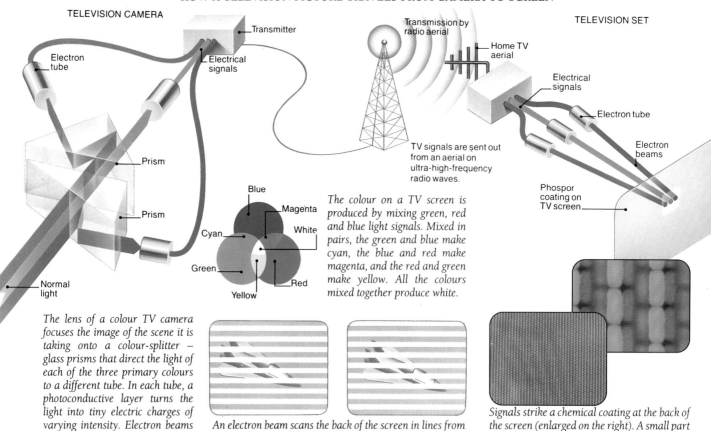

TELEVISION CAMERA

Electron tube
Transmitter
Electrical signals
Prism
Prism
Normal light

Transmission by radio aerial
Home TV aerial
TV signals are sent out from an aerial on ultra-high-frequency radio waves.

TELEVISION SET
Electrical signals
Electron tube
Electron beams
Phospor coating on TV screen

Blue
Magenta
Cyan
White
Green
Red
Yellow

The colour on a TV screen is produced by mixing green, red and blue light signals. Mixed in pairs, the green and blue make cyan, the blue and red make magenta, and the red and green make yellow. All the colours mixed together produce white.

The lens of a colour TV camera focuses the image of the scene it is taking onto a colour-splitter – glass prisms that direct the light of each of the three primary colours to a different tube. In each tube, a photoconductive layer turns the light into tiny electric charges of varying intensity. Electron beams translate the charges into electrical signals for sending through a circuit to a transmitting station.

An electron beam scans the back of the screen in lines from top to bottom, first the odd-numbered lines, then the even-numbered lines, to produce a whole picture every twenty-fifth of a second.

Signals strike a chemical coating at the back of the screen (enlarged on the right). A small part of the picture is shown actual size on the left. It consists of dots of colour varying in intensity that merge in your eye.

used, must be in a straight line with the receivers – they cannot beam signals over the horizon. This limits their range to about 40 miles (65km), so a network of transmitters is used. In countries with scattered populations – or tall buildings that interfere with reception – such a network presents problems. So TV companies are increasingly turning to communications satellites to relay signals.

Receiving the picture

When you press the channel button you want, it completes a circuit in the selector mechanism, and this electronically tunes the receiver to the right frequency for reception. The broadcast signals are picked out of the air by your television aerial.

The signals from the aerial are very weak and have to be amplified. Then they are demodulated (separated from the radio carrier wave) and fed into the picture tube.

The picture tube works like a camera in reverse, changing the electric signals into a pattern of coloured light. At one end is an electron gun, and at the other end the screen. The electron gun contains three separate tubes, one for each primary colour, each firing electron beams. The back of the screen is coated with vertical stripes of fluorescent materials called phosphors, alternating red, green and blue. Behind the screen, an aperture grille with vertical slots lines up with the stripes, allowing each primary colour beam to strike only its own colour of phosphor.

The incoming picture signals are fed to the electron gun, and its electron beams scan the screen in the same way that the camera tube scanned the target. As the electron beams vary in strength according to the picture signals, they hit the screen in points of varying brightness, tracing the same light pattern that was picked up by the camera. This merges in your eyes to give a picture of the original scene.

Information on call

In the mid-1970s the television set became much more versatile following the introduction of teletext and viewdata systems, often called videotext. The pioneering work on both was done in Britain, where a service began in 1974.

Teletext sends information to the television set via coded signals broadcast in spare scan lines (some are unused in every field when the scanning beam moves back to the top of the picture). Viewers with a decoder on their set can call up teletext information, which includes news and weather forecasts, with a remote control.

Viewdata subscribers can call up information on a vast range of topics, from package holidays to livestock feed prices. The information is sent by telephone lines from a computer data bank to the screen of a specially adapted television set.

The march of time *A painter's impression (below) shows the end of the* Titanic, *which sank off Newfoundland in 1912. The wreck was found 13,000ft (4000m) down in 1985, by a French-American expedition. They later took photos by guiding a robot from a three-man submarine. Pictures such as the rusty prow (left) were shown on TV.*

From spinning discs to space satellites

Although television is thought of as a 20th-century invention, its beginnings date back to the 1880s. The first ideas about transmitting pictures over a distance were considered in the years following the introduction of the telephone. If voices could be sent over a long distance, why not pictures?

From the beginning, it was realised that pictures could not be sent as an entity, and ways of breaking down and then reconstructing a picture were suggested by a German inventor, Paul Nipkow, in 1884. Nipkow used spinning perforated discs to dissect and then resurrect a black-and-white image.

In 1906, a Russian scientist, Boris Rosing, put together the scanning principle of the Nipkow disc and the display possibilities of the cathode-ray tube – invented by a German, Ferdinand Braun, in 1897 – to create the first crude television system. The cathode-ray tube is still the vital component of modern television.

Experimental broadcasts were begun in America in 1928, but the first practical television system was set up by the eccentric Scottish inventor John Logie Baird in London. He opened the first television studio in 1929, and used Nipkow discs for scanning in both transmitter and receiver. Within a few years, however, Baird's mechanical disc-scanning system was overtaken by the electronic camera invented by the Russian Vladimir Zworykin, who produced the first practical one in 1931.

The first three-day-a-week television service began in Berlin in 1935, operated by Fernseh, a German company with which Baird was involved. Britain's BBC opened the first public high-definition service in 1936, and RCA began transmission in America in 1939. Colour transmission started experimentally in the USA in 1951.

Cable television began in the United States in the 1950s, with commercial companies sending programmes to subscribers along cables. This allows more channels than radio transmission. In Britain and Europe, cable television did not arrive until the 1980s.

Sometimes cable television is also partly satellite television, programmes being relayed by satellite to company dish aerials at a central station, then sent out to homes through the cables.

Other television systems introduced or under review in the late 1980s included microwave television carrying up to 60 channels over short distances, high-definition television (HDTV) using over 1200 screen lines, and direct broadcasting by satellite (DBS) to small domestic dish aerials. For this the transmitting company has to code the signals so that only a subscriber with a decoder on the set can receive them.

Remote controls: operating switches from a distance

The coming of the computer and the exploration of space sparked the need for increasingly complex yet small, durable, and often remotely operated controls. This has brought about the age of microelectronics, which began in the 1950s centred round the transistor and silicon chip. It is a silicon chip that is the heart of the remote control that you use to switch on your television set from the armchair.

When you press a button on the remote control, the chip – which contains a microelectronic circuit – sets off an electronic oscillator (vibrator). This produces an infrared beam, which is made up of electromagnetic waves (page 217).

The beam carries a coded signal, the code varying according to the button pressed – switch on, change channels, or raise volume, for example. The code – based on binary digits (page 241) – is superimposed on the beam in the same way that a radio signal is superimposed on a carrier wave.

In the television set, the coded beam is received by a device sensitive to infrared waves. The incoming signals are amplified and fed to another silicon chip that identifies the code. The chip then feeds the appropriate signal to an electronic switch that carries out your instruction.

Ultrasonic remote controls can be used to open or close garage doors. They emit high-frequency sound waves that are directed to a receiving microphone. This sends signals to an electric motor that operates the doors. However, an ultrasonic control must be operated in a direct line to the doors, so radio control is now more often used. A hand-held radio control is a miniature transmitter that can open garage doors fitted with a receiver from anywhere in the vicinity. The radio waves switch on an electric current to the motor that operates the doors.

A more complex radio-control system is used to operate model aeroplanes and boats. The hand-held transmitter sends out beams of coded radio waves. A miniature receiver on the model decodes the signals, separating them from the radio wave. The decoded signals are fed to tiny electric motors, called servos (short for servo-mechanisms, which increase their power). The servos open and close the engine throttle, raise and lower the landing gear, and operate the control surfaces – such as ailerons and rudder – on the wings and tail.

Video: recording pictures on magnetic tape

A home video recorder picks up electrical signals from the television station at the same time as your television set. But instead of converting the signals directly to pictures, the video stores them on magnetic tape in the same way that a tape recorder stores sound signals. Because television signals carry pictures as well as sound, home video tape is generally four times the width of a sound cassette tape.

As the video recorder is connected directly to the aerial, it picks up television broadcasts when switched on, whether or not the television is on. Both can be tuned to pick up different programmes at the same time.

The two main video cassette recording systems available are Betamax, introduced by the Japanese company Sony in 1975, and VHS (Video Home System), pioneered by JVC (Japan Victor Company) in 1976. Each system needs different cassettes and different recorders. Betamax produces slightly better quality pictures, but VHS tapes can run longer – up to four hours. VHS has proved the more popular of the two, and new Super VHS has better-quality pictures than either of the standard systems.

Recording and playback

When a video tape cassette is fitted into the video recorder and the record button pressed, the machine draws a loop of tape from between the two reels in the cassette and wraps it round a rotating drum driven by an electric motor.

The picture recording heads, usually two, are mounted on the drum facing outwards, and imprint the signals on the tape as they rotate with the drum. The heads are tiny electromagnets, and operate in the same way as for sound tape recording.

The tape runs past the drum at an angle. The picture signals are recorded in the central area as a series of sloping tracks, and the accompanying sound signals are recorded as lengthways tracks along one edge of the tape.

As with a tape recorder, playback is a reversal of the recording process. When the tape is loaded and the play button pressed, the stored signals on the magnetic tape produce electrical signals in the playback head. This feeds the picture and sound signals to the television set, where the recording is re-created on the screen.

Television and video recorder

A video recorder is connected to the TV aerial. It picks up the programme being put out on the channel it has been tuned to. When you load the tape and press the recording switch, the video machinery draws out a loop of tape from between the cassette's two reels. The tape then winds round a rotating drum and is drawn past the recording heads.

HOW A HOME VIDEO RECORDS TV PICTURES

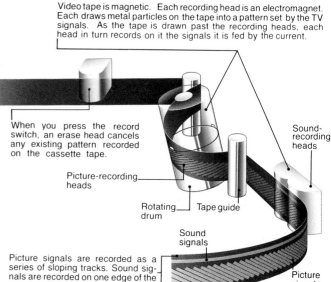

Video tape is magnetic. Each recording head is an electromagnet. Each draws metal particles on the tape into a pattern set by the TV signals. As the tape is drawn past the recording heads, each head in turn records on it the signals it is fed by the current.

When you press the record switch, an erase head cancels any existing pattern recorded on the cassette tape.

Picture-recording heads

Sound-recording heads

Rotating drum

Tape guide

Sound signals

Picture signals are recorded as a series of sloping tracks. Sound signals are recorded on one edge of the tape lengthways.

Picture signals

Magnetic tape

Tape recording: storing sounds as magnetic patterns

As a child at school you may have made patterns with iron filings on a thin sheet of paper by moving a magnet underneath. Tape recorders work in a similar way – they set up a pattern of magnetised metal particles on a tape, a pattern that corresponds to the sounds of the instruments and voices being recorded.

The tape consists of a thin layer of powder-like metal particles (commonly iron and chromium oxides) in a plastic coating on polyester ribbon. The recording head which creates the patterns is a tiny electromagnet.

To record a tape of anything from a solo singer or speaker to a full orchestra, the sound is directed at a microphone where its pressure waves are converted to weak, variable electrical signals. The signals are fed to an amplifier to boost their strength, and then to a recording head in the tape recorder.

Here, they flow through the coils of the electromagnet and produce a magnetic field. When the tape is carried past the recording head, each particle is magnetised – it becomes a tiny magnet and is attracted more or less towards the electromagnet according to the strength of the signals. So the particles become, as it were, a code for the original sound.

The electrical signals used to create the pattern may be fed from a microphone, or from a radio, compact disc, record player or another tape recorder. Tapes are now normally recorded in stereo (page 223). With digital audio tape (DAT), the electrical signals from the microphone are converted into numerical values represented by binary numbers (see *Computers*, page 241). This system is more precise, and produces a more faithful recording.

Most modern tape recorders use the same head for recording and playback. For recording, the tape must be wiped clean of all previous patterns before it reaches the head. This is done by an erasing head, an electromagnet fed with high-frequency current that upsets the existing alignment of the particles on the tape. The erasing head is switched on automatically when the recording button is pressed.

To play back a recording, all that is needed to reproduce the coded sound is to reverse the process. When the tape is played back, its magnetic pattern sets up an electric current in the electromagnetic head. The current is fed to an amplifier and then to loudspeakers that produce pressure waves, which vibrate your eardrums in the same way as the original sounds.

Getting rid of background noise

One of the drawbacks of sound reproduction on tape is the background hiss that results from the magnetic action, which becomes most noticeable during quiet passages. To combat hiss, a noise reduction system known as Dolby (after R.M. Dolby, its American inventor) is widely used.

In quiet passages, electronic circuits automatically boost the signals before they reach the recording head, so helping to drown the hiss.

On playback, the signals are reduced to their correct level for feeding to the speakers. The hiss is reduced at the same time, becoming inaudible.

PUTTING SOUNDS ON MAGNETIC TAPE

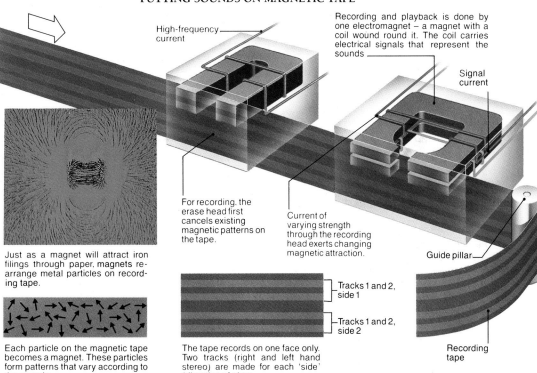

High-frequency current

Recording and playback is done by one electromagnet – a magnet with a coil wound round it. The coil carries electrical signals that represent the sounds

Signal current

For recording, the erase head first cancels existing magnetic patterns on the tape.

Current of varying strength through the recording head exerts changing magnetic attraction.

Guide pillar

Just as a magnet will attract iron filings through paper, magnets rearrange metal particles on recording tape.

Each particle on the magnetic tape becomes a magnet. These particles form patterns that vary according to the sounds.

Tracks 1 and 2, side 1

Tracks 1 and 2, side 2

The tape records on one face only. Two tracks (right and left hand stereo) are made for each 'side' (direction of play).

Recording tape

MAGNETISM AND ELECTRICITY

Iron and its alloys, such as steel, are naturally magnetic. They draw other magnetic substances towards them if they are within a certain range, known as the magnetic field. All magnets have a north and south pole, and it is opposite poles that attract each other.

A magnet's attractive power relies on the arrangement of its atoms. All the atoms are tiny magnets formed into groups, known as domains. The magnetic strength is increased if the domains are induced to fall into line by the action of another magnet.

A bar of iron placed inside a coil of wire carrying an electric current will be magnetised for as long as the current flows. This is because an electric current has a magnetic field that acts at right angles to its direction of flow – in the same way as naturally occurring electromagnetic radiation (page 217). The strength of the magnet depends on the strength of the current.

These 'electromagnets' can be much stronger than ordinary magnets, and can be easily magnetised or demagnetised by switching the electric current on or off.

Conversely, moving a magnet in and out of a coil of wire will set up an electric current in the wire for as long as the magnet is moving. This was how the first electric generator was produced after the principle (electromagnetic induction) was discovered by an Englishman, Michael Faraday, in 1831.

How a needle makes sounds on a revolving record

When you play a record, the sound you hear is caused by vibrations in the loudspeakers setting up vibrations in the air that impinge on your eardrums. Similar vibrations were created by the pop group or orchestra that played the music in the first place, and were stored on the record so they could be reproduced over and over again.

The storage process begins when the sound of the original music enters a microphone and causes its diaphragm to vibrate, just like an eardrum. The vibrations are converted into weak, variable, electrical signals. All microphones have a diaphragm that works on the same principle as the one in the telephone mouthpiece (page 214), but there are various other devices for converting the vibrations to electric current.

The electrical signals produced by the microphone are boosted by an amplifier, taped, and fed to a recording lathe that cuts a master disc. When you play a record (a replica of the master disc), the vibrations of the stylus (needle) reproduce the electrical signals, and the loudspeakers convert them back to the original sounds.

Making a master disc

To make a master disc for reproduction, the sound is picked up by a number of microphones and the electrical signals are recorded in from 2 to 48 separate tracks on magnetic tape.

The tape is then edited on a complex electronic mixer on which the recording technician can modify the tonal quality and loudness of each track. The producer may wish to increase the volume of a particular instrument, for example. In this way, the multi-track recordings are mixed to produce a two-track master tape with the sounds blended and balanced for the best effect from the left and right stereo channels (facing page). The master disc is then cut with electrical signals fed from the master tape.

On the disc-cutting lathe, a chisel-shaped cutting stylus vibrates and cuts a wavy groove in the recording surface (generally a layer of lacquer on a flat aluminium disc), in a spiral from the edge to the centre. The disc is spun at precisely 33⅓ revolutions per minute (rpm) to make a long-playing record, or 45rpm for a short single record, but the speed of the cutting head varies with the strength of the signal, and is faster when the signal is louder.

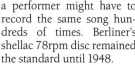

Birth of the record player

The first sounds were recorded and reproduced by the American inventor Thomas Alva Edison in 1877, in a contraption he later refined and marketed as the phonograph ('sound writer'). It used a horn with a diaphragm at the narrow end as both a microphone and loudspeaker. When someone spoke or sang into the horn, the diaphragm – and a steel needle attached to it – vibrated up and down. The record was a sheet of tinfoil wrapped round a cylinder with a spiral groove cut in its surface. To record, the cylinder was turned by a handle. Sounds entering the horn vibrated the needle, which moved along the spiral groove and indented the tinfoil as it did so. To play the recording, the cylinder was turned again, and as the needle followed the indentations in the tinfoil, it vibrated the diaphragm, causing sounds to emerge from the horn.

German-born Emile Berliner, working in the United States, made the vital breakthrough in sound recording in 1888 when he introduced the record disc. It was played on a turntable using the same type of horn and needle as the phonograph. Berliner called his machine the gramophone. Four years later he pioneered the technique of copying discs by electroplating and stamping. Previously, each disc or cylinder had to be recorded separately – a performer might have to record the same song hundreds of times. Berliner's shellac 78rpm disc remained the standard until 1948.

Live performance

In the early days of recording, as at this session in France in the early 1900s, the technology for master-disc making was in its infancy. The turntable mechanism had to be wound up by hand for each disc cut. As the needle was set on disc, the performers, who were grouped round the horn, began to play. The equipment for making the recording was mounted on an isolated concrete block, so that vibrations other than the sound waves from the performance would not affect the needle as it cut the disc. Earlier types of recording using a wax cylinder (pictured above), had to be individually made.

HOW A RECORD NEEDLE REPRODUCES THE SOUND

The needle, or stylus, is an artificial sapphire or diamond with a rounded or elliptical tip. The groove (shown 1000 times enlarged) is a different shape each side, one for the right-hand stereo signals and one for the left-hand signals.

The needle vibrates as it runs along the uneven groove walls, setting up electrical signals in the pick-up head. The signals are amplified and then converted to sound by cones (diaphragms) vibrated by electromagnets in the loudspeakers.

In a moving-magnet type of pick-up head, the needle is linked to a magnet. As the needle vibrates, the magnet's movements induce electrical current in two wire coils, creating the signals fed to the two stereo speakers.

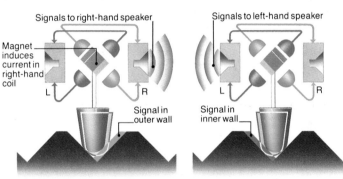

The stereo groove causes the moving magnet to induce different signals in each coil. If only the outer groove wall contains a signal, then only the coil corresponding to the right-hand speaker will produce current. Or if only the inner groove wall contains a signal, only the left-hand speaker will receive current.

The stereo signals force the stylus to vibrate so that it cuts a different pattern in each wall of the V-shaped groove. The groove walls are at 45 degrees to the disc surface but at right angles to each other. There may be up to 350 grooves to 1in (140 to 1cm) – the number varies according to the loudness of the recording. A loud passage needs more space because the stylus vibrates more, so produces fewer but wider grooves.

After the sound groove has been cut in the lacquer, the master disc is electroplated with nickel and processed to eventually produce a very thin reverse-image nickel disc, called the stamper, which is the mould for making records for sale.

The records you buy are moulded PVC (polyvinyl chloride). Granules of PVC are simultaneously pressed and heated between two separately recorded stampers – one for each side of the disc – then cooled. Each long-playing record pressing takes about 25 seconds.

The record player and speakers

In the best hi-fi systems, the turntable is heavy and usually belt-driven to isolate it from the vibrations of the motor.

The stylus has a rounded tip and is usually made of synthetic sapphire or diamond. It is fitted into a pick-up head that also contains an electromechanical transducer, a device that converts the vibration of the stylus as it moves along the disc groove into electrical signals. The transducer is commonly magnetic – as the stylus travels around, it moves a magnet inside a wire coil and induces an electric current in the coil.

Two coils are used, a different one to sense the vibrations of each stereo track and produce current for the left-hand and right-hand output signals. These signals are replicas of those that operated the cutting stylus on the master disc.

The output signals coming from a pick-up are very weak, and have to be boosted in the electronic circuits of an amplifier. Some of these circuits control volume, tone and balance.

From the amplifier the boosted signals are fed to each of the loudspeakers, where an electromagnet vibrates a cone-shaped diaphragm to convert the signals back into sound waves. A simple speaker has a single cone, but speakers in hi-fi systems have two or three separate, different-sized cones because each size is best for reproducing a different range of sounds (or frequencies – the higher the sound, the greater the vibration frequency).

Sounds from two directions

Stereophonic sound helps to give a sense of direction and feeling of depth to radio broadcasts or recordings. When you hear an orchestra playing on the radio, for example, you can tell where the violins, woodwind and drums are positioned.

Many VHF radio programmes are now broadcast in stereophonic sound – a system pioneered in the United States by Zenith and General Electric in 1961. The programme is recorded using a number of microphones, and edited to produce sounds from the right and left of the broadcast studio on two separate tracks.

The transmitter sends out two sets of radio signals over the air. One set carries the combined output of the microphones so that it can be received on ordinary (mono) receivers. The other set carries coded signals for a stereo receiver. It has a decoder that can sort out the coded set into left and right channel signals. These are amplified separately, and fed to separate left-hand and right-hand loudspeakers.

Thomas Edison: the 'wizard' who lit up the world

At precisely 3pm on September 4, 1882, the 35-year-old inventor Thomas Alva Edison embarked on what he called 'the greatest adventure of my life'. Power was turned on in New York's first central generating station in Pearl Street – and 85 houses, shops and offices in the area suddenly blazed with the light from 400 incandescent lamps.

Edison and his fellow directors of the Edison Electric Light Company had gathered in the Wall Street office of one of their main backers, the millionaire financier J. Pierpont Morgan. Morgan's office was among those to be illuminated on that autumnal afternoon. And by seven o'clock, as it started to grow dark, the electric light made its impact in the nearby offices of the *New York Times*.

For months beforehand, Edison had supervised the start of New York's conversion from gas to electricity. He chose the site of the power station near the East River because it was in the city's financial area and he wanted to impress potential backers. He organised a house-to-house survey of the district, and arranged the installation of such things as mains, junction boxes, switchboards, meters, fuses and lampholders.

Eleven months later – in August 1883 – more than 430 buildings in the city were being lit by some 10,000 lamps. Edison's work with electricity bore out his policy of inventing only things that people wanted and that would make life easier for them.

He had put this principle into practice in May 1876, when together with about 20 handpicked 'friends and co-workers' he opened a new laboratory – or 'inventions factory' – in the hamlet of Menlo Park, New Jersey.

The factory was a two-storey wooden building set in rich farmland and it became, in effect, the world's first industrial-research laboratory. It was equipped with a steam engine, a forge, storage batteries, photographic equipment, copper wire, induction coils, and measuring instruments such as an electrometer and a galvanometer.

At the time, the inventor and his team were trying to perfect the incandescent lamp – which inventors had been working on since the 1830s. In 1878, Edison formed the Edison Electric Light Company, but it was not until the end of the following year that, stage by laborious stage, he finally produced a practical electric light bulb. (Coincidentally, a successful light bulb was developed at around the same time in England by the physicist and chemist Joseph Swan.)

Edison showed his invention to the public on New Year's Eve, 1879, when he lit up Menlo Park's road, laboratory and library by means of a dynamo and about 40 lights. Some 3000 onlookers attended this demonstration of genius by the so-called 'Wizard of Menlo Park'.

Born in Milan, Ohio, on February 11, 1847, Thomas Alva Edison was aged seven when his family moved north to Port Huron, Michigan. His formal education ended after three months, when the village schoolmaster expelled him as retarded. In fact, the youngster was suffering from partial deafness – the result of an attack of scarlet fever.

It was left to Mrs Edison to encourage the youngster's growing interest in science, particularly steam engines and mechanical forces. Tom set up a small chemical laboratory in the cellar of the Edisons' home. There he produced his own electrical current from voltaic cells, or batteries, and made and operated a primitive telegraph set.

A short while later, while working as a newsboy and candy salesman on the railroad between Port Huron and Michigan, Ohio, he built a modest laboratory in the baggage car. He also installed a secondhand printing press on which he produced a weekly newspaper, the *Grand Trunk Herald*, for sale on the train.

Tramp telegrapher

Between the ages of 16 and 21 he worked as what he called a 'tramp telegrapher' throughout the Midwestern and Southern states.

In 1869 he was in New York, sleeping in a basement in Wall Street. One day that summer he chanced to be in the nearby Gold Indicator Company's offices when the telegraphic gold-price indicator failed. He repaired it on the spot and was taken on as assistant to the company's chief engineer. He later created the more reliable Edison Universal Stock Printer – which he sold to Western Union for $40,000.

Edison used the money to open and equip his first proper workshop – in Newark, New Jersey – where he manufactured the ticker-tape machine in the early 1870s. In 1876 he moved to the outlying district of Menlo Park, where he devoted himself to life as a full-time inventor.

The following year he produced an alternative transmitter for Alexander Graham Bell's telephone. In Bell's instrument, the sound vibrations of the human voice were converted directly into electrical impulses. But the sound reproduction was faint, especially over longer distances when it all but faded away.

Edison's transmitter used pieces of carbon to make a contact whose resistance was changed by the pressure of the sound waves. This

Birth of electric light *Edison's generator, the 'Long-waisted Mary Ann', is attached by belts and pulleys to his dynamometer – which measured the power produced by steam engines in the back room. The engraving shows his 'inventions factory' in Menlo Park in 1879 – the year he produced his incandescent lamp (right).*

Five sleepless days *Edison claimed to have worked for five days without sleep on the improved model of his phonograph when this photograph was taken in his West Orange workshop (left). It was then around dawn on June 16, 1888, and later that day he was pictured with members of his work team (below), looking less dishevelled.*

advantage will be at once detailed for the work, and thus the working model will be brought out in a very short time.'

Improvements were then made, working drawings were prepared and the necessary patterns and castings created. The complete, full-sized machine or apparatus was then built and tested. Next, provided it met Edison's demands and expectations, it was taken to another workshop to be reproduced.

'Inventions of sufficient magnitude . . . will be launched as the bases of separate industries,' the article concluded.

Among these, in 1889, was the Kinetoscope, or 'moving picture machine', which Edison declared would bring the worlds of politics, art and sport to the man and woman in the street. Edison's peephole Kinetoscope gave the illusion of movement by flashing a series of photographs onto a screen in the machine.

From shorts about ballet dancers and boxers, Edison moved on to produce cinema feature films – including *The Great Train Robbery*, made at the Edison studios in West Orange in 1903. With a running time of ten minutes, it was one of the longest motion pictures so far made and his last major triumph.

Edison died on October 18, 1931, at the age of 84. Three days later he was buried near his West Orange home, mourned by millions of his fellow Americans.

controlled the current from a battery, and much stronger electrical signals could be sent than with Bell's telephone. The caller's voice could be heard over a much greater distance.

With Bell's telephone, the mouthpiece also served as the earpiece, so that the user had to alternately talk and listen to the same outlet. Edison separated the transmitter from the receiver, making the telephone much easier to use.

On perfecting the 'loud-speaking telephone', Edison turned to the invention of the phonograph – the forerunner of the gramophone and modern record player. In December 1877, Edison demonstrated the machine to his employees at Menlo Park. As the phonograph cylinder slowly turned, his high-pitched voice was faintly heard reciting a nursery rhyme: 'Mary had a little lamb, its fleece as white as snow . . .'

He patented the phonograph in February 1878 and nine years later moved to a spacious new home and research laboratory in West Orange, New Jersey. By then he had made an estimated million dollars out of his various inventions (altogether he took out 1093 patents for inventions, from an electrical pen to

low-cost, poured-cement houses). He employed up to 5000 workers in various shops and factories.

Edison once outlined his working methods to a writer from the *Scientific American*, who reported: 'Rough sketches will be submitted to model makers, who will secure from the vast supplies of material blanks for the necessary parts, or possibly completed pieces for the apparatus, and as many workmen as can be employed to

Moving pictures *Edison's Kinetoscope flashed a series of photographs on a continuous strip of film onto a screen – so giving the appearance of moving pictures. The pictures were seen through a viewer on top of the machine, which coin-operated. The films lasted for only about 15 seconds.*

Compact discs: playing music by laser beam

A compact disc is only 4¾in (120mm) across, but it holds 3 miles (5km) of playing track and plays for about an hour. CDs are played on one side only, and do not get scratched during play, or wear out, because no needle or stylus touches the surface. Instead a light beam from a low-powered laser reads the disc from the underside, and interprets microscopic pits and flat areas on the playing track that spirals out from the centre of the disc. Just as the Morse code operates by dots and dashes, so the pits and flats are a digital code, waiting to be interpreted into sound.

Digital codes work by forming patterns using just two digits – 0 and 1. From these two, a code can be compiled that represents an infinite richness of patterns and sounds. Any sound within the range of the human ear – from a single drumbeat to a full orchestra in crescendo – can be faithfully reproduced upon decoding.

As the laser beam scans the rotating disc, the various pits and flats affect the beam's reflection, which falls on a light-sensing device called a photodiode. This device converts the information that falls on it into electrical signals. These signals are decoded electronically into variable electric current, and then amplified and fed to the loudspeakers, which reproduce the sound waves that led to the creation of the pits and flats in the first place.

Putting the code on disc

As with other forms of sound recording, a compact disc begins when a microphone converts the sound waves into electrical signals. The voltage of those signals is measured and coded electronically into binary digits (page 241). The digits then undergo further coding to link the two stereo channels into one pulse train, and to overcome damage to the signals from scratches or fingerprints that might occur during handling.

As a blank glass disc coated with a light-sensitive resin is spun under a laser beam, the coded signals are fed to the laser as electrical pulses. It emits them as light flashes that cause a pattern of pits and flats on the coating – revealed once the coating is chemically developed. This gives far more accurate recording than with even the best conventional method.

The master disc provides a mould for reproduction. Each disc is given a thin aluminium coating to make it highly reflective, then lacquered for protection.

Compact music *The pits and flats that are the coded sound on a compact disc can be clearly seen, 930 times their actual size, on the magnified picture (right) of a disc with its outer plastic covering drawn back.*

Coded track *A laser beam scans the pits and flats. It converts them to On and Off flashes of light.*

Coded signals *The light flashes are converted to a coded string of pulses of electric current. This represents the binary digits (top right) for the numerical values (bottom right) that convert the electric current to a continuous wave.*

Decoded signals *Each of the numerical values is a measurement of current strength at points along the wave. It was sampled during the recording 44,100 times each second, so accurately represents the original sounds. The system of binary coding provides 65,535 possible sound levels for each of the sample measurements.*

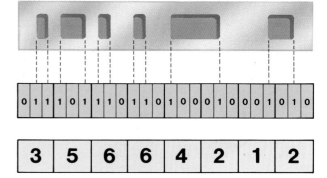

| 0 | 1 | 1 | 1 | 0 | 1 | 1 | 1 | 0 | 1 | 1 | 0 | 1 | 0 | 0 | 0 | 1 | 0 | 0 | 0 | 1 | 0 | 1 | 0 |

| 3 | 5 | 6 | 6 | 4 | 2 | 1 | 2 |

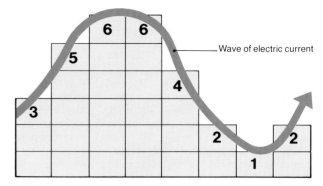

Wave of electric current

Emerging sound
When the varying electric current is amplified and fed to a speaker, it is changed to sound waves that reproduce the recording.

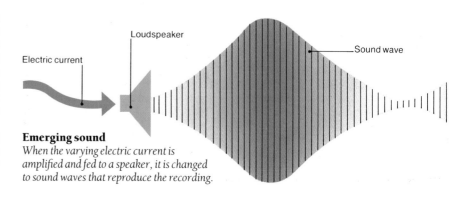

Electric current

Loudspeaker

Sound wave

How a synthesiser makes electronic music

When you listen to music, what you hear is a blend of regular vibrations – of a violin string, the reeds in an oboe, or the column of air in a trumpet, for example. The greater the rate of vibration (the frequency), the higher the sound, or pitch.

When a violin, an oboe, and a trumpet play the same note, they all produce a pure (fundamental) vibration of the same frequency. What makes instruments sound different are the overtones (harmonics) that result from fractional vibrations on top of the fundamental vibration.

A violin string, for instance, vibrates along the whole of its length to produce the fundamental pitch, but each half and quarter of the string vibrates as well to give overtones. Instruments bring out different mixtures of overtones according to their shape and materials, and the vibrations resound in the body of the instrument to create its distinctive quality.

An electronic synthesiser makes music by generating electric current in a wide range of frequencies. When the current is fed to a loudspeaker, the fundamental sounds and overtones of all sorts of instruments are simulated, as well as many sound effects. As a synthesiser can rarely simulate all the continually changing overtones of a conventionally played instrument, it generally lacks the same richness, but modern types get very close.

Synthesisers are used by pop musicians in company with conventional instruments

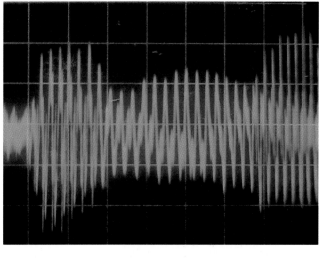

A vision of sound
Swelling notes from a piece of orchestral music are seen here as green, vibrating electronic signals on a screen. The even wave of the pure sound can be seen darker and more compact below the varying overtones.

to make 'live' electronic music. They can be linked with microphones and other synthesisers, or they can be played by a tape recorder or computer. Some can be fed with patches (push-in computer program discs or boards) that create different sounds. Some modern digital synthesisers have built-in computers and can produce complex overtones. Some use FM (frequency modulation) synthesis, a process similar to modulating radio waves.

With modern synthesisers that use a computer-connection system called MIDI (Musical Instrument Digital Interface), the player can feed in sounds from various instruments or another computer or synthesiser to obtain a wide variety of effects. With a digital electronic instrument known as a sampler, sounds can be fed in and replayed at all pitches across a keyboard.

Synthesisers are also used for composing music. Herbert Eimert and Karlheinz Stockhausen set up the first electronic music studio in Cologne, Germany, in 1953, and Stockhausen is one of the foremost composers of electronic music. Others include the Americans Milton Babbitt and Morton Subotnik. Subotnik's *Silver Apples of the Moon* (1967) was the first electronic work to be composed for recording. The score for *Koyaanisqatsi*, a 1982 film based on North American Indians, included electronic music by the American composer Philip Glass.

Shaping electronic sounds

There are three main stages in producing electronic music – generating current, filtering it, and amplifying it.

In the generator, a device called an oscillator gives the current its vibrating waveform. The rate of vibration (the frequency) is controlled by varying the voltage to the generator circuits. For the pure (fundamental) pitch, the wave is generated as regular loops – know as a sine wave. Other waveforms generated include square waves and sawtooth waves, which produce basic sounds and some overtones.

Various filter circuits are used to further shape the vibrating waves. Filters let through certain frequencies only, and block the rest. They alter the quality of the sound and create different effects. Amplifying sounds is achieved by increasing the voltage to the loudspeaker circuits.

A synthesiser has a keyboard like a piano, but the keys simply change the voltage that goes to the generator circuit, and so produce sounds of a different pitch. Other knobs, dials or slides control the route through the various circuits.

To change the intensity and duration of a sound, the player operates a control called an envelope generator, which alters the way in which the voltage is applied to several circuits at the same time. A sound can be switched in suddenly and briefly, for example, or brought in with gradually increasing volume and slowly faded out.

The growth of electronic sounds

The first person to attempt to create sounds electronically was an American inventor, Thaddeus Cahill. He invented an instrument called a telharmonium in 1906, which used electric motors and telephone receivers to produce sounds, but without much success. By 1920, a Russian scientist named Leon Theremin generated electronic sounds using two radio-wave oscillators; it was played by moving the hands round its aerials. This altered the circuit tuning and produced sound – varying according to the hand position – from the loudspeakers. The instrument was called a Theremin.

The forerunner of today's synthesisers was built for acoustical research by the Radio Corporation of America (RCA) at Princeton, New Jersey, in 1955. It was fed with punched paper tape, and the punched code activated the sound generators, filters and amplifiers. The music was recorded on tape.

Because the RCA synthesiser circuits used thermionic valves – electronic vacuum tubes – it was large enough to fill a room. In the 1960s, an American physicist, Robert Moog, developed the Moog synthesiser with circuits based on transistors. Further developments in electronics brought the modern synthesiser down to portable size.

FM synthesis, the basis for the digital synthesisers of the 1980s, was invented by Dr John M. Chowning of Stanford University, California. The idea of sampling, on which most modern synthesis is based, was introduced by Australians Peter Vogel, Kim Ryrie, and Tony Furse with their Fairlight Computer Musical Instrument (CMI).

Fibre optics: carrying sounds on light beams

Strands of the purest glass, some of them ten times finer than a human hair, are taking over from copper wire in cables used for transmitting telephone and television signals. The glass is so pure that you would be able to see through a block 12 miles (20km) thick as if it were a windowpane.

These fibre-optic cables can carry more information at higher speeds than copper cable, transmitting it as flashes of light. And they occupy only about one-tenth of the space of copper cable. Optical cables now in use can carry nearly 20,000 telephone calls at once. Sound, pictures and computer information can all be carried in the same cable, and the signals do not fade away as easily as they do in copper wire, so the cable needs fewer signal boosters.

When light is shone into one end of a fibre, it is internally reflected many times – some 15,000 times per yard. Scarcely any light leaks out of the sides, because every fibre has an inner core that channels the light along it and an outer cladding that

reflects it back into the core.

There are two main types of fibres. The finest, known as mono-mode fibres, transmit light as a single wave pattern, and the light signals can travel up to about 120 miles (190km), without being boosted.

In the thicker fibres, which are known as multimode fibres, up to 1000 wave patterns can be transmitted at different intervals, but some light is lost and so the signals need boosting about every 10 miles (16km).

How messages are transmitted

In a fibre-optic telephone system, the electrical current produced by the telephone in response to the vibrations of the voice is first fed into an encoder. This measures the current strength about 8000 times a second and converts it into digitally coded electrical signals representing binary numbers – a series of ones and zeros.

The light transmission is by lasers (opposite page). The type used in optical-fibre transmission is a semiconductor laser that produces invisible infrared light. This has a much higher frequency than the electric current in copper cable, so can carry much more information.

The electrical signals switch the laser rapidly on and off, producing digitally coded light pulses which pass into the optical fibre through a lens. At least 2400 million bits (binary digits) can be transmitted through a single fibre every second

– equivalent to about 32,000 simultaneous telephone conversations. Because there are gaps in the signals of one call, numbers of calls are sent together, slotted between each other. This is known as multiplexing.

At the receiving end of the fibre cable, the light pulses are picked up by a photodetector, which converts them back into electrical signals, and fed to a decoder. This changes them back to the pattern of electrical current transmitted from the telephone mouthpiece.

The transmitters and receivers used are so small they could both fit together inside a matchbox, and the laser generators are no bigger than grains of salt.

THE FIBRE-OPTIC REVOLUTION

Telephone cables carrying messages at the speed of light have given a new lease of life to telecommunications. The amount of information now transmitted – telex, fax and computer data as well as telephone calls – was straining the copper-cable system to the limit. Fibre-optic cables, with their high capacity, small size and freedom from electrical interference, are the key to development.

The first uses of optical fibres was in medicine in 1955, for lighting up parts of the inside of the body. The light loss through the fibres was at first too great for many other uses. But in 1966, Dr Charles Kao and Dr George Hockham, two scientists working in Britain at the Standard Telecommunications Laboratories, discovered that the loss was due to impurities in the glass. By 1970, an American firm, Corning Glass, had produced fibre optics good enough to transmit telephone signals.

Fibre-optic cables are now gradually replacing copper ones between exchanges. The first transatlantic fibre-optic cable, TAT-8 – jointly laid by American, French and British companies – began service in 1988. Its capacity of around 40,000 simultaneous telephone calls is three times as great as the seven existing copper transatlantic cables put together.

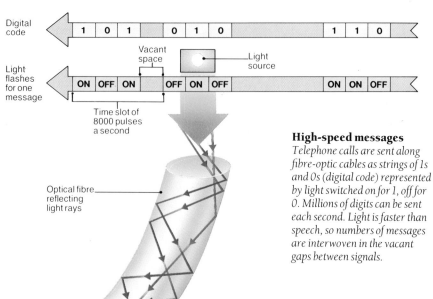

Digital code 1 0 1 0 1 0 1 1 0

Vacant space

Light source

Light flashes for one message ON OFF ON OFF ON OFF ON ON OFF

Time slot of 8000 pulses a second

Optical fibre reflecting light rays

High-speed messages

Telephone calls are sent along fibre-optic cables as strings of 1s and 0s (digital code) represented by light switched on for 1, off for 0. Millions of digits can be sent each second. Light is faster than speech, so numbers of messages are interwoven in the vacant gaps between signals.

Seeing round corners *A fibre-optic 'image guide' is rather like a bee's eye, which sees a whole picture through about 9000 tiny lenses. The guide is a cable carrying about 27,000 glass fibres, each finer than a human hair. They can transmit light to inaccessible places and reflect an image back to the eye. Doctors use image guides for internal examinations or for surgery, and engineers to look inside engines.*

Holograms: three-dimensional pictures on a flat surface

What are credit cards, fashion-house clothes labels, and aircraft tyres increasingly likely to have in common? The answer is holography – a way of producing three-dimensional pictures. Holograms are used on credit cards and clothing labels as security devices, because the pictures are almost impossible to forge.

Holograms are also in widespread use for testing products such as aircraft tyres. Technicians make holograms of new tyres before and after subjecting them to stress. Superimposing one hologram on the other shows up minute flaws.

Professor Dennis Gabor, a Hungarian-born British scientist, was the inventor of holography in 1947. He named the technique from the Greek words *holos* and *gramma*, meaning the 'whole message', because it produced an image in the round.

But it was not until 1961 that two American scientists – Emmet Leith and Juris Upatnieks of the University of Michigan –

produced the type of hologram from which modern holography has developed. They used a laser because it gave the strong, pure light that was needed.

You normally see an object in three dimensions because light waves are reflected from all round it – the collections of light waves are known as wave fronts. Reflected light waves overlap and interfere with each other, and their interactions are what gives the object its light, shade and depth. A camera cannot capture all the information in the wave fronts – only light and shade – so it produces only two-dimensional pictures. Holography captures the depth as well, by measuring the distance light has travelled from the object.

Making a hologram

One of the simplest kinds of hologram is made by splitting the laser light into two beams through a partially silvered mirror.

One beam, called the object beam, lights up the subject of the hologram, and the light waves are reflected onto a photographic plate – a glass plate with light-sensitive emulsion on one side. The other beam, called the reference beam, is reflected directly onto the photographic plate. The two beams coincide to create an interference pattern, which is recorded on the photographic glass plate.

If the photographic plate, when developed as a hologram, was examined under a microscope, it would show a meaningless jumble of lines. This is the interference pattern. When laser light is projected through the developed hologram at the same angle as the original reference beam, but from the opposite direction, the pattern scatters the light to create a projected three-dimensional image of the original object, hanging ghost-like in space.

Embossing the image

To make a three-dimensional print of the hologram, the ghost-like image is used as the object for a second hologram. For making the second hologram, the photographic plate has a special coating that can be processed to form an ultra-thin relief

Science illustrated *This hologram at the Palace of Discovery at La Villete in Paris projects a model of the future Paris Museum of Science and Technology.*

surface of the image suitable for embossing.

The laser light for the second hologram is directed at the object through a horizontal slit. This limits the wave fronts to give a view of the object from a fixed vertical viewpoint, but allowing a horizontal 'look around'. This restriction makes it easier to see the three-dimensional image in ordinary light. The embossed hologram is called a rainbow hologram because, when viewed in ordinary light, it reflects white light to re-create the colours that make up white – as if the light had passed through a prism. The final picture looks different when viewed from different horizontal positions, but shows a rainbow effect when the viewer's eyes are moved vertically.

WHAT IS A LASER?

The word 'laser' is made up from the initials of the words that describe its action, Light Amplification by Stimulated Emission of Radiation. An American physicist, Theodore H. Maiman, invented and first demonstrated it in 1960.

One of the earliest types of laser was the solid ruby laser, made from a ruby crystal or an artificial ruby rod. The chromium atoms in the ruby are stimulated to emit the laser light. An electronic flash tube coiled round the rod gives out intense bursts of light that excite the chromium atoms from a low-energy to a high-energy state.

After a few thousandths of a second, the atoms revert to their normal state, spontaneously emitting an energy package known as a photon. When a photon strikes another chromium atom still in a high-energy state, it stimulates it to emit an identical photon.

The pairs of identical photons travel together in the same direction and exactly in step. The beam is built up by millions of them being reflected back and forth between mirrors at each end of the ruby rod. It finally emerges through a half-silvered mirror at one end, in bursts (pulses) of red light of about one-thousandth of a second.

The laser's power lies not in the amount of its energy, but in the concentration. The beam is very straight, and the photons – all on the same wavelength – all strike the same surface at the same moment. A laser beam can be powerful enough to burn a hole in a steel plate, or delicate enough to be used in eye surgery.

The smallest lasers now in use are semiconductor lasers. They produce an invisible infrared beam when charged with an electric current.

Fax: sending photocopies by telephone

With a fax machine linked to the telephone system, an exact copy of a document or picture can be sent across the world in seconds. Fax – short for facsimile transmission – is now used extensively. In 1988 there were about 4 million machines worldwide.

Fax transmissions are charged at the same rate as an ordinary telephone call, but material can be sent much quicker than it could be dictated. Automatic machines can receive information round the clock, and can be programmed to send documents after office hours, making use of cheaper telephone rates. On some machines the same document can be sent to many different terminals one after the other – this is called sequential broadcasting.

To transmit a document or picture, the user puts it on the machine, and dials the number on the machine key pad. The machine then takes over and signals when it has made a connection.

The document or picture being sent is moved across a light source, usually a fluorescent tube. Light from the tube is reflected off the document and passed by mirrors through a lens onto a device called a CCD (charged coupled device). The CCD is made up of thousands of tiny cells that convert light into electric current, the voltages varying according to the light each cell detects.

These varying voltages are converted to digital signals that are fed to a unit called a modem (modulator/demodulator), which combines them with a carrier wave of electric current for sending along telephone lines.

The modem also tests the quality of the telephone line before feeding in the signals. If the quality is not good enough, the machine will not transmit because the information would be scrambled. Instead, it displays a message telling the user to send the document again. The latest machines can retransmit corrupted data until it is free of error. This is known as ECM (error correction mode).

When the signals arrive at the telephone receiver, they are demodulated – separated from the carrier wave – and fed to a printer that re-creates the document in horizontal chains of dots built up into lines.

Most fax machines use thermal printing, and have a thermal print head consisting of hundreds of pinpoint heaters, which operate in patterns. They print onto thermal recording paper, which has a chemical coating that is changed to a black image where the heat falls on it.

Some machines can print onto plain paper, an advantage because plain paper can be stored longer without fading. They may use a laser printer, in the same way as a photocopier. Or they may use thermal transfer, in which an ink sheet is used between the thermal print head and the plain paper. The heaters melt the carbon on the ink sheet, and it sticks to the plain paper to produce a black image, which dries immediately.

FAX GETS FASTER

Newspapers have been using facsimile machines to send photographs (wire photos) since 1907, when a photo from Paris was wired to the *Daily Mirror* in London. In 1959, a Japanese newspaper *Asahi Shimbun* ('Morning Sun'), sent whole pages from its main office in Tokyo to a printing works at Sapporo 600 miles (960km) away. Now it sends a complete copy daily by satellite link to London, where it is printed, for sale in Europe.

In recent years, technological advances have resulted in cheaper machines able to give good quality reproduction. Newspapers and business firms are not the only users. Police forces can send each other copies of fingerprints and photofit pictures.

The earliest fax machines took about six minutes to transmit a document the size of an A4 typing sheet. Later machines cut the time by half. Modern machines take less than 30 seconds. They code the information digitally although it is transmitted as analogue (like sound-wave) signals. Machines available in the 1990s will both code and transmit digitally, cutting A4 sheet transmission time to four or five seconds.

Around the world in seconds *After Mount St Helens erupted in the USA in May 1980, a US army officer is pictured searching for bodies in a damaged truck. The enlargements show how the facsimile is made up of tiny dots. They are coded as digital signals, and sent by phone all over the world in seconds.*

The bleep that means you are wanted

Busy executives and technicians can carry their own personal buzzer – rather like a pocket electric bell – to warn them when they are wanted. Doctors on their rounds in a sprawling hospital, for example, can be called to a particular ward, or firemen on routine duty to a fire alert.

The pocket alarm, known as a bleeper (or beeper) because of the sound it emits, is a battery-powered miniature radio receiver tuned to one station. The bleep is made by a tiny crystal that vibrates to produce sound when electric signals are passed to it. The signals are generated in the bleeper's electronic circuits, triggered by a radio signal transmitted at the touch of a button from the control unit.

The simplest bleeper can emit several different signals, rather like the dots and dashes of Morse code. Four long bleeps, for example, could mean 'Ring the office', or interspersed long and short ones 'Come to reception'. More advanced types can display a short message, or can store messages.

The system is known as radio-paging. A small network can call up to about 100 receivers, either separately or simultaneously in a group. Each receiver has a number, and the controller makes contact by sending the receiver number and then the required message.

Long-range paging services are operated by commercial companies who transmit messages to their subscribers' bleepers from a control room. The world's largest paging network is operated by British Telecom, who have transmitters covering various zones throughout the country.

Radio-paging systems all have to be licensed, and are allocated a frequency, generally around the 27mHz waveband. The operating range varies according to the power of the transmitter, but is typically 30-40 miles (48-64km).

How photocopiers print without ink

Until the 1940s, making copies of a document or a drawing was a laborious and often messy task. It generally involved either photography or cutting a master stencil for a copier with an inked pad.

Modern photocopiers make use of static electricity – no ink is involved. They can produce up to 135 black-and-white copies a minute, and can also make the copy larger, smaller, darker or lighter than the original. At the touch of a button that controls an electronic microprocessor, they can be made to print copy on both sides of the sheet, and sort sheets into sets.

Today's electrostatic copiers are the descendants of a machine invented in 1938 by an American physicist, Chester Carlson, in New York, which came into use in 1947.

He called the process *xerography*, from the Greek for 'dry writing'.

In old-type copiers, the stencil was fitted round a rotating drum. Most modern copiers still use a rotating drum, but an image of the document to be copied is projected onto the drum by mirrors and lenses. It is this optical system that allows the image size to be changed.

The drum is charged with static electricity, and coated with a thin layer of material, such as powdered silicon, which conducts electricity when light shines on it. The blank, or white, parts of the original reflect the light onto the drum, so the charge is removed. The black parts of the original do not reflect light, so the charge on the drum remains. These charged parts attract a fine black powder, called toner, that forms the image on the copy paper.

In a colour copier, the original is scanned three times and exposed onto the drum through three filters that split it into different strengths of the three primary colours of light – red, blue and green. The colours are re-created on the copy by using toners of the three secondary colours – magenta, cyan and yellow – as well as black.

As with colour printing, the image is overprinted in four stages – first the yellow parts, then the magenta parts, then the cyan parts, and finally the black parts.

The latest laser colour copiers give more precise colour reproduction. The three-times scanned original picture is projected to a bank of photosensitive cells, known as charge-coupled devices (CCDs). They convert it to digitally coded electrical signals. The signals are fed to a laser that emits them as light signals and builds up the image line by line on a charged photoconductive drum.

HOW A PHOTOCOPIER WORKS

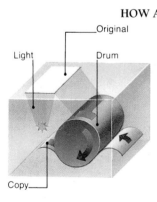

A fluorescent or halogen light shines on the original, which is scanned by a mirror moving back and forth underneath it, projecting the image onto an electrically charged rotating drum. The drum is coated with a photoconductive material – one that conducts electricity when light shines on it.

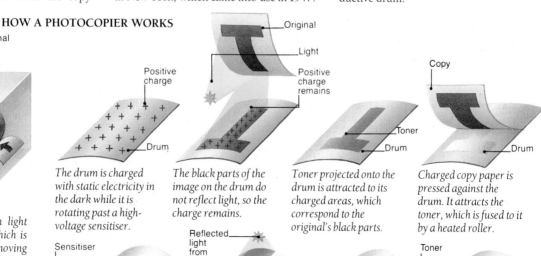

The drum is charged with static electricity in the dark while it is rotating past a high-voltage sensitiser.

The black parts of the image on the drum do not reflect light, so the charge remains.

Toner projected onto the drum is attracted to its charged areas, which correspond to the original's black parts.

Charged copy paper is pressed against the drum. It attracts the toner, which is fused to it by a heated roller.

How a camera captures a fleeting moment

Giant camera *Chicago Railway Company in the USA used this camera to take a picture of a luxury train in 1900. It was the only way they could get it all in. The camera, which travelled in its own railway carriage, was 12ft (4m) long and took photos about the size of a door.*

With a modern camera, you need do no more than press a button to take a photograph – to snap the action of a sporting event or record the beauty of a prizewinning rose, for example – and make a permanent record of a fleeting moment.

Technology has taken the guesswork out of picture-taking, there are now computerised automatic cameras that focus themselves, set their own controls, and wind-on the film after each shot. In contrast there are also simple throwaway cameras that are disposed of once the film has been processed.

All cameras, no matter how sophisticated or how simple, work in much the same way. When you click your camera to take a picture, you are opening the shutter for a brief moment to let light through the lens to a dark interior. In this moment, the light rays form an inverted image of the scene in front of you on the light-sensitive film at the back of the camera.

Processing the film completes the chemical changes begun by the light striking the film, and printing the film provides a picture of the scene you snapped.

The camera's parts

The glass lens is the camera's eye. When light rays pass through glass, they slow up because glass is denser than air, and all except those that strike it at 90 degrees are bent (refracted). In a camera lens the glass is shaped in such a way that light rays are made to bend inwards. They meet, or focus, a short distance behind the lens at what is called the focal point.

When you take a picture, you must be at the right distance from your subject for the light rays entering your camera to focus on the film, and so give a clear image. The right distance depends on the focal length of the lens – the measurement from its centre to its focal point.

Most manual cameras have a control for focusing by moving the lens backwards or forwards to allow for different distances between camera and subject. There is usually a distance scale on the camera. Automatic cameras focus themselves.

Subjects just slightly nearer to, or farther from, the camera than the one in focus will be reasonably well defined on the film. This area is known as the depth of field.

Modern cameras have compound lenses – an assembly of lenses of different glasses and shapes – that iron out the distortions likely with a single lens.

On the common 35mm camera – 35mm (1⅜in) is the film width – the focal length of the standard lens is generally around 2in (50mm) and its angle of view is about 45 degrees. Many cameras can be fitted with interchangeable lenses with different focal lengths, or have zoom lenses with an adjustable focal length.

For a picture that is neither too pale nor too dark, the film must have the right amount of exposure to light. This is controlled by the aperture and the shutter. The aperture in the centre of the compound lens has a device, called an iris diaphragm, with overlapping leaves that can form a larger or smaller opening. The size is controlled by an external ring with the aperture size shown on a scale expressed by f-numbers. The f-number gets higher as the aperture size decreases.

On a typical 50mm lens the f-number scale reads: f 22, 16, 11, 8, 5.6, 4, 2.8 and 2. Each aperture lets in twice as much light as the next higher number – for example, f5.6 admits twice as much light as f8.

The shutter that opens to let in the light is between the lens and the film. The length of time it stays open is known as the shutter speed. This can range from as fast as 1/4000th of a second to as slow as several minutes. Fast speeds are needed for quick action photography, such as motor racing, so that you can 'freeze' the motion to prevent blurring the image. Fast films are often used with fast shutter speeds, to make the maximum possible use of the small amount of light that enters.

Slower shutter speeds are suitable for taking pictures of dim scenes in which there is no movement. Some cameras have a 'B' setting for time exposures, in which the shutter can be locked open for any length of time. Long exposure times are sometimes chosen to blur moving subjects

HOW A CAMERA USES LIGHT

When you take a photograph, the subject that you see through the viewfinder is recorded on the film during the brief moment that the shutter opens to let in light through the lens. The film is coated with an emulsion that is chemically affected by light. 'Fast' films are more sensitive to the light than 'slow' films, so can be used in duller conditions. The speed of the film is indicated on the box and the spool by the ISO number. The higher the number, the faster the speed.

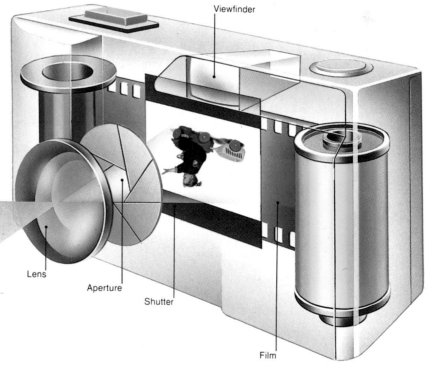

Viewfinder

Lens

Aperture

Shutter

Film

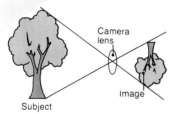

Camera lens

Image

Subject

The camera lens concentrates light from the subject of the photograph and projects an inverted image of it onto the film at the back of the camera.

Small aperture

Large aperture

The diaphragm has overlapping leaves that form an aperture which can be made larger or smaller. A big aperture lets more light enter the camera.

A common type of shutter has two blades that open to form a slit that crosses the film. The smaller the slit, the faster the shutter speed.

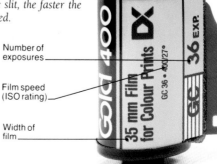

Number of exposures

Film speed (ISO rating)

Width of film

233

into abstract shapes. Different aperture and shutter combinations can give the same exposure. For example, as f5.6 lets in twice as much light as f8, using f5.6 at a speed of 1/250th of a second is the same as using f8 at 1/125th of a second, but the picture taken with the f5.6 combina-tion will be less blurred and have less depth of field. Most modern cameras have built-in electronic exposure meters that make suitable combinations of aperture and shutter settings for the brightness of your subject and the type of film.

Although you can often take photo-graphs in artificial light with some fast films, an electronic flash is normally needed. Some cameras have a built-in flash unit, others have one that can be fitted into

f/5.6　　　　f/11　　　　f/22

Diaphragm aperture *The three sections of this negative have been exposed at f5.6, f11 and f22, letting in less light at each setting.*

Range of shutter speeds

1/15　　　　1/60　　　　1/250

Shutter speed *This negative was exposed at shutter speeds of 1/15sec, 1/60sec and 1/250sec, allowing the light less time to act on the film in each case.*

Final result *Combining the apertures and the shutter speeds shown on the left, produces a photograph with three different exposures, ranging from overexposed to underexposed. The best result was obtained at 1/60sec at f11.*

Shutter effects *A slow shutter speed has provided enough light to record the night scene above. Car lights appear as long ribbons of white. On the right, a pole vaulter has been 'frozen' in six positions by keeping the shutter open during the jump and illuminating him six times with a high-speed flash. This gives a similar effect to opening the shutter six times very rapidly.*

a 'hot shoe' on the camera. The flash must synchronise with the shutter opening – most do so automatically.

How a film works

The film that captures the light rays is a strip of transparent plastic (polyester or tri-acetate) covered with a light-sensitive coating. The coating is a compound of silver salts and a halogen element forming tiny silver halide grains, suspended in gelatine. Exposure to light makes the silver halides start to break down, to eventually form an image in silver.

For the best result, there must be exactly the right amount of light. Too little will result in underexposure, lacking detail because the print or slide is too dark. Too much will produce an overexposed result, lacking detail because it is too light.

Films with large light-sensitive grains are quicker to react and are termed fast films. Slow films have small grains and need extra light for exposure. Films are graded for speed on the ISO (International Standards Organisation) scale. The higher the ISO number, the faster the film.

Processing black-and-white film

Developing the first stage in film processing amplifies the chemical changes begun by the light. It is done in the dark as the film is still light-sensitive.

In the darkroom, the film is immersed in developer, a fluid chemical mixture that reveals the image as a negative, so called because it is darkest where most light has reached the film. This is because the developer reduces the exposed silver halide grains to fine particles of metallic silver, which appear black. Before the developed film can be handled in the light, it has to be fixed – that is, unexposed silver salts are removed by immersing it in a chemical such as 'hypo' (sodium thiosulphate).

To make the negative into a positive print of the original scene, it is put in an enlarger and focused on silver halide coated light-sensitive printing paper. The enlarger projects the negative image on the paper at the size required, and exposes it to light. The paper retains the image in the same way as the film, but the darkest parts of the negative let through the least light, so the original light pattern is re-created. After exposure, the print is developed and fixed in a similar way to the negative.

Colour photography

Colour films go through a similar process, but can produce two different results, depending on the type. A transparency (or slide) gives a direct positive image for projecting on a screen or looking at with a hand-held viewer. Colour prints go through two stages. The film forms a colour negative, which is printed onto photographic paper (see box, right).

THE TRICK OF LIGHT THAT GIVES A COLOUR PRINT

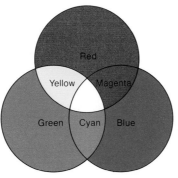

Composition of light *Natural 'white' light contains three primary colours – red, green, blue. Combined in pairs, they give secondary colours – magenta, yellow, cyan. Combining pairs of secondaries (below) produces the primaries again. Colours opposite each other on the chart are termed 'opposites' or complementaries.*

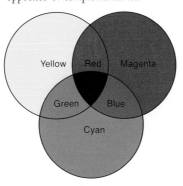

Recording light on paper

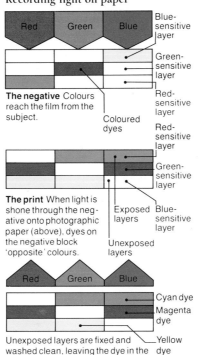

The negative Colours reach the film from the subject.

Blue-sensitive layer
Green-sensitive layer
Red-sensitive layer
Red-sensitive layer
Green-sensitive layer
Blue-sensitive layer
Coloured dyes

The print When light is shone through the negative onto photographic paper (above), dyes on the negative block 'opposite' colours.

Exposed layers
Unexposed layers

Cyan dye
Magenta dye
Yellow dye

Unexposed layers are fixed and washed clean, leaving the dye in the exposed layers. Dye combinations re-create the original colours.

Sunlight is broadly made up of the three primary colours of light: blue, green and red (left). All colours can be made by different mixtures of the three. Pairs of primary colours produce secondary colours: magenta (blue and red), yellow (green and red), and cyan (green and blue). If secondary colours are paired, they reproduce the primary colours (below left). Magenta and yellow make red, cyan and yellow make green, cyan and magenta make blue. Each of the six colours takes no part in making up the colour opposite to it in the charts. Blue and yellow are 'opposites', so are green and magenta, and red and cyan.

Negative and print

A colour film has three layers, each sensitive to one of the primary colours. When a photograph is taken, each layer records a primary colour but forms an image in dye of the opposite colour to the primary. So the image of the blue wheel in the picture below is recorded in the blue-sensitive layer in a yellow dye.

The negative is then printed by light in a darkroom on paper that contains similar colour-sensitive layers. When normal light passes through the blue wheel on the negative, the yellow dye blocks the blue rays but lets through the red and the green. The paper records the red and green as cyan and magenta dyes (their 'opposites'). When you look at the photograph the combination of cyan and magenta appears blue. All the other colours are produced in the same way.

Colour change-over *The colour negative above, with images showing up in their opposite colours, produces the print shown below. To overcome deficiencies in some dyes, negatives have a slight orange tint.*

Angles on Sunset Boulevard *A section of Sunset Boulevard, the main thoroughfare in Hollywood, was photographed from about 70yds (64m) away, using different lenses. The top picture was taken with a telephoto lens with a focal length of 180mm. A telephoto lens has a narrow angle of view (this one gives 14 degrees), but gives a magnified image. The centre picture shows the same scene taken with a standard lens of 50mm focal length. The angle of view is 45 degrees, much the same as your eye, and it brings in more of the street scene. As the focal length decreases, the angle of view increases.*

A telephoto lens is one of several types of interchangeable lens that give a range of focal lengths and angles of view, allowing you to include different amounts of a scene from the same position. A zoom lens allows the same scope without changing the lens, as its focal length can be varied.

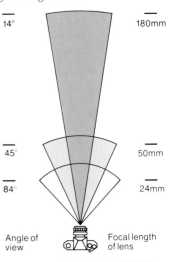

14°   180mm

45°   50mm

84°   24mm

Angle of view   Focal length of lens

Broad view *A lens with a wide angle of view takes in a wider range than your eye. This view of Sunset Boulevard (right) was taken with a wide-angle lens of 24mm focal length, giving an 84 degree angle of view. The wide angle makes the statue and distant buildings look smaller than if you were viewing the scene through your own eyes.*

One of the uses of a wide-angle lens could be to take a photograph across a room where, with a normal lens, you could not get in all of the scene that you wanted. But a group of people pictured from too close a view might appear distorted. Wide-angle lenses are most often used for special effects. A lens with a very wide angle of view – 180 degrees or more – is called a fish-eye lens. It gives an image that is distorted at the edges.

Two types of camera

Two of the most widely used cameras are the compact and the single-lens reflex (SLR). Both use 35mm film, although a few SLRs, including the Hasselblad, use 120 film – 2¼in (60mm) wide – which needs less enlarging so gives better definition.

The two types differ in two main ways. First, most compacts have one built-in lens whereas the SLR can be fitted with a variety of interchangeable lenses. Secondly, the compact has a separate viewfinder whereas the SLR has a reflex viewfinder which 'sees' through the camera lens.

With a separate viewfinder, the photographer's view does not coincide exactly with that of the lens (this is known as parallax error), so some compensation is needed for close-ups. With a reflex viewfinder, the photographer can see exactly the image that will be thrown onto the film, because light entering the camera lens is reflected by a mirror through a pentaprism (a five-sided prism) to the viewfinder eyepiece. The pentaprism reverses the mirror image and presents it to the eye the right way round. When the shutter release is pressed, the mirror springs upwards to let the light from the image onto the film.

The compact is smaller than the SLR, is easy to operate, and has few controls. The most expensive models have automatic focusing, automatic exposure, a zoom lens, built-in flash, and motor-driven film wind-on. They can take pictures comparable in quality to many SLRs.

SLR cameras can be programmed for auto-exposure in different ways – for example, a suitable aperture is automatically chosen for a manually selected shutter speed, or the other way round. Often the exposure meter has an indicator in the viewfinder to show the combination of aperture and shutter speed being set for optimum exposure.

The latest SLR models have built-in microprocessors controlling auto-focusing, auto-exposure and motor-driven wind-on. They can be fitted with a range of interchangeable backs offering different features, such as using different film and printing various information on the film.

DATING THE PICTURE

It is easy to forget when a photograph was taken, but a camera fitted with a data back can record the date on the film for you.

The unit has a built-in clock with the date displayed by a light-emitting diode (LED). This can be exposed onto the film directly with the image, or by means of a tiny internal flash unit, so that it is recorded on the negative. If you wish, it can be printed on the photo margin.

Producing photographs on the spot

In 1944, a child's disappointment at having to wait several days to see the photograph her father had taken led him to devise a quick method of film processing.

He was an American, Dr Edwin Land of Cambridge, Massachusetts, and in just a few months he had come up with a solution. Within three years the first instant-picture camera came on the market, capable of producing a finished black-and-white picture in about a minute. He called it the Polaroid-Land camera.

Today, a Polaroid camera can produce a black-and-white print in as little as ten seconds and a colour print in only a minute. The secret behind instant photography lies in the film, not in the camera. The film not only has a coating of light-sensitive emulsion like a normal photographic film, but also carries the chemicals necessary to process it.

The film pack has both negative and positive sections – in a colour film each is many-layered, with dye developer layers alongside each colour-sensitive negative layer. The processing chemicals that trigger off the developing and printing process are in jelly-like form in a tiny plastic pod between the negative and positive sections.

The pod bursts when the film is removed from the camera through a pair of rollers. The chemicals are spread evenly over the film, and diffuse through it to set the picture processing in motion. The sandwich of film and print material develops in daylight outside the camera, and a positive picture is revealed when the negative and positive layers are pulled apart.

How a camera focuses automatically

In the split second between the pressing of the shutter release and the opening of the shutter, an automatic camera measures the distance between the lens and the subject and positions the lens to give sharp focus.

Most compact cameras have a tiny electric motor driving a transmitter that emits a beam of infrared light. The transmitter is linked to the lens, which moves in or out as the beam scans – focusing from near to far. The beam reflects back from objects to the camera, and a sensor monitors its signals and stops the transmitter when the strongest signal shows that the lens is in focus. This automatically triggers the shutter.

Some instant cameras have ultrasonic focusing similar to the echolocation scanning system bats use to navigate. A gold-plated disc (the transducer) sends out 'chirps' too high to be heard by human ears, each lasting 1/1000th of a second. The disc receives the chirp echoes from the subject, and a built-in microcomputer measures the time each chirp takes to go out and come back. From this it calculates the distance to the subject.

SLR (single-lens reflex) cameras with an auto-focus use what is known as an electronic phase detection system. In this, light entering through the lens is separated into two images. A sensor measures the distance between the two images, which are a specific distance apart when the lens is in focus. If the distance is not correct, the sensor causes a motor to move the lens.

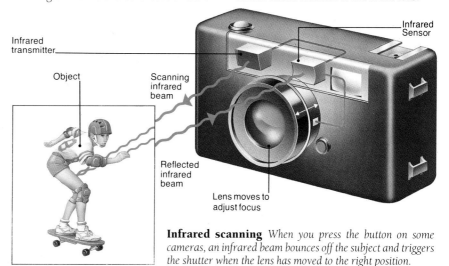

Infrared scanning *When you press the button on some cameras, an infrared beam bounces off the subject and triggers the shutter when the lens has moved to the right position.*

The wizardry of a silicon chip

Within an area no bigger than a shirt button, a microchip holds as many as 450,000 electronic components. They are linked into electric circuits and are visible only under a microscope.

Microchips have transformed modern life and made some of the science fiction of the past into reality. They regulate digital watches, set programs on washing machines, and beat us at video games. They also manipulate robots on car-production lines and control national defence systems.

Electronically, the circuits that make up a microchip are not particularly complex – many are just switches. Their wizardry lies in their minute size, which allows signals to flow through at lightning speed. So they can carry out up to 250 million calculations in a second.

Most microchips are made of silicon, one of the most abundant elements on earth, and easily obtained from sand and rocks. A few are made from gallium arsenide – a compound of arsenic and the metal gallium, found in minerals such as coal.

Chips for everything

There are various kinds of microchip. A microprocessor chip can be a computer in itself – in a washing machine, for example. Or it can be the nerve centre of a larger computer, controlling all its activities.

Memory chips store information in computers on sets of identical circuits – either permanently or temporarily. Interface chips translate the signals coming into the microprocessor from outside – such as from a keyboard – into binary code (page 241), so that the electronic circuits can handle it. They also translate the outgoing signals back into figures or words for the computer screen.

Clock chips provide the timing needed for all the computer circuits to process electric signals in the right sequence. Each is linked to a quartz crystal that vibrates at a precise frequency.

How the silicon conducts electricity

Pure silicon is an insulator – it does not conduct electric current. However, if it is impure – containing certain other elements – it will conduct a weak current. So it is called a semiconductor, halfway between an insulator and conductor. Semiconductors allow the delicate control of current needed for electronic devices, such as transistors, to an extent impossible with full conductors such as metals.

A semiconductor is made by adding elements – usually phosphorus or boron –

Bee tracking *'Killer bees' from Brazil, which migrate north and destroy domestic honeybees, are under surveillance by an American laboratory. Captured bees have a microchip with an infrared transmitter glued to them, and are then released. Scientists pick up the transmissions and study the bees' movements to try to control migration.*

to the silicon. If a small amount of phosphorus is introduced as a gas while the silicon crystal is being formed into a chip, the phosphorus atoms bond together with some of the silicon atoms. Four electrons (see *What is electricity?* page 12) in the outer layers of each type of atom pair off, but one phosphorus electron is spare, so it is left free to form an electric current when a voltage is applied. Electrons are negatively charged, so this type of crystal is called an n-type (negative) semiconductor.

If a small amount of boron is mixed with the silicon, there is one electron short in the bonding system, leaving a hole that attracts free electrons. Free holes create a positive charge, so the crystal is called a p-type (positive) semiconductor.

These two types of semiconductor are formed in sections within one crystal for most microchip components.

How a transistor works

Transistors are the commonest components in a microchip. They are used mostly as switches, letting current through to represent the binary digit 1, or cutting it off to represent 0.

A widely used type of transistor has two islands of n-type semiconductor in a larger base of p-type. While the transistor is

switched off, the free electrons from the n layers drain into the p layer and are absorbed by the free holes. The transistor is switched on by applying a voltage from a separate low-power circuit to an aluminium gate above the p base. This voltage attracts the free electrons from the p base towards the gate. They then form a bridge between the two n islands and provide a path for the current through the circuit in which the switch is operating.

The transistor is switched off by cutting off the power. The free electrons then drain back to the p base and are absorbed by the free holes. Without the bridge they formed between the islands, current cannot flow through the circuit.

Making a microchip

Chips are produced several hundred at a time on a slice of ultra-pure, artificially formed silicon crystal, so thin that it would take about 250 slices to form a piece 1in (25mm) thick. Layout diagrams for circuits are prepared on a computer, then each reduced to chip size and set out side by side on a glass plate known as a mask. Because switches and other components are built up in separate layers on the chip, a mask is made for each operation. The masks – which block out the unwanted parts – are

Designing a chip
A computer is used to design the layout of each electronic circuit. A designer can manipulate the screen image by using a light pen (above), and check the overall layout on a computer print-out (top right). Masks for covering unwanted areas on each layer of the chip are made using a master negative (bottom right) that is about 250 times larger than the actual chip size. It is reduced photographically and then printed on the silicon – in hundreds side by side on the same sheet – as a guide to processing. The sheet is sliced under a microscope with a diamond cutter.

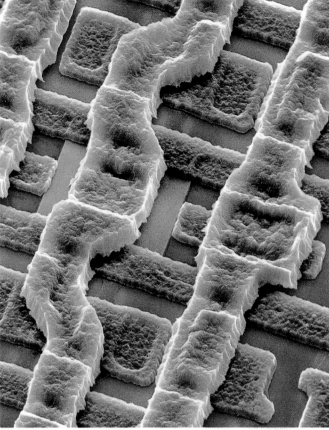

Memory lines *The electronic switches and conductors shown here are enlarged 4000 times. They form part of a memory microchip capable of storing 256,000 binary digits as short bursts of electric current.*

made many times larger than the chip and reduced photographically.

The chips are built up by forming each layer – p-type or n-type layers or insulating layers of silicon dioxide – and etching out the unwanted parts. This is done by treating the layer with a coating sensitive to ultraviolet light, masking it, then exposing it to ultraviolet light. The exposed parts become resistant to acid, but the blocked-out parts do not – they are etched away when the layer is coated with acid.

Parts such as aluminium contacts are deposited in the areas etched for them as a vapour. When hardened, the aluminium is etched to add the required circuit connections, which lead to contact pads at the edges of the chip.

All completed chips on a slice are tested with delicate electrical probes to check that they are working properly. About 70 per cent prove faulty. They are marked as rejects and thrown away. After testing, the slice is cut into individual chips under a microscope with a diamond-tipped cutter. The good chips are each mounted in a frame that is encased in plastic. The contact pads are linked to metal connectors with fine wires of gold. The metal connectors are in turn linked to protruding legs, or pins, that plug into the external circuit.

Computers: machines with memories

Computers started life as adding machines in the 19th century. Today they do far more than add up – they control washing machines and robots and fly aeroplanes, for example. They have memories that can store an incredible amount of information, and they can be programmed to 'think'.

A computer 'thinks' by continually choosing between two alternatives to arrive at a logical decision. It does this whether it is working out an involved mathematical calculation, finding the vacant seats still available on an airline flight, or playing a game of chess. Although it can think only within the limits of its program, it can evaluate a massive amount of information much faster than a human brain.

Computers channel information by switching electric current into various paths. Until the advent of the silicon chip in the 1970s, machines were much larger and slower because their switches were thousands of bulky valves, which looked rather like lamp bulbs. Memories, stored on magnetic drums, could fill several rooms. By comparison, modern computers are the

size of an overnight case and can carry out millions of operations a second.

Another factor that has helped to speed up computers is the use of binary numbers (see overleaf). The first electronic computers had a decimal system, and had to use many more components to represent a number. But since the late 1940s, machines have generally coded both numbers and words into binary numbers, stored as electrical charges. A pulse of current represents 1 and a gap in current 0.

The workings of a computer

A typical personal computer looks like a television set with a keyboard below the screen. The program, a list of instructions to the computer for the task to be carried out – word processing, for example – is usually set out on a magnetic disc that is inserted into a slot in the machine. Then information is fed in via the keyboard.

Programs – sold in sets, or packages – are termed software. The keyboard, screen and working parts of the computer are known as hardware. Programs are written in various computer languages, such as BASIC (which stands for Beginner's All-purpose Instruction Code), COBOL (Common Business Oriented Language) and FOR-TRAN (FORmula TRANslation), used for scientific and mathematical problems. The languages are simple words and abbreviations, and have to be compatible with the machine code of the computer they are used in (facing page).

The heart of the computer is a microprocessor chip, which controls the operations of the memory (or information store) and the arithmetical and logic unit (facing page) that processes the information. A clock chip synchronises all the actions and another interface chip turns the binary numbers back to ordinary numbers or characters to be read on the screen.

The processed information can usually be printed out on paper, typically by a line printer. This has a wheel or chain that impresses the characters onto the paper, and prints them out a line at a time, at the rate of about 2000 characters a minute.

The computer memory

The computer contains two built-in memories, both consisting of microchips. The main memory temporarily stores what is being processed and is known as the random access memory (RAM). It has a read/write control that allows the person using the computer to alter information as well as read it. This memory is erased once the job is done and the power switched off.

The computer's second memory, its read-only memory (ROM), is its permanent store, and the contents are not lost when the computer is switched off. Information in the read-only memory, such as the machine language and any built-in programs, cannot be altered.

Although it is as thin as a hair and no bigger than a shirt button, a memory chip can hold around 450,000 electronic devices linked by circuit connections so fine that it would take 59 million to fill a 1in (25mm) thickness. There are now chips that can store up to 1,048,576 binary digits (bits). In computer jargon, its capacity is 1024-K – K is for Kilo, representing 1024.

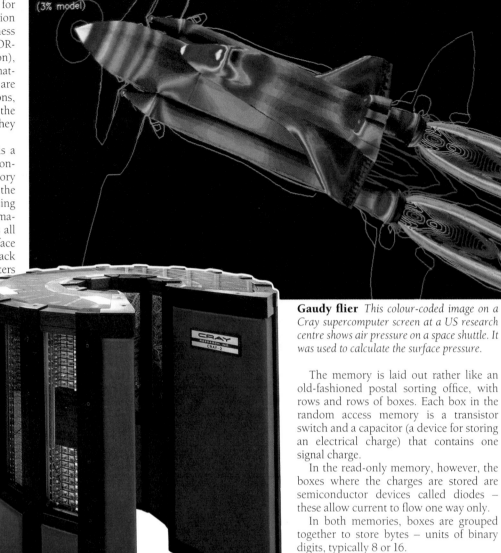

Gaudy flier *This colour-coded image on a Cray supercomputer screen at a US research centre shows air pressure on a space shuttle. It was used to calculate the surface pressure.*

The memory is laid out rather like an old-fashioned postal sorting office, with rows and rows of boxes. Each box in the random access memory is a transistor switch and a capacitor (a device for storing an electrical charge) that contains one signal charge.

In the read-only memory, however, the boxes where the charges are stored are semiconductor devices called diodes – these allow current to flow one way only.

In both memories, boxes are grouped together to store bytes – units of binary digits, typically 8 or 16.

Each box can be located by an address code that is similar to a map reference. When the computer receives its instructions, it sends a message to the necessary box. The bits (electrical signals) leave the memory for the processing unit on a transfer system termed a data bus.

Warm work *There are more than 200,000 microchips at work in the supercomputer processor (above). It took 20 hours to handle the data for the space shuttle launch (top). The working rate of a billion operations each second is so fast it generates enough heat to melt the machine. So it is continually washed with coolant while operating.*

Super simulator *Supercomputers, with processors like the one on the right, can do billions of calculations fast enough to build the pictures of changing atmospheric conditions needed for global weather forecasting.*

WHAT ARE BINARY NUMBERS?

Because we have eight fingers and two thumbs, it seems natural for human beings to count in tens. It is just as natural for a computer to count in twos, for it has to decide between 'yes' or 'no' for every step in a process.

In everyday numbers, the digits from 0 to 9 are read from left to right and are based on the power of ten. For example, 110 is one hundred, one ten, and no units.

The binary system uses only two digits: 0 and 1. Numbers are read from right to left and are based on the power of two. Moving from the right, each digit doubles in value, 1, 2, 4, 8, 16, and so on. So in the binary system, the digits 110 equal 6 (0 + 2 + 4), and the number 110 is as shown below.

Ordinary number 110 in binary code

Binary values

| 128 | 64 | 32 | 16 | 8 | 4 | 2 | 1 |

Binary digits

| 0 | 1 | 1 | 0 | 1 | 1 | 1 | 0 |

Calculation

64 + 32 + 0 + 8 + 4 + 2 + 0 = 110

Words fed into a computer are stored as binary numbers. If text such as LOAD"FILE in BASIC computer language is keyed in, the word LOAD could be processed as shown below.

BASIC	Binary number
L	1 0 0 1 1 0 0
O	1 0 0 1 1 1 1
A	1 0 0 0 0 0 1
D	1 0 0 0 1 0 0

Computers also have back-up storage for extra information. This, like programs, is usually on magnetic discs that are inserted into the machine. The information is in a magnetic pattern, the computer reads the disc or writes on it with an electromagnetic head, like the recording head in a tape recorder.

There are two types of disc – hard discs made of metal and floppy discs made of plastic. Hard discs can carry 10-30 times as much information as floppy discs, and can respond about 100 times faster, but they are more expensive.

Magnetic tapes can also be used to build up a large computer store, but the information takes longer to extract. The whole tape has to be run if you want the piece of information at the end. Tape storage is used for huge filing systems such as the records of insurance companies and tax authorities.

How calculators use logic to add up

A modern pocket calculator is as powerful as a room-sized computer of the 1970s, and the smallest types operate on pill-sized batteries or a panel of solar cells.

The calculator's astonishing capabilities depend on a ¼in (6mm) square silicon chip carrying around half a million electronic signals that represent the numbers involved in the calculations. Up to about 400,000 operations per second are possible, regulated by a quartz crystal clock that is switched on with the calculator.

When you tap a key marked with one of the digits from 0 to 9, the circuits automatically convert it to binary numbers (left). The number keys send electronic pulses to a part of the chip called the register, for temporary storage. When you press a function key, such as 'plus', it sends a signal to the control circuits in another part of the chip. Pressing the 'equals' key for the answer triggers off the control circuits to send the number signals into the arithmetic logic unit, which does the calculations.

This sends the numbers through its circuits by means of switches, known as logic gates, that switch on for 1 or off for 0. These gates operate according to the rules of Boolean algebra, devised by the English mathematician George Boole in the 1840s. The essence of this is that every statement is either true or false, and that when two statements are combined, either both are true, or one or both are false.

The calculator uses three basic types of logic gate to evaluate each step in its calculations as either 1 or 0 – comparable to true or false. Two of the gates, the AND gate and the OR gate, are each fed a pair of digits

HOW THE LOGIC GATES ADD UP 3 AND 2

Adding 3 and 2 in binary numbers can be set out on paper as shown below.

Value of digit		8	4	2	1	
Binary number	3	0	0	1	1	(2 + 1)
Binary number	2	0	0	1	0	(2 + 0)
Answer	(5)	0	1	0	1	(4 + 1)

In every binary addition, there are four possible answers:

0 + 0 = 0 (carry 0)

0 + 1 = 1 (carry 0)

1 + 0 = 1 (carry 0)

1 + 1 = 0 (carry 1)

So in column two of the sum above, 1 + 1 = 0 because it represents 2 + 2 in everyday addition, and the answer, 4, is carried to the third column.

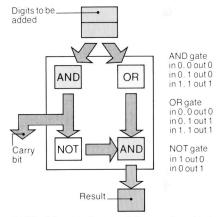

AND gate
in 0. 0 out 0
in 0. 1 out 0
in 1. 1 out 1

OR gate
in 0. 0 out 0
in 0. 1 out 1
in 1. 1 out 1

NOT gate
in 1 out 0
in 0 out 1

Half adder Each pair of digits to be added goes through AND, OR and NOT logic gates to an AND gate. The first AND gate produces the carry bit.

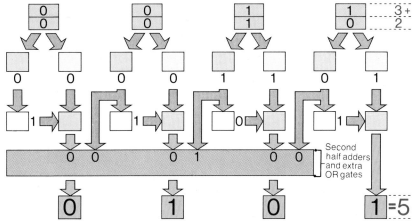

Full addition Full adders are made up of two half adders and an extra OR gate that carries digits to the next column. The second half adder takes in the carry bit and the result from the first half adder. They are processed (not shown in detail) in the same way as in the first half adder.

and put out one. The AND gate outputs a 1 only if it is fed two 1s, the OR gate if it gets 1 in the pair. The third gate, the NOT gate, is fed only one digit, which it inverts.

These three gates in combination can add up, which is the basis of all calculations – subtraction is negative addition, multiplication is repeated addition, and division is repeated subtraction. The logic gates are in units called half adders, linked to form full adders. By processing the signals through the adders, the calculator can tackle the most complicated sums. Thousands of logic gates are used each time, but the signals pass through so fast that the answer appears in a matter of moments.

From pebbles to chips

The abacus, which probably originated in China thousands of years ago, was the first calculator, and it is still widely used in Asia. Counting is done by moving beads across a wire frame. The name is derived from *abax*, Greek for 'slab', probably because counting was once done with pebbles placed in a hollow in a slab or the ground.

The slide rule, devised in the 1620s by the English mathematician William Oughtred, made use of the logarithms that had been invented by the Scotsman John Napier earlier in the 17th century. Blaise Pascal of France patented the first mechanical calculator in 1647, when he was only 24 years old. It had a system of interlocking rotating cogwheels. Gottfried Liebniz of Germany improved on this calculator in 1673.

The ultimate calculating machine was Charles Babbage's analytical engine, designed in the 1830s but never built. Babbage was a professor at Cambridge. His machine could in theory perform all kinds of mathematical calculations, and in 1843 Lady Ada Lovelace published programmes for its use. It was the forerunner of today's computers.

Totting up *This 16th-century engraving shows a money changer using a folding abacus to check his takings.*

How banks store cash safely

Life is getting tougher all the time for safe-breakers. Whether they use hammers, explosives, diamond-tipped power drills, oxyacetylene torches or thermic lances that can burn holes in stone and concrete, modern safes are designed to resist them all.

The body of the safe is a tough sandwich up to 4¾in (120mm) thick, consisting of hard steel-alloy plates welded together, with a filling of ceramic materials or special concrete. There may also be layers of tough fireproof material bonded to the inside of the steel layers, and the filling may be reinforced with carbon-steel wire. Sometimes it also contains very hard chunks of ceramic material designed to blunt drills.

Not only is the safe door locked: it has strong steel bolts that slide into all four edges of the door opening. The bolts are pushed in and out with one handle – known as a throwing handle – that will work only when the door is unlocked. Some safes also have a mechanism that disconnects the bolts from the throwing handle once the door is locked.

Many safes have anti-explosive devices (AEDs). If anyone attempts to blow the safe open, the devices automatically trigger a mechanism that locks the bolts in position so they cannot be withdrawn.

There are two types of AED: 'live' types have to be primed each time the door is locked, but 'dead' AEDs do not – they are set off only by an explosion or by heat.

Under lock and key

Safes are generally locked with combination locks because keys can be duplicated and key locks are easier to pick. Also because keyholes are a good place to pack explosives. Some have both key and combination locks.

Most safes have a four-wheel combination lock with 100 numbers on each wheel. Setting the correct numbers in line on the wheels lines up notches that allow the bolt to be withdrawn from the lock. The operating number can be changed at will from the 100 million combinations that are possible.

Safe-breakers who try to open a safe by listening, perhaps with a stethoscope, to detect the click of a wheel lining up as it is turned, rely on there being some play in the mechanism. Modern combination locks on safes are so precisely engineered that there is no play in the moving parts.

Bank vaults usually have combination locks linked with time locks. Not even the right combination will open the door, except at the times set on the time lock.

Tough proposition *This massive stainless-steel door guards a treasury or bullion store. The bolts that slide into the door posts are clearly shown. The grille behind the door protects staff working in the store when the door is open.*

How plastic cards give you cash and credit

When you push your plastic card into a cash dispenser, a scanning device – an electromagnetic recording and erasing head – checks the dark brown strip on the underside. This strip is magnetic tape similar to that used in tape recorders, and it carries three tracks holding up to 226 letters or numbers. One track gives your account number, another gives any weekly cash limit, and the third checks that your PIN (personal identification number) is correct.

If you tap in the correct PIN on the keys, the dispenser, which is linked to the bank's computer, checks that the weekly limit has not been exceeded, that your account is not overdrawn, and that the card has not been reported lost or stolen. If all is in order, it subtracts the amount you ask for from the existing balance and inserts the new balance before dispensing the cash.

Phonecards work in much the same way – a scanner inside the telephone checks tracks on the card to see if it still has any unused units. The appropriate number of units are erased as you make a call.

The electronic vending machines of the future will not take coins at all. They will be operated by debit cards, which will have a certain amount of credit indicated on a magnetic strip.

Electronic fund transfer

New-style credit cards carry your name, account number, and an expiry date. When the card is put in the retailer's machine, it feeds the details through to the credit-card company's computer, which takes about 15 seconds to check that the card has not been reported lost or stolen and that you have not exceeded your credit limit. If all is in order, the computer authorises the transaction and a receipt for you to sign appears on a slot in the machine.

This method of credit-card processing is known as EftPos (electronic funds transfer at point of sale). It became available in some places in 1988. EftPos systems include debit cards – bank cards that can be used for payment instead of cheques, and which instantly debit the holder's bank account. Before electronic transfer was available, credit-card details had to be checked by telephone if purchases cost more than a certain limit.

The electronic transfer system can cut down the amount of credit-card fraud, because the computer can cancel further transactions immediately a card loss is reported, and will not accept a forged card.

But magnetic strip cards are giving way to smart cards, which should make fraud even more difficult.

Smart cards are cards that contain miniature electronic brains. They were invented in 1974 by a Frenchman, Roland Moremo. By 1988, nearly 4 million were in use in France, and more were on trial in Britain and other parts of Europe, the USA and Japan.

The smart card's brain is a tiny, wafer-thin silicon chip (see *Microchips*, page 238). This chip carries a record of the cardholder's credit limit, and contains details of previous transactions.

When you pay with the card, the retailer puts it into a counter terminal and the card's brain carries out its own checking – it does not need to refer to the company's computer. The counter terminal carries details of lost and stolen cards, so if a listed card is put through, the transaction is automatically cancelled and the card neutralised so that it cannot be used again. The counter terminal passes details of the transaction to the company's computer.

Although smart cards carry all the details of the cardholder's transactions, the cardholder has no way of consulting them, except at a special dispenser. The supersmart card overcomes this disadvantage. It looks like a solar-powered calculator, and has a small display screen and keyboard on which the holder can check the transactions and the credit balance on his account.

How supermarket checkouts read bar codes

Every successful shopkeeper needs to know which goods are selling well and which are going slowly, so that he can restock or phase them out, as appropriate. For the small shop, tidy bookkeeping and a glance at the shelves may give all the information necessary. But supermarkets and other big stores need quick and accurate records of a much larger flow of merchandise. That is why they use bar codes, which are printed on the packaging.

A bar code can be read by a laser scanner, which passes it to a computer. This supplies the details and price of the goods, totals the bill, and feeds the information to the cash register which prints out a receipt. The computer also records the sale for stockkeeping.

Common bar codes are European Article Numbers (EAN), based on a number with 13 digits, and Universal Product Code (UPC), based on a number with 12 digits. Each digit is represented by a series of parallel straight lines and white spaces. The laser scanner translates the information into binary digit signals (page 241), which it feeds to the computer.

The code gives the manufacturer details of the product and the package size, and includes a security code that prevents anyone altering it or the scanner misreading it. The computer supplies the price from the product information. So the only way to change the price of an item is by altering it in the computer.

A laser scans a bar code with a beam of light passed from one end to the other. It is sensitive enough to read from left to right or right to left. Although the bar codes are usually printed in black on a white background, a laser can read a bar code which is printed in any dark colour except red, and the background can be any pale or pastel colour. Some of the lasers used scan with red light, so cannot pick up a reflection from red.

Bar coding is faster and more accurate than other systems. Human error is limited because staff do not have to mark a price on every item, and checkout assistants do not have to key in prices at the till.

However, another kind of error can occur. Because the computer supplies the prices at the checkout, the store management has to ensure that the goods on the shelves display the same prices. Also that the shelf price is changed if a computer price is altered, or a customer may appear to be charged the wrong price.

CARDS THAT RECORD YOUR HEALTH – AND EVERYTHING ELSE

American motorists were able to buy petrol with oil company credit cards before the First World War, but the age of the credit card dawned in 1950 with the introduction of the Diners Club charge card by American businessman Frank McNamara. The idea came to him after dining in a New York restaurant and discovering he had mislaid his wallet. The Diners Club card is not strictly a credit card because the whole bill has to be paid when the invoice is received – most other cards carry forward a debit balance.

Today there are more than 350 million credit or charge cards in use in the United States alone. Worldwide, cards are numbered in billions.

Smart cards are likely to have a wider use than for money transactions. In the late 1980s some medical authorities in parts of Europe, the USA and Japan began trials with medical identity cards – smart cards carrying the holder's medical history. The cards save time and paperwork, as they can be consulted by doctors and chemists in computer terminals at hospitals, surgeries and pharmacies, and updated each time the patient is seen. The European trial programmes aim to produce a standardised EEC care or health smart card for use in the 1990s.

Also available are laser cards, developed in the USA, in California. They are not as smart as smart cards, but are able to carry a much larger store of personal information, contained in a pattern of tiny holes – only a thousandth of a millimetre across – on a photosensitive strip. The dots, like the pits and flats on a compact disc, can be read by a laser scanner in a special terminal.

The card can hold coded identification details, including fingerprints, signature, voiceprint, and even a photograph, as well as various hidden security codes making it virtually impossible to counterfeit. Its information storage space is so vast there is plenty of room for such things as bank accounts, medical history and educational attainments. Information is filed on the card under separate access codes, so the bank, for example, could read out only financial information and the doctor only medical information.

How a quartz watch tells the time

The exquisite workmanship of the traditional mechanical wristwatch has given way to the magic of the microchip. In the quartz watch, a vibrating crystal has taken over the role of timekeeper from the traditional finely tuned balance wheel and hairspring. Minute electronic circuits control its operations.

A quartz crystal vibrates at an unvarying rate when an electric current is passed through it. The man-made quartz crystals used in watches are usually designed to vibrate 32,768 times a second when stimulated by the current from a battery.

ALL DONE BY CRYSTALS

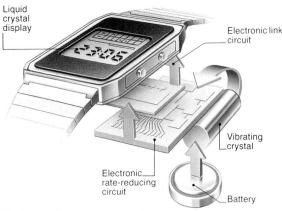

Liquid crystal display

Electronic link circuit

Electronic rate-reducing circuit

Vibrating crystal

Battery

The heart of the quartz watch is a vibrating quartz crystal charged with electric current from a battery. A microchip converts the vibrations to one-second pulses that advance the time displayed by liquid crystals.

These vibrations produce electric pulses, and as the pulses travel through the electronic circuits of the microchip, their rate is successively halved in a series of 15 steps. The result is one pulse per second. Each one-second pulse triggers the chip to send signals to the digital display to advance the numerals one second.

The chip also uses the pulse as a base for other counting circuits, such as those that display hour and date, and to control the alarm signal.

Many modern quartz watches display the time in digits on a liquid crystal display (LCD). The liquid crystals are sandwiched between a reflective bottom layer and a top layer of polarised glass, and transparent electrical conductors separate them into segments. Each digit is formed from segments – up to seven are normally used, all seven being used for the figure 8.

The liquid crystals rearrange their molecules according to their electrical state. Where the conductors carry no charge, light through the sandwich is reflected out again, so the display is blank. When the conductors are charged by an electric pulse, the molecules in the affected segments realign and twist the light away from the reflective surface, so the segments appear dark.

HOW LONG IS A SECOND?

Since 1967, the standard international definition of a second, established by the International System of Units (SI System), has been the radiation frequency of a caesium atom – that is, 9,192,631,770 hertz (cycles per second). This frequency is measured by a caesium clock regulating a quartz clock.

Master atomic clocks at various national laboratories are synchronised through the International Time Bureau in Paris.

into vapour. Caesium is a silvery-white metal similar to sodium, with a very low melting point of 83°F (28.5°C) compared to iron's 308°F (153.5°C) melting point.

Like all atoms, the caesium atom has a nucleus surrounded by orbiting electrons (see *What is electricity?* page 12).

These electrons can be manipulated in an electromagnetic field. When this happens, the atom's energy level is changed to a lower or higher state, and it either absorbs or radiates electromagnetic energy. The radiation frequency is absolutely constant.

The vaporised caesium is subjected to an electromagnetic field inside a resonator, causing sharply defined vibrations with a frequency of 9,192,631,770 hertz (cycles per second).

This is the precise frequency at which the atoms change their energy state.

The quartz clock is used to keep the resonator vibrating at this frequency, its normal quartz frequency of 100,000 hertz being multiplied electronically.

As long as the quartz clock is accurate, the caesium atoms will all resonate uniformly. They are focused on a detector that senses any change in their energy concentration. If there is a change, this detector sends an 'error' signal through the circuit to the quartz clock.

Atomic clocks as ultimate timekeepers

No clock, it seems, can be relied upon to keep perfect time. The best mechanical timepieces gain or lose about four seconds a year, and even modern quartz crystal clocks are accurate only to about one second in ten years. But an atomic clock is reckoned to be accurate to one second in at least 1000 years.

Every clock measures time by counting the regular vibrations of something. Early clocks used the swing of a pendulum, and early watches the constant oscillation of a balance wheel. Quartz clocks have crystals made to vibrate at 100,000 cycles a second when electric current is applied.

Atomic clocks keep time by the vibrations of their atoms – more than 9 billion vibrations a second in the most commonly used caesium atomic clock. And unlike

mechanical clocks, which are upset by such things as temperature and friction, atomic clocks are virtually unaffected by outside conditions. They have no dial or any sort of display by which you can read the time – what they do is regulate quartz clocks to keep them highly accurate.

The main housing of the caesium clock is a vacuum tube with a small electric oven at one end in which a piece of caesium is melted and turned

Old timer *The caesium atomic clock used at Greenwich Observatory until 1962 was accurate to one second in 300 years. It is now in London's Science Museum.*

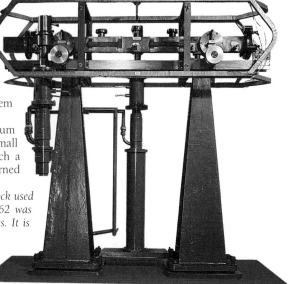

With this feedback, the quartz clock is electronically adjusted to correct the vibration of the resonator.

Using atomic clocks

Atomic clocks are used to calibrate other clocks and for scientific research in observatories and space laboratories. They are also used on high-speed aircraft for synchronising with radio-frequency navigation signals.

Other materials besides caesium can be used for atomic clocks. Ammonia was used in the first atomic clock built in 1947 at the National Bureau of Standards in Washington DC, in the USA.

The most accurate atomic clocks now use hydrogen, which has a radiation frequency of more than 1420 billion hertz. They are said to be accurate to about one second in nearly 2 million years. And American scientists are developing a mercury atomic clock which they expect to be accurate to one second in 10 billion years!

The microscope that is used to explore inner space

When you look at a tiny object such as a drop of pond water under an ordinary microscope, it is enlarged enough for you to distinguish tiny creatures that you could not see with the naked eye. An ordinary microscope, also called an optical microscope, works by bending light waves through lenses, and there is a precise limit to the resolving power – the amount of detail it can show. Just as the human eye cannot distinguish the details of minute objects, so the optical microscope cannot show up the details of objects that are less than half the wavelength of light apart – that is, about 0.00025mm.

The best optical microscopes cannot magnify more than about 2500 times, and this is not large enough for some detailed scientific study.

An electron microscope can magnify an object up to a million times, allowing scientists to study the very molecules that make up the Universe.

It works by sending out a beam of electrons from an electron gun similar to the type that is used in a television tube.

The electrons are accelerated through a powerful electric field (several million volts in the most advanced types) and focused into a beam by means of magnetic coils, called magnetic lenses. The beam has to travel through a vacuum, because air molecules would interfere with it.

There are two types of electron microscope. The transmission electron microscope (TEM) transmits the beam through a thin slice of the specimen being studied. This type, used for such tasks as examining sections of cell or tissue, can magnify up to a million times.

The scanning electron microscope (SEM) scans the specimen – that is, it travels back and forth to cover its entire surface. As the beam is reflected, so the microscope builds up a specimen of the picture, line by line. It can magnify up to about 200,000 times, and its uses include scanning cancer cells and forensic specimens such as spent bullets and clothing fibres. Because of the very short wavelength used, it can scan in three dimensions.

An electron beam is not visible to the human eye, but the image is projected onto a fluorescent screen, rather like a television screen, which glows where the electrons strike it. The picture produced can be recorded on photographic film.

Seeing the unseen *Specimens viewed by an electron microscope can be photographed as they appear on its screen. The two shown have been coded with false colours to simplify viewing. On the right, a weevil emerging from a wheat grain is seen through a scanning electron microscope about 32 times larger than life. The slice of human nerve sheath pictured below is seen through a transmission electron microscope about 250,000 times its normal size.*

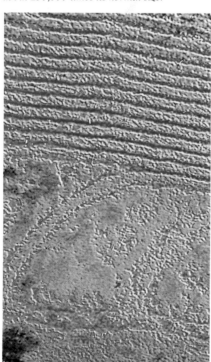

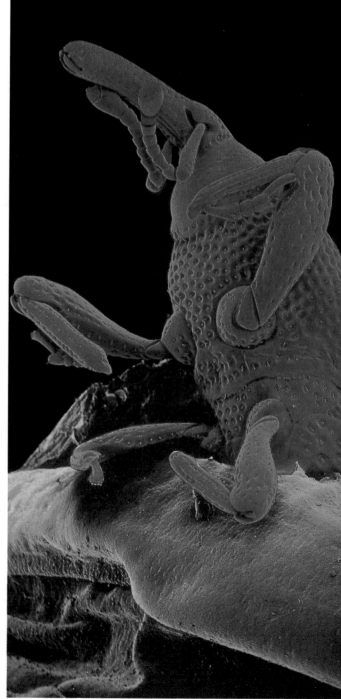

How do robots put their electronic brains to work?

The popular idea of a robot is a machine that acts like and resembles a human being. But the robots that are increasingly being used for a wide range of tasks do not look man-like at all.

The robots that wield welding guns in car factory production lines look something like cranes. The mobile robots used by army bomb-disposal squads look like wheelbarrows on tracks. And children have likened a mobile robot used in school to teach them computer programming to a giant sweet.

Robots do, however, resemble human beings in the range of actions they can carry out. Instead of repeatedly performing just one action, like an automatic machine, a robot can perform a chain of different actions. Its movements are controlled either hydraulically or pneumatically (by oil or air pressure) or by electric motors. And its brain is a small computer that directs its movements.

Inside the computer's memory are the instructions for carrying out a task – picking chocolates from a container and putting them in the right part of a display box, for example. By changing the program, the robot can be made to vary the task, or do something different within the limits of the activities it is designed for.

Most robots are the equivalent of an arm that can lift and move in several directions, and a hand that can pick things up. But the robot's hands are normally much simpler than a human hand, and – depending on the job it is built for – may be just a two or three-clawed gripper, a suction pad or a magnet. Some robots are strong enough to lift a heavy load across a factory floor.

Others do delicate precision work such as assembling computers.

There are two ways of instructing a robot to do its job. One way is to work out the precise movements needed and write them as a computer program. The other is to literally show it what to do.

Fiction and fact *The robot known as Robby (right), which appeared in* The Forbidden Planet, *a 1956 American film, is everyone's idea of a robot. The real thing is usually less theatrical but more impressive, like the hands and arms below, which are designed to pour drinks for disabled people. Some robots are used for bomb disposal and some for teaching school-children geometry. Others can read music, and in future robots may respond to spoken orders.*

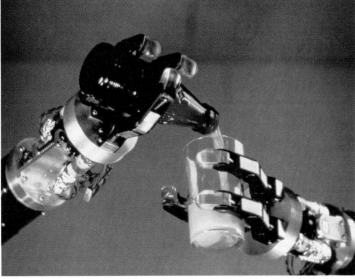

The engineer guides the robot's arms through the movements he wants it to make – spray-painting a section of a car body, for example – while the robot's computer brain memorises the action. After that, the robot can repeat the exact movements over and over again.

Robots that can see

Some robots can be fitted with vision equipment that increases their abilities. With welding, for example, a robot that cannot see must have the parts always placed in the right position. A robot that can see can check the positions of the parts and guide the robot arm accordingly.

Nottingham University in England developed the first seeing robot in 1970, under the direction of Professor Wilf Heginbotham and Professor Alan Pugh, but the idea was taken up and marketed in America. Vision equipment is still limited, but researchers in many parts of the world are continuing to improve it.

The robot is linked to a television camera that scans the job by means of two computers. One computer assesses the camera information and passes it to the other, which controls the robot. But such systems are expensive, and are limited in use because of the time taken to analyse the

Selected assortment *Adept One, a computer-controlled American robot, can recognise the chocolates shown on the TV screen and pick out the right ones for packaging.*

information and instruct the robot to move accordingly. Some jobs are more economical and quicker done by a human. Also, object recognition is more limited than the human eye, although researchers are using advanced computer techniques to develop improved methods of shape recognition.

Robots for fun

The Japanese are not only world leaders in robot technology (they had 118,000 in use at the end of 1987), they also enjoy them. Japanese businessmen can buy robot

executive toys, Japanese children can see robots that sing and talk at Tokyo's Science and Technology Museum. And Japanese of all ages can enjoy an 18th-century-style doll that walks across the table, bows and offers a cup of tea. But fun robots are not confined to Japan – an American company sells a robot that hands out drinks to guests from the bar.

Professor Ichiro Kato, of Waseda University in Japan, has developed a humanoid (man-like) robot that can read music and play the organ and one that can walk on two legs, as well as a spider-like robot that can climb stairs. But these are not just for fun, they are experiments that can lead to practical use. The spider, for example, may be adapted for use in the building industry, and the walking robot was a step to the development of an artificial leg with a microcomputer to direct its movements.

Schoolchildren in many parts of the world also learn about computers and programming with robotic toys, such as the British-made remote-controlled Turtle, which also teaches geometry, and the Roamer (the giant sweet), which has a built-in microprocessor and can be programmed to move about and produce electronic music.

Robots as competitors or servants?

The Czech playwright Karel Capek introduced the name robot in the early 1920s. He wrote a play called *Rossum's Universal Robots* in which an army of industrial robots became so clever that they took over the world. Capek coined the word robot from the Czech *robota*, which means 'slavery'. Since then men have worried not so much about robots taking over the world, but more about robots taking over their jobs.

Robots have indeed taken over some jobs – dull, mechanical, routine work. They save costs because there is no need for them to change shifts, they do not tire or lose concentration, they do not take tea or coffee breaks, they do not fall ill (although they may need repairs), and they do not go on strike. But even though American and British researchers have produced robotic four-fingered hands capable of picking a flower, robots are still a long way from having the perception, dexterity or flexibility of human beings.

It is, however, generally accepted that the responsible use of robots in industry is beneficial because it saves people from doing dull and dangerous jobs. Robots were used to clear up the radioactive debris after the Three Mile Island nuclear accident in America in 1979. They are also being developed for inspecting and manufacturing nuclear plants, fighting fires, felling forest trees, and acting as security guards – walking burglar alarms that can warn human guards of an intruder. And a four-legged, 72 ton robot was used to roll boulders to build up the sea wall in Tokyo Bay, Japan, in 1986 – saving 50 divers from the risky task.

Experiments are also under way with robots that can help infirm and disabled people to be independent. Researchers in Britain and America are developing robots that can respond to

spoken commands. They will be able to undertake such tasks as brushing teeth, serving soup, loading a computer, opening filing cabinets and picking up mail.

Safe viewing *Robin, an American walking robot for inspecting nuclear power plants, will save its operator from entering a dangerous radioactive area. It carries lights and a TV camera.*

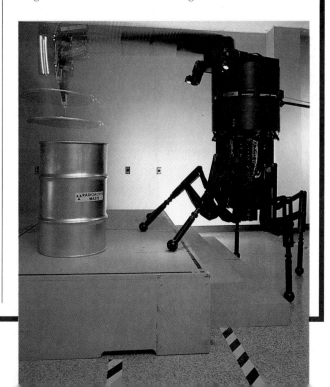

How does a car engine make the wheels go round?

Before a typical car engine can make a car move, it has to convert the up-and-down movement of pistons driven by fuel combustion to the rotary movement of a shaft that turns the wheels.

Developing engine power

In the commonly used four-cylinder engine, power is developed when a mixture of petrol and air is compressed and ignited inside the engine cylinders. As the fuel mixture ignites, the hot gases that are produced force a piston down its cylinder. The cylinders are phased to fire one after the other to give continual running power.

The pistons are connected by rods and bearings to the main engine shaft, the crankshaft, and as the pistons go down, they force the crankshaft to rotate.

The crankshaft has a heavy flywheel fitted at one end, to keep it turning steadily and to smooth out the motion of the pistons. The flywheel also links the engine to the transmission – the system that conveys the power to the car's wheels.

Transmitting the power

There are two main types of transmission system. The traditional one has the engine at the front of the car driving the two rear wheels. In the increasingly common front-wheel-drive system, the engine is at the front driving the front wheels. Some vehicles have a rear engine driving the rear wheels, and some – mostly those for use in rough terrain – can have just two or all four wheels driven. In normal conditions, only the two rear wheels are driven, but the drive can be switched to the front wheels as well by using an extra gear lever.

In a front-engined rear-wheel-drive car, the engine transmits the drive to the rear wheels through a clutch, gearbox, propeller shaft and the final drive.

A front-wheel-drive car has no propeller shaft because the engine is close to the driving wheels. The clutch, gearbox and final drive are usually incorporated into a single unit.

The clutch is incorporated with the flywheel, and allows a smooth and gradual take-up of motion from the turning crankshaft through the gearbox to

Tough going *When a rally car completes about 2000 miles (3200km) of hard driving, its wheels will have made over 2 million revolutions and its pistons moved up and down more than 8 million times.*

Spark plug

Inlet valve

INTAKE

0·33 ms

0·67 ms

1·00 ms

1·33 ms

1·67 ms

2·00 ms

HEAT TURNED INTO MOVEMENT

A piston is driven down its cylinder to turn the crankshaft by the expansion of hot gases given off from burning petrol and air. The petrol and air is mixed in the carburettor. It enters the cylinder through an inlet valve, and is set alight by a spark plug in the top of the cylinder (left). Firing and gas expansion take two thousandths of a second. The piston action is in four strokes – a power stroke down after firing, an up-stroke that pushes burnt gases out through a valve, down again to draw in fuel, then up to compress fuel before the next firing. The pistons are phased so each makes a different stroke at the same time.

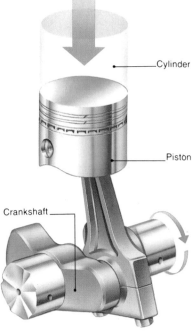

Cylinder

Piston

Crankshaft

One up and down movement of a piston gives one revolution of the crankshaft. A piston may go up and down 6000 times a minute to turn the engine at top speed.

Rear-wheel drive *In a traditional car, the engine at the front has a propeller shaft to take the drive to the rear wheels. The drive has to turn a right angle to get to the wheels.*

Front-wheel drive *Many cars have an engine at the front of the car to drive the front wheels. As it is in line with the axles, the drive does not have to turn a right angle.*

Four-wheel drive *On some cars, the drive can be directed to all four wheels to give better grip in bad conditions. The drive turns a right angle at both ends of the car.*

the stationary propeller shaft when the car starts moving.

A simple clutch consists essentially of a driven plate and a pressure plate. In normal driving the driven plate is sandwiched against the flywheel by the pressure plate. When the driver presses the clutch pedal, the pressure plate is sprung away from the driven plate, which moves out of contact with the flywheel, so drive to the gearbox ceases. When the driver releases the clutch pedal, drive through the gearbox is resumed. The clutch is operated either mechanically by means of a cable or hydraulically by liquid pressure.

On a car with manually operated gears, the clutch acts as a kind of switch, allowing the driver to disconnect the engine from the rest of the transmission when changing gear. A car with automatic gears does not have a normal clutch; it uses a device called a torque converter, in which whirling oil is used to transfer motion from the flywheel.

A gearbox is needed to help the engine apply more turning effort when necessary.

Car engines develop their maximum turning effort when the crankshaft reaches a certain number of revolutions per minute. This number is not the same for all cars. For example, a car designed for high-speed driving develops its maximum effort at a high number of engine revs, but a car designed to have pulling power develops it at a lower number of revs.

With any car, more effort is needed to get it moving than to keep it going once it has picked up speed. And more effort is needed to drive it uphill than on the flat.

In bottom gear, the propeller shaft turns about three times slower than the crankshaft, in second gear about twice as slow, and in third gear just slightly slower. This gives the engine more push, because the same power applied at a slower speed has greater force – just as it takes more effort and slower winding to raise a heavy bucket from a well than a light one. When reverse gear is engaged, the propeller shaft turns about four times slower than the engine.

The exact difference in turning relationships between the engine and the propeller shaft depends on the design of the car, and is known as the gear ratio. In top gear, the propeller shaft turns at the same speed as the crankshaft, so the gear ratio is 1 : 1. This is because by the time the car reaches top gear, the engine is near its maximum effort and the car has gained sufficient speed for extra effort to be unnecessary.

Inside the gearbox, the change in speeds between the two shafts is brought about by locking together different-sized gear wheels with toothed outer edges. For example, if one gear wheel is locked with another that has twice the number of teeth, the smaller wheel makes two revolutions for each revolution of the larger wheel.

In a manual gearbox, the driver makes

HOW GEARS WORK

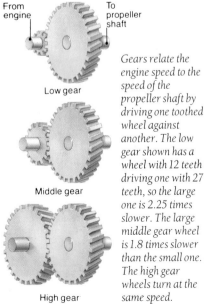

From engine

To propeller shaft

Low gear

Middle gear

High gear

Gears relate the engine speed to the speed of the propeller shaft by driving one toothed wheel against another. The low gear shown has a wheel with 12 teeth driving one with 27 teeth, so the large one is 2.25 times slower. The large middle gear wheel is 1.8 times slower than the small one. The high gear wheels turn at the same speed.

the adjustments by operating the gear lever. In an automatic gearbox, the changes are brought about by oil pressure.

The oil pressure is regulated by valves known as shift valves. They work either by pressure from throttle when the driver pushes down the accelerator pedal, or by a device called a governor that is sensitive to road speed, and is located on the gearbox output shaft. The governor takes control from the throttle pressure once the car reaches a predetermined road speed. When the car drops below the predetermined speed, the throttle pressure takes over again.

Carrying the drive to the wheels

The gearbox and rear axle of a front-engined rear-wheel-drive car are almost the car length apart, so need to be linked by a propeller shaft, which passes on the engine power to the rear axle. A propeller shaft is made of hollow steel and has flexible couplings at each end, called universal joints. These joints allow the shaft to change angle – over road bumps, for example – while still transmitting power. The shaft can also change length slightly by sliding backwards and forwards on splines on the gearbox output shaft.

The propeller shaft ends at the final drive, a complicated set of gears in the middle of the rear axle. The final drive turns the drive through a right angle to rotate the half-shafts attached to each rear wheel. This is done by the propeller-shaft pinion and the crown wheel, which both have bevelled teeth. The crown wheel has a much larger circumference, so turns slower than the pinion, thus reducing the speed of the wheel half-shafts.

The final drive also gears down the speed of the propeller shaft to the speed of the wheels. Because of their larger circumference, the wheels turn only once for every three to six turns of the crankshaft. For example, if a car is travelling at 60mph (96km/h), the wheels are turning at probably only 1000 revolutions a minute while the crankshaft is turning at about 4000 revolutions per minute.

Also incorporated in the final drive is a mechanism called the differential, which allows the rear wheels to revolve at different speeds when cornering. If both wheels revolved at the same speed, the inner one would skid at every corner.

On each half-shaft there is a bevel gear that meshes with two small bevel pinions on the inside of the crown wheel, one at the top and one at the bottom. While the car is driving straight, the force on each bevel pinion is equal. If one road wheel starts to drag – the inside wheel when the car takes a bend, for example – its half-shaft bevel gear becomes harder to turn, so the pinions drive the other half-shaft gear faster, increasing the speed of the other wheel.

How do anti-lock brakes work?

Most drivers have experienced the frightening moment when the wheels lock and the car slides uncontrollably towards the vehicle in front. Although drivers are taught to leave a sufficient gap for braking, and to take extra care on wet or icy roads, the huge number of rear-end collisions every year is ample evidence they do not.

Skidding and sliding happen because the behaviour of a car changes rapidly when the wheels begin to lock. Up to a point, pressing the brake pedal harder produces greater deceleration. But once the wheels have locked, their grip on the road is lost, they begin to slide instead of turn, and the driver can no longer control the car's direction. Panic follows, and the natural reaction is to stamp ever harder on the brake, which makes things worse.

Advanced driving manuals recommend cadence braking, in which the brake pedal is pumped up and down in quick succession to ensure that the wheels never lock. But, in practice, few drivers have the skill or experience to do this in an emergency.

Anti-lock brakes are designed to automate the technique of cadence braking, taking the skill out of the hands and feet of the driver and entrusting it to a package of electronics and hydraulics. They consist of two parts: an electronic sensor that can detect how rapidly the wheels are decelerating, and a system for automatically controlling the hydraulic pressure on the brakes to achieve the best and safest deceleration.

The sensor consists of a slotted or toothed exciter disc attached to an axle or inside a brake drum. As the axle turns, each tooth and gap in this disc pass close to a monitor and generate a current, which varies according to the rate at which the disc is rotating.

The signals are interpreted by electronic circuits, which determine both the speed of the disc and the rate at which it is decelerating. If the disc is slowing down too rapidly and is about to lock, the circuits instruct the hydraulic controls to reduce brake pressure, preventing a skid. As the driver continues to press the brakes, pressure rises again, and the system repeats the operation until the vehicle has stopped. The system can produce up to 45 cadences a minute, if required.

The details of how the electronic signals are used to control brake pressure depend on individual designs. Some of the earliest non-skid brakes, in the 1960s, were fitted to trucks, which use air under pressure to activate their brakes. In these systems it is relatively simple to bleed off some of the air through a valve to reduce pressure. The air

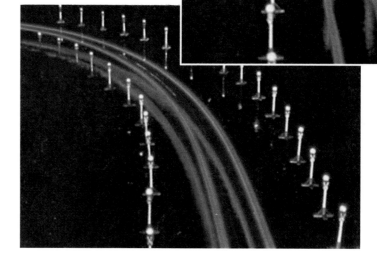

Controlling a turning car
Time-exposure photographs show what happens when a car's wheels lock on a bend (right) and when they keep turning (below). Locked wheels can cause a car to slide erratically, and even leave the road, in wet conditions. Anti-lock brakes prevent this, allowing the driver to steer smoothly around the bend as they pump on and off 45 times a second.

lost can easily be replaced by drawing on air stored under pressure in the vehicle.

The same simple arrangement cannot be applied to cars, which use hydraulic fluid. This is because there is little fluid in reserve, and also it would be both expensive and dangerous to spill bled-off hydraulic fluid all over the road. One alternative is to reduce pressure by briefly increasing the volume of the hydraulic system – with a piston arrangement, for example – and then to restore pressure again. Among the systems that have been developed are some that even allow sharp turns to take place safely during heavy braking.

Although anti-locking brakes were originally available only on the most expensive cars, they are increasingly becoming standard, or optional, on most new cars.

How a seat belt protects its wearer

When you are travelling in a car, you and the car are moving at the same speed. If the car stops abruptly, your body keeps moving forward. This is an illustration of inertia – the tendency of a moving object to keep moving, or of a stationary object to remain at rest.

An inertia-reel seat belt works on the same principle. Its mechanism includes a pendulum, which hangs vertically under ordinary driving conditions. But if the car stops abruptly it swings forward, and a locking lever resting on the pendulum is released. The lever engages a toothed ratchet that locks the shaft round which the belt is wound. The locked seat belt then prevents your body from being flung forward.

When you fasten a seat belt, it winds out from the reel against slight tension from a spring. This keeps it taut during normal travelling, but allows enough free movement for a driver to reach forward as necessary. But if you tug abruptly on the belt while winding it out, the locking mechanism will engage and stop the action of the spring. Slackening the belt releases the spring and the locking lever.

Why racing cars have smooth tyres

Car tyres are not just cushions for the wheels. They are there to give the car a good grip on slippery roads, and stop it sliding about when braking or cornering.

The tread pattern running all round the tyre has thin cuts (known as sipes) in the rubber to sponge up surface water, and zigzag channels to pump the water out behind as the car rolls forward. On a wet road, a tyre has to move more than 1 gallon (5 litres) of water a second to give an adequate grip.

On a perfectly dry road, the treads are not needed. A smooth tyre gives the greatest possible area of contact with the road. But if smooth tyres are used in wet weather, the film of water on the road builds up in front of them and underneath them and actually lifts them off the road surface – this is known as aquaplaning. When aquaplaning occurs, the driver loses control.

Most cars have to function in all weathers, so must have tyre treads, but racing cars make comparatively few outings a year. If the track is dry, they run on smooth tyres, called slicks, to get the best grip on the roads. The extra wide tyres and wheels give more grip than the average car. In wet weather, however, the slicks have to be changed for treaded tyres.

Gripping the road *A racing tyre for completely dry roads has no treads (above). A domestic car tyre has to travel in all conditions, so it has treads to sponge up and pump out water as it moves (below).*

Breathalysers: detecting alcohol by colour changes

When someone blows into a breathalyser bag, any alcohol in their breath is turned into acetic acid (vinegar). This chemical reaction changes the colour of the crystals in the blowing tube. The more crystals that change colour, the more alcohol they have in the body.

The first breathalyser was developed by an American doctor, Rolla N. Harger (he called it a 'Drunkometer'), and it was introduced by the Indianapolis police in 1939. Similar breathalysers began to be widely used by the police in many countries in the 1960s, as a yardstick for judging a driver's ability to drive. A high intake of alcohol dulls the nervous system and slows up coordination.

To begin with, the commonest type of breathalyser was a plastic bag, similar to a balloon, with the crystals in the blowing tube, and the driver was asked to inflate the bag. If the crystals changed colour as far as a level marked on the tube, the driver was possibly 'over the limit', and needed further tests. The crystals used were an orange-yellow mixture of sulphuric acid and potassium dichromate. They turned the alcohol into acetic acid (vinegar), and in doing so they were changed into colourless potassium sulphate and blue-green chromium sulphate.

The breathalysers used by the police today, however, are usually electronic, and much more accurate than the inflatable-bag type. They use the alcohol blown in through the tube as fuel to produce electric current. The more alcohol the breath contains, the stronger the current. If it lights up a green light, the driver is below the legal limit and has passed the test. An amber light means the alcohol level is near the limit, a red light above the limit, and in both cases the driver has failed the breath test and needs further testing.

This type of breathalyser is about the size of a TV remote control, and contains a fuel cell that works like a battery. Breath from the tube is drawn into the cell through a valve, and meets a platinum anode (a positive plate), which is against a spongy disc impregnated with sulphuric acid.

The platinum causes any alcohol in the breath to oxidise into acetic acid – that is, its molecules lose some of their electrons. This sets up an electric current through the disc, and it flows to a cathode (a negative plate) on the other side.

How an aerosol sprays

When you press the button of an aerosol spray, you open a valve at the top of the spray tube and expose a hole in the spray nozzle. Normally, the valve is held shut by a coil spring. Opening the valve allows gas pressure within the can to force the can's liquid contents up through the tube and out through the nozzle.

In the factory, an aerosol can is partly filled with a concentrated form of the product to be sprayed – such as paint or insecticide – and then pressurised with propellant gas. The propellants now mainly used are hydrocarbons such as butane. These substances boil at a low temperature, and change easily from liquid to vapour or vapour to liquid. In the container the propellant exists mainly as a liquid, and acts as a solvent or carrier for the product.

As the can contents are squirted into the

Spray can *Pushing the button down opens a valve and allows gas pressure to force the liquid through a tube to the nozzle.*

Push button opens valve

Mixture disperses as fine spray

Gas pressure forces mixture up tube

Propellant and product mixture

air, the small amount of liquid propellant in the mixture vaporises because the atmospheric pressure is lower than the pressure in the can. So the product is dispersed as a spray of fine droplets. This spray is technically termed an aerosol – that is, liquid or solid particles suspended in gas. Fog, for example, is a natural aerosol. In foam aerosols, the propellant actually forms the bubbles.

Once the spray has been used, the pressure inside the can is lower so gas starts to build up again from the liquid propellant still in there, to restore the pressure.

Breaking down the ozone layer

A group of substances called chloro-fluorocarbons (CFCs), which are organic compounds containing only chlorine and fluorine, were widely used in aerosol sprays from the 1950s until the late 1980s, but they are now being phased out of use. Unfortunately, CFCs drift high into the atmosphere where they accumulate, and sunlight causes them to break down into chlorine atoms. These atoms in turn break down ozone atoms in the ozone layer into oxygen. Scientists measured a temporary hole as big as the United States in the ozone layer over the Antarctic in October 1987, and severe thinning of the ozone layer over the Arctic was detected in 1989.

The ozone filters most of the harmful ultraviolet light from the sunlight reaching Earth. An increase in ultraviolet radiation can damage human cells and lead to skin cancer and eye cataracts. It also affects plants, which may produce less seed.

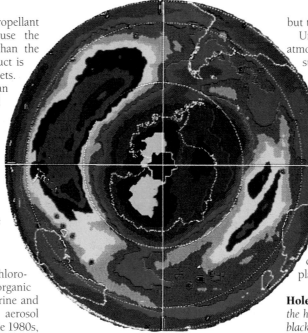

Hole in the ozone *This satellite map shows the hole in the Antarctic ozone layer as pink, black and purple.*

Why selective weedkillers do not destroy crops

Weeds are plants growing in the wrong place. Farmers and gardeners have to remove them because they compete for space, light and soil minerals with cultivated plants, and either stunt their growth or choke them out altogether.

At the end of the 19th century, farmers turned from the traditional methods of weed control, such as hoeing and crop rotation, and started to use chemical weedkillers – a method pioneered in France in 1896. Poison such as copper sulphate, for example, was sprayed on young cereal plants to kill the prolific yellow-flowered weed charlock, which is common in cornfields. The poison was selective because it had little effect on the narrow, erect leaves of the cereal, which deflected most of the droplets, but the broad, horizontal leaves of the charlock took a larger dose and were withered.

Today's chemical weedkillers destroy a weed by exploiting its own growth system. They use chemicals that simulate the

Spraying crops *A strip of mayweed stands in a field of barley which has been sprayed with a weedkiller. Crops are usually sprayed by tractors driving up and down the fields. Although the selective weedkiller used here killed most of the mayweed, this strip was missed.*

weed's hormones – its natural growth substances – to trigger off such rapid growth that the plants exhaust themselves and soon die.

Such hormone weedkillers have been developed since 1945, and two that are widely used are MCPA and 2,4-D – the names are short forms for the chemicals used. These two are selective because they are effective against broad-leaved plants, but have no effect on grass or cereals, which have different hormones.

But peas and beans are broad-leaved plants, so MCPA and 2,4-D cannot be used to kill weeds among them. Scientists have therefore developed chemicals that turn into MCPA and 2,4-D inside broad-leaved plants – but not in peas and beans. These weedkillers are known as MCPB and 2,4-DB. The B indicates that they contain butyric acid, which is converted into active weedkiller inside susceptible plants.

Wild oats among a cereal crop cannot be destroyed by either of the two types of hormone weedkiller because their hormones are similar to those of the cultivated crop. For this, scientists have developed a weedkiller that makes use of differences in the way the wild and cultivated plants grow from seed. The weedkiller, PCP, is put into the top layer of soil after sowing. The wild oat sends up its growing tip early, and enters the poisoned layer while it is most toxic. The weedkiller attacks the growing tip and kills the plant. The cultivated grain reaches the poisonous area later, after the shoot has grown a protective sheath and when the weedkiller has become less toxic.

By investigating plant structure and growth, scientists have come up with hundreds of different weedkillers that are selective between different plants – not just between broad-leaved and grassy types. Some can distinguish between different grasses, for example. In a lawn, annual meadow grass can be eliminated by a weedkiller known as bensulide, but the lawn grass is untouched.

The greenfly pesticide designed to spare the bees

Greenfly are just one type of the sap-sucking aphids that often cluster in their thousands on rose bushes. Blackfly on beans are another pest. In summer, female aphids can reproduce without males – a process known as parthenogenesis. Given warm weather and strongly growing juicy plants, one lone female could multiply into a plague of 100,000 within a month.

Many insecticides are effective against aphids, but they also destroy the insects that prey on aphids, and destroy pollinating bees, if not used carefully.

One insecticide that kills aphids, however, is designed to spare ladybirds, lacewings and bees. It is a complex man-made chemical called pirimicarb. When it is sprayed on and seeps through the greenfly's skin, its molecules fit like a glove against those of a vital enzyme in aphids called acetylcholinesterase. This enzyme breaks down poisonous substances formed by the insect's nervous system. Blocking its action causes rapid

Killing the right insects *Greenfly feast on a stinging nettle, and ladybirds feast on the greenfly. Pirimicarb can kill the greenfly but not the ladybirds, which perform a useful function in controlling the pests. The pirimicarb also penetrates the plant to prevent reinfestation.*

death. Lacewings and ladybirds have different-shaped enzymes, so are less likely to be affected.

Pirimicarb not only kills aphids on contact, it will pass through leaves to kill those underneath as well, and also gives off fumes that poison them. What is more, it penetrates into the sap of the plants, so will kill aphids eating the sap for up to two weeks after spraying.

Because pirimicarb acts against the nervous system it can have adverse effects on humans, animals and birds. It must be used sparingly, carefully following the instructions on the dispenser.

How can metals be made to remember shapes?

When lightning struck the roof of York Minster, one of Britain's finest medieval cathedrals, in 1984, it started a fire that was trapped between the ceiling and the wooden roof. Firefighters could not get into the area, and the enormous heat that built up destroyed most of the roof.

If lightning should strike York Minster twice, space-age science has ensured that the same type of damage will not happen again. The new roof is fitted with trap doors to let the heat out and the firefighters in, and the doors have latches operated by springs made from memory metals, which will open automatically if they get hot.

Memory metals have two different shapes they can 'remember', and will switch from one to the other under certain conditions. The York Minster trap-door springs are made to remember a certain temperature, at which they will expand and withdraw the bolt, releasing the door.

One of the first uses of memory metals has been for hydraulic pipe couplings in aircraft, which came into use in 1971. The couplings are made too small to fit at a certain temperature, and are then cooled to well below room temperature and stretched to fit. When they warm up to their normal operating temperature, they shrink to the first shape, forming a tight joint. The same idea is used in surgery, with metal couplings to bind together broken bones. Body heat keeps them constantly tight.

Metals that change their shape under heat now have all kinds of uses, such as operating switches and valves in automatic coffee machines, and opening greenhouse windows when it is hot and closing them when it is cold.

Most metals are made up of crystals (arrangements of atoms). When two or more metals are combined into an alloy, the alloy can form different crystal structures under different conditions.

Some alloys, if they are cooled rapidly, will undergo an abrupt change to a different alignment of crystals at a certain temperature. This transition temperature varies with the make-up of the alloy. The changed structure it brings about is called martensite, after the German metallurgist Adolph Martens who first identified it.

If such an alloy is shaped by heat treatment so that it becomes martensite at, for example, 122°F (50°C), it will change its shape at that martensitic temperature, but revert again at a different temperature.

Shaped for shaping
A Japanese company has found an unusual use for memory metals – as a super-elastic wire frame in brassieres. The alloys used will stretch up to ten times more than ordinary metals. When stretched in use, the bra wire gradually returns to its original bust-supporting shape.

Another use for super-elastic wire is in straightening teeth. Conventional stainless-steel wires have to be regularly tightened, often by turning a tiny key. Super-elastic alloy wires exert a continuous gentle pressure ideal for coaxing teeth in the right direction.

How does a digital clock turn on the oven?

When your clock radio starts playing music first thing in the morning, or the oven automatically comes on to cook a meal, the switch has probably been operated by a digital clock.

At the heart of the switch is a quartz crystal which vibrates at a fixed frequency when connected to a source of electrical power – battery or mains. The vibrations produce regular electrical pulses, which travel through circuits in a microchip to operate the digits on the clock.

The switch also has a memory, in the form of a microprocessor, which stores the times when the radio, oven or central heating system has to be turned on. The microprocessor constantly compares the stored time with the real time as measured by the clock.

When the turning-on time comes, it sets off a low-voltage electronic signal. This signal is amplified by a transistor circuit and flows through a relay, an electronic device in which a small current causes a metal contact to move, switching on the main current.

How do hidden defences detect burglars?

Medieval castles had all sorts of traps and pitfalls to keep out intruders. Homes of today can have an equal number of defences, without having to resort to boiling pitch. Modern defence devices include floodlights or alarms that are triggered when an intruder upsets a circuit monitored by hidden magnets or microchips, or by invisible beams.

The outer defences
The modern burglar might first have to face a strategically placed invisible infrared detector that is affected by temperature changes caused by body heat. When anyone approaches the house, a sensor in the detector switches on floodlights. If the caller is legitimate, the lights show the way, but anyone planning burglary will feel very exposed and less likely to continue.

The sensor is pyroelectric – that is, made from a ceramic material such as tourmaline, which, when heated, generates a voltage across it. The system is designed so that the sensor will respond to a temperature change caused by human body heat, but is less likely to be set off by changes in the weather.

A burglar who dodges a floodlight barrier may then face a door connected to a noisy alarm. A magnetic switch is inserted between the door and its frame. When the door is shut, two contacts keep the switch circuit closed. This switch circuit is monitored electronically by an alarm circuit. If the door is opened and the switch circuit is broken, the alarm circuit triggers the alarm.

But a resolute burglar, out of sight of passers-by, might attack the door with a chisel or drill. This type of attack can be foiled by a vibration detector fitted to the door. This is a device in which a ball is disturbed by vibrations. The ball rests on sharp metal points wired to a microchip that is programmed to accept certain vibrations – such as those caused by wind or passing traffic – as normal. If the ball bouncing on the points sets up vibrations not in the program, it sets off the alarm.

The inner defences
If the burglar succeeds in getting through a door or window, he may face a battery of inner defences. These include pressure pads concealed under the carpet and linked to an alarm circuit. They have two metal plates or foil sheets separated by a layer of spongy plastic. The two plates are

pressed together if anyone treads on them, and this sets off the alarm.

Anyone who prowls around inside the house may be caught by a 'magic eye'. This is a photoelectric cell with an invisible infrared beam shining onto it. If the beam is interrupted, the photocell triggers an alarm.

Other types of indoor detector use either ultrasonic waves (too high pitched for humans to hear) or microwaves (high-frequency radio waves) transmitted by

devices called transducers. They transmit the waves at a certain frequency (a given number per second), and the waves are reflected back to the unit from objects in the room. If anyone moves through the room, the reflected waves get bunched up or pulled apart, so their frequency is altered. The sensor detects the frequency change and feeds signals to a microchip which assesses the speed and bulk of the intruder. Anything assessed as typically man-sized makes it set off the alarm.

A commoner type of indoor detector uses an infrared system similar to the outdoor floodlight type. In the detector, a many-faced mirror or special lens creates a number of sensitive zones. If anything moving in and out of these zones is at a different temperature to the room surroundings, it generates a voltage. The detector electronically monitors the voltage, and is designed to set off the alarm if the temperature increase is likely to be caused by human body heat.

How a sewing machine uses two threads to make a stitch

A French tailor, Barthélémy Thimmonier, made the first practical sewing machine in 1830, and in 1848 he sold the patent of a machine to a Manchester company. This machine made chain stitches – a series of interlocking loops formed from one thread. In 1833 an American inventor, Walter Hunt, designed a machine that produced a lock stitch from two threads. This was the ancestor of the treadle machine designed by another American, Isaac Merritt Singer, in 1851. Singer's machine was a runaway domestic success.

Modern domestic machines use the same basic features as Singer's machine. The machine needle has its eye at the sharp end, and carries thread from a reel at the top of the machine. The other thread comes from a bobbin in a shuttle at the bottom of the machine. The bobbin thread stretches

along the underside of the fabric, and is continually locked into loops of thread brought down through the fabric by the needle.

All the moving parts of the machine are driven by cranks powered by an electric motor, which is controlled by the foot pedal. Modern machines are programmed by silicon chips, and can be made to sew on buttons, finish off seams, insert zips, and embroider, darn or tuck, using 20 or more different types of stitch.

All the stitches are based on three types – the basic lock stitch, a zigzag stitch and a stretch stitch. The zigzag stitch is made by a swing needle that moves diagonally from side to side each time it pierces the fabric. The stretch stitch is formed

by moving the fabric backwards and forwards during stitching.

Today's domestic sewing machines have increased in speed from the original 20 stitches per minute to around 800-1000 per minute. But in factories, Thimmonier's original chain stitches are preferred because of their faster rate – about 7000 stitches a minute.

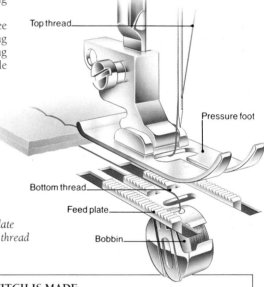

The basic mechanism
The fabric is sandwiched between the pressure foot and the feed plate of the sewing machine, and is fed through the two by the movement of the feed plate which grips it with its teeth. The needle moves through a slit in the feed plate and supplies the top thread. The bottom thread is provided by the bobbin.

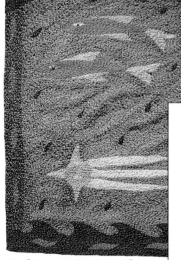

Machine art *Sewing machines can be used to create elaborate embroidery. In this work, the direction of the stitches could be varied at will by disengaging the feed plate. Altering the tension produced very loose stitches.*

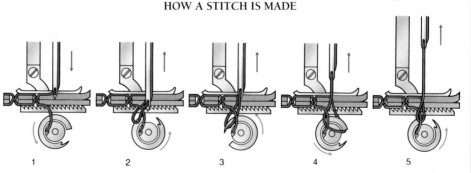

HOW A STITCH IS MADE

1 2 3 4 5

The needle loaded with thread passes down through the fabric until it gets to the level of the bobbin (1). When the needle is pulled up, it leaves a loop of thread (2). The rotating hook which surrounds the bobbin takes the loop behind and around the bobbin thread (3). When the hook reaches a certain position the thread slips off it (4). The still-ascending needle tightens the thread (5).

Why do steel ships float?

The Greek mathematician Archimedes was getting into the bath one day some 2200 years ago when he discovered the principle of buoyancy – the reason why steel ships weighing thousands of tons can float on water.

He noticed, as he lowered himself into the tub, how the water displaced by his body spilled over the sides, and realised in a flash that there was a relationship between his weight and the volume of water displaced. He was so excited that he rushed naked into the street yelling 'Eureka!' (I found it!), or so it is said.

But Archimedes was not pondering the question of ships at the time. What he had found was the answer to a thorny problem which he had been asked to solve by King Hieron II of Syracuse, where Archimedes lived. Syracuse in Sicily is part of modern Italy but was Greek in ancient times.

The king had a new crown and wanted to know if it was pure gold or partly silver. Archimedes realised that if the crown was partly silver, it would take up more space than a pure gold crown of the same weight because silver is not as dense as gold. By comparing the crown's volume (measured by the amount of water it displaced) with the volume of equal weights of gold and then silver, he was able to tell the king his crown was not pure gold.

The buoyancy principle

Archimedes went on to do further experiments, from which he formulated the buoyancy principle – that an object such as a ship will float when the weight of water it displaces equals its own weight.

A steel ship's ability to float depends, however, upon how its weight is distributed. For example, a solid lump of steel put on the surface of a pond will sink, but steel of the same weight shaped as a bowl will float. This is because the bowl's weight is spread over a wider area, allowing it to displace its own weight of water before it reaches the point of being submerged.

A steel ship, like the bowl, floats because it is hollow, and so its weight is widely distributed over the water. The depth of the keel below the water line is known as the draught. Ships have loadlines to show the maximum draught that is permissible.

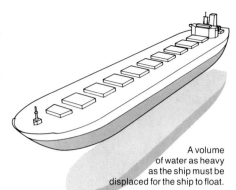

A volume of water as heavy as the ship must be displaced for the ship to float.

Displacement *Archimedes was the first to realise that anything will float if it is shaped to displace its own weight of water before it reaches the point where it will submerge.*

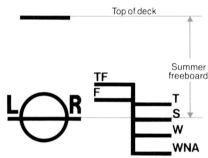

Loadlines *These lines show the maximum draught to which a ship may float, and are assigned by classification societies, such as Lloyd's Register of Shipping, for governments. The picture shows a line assigned by Lloyd's (LR). The centre of the circle is in line with the summer loadline (S) on the ship's side. Other marks include lines for calm tropical (T) or rough winter (W) waters.*

Sea giant *The Berge Stahl was the largest cargo ship in the world when she was launched in 1986. She is 1125ft (343m) long and has a carrying capacity of over 360,000 tons.*

WEIGHING UP SHIP SIZES

The world's biggest aircraft carriers, of the US Navy's *Nimitz* class, are 1092ft (333m) long and have a 'displacement tonnage' of nearly 91,500 tons. This represents the total weight of the ship and everything on board. Only naval ships are measured in this way. Cargo ships and passenger ship sizes are both expressed differently.

The world's largest dry cargo vessel, the Norwegian *Berge Stahl*, for example, is just over 1100ft (340m) long and is described as over 364,700 tons dwt (deadweight). This tonnage refers to the ship's carrying capacity – it does not take into account the weight of the vessel itself.

The world's largest passenger liner, *Sovereign of the Seas*, is described as 73,200 grt (gross registered tons). Gross registered tonnage is not the ship's weight at all – it is the volume of almost all the enclosed space, with 100cu ft (about 3cu m) being assessed as equivalent to 1 ton.

The Berge Stahl is nearly 130ft (40m) longer than the height of the Eiffel Tower.

How a submarine stays submerged for weeks at a time

Nearly 160 years separate the first *Nautilus* submarine, invented by an American, Robert Fuller, in 1800, and the first nuclear submarine, USS *Nautilus*. The first *Nautilus* had a crew of three and could submerge for four hours. Its nuclear namesake, with over 100 on board, could stay down for weeks.

In the Second World War, the German U-boats that hunted the Atlantic convoys were powered when on the surface by diesel engines – which need an air supply – and by battery-powered electric motors when submerged. The foremost German submarine of the period, the Type XXI, could stay below for two days at a speed of 6 knots – 7mph (11km/h) – or four days if it moved more slowly. Then it had to surface and run the diesel engines to recharge the

batteries. In 1944 the Germans began to use the 'schnorkel', an invention captured from the Dutch. It drew air from the surface so that diesel engines could be used with the submarine at periscope depth. This extended underwater time a little.

The development of nuclear propulsion changed everything. A nuclear reactor needs no air, and only very small amounts of fuel. The USS *Nautilus* went into service in January 1955, and could travel submerged at 20 knots – 23mph (37km/h). Like its successors, it had a small, pressurised water-reactor refuelled by removing the uranium core and replacing it with a new one. A single core provides enough power for about ten years of operation.

Heat from the reactor provides steam for

Submarines new and old *USS* Whale *breaks through the ice to surface at the North Pole in 1969 (above). This nuclear-powered vessel can stay underwater for weeks, unlike the steam-powered submarine of 1879 (inset), which could stay down for only about an hour and travel just a few miles.*

propulsion and to generate electricity, and fresh water is distilled from sea water. Air for breathing is continuously purified by machinery, and the oxygen content is replenished from sea water – by passing an electric current through it to separate oxygen and hydrogen atoms. Compressed air for operating machinery and torpedo tubes, and for blowing ballast tanks to surface, is carried in tanks.

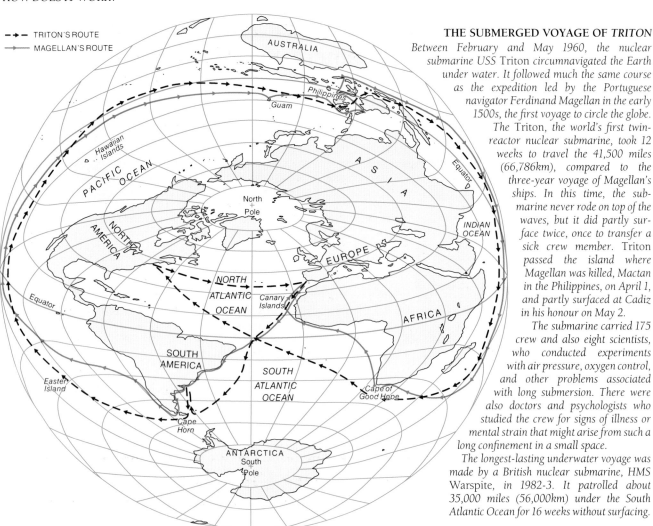

TRITON'S ROUTE
MAGELLAN'S ROUTE

THE SUBMERGED VOYAGE OF *TRITON*

Between February and May 1960, the nuclear submarine USS Triton *circumnavigated the Earth under water. It followed much the same course as the expedition led by the Portuguese navigator Ferdinand Magellan in the early 1500s, the first voyage to circle the globe.*

The Triton, *the world's first twin-reactor nuclear submarine, took 12 weeks to travel the 41,500 miles (66,786km), compared to the three-year voyage of Magellan's ships. In this time, the submarine never rode on top of the waves, but it did partly surface twice, once to transfer a sick crew member.* Triton *passed the island where Magellan was killed, Mactan in the Philippines, on April 1, and partly surfaced at Cadiz in his honour on May 2.*

The submarine carried 175 crew and also eight scientists, who conducted experiments with air pressure, oxygen control, and other problems associated with long submersion. There were also doctors and psychologists who studied the crew for signs of illness or mental strain that might arise from such a long confinement in a small space.

The longest-lasting underwater voyage was made by a British nuclear submarine, HMS Warspite, *in 1982-3. It patrolled about 35,000 miles (56,000km) under the South Atlantic Ocean for 16 weeks without surfacing.*

INSIDE A NUCLEAR SUBMARINE

Modern nuclear submarines are nearly as long as a football pitch – around 300ft (91m). They carry a crew of about 140, who work in shifts. There is room to store enough food for several months, and the canteen doubles as a games room or cinema outside mealtimes.

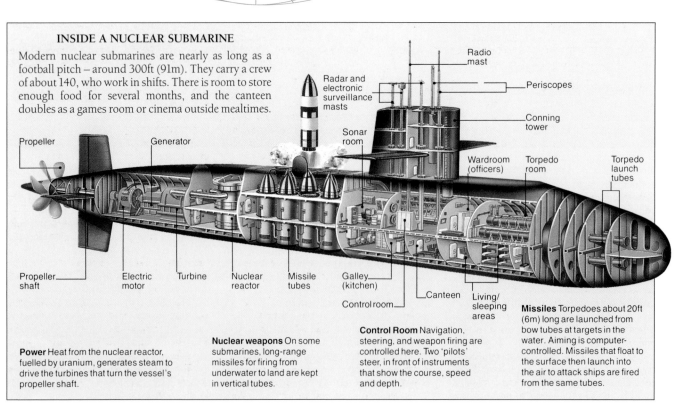

Power Heat from the nuclear reactor, fuelled by uranium, generates steam to drive the turbines that turn the vessel's propeller shaft.

Nuclear weapons On some submarines, long-range missiles for firing from underwater to land are kept in vertical tubes.

Control Room Navigation, steering, and weapon firing are controlled here. Two 'pilots' steer, in front of instruments that show the course, speed and depth.

Missiles Torpedoes about 20ft (6m) long are launched from bow tubes at targets in the water. Aiming is computer-controlled. Missiles that float to the surface then launch into the air to attack ships are fired from the same tubes.

How does a submarine's crew navigate underwater?

Submarines often travel in the ocean depths for weeks on end. They do not need to surface to check their position by the Sun, Moon or stars, because the latest navigation systems allow them to know where they are to within less than 320ft (100m) of their actual position while still submerged.

These systems are known as inertial navigation systems and are computer-controlled. There are usually at least two on a submarine, operating independently. They are a modern version of 'dead reckoning' – calculating where you are by measuring exactly how far you have come from your starting point, and in what direction.

The inertial navigation system is held absolutely horizontal and pointing in a fixed direction by gyroscopes, whatever the attitude of the submarine.

At the start of the voyage, the instruments are fed with the submarine's exact position. An accelerometer then measures movement in every direction, and the computer works out the overall distance and direction travelled, thus establishing the present position.

Sonar (page 154) is used to determine the water depth below the vessel to prevent it running aground.

Inertial systems are on the whole accurate, but the small errors they do make gradually accumulate. They have to be realigned regularly. This is done by picking up radio signals from satellites in space, which form part of the American NAV-STAR Global Positioning System (GPS). The submarine has to partly surface.

The satellites transmit a radio message which contains precise details about their orbit, and a time signal controlled by an atomic clock. In effect, the signal says 'It is now time X'. The submarine uses its own clock to calculate how long it takes the signal to arrive. As radio waves travel at 186,000 miles (300,000km) per second, the navigators can calculate the submarine's distance from the satellite by the time the signal takes. By calculating the distance from three GPS satellites, the ship's position can be pinpointed on a chart.

During the 1990s, the last of 18 satellites in the GPS system will be placed in orbit at a height of 12,500 miles (20,000km), orbiting the Earth at 12-hourly intervals. They will ensure that at any time at least four satellites will be available for navigators to calculate their position to within 550yds (500m).

The GPS system has virtually replaced older forms of submarine navigation such as the OMEGA system, but submarines still carry it as a back-up. This system detects radio signals broadcast from eight stations dotted around the Earth's surface – in Japan, Hawaii, Australia, Argentina, North Dakota, Norway, Liberia and Réunion Island. These stations broadcast at very long wavelengths, so their signals carry all around the world. The signals are synchronised, and by measuring the time differences in their reception, a submarine's position can be estimated to within about 2 miles (3.2km).

Inertial navigation is also mounted in long-range intercontinental missiles launched from submarines.

Providing precious air high above the clouds

If you were able to float up into the sky in a balloon, without any special protection, you might start to get a headache and feel breathless after the balloon reached about 10,000ft (3000m). The symptoms would be caused by the decrease in air pressure as you rose higher.

By 18,000ft (5500m), your headache would be quite severe and you would be breathing hard.

At 25,000ft (7600m) you would be struggling for breath, and gases might begin to bubble out of your blood, causing the agony of 'the bends'.

Above 30,000ft (9000m), the shortage of oxygen in the air would cause you to lose consciousness. However, if you had taken an oxygen supply with you, you could continue on to 40,000ft (12,000m) before blacking out.

If the balloon continued to carry you up, you would reach the point – at 63,000ft (19,000m) – where the air pressure is so low that the boiling point of water drops to 98.6°F (37°C), which is normal body temperature. And then your blood would boil.

So how is it that jet airliners constantly carry passengers at altitudes of 35,000ft (10,500m) without causing them harm?

Airliners fly at these heights to avoid the bad weather lower down, and because jet engines operate more efficiently in thin air.

However, people are used to breathing air at a pressure of about 14.7lb per square inch (1kg per square centimetre). At that pressure, oxygen is absorbed into the blood and circulated to every cell to keep the body functioning properly.

As you climb higher above sea level, the air gradually becomes thinner, and the pressure falls. There is less oxygen present and less pressure to force it into the blood. So the body begins to be starved of oxygen.

Airliners, therefore, are supplied with air under pressure so the passengers can breathe easily. The passenger cabins are made airtight and strong enough to withstand the pressure difference between the inside (high) and outside (low). To limit the stresses on the fuselage, the air in the cabin is not kept at sea-level pressure, but at a pressure equivalent to about 8000ft (2400m). It is gradually reduced to this level after takeoff, and increased back to sea-level pressure just before landing.

The supply of air to build up the cabin pressure is obtained from the compressor sections of the jet engines. It is cooled by a refrigeration system and its pressure is regulated by valves before it is piped into the cabin. After circulating through the aircraft, the air is gradually allowed to leak back through other valves into the atmosphere. It is continually replaced by fresh air from the compressors.

If an airliner should suddenly lose air pressure, emergency oxygen masks drop down in front of the passengers, who can use them to breathe until the plane has descended to a safe altitude.

Down in the deep

The problem in submarines and other underwater craft is the reverse – the pressure outside the craft is greater than inside.

Water pressure increases by roughly the pressure of the atmosphere for every 33ft (10m) you go down. The pressure at 100ft (30m), for example, is four 'atmospheres'.

Deep-sea craft are constructed with a hull that is able to withstand the external pressure which would otherwise crush it, and the air inside the craft is usually maintained at sea-level pressure. Oxygen is supplied from pressurised bottles, and the air is constantly filtered through lithium hydroxide, which absorbs the carbon dioxide breathed out by the crew.

Nuclear submarines have a much more sophisticated air conditioning system (page 257).

George Stephenson: the man who made the trains run

They came from miles around – on foot, on horseback and in donkey-drawn carts – to see the opening of the world's first public steam railway. Some of the country folk, known as 'Johnny Raws' by reporters covering the event, thought that the engine literally would be an 'iron horse'.

'Excitement in many minds took the form of disappointment,' wrote a railway historian, 'when it was found that the locomotive was not built after the fashion of a veritable four-footed quadruped . . . an automatic semblance of a horse stalking along on four legs.'

Even so, the spectators were sufficiently awestruck at the sight, and sound, of George Stephenson's pioneer steam engine, *Locomotion*. Although it carried passengers, the railway was mainly meant to take coal from inland pits to wharves at Stockton-on-Tees.

The locomotive's inventor was at the controls on the morning of September 27, 1825, as the train – with its 32 open wagons carrying over 300 people and 12 coal wagons with people perched on top – set off on the 20 mile (32km) run from Shildon colliery to Darlington, and on to Stockton.

At first, the way was led by horsemen carrying flags with which they warned of the locomotive's approach.

Gradually, as the train reached speeds of up to 15mph (24km/h), the horsemen parted and were left behind. Their place was taken by scarlet-coated huntsmen, also on horseback, and by a coach-and-four, which was also outpaced.

By the time the *Locomotion* reached Stockton – where more than 40,000 people had gathered and a brass band played the national anthem – the days of horse travel

Raising steam *This replica (right) of Stephenson's 1825 steam engine* Locomotion *travels the tracks at Beamish North of England Open-Air Museum in County Durham.*

were numbered. The age of the steam train had come.

Born in the Northumberland mining village of Wylam, near Newcastle upon Tyne, on June 9, 1781, George Stephenson was the self-educated son of a colliery mechanic. His fascination with steam started in 1813 when – as the chief mechanic of Killingworth colliery in Northumberland – he examined one of the 'steam boilers on wheels' designed by a mine manager, John Blenkinsop, and used for carrying coal at several north-eastern collieries.

The following year Stephenson built his own steam locomotive: *Blücher*, named after the Prussian field marshal who played a crucial role in the Napoleonic Wars.

Unlike Blenkinsop's engine, which had cogged wheels that engaged with cogs on the side of the rails, *Blücher* had rimmed wheels which ran on smooth-edged rails,

Private figure *Quiet and retiring, George Stephenson refused most of the honours offered to him in old age – including a knighthood and a seat in Parliament.*

giving a faster and smoother ride. *Blücher* began work at Killingworth in 1814, but kept on breaking down.

For months, George Stephenson modified and improved his engine. Then he

made his key development: the steam-blast technique. This redirected exhaust steam into *Blücher*'s chimney through a narrow blast pipe. The steam pulled air in after it, increasing the draught in the furnace and so providing more power and speed.

His subsequent success with *Locomotion* led to his appointment, in 1826, as the engineer of a proposed passenger and freight railway link between Liverpool and Manchester. For this, he and his son Robert designed and built a revolutionary new engine, the *Rocket*, at their Newcastle workshop. It featured a multi-tubular boiler, in which the water was turned to steam by contact with 25 copper tubes – each 3in (76mm) in diameter – heated from the firebox.

The Liverpool and Manchester Railway opened on September 15, 1830, when more than 50,000 spectators gathered at the starting point, the engine yards at Liverpool. A cannon was fired, and eight locomotives – including the *Rocket* – steamed off. They were headed by the *Northumbrian*, the Stephensons' latest and most powerful 'iron horse', driven by George Stephenson himself.

Travelling in the *Northumbrian*'s carriages were the prime minister, and hero of Waterloo, the Duke of Wellington; the Austrian ambassador, Prince Paul Esterhazy; and one of the railway's staunchest supporters – the Tory MP for Liverpool, William Huskisson.

The procession moved ahead without incident until the *Northumbrian* stopped at Parkside, about 18 miles (30km) from Liverpool, to take on fuel and water. Two of the following trains, the *North Star* and the *Phoenix*, caught up with and passed the *Northumbrian* on a parallel track.

Prince Esterhazy and the lanky Mr Huskisson got out to stretch their legs by the side of the train. The Duke of Wellington waved to the Member of Parliament and opened the door of his gilt and crimson-draped carriage. Huskisson hurried forward, shook hands with Wel-

First home *Driven by Stephenson himself (below), the locomotive* Rocket *outpaced and out-powered its rivals at the railway trials held at Rainhill near Liverpool in 1829.*

lington, and the two men were chatting when the *Rocket* thundered into view on the other track.

Prince Esterhazy, small and slightly built, was hauled bodily into one of the carriages. But the 60-year-old Huskisson, who was partly paralysed down one side, was less agile. In his attempt to find safety, he stumbled and fell into the path of the oncoming engine. Unable to brake in time, the *Rocket* passed over Huskisson's thigh, crushing it terribly. 'I have met my death!' the victim cried out in agony.

One of the railway's guests hastily applied a handkerchief tourniquet to the badly bleeding man. With great presence of mind, George Stephenson ordered all but the leading carriage of the *Northumbrian* uncoupled. He put Huskisson into the carriage, resumed control of the engine, and set off at full speed for the village of Eccles, 15 miles (24km) away on the outskirts of Manchester. He arrived there in a record 25 minutes, but Huskisson died in the vicarage that evening – the first passenger victim of a railway accident.

The next morning the first fare-paying passengers, 130 of them, left Liverpool for Manchester. By 1840, Britain was networked with 1500 miles (2414km) of railway lines; and by the 1890s the ever-growing railway had spread worldwide, opening up undeveloped areas in North and South America, Australia and southern Africa.

Known as the 'Father of Railways', Stephenson worked

Treasured survivor *The modified remains of the Stephensons' revolutionary* Rocket – *with the original smokestack in a different position since the Rainhill trials – are now at the Science Museum, London.*

as an adviser and consultant on numerous railroad projects in Britain and Belgium and other parts of the Continent.

In 1838 he retired to Tapton House near Chesterfield in Derbyshire. The house overlooked a stretch of the North Midland Railway, and it allowed him to watch his beloved trains go by. He spent his last few years enjoying his garden. He died on August 12, 1848, at the age of 67.

Tickets to ride *The passenger's half of an 1832 railway ticket for the Liverpool and Manchester Railway (below). For a few, there were also free passes (bottom).*

How does a giant airliner lift itself into the air?

A Boeing 747 'jumbo jet' fully loaded with fuel and some 500 passengers weighs more than 350 tons. Yet it can take to the air and fly. How does it take off and stay up?

The key lies in the cross-sectional shape of the wings, which are rounded at the front, fairly flat underneath, curved on top, and tapered sharply to a point at the rear. This shape is known as an aerofoil, or airfoil, and it enables the plane to lift itself off the ground. The wings push the air aside as they move forward, and as the air passes over the curved top surface, it speeds up. When air moves faster, its pressure drops, and the wing tends to lift.

Lift and weight are two of the major opposing forces acting on an aeroplane in flight. The other two are thrust – the forward force produced by its engines – and drag – the air resistance it encounters.

The lift developed by a wing increases as the air speed increases. Increasing the wing area and the curvature (or camber) of the wing also increase the lift. Low-speed planes therefore need large cambered wings to generate enough lift. High-speed planes need smaller wings only slightly cambered.

Lift is also influenced by the angle at which the wings meet the airstream. Planes are designed so that their wings are inclined at a small angle – called the angle of attack – in level flight. As a plane flies slower and slower, its height can be maintained by raising the nose and angling the wings more and more into the

airstream, increasing the angle of attack. But if the angle is increased to more than about 15 degrees, the smooth air flow over the wings breaks down, lift is lost, and the plane stalls. The speed at which this happens is called the stalling speed.

As an aeroplane's weight directly opposes its lift, it is vital to make the plane as light

A jumbo takes off *To become airborne, a plane has to travel at speed along the ground, getting faster and faster until the lift developed by its wings becomes greater than its own weight. A heavily loaded Boeing 747, pictured taking off below, has to reach a speed of about 180mph (290km/h) before it can take off.*

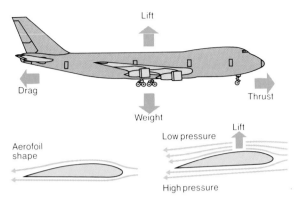

THE FORCES OF FLIGHT

For a plane to fly, it has to overcome its weight and drag (air resistance) with lift and thrust.

When an aerofoil moves through the air, different pressures develop in the air-streams over and under it.

Air over the curved top of the wing goes faster. The result is that its pressure drops and the wing begins to lift.

The faster the speed, the less the pressure. A plane lifts when pressure below the wing exceeds that above it.

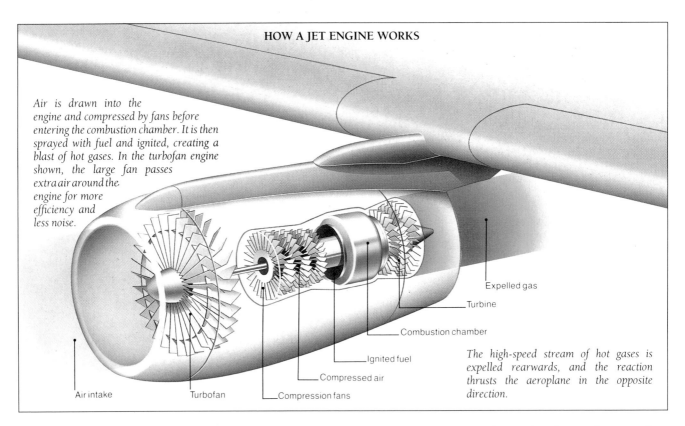

HOW A JET ENGINE WORKS

Air is drawn into the engine and compressed by fans before entering the combustion chamber. It is then sprayed with fuel and ignited, creating a blast of hot gases. In the turbofan engine shown, the large fan passes extra air around the engine for more efficiency and less noise.

Expelled gas

Turbine

Combustion chamber

Ignited fuel

Compressed air

Compression fans

Air intake

Turbofan

The high-speed stream of hot gases is expelled rearwards, and the reaction thrusts the aeroplane in the opposite direction.

as possible, but this must be done without sacrificing strength. A light but strong airframe is produced by constructing it in aluminium alloys. Carbon fibre materials are also being increasingly used.

Developing thrust

Thrust – the forward force that keeps the plane moving through the air – is produced by the engines.

Most aeroplanes of today have jet engines, which create thrust by burning kerosene fuel and ejecting the hot gases produced at high speed. As the jet of gases shoots backwards, the plane is thrust forwards by reaction – like the kick of a rifle after a bullet is fired. The gases do not push against the air, as some people think – indeed, the presence of air reduces the thrust by slowing down the gas jet. This is one reason why jet planes cruise at high altitudes, where the air is thinner.

Two main types of jet engine are in use – turbojets and turbofans. In a turbojet, air is taken in and compressed by a fan, or compressor. Fuel is then sprayed into the compressed air and ignited. The hot gases that are produced spin the blades of a turbine before escaping at the rear through the engine nozzle. The turbine drives the compressor.

The turbofan engine works on the same principle but it has another large fan in front of the compressor. This drives air around the engine as well as through it. A turbofan engine pushes out more air at slower speed than the turbojet. It is more

efficient for slower aircraft – such as passenger airliners. Turbojets suit faster aircraft such as fighters and Concorde.

Some planes still use propellers for propulsion, as all the early planes did. A propeller has a number of cambered blades that, like wings, also have an aerofoil cross-section. When the blades spin in the air, they generate a forward thrust in much the same way that a wing develops lift. The propeller is often called an airscrew because pioneer aviators thought it pulled itself through the air in something like the way a screw pulls itself through wood.

Modern propellers have a variable pitch. The angle at which they meet the air is changed automatically according to the conditions of flight. For takeoff the blades need a fine angle to build up maximum thrust at a slow speed, rather like a car in low gear. When in flight, the angle is broader to give the plane as much forward movement as possible for each revolution of the blades.

Many propeller-driven aeroplanes are powered by petrol engines that work much like car engines. Others are powered by a turboprop – a modified jet engine with an extra turbine in the jet exhaust to drive the propeller.

Streamlining and stability

Air resistance – drag – must be kept at a minimum for economical flight. This is done by careful design and construction. All the plane's surfaces are made as smooth or as 'slippery' as possible, so there are no

raised or rough surfaces to obstruct airflow. The plane is also streamlined – its cigar-like fuselage (body) is shaped to cause minimal air resistance. Designers are constantly experimenting with shapes that will decrease drag (page 147).

A plane needs a tail for stable flight just as a dart or an arrow needs a tail (or flight) to keep it travelling true. The tail has two sections – the tail fin and the tailplane. The upright tail fin corrects any tendency of the plane to yaw, or slew from side to side, as it travels through the air. The tailplane corrects the tendency of the plane to pitch or rock up and down. These two tail surfaces are often called the vertical and horizontal stabilisers.

A plane also has a tendency to roll, or rock from side to side as it flies. Rolling is reduced by inclining the wings at a dihedral angle – tilted slightly upwards so that the wings viewed from in front or behind make a V shape. This is particularly noticeable in light, low-speed planes. A plane's wings are flexible enough to flap up and down slightly in flight in response to air turbulence. This prevents them snapping under the strain.

How the pilot steers the plane

To climb, descend, or turn, the pilot manipulates control surfaces at the rear, or trailing edges, of the wings and tail. The control surfaces are hinged panels that can be moved up and down or from side to side by means of a control column (or wheel) and foot pedals.

On the wings, the main control surfaces are the ailerons – one on each wing, often near the wing tip. Moving the control column to the right raises the right-hand aileron and lowers the left-hand one. This makes the right-hand wing dip and the left-hand wing rise, a manoeuvre called banking. Moving the control column to the left makes the plane bank to the left.

To turn the plane's nose left or right, the pilot moves the rudder, a hinged surface on the vertical tail fin, by using foot pedals. Pressing the left-hand pedal swings the rudder left, so the nose swings left. Pressing the right-hand pedal swings the rudder and thus the nose to the right.

Use of the rudder alone does not make the aeroplane turn. It simply changes the position, or attitude, of the plane in the air – because of its considerable tendency to keep straight, the plane side-slips, or 'skids'. To turn without side-slipping, the pilot uses a combination of ailerons and rudder, a manoeuvre known as bank and turn.

To move the plane's nose up or down, the pilot operates the control surfaces on the tailplane, which are called the elevators.

Pulling on the plane's control column makes the elevators hinge up, causing the nose to rise. Pushing on the column makes the elevators hinge down and the nose dip. But to make the plane

Skymasters *Team aerobatics and formation flying in high-speed jets call for great precision and coordination. As the Royal Air Force display team, the Red Arrows, go into action red, white and blue jet streams from the seven aircraft paint a pattern in the sky.*

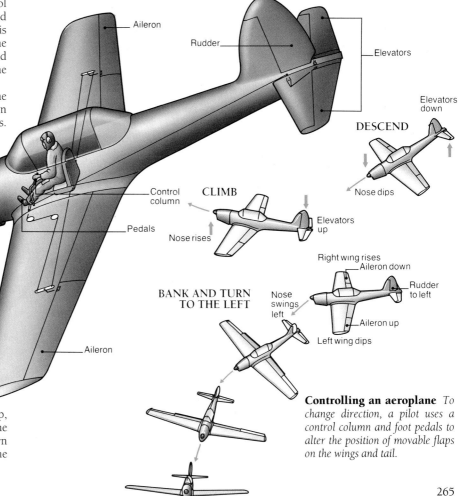

Controlling an aeroplane *To change direction, a pilot uses a control column and foot pedals to alter the position of movable flaps on the wings and tail.*

265

climb or descend, the engine throttle must be operated as well. To climb, the pilot opens the throttle to admit more fuel to the engine and increase speed, and at the same time raises the elevators. Greater speed means greater lift, so with its nose pointing upwards the plane climbs. To descend, the elevators are lowered while the throttle is eased back. Lower speed means less lift, so the plane loses height.

Power-assisted controls

On modern aircraft, the controls are power assisted, operating by hydraulic pressure. This gives the force needed to move control surfaces against the airflow at high speed. Most modern planes fly on autopilot – an automatic control system often nicknamed 'George' – for much of the time. This is computer-controlled from data fed in by measuring instruments that sense changes in conditions, such as wind speed, deviation and pitch. Once the autopilot has been set for a particular course, height and speed, it will manipulate the throttle and control surfaces as necessary.

Taking off and landing

Takeoff and landing are the two most critical flight manoeuvres. Because the plane must be travelling more slowly, the wings develop less lift.

To increase the lift at low speeds, the wings have other control surfaces – flaps at the rear and slats at the front. The flaps extend out and down on tracks, and as they extend they increase the wing area and exaggerate its camber, increasing the lift.

The slats, fitted on the leading edge of the wings, are movable curved surfaces. When they open, they improve the airflow around the wing, again increasing the lift.

After the plane has touched down, the problem is not to increase lift, but to kill it. This is done by means of spoilers (or speed brakes) – hinged surfaces usually located in front of the flaps. They are opened immediately on landing and hinge upwards at right-angles to the wing. This increases drag, breaking up the airflow over the top of the wings so that the wing loses all its lift. Initial braking is effected by applying reverse thrust – a jet engine has a mechanism that can deflect the exhaust gases forward.

Once the plane is travelling slowly enough, the pilot applies the wheel brakes.

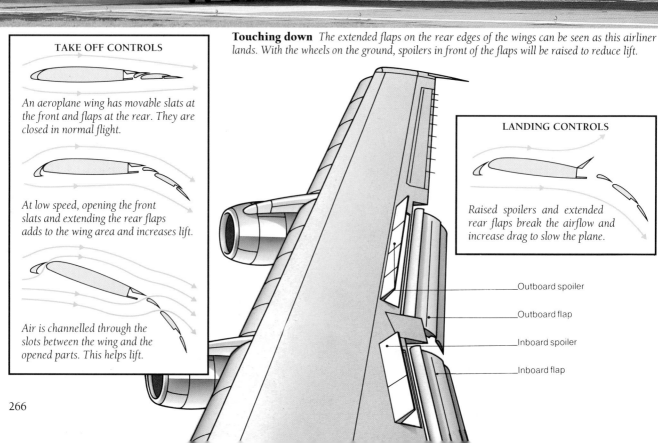

Touching down *The extended flaps on the rear edges of the wings can be seen as this airliner lands. With the wheels on the ground, spoilers in front of the flaps will be raised to reduce lift.*

TAKE OFF CONTROLS

An aeroplane wing has movable slats at the front and flaps at the rear. They are closed in normal flight.

At low speed, opening the front slats and extending the rear flaps adds to the wing area and increases lift.

Air is channelled through the slots between the wing and the opened parts. This helps lift.

LANDING CONTROLS

Raised spoilers and extended rear flaps break the airflow and increase drag to slow the plane.

Outboard spoiler

Outboard flap

Inboard spoiler

Inboard flap

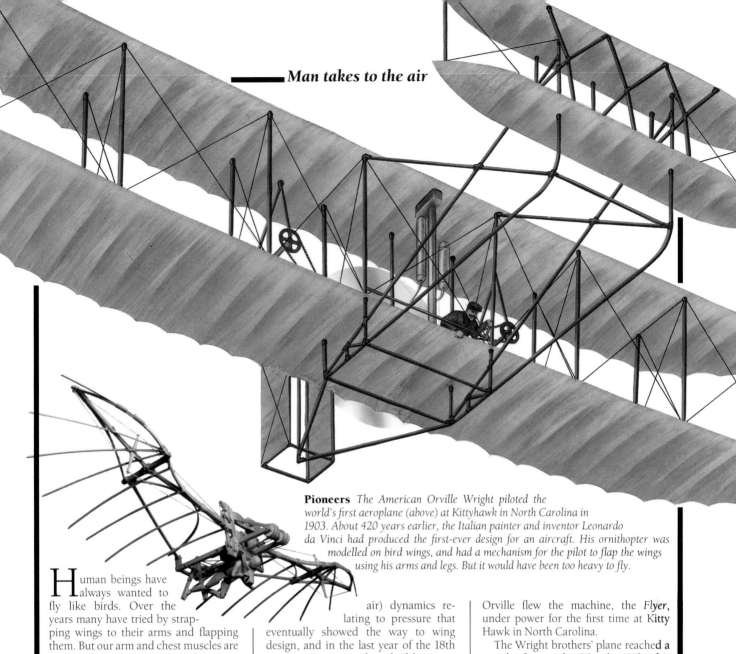

Man takes to the air

Pioneers *The American Orville Wright piloted the world's first aeroplane (above) at Kittyhawk in North Carolina in 1903. About 420 years earlier, the Italian painter and inventor Leonardo da Vinci had produced the first-ever design for an aircraft. His ornithopter was modelled on bird wings, and had a mechanism for the pilot to flap the wings using his arms and legs. But it would have been too heavy to fly.*

Human beings have always wanted to fly like birds. Over the years many have tried by strapping wings to their arms and flapping them. But our arm and chest muscles are not nearly strong enough. When man eventually did learn to fly, in 1783, it was in balloons filled with hot air or hydrogen.

Fascination with flying persisted, however. In 1738, the Swiss scientist Daniel Bernoulli had put forward the fundamental law of fluid (gas and air) dynamics relating to pressure that eventually showed the way to wing design, and in the last year of the 18th century one man at least had begun to appreciate the forces involved in heavier-than-air flight. He was the English engineer George Cayley, who sketched these forces on a silver disc in 1799. On the reverse of the disc, Cayley sketched a design for a glider, and five years later he built a model of it. But not until 1853 did he build a full-sized glider that could actually fly and carry the weight of a man.

Otto Lilienthal in Germany, and Octave Chanute and the Wright brothers (Orville and Wilbur) in the United States, in turn advanced the science of flight. It was the Wright brothers who took the next logical step and fitted a lightweight petrol engine of their own design to one of their gliders. On December 17, 1903, Orville flew the machine, the *Flyer*, under power for the first time at Kitty Hawk in North Carolina.

The Wright brothers' plane reached a speed of scarcely 30mph (50km/h), climbed only a few feet in the air and remained airborne for only a matter of seconds, travelling about 120ft (37m). There would virtually have been enough room for the entire flight to have taken place in the fuselage of a modern jumbo jet. Yet half a century later, flights of many hours became routine, and now supersonic airliners are flying twice as high as Mt Everest and transporting hundreds of passengers at speeds as fast as a rifle bullet.

Cayley's glider *British engineer Sir George Cayley (inset) designed the first workable aircraft, a model glider in 1804. In 1853 a full-sized glider was flown 500yds (460m) by Cayley's coachman.*

Hang-glider *In the 1890s, the German engineer Otto Lilienthal was flying gliders he had built of willow wands and waxed cotton cloth. After taking off from a hilltop, he was able to glide up to 750ft (230m).*

Helicopters: aircraft with spinning wings

The helicopter's spinning blades not only lift it into the air, they are also its means of propulsion – rather like a combined wing and propeller. And if the engine fails, the blades can be kept spinning to glide the machine to the ground (this is known as autorotation).

Each of the long, thin blades – the number varies from two to six – has the aerofoil shape of an aircraft wing (page 263) and the leading (front) edge is angled upwards.

To lift the aircraft off the ground the blades are rotated and their pitch – the angle at which they meet the airstream – is gradually increased. As a result air pressure decreases above each blade and increases underneath it, providing an upward force. When the lift beneath the blades is greater than the weight of the helicopter, it rises into the air.

Once the helicopter is airborne, flight is controlled by adjusting the amount and direction of lift by altering the pitch of the blades. The pitch can be altered by two controls – collectively by the collective pitch lever, or separately by the cyclic pitch column.

The collective pitch lever angles all the blades at the same pitch. It is used by the pilot for vertical ascents and descents. As the pitch is increased and more lift is generated, the throttle is usually opened up automatically to provide the necessary extra engine power.

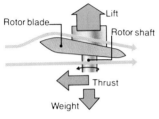

Aerofoil shape As each blade's pitch is raised it gives more lift.

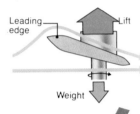

HOW HELICOPTER BLADES CREATE LIFT
The blades of a helicopter are like the aerofoil shape of aircraft wings. When they spin and their pitch is gradually increased, air pressure decreases above them and increases underneath – giving the helicopter lift.

Swashplate A hinged socket called a swashplate allows the rotor to tilt in any direction.

Cyclic pitch column

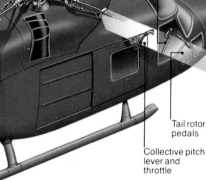

Tail rotor A small, vertical tail rotor stops the helicopter's body from spinning.

Tail rotor pedals

Collective pitch lever and throttle

Controls Two foot pedals control the tail rotor. One lever governs collective pitch, and a second controls cyclic pitch.

Blade The blades' pitch can be changed all together by the collective pitch lever or individually by the cyclic pitch column, causing the whole rotor to tilt – propelling the craft in that direction.

HOW HELICOPTERS MANOEUVRE
The cyclic pitch column changes the blades' pitch individually as they sweep round. This creates more lift on one side than the other, making the rotor tilt. The craft is propelled in the same direction in which the rotor is tilting.

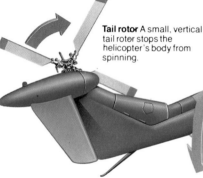

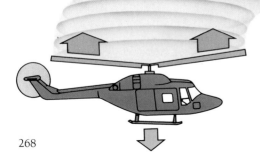

Takeoff *To increase lift, the pitch of all the blades is raised by the collective pitch lever. The throttle usually opens up automatically to provide the extra power needed for takeoff.*

Gaining height *Applying more engine power increases the collective pitch of the blades and lifts the craft. To move forwards, the rotor is tilted using the cyclic pitch column. The movements are coordinated to make a smooth transition to forward flight.*

Stability *Twin rotors are used to prevent the fuselage from turning. On the Chinook (above), gearing stops the intermeshing rotors hitting one another. The Russian Mil Mi-26 (left) has two rotors on the same axis turning opposite ways. The world's largest helicopter is the 100 ton Mil Mi-12 (right). The overall span of its rotors is only slightly less than a jumbo jet's wingspan.*

Flying forwards *Easing the cyclic pitch column forwards gives more lift over the tail of the helicopter. The rotor tilts and propels the craft forwards at a constant altitude.*

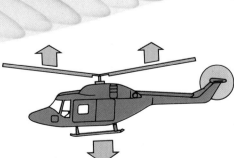

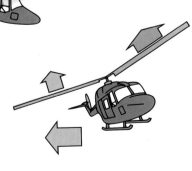

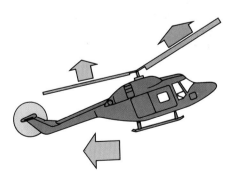

Hovering *To hover, the pilot adjusts the pitch of all the blades with the collective pitch lever so that the amount of lift just exceeds the weight of the helicopter.*

Flying sideways *The pilot moves the cyclic pitch column in the direction he wants to go, causing the blades to give more lift on one side than the other. The rotor tilts and propels the helicopter in the chosen direction.*

Flying backwards *By easing back the cyclic pitch column, the blades are given more lift as they pass over the front of the craft than over the back, so the rotor tilts backwards enabling the helicopter to reverse.*

Running the gauntlet *During a war, helicopters often provide the safest means of transport for supplies and men. Here, a Russian army helicopter is pictured operating in Afghanistan. To protect the craft from heat-seeking missiles, a flare is fired to act as a thermal decoy – luring missiles away.*

Air-sea rescue *US coastguards winch a sick man on board their hovering helicopter, which is equipped to give him treatment on the way to hospital.*

The cyclic pitch column adjusts the pitch of each blade individually as it sweeps round. If the column is moved forwards, each blade's pitch increases as it passes over the tail and decreases as it passes over the front of the helicopter.

This creates more lift over the tail than over the front of the craft which makes the whole rotor tilt forwards. The helicopter is propelled in whichever direction the rotor is tilting. So if the rotor is tilting forwards the craft flies forwards. To change direction while hovering, the pilot can use two foot pedals to change the thrust of the tail rotor and swing the craft's tail round.

The tail rotor provides directional control at low speeds and in autorotation, and when the helicopter is hovering it counteracts the tendency of the fuselage (body) to move in the opposite direction to the blades – this is known as torque reaction.

For single-engined helicopters a tail rotor is essential to eliminate torque reaction. Some helicopters cancel it out by having twin rotors turning opposite ways.

The twin rotors may be arranged in a number of ways. The Russian Kamov KA-25 Hormone and the German Wagner Sky-Trac have them revolving about the same axis. The American Boeing/Vertol CH-47 Chinook has them located fore and aft. The Russian Mil Mi-12 Homer has them mounted side by side at the ends of rudimentary wings projecting from the fuselage. The Homer is one of the world's biggest helicopters, measuring some 220ft (67m) across the rotors. US Air Force rescue craft, Kaman HH43 Huskies, have twin rotors side by side, with blades intermeshing.

Versatile but not speedy

The maximum speed a helicopter is capable of is about 250mph (400km/h). This is because, at that speed, the rotor's advancing blades are travelling at a speed approaching the speed of sound (about 760mph/1200km/h), at which point all normal aircraft encounter drag and lift problems. The retreating blades, however, are travelling at less than the forward speed of the aircraft, and can scarcely generate any lift. So flight becomes impossible to sustain. In practice, the top speed of a helicopter is generally no more than 185mph (300km/h).

Most helicopters are powered by gas turbines, with one or more gas engines driving the rotors at a constant speed. Although the engine provides abundant power, most of it is used for lift. An airliner with a similar engine could fly much farther and much faster for the same fuel consumption.

Further development in helicopter design therefore seems to lie in a hybrid craft – part helicopter, part plane – known as a tilt-rotor craft.

From whirligig to whirlybird

Man and machine *Igor Sikorsky, inventor of the first successful single-rotor helicopter, pilots his machine in America in September 1939.*

Mountain rescue *Helicopters are invaluable in finding lost or injured climbers and lifting them to safety.*

Although the helicopter in its present form is scarcely 50 years old, the principle of the rotary wing has been known for centuries. The Chinese used it some 2500 years ago for their flying top – a stick with propeller-like blades on top which was spun into the air. And Leonardo da Vinci actually sketched a helicopter in 1483. The English flight pioneer Sir George Cayley was among several people to design a model helicopter in the late 1700s, but the first man-carrying helicopter, which rose a few feet in the air, was not built until 1907 – by a Frenchman, Paul Cornu, at Lisieux.

Problems with stability and other design aspects led to helicopters being abandoned for nearly 30 years in favour of fixed-wing aircraft. Many of the design problems were, however, solved by the Spanish inventor of the autogiro, Don Juan de la Cierva, in 1919. This aircraft had a large rotor that was not driven by the engine but turned freely in the airflow. It could not take off vertically – it had to taxi to get the rotor turning enough to lift it.

Not until 1936 did the German Professor Heinrich Focke, of the Focke-Wulf Company, design a practical helicopter with twin rotors. Three years later a Russian-born engineer, Igor Sikorsky, produced a successful single-rotor helicopter, the VS-300, in the USA. This was the true ancestor of the modern rotorcraft – the most versatile of aircraft.

The development of jet engines in the 1950s led to the adoption of turboshaft engines that have considerably increased the range and speeds possible. Today the helicopter is invaluable not only as a military transport, hedge-hopping patrol plane and sky crane – for lifting steeples onto churches, for example – but also for rescuing people from remote mountainsides, sinking ships and burning buildings.

Hydrofoils: riding on underwater wings

Compared with other forms of transport, ships and most boats are very slow. Even fast ocean liners do little more than 30 knots – about 35mph (56km/h) – and most freighters limp along at less than 20 knots (23mph/37km/h). This is not much faster than you can pedal on a bicycle! Hydrofoils are by far the fastest boats around; they skim the water, supported by underwater wings, at speeds of 50-60 knots – 60-70mph (96-113km/h).

A ship's speed is slow because much of its hull is under water and subject to a considerable amount of drag – first because of the friction between its sides and the water, and second because of its resistance to the waves. The higher the speed through the water, the greater the drag.

The hydrofoil boat takes its name from its underwater wings, called hydrofoils, or often just foils. Each wing has the same aerofoil shape in cross-section as an aeroplane wing – thick in front, curved on top, rather flat underneath and tapered sharply at the rear.

Just as an aeroplane's wing develops an upward force called lift as it moves through the air, so a hydrofoil develops lift when it moves through the water. Because of the aerofoil shape, the water travels faster above the foil than underneath, causing a drop in pressure. The higher pressure underneath the foil forces it to rise up through the water.

In a hydrofoil boat the hull is mounted on foils fore and aft. At rest, the hull floats in the water like an ordinary ship or boat. But as the boat moves forward the foils start to develop lift and begin raising the hull out of the water. Lift increases with speed, raising the hull higher and higher until it is completely clear of the water and is free from most of the speed-sapping drag.

Because lift increases with fluid density, and water is more than 800 times denser than air, foils are smaller than aeroplane wings but have to be much stronger. Two main types of foil are used – the V-foil and the fully submerged foil. Some craft have both types – a V-foil at the front and a fully submerged foil at the rear. Most hydrofoils are driven by propellers.

The most widely used foil, the V-foil, extends above the surface. The ride is self-adjusting, because if the foils sink deeper into the water, more lift is generated and they rise again. If they rise too far, they generate less lift and sink again.

V-foil hydrofoil boats operate best in comparatively calm water. Rough water causes them to pitch up and down a lot, so they are used mostly on calm inland and coastal waters.

Riding on water *The submerged foil (above) and V-foil (below) are both types of hydrofoil. They provide the lift for passenger boats and for hydroplanes (right), the fastest boats in the world. The highest speed reached by a hydroplane is 345mph (555km/h).*

Craft with fully submerged foils give a much smoother ride, but need an elaborate control system to do so. They are not self-adjusting; they achieve lift by changing the angle of the foil to the water – lift increases as the angle increases. To keep them stable, the foil angle has to be adjusted according to changes in motion and the height of the hull above water. Measurements are made with sonar apparatus, and electronic signals are used to control the foils.

Jetfoils work on high-speed jets of water that discharge from nozzles at the rear and propel the boat through the water. The craft is thrust forward by the force of the reaction.

The boat takes in the water it is travelling on, scooping it up through an inlet in the centre of the rear foil struts. The powerful pumps, driven by gas-turbine jet engines, step up the water pressure before discharging it. They need to pump about 24,000 gallons (109,200 litres) of water a minute to keep the boat at a cruising speed of 50mph (80km/h).

The jetfoil operating as a cross-Channel ferry between Dover and Ostend takes about 1½ hours – less than half the time of the traditionally built ferries.

Although hydrofoils are the fastest vessels afloat, they are unlikely ever to be the largest. The weight of an ocean liner, for example, is such that the foils needed to give it lift would be impossibly heavy. This is because the weight of a foil trebles each time its size is doubled.

HOW V-FOILS AND JETFOILS GET THEIR LIFT

The V-foil, at the front, extends above the surface. The ride is self-adjusting because if the foil sinks deeper into the water, lift is generated, making the boat rise again.

A jetfoil discharges high-speed jets of water from nozzles at the rear of the boat, propelling it forward. The boat draws in the water and feeds it to pumps on the foils.

Hovercraft: boats that fly on a cushion of air

Although it travels on water, a hovercraft is not really a boat. And although it flies through the air, it is not really an aircraft. It is an amphibious craft that moves on a cushion of compressed air, and can travel easily over land and water – above mud and marsh, rocks and scrub, or ocean waves. Hovercraft is its British name, but it is also known as an air-cushion vehicle (ACV).

The air to lift the hovercraft off the ground is sucked in by its powerful fans, which compress it and direct it underneath. In many hovercraft, the compressed air is channelled first into an inflatable bag. Known as the skirt, the bag fits round the edge of the underside, and is up to about 16ft (5m) deep at the bows.

The compressed air escapes through holes in the inner wall of the rubbery fabric of the skirt to maintain a cushion of air, which, although its pressure is only about one-sixtieth of the pressure of a typical car tyre, lifts the craft off the ground. Separate flexible segments – known as fingers – hang down from the outer edges of the holes to touch the surface. They seal the air in effectively, even on a rough surface.

The world's largest civil hovercraft is the

Putting on the pressure

An experiment with two tin cans, a pair of scales and an industrial air-blower led Christopher Cockerell to design the hovercraft in 1954. An English electronics engineer who had turned to boat design, he was looking for ways to reduce friction between a boat hull and the water. The idea of an air cushion had been explored by Sir John Thornycroft in the 1870s, but never got beyond an experiment.

Cockerell thought that an air cushion could best be formed if the air, instead of being pumped straight into the cushion, was pumped under the hull from a narrow slot round the edge, and directed inwards. He tested his idea by blowing air against kitchen scales, first through an open-ended tin can (as if blown straight into the cushion), then through the slot between two tin cans, one inside the other (as if round the edge of the cushion). The second method produced more force.

Only a year later, he patented the design for the hovercraft, and the 4 ton SRN-1, the first full-size hovercraft, made its debut at Cowes in 1959. It crossed the Channel for the first time on July 25 the same year, 50 years to the day after the French aviator Louis Bleriot made the first cross-Channel aeroplane flight. Christopher Cockerell was knighted in 1969.

Hovercraft are now in use worldwide. And the hover mower uses the same principle.

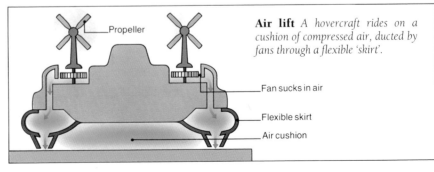

Cockerell's experiment *An air-blower mounted on a stand blows air through the gap between two tin cans, one inside the other, against a pair of scales. This proved to Christopher Cockerell that he could lift a vessel on an air cushion inflated by air pumped in from jets round the edge.*

305 ton SRN-4 Mark III, which carries more than 400 passengers and 60 cars across the English Channel. It has four fans, each 11ft 6in (3.5m) across, driven by gas-turbine engines. On the SRN-4, the same engines turn the four propellers that drive the craft forwards. Some craft have separate engines for fans and propellers.

The propellers are mounted on pylons on top of the hull. On the SRN-4 Mark III, the propeller blades are 21ft (6.4m) across. The hovercraft is thrust forwards by reaction – its propellers accelerate the airstream round them backwards, and this propels it forwards. The propellers are variable-pitch, which means that the pitch, or angle, of the blades can be altered. Although the propellers run at more or less constant speed, the speed of the airflow, and thus of the hovercraft, is altered by changing the pitch of the propellers.

This system gives the SRN-4 a top speed of more than 65 knots – 75mph (120km/h) – nearly twice the speed of the fastest ocean liner. The driver, known as the commander, controls the craft in much the same way that a pilot controls an aircraft. The rudder is the hinged rear edge of the vertical tail fins positioned in the propellers' slipstream.

Amphibian *The hovercraft, also called an air-cushion vehicle, can travel over land or water. The compressed air it rides on allows it to negotiate uneven ground or choppy waves.*

Air lift *A hovercraft rides on a cushion of compressed air, ducted by fans through a flexible 'skirt'.*

Propeller

Fan sucks in air

Flexible skirt

Air cushion

Wonders of the medical world

Since the Second World War medical science has transformed the treatment of disease and made possible previously unthought-of operations. Surgeons work with laser beams and with the help of microscopes. Artificial organs provide renewed life. And babies are conceived outside their mother's body.

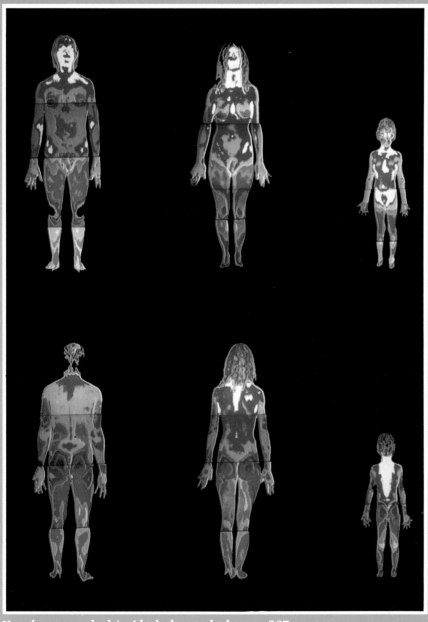

How doctors can look inside the human body, page 287.

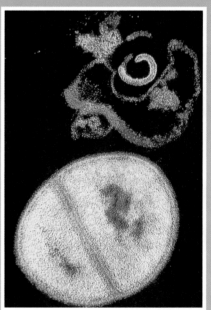

How antibiotics kill harmful bacteria, page 288.

How 'test-tube babies' are conceived and born, page 276.

Creating a test-tube baby

On July 25, 1978, Mrs Lesley Brown, a 30-year-old Englishwoman, gave birth to the first child ever conceived outside the human body – a 'test-tube baby'.

Her daughter Louise was conceived on a laboratory bench in Oldham, Lancashire, with the help of pioneering research scientists Dr Patrick Steptoe and Mr Robert Edwards. It was not until nearly two years later that their remarkable achievement was repeated – this time by Australian scientists, when Candice Reed was born in the Royal Women's Hospital, Melbourne, on June 23, 1980.

In fact, neither of the babies was produced in a test tube. Conception, now more accurately referred to as 'in vitro fertilisation' (IVF), takes place in a glass dish (*vitro* is Latin for glass).

The technique for fertilising a human egg outside the body allows women who have been unable to conceive – because the male sperm cannot reach the female egg – to have their own babies. Lesley Brown could not become pregnant because her Fallopian tubes, through which the female egg passes into the womb, were blocked.

IVF works only for the relatively small number of women whose infertility is caused by blocked Fallopian tubes, and whose wombs are otherwise healthy. So before IVF is considered, infertile couples must undergo rigorous testing to establish whether they are suitable cases for treatment.

The first step in the IVF process is to determine the precise moment in the woman's menstrual cycle at which the egg is released from the ovary. Then the woman is put on standby for a minor operation that will take place just before the egg is due to be released. The mother will probably have had a course of hormone treatment before the operation to encourage several eggs to be released, so that there are some 'spares'.

The surgeon inserts a periscope-like device called a laparoscope through a small slit in the abdomen. This instrument allows him to see not only the reproductive organs, but also the actual egg – or eggs. The surgeon removes the eggs, using a fine, hollow syringe to suck them up through the laparoscope.

The eggs are then put in a dish containing nutrients to help them survive, and are stored in an incubator for a few hours. Meanwhile, a sample of semen,

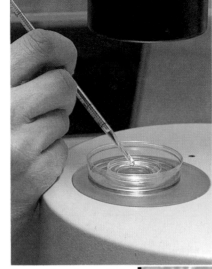

Conception in a dish
In in vitro *fertilisation, eggs and sperm are placed in a salt solution in a glass dish. Here eggs are being examined to see if they have been fertilised.*

Incubation *Before fertilisation the eggs are stored in a nutrient-rich substance in an incubator. Here a laboratory technician is removing the eggs from the incubator to prepare them for fertilisation.*

containing millions of male sperm from the father, is put in a salt solution which keeps the sperm in prime condition ready for the fertilisation process.

The eggs are then removed from the incubator and mixed into the semen-and-salt solution. Individual sperm must unite with a female egg within 24 hours to form the very beginnings of a new human being. Once fertilised the egg becomes resistant to penetration by another sperm.

The newly fertilised egg now begins a process of cell-splitting and multiplying as

Sperm and egg meet *Enhanced with false colours and magnified 6570 times, this electron microscope photograph shows a sperm penetrating the outer membrane (zona pellucida) of a woman's egg. Once this has happened, the membrane thickens to prevent other sperm from entering. Fertilisation occurs when the nucleus in the head of the sperm fuses with the nucleus of the egg.*

it begins to develop into the increasingly complex embryo. When, many hours later, the egg has divided into about eight individual cells, it is transferred to the mother's womb.

With the aid of a powerful microscope, a gynaecologist identifies which of the *in vitro* eggs have been fertilised, and draws

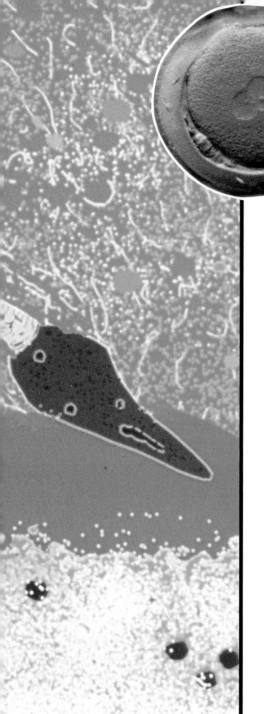

Beginning of life
Once male and female nuclei merge (left) the egg cell will start to divide, creating new cells which will specialise and eventually form a baby. Louise Brown (below) was the world's first 'test-tube baby'.

How optometrists test your eyes

An optometrist can get a good idea of your state of health by looking into your eyes. Closer examination can often determine your age within an astonishingly accurate couple of years, or even pick up the first signs of a serious disorder affecting another part of your body, such as a brain tumour or diabetes. This is because the eyes are the only part of the body where blood vessels and the end of a nerve (the optic nerve) can be seen clearly without surgery – and where slight changes in health can be picked up.

The optometrist's principal function is to assess – to a fine degree – how well your eyes work, to prescribe corrective spectacles or contact lenses if necessary, and to refer any more serious disorder for treatment by an eye specialist.

The starting point of an eye examination is still – more than 120 years after its introduction by Dutch eye specialist Dr Hermann Snellen – the familiar letter chart. The optometrist relies on the patient telling him just what can or cannot be seen with each eye. The letters are deliberately meant to confuse – similar shapes, like P and F, may be placed together, for example, so that the patient's ability to distinguish between the letters and the gaps between them is really put to the test. Cheating – by screwing up your eyelids to reduce the aperture and so improve your depth of field, for example – is possible, but it is not allowed.

The Snellen Chart gives only a rough idea of sharpness of vision. In other tests, which may be as simple as following a moving object with your eyes, the opto-metrist checks the strength of the eye muscles and whether both eyes are working together efficiently. He checks the reflex action of the pupils – that they respond to light – and that you have a good overall field of vision.

Many of the tests are used in tandem with a 'trial frame', like a heavy spectacle frame adjusted to the patient's exact eye measurement, in which the optometrist puts different combinations of lenses. It is a fine-tuning process; any weaknesses are identified by a process of elimination. From a tray of maybe 200 different lenses, each of which has a different function or strength, there are thousands of possible combinations, and the perfect one for a given individual can be found to a high degree of accuracy.

The optometrist backs up the tests by looking at the eye with a small, hand-held device called a retinoscope which shines a beam of light through the pupil onto the retina at the back of the eye. The retina contains special cells called receptors, which convert light waves into nerve impulses. These bounce back a pattern of light as the retinoscope scans the eye, giving the optometrist an idea of the shape. An eyeball which is too long from front to back is a sign of short-sightedness; one which is too short is a sign of long-sightedness. If the cornea, the transparent outer surface of the eye, is squashed, it means that images are distorted (astigmatism). If the beam of light doesn't reach the retina at all, there is probably some obstruction, such as the milky film known as a cataract.

The optometrist now has an idea of the eyes' shortcomings, but he needs to examine the interior of the eyes more closely to find any dangerous defect.

An ophthalmoscope – another hand-held instrument – lights up the transparent centre and back of the eye with a fine beam of light directed through the pupil. This combined with a series of lenses that are adjusted by turning a small wheel at the side of the instrument, enables the optometrist to focus on different parts of the eye. If the eye is healthy, he will see a circle of clear pink-orange, crossed by a tracery of nerve tissues and blood vessels (this is the point where the general health of the patient's nervous and circulatory systems can be gauged). Any age-related changes will be detected too, for example if the fluid washing through the eye is being trapped.

The extent of any fluid blockage is gauged by measuring the pressure build-up in the eyeball using a tonometer. The instrument is placed lightly against the eye, and gives a pressure reading in millimetres of mercury. Another type of tonometer releases a puff of air against the eye; the speed at which the air bounces back indicates the amount of pressure.

them up into a fine, hollow tube. This is then inserted along the woman's vagina, and the embryos are discharged into the womb to continue their growth.

To avoid the risk of multiple births, only a limited number – possibly three – of the fertilised eggs will actually be implanted.

From now on, an embryo is fighting for survival as much as in a normal pregnancy. It must attach itself to the wall of the mother's womb to gain the necessary nutrients to survive and grow. There is only a one-in-five chance that this will happen – so if more than one IVF embryo is 'planted' in the womb, the greater the likelihood is of the mother giving birth to a healthy baby nine months later.

How glasses sharpen your vision

If you have perfect vision, the light rays entering the pupils of your eyes will converge exactly on the retina at the back, and the sharply focused picture will be relayed to the brain.

Most people's vision is at its sharpest at about the age of one year. Problems often develop at around puberty. The eyeball grows too long from front to back, or not long enough, or it becomes misshapen. These are the three most common reasons why people need to wear glasses to correct the eye's focal length.

In early life, a person's potential sight problems may be compensated for by the strong action of the ciliary muscles attached to the iris of the eye's lens. These muscles increase or decrease the curvature of the lens so that it is possible to focus on things close up or far away.

But if the ciliary muscles weaken, as often happens in middle age, the lens can no longer be made thick enough to focus on close-up objects, such as small type on a printed page. A person who at the age of ten could focus on the tip of his own nose may suddenly find that he cannot read a book unless he holds it at arm's length.

The three main causes of blurred vision are long-sightedness, short-sightedness and astigmatism, and glasses of different types are used to correct them (see right). Tinted lenses help wearers whose eyes are sensitive to light or reflections from clear lenses. An anti-reflection substance can also be used to coat lenses and help to make vision sharper.

Spectacle lenses are made of either glass or plastic. Glass is heavier but is also more resistant to scratching.

How contact lenses are made

Leonardo da Vinci described the principle of fitting an artificial lens directly onto the surface of the eye in 1508. Nearly 400 years later, in 1888, a German eye specialist, Dr Adolf Fick, made plaster-cast impressions of the eyes of corpses to use as moulds for the first glass contact lenses.

Today's contact lenses are tiny, transparent plastic discs which float on the film of moisture that covers the front surface of the eye. They are prescribed by an optometrist (also known as an ophthalmic optician) to fit the patient's eye size and shape precisely. Virtually invisible when worn, they actually move with the eye, giving a much more natural vision than that achieved with spectacles.

To make up a prescription for contact lenses, the optometrist determines what sight defects need to be corrected (see *How optometrists test your eyes*, page 277) and makes detailed measurements of the eye's outer surface using a keratometer. This device registers a light image of the eye (rather like the reflection on a Christmas tree bauble), gives measurements to 0.01mm and calculates the curve of the eyeball.

Modern contact lenses are made from plastic rather than glass and may be rigid or pliable. The material prescribed depends on the patient's eye sensitivity, allergic reactions and special needs or activities.

The sight defect is actually corrected by the shape of the front surface of the lens – a flat curve adjusts short-sightedness, a steep curve long-sightedness, and a distorted curve corrects the imbalance of astigmatism. The hard lens, which until the late 1970s was the most common but is now used by only about 10 per cent of patients, is hand-lathed to the precise size and shape required from small circular blocks of solid Perspex. These lenses are the most durable and easy to care for, but can cause dryness and irritation. To counter this problem, gas-permeable (or oxygen-permeable) hard lenses have fluorocarbons and silicon mixed in with the Perspex to give a more porous material. Oxygen can filter through to the surface of the eye and waste gases can escape.

Soft, or hydrophilic (water-loving), lenses are even more permeable – and comfortable to wear. They consist of almost jelly-like plastic with between 38 and 85 per cent water content. A mould of the prescribed shape and size is filled with the molten water-plastic mixture, and when this has cooled and solidified, the lens is removed and polished. Shapes do not vary a great deal between individuals – a range of only five different fittings is suitable for 80 per cent of patients – and because soft lenses are so flexible, they can often be bought off the shelf.

Tinted plastic is sometimes used to make contact lenses easier for the wearer to find when they have been taken out, to reduce sensitivity to light, or for cosmetic reasons – to make grey eyes look blue, for example. To ensure that the correct lens is fitted into the correct eye, tiny distinguishing dots can be marked on one or both lenses.

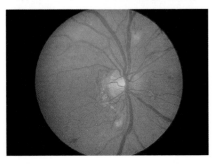

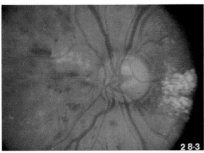

Examining the eye *When an optometrist examines an eye through an ophthalmoscope (top), he sees the retina at the back of the eye (centre) and can identify any damage or disorders which may result from disease. In the photograph at the bottom, the dark red spots and pale yellow areas are haemorrhages and deposits caused by diabetes.*

One of the earliest warnings of glaucoma can be seen with the slit-lamp microscope, which magnifies up to 50 times and is combined with a lamp that provides a narrow beam of light through a tiny slit.

The microscope is used to examine the front surface of the eye, where the angle between the iris (the coloured part of the eye) and the cornea can be seen clearly. It is here that the very first signs of fluid blockage can be seen. The optometrist can also detect the tiniest of scratches – caused perhaps by contact lenses – old scars and any damage to the cornea, iris or lens caused by a foreign body.

Short sight *Short-sighted people cannot focus far away, because the eyeball is too long and the rays of light converge in front of the retina. Concave lenses alter the angle of the rays so they converge on the retina.*

Long sight *Vision is clear at distances but not close up because the eyeball is too short from front to back and light rays have not converged when they reach the retina. Convex lenses shorten the focal length.*

Astigmatism *Vision is out of focus on either the horizontal or vertical plane because the eyeball is irregular. Astigmatism is treated with lenses shaped like a lengthways slice from a tube.*

Normal *A person with normal sight can focus on an eye chart at 20ft (6m) and closer. The eyeball is the right shape for light rays to converge exactly on the retina. It also reacts fast to changes in light.*

How do blind people learn to read and write?

In 1829, a French population census listed 15-year-old Louis Braille, a pupil at the Paris Institute for the Young Blind, as 'unable to read or write'. Yet in the same year, the young Braille published a new 'language' which provided the key to reading and writing for blind people.

He devised a completely new alphabet – a code of raised dots (which are much easier to feel and identify than a continuous line). The dots are arranged in domino-like combinations to form characters that correspond with letters of the alphabet, punctuation marks and common words such as 'and' and 'the'.

The Braille 'language' is touch-read by running the tips of one or two fingers over the embossed text. In 1932, more than 100 years after the system was first published, Braille was adopted as the standard language

Louis Braille
He invented Braille printing in 1829.

for the blind in the English-speaking world. The original, 63-character, letter-by-letter system has since developed into a more advanced, contracted form in which the dot symbols represent common letter combinations such as 'ow', 'ing', and 'ment', making it quicker to read and write, and less space consuming. Now there are Braille adaptations for every major language in the world, and for music, mathematics and science.

Braille can be 'hand-written', using a stylus to press out the dot characters onto a sheet of paper clamped into a metal frame. The writer works on the back of the sheet, from right to left, so that when the paper is turned over the dots are raised, and read from left to right in the normal way.

Braille typewriters and computers with Braille print-out facilities are in common use, and the printers' latest embossing machines can imprint both sides of a single sheet of paper without the dot patterns on either side conflicting.

Braille is used mostly by people who are born blind or who lose their sight at an early age. Many people, however, become blind in their 60s, after many years of reading conventional print – and may also, because of age, diabetes or arthritis, have reduced sensitivity in their fingers. For them, the adaptation to touch-reading dotted symbols can be difficult. Some depend totally on taped books. Others learn to touch-read the alternative 'Moon' system of raised letters – the stronger, simpler outlines reflect standard letter shapes, and are easier to learn.

Invented in England in 1847 by Dr William Moon of Brighton, 'Moon' is a letter-by-letter system with nine basic characters, whose interpretation depends on which way up or round they are used. The lines of text are read alternately from left to right and then from right to left, in a continuous flow. Moon is used in the English-speaking world only, and is much less established and versatile than Braille. The range of texts is limited, as printing technology responded more readily to embossing the dotted characters of Braille than the Moon lines and circles.

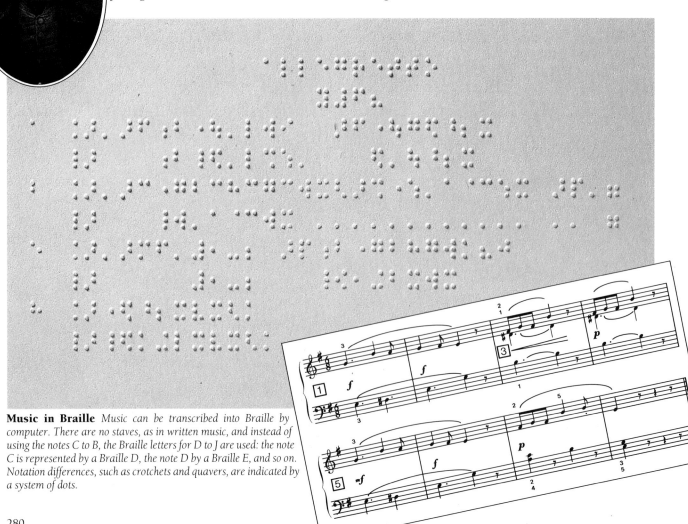

Music in Braille *Music can be transcribed into Braille by computer. There are no staves, as in written music, and instead of using the notes C to B, the Braille letters for D to J are used: the note C is represented by a Braille D, the note D by a Braille E, and so on. Notation differences, such as crotchets and quavers, are indicated by a system of dots.*

How your intelligence may be measured

Even the experts cannot agree on exactly what intelligence is, but that has not stopped attempts to measure it.

Your intelligence is likely to be tested at all stages of your life – at school, if you enter the armed or civil services, even sometimes when you apply for a job. These tests are designed to measure your ability to solve problems, and contain questions about numbers, language and shapes.

The first tests of intelligence were produced in 1905 by Alfred Binet, at the request of the French government. They wanted to identify children with learning difficulties, so extra tuition could be given.

In 1916, the American psychologist Lew Terman, who was working at Stanford University in California, adapted the Binet tests, and coined the term 'intelligence quotient', or IQ. These tests became known as the Stanford-Binet tests.

The original Stanford-Binet tests asked a series of questions relating to numbers, words and objects, to determine the mental age of the person doing the test (as opposed to his or her actual age). The tests were given to a large number of people of the same age at the same time. The average number of right answers achieved was the average mental age of that group, and each member of the group was judged against its average.

The mental age of a person was then divided by his or her actual age, and multiplied by 100 to calculate the IQ. So, if your mental age was 16 and your actual age was 15, you had an IQ of 106. These tests were given to children up to the age of 18. After the age of 15, the rate of development skills slows down, so the comparison of mental age to actual age becomes less relevant.

New tests have been produced since the original Stanford-Binet, which more accurately measure the intelligence of today's population. But they still work on the same basic principles as the original tests.

The average score is 100. Fifty per cent of people tested have an IQ of between 90 and 110. If your IQ is over 100, it means that according to the tests, you are more intelligent than average. But in fact, your score only reveals how well you complete intelligence tests.

Different IQ tests also produce various results for the same person. For example, a test of verbal ability (reading and language) might give quite different results from a test of reasoning or maths. Although this is

TESTING YOUR INTELLIGENCE

Intelligence tests measure what a person has learned as well as his or her ability to solve problems in different areas, such as maths, language, logic and spatial perception. But since some people's aptitudes lie predominantly in one area rather than another, and some tests are culturally influenced, these tests cannot determine a person's general level of intelligence. On the right and below are examples of the kinds of problems set in these tests.

6	2	4
2	?	0
4	0	4

1. Arithmetic crossword *Two numbers in a line going across and down each produce the third. Try to work out the missing number.*

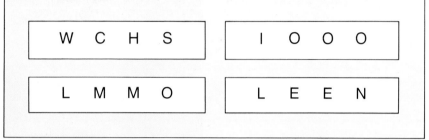

2. Mismatched letters *In a playground scuffle, a message written by a little girl to her mother – in a slightly unusual way – was accidentally torn into four pieces. By rearranging the pieces, can you work out what the message says?*

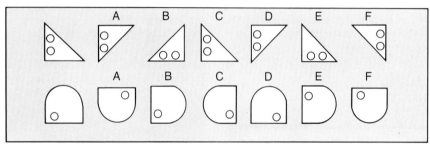

3. Seeing dots *In each row there are several shapes with dots that are the same as the first shape in the row, except that they might have been swivelled around. The task is to identify them. This is a test of spatial perception and can be done well by an uneducated person.*

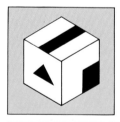

4. Three-dimensional teaser *This teaser is another which tests your spatial perception, and involves working out which of the four patterns corresponds to the box when it is unfolded.*

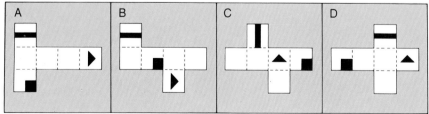

1. The answer is 2. In each vertical and horizontal row, the second number is subtracted from the first.

2. Message reads 'WILL COME HOME SOON'.

W	C	H	S
I	O	O	O
L	M	M	O
L	E	E	N

3. First row: B, C, F. Second row: A, C, E.

4. The D answer is the correct one.

connected to your ability to do things in real life, there are many other influences.

Research has shown that cultural background, motivation (or lack of it), class differences, changes in family structure and home conditions, and even the rapport between the tester and the person being tested, all affect the final IQ score achieved.

The intelligence tests described here are a comparative measure – they compare the person being tested with a standardisation sample. People with very high and very low ability are 'off the scale'. There are no standards to measure their ability against because no large sample of that ability has been tested. So reports of children with IQs of 170 or 220 are only assessments.

Binet was convinced that a person's intelligence changes in their lifetime, but there are many who believe intelligence is inherited and does not vary.

New Stanford-Binet tests are now used in conjunction with a variety of others, such as the British Ability Scales. These systems are designed specifically for adults (where age is not necessarily taken into consideration), schoolchildren and pre-school children, whereas the Stanford-Binet tests were created primarily for schoolchildren. Systems other than Stanford-Binet are also geared to a more accurate assessment of cultural minorities, whose scores were lower than they should have been on the Stanford-Binet tests, which were designed for white, Westernised children.

How do you remember?

In Rangoon, Burma, in 1974, a man called Bhandanta Vicitsara recited 16,000 pages of Buddhist text from memory. That sort of memory is phenomenal, but almost everyone is able to remember surprisingly large amounts of information. Despite this, you forget a new telephone number almost immediately after you dial it.

This apparent contradiction occurs because people have two types of memory. Short-term memory can retain only six or seven items for up to a minute. Long-term memory can retain much more complex information for years and even decades.

Scientists have discovered that short and long-term memory are located in different parts of the brain. Short-term memory is found in the middle of the brain, but long-term memory is located all over the outer part. This is why, when a disease or stroke affects the inner part of the brain, and results in memory loss, the victim can remember events leading up to his memory loss, because they are part of his long-term

memory, but cannot store new memories.

Psychologists know that memory is linked to the five senses. During the learning phase, a child who has reached the age of six has a vocabulary of 6000 words. Throughout the rest of his life the average person will acquire only another 14,000. Yet the foundations are laid before he can read, so he has learned these sounds by their meaning, rhythm and tone, and by association.

When information is held in the long-term memory, it is probably translated into some kind of picture and stored in the nerve cells in the outer part of the brain. There are more than 100,000 million such cells, each of which has 10,000 connections to other cells, making the network unbelievably complex.

The information in the cells is probably stored by chemicals which alter the way the cells work and the way they are connected to each other.

Something in a person's short-term memory can be transferred to his long-term memory by repetition and learning. The information is actually transferred by

chemical messengers. These messengers are molecules which travel from one brain cell to another. Each molecule causes a specific action, and so 'transmits' a message.

So even though you may forget a telephone number you have just dialled, you can eventually store it in your long-term memory if you are going to need it in the future.

How does hypnosis work?

Hypnosis is rarely performed on stage today (at least in the Western world) because its use as entertainment has been restricted by law. Most hypnotists are actually doctors or hypnotherapists, who treat anxiety and psychosomatic disorders such as stress-induced asthma or rashes, or addictions such as smoking or alcoholism.

A hypnotist may begin a session by

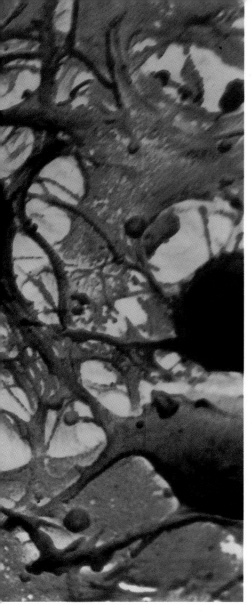

Storehouses of memory *Magnified 1000 times, the nerve cells in the outer part of the brain are clearly visible. It is in these cells that long-term memory is stored.*

anyone against their will, and no one in a trance can be made to do anything he considers wrong. Even so, about 80 per cent of people can be hypnotised into the light trance that is needed for most hypnotherapy.

Before anaesthetics became widespread in the mid-19th century, hypnosis was used in surgery in Paris, France, by the Austrian doctor Franz Mesmer (1734-1815). He performed his first operation there using hypnosis in 1778.

An innovative English surgeon, John Elliotson (1791-1868), introduced hypnosis to London in 1837. He operated on hundreds of patients successfully, numbing them by hypnosis, but was rejected by the medical establishment. He lost his professorship the following year.

His colleague, John Esdaile, however, met no opposition to hypnotism while he was medical officer to the East India Company. He performed hundreds of serious operations, including amputations, on patients under mesmeric trances, and thousands of minor ones, painlessly and with few fatalities.

In America today hypnosis is becoming increasingly popular in surgery as an alternative to anaesthetics, which can have unpleasant and dangerous side effects. It is often used during dental treatment or to reduce the agony of burns.

The technique is also being increasingly used to relieve the pains of childbirth. Some antenatal clinics offer classes in self-hypnosis so that an expectant mother can learn to numb parts of her body by her own powers of mental suggestion.

asking a patient to count backwards from, say, 300 while gazing steadily at a fixed point. The aim is to concentrate the mind of the patient and induce a feeling of relaxation so he responds to suggestion.

The hypnotist may then repeat simple, encouraging directions in a soothing and rhythmical tone. Gradually the patient enters a sleep-like condition which allows him to accept the hypnotist's influence. He begins to fall into a trance. His temperature goes down, his pulse rate slows and his blood pressure falls. There may be signs of rapid eye movements. As he relaxes, he may talk about anxieties that he has been suppressing, and the hypnotist may discover the underlying cause of the problem.

The patient always returns to the waking state. If the hypnotist fails to bring him out of his trance, he will simply fall asleep naturally, and later wake up.

For hypnosis to work, there must be a feeling of trust between patient and therapist. People who are imaginative and can picture vividly the ideas suggested by the hypnotist are the best subjects.

It is virtually impossible to hypnotise

How athletes train to break records

On May 6, 1954, at the Oxford race track, sporting history was made by a young medical student, Roger Bannister. He ran 1 mile in less than four minutes. Today his record of 3 minutes 59.4 seconds has been beaten by more than 13 seconds.

The Soviet weightlifter, Vasily Alekseyev, also won a place in the record books when he broke 80 world records and reigned as world champion for eight years, from 1970 to 1977. How is it that his records too – seemingly impossible when they were set – are now regularly being broken?

Better training facilities, scientific analysis of performance, sports psychology, improved diet and more competitions mean that athletes today are stronger, faster and more agile than their predecessors were 30 years ago.

Scientific training

Apart from good health, top athletes tune their bodies to perfection for their particular sport – and they tune them like machines. At training centres around the world, such as the centres sponsored by the US Olympic Committee at Colorado Springs and Lake Placid, doctors analyse athletes' performances using the principles of mechanical engineering. They regard the muscles as levers and pulleys subject to the same laws of physics. By making the body's movement more efficient, they can make it achieve more.

One technique is to place electrodes on the body, linked up to a device which makes a noise when the athlete tenses. This makes him aware of the tendency and he can relax the area pinpointed.

Athletes also train with light-emitting electrodes attached to them. The lights are captured by a camera linked to a computer, which analyses the athlete's technique and relays the results immediately onto a screen. The athlete gets instant feedback on the efficiency of his movements and, therefore, areas of improvement.

The doctors working in these training laboratories have discovered that for some sports, such as archery, it is important that the intuitive side of the brain (the right side) takes over, and that for other sports, such as rowing, the analytical side (the left side) is vital. They are investigating ways of stimulating and reducing the electrical activity of the brain so that the important side can take over at the crucial moment in an event. But how much of their success is due purely to psychology is difficult to say at this stage.

Athletes are also taught to pace their oxygen needs. Running on a treadmill, their maximum intake of oxygen is monitored. The average man takes in 40-50ml of oxygen per kg of his weight every minute; a male long-distance runner or skier can take in 85ml per kg each minute. So runners, for example, are taught to identify the point at which their oxygen supply becomes insufficient for their needs, and to pace themselves so that they run as close to maximum oxygen consumption as possible.

Doctors are bringing hormones into their investigations, too. They have found that there is a daily fluctuation in hormone production, which means that the body performs better at certain times of the day. By training at these particular times, athletes can come even closer to their optimum performance.

Higher and higher *In 1936 Cornelius Johnson of the USA (left) reached 6ft 9½in (2.07m); in 1960 John Thomas of the USA (right) reached 7ft 3¼in (2.22m); and in 1987 Patrik Sjoberg of Sweden (below) cleared 7ft 11¼in (2.42m).*

HOW THE WORLD RECORD GREW FROM 1854

HEIGHT	NAME	DATE	
1.675m	John Gilles (GB)	7/9/1854	
1.97m	Michael Sweeney (USA)	21/9/1895	(to end 1908)
2.01m	Edward Beeson (USA)	2/5/1914	(to end 1918)
2.03m	Harold Osborn (USA)	27/5/1924	(to end 1928)
2.09m	Melvin Walker (USA)	12/8/1937	(to end 1938)
2.11m	Lester Steers (USA)	17/6/1941	(to end 1948)
2.16m	Yuriy Stepanov (USSR)	13/7/1957	(to end 1958)
2.28m	Valeriy Brumel (USSR)	21/7/1963	(to end 1968)
2.34m	Rudolf Povarnitsin (USSR)	16/6/1978	(to end 1978)
2.43m	Javier Sotomayor (CUB)	8/9/1988	(to end 1988)

The technique's a flop *From the earliest documented high jumps, in 1854, the world record was being improved all the time. From 1854 to 1988, men have jumped 2ft 6in (0.76m) higher. Apart from better diets and training, the improvement is due to changes in technique. The bar was jumped by means of a roll or a straddle jump until, in the mid-1960s, Dick Fosbury invented the Fosbury Flop. This method of high jumping involved jumping over the bar backwards and flicking the legs over it together, as the last part of the movement.*

Record-breaking diets

One way to ensure that an athlete's body is in prime condition is a good diet. The evidence now is that a diet high in raw fruit and vegetables and unrefined carbohydrates (wholemeal bread and pasta, brown rice and pulses), and low in fat, sugar and salt, can improve performances by more than 5 per cent. Fresh fruit and vegetables increase the oxygen intake of muscle cells, whereas the effort of processing sugar, fat and salt can rob the body of essential nutrients.

One myth athletes are particularly prone to is that a high intake of protein is necessary for greater strength and muscle power. Even though this was scientifically disproved early this century, it was not until the beginning of the 1980s that sports institutions accepted the benefits of low-protein diets.

There is hard evidence that higher levels of performance can be achieved by taking in no more than 1¾oz (50g) of protein a day (the equivalent of 5oz of grilled steak, there being 10g of protein in 1oz of meat). This compares sharply with the 200g or more of protein (about 1¼lb of grilled steak) that some athletes will eat each day.

It has also been found that loading up on carbohydrates for a short period before an event increases energy levels (see box).

Sports psychology

Good health and regular training merely make for a good athlete – they do not necessarily mean that records can be broken. One difference lies in a positive attitude of mind. There are now psychologists who specialise in 'psyching up' athletes to achieve their goals. This includes getting them to listen repeatedly

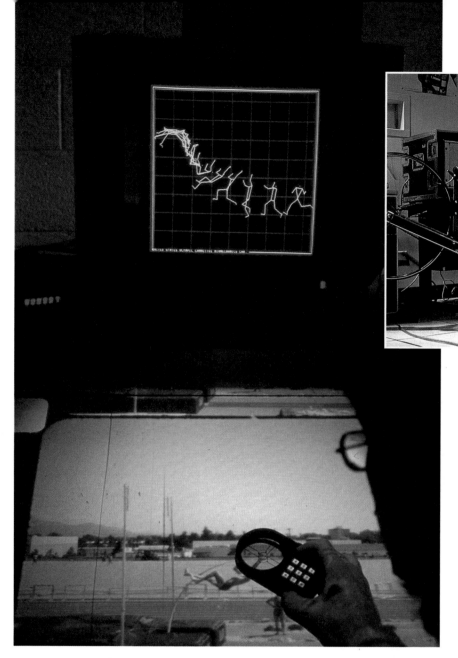

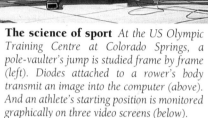

The science of sport *At the US Olympic Training Centre at Colorado Springs, a pole-vaulter's jump is studied frame by frame (left). Diodes attached to a rower's body transmit an image into the computer (above). And an athlete's starting position is monitored graphically on three video screens (below).*

to tape recordings encouraging them to persevere, and teaching them how to improve their concentration, to relax and 'visualise'. The last is almost a form of meditation and involves the athlete relaxing completely and imagining step by step an event in which he or she wins. This way the winning strategy becomes automatic.

The financial rewards of athletic success can be high, and some athletes are tempted to build muscle and improve performance by taking drugs such as anabolic steroids. But the side effects of drugs are so harmful – for example, they increase the risk of heart disease – that their use is prohibited.

The question everyone asks is – where is the limit? Some doctors believe that athletes specialising in events which require short bursts of energy are reaching the limits of their performance. But they say that records in endurance events, such as marathons, will continue to improve as the human body learns to adapt.

CARBOHYDRATES AND EXTRA ENERGY

There is one dietary regime which has been shown to boost athletes' energy levels significantly.

Known as carbohydrate loading, it increases the level of glycogen in the muscles. Glycogen is a form of glucose which is broken down to release energy. By building up the amount of glycogen they contain, the muscles can work hard for longer.

The programme usually starts a week before a competition. On the seventh day before the event, preferably in the evening, the athlete performs a strenuous training routine to deplete the glycogen stored in his muscles, and eats a low-carbohydrate meal.

During the following three days he trains less and continues with low-carbohydrate meals.

On days three and two the athlete eats a high-carbohydrate diet and eases the training further.

On day one the carbohydrate intake is increased again, and the athlete rests, in preparation for the event the following day.

The principle behind this programme is that when a high level of carbohydrates is introduced to muscles low on glycogen, the muscles overcompensate and take in a higher than normal level of glycogen over a short period. It is these surplus stores that the athlete draws on during his event, which keep him going longer.

Following this dietary routine, some top-ranking marathon runners have found that their performances have improved significantly.

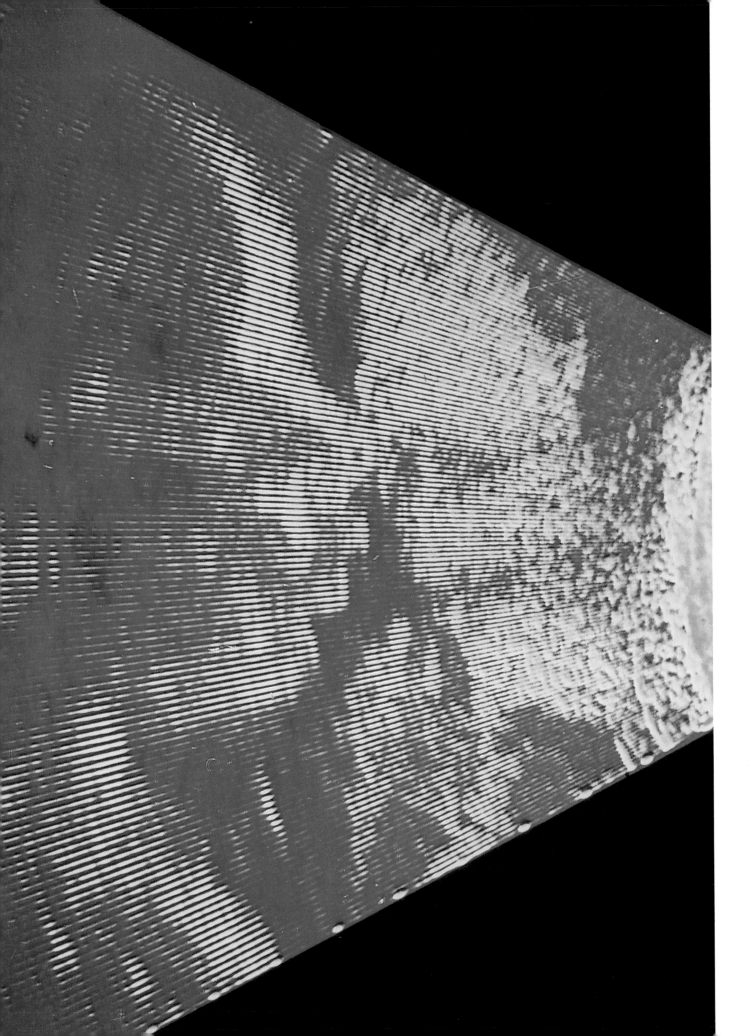

How can doctors look inside the body?

Without lifting a knife, doctors looking at the body today can see the tiniest cracks in bones, tell whether a tumour is malignant or benign, even identify certain chemicals in the brain. This is all possible with cameras and computer screens. This new perspective on the inside of the body started with the discovery of X-rays. They were discovered on November 8, 1895, quite by chance, by the German physicist Wilhelm Röntgen. He called them X-rays because he neither knew what they were nor understood their properties. Scientists now know they are electromagnetic waves, like light and radio waves, but with a shorter wavelength.

X-rays can pass through objects or substances with a low density, but are stopped by heavier or denser materials. So whereas skin and muscle allow the rays to pass through them, solid bone reflects them. Within a few months of Röntgen's discovery, X-rays were being used to take photographs to aid medical diagnosis of bone fractures, tumours and dental cavities.

Photographic negatives are produced by directing X-rays through the body and onto a negative plate. The rays appear as areas of white on the negative. Any diseases or structural faults in the bone can be seen. Radiologists, who are specialists in reading X-ray photographs, can even spot non-bone disorders, such as fluid in the lungs, by looking for various shadows on the film, which are a sign of disease.

Because conventional X-ray photographs depict the body in two dimensions only, they cannot reveal the shape or depth of a diseased area. In 1973 a new method of observing the body was introduced, which produced a three-dimensional image of the body's organs. It is known as a CT, or CAT, scan, which stands for Computerised Axial Tomography.

The CT system shows cross-sections, or 'slices' of the body, on a screen. By using a series of these images, a three-dimensional picture of the body, or a part of the body, can be built up.

When a CT scan is taken, the patient is laid on a table surrounded by a doughnut-shaped metal ring which rotates around the patient's body. The scanner has X-ray tubes around one side, and detectors opposite them. As the scanner moves round, the X-ray tubes shoot thin beams of rays through the patient's body. Small amounts of the rays are absorbed by the body's tissues. When the beams pass out of the other side of the body, they strike the detectors, which convert them to electronic signals. A computer analyses the amount of radiation that has been absorbed.

The computer's analysis is coded into colours which indicate the relative density of tissue – the denser the tissue, the more radiation it will have absorbed. This coloured image, called a tomogram, is projected onto a screen for analysis.

The CT takes one 'slice' through the brain in five seconds. A similar machine, called a Dynamic Spatial Reconstructor, which portrays an organ on a video screen, can produce 75,000 cross-sections in the same time. It allows scientists to observe an organ moving and responding to stimuli and see if it is working normally.

Another kind of scanning device, which produces similar images of horizontal slices through the body, is called a PET scan (Positron Emission Tomography). This method involves injecting a radioactive chemical into a patient. The chemical is absorbed by some organs of the body, and emits positive electrons (positrons) which collide with negative electrons in the organs' cells. The collision causes gamma rays to be released, which are recorded by a computer.

Some diseased parts of organs do not absorb the chemical and this shows up on the image produced by the computer, allowing medical scientists to diagnose the sites of diseases such as cancer. The PET scanning system can also be used to detect the accumulation of certain chemicals in the brain which are a sign of mental illnesses such as schizophrenia, manic depression and epilepsy.

An even more advanced way of taking a picture of what is happening inside the body is called Nuclear Magnetic Resonance

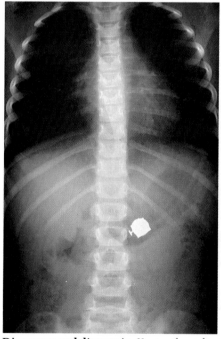 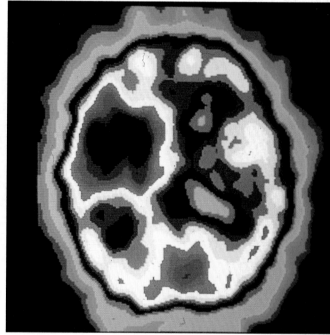

Discovery and diagnosis *X-rays, the earliest way of seeing inside the body, were used in the case on the left to locate an accidentally swallowed wristwatch in a patient's stomach. A Positron Emission Tomography (PET) scan uses a radioactive substance to show up a brain tumour (the red/black areas).*

Imaging (NMR). This involves large magnets which beam energy through the body causing hydrogen atoms in the body to resonate. This gives out energy in the form of tiny electrical signals. A computer attached to the scanner detects these signals, which vary in different parts of the body and according to whether an organ is healthy or not. The variation enables a picture to be produced on a screen. Because NMR does not involve radiation it can often be used where X-rays would be dangerous.

Ultrascan, or ultrasound, which may be used to monitor development of the foetus in pregnant women, uses high-frequency

Life before birth *Ultrascan reflects sound waves from different tissue depths. It can be converted by computers into images, like this foetus after seven months (left).*

sound waves beyond the audible level. The sound is reflected from different depths within the body – and a computer converts the signals into pictures. In this way such factors as growth and deformity can be checked.

There are still some conditions, such as stomach ulcers, which scanners of different types do not reveal adequately. However, doctors can look directly into the body through an endoscope.

An endoscope is a flexible tube which is inserted into the body. Two glass-fibre tubes which transmit light waves are inserted into the endoscope, allowing the doctor to see directly inside the patient. One fibre is used to shoot a beam of light down the tube, the other is fixed to a camera, or an eyepiece. The light bends, so that the doctor can see around twists and curves.

Endoscopes have even been used to photograph the development of a foetus inside its mother's womb. They are also used in the frontiers of surgery where, instead of the knife, surgeons operate by laser (page 292).

Other types of monitoring the body include: Doppler scans using sound waves to seek out blood clots; echocardiography, which checks heart disease and efficiency; and electrocardiography (ECG), in which electrodes on the skin create a graph that can show up signs of heart trouble.

How antibiotics kill bacteria

The most widely prescribed drugs in the world are antibiotics, a term which ironically, means 'against life'. Antibiotics are used to treat infections and diseases, such as diphtheria and tuberculosis, that only 50 years ago were killing tens of thousands of people every year.

During the First World War many soldiers died because their wounds became infected, or dysentery weakened them. When the war began there was only one drug which could attack bacteria. It was an arsenic compound, Salvarsan, used to treat syphilis.

Antibiotics were discovered in 1929, when the British scientist Alexander Fleming noticed that the bacteria he was growing on a dish in his laboratory stopped growing after a mould called *Penicillium* found its way into the dish. He tested it on various bacteria and recognised its potential, but was unable to develop it further.

Ernst Chain, a German biochemist, and Howard Florey, an Australian pathologist, who were both working in Oxford, took up Fleming's discovery in 1938. Two years

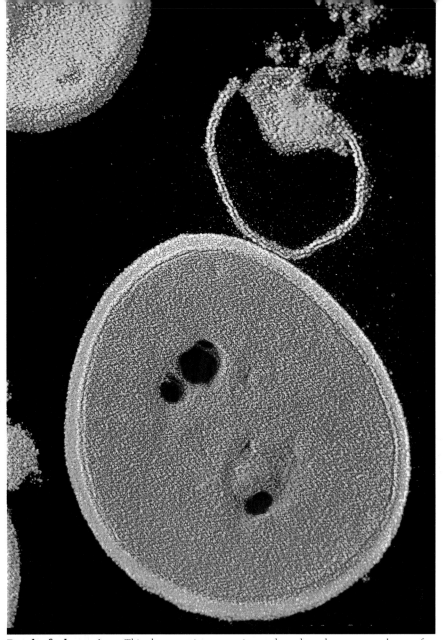

Death of a bacterium *This electron microscope picture shows how the outer membrane of a bacterium is destroyed (top right) by antibiotics, releasing its inner cellular structure. The larger bacterium (centre) is still complete and unaffected by antibiotics.*

later they produced the first penicillin antibiotic. Their first patient was a policeman who had a severe bacterial infection of the head, face and lungs. His recovery was astoundingly fast – after only five days of treatment his condition improved immensely. But not enough of the antibiotic had been produced to sustain the treatment, and a month later he died.

In 1940, when the invasion of Britain by Germany was a worrying possibility, Florey and Chain smeared some of the *Penicillium* culture onto the inside of their coats, so that if they were forced to move, either of them could carry on their research elsewhere.

The Second World War gave impetus to the large-scale production of the drug, but lack of money in the United Kingdom meant that penicillin had to be manufactured in the United States. By 1943 there

was enough available to treat war casualties, and by 1950 there was sufficient to meet worldwide demand. Among the diseases it was used to treat successfully were pneumonia, diphtheria, syphilis and meningitis.

There is now a wide range of antibiotics, and they are still increasing – even in the late 1980s, synthetic antibiotics known as quinolones were being introduced to treat infections of the chest and bladder. These antibiotics have the added benefit that bacteria do not seem to be able to develop resistance to them.

Antibiotics work by killing bacteria in a sick person's body. Infections take hold on the body only if the bacteria that cause them are allowed to reproduce. It is the mass reproduction of bacteria that causes the symptoms of the infection.

Penicillin interferes with the structure of

bacterial cell walls as the bacteria are being reproduced, so that the cell contents leak out and the bacteria die.

Other antibiotics poison the parts of the bacteria that make the proteins they need in order to reproduce. Yet other types of antibiotics interfere with the genetic codes in the bacteria that allow them to multiply. Scientists who produce new strains of the drugs must ensure that the antibiotics do not harm the body's cells as well as bacterial cells. If they do, the patient suffers side effects such as diarrhoea or dizziness. And, although antibiotics are designed to be selective in the bacteria they kill, some also kill useful bacteria that the body needs to keep harmful microorganisms at bay. Consequently, a secondary infection can set in. For example, penicillin frequently kills the bacteria that ward off the yeast *Candida*, which causes thrush, a disorder of the mouth, vagina or skin.

But the most worrying problem scientists have is that bacteria evolve continually and develop new ways to combat attempts to stop them from multiplying. The bacteria responsible for wound infections and sexually transmitted diseases, for example, repeatedly develop resistance to antibiotics. So the search for newer and better antibiotics will never stop.

How do doctors perform microsurgery?

On Christmas Eve in 1986, Beatrice Ramos threw herself and her 13-month-old son, Vladimir, under a subway train in New York. Both were badly hurt. Vladimir's right foot and left leg were injured beyond repair. But to spare him from having two false limbs, surgeons at Bellevue Hospital performed a pioneering operation in which they attached his left foot to his right leg.

Only ten years earlier, such an operation would have been thought impossible. Now, operations to save limbs are much more common.

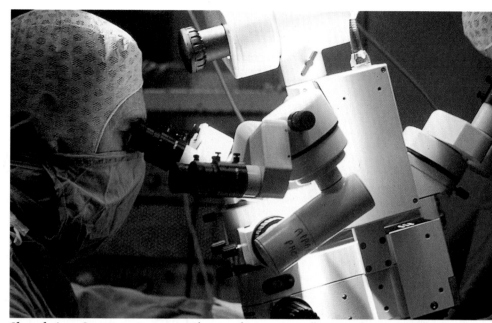

Shared view *Operating microscopes with two or three eyepieces allow more than one surgeon simultaneous views of the areas to be operated upon. Because restoring severed nerve fibres and tiny blood vessels takes hours, doctors work in relay teams.*

Microsurgery involves working on the tiniest structures in the human body, such as nerve fibres, veins and fine arteries. When sewing back a severed part of the body, it is not sufficient simply to sew it on. Without connecting blood vessels the part would die from lack of oxygen, and if the nerves were not connected, it would have no nervous stimulation and would be useless.

Since the structures involved are so fine – an artery in a finger is about ⅟₁₆in (1-2mm) wide and a nerve fibre varies from .002mm to .02mm – microsurgery is possible only with high-powered microscopes. These instruments have a magnification from × 6 to × 40, allowing surgeons to see the tiny structures that need joining up. Microscopes with two or three heads have been developed, which allow more than one surgeon to work at the same time.

When stitching nerves, surgeons have to make sure that they join matching bundles. They are usually identified before surgery.

The surgeon works with a needle which is only 50 microns (.05mm) thick, with 18 micron (nearly .02mm) nylon thread.

When stitching two blood vessels together, a surgeon normally uses a method known as triangulation. Three stitches are made 120 degrees apart at the end of the blood vessels, and then the surgeon sews all the way around their circumference, a third at a time.

It can take 15 to 30 minutes to stitch one vein to another. Stitching back a hand can take 19 hours.

Sometimes blood vessels can be joined together without intricate sewing. By using electrical probes to heat up the severed ends the surgeons can literally weld them together.

After surgery, physiotherapy is essential to restore the replanted limb to working order. For a replanted hand it takes about 200 days for the nerve and blood vessel tissues to regenerate. It takes longer, however, for the part to function normally.

Apart from repairing injuries, microsurgical techniques can be used for a host of other problems. Eye operations, for example, involve microsurgery. An eye operation called 'radial keratotomy', which was pioneered by Russian surgeons, can sometimes cure short sight. The surgeon makes a number of slits radiating from the centre of the cornea, the surface of the eye. The cuts change the shape of the cornea, which alters the distance between the front of the eye and the retina, bringing objects into focus which previously were not.

Brain surgeons use operating microscopes to place their instruments with much greater precision, so improving the chances of success in removing tumours. The microscopes enable surgeons to remove the tumour without cutting away any normal brain tissue.

Precision work *The ultra-fine, curved needle that surgeons use for microsurgery is slightly thinner than the two human hairs in the photograph. The thread, which is attached to the needle, is much finer than hair.*

Marie Curie: miracle in a store-shed

For more than four exhausting years, the Polish-born chemist Marie Curie and her husband, Pierre, worked in a large dilapidated wooden shed near their Paris lodgings. It was there – late on a September night in 1902 – that they finally discovered the radioactive element which they named 'radium' – from the Latin word *radius*, meaning 'a ray'.

Radium provided the first effective treatment for some types of cancer, destroying the diseased human cells by bombarding them with radioactive particles.

Honoured *Marie Curie, winner of two Nobel prizes.*

The Curies had spent the historic day pouring measures of purified pitchblende into the last of some 6000 evaporating bowls. Marie Curie believed that the black mineral ore contained a completely new and dynamic element whose rays could destroy unhealthy body tissue. By constantly filtering and re-filtering the pitchblende, she hoped that the elusive element would become crystallised in the bowls.

When they went home that evening the miracle still had not occurred. Then, just as they were about to go to bed, Marie decided to have another look at the particles in the bowls. She and Pierre hurried through the dimly lit streets.

They let themselves into the darkened shed – with its rows of wooden tables and clutter of laboratory equipment – and Marie asked Pierre not to light the lamps. They moved cautiously forward and there, all around them, rays of light came from inside the small, glass-covered bowls. Marie turned to her husband and said quietly, 'Do you remember the day when you said to me: "I should like radium to have a beautiful colour"? Look ... Look!'

The bowls which lined the tables and the shelves on the walls gave off a soft, bluish-purple glow. Too moved to speak, Marie watched the unwavering rays. 'She was to remember for ever this evening of glow-worms, this magic', wrote her daughter Eve Curie afterwards.

The Curies had met in 1894 when Marie – who was born Manya Sklodowska in Warsaw on November 7, 1867 – was studying at the Sorbonne in Paris. She had little money to spend on food, and on one occasion she fainted from weakness in the lecture hall. Even so, she passed top of her class with honours in physics and mathematics.

Unable to afford a laboratory of her own, she was invited by Pierre – a respected but impoverished scientist at the School of Physics and Chemistry – to share his workshop with him. They were married in July 1895, and so began their short but fruitful scientific collaboration.

They were inspired by the work of the eminent French physicist Henri Becquerel, who in 1896 discovered rays of an unknown kind which were spontaneously emitted from uranium.

Marie became fascinated by the emission of similar rays from pitchblende, which were four times stronger than those given off by the uranium it contained. She felt

The happiest years *Marie Curie and her husband Pierre conducting an experiment in their makeshift laboratory. They converted it from a derelict shed (above), which was dominated by a blackened cast-iron stove with a rusty pipe. 'It was in this miserable old shed that the best and happiest years of our life were spent, devoted entirely to work', she recorded.*

Measuring implement *Among the Curies' equipment was this complex metal-and-wood device for measuring radioactive intensities.*

they could only be explained by the presence in the ore of a hitherto unknown substance which she determined to discover.

Through Pierre's influence, she was given the use of an abandoned store-shed at the school. It had a leaky skylight and an earth floor.

'We had no money, no proper laboratory and no help in the conduct of our important and difficult task,' she wrote later. 'It was like creating something out of nothing. I sometimes passed the entire day stirring a boiling mass, with an iron rod nearly as big as myself. In the evening I was broken with fatigue.'

During the Curies' years of research they had noted how the pitchblende – which consists mostly of radioactive uranium oxide – burned Marie's fingers, causing red and irritating sores. Slowly the sores healed, which made Marie think that if the radiation could destroy healthy cells with-

out any lasting ill effects perhaps it could be used to eradicate malignant cells.

In 1898 she announced that spontaneous rays, which she described as 'radioactive' – that is, emitting atomic radiation – also came from the metal thorium. She felt that she was on the track of the elusive radioactive element in pitchblende. To have escaped scientific detection for so long it must exist in extremely small quantities – probably no more than a millionth part of the ore itself.

Much of Europe's pitchblende came from the St Joachimsthal mines in western Czechoslovakia, where the uranium salts extracted from it were used in the making of glass. The residue was dumped in a nearby pine forest – and, with the help of the Austrian government, a ton of the residue was sent to the Curies by rail.

The hardest task of all was now before them: refining the ore into its various elements. Pierre conducted the delicate laboratory work of studying the radioactive substances, which included uranium and polonium (which Marie had discovered earlier that year and had named after her native Poland). Meanwhile, wearing an acid-stained, dust-covered smock, Marie toiled in the yard, stirring large pots of pitchblende and ensuring that the fires beneath them were kept alight day and night.

The work continued non-stop for another four years – until success finally came on that autumn night in 1902, when Marie first saw her 'magical, blue glow-worms'.

Once the radium had been successfully isolated, Pierre deliberately exposed his arm to the rays. To his scientific delight, a burn appeared. Almost eight weeks later

the burn was no more than a tiny grey mark – and he then repeated the experiment on animals. The radium acted in the same way and he, too, was convinced that by destroying diseased cells the powerful rays could cure cancerous growths.

In 1903 the Curies shared the Nobel prize for Physics for the discovery of radioactivity with Henri Becquerel. Two years later, radium was a standard commercial product as a weapon against cancer and was being manufactured in factories across Europe. The Curies stood to make a fortune from their discovery, but Marie resolutely refused to patent it.

'If our discovery has a commercial future,' she stated, 'that is an accident by which we must not profit. Radium is going to be of use in treating disease. It seems to me impossible to take advantage of that.'

But the Curies' partnership did not last for much longer. In April 1906, Pierre was knocked down and killed by a horse-drawn wagon in Paris.

Five years later Marie was awarded the Nobel prize for Chemistry for the discovery of radium and polonium and the isolation of pure radium. She died on July 4, 1934 – partly as a result of her long exposure to radiation.

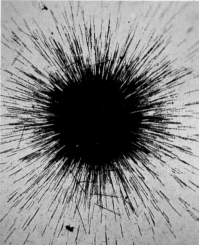

Radium rays *A dramatic example of radium's radioactivity. A speck of radium salt was placed on an emulsion on a photographic plate. When developed, the emulsion showed the dark track of atomic particles emitted by the radium.*

Separating radium *Until their discovery of radium in 1902, the Curies worked alone in their shed – with Marie doing her full share of 'man's work'. Later, however, she employed male assistants for the arduous job of separating radium from pitchblende contained in large, brick-built vats.*

How surgeons do bloodless operations with just a beam of light

Beaming into the inner ear
Looking through a microscope, a surgeon directs an argon laser beam into a human ear (above). The beam drills through the bones of the inner ear (left) to counteract an abnormal growth of bone which is preventing sound waves from reaching the inner ear.

Until laser surgery was invented in 1963, someone with a growth, a cancer or a cataract, needed a major operation to have it removed. Now, laser beams can be used in 'bloodless' operations to remove growths and even repair tissues, without cutting, less painfully and more safely.

In laser surgery to remove a growth from the throat, for example, a small tube, or endoscope, is passed down the patient's throat, under local anaesthetic. A laser beam is directed down the tube along an optical fibre and is focused on the growth. All laser surgery works on this principle of passing light down an optical fibre. The beam is a form of light which carries a great deal of energy. The energy is absorbed by the tissues of the growth, or the skin tissues to be removed, which become hot. By controlling the heat intensity, doctors can burn off – literally vaporise – unwanted cells.

In this way, laser beams are used to cut away cancers, vaporise the dyes in tattoos or get rid of birthmarks.

Another use of laser beams is to heat tissues sufficiently to 'weld' them together – to stop blood vessels bleeding, for example. The operation might be performed on a patient who is bleeding from a stomach ulcer.

The wavelength of the laser beam affects the way in which tissues respond to it. Lasers that use carbon dioxide produce beams of light which are absorbed by tissues at a depth of only 0.1mm. This means that they can be used to make fine cuts in tissue, as a sort of 'laser scalpel'. Such precision cutting might be used when making incisions in the cornea of the eye to correct defects in sight, or in removing throat tumours.

Lasers using a metal-based chemical called neodymium produce light which is absorbed by a greater depth of tissue, making it useful to destroy cancers.

Those lasers that use the gas argon produce a distinctive blue-green light, which is absorbed by haemoglobin – the chemical in the blood that gives it its red colouring. Argon beams can therefore be used where haemoglobin levels are high, as in birthmarks.

A further benefit of laser beams is that they allow doctors to reach areas of the body previously hard to get at with a scalpel and to perform operations that were impossible before: to rid arteries of blockages of fatty deposits; to sew back detached retinas; to cut a hole through a cataract in a lens and so restore vision; and to cure cancer of the cervix.

How do anaesthetics numb pain?

Less than 150 years ago, surgery was performed without any anaesthetic. A patient was held down by strong men as he battled to escape from the pain of the surgeon's knife. Surgeons even resorted to stupefying their patients with alcohol, knocking them unconscious, or freezing the part to be operated on with ice.

The first time an anaesthetic was used was on March 30, 1842, in Jefferson, Georgia, USA, when Dr Crawford Long removed a tumour from the neck of James Venable, who first inhaled ether. But it was only following William Morton's public demonstration in Boston of the extraction of a tooth under ether, in 1846, that ether became widely adopted as an anaesthetic.

At around the same time in the United States, nitrous oxide, also known as laughing gas and used as a music hall entertainment, was being inhaled as an anaesthetic for dental surgery. In Britain, research was being done on the uses of chloroform, particularly to relieve the pain of childbirth.

Without these early attempts at the use of anaesthetics, many of today's surgical procedures would not be possible. Now, major operations, such as heart transplants, cosmetic surgery and removal of cancer, are possible without pain. But just how do anaesthetics allow people to slip off into a world where pain does not exist?

Anaesthesia derives from the Greek

word for 'lack of feeling'. All anaesthetics induce this condition by blocking the pathway of pain signals to the brain. However, how they actually work is not yet fully understood.

Anaesthetics take two forms – general, which put the patient 'to sleep', and local, which affect only part of the body.

Loss of sensation, or analgesia, may be provided by nitrous oxide, but this does not put the patient to sleep. It may cause mental or physical excitement. Sleep is usually induced by an injected barbiturate. The muscles are then relaxed with a neuro-blocker, or muscle relaxant, such as curare.

During surgery, the patient is watched carefully, so that any changes in circulation, breathing or kidney function which may result from the anaesthetic can be regulated.

Local anaesthetics are given as an injection to remove all sensation from a localised area. The patient is conscious and can cooperate with the surgeon.

There are three principal uses of local anaesthetic. Topical anaesthetics remove the sensation from nerve endings in mucous membranes such as those in the eye, the nose and the mouth. They are used, for example, to remove a foreign object from the eye. Nerve-block anaesthetics are injected into a nerve to anaesthetise a small area, for example, to enable a tooth to be extracted. Other anaesthetics are injected into a large nerve group to numb a larger part of the body, such as an arm.

Atoms that transmit pain

A clue to the way general anaesthetics work comes from research into local anaesthetics. These are known to interfere with the way nerve impulses are transmitted along the nerve fibres. Sodium and potassium atoms play an important part in sending these impulses to the brain. If you stub your toe, for example, the sodium and potassium atoms pass in opposite directions across the membrane of the nerve cell causing the next cell to do the same and so on until the signal reaches the brain, when you feel pain. But local anaesthetics stop the atoms from passing in and out of the nerve cell, so no pain signal reaches the spinal cord.

Scientists think that general anaesthetics may cause unconsciousness by suppressing the activity of certain enzymes in the nerve cells, or changing the properties of the nerve-cell membranes, or even by interacting with water molecules in the brain to form small crystals which affect the path of a signal along a nerve cell.

Research continues into the exact mechanism, but what is certain is that without anaesthetics a great deal of surgery could never be performed.

How a pacemaker helps a heart patient to lead a normal life

The human heart beats 3000 million times in an average lifetime, pumping the equivalent of 48 million gallons (218 million litres) of blood around the body.

The regular rhythm – on average, 72 beats each minute – is controlled by the sino-atrial node, a tiny rounded organ located in the top left corner inside the heart. This is the heart's natural pacemaker, which sends electrical impulses to the heart's tissues. The heart contracts and expands in response to these impulses, producing the heartbeat.

Occasionally, the heart's electrical conducting system can be disturbed by illness, such as angina or a heart attack. Sometimes it just fails completely. If this happens, the heart can be stimulated electrically to continue beating regularly.

If the heart stops it can sometimes be restarted with an electrical shock from a machine called a defibrillator. If the normal beat does not resume immediately, sometimes a temporary pacemaker can be fitted outside the body – it is usually strapped to the waist. For those suffering from other irregularities of the heart beat a pacemaker is surgically placed inside the body, implanted in the chest.

All pacemakers, inside and outside the body, work in the same way. An electrode on the end of a wire, called the pacing lead, is attached to the wall of the heart's right ventricle (chamber), either directly

The heart's little helper
An X-ray of a patient's chest reveals the pacing box and lead of a pacemaker fixed in position near the heart (right). Made of lightweight titanium, a heart pacemaker is small enough to fit into the palm of a hand (below). The battery may last for as long as 12 years.

through the chest, or threaded through a vein. The electrode is powered by the pacing box, a miniature generator operated by lithium batteries. Modern pacemaker batteries last at least five years, and some last up to 12 years.

Powered by the pacing box, the electrode produces electrical impulses which stimulate the sino-atrial node and make the heart beat. The pacing box is set to maintain the intervals of the impulses at a given rate, usually one beat per second, which is a little slower than the average heart rate. However, the box functions only when the heart is not producing its own electrical impulses at the correct intervals. It is sensitive enough to detect these delays and by filling in the gaps, maintains a normal rhythm. Some models include a radio transmitter and receiver, which means that a doctor can adjust the rate of the pacemaker from outside the patient's body.

The first successful pacemakers were

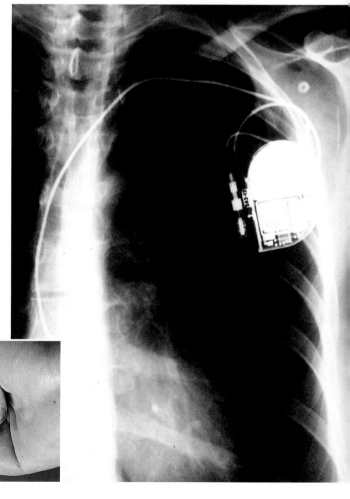

used by Dr Walter Lillehei, a cardiac specialist at the University of Minnesota, USA, in the late 1950s. They consisted of an electrode on a wire fed to the heart through the chest and attached to a battery pack strapped around the waist. The pack was about the size of a cigarette packet. Although the system was convenient because no surgery was needed to replace the batteries, the opening in the chest for the wire repeatedly became infected. External pacemakers are now used for temporary heart problems only, or until an internal pacemaker can be fitted.

The pacing box of the most commonly used internal pacemaker is about the size of a matchbox and weighs about 1oz (25g). It is usually made of lightweight titanium.

The box is implanted in the body, usually just inside the skin of the chest wall. It must be in the best position for threading the tube through the large vein to the heart and attaching the electrode, which is the size of a match head, to the heart wall. The body does not reject it because it is not living material.

The implanting operation is done while the patient is under general anaesthetic, but surgery to replace the batteries can usually be done with only a local anaesthetic.

A person wearing a pacemaker needs to be examined by a doctor frequently to make sure that it is functioning properly. Also, some wearers have to take care that their pacemakers are not affected by certain electrical circuits, such as magnetic detectors in airports or libraries.

New electronic technology may produce even smaller pacemakers which can be attached to the heart wall, eliminating wires and large battery packs, although they are still powered by batteries.

Another development is the rate-responsive pacemaker, which is sensitive to the patient's activity. Instead of providing an impulse once a second, it will increase the impulses when he is active and slow them down when he is resting – like the heart's natural pacemaker.

Since the first successful pacemaker was developed, more than 5 million people with serious heart disease have been helped to live more comfortable and active lives.

Spare-part surgery: how surgeons transplant organs

History was made on June 17, 1950, at the Little Company of Mary Hospital, Chicago, when the first successful organ transplant operation was performed by Dr Richard H. Lawler. The organ was a kidney and the patient was Ruth Tucker, aged 49. The donor, a woman of the same blood type, age and general physical characteristics as Mrs Tucker, had died moments before of a chronic ailment. Ruth Tucker died five years afterwards from a coronary thrombosis. More than a decade later in the Groote Schuur Hospital in Cape Town, South Africa, on December 3, 1967, Dr Christiaan Barnard carried out the world's first human heart transplant (page 296).

Now, kidney and heart transplants are so commonplace that they rarely attract more than local attention. They have been so successful that many other organs are also being replaced, including the liver, the lungs, the pancreas and the cornea. Even bone marrow is being transplanted, to combat diseases such as leukaemia, and portions of brain tissue are being grafted for the treatment of rare conditions such as Parkinson's disease.

Removing a living organ from one person and placing it in another is fraught with difficulties. The first problem to overcome is the rejection of alien tissues by the person receiving the transplant. The body's immune system attacks anything 'foreign' that is introduced into the bloodstream. This includes tissues as well as bacteria and viruses. White blood cells surround the foreign tissues and prevent them from functioning. If the body's defence system attacks, or rejects, the tissues of an organ, the organ dies.

To reduce the problem, organs are obtained from 'matched' donors – people with the same tissue type as the patient. The organs of matched donors have chemical properties so similar to those of the recipient that the recipient's defence system is foiled into believing that the organ is not foreign.

Donated organs must be healthy and preferably young. Surgeons rely on the relatives of a dead person giving permission for the removal and transplantation of the deceased's organs.

The list of patients who need transplants is now computerised. The computer records details of their tissues as well, so that when a donor becomes available – often following a fatal accident – the details can be matched by the computer.

In the Netherlands there is a central computer called Eurotransplant. It covers the whole of Europe, including the UK, and is run jointly by various health agencies. When a person dies who has agreed to be a donor, his or her tissue details are sent immediately to the computer. It then locates a suitable recipient and the transplant teams go into action.

The first job is to remove the organ from the dead donor as soon as possible; it becomes unusable after 30 minutes. Surgeons remove the organ and pump fluid through it to keep the blood vessels open and prevent clots from forming. The organ is then put into a polythene bag packed with ice, and placed in cold storage at 41°F (5°C) to keep it fresh.

Meanwhile, the computer selects a recipient who is contacted and told to attend his or her hospital immediately. The donor organ has to be transplanted as soon as possible because it will survive only a few hours, even in cold storage. A heart can be kept for three to five hours, a liver for ten, and a kidney for 24 to 48 hours.

Once the recipient is in the operating theatre, the surgeons remove the diseased organ in preparation for transplanting the new one. Transplant operations take a number of hours to perform. Even the simplest take at least four hours.

Corneal replacements are among the easiest transplant operations. They are performed to repair damage to the surface of the eye and restore sight. They are relatively free of complications because the cornea has no blood, so is not affected by

TRANSPLANTING A HEART

When a heart becomes available, a suitable recipient is quickly located and told to get to the hospital immediately. At the same time, a combination of police, ambulance and helicopters race the donated organ to the hospital. A heart may travel hundreds of miles from donor to recipient, sometimes across international boundaries. But to save time, the European computerised system, Eurotransplant, tries to locate recipients who live as close to the donor as possible.

To prepare a patient for a heart transplant, the surgeon cuts into the chest and ties off the blood vessels leading to and from the recipient's heart. The recipient's blood supply is then redirected through the heart-lung machine, which replaces the function of the patient's own heart and lungs.

The faulty heart is taken out, and the new organ is placed in the space. The new heart is then connected to the major veins and arteries before the recipient's blood is diverted through the new organ. The surgeon then sews up the chest and the operation is complete.

Transformation *In 1988, the 56-year-old British actress and journalist Molly Parkin entered a Harley Street clinic for cosmetic surgery to revive her ageing skin. Three days later, after blepharoplasty and a brow, neck, and face-lift, she was transformed (right). The loose skin of her eyelids, and the bags under her eyes, had gone. Her upper lip had been given more fullness with a skin graft, and the fat on her jaw had been removed by suction, making the jawline more defined.*

the body's defence system. Also, corneal tissues can be stored in tissue banks for longer than most other tissues.

Once a transplant operation is over, its success still depends on the accuracy of the tissue matching. Even if the match is exact, the body's defence system may still reject the donated organ. To prevent this, drugs which lower the effectiveness of the defence system are used. However, they can also make transplant patients more prone to infections. Some patients have to take anti-rejection drugs for the rest of their lives, so doctors monitor them carefully for signs of infection.

Despite the difficulties, transplant surgery has provided many people with a new lease of life. More than 70 per cent of liver-transplant patients live longer than a year; and 80 per cent of heart-transplant patients survive a year after their operations, whereas ten years earlier only 66 per cent lasted a year. Between 91 and 96 per cent of kidney and cornea transplants are successful.

The problem for surgeons is finding enough donor organs to meet the demand. They are already experimenting with transplants of animal organs, such as baboons' hearts and pigs' kidneys. But the main problem is that the human tissues reject the animal tissues.

Research is also being done into the use of synthetic organs. Apart from being easily available, they will eliminate the problems of storage and short life.

Face-lifts: how surgeons smooth away the wrinkles

As the skin ages, some of the subcutaneous or underlying fat which supports and pads it dissolves away. And one of the skin's main constituents, called collagen, loses its ability to retain moisture, making the skin less elastic and drier. The result is sagging skin and wrinkles.

Most people accept wrinkles as part of growing older. For others, particularly those in the public eye like entertainers and politicians, ageing skin can be a problem. The only answer is cosmetic surgery.

There is more to cosmetic surgery than a face-lift – which, as its name suggests, means pulling the skin up over the face. Its cosmetic effects are, for the most part, restricted mostly to the chin and neck. Wrinkles around the eyes, the side of the nose, and across the forehead have to be dealt with in separate operations, such as an eyebrow or forehead lift, or a nasal fold removal. In blepharoplasty, excess loose skin is removed from the upper and lower eyelids.

Minor nips and tucks are done under local anaesthetic, but a face-lift is a major

operation, and is usually done under general anaesthetic. The surgeon first makes an incision into the skin around each ear. He starts the cut well within the hairline above the ear, and continues it around the bottom of the ear and then up behind it. The cut is then taken horizontally towards the back of the head. Most of the cut is within the area covered by hair, so that the scars will be hidden.

Once the cuts are made, the surgeon carefully separates the skin below the line of the cut from the underlying fatty layer. He then pulls the loose skin towards the back of the head. The thin layer of muscle tissue in the neck is lifted and tightened. The excess skin is cut off and the incision sewn up.

It often takes two to three weeks to recover from the slight inflammation of the face caused by the operation. The scars, which can be camouflaged by make-up a week after the operation, fade in time.

No face-lift retards ageing permanently. The ageing process continues from the time of the operation at the normal rate. More face-lifts can be performed on the same person but there is always a limit, because each time the surgeon removes more skin. When the skin is stretched to its tightest limit without hindering normal functions, such as smiling, there is no excess available and further operations become impossible. Not all operations are a success and some people have been left with badly scarred faces.

Christiaan Barnard: the surgeon who performed the first heart transplant

The phone call that helped to make medical history came as Dr Christiaan Barnard was taking an after-dinner nap in his home in Cape Town, South Africa. The caller – a sister at the city's Groote Schuur Hospital – told him that a young woman, the victim of a road accident that day, had been brought in suffering from irreparable brain damage. If she died, then her heart could be used in the world's first heart transplant operation. She was the right blood group and her father was ready to give his permission.

'I always pray before any major operation,' Dr Barnard wrote later, '– usually in the car on the way to the hospital because I am alone then. And now, as I drove through the night, I felt more than ever the

need for it. Yet I could not pray. Each time I began, my thoughts broke in on me ...'

So far, he had only transplanted the hearts of laboratory dogs. Now – on Saturday, December 2, 1967 – he was about to transplant a heart from one human being to another. The donor was a 25-year-old woman, Denise Darvall, from Tamboers Kloof, Cape Town. The recipient was Louis Washkansky, a 53-year-old wholesale grocer in the city whose 'shattered and ruined' heart, as Barnard described it, would give him only a few more weeks of life at most.

Washkansky had already survived several heart attacks. However, he had difficulty in breathing, his kidneys and liver were beginning to fail, his legs were badly swollen, and he had diabetes.

He was not supposed to eat or drink anything sweet, yet he encouraged his wife, Ann, to smuggle in lemonade and cherries for him. He seemed more interested in reading cowboy novels and thrillers than in considering the circumstances of his case. But he showed his courage when Barnard told him of the possibility of saving his life. He shrugged and said, 'So they told me. So I'm ready to go ahead.'

By an uncanny coincidence, Mrs Washkansky had been driving home late that afternoon from visiting her husband when she saw a crowd of people gathered around a street accident. As the police waved her on, she noticed the covered body of a woman lying on the ground. Although she did not know it then, the body was that of Denise Darvall.

So, at around 9 o'clock that night,

The donor *Denise Darvall's heart gave new life to Louis Washkansky. She was knocked down by a car while shopping with her mother, and was fatally injured.*

The surgeon *Concerned but quietly confident, Dr Barnard gave Louis Washkansky's heart operation an 80 per cent chance of success.*

The patient *Louis Washkansky sits beside his wife Ann, elegant in jewellery and furs, at a smart social function in Cape Town.*

Dr Barnard – the man who had pioneered open-heart surgery in his native South Africa – stood looking down at the dark-haired Miss Darvall. Clinically speaking, she was no longer alive. Her heart, however, was still healthy and sound.

Barnard wasted no more time. An orderly began to shave the hair on Washkansky's chest, and one of the nurses brought in the hospital's heart-lung machine. The machine – which would take over from Washkansky's own heart and lungs to make the transplant possible – had been brought back from the USA by Dr Barnard after his surgical training at the University of Minnesota, in Minneapolis.

He showered, swabbed himself with antiseptic, scrubbed his hands, put antiseptic ointment up his nostrils, and donned a germ-free gown, cap and face mask – as well as sterile rubber boots. He entered the operating theatre, where Washkansky was sitting casually on the table, propped up by some pillows. He looked at the surgeon and – although he barely had the breath to talk – said jokingly, 'So it's out with the old and in with the new. Auld Lang Syne!'

A short while later Washkansky was under the anaesthetic, and at midnight the revolutionary operation began. Under Barnard's skilled direction, his chief assistant, Rodney Hewitson, cut open the patient's chest.

'Louis Washkansky's heart came into full view,' wrote Barnard later, 'rolling in a rhythm of its own like a separate and angry sea, yellow from the storms of half a century, yet streaked with blue currents from its depths – blue veins drifting across

the heaving waste and ruin of a ravaged heart. On the right, its purple atrium (chamber) slid back and forth with each contraction – struggling as would a monstrous fish tied to the shoreline of the yellow sea.'

Meanwhile, in another theatre just 31 paces away, Denise Darvall was being kept 'alive' by a respirator. Barnard hurried in there and switched the machine off. His fingers were already thickening with the arthritis that was to put a premature end to his work as a surgeon. But a short time later he cut into Denise's chest and removed her heart. He placed it into a basin of ice-cold salt solution and carried it into the main theatre – where it was linked to a small pump circulating blood from Washkansky's heart-lung machine.

Next, Barnard removed the bulk of Washkansky's oversized heart, leaving a flap to be sewn to the donor heart. The 'new' heart was then placed in Washkansky's empty chest and Barnard looked at it with awe. A woman's heart is usually 20 per cent smaller than a man's – and the cavity in Washkansky's chest was twice the normal size.

Using silk and two needles, he then began the delicate task of stitching the donor heart in place. The pump supplying the heart with blood was cut off – and almost at once the organ lost its healthy pink colour and started turning blue. As Barnard continued his needlework – stitching first one way, then the other – he glanced at the theatre clock. It was 5.30am and the heart had been denied blood or oxygen for 15 minutes. Four more minutes crawled by. The last suture was tied; the

blood was allowed to return; and the heart began to twitch.

To start it beating, a powerful electrical charge was passed through two discs cupped around the heart. Washkansky's unconscious body twitched convulsively and, as Barnard and his 20-strong medical team looked anxiously on, the heart began to steadily pulsate. The heart-lung machine was withdrawn and, more than eight hours after the operation had begun, Washkansky – his body bristling with 18 essential lifelines connected to a variety of monitoring instruments and machines – was wheeled into his sterilised room and placed under a plastic tent.

Now started the fight against post-operative infection and the body's rejection of its new heart – which it regarded as an alien object which must be destroyed. Washkansky was given anti-rejection drugs and, once the initial danger period was over, he enjoyed five wonderful days of good health.

Then on December 15, 12 days after his operation, an X-ray showed that he had a shadow on the lung. His wife had already noticed that he seemed to have a slight cold; in fact, double pneumonia had set in. Ironically, the anti-rejection drugs he was taking had weakened his body's immune system and he was helpless against the germs which invaded and inflamed his lungs.

Despite everything that Barnard and his colleagues could do, Louis Washkansky died of pneumonia shortly after dawn on December 21. His new heart – implanted in him 18 days before – worked perfectly up to the end.

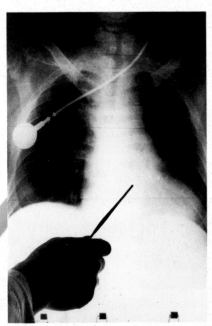

Safely in place *The first X-ray photograph of Louis Washkansky's new heart. The pointer indicates the heart.*

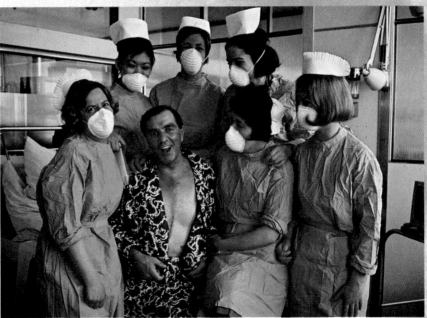

High hopes *Jubilant and optimistic, Louis Washkansky is surrounded by delighted nurses after his operation. He said he had never felt better or happier in his life, and spoke hopefully of spending Christmas at home with his family. However, 18 days after his operation, he died of pneumonia.*

How do artificial kidneys work?

Toxic wastes produced by the breakdown of food in the body are normally removed by the kidneys. The kidneys also regulate the body's fluid and salt content. If they go wrong, the poisonous wastes accumulate in the blood and fluid builds up, which eventually causes uraemia, a disease which kills thousands of people each year.

Kidneys can sometimes fail without warning, but more common is 'chronic kidney failure', in which the kidneys deteriorate gradually. The only ways of dealing with kidney failure are either to transplant a healthy kidney (page 294) or to remove the waste products artificially.

Waste removal is done by a dialysis machine which acts as an artificial kidney, filtering the wastes out of the blood. The process is often performed at home by patients trained to use the machine. One method, haemodialysis, involves inserting two needles into the patient's arm or leg – one in an artery, the other in a vein. Each needle is connected by a piece of tubing to the dialysis machine.

Blood flows from the patient's artery into the machine, where it is mixed with a drug called heparin to stop it from clotting. It is then passed through a semipermeable coiled Cellophane tube, which is immersed in a warm chemical bath. The perforations in the Cellophane are large enough for the small molecules of waste to filter through them, but the blood cells, which are larger, remain inside the tube. Once the waste products have been filtered out, the cleansed blood is mixed with an agent which counteracts the heparin and is pumped back into the patient through the needle in the vein.

Three sessions a week

Someone who requires this mechanical form of waste removal has to undergo three eight-hour sessions a week, connected to the machine.

Another filtering system, called peritoneal dialysis, does not require the machinery used in haemodialysis. The peritoneum is a large protective sac of flexible tissue, surrounding the abdominal organs. These organs have a plentiful blood supply, and being close to them the peritoneum is well situated to act as a filter for unwanted molecules.

In peritoneal dialysis, the patient has a small piece of tubing inserted through the abdominal wall into his or her peritoneum. A special liquid known as dialysing fluid is then poured into the abdominal cavity via the tube. The fluid attracts the waste products from the blood in the abdominal organs, and is then sucked out. The whole process takes up to 12 hours and is performed two or four times a week.

The type of dialysis that patients receive depends on a number of factors, including age, the availability of machines, and their ability to insert needles into themselves. In some countries, the cost of machines is also a consideration.

How doctors can sometimes cure baldness

More than 90 per cent of men succumb to some degree of baldness. And some women, particularly after the menopause, also find that their hair thins and recedes. The problem is entirely genetic – bald fathers have sons who are likely to become bald. And it doesn't just affect humans either: monkeys become bald as well.

The exact genetic code that causes baldness and thinning still eludes researchers, but they know it has something to do with male sex hormones called androgens. These hormones suppress the activity of certain hair follicles on the scalp, so that the life span of the hair that grows from them is reduced. Normally, a hair allowed to grow uncut will last from two to six years. But as baldness sets in, the hair in some areas of the head falls out more often. The overall effect is that the hair in those places gets thinner and shorter, until it is reduced to fuzz.

Men have more androgen than women, which is why more men than women suffer from baldness.

One solution to baldness is a 'scalp transplant', which is carried out by a cosmetic surgeon. But only some people are suitable. Their baldness should be stable, that is, not getting worse each year, and should occur mainly at the front and top of the scalp. The remaining hair needs to be dark to hide the effects of the surgery. It also needs to be healthy and abundant because it is this hair that will be transplanted. In hair transplant surgery there are no donors, the patient's existing hair is simply redistributed.

First the patient's hair is trimmed closely. Then, usually under local anaesthetic, circular sections of scalp are removed from the side or back of the head. These sections are ⁵⁄₃₂in (4mm) in diameter and contain from 12 to 18 hair roots. Each section is removed with a hole punch device, from as wide an area of hairy scalp as possible, so that the gaps that are created will be covered by existing hair. The sections are then punched into the bald area of the head using the same instrument.

The number of circular sections required varies, depending on the baldness. In the worst cases, more than 250 are needed.

The time taken for the operation depends on how much hair is being transplanted. Usually, several sessions are necessary, because only up to 20 grafts are made at a time. This process takes from one to one and a half hours.

The holes left where the scalp has been removed take about two weeks to heal, and shrink in the process. Overlying hair soon disguises them.

The sections of implanted scalp lose their hair after the operation and it does not start regrowing for about three to six months. It can take a further year or so before the bald area is covered with hair. In time, however, the transplanted follicles may also be affected by androgen, so the transplant is not necessarily permanent.

How people survive a bolt of lightning

An American park ranger, Roy Sullivan, who lived in Virginia, was reputedly struck by lightning more times than anyone else in the world. He was first hit in 1942, and received his seventh strike on June 25, 1977. On each occasion Sullivan was injured. He first lost a toenail, then had his eyebrows burnt off, his shoulder was seared, his hair was set alight and his legs were burnt. But he survived.

Lightning can travel between 100 and 1000 miles per second (160 to 1600km per second), and the temperature it generates can reach 54,000°F (30,000°C), six times hotter than the surface of the sun. So what is remarkable is that many people hit by this awesome force do not die, although they are usually burnt quite badly.

Lightning is a spark of electricity caused by the difference in energy between the clouds and the surrounding air or the ground. In cloud-to-ground lightning the energy seeks the shortest route to earth, which may be a person out in the open.

This shortest route could be through the shoulder, down one side of the body, through the leg and into the ground. On the way it will cause pain, shock and burns, but the bulk of its energy is discharged into the ground. As long as the lightning does not pass across the heart or spinal column, the victim will probably not die. But if the force crosses the heart, there is a great risk that it might be damaged, or stop, resulting in instant death.

Building things up
and knocking them down

*Massive dams, bridges across wide estuaries and
tunnels beneath the sea – all are modern miracles of construction.
Just as dramatic is the demolition of skyscrapers and nuclear
power stations when they reach the end of their lives.*

*How a giant bridge is
built, page 306.*

How great rivers are dammed, page 308.

*How demolition experts blow up
skyscrapers, page 304.*

How did they build a skyscraper in the middle of a city?

The 47-storey Hong Kong and Shanghai Bank was built in one of the world's most crowded cities. Twenty-storey skyscrapers and one of Hong Kong's most historic buildings – the Courts of Justice – flanked the site.

Conditions for high-rise building vary from city to city, dependent on terrain, prevailing local weather conditions and existing underground service systems, such as sewers and power lines.

In Hong Kong's case, the new bank had to be built on reclaimed foreshore land that is soft and waterlogged. But if the whole area had been drained it would have caused severe subsidence and the surrounding buildings and roads would have collapsed.

The bank was built on a site that comprised 100ft (30m) of waterlogged rubble and fill covering the solid bedrock.

A way had to be found to drain the ground beneath, without disturbing ground water in the surrounding area.

Even if adjacent buildings settled by as little as 2in (50mm), large cracks would have appeared in plasterwork and serious structural damage would probably have resulted. How did the structural engineers, Ove Arup, put up such an enormous building without causing any damage?

Digging a huge waterproof pit

First, the space that the bank's basement would occupy had to be made waterproof by huge concrete walls, penetrating down to the solid bedrock. Because the ground was so soft, the walls had to be built section by section.

A clamshell grab (a large dredging bucket made of two hinged jaws) was used to dig a short, narrow trench, just wide enough for it to operate in. During the excavation the trench was kept full of a heavy clay slurry to prevent it caving in.

A special sort of clay, bentonite, which stays liquid when it is stirred, was used. If it is allowed to stand it thickens. The slurry was circulated continuously, but any clay that became stagnant in nooks and crannies helped to strengthen the trench walls.

The grab was laboriously hauled up with its load of rubble through the slurry, emptied and then plunged back down, until the trench had reached a maximum depth of 118ft (36m). Then a pipe was lowered to the bottom of the trench, and concrete was poured down it. The concrete displaced the slurry from the bottom of the trench upwards.

More trenches were dug and filled until the area was completely enclosed with an enormous underground concrete wall the height of a 12-storey building.

To prevent any seepage of ground water, the walls were sealed to the granite bedrock with wet cement. With the walls completed, the area, which is about 67yds (61m) square, was completely sealed off.

Building the basement – downwards

The four-level basement could then be built to house the vaults and safe deposits. To support the top of the underground walls when the earth was removed from inside them, the basement was built from the top downwards. The concrete floor of the storey immediately beneath street level was built first. Openings were left in the floor so that mechanical diggers and workmen could excavate and build the next floor down. This process was repeated until the bottom floor was finished.

Even with these careful precautions, some ground movement was inevitable. Two 20-storey buildings, the Bank of China and the Chartered Bank Building, were only 33ft (10m) from the new building. Both settled ½in (13mm) and tilted very slightly towards the excavation site, but there was no sign of any damage.

Above ground, the building is supported by eight giant steel columns each consisting of four steel tubes, linked at each storey level by beams. To support each column, four wells were sunk in the bedrock below the basement and filled with concrete. The wells were about 10ft (3m) wide and were

High rise *In heavily populated cities like Hong Kong the only way to build is up. But local conditions such as climate, terrain and below-surface utilities vary wherever new buildings are planned.*

blasted 16½ft (5m) down into solid granite. Much of the work was done by Chinese families, the men digging by hand in the bottom of the well and the women operating the electric hoists that took away the rubble.

Putting up the superstructure

The building rises to 590ft (180m) above ground level. The eight steel columns each weighed over 1000 tons. They were made up of sections called 'Christmas trees' using steel 4in (100mm) thick. They consisted of segments of the four tubes, 25½ft (7.8m) tall, linked by four crossbeams. Fifty Chinese workmen were specially trained to weld them together – gradually building up the columns. The Christmas trees were protected by a rubber-cement mixture to prevent corrosion and a ceramic fibre blanket to protect them against fire. According to local custom, they were given an extra form of protection – joss sticks were burnt around them to ensure the building's good fortune. Finally they were sealed in a thin aluminium casing for visual appeal.

All the floors of the building are suspended from giant beams stretching between the columns at five levels. Each beam consists of twin triangular frames covering a depth of two storeys. Each one has 'hangers' to which the floors are attached.

While the columns were being erected, the floors were already being built – supported by temporary props. This saved valuable time. As soon as the beams were in place, the hangers were attached to the completed floors and the props were moved up to support the construction of another floor.

Most of the bank's external walls are taken up by large windows made from ½in (13mm) thick tempered glass. The rest of the building is clad in aluminium panels.

Sections from around the world

After four years of building, the bank was completed in 1985. To speed up construction and minimise any inconvenience to people working in offices near the site, a great deal of the building was prefabricated.

In a triumph of international coordination, completed parts of the building were shipped in from all over the world. The Christmas trees were made at Ravenscraig in Scotland, the windows were made in Austria and the cladding for the exterior walls came from the USA. Other components came from West Germany and self-contained modules of air-conditioning plants and toilets came from Japan.

Cranes were specially designed to lift the prefabricated steel elements and modules into place. Cloakrooms and toilets for a whole floor arrived in modules weighing up to 40 tons. The external walls of the modules were already finished in aluminium, matching the rest of the cladding, so that when they were lifted into position they instantly blended with the building.

Floor supports *As the building rose, giant double triangle-shaped frames were built into the structure to hold up the floors.*

Mainstays *Eight columns, each made of four tubes, are the key supports of the Hong Kong and Shanghai Bank (left).*

Clear view for the staff *Most of the bank's outer 'walls' are made of thick, tempered glass (below).*

Multinational *Components of the bank were supplied by many different countries.*

How the world's tallest building rose into the sky

The fastest method of erecting tall concrete buildings is called slip forming. It is widely used for grain silos, chimneys and offshore oil platforms. But the most spectacular example of slip forming is the CN Tower in Toronto, Canada. It is the world's tallest self-supporting tower at 1815ft (553m).

The usual way of building a high concrete wall is to pour wet concrete into a mould, called 'shuttering' or 'formwork', and compact it. Once the concrete has set, the shuttering is dismantled and re-erected on top of the new piece of wall, and the next layer of concrete is poured into it.

In slip forming, the shutters are not dismantled but slide continuously up the wall, hanging on vertical steel rods. Quick-drying cement is used which is soon strong enough to support the shutters as they move up.

Hydraulic jacks are fixed to the steel rods, which lift the shuttering up in frequent small steps, 1in (25mm) at a time. The CN Tower was built at an average speed of 20ft (6m) a day.

Slip forming can be used only on buildings that are suitably shaped; circular walls are the simplest. The concrete has to be exactly the right quality, placed evenly and compacted immediately. It is difficult to get the slip going, so once it has started the work usually continues day and night, until the building is finished.

Concrete takes days to harden completely. Although it can support the weight of the shuttering and the fresh concrete above, it is still relatively soft. This resulted in the CN Tower being twisted by the force of the Earth in rotation, and engineers had to use steel ropes to pull the tower through six degrees back to its correct shape.

Another method of continuous construction using jacks is the jackblock system. The top floor is built first, then it is jacked up, allowing the next floor to be built under it. The jacks then lift the two completed floors, and the next storey is built underneath them, and so on.

A Dutch insurance company's head office in The Hague was built using the jackblock system, and the final weight lifted by the jacks was 32,000 tons. This method of building allows work to be done inside the building as it rises, so the top floor is finished first.

Towering over Toronto *The CN Tower, an arresting slip-formed construction, is the world's largest free-standing building.*

BUILDING THE CN TOWER

In 1975, two-and-a-half years after the tower was begun, the Space Deck (above) was built 1465ft (446m) above the streets of Toronto.

Materials were hoisted by crane up to 1150ft (350m) (above); at this level slip forming was completed.

The building rose at the rate of 1in (25mm) of concrete every minute, and the base of the tower was finished in three months (below).

How does cement set underwater?

For most cements to set hard the amount of water added to them has to be just right. So how can Portland cement set underwater when used to build a dam or bridge?

Cement sets, not because the water it is mixed with evaporates, but because of a chemical reaction with water. Portland cement, which is used underwater, actually controls the amount of water that can react with it because of the way its grains are made up, so it does not matter how much water is added. It was patented in 1824 by the English engineer Joseph Aspdin.

He mixed limestone or chalk (calcium carbonate) with clay (aluminium silicate) and heated them until they combined to create two forms of calcium silicate. One type, tricalcium silicate, reacts with water quite quickly. The other type, dicalcium silicate, reacts more slowly, producing the final hardness after a month or more.

When water reacts with the outside of the grains of cement, the tricalcium silicate forms a coating that limits the amount of water that can seep through. This stops the cement becoming too diluted.

Portland cement's qualities of strength and water resistance are still used to build the concrete foundations of most structures that are built in water, such as lighthouses, port installations, dams, oil rigs and bridges. Concrete is poured down large tubes onto the seabed or the bottom of a river, where it sets.

WHAT MAKES CONCRETE SO HARD?

When water is added to cement, the water reacts with the surface of the cement grains to make a jelly-like material which holds the grains together.

Three or four hours later the gel starts throwing out tendrils, radiating from each grain of cement. The tendrils from neighbouring grains intertwine, trapping any sand or gravel mixed with the cement.

Over a period of days or even weeks the tendrils harden – locking the grains together in a way that makes cement almost impossible to crush. However, the tendrils are quite easy to pull apart, and because of this weakness concrete is usually reinforced with steel bars.

How concrete is compressed to make elegant buildings

Many of the world's most elegant modern buildings have been constructed with a material bearing the unromantic name of prestressed concrete. Skyscrapers, graceful bridges, slender dams, even the Sydney Opera House, all rely on its enormous strength.

Prestressed concrete has steel cables running through it that have been stretched by hydraulic jacks. As the cables try to contract to their original length, they pull inwards – compressing the concrete.

The idea of prestressed concrete was first used effectively in 1928 by the French civil engineer Eugene Freyssinet. He developed two sorts – pre-tensioned concrete in which the wires are stressed before the concrete has set, and post-tensioned concrete, stressed after it has set.

In bridge construction today, steel cables are threaded through ready-made holes in precast concrete blocks. Then the cables are stretched and anchored with conical plugs in the blocks at each end of the bridge to maintain their tension. The principle is the same as picking up a row of books by squeezing the ends together. In effect the books create a beam, and the harder you squeeze the stronger the beam becomes. And within limits, the more a bridge's concrete blocks are compressed, the stronger the bridge will be.

Pre-tensioned concrete is made in factories. Wet concrete is poured over stretched steel wires while they are held under tension. Once the concrete has set, the wires can be cut off at each end of the concrete block, pulling it together. This method is used to produce railway sleepers and strong concrete beams anything up to 150ft (46m) long.

Demolishing a structure built with prestressed concrete can be dangerous and quite unpredictable. When the building does start to collapse, the locked-up forces and tension in the cables often sends rubble in all directions.

Concrete elegance *The billowing shapes of the Sydney Opera House show off the grace of prestressed concrete.*

How to collapse a skyscraper within its own walls

Van Eck House, a 20-storey skyscraper built in 1937, was for many years the tallest building in South Africa, standing out on the skyline of Johannesburg. In 1983 it was demolished in 16 seconds.

Although it stood in the densely built-up city centre, no damage was done to any other building – even plate-glass showroom windows on the other side of the street were unharmed.

Dropping a building so that every piece of rubble falls within its own walls is called 'implosion' by Mike Perkin, the explosives engineer of Wreckers (Pty) Ltd who carried out the feat. His first task was to study the structure of the building and assess its condition. He was then able to plan how to place explosive charges that would destroy vital points of structural support.

Before the blast came two months of preparation. Internal partitions were removed, together with any other non-structural parts of the building that might obstruct it from falling freely. Protective sheeting was placed around the building to stop debris flying out. It was also necessary to make sure that the vibrations, caused by the explosions and the building crashing to the ground, would not damage surrounding buildings. Perkin timed the explosions so that the rubble from the first blasts at the bottom of the building cushioned the fall of the remaining material.

His team drilled nearly 2000 holes between 4 and 30in (100 and 760mm) deep to take the charges, and laid 6 miles (10km) of wiring. Most of the charges were placed in groups of five holes drilled into walls or supporting columns. On every floor 50 charges were needed for the walls of the lift shaft and 60 charges for the walls of an interior well. The charges in the columns were twice the size of those for demolishing the less robust walls.

The charges were fired electrically. The series of explosions started when Perkin pushed down the plunger, sending current to the detonators – caps of high explosive placed in every cartridge. They exploded either at once or after a set delay, sending a ripple of blasts through all 20 storeys of the building.

The end of a landmark *The 20-storey Van Eck House was reduced to rubble in 16 seconds. At the far left, the doomed building stands for the last time as a South African landmark. The building starts to collapse when the first charges explode in the interior walls of the lower floors. A split second later the columns close to them are blown up, removing all the building's internal support from the middle outwards. The chain of explosions continues upwards floor by floor. Free from any obstruction, the outside walls are twisted inwards by the collapsing floors.*

Clouds of concrete dust are created as the shattered building falls as rubble. The timing of the charges has to be exactly right. Delays from a fraction of a second to several seconds between exploding charges ensure that every piece of the building falls freely. Van Eck House was built of reinforced concrete. The charges had to blast through the reinforcing rods embedded in the structure to make a clean fracture. Otherwise a tangled mass of steel rods supporting large pieces of concrete would have remained. Sixteen seconds later, the building is a pile of rubble, lying almost exactly in the space it occupied when standing.

The long-term job of demolishing a nuclear power station

Some large buildings can be demolished in a few days, but to remove a nuclear power station may take a century or more, because of the danger from radioactivity.

When a nuclear power station is shut down, the first step is to remove all the nuclear fuel. It is taken out of the reactor – the heart of the power station – by the same machinery that has been used throughout its operating life to regularly replace old fuel with new. This remotely operated equipment places the old fuel into special containers for taking to a reprocessing plant. There it is turned into enriched fuel for use in other reactors. A small amount of radioactive waste is also produced and stored for future disposal (page 122).

As a reactor contains anything from 23,000 to 43,000 highly radioactive fuel rods – depending upon its design – and each has to be removed separately, this part of the job may take up to five years. But with the fuel gone, 99 per cent of the site's radioactive content has been removed.

The next stage is to remove all the conventional plant, equipment and build-ings. This will involve some radioactivity – in the boilers, for example – and will take another five to seven years to finish.

The final stage is the most controversial, and plans vary from country to country. Usually, a sealed reactor will be left for 100 years or more to 'sleep it off', so that the radioactivity inside it can decay. Although remote-controlled robot equipment already exists to demolish the reactor from the inside out, other robots would be needed to service and maintain them. In 100 years' time, radioactivity will be low enough for human maintenance teams to look after the robots in the reactor. So in most cases the reactor will remain encased in concrete like some ancient monument 160ft (50m) high. By 1986, 34 nuclear power stations had been taken out of service round the world. Most are begin-ning to 'sleep off' the radioactivity.

French nuclear specialists are content to leave their 'sleeping' reactors to be dealt with by a future generation with more advanced techniques.

The British, however, are undertaking a demonstration project to show that a reac-tor can be dismantled faster. At Sellafield in Cumbria, the Windscale advanced gas-cooled reactor is planned to be returned to 'green-field' status by 1996. Work began in 1982. Dismantling is being carried out inside the steel dome under reduced air pressure so that radioactive gas cannot leak. A remote-controlled manipulator – like a giant arm and hand – will be lowered down inside the reactor to cut it into pieces weighing about a ton, using oxypropane cutting equipment. The operations will be monitored on closed-circuit television.

Each piece will be carried to a 'sentenc-ing cell', where it will be weighed and its radioactivity measured. It will then be lowered into a reinforced concrete box, and the remaining space will be filled with concrete to form a 50 ton cube.

Nearly 1900 tons of radioactive waste will have to be dealt with in this way. The cubes will be kept in a building on the site until a repository is built for the waste. Methods of breaking up the concrete shield remotely are still being tried out.

The cables that could bind up the world

The Humber Bridge has the longest single span in the world – 4625ft (1410m). It is held up by two mammoth cables, each nearly 1½ miles (2.3km) long and weighing 5500 tons. The cables are made up of a total of 43,000 miles (70,000km) of steel wire which would stretch more than one-and-a-half times around the world.

The bridge, which crosses the Humber estuary in the north-east of England, is supported by twin towers 510ft (155m) high – the height of a 50 storey building. They are so far apart and so tall that the curvature of the Earth makes the distance between them greater at the top than at the bottom.

The Humber Bridge was opened in 1981, after 7 million man-hours of work. How did engineers set about building such an enormous structure?

The first stage was to build the foundations for the towers and the two anchorages, where the cables would be secured at each end of the bridge.

The bridge's reinforced concrete towers were built by the slip-forming technique (page 302). Men working around the clock in 12 hour shifts completed the south tower in just ten weeks.

Steel saddles, weighing 45 tons, were hoisted onto the top of each tower – ready to take the load from the cable and spread it evenly onto the tower.

The anchorages for the cables are massive concrete blocks set deep into the ground. The concrete anchor block at the north end of the bridge is founded in a bed of chalk and weighs 190,000 tons. On the south side the chalk is covered by alluvia and a clay bed so the anchorage had to be larger and heavier – it weighs 300,000 tons. Steel castings, called strand shoes, were bolted into each block – ready to anchor the 37 strands that were to make up each of the bridge's massive cables.

To lift the finished cables into position high above the water would have been impossible, so they were manufactured in position.

Bridging an estuary *At 4625ft (1410m), the Humber Bridge has the longest single span on Earth. It is suspended on two huge steel cables which are anchored at each end in massive concrete blocks embedded deep in the ground. Men worked day and night (inset) in two 12 hour shifts, building the concrete towers which support the cables. The bridge can carry a maximum of about 5000 cars.*

Before this process could begin, steel ropes were used to pull the top of each tower towards the river bank, pulling them away from each other by a calculated amount. Later on, the weight of the bridge deck would pull the towers back to a vertical position.

The first link between the two towers was created by two temporary catwalks made from steel mesh and wire ropes. The ropes were winched across the river and slung between the top of each tower – following the curved path that the cables would take. Above the catwalks a 'tramway' was built ready to pull the wire across the

bridge – gradually building up the cables.

Each cable is made up of 14,948 galvanised steel wires – 404 wires for each of the 37 strands. The wires run parallel to one another – with no twisting or weaving. Each time a wire was laid its sag was carefully checked – every wire had to take up its share of the bridge's load. Each wire is $\frac{3}{16}$in (5mm) thick and can withstand a tension of 3 tons, but in practice the weight of the bridge only exerts about 1 ton on each wire.

The process of pulling the wire across the catwalk on the tramway took several months. The wire was stored on large

drums, and every time one drum was finished, the end of the wire had to be joined to the next. This was done by a special 'union' – a device that is squeezed onto the two ends of wire with a hydraulic press, making a join stronger than the wire itself. Bad weather, especially biting winds, caused long delays while the cable was being made.

The completed cables are 27½in (700mm) in diameter. Steel bands were clamped around them to carry the steel ropes called hangers that support the bridge's deck.

The parts for the 16,500 ton steel deck were made in many places all over Britain. They were carried by rail to a disused marshalling yard downstream from the

Link up *A worker (left) reaches for a wire to lay it into one of the 37 strands, each containing 404 wires, making up each cable. One of the 124 roadway sections (below) is hauled up to join those already in place.*

bridge, and there they were put together.

The massive sections, which are 60ft (18m) long and 95ft (29m) wide, were floated up the river on pontoons pulled by tug boats.

Four gantries with lifting tackle were built with wheels that fitted over the cables so that they could be moved along the bridge. Working from the middle of the span outwards, the gantries lifted the 124 sections of the deck into place, where they were attached to their hangers.

When the first sections of the deck were hung in place, the cables sagged a further 33ft (10m). As more sections were added,

the profile of the cables changed until they took their final shape. Only when all the deck sections were in place, and the final alignment was achieved, could the deck be permanently welded together. The cables were then painted with red lead and mechanically wrapped with galvanised wire to prevent rusting.

Once the steel deck had been completed, the roadway was surfaced with 3500 tons of mastic asphalt, which is tough, waterproof and can stretch without cracking. The road surface must be flexible because high winds can cause the bridge to twist and sway sideways by up to 15ft (4.5m).

The potentially damaging effects of the wind were allowed for after testing models in a wind tunnel. The deck was built so that the wind flows smoothly over or under it – like an aircraft designed for zero lift. The bridge is designed to carry a traffic load of about 4750 tons, or about 5000 cars, which would cause it to sag an extra 10½ft (3.2m). A rise in temperature can also cause the cables to stretch, but all these movements are perfectly safe.

At each end of the main span there is an expansion joint that works like a roll-top desk. A short stretch of paved deck continues under the permanent roadway, and when the bridge sags this overlap is pulled out. When the bridge's load decreases it is pushed back underneath.

BRIDGE MOUNTAINEERING

Every two years, combining engineering expertise and mountaineering skills, experts are called in to inspect the Humber Bridge's towers and cables. A lift in the towers' main legs takes them up to a platform near the top, then they climb a ladder the rest of the way. With safety lines tethered to harnesses, the men climb out along the cables, often suspended 500ft (150m) over the river, checking for such things as structural faults and doing maintenance work on cables.

Maintenance *Wearing safety harness, technicians clamber over the Humber Bridge to do maintenance work.*

How do they dam great rivers?

Water is the world's most precious resource. It is essential for all life and most industrial processes, but in many places the water supply is insufficient or erratic. Rivers can dry up or can cause disastrous floods that devastate large areas of land.

Dams allow water to be stored in reservoirs, enabling the water supply to be controlled throughout the year. And water from a reservoir can be used to drive turbines which provide electricity. The electricity can then be used to pump water to a distant city.

Dams have to withstand more pressure or weight than any other man-made structure. In the 20th century, dam-building represents the peak of engineering skill and imagination. It has produced structural forms as daring and original as any the world has seen.

Gravity dams

The weight of the gravity dam resists the horizontal force of the water pushing against it. Some early ones were built of stone, but today they are made of concrete. The pressure of the water tends to tip the dam over, lifting the bottom of the dam, if it is not heavy enough.

Concrete can withstand great pressure, but it is not so strong if it is being pulled or stretched in any way. Dams are built in a way that minimises any tension (pulling force) by ensuring that the pressure of the water and the weight of the dam combine to make a force that falls on the middle third of its base.

Hollow dams

The weight of a gravity dam can be used more effectively by changing its shape and leaving hollow spaces inside its walls. This can save up to a third of the concrete used in a normal gravity dam. The main dam at Itaipu (overleaf) is a hollow gravity dam.

Buttress dams

Another way of economising on the amount of concrete used is to build the dam as a series of connected buttresses, like the 'right-wing dam' at Itaipu. To build solid gravity dams at Itaipu, instead of the hollow and buttress dams, half again as much concrete would have been needed.

Arch dams

At sites with steep valleys of strong rock, even greater savings of material can be made by using arch dams, which transfer the pressure of the water to the sides of the valley. Cabora Bassa Dam, completed in 1975, on the Zambezi River in Mozambique, is 525ft (160m) high and used just

over a million tons of concrete, which is only about a quarter of the amount needed for a gravity dam in the same position.

Overhung dam

The design which uses least concrete of all is the overhung or doubly curved arch dam, which uses a three-dimensional arch like part of a dome. The Coolidge Dam built in Arizona in 1929 is an example of a 'multiple dome' – three part-domes with buttresses in between.

Embankment dams

Modern earth-moving equipment has made it easier to move large amounts of material. Making an embankment of millions of tons of rock or earth is often cheaper than building a slender arch of concrete. In 1980 the world's tallest embankment dam, the Nourek Dam, was completed on the Vakhsh River in Tadjikistan, USSR. It is 1040ft (317m) high and contains enough fill to make a cube taller than the Empire State Building.

Arch-gravity dam *The Hoover Dam on the Colorado River was completed in 1936. It is 577ft (176m) high and relies on its weight (gravity) and its shape (an arch) to hold 38 billion tons of water.*

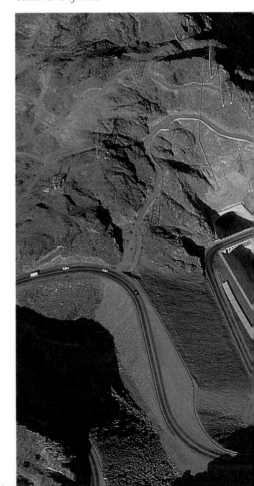

Hollow dam *In 1985 the massive walls of the main dam at Itaipu in South America (see overleaf) were nearing their full height – 590ft (180m). Itaipu is the largest concrete dam in the world. Although there is a space the size of a giant aircraft hangar inside it, the dam's weight is still able to resist the huge pressure of the Parana River, the fifth largest river in the world.*

Embankment dam *The Pantabangan Dam on the Pampanga River in the Philippines was made by building an enormous earth embankment and facing it with stone and concrete. Its reservoir displaced a whole town, and it now supplies water for vast areas of farmland.*

Building the world's largest concrete dam

In October 1988 the world's largest hydroelectric scheme was completed after nearly 14 years of work by 40,000 men. It involved damming the fifth largest river in the world, the Parana River in South America, where it forms the border between Brazil and Paraguay.

Itaipu Dam is the largest concrete dam in the world, made from over 28 million tons of concrete – enough to build a six-lane motorway 400 miles long. It is nearly 5 miles (8km) long and 590ft (180m) high – raising the river's level near the dam by 330ft (100m).

Before it could be built, the Parana River had to be diverted from its age-old natural course. The diagrams on the right show how this was done.

Digging a new course

1. A diversion channel was dug parallel to the river on the Brazilian side. It was 1.3 miles (2.1km) long, 490ft (149m) wide and 300ft (91m) deep. About 50 million tons of rock were excavated in 32 months.

A concrete cofferdam (a temporary dam to keep water out while construction was in progress) was built at each end of the diversion channel.

2. While the river continued to flow along its original course, the first section of the permanent dam (the control dam) was built in the new channel with 12 sluices, each 22ft (6.7m) wide and 72ft (22m) high.

The river banks were excavated to bring the water up to the cofferdams. The two cofferdams were then destroyed with explosives, and water poured into the diversion channel and through the sluices.

Diverting the flow

3. The next stage was the gigantic operation of stemming the flow of the river along its natural course so that the main section of the dam could be built. This dangerous task was a race to close off the river before the flood season arrived.

Working 24 hours a day for ten days, 100 dump trucks and 20 tractors tipped two 'tongues' of rock across the river, forming the base of two more cofferdams or barrages, one upstream and one downstream of the main dam. The river in flood would have scoured this material away

HOW THEY DIVERTED THE PARANA RIVER

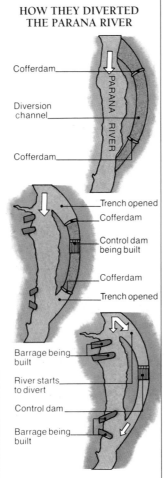

Cofferdam

Diversion channel

Cofferdam

PARANA RIVER

Trench opened

Cofferdam

Control dam being built

Cofferdam

Trench opened

Barrage being built

River starts to divert

Control dam

Barrage being built

A diversion channel was dug with a temporary dam at each end. A control dam was built across it. Two barrages built across the river forced the water to flow through the channel.

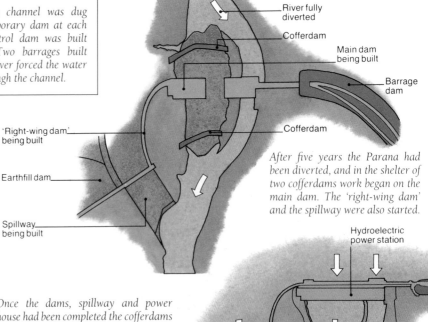

Nearing completion *The Itaipu Dam stretches across nearly 5 miles (8km). The spillway, with its giant shoots, is on the left of the photograph and the curved 'right-wing dam' is in the centre. On the right, the main dam stands in the empty river bed as the Parana River sweeps through the diversion channel.*

BUILDING THE MAIN DAMS

River fully diverted

Cofferdam

Main dam being built

Barrage dam

'Right-wing dam' being built

Cofferdam

Earthfill dam

Spillway being built

After five years the Parana had been diverted, and in the shelter of two cofferdams work began on the main dam. The 'right-wing dam' and the spillway were also started.

Hydroelectric power station

PARAGUAY

BRAZIL

Spillway for surplus water

Once the dams, spillway and power house had been completed the cofferdams were destroyed and the sluice gates in the control dam were shut. For 40 days the river was blocked – forming a reservoir that covered 600sq miles (1550sq km). Then at last the water was allowed to flow through the turbines and generate electricity.

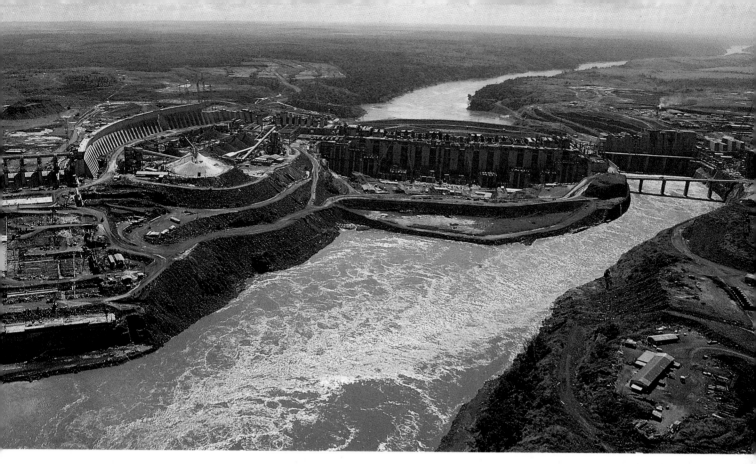

faster than it could have been put in place.

The tipped rock forced all the water through the diversion channel, leaving a stagnant pool between the tongues of rock. The two cofferdams were completed safely, and the water was pumped out. The cofferdams were enormous – each 328ft (100m) high and 1800ft (550m) long, and designed to withstand a flood that was likely to occur only once in 100 years.

4. The main dam and the power station were built within the shelter of the two cofferdams. All the concrete was supplied by three concrete works specially constructed near the dam.

A large spillway was built for any excess water to flow over. It was linked to the main dam by a curved concrete buttress dam – the 'right-wing dam'.

The giant reservoir

5. When the main structures had been built, the sluice gates in the diversion channel were lowered to stop the flow of the river. For the next 40 days it backed up behind the dam, forming a reservoir that filled 100 miles (160km) upriver and spread over 600 sq miles (1550sq km).

At last the water began to flow through the hydroelectric turbines. Itaipu has 18 generators with a capacity of 12,600 megawatts. They are able to supply the whole of Paraguay and the great Brazilian cities of São Paulo and Rio de Janeiro.

The diversion channel had served its purpose and the 12 sluices were concreted solid. Any surplus water flows over the spillway.

How they build to resist the wind

In 1940 the world's third longest suspension bridge collapsed during a gale at Tacoma Narrows in Washington State, USA. In the four months since the bridge had opened, light winds caused its deck to ripple and oscillate. Cars crossing it looked like ships in a heavy sea – giving the bridge the nickname 'Galloping Gertie'. It finally broke up in a 'moderate gale' of 42mph (68km/h). Fortunately there were no casualties.

The larger a structure is, the more vulnerable it becomes to the wind. But by using modern technology and materials,

Narrow escape as 'Galloping Gertie' collapses *The Tacoma Narrows Bridge in Washington State was called 'Galloping Gertie', because its deck rippled and oscillated so much. In 1940 'Gertie' broke up in winds of only 42mph (68km/h). The car on the bridge (right of centre) belonged to a journalist who crawled 500ft (150m) to safety.*

engineers have built taller skyscrapers and longer bridges which can withstand even the fiercest gale by swaying with it.

Some buildings are designed to sway more than others. The top of Moscow's concrete television tower, which is 1762ft (537m) tall, sways as much as 19ft (5.8m) in high winds. But the Sears Tower in Chicago, which is 1450ft (442m) tall, has a more rigid steel frame that should never sway more than 3ft (1m).

In high winds, people standing at the base of a skyscraper can see the building move, and people on the top floors will probably be able to feel some movement.

Before a skyscraper is built, scale models of the building in its surroundings are tested in wind tunnels to see if it will move dangerously in powerful gusts or eddies of wind. Computers are used to simulate hundreds of tests with varying strengths of gales coming from all directions. The computers can also predict probable stresses caused on the building.

In Hong Kong there are usually three typhoons a year and yet over half the population lives above the ninth floor. Not surprisingly the city has its own strict guidelines for the construction of tall buildings – the Hong Kong Wind Code.

In 1980, models of the 47-storey Hong Kong and Shanghai Bank underwent some of the most extensive tests ever carried out. They revealed that strong gusts would be funnelled through an open space at the base of the building, so glass walls were incorporated into the design to stop the wind rushing through the area. And the windows and external panels were fixed with flexible adhesives to stop them popping out when the building flexed.

Many large buildings have a 'design load' able to withstand winds that occur in the area once every 1000 years. In most parts of North America and Europe the strongest winds expected would be about 120mph (193km/h), but in a few places in the world winds of 200mph (320km/h) have been measured. Buildings also have a 'limit load'. For the Sears Tower, it is 1.8 times greater than the 'design load' – the equivalent of withstanding winds expected once every 10,000 years. If the limit load is approached the building would probably suffer permanent damage, but its main framework should remain intact.

The slender design and exposed locations of suspension bridges make them particularly susceptible to the effects of wind. The deck of a bridge can be lifted up or pressed down with terrific force. In fact, the load caused by the wind can be far greater than the weight of traffic.

Modern engineers have reduced the effect of the wind by designing bridge decks with a streamlined cross-section, so the wind flows over them with the least possible resistance.

How are giant cranes erected?

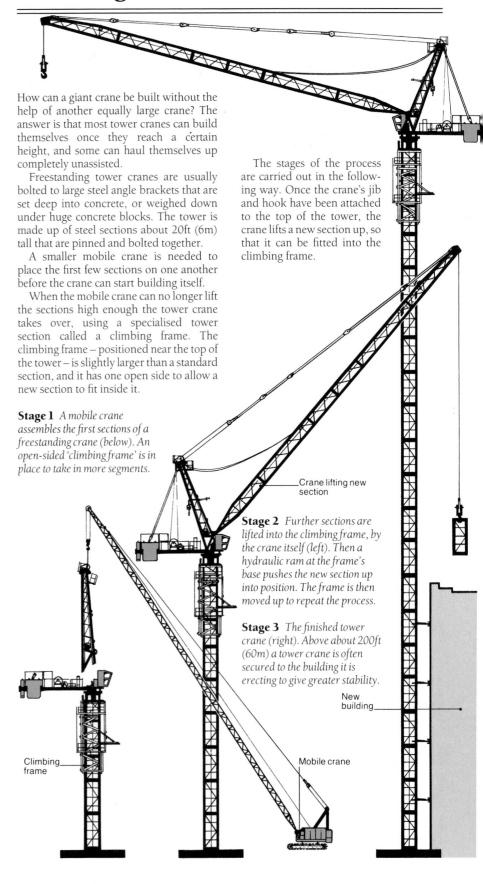

How can a giant crane be built without the help of another equally large crane? The answer is that most tower cranes can build themselves once they reach a certain height, and some can haul themselves up completely unassisted.

Freestanding tower cranes are usually bolted to large steel angle brackets that are set deep into concrete, or weighed down under huge concrete blocks. The tower is made up of steel sections about 20ft (6m) tall that are pinned and bolted together.

A smaller mobile crane is needed to place the first few sections on one another before the crane can start building itself.

When the mobile crane can no longer lift the sections high enough the tower crane takes over, using a specialised tower section called a climbing frame. The climbing frame – positioned near the top of the tower – is slightly larger than a standard section, and it has one open side to allow a new section to fit inside it.

Stage 1 *A mobile crane assembles the first sections of a freestanding crane (below). An open-sided 'climbing frame' is in place to take in more segments.*

The stages of the process are carried out in the following way. Once the crane's jib and hook have been attached to the top of the tower, the crane lifts a new section up, so that it can be fitted into the climbing frame.

Crane lifting new section

Stage 2 *Further sections are lifted into the climbing frame, by the crane itself (left). Then a hydraulic ram at the frame's base pushes the new section up into position. The frame is then moved up to repeat the process.*

Stage 3 *The finished tower crane (right). Above about 200ft (60m) a tower crane is often secured to the building it is erecting to give greater stability.*

New building

Climbing frame

Mobile crane

View from the top *This giant crane rears high over Washington DC on a 1 million sq ft (93,000sq m) office site, begun in 1982.*

A hydraulic ram at the base of the climbing frame then pushes up the new section until it locks into position above.

Another new section is slotted into the now empty climbing frame and fixed in position.

The climbing frame then moves up around the section it has just raised, and again pushes it up, together with the rest of the top of the crane. It is once again empty to receive a new section, and the whole process is repeated. It can sometimes take a whole day to add three new sections to a crane.

When the crane has reached its final height the climbing frame is usually removed from the tower. But sometimes the crane will operate with the frame still in place. And if the crane's height needs to be altered regularly, the frame may remain on the tower the whole time.

To dismantle a crane the process is reversed – the climbing frame is used to lower the sections rather than raise them.

How do they weld metal underwater?

Welding is the fastest and cheapest way of making a repair underwater. In the past, damaged oil platforms or pipelines had to be brought to the surface before they could be mended. Now divers can weld at depths up to 1000ft (300m), but it can be dangerous and difficult.

Welding works by generating heat intense enough to fuse metals together. There are several ways of providing the heat to melt the metal, but only one of them – electric arc welding – can be used underwater.

By using a strong electric current an electrical discharge, or arc, can be made to cross a small gap between two electrodes. In the case of welding, the charge travels from an electrode at the end of a cable to the metal which needs repairing and in effect is the other electrode. The heat produced by the charge has to be sufficient to melt the metal.

People have known that welding underwater was possible since 1802 when the British scientist Sir Humphry Davy discovered that an electric charge would arc underwater. But although the method was used to temporarily repair ships in the Second World War, it has only been widely used since the 1970s, when an increasing number of underwater repairs needed to be carried out on oil platforms and pipelines.

There are two different sorts of underwater welding. The simplest method is 'wet water' welding, for which a generator on the surface provides a large current of about 500amps which is fed through an insulated cable to the diver who does the welding. To prevent the current 'leaking' into the water and becoming weaker, the electrodes are coated with wax or waterproof paint.

The major problem with wet water welding is that the water cools the metal being welded very quickly, which makes the weld hard but also very brittle. Oxygen and hydrogen gas, produced from the water by the heat of the weld, penetrate the weld when it is hot, which can weaken it further. Another limitation of wet water welding is that it cannot be carried out at depths of more than 300ft (90m), because the pressure of the water becomes too great for the electric charge to arc.

The second method of underwater welding – dry chamber welding – can be used at greater depths and also produces better quality welds, but it is expensive.

First, the area that needs repairing is surrounded with a tough, transparent plastic jacket or box. Then the water is displaced by blowing compressed gas into the box so that the area of metal around the weld is dry.

The bottom of the chamber is open, so the diver can reach inside to use the welding torch. The gas trapped inside the box prevents the water getting in. Divers sometimes have difficulty seeing how their work is progressing because smoke and steam generated by the weld can obscure their view.

Even more ambitious welds can be carried out by surrounding the whole area with a high-pressure chamber large enough to accommodate the diver as well. This produces better results, comparable with welds above the surface, but it is expensive because the chambers usually have to be specially designed to fit over the area of pipeline or joint which needs repair and costly seals have to be made. At least one support ship is needed, together with a barge crane to raise and lower the chamber.

Some of the largest chambers have room for several divers to work and even rest between shifts. They have been used at depths of 1000ft (300m) or more.

With oil companies drilling deeper and deeper, there is a need for underwater welding at anything up to 2000ft (600m). Engineers believe this will soon be possible using the dry chamber technique. But for welding at such great depths it is likely that divers will be replaced by remote-controlled robots.

How they cut metal underwater

When divers cut through parts of British Petroleum's Magnus platform in one of the deepest parts of the North Sea, they were further in time from the Earth's surface than astronauts on the Moon. They were carrying out repairs at depths up to 660ft (200m), and to avoid getting the 'bends' they had to spend more than eight days in decompression, before they were able to come to the surface.

Underwater cutting is often necessary for building or repairing oil platforms or

Fire below the sea *Since the 1970s, giant oil rigs have sprouted from the ocean floors, as in the Brent Field of the North Sea (right). They have created a new race of deep-sea divers who can weld and cut metal in the ocean depths (left). Teams of divers may work together inside high-pressure chambers at depths of 1000ft (300m). To avoid getting the bends – the agonising condition that can cause the blood to boil – they have to spend eight or more days decompressing before they are able to step out again into the open air.*

pipelines. For example, a damaged pipeline has to be cleanly cut before a new section can be welded to it, otherwise the weld would not hold.

There are two basic methods for cutting metal underwater; one is oxy-arc cutting, the other uses explosives. Oxy-arc cutting is a similar process to arc welding except that a supply of oxygen and a stronger electrical current are used to provide enough heat to cut right through the metal rather than just melt it.

For cutting through large pieces of metal, such as the leg of an oil platform which is being dismantled, the oxy-arc method is used to make grooves in the metal into which plastic explosives are placed. As long as the right amount of explosive is used and it is positioned correctly, there should be no damage to the leg apart from a clean cut.

The hazards of digging a tunnel underwater

Tunnelling underwater was considered impossible until the French-born engineer, Marc Brunel and his son, Isambard, built a tunnel beneath the Thames between Rotherhithe and Wapping in 1841. In the nine years it took to complete, it was flooded five times, killing at least 12 men. Water seeped through the riverbed and poured into the tunnel when the roof gave way.

The Brunels were successful only after they invented the shield, which was a movable framework that supported the tunnel face and the earth immediately behind it. The workers would excavate a few feet of tunnel, then jack the shield forward against the new face. The newly exposed part of the tunnel was lined with bricks and the process would be repeated until the tunnel was finished.

Lining a tunnel right up to the shield meant that, in theory at least, the only place where a leak could occur was at the face. And shields were designed so they could be made watertight and stem a potential flood. In practice, there were still fatalities.

In 1908 the first attempt to drive the Lotschberg Tunnel through the Swiss Alps, under the Kander River, proved disastrous. Geologists had predicted that the tunnel would be going through safe bedrock, but the roof collapsed near the face and the tunnel quickly filled with soil and water, killing 25 men. The tunnel was rerouted and successfully completed upstream where the bedrock proved sounder.

Underwater tunnelling is still one of the most difficult and dangerous feats of engineering. The problems vary enormously depending on the nature of the ground. Water only trickled into the English end of the Channel Tunnel, because the ground is virtually impervious to water, but at the French end engineers had to contend with the full sea pressure.

Various techniques have been used to reduce the risks of flooding. By filling the tunnel with compressed air, the flow of water can be held back until there is time to erect the lining. If the pressure inside the tunnel equals the pressure of water outside, no water can get in – just like a diving bell. This method was used for many of the tunnels built in the 19th century, but it has drawbacks. A large compressor plant is needed with standby equipment to insure against a loss of pressure. It can also give workers 'the bends' when they emerge into normal atmospheric pressure.

At a pressure of three atmospheres (44lb per square inch) a man can work only one hour a day and has to spend six hours in a decompression chamber. All the tools and spoil have to be passed through a complex system of air locks.

High-pressure tunnelling is avoided whenever possible and other techniques are used. The ground ahead of a tunnel is often strengthened before digging by injecting it with a cement-like compound called grout. Grouting also makes the ground more resistant to water by filling and sealing small fissures.

The biggest aid to modern tunnelling are moles – massive machines that not only burrow through the ground but also provide protection for workers by acting as a shield. Moles can also trail an erector arm that lifts heavy precast concrete segments which are used to line most tunnels.

Making tunnels meet in the middle

Like most tunnels, the Anglo-French Channel Tunnel is being drilled from both ends. But if one of the tunnelling machines digging it should stray even one degree off course, after 15 miles (24km) it would miss the other half of the tunnel by over a quarter of a mile (400m).

To keep the machines on line a laser guidance system has been installed at both ends of the Channel Tunnel. A thin pencil of light shines down the tunnel hitting the target on the back of the boring machine. The guidance system has a computer that is designed to measure how far the machine has gone, whether it has moved up or down and whether it has rolled or turned to the right or left.

All tunnelling machines, or 'moles', have a tendency to deviate in one direction or another. As soon as the computer detects any deviation from the correct line it automatically steers the machine back on course. It sends signals to the steering 'shoes' which are hydraulic pads that control the machine's direction by pushing off the ends of the tunnel lining. The signals sent to each shoe will adjust the direction of the mole so that the tunnel can be built in a curve or on rising or falling gradients, or straight, as the engineers require.

Since the laser can only operate in a straight line it has to be moved to a new site as the tunnel changes direction. The laser has to be positioned with great accuracy – any mistake will mean that it could be guiding the mole in the wrong direction. Usually the laser is positioned near the top of the tunnel where it is less likely to be disrupted by the clouds of chalk dust caused by tunnelling.

In the past engineers have had to rely on conventional surveying methods. Theodolites are still used to measure horizontal and vertical angles. They are like a small telescope mounted on a secure base. The surveyor looks through the theodolite and focuses on a target farther down the tunnel. He can then calculate by how much the tunnel is rising or falling, or veering to the left or right, and make the appropriate corrections.

One of the most convincing demonstrations of the effectiveness of these traditional methods was the two tunnels bored by the Canadian Pacific Railroad through the Rockies between 1907 and 1909.

The purpose of the two tunnels was to bypass the steepest stretch of track in North America, the 'Big Hill' between Kicking Horse Pass and Mount Stephen, just west of the border between Alberta and British Columbia. It used to take four engines to haul a train up. Coming down was even worse. Men were posted along the line ready to operate points to divert the trains travelling too fast up specially built spurs running steeply uphill.

The hill was bypassed by drilling two spiral tunnels with low gradients into the mountains. Both curved steadily round, rising slowly for more than 3000ft (914m), and both were built by drilling from each end. When the two halves of the first tunnel met they were only 2in (50mm) out.

How *was* it done?

Many of the great feats of the ancient world remained unexplained for centuries. Now archaeologists use computerised techniques to reconstruct the working methods, the crops, and even the appearance of people who lived before the birth of Christ.

How Stone Age artists painted by lamplight, page 347.

How archaeologists study the health of ancient Egyptians, page 324.

How the giant statues of Easter Island were put in place, page 328.

How the Great Pyramid was built

For more than 4000 years the Pyramids of Giza have been regarded as one of the wonders of the world. Perhaps the greatest wonder of all is how their builders managed to erect them with only the simplest of tools – not even the wheel, which came into use in Egypt several hundred years after the Pyramids of Giza were finished.

There are three major pyramids at Giza, near Cairo, and they were built as the tombs of three Egyptian pharaohs, who had the status of gods on Earth. The first and largest, known as the Great Pyramid, was the monument of Pharaoh Khufu (Cheops to the Greeks), who reigned from about 2590 BC to 2567 BC. The Great Pyramid is 480ft (146m) tall. Its base covers over 13 acres (about 5.3 hectares) and is 750ft square (229m). The pyramid is built of about 2,300,000 blocks of stone, weighing an average of more than 2½ tons each. Some weigh more than 15 tons and the granite roof slabs of Khufu's burial chamber weigh 50 tons.

Until recently, before it was decided that too many tourists had had accidents, visitors were allowed to climb up one corner of the Great Pyramid to the top. This, more than anything, was the way to comprehend the enormous size of the stones. They form a giant staircase, each step of which is about the height of a family dining table. In their day though, the pyramids had a smooth and dazzling casing of limestone which was later prised off for use on other buildings.

The pyramids are built on a slight hill on foundations of solid rock. A nearby outcrop of rock forms the lower part of the Great Sphinx. Today the outskirts of the city of Cairo reach virtually to the foot of the pyramids, but when the pyramids were built, the site was out in the desert.

Accommodation for the workers had to be provided on site, and all their supplies had to be packed on the backs of donkeys or men, or dragged over the ground on sledges. There were no camels or horses in use in Egypt at that time.

The idea of pyramid building was not new when the three great monuments at Giza were erected. The earliest Egyptian pyramid was built in a series of steps at Saqqara in about 2660 BC and the first true pyramid, built with smooth sides, was built by Khufu's father at North Dahrhur. But the Pyramids of Giza were exceptional – so

much so that Diodorus Siculus, a Greek historian who lived in the 1st century BC, said that 'The Pyramids . . . by the immensity of the work and the skill of their construction strike those who see them with wonder and awe'.

A house for the spirit of pharaoh

The ancient Egyptians believed firmly that after death their spirits would live on, and they took the utmost pains to ensure that they would benefit from the afterlife. The more important the person, the more care was taken. The most elaborate preparations for the afterlife were naturally those for the pharaoh.

The first act of a new pharaoh was to commission his tomb. Depending on how elaborate he made it, work on the tomb could go on until the day of his death. This explains why so many royal tombs in Egypt are incomplete; work stopped when the pharaoh died, except for preparing the tomb to receive his body.

The tomb would be a house for his *ka*, spirit, which was an invisible double of the living body. The Egyptians thought that the survival of the *ka* depended on the continued existence of the earthly body. For this reason, they embalmed the bodies of their dead to preserve them. For the afterlife the *ka* also needed the objects which the dead person had used in earthly life – offerings of food were especially important.

The tomb's chief role was to protect the body and goods within it from grave

The Pyramids of Giza *Rising from the Sahara desert into the evening sky – the monuments to Khaf-Re, Khufu (the tallest of all) and Men-kau-Re.*

Cutting the stone *Grooves like giant teethmarks show how workers used large wooden wedges to split off massive granite blocks at the Aswan quarry.*

BEFORE THE WHEEL

The Giza pyramids are still among the world's largest structures – as tall as a 48-storey skyscraper, yet they were built centuries before the wheel was invented. The Egyptians only had primitive tools to quarry the massive blocks of rock and cut them to size. Hauling the blocks weighing up to 50 tons from the quarries and positioning them had to be done by a few oxen and gangs of men with names like 'Boat Gang', 'Vigorous Gang' and 'North Gang'. These names are still marked in red ochre on some of the blocks. Only

Copper chisels were used to shape the stone. No other metal was available for tool-making.

two metals were known to the Egyptians – gold and copper. Gold was too soft and too precious to use to cut stone, so the work-men used either cop-per tools or a very hard rock known as dolerite. Dozens of metalwor-kers were kept busy manufacturing and sharpening copper saws, chisels and drills. Handles for the tools were made of strong seasoned wood. Levelling and measuring devices were usually made from twine or strips of hide attached to wooden rods.

Granite pounders
Marks made by the dolerite balls used in quarrying the granite from the rock can still be seen.

Mallet *Wooden mallets were used to hit the copper chisels. They were also used to drive wooden or copper wedges into granite to split it from the bedrock.*

Saw *Copper saws were used to cut soft stone blocks. Carpenters also cut the large posts that were used to lever the stone blocks into place.*

Adze *Egyptian carpenters used an adze with a copper blade in the same way as a plane. Wooden objects could be smoothed and shaped to the correct finish.*

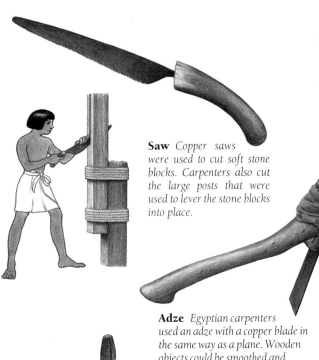

Rods and rockers *Wooden rods joined by strips of twine were used to check that the blocks' surfaces were flat. On site, blocks were placed on wooden rockers so that they could be moved more easily into position (below).*

Drill *Copper drills were spun by twine attached to a cross-piece that was moved back and forth like a fiddler's bow. They were used to make furniture and other wooden tools.*

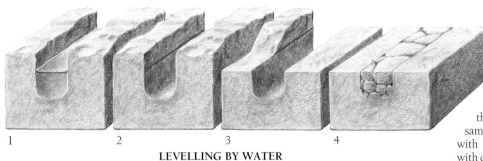

1   2   3   4

LEVELLING BY WATER

The Egyptians knew that water finds its own level, so they dug a network of channels across the site of the pyramids and filled them with water (1). Then the water level was marked along the channels' sides (2). After the water was drained the sides were cut down to the lines (3) and filled with rubble (4).

robbers. But the pyramids were also built to display the power and wealth of their occupants. The pharaohs were sent into the afterlife with fabulous treasures. Nobles also had rich grave goods, and even comparatively lowly people were buried with a few pots of food.

An army of peasants

Whatever else they lacked, the Egyptian pharaohs had two things on their side: time, and virtually unlimited manpower. The Greek historian Herodotus says that 100,000 labourers were engaged on the task, working for three months at a time. Herodotus was quoting what he was told by Egyptian priests of his own day (about 450 BC), but there is support for this story. For three months of the year the Nile flooded the arable land, and the Egyptian peasants could not work on it. During that period there was a vast reservoir of unemployed workers available.

Herodotus says that the building of the Great Pyramid took 20 years. This was on top of ten years spent preparing the site, and building two funerary temples and a causeway connecting them, which was also used to carry stone from the Nile. Probably about 4000 skilled men were employed at the actual site at any one time, but many others would have been working at the quarries and hauling the stones to Giza.

The work of building the pyramids began with quarrying the stone blocks and dressing them to size. The main stone used was limestone. Some of it was quarried close to the site, but fine white limestone used for the outer casing of the pyramids came from cliffside quarries at Tura, about 8 miles (13km) away on the other side of the Nile. Granite was used for lining the interior chambers, and that came from quarries at Aswan, 600 miles (960 kilometres) upstream.

The way these ancient quarries were worked can be seen from marks left in the rock. The quarrymen used copper chisels, hardened and tempered by heat and quenching, to cut their way down into the limestone, gradually separating block after block from the rock face.

Limestone is a sedimentary rock which tends to split along its bedding planes, or horizontal layers, and it also tends to form vertical fissures. Both of these characteristics helped the quarrymen.

Granite is an igneous rock which does not have the same kind of natural cleavage lines as limestone. Fires were built on the surface of the granite and when the stone was really hot, cold water was poured over it. The sudden cooling caused the flawed surface granite to split off and reveal better-quality granite underneath.

Each block had to be separated on all four sides by pounding it with balls of dolerite – a stone even harder than granite. Next the granite blocks were freed from the stone beneath them. The masons cut grooves along the base of the blocks and hammered in large wooden wedges. The wedges were then soaked with water to expand the wood and split the rock.

Further trimming and shaping of the blocks of limestone and granite was done partly with the aid of copper chisels, which would soon become blunt, and partly with dolerite balls. Several of these dolerite balls have been found in the quarries at Aswan.

Rough dressing would have been done at the quarries, but the finishing was undertaken at the site, where the skilled masons worked. The huge blocks of stone

were mounted on wooden rockers and rocked into position on the site.

While the stones were being quarried, the site for the pyramid had to be prepared. Levelling the site would have been done in the same way as the quarrying of the stone, with dolerite hammers at first, and then with copper chisels. It was probably carried out by gangs of skilled masons.

The Egyptians had no spirit levels, but they did know that water always finds its own level. So they ran a channel around the hill on which the pyramids stand, fed by water from the Nile brought along a canal dug for the purpose. Herodotus says the water turned the hill into an island.

The actual site of the pyramid could then be enclosed with banks of mud and flooded with water. The water would be raised from the Nile-fed channel by means of *shadufs*, the bucket and counterweight devices still in use in present-day Egypt.

The workers then dug a series of channels across the site and cut the channels down to water level so that the whole site could be levelled (see diagram). In fact, in the case of the Great Pyramid, they did not bother to level the entire area; a part of the hill was left in the centre and the pyramid was built around it.

There is a small error in the level of the platform under the Great Pyramid: it slopes upwards very slightly from the north-west corner to the south-east corner. It has been suggested that the error could have been caused by a strong wind blowing on the day when the levelling points were set out – piling up the water in the channels.

Great care was taken over the orientation of the pyramids. The Great Pyramid, in particular, is sited so that its sides face almost exactly north, east, south and west. Egyptian astronomers had considerable skill, and they obviously lined the site up

HOW THE BLOCKS WERE RAISED

The blocks were dragged up a massive ramp made from mud, brick and rubble.

The ramp grew up with the pyramids – layer by layer. As the ramp became higher it also became narrower. It is not clear how many ramps were used – probably just one, or perhaps four – one for each corner.

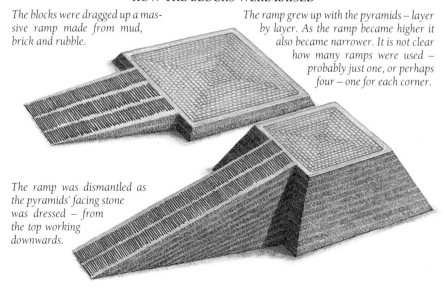

The ramp was dismantled as the pyramids' facing stone was dressed – from the top working downwards.

on a prominent star. Modern astronomers think it was Alpha Draconis, a star then close to the north celestial pole.

Setting out right angles at the corners of the pyramids would have been no difficulty for the Egyptians. They were already familiar with the fact that a triangle with sides of three, four and five units automatically yields a right angle, and they would have had wooden builder's squares, similar to those used by builders and masons today. In the same way they could make sure the stones used for building were perfectly square at the corners. Strings would have been used to mark out the sides of the pyramids.

So well did Khufu's surveyors do their work that the sides of the Great Pyramid are not more than 7in (180mm) different in length out of 750ft (230m). Strings would also have been used to check straightness while building, and plumb lines would have kept the structure vertical.

The original height of the Great Pyramid was 481ft (146.6m). It has lost the top few courses, as well as its outer casing, and is now about 450ft (137m) tall, with a square platform on top instead of a point.

Before erection of the structure began, a burial chamber was cut out of the rock beneath the site. This was probably a precaution in case Khufu died before the pyramid was built.

With only a few donkeys and possibly some oxen available, moving the huge stones from quarry to building site had to be accomplished by human muscle power. Wall pictures from Egypt show that huge gangs of men were employed to haul heavy loads, or to trudge along the river banks pulling barges.

Gangs of men hauled the stones along causeways from the quarries on wooden sleds to the nearby waters of the Nile. Most of the blocks were probably transported when the Nile was flooded so that most of the journey was over water.

With ropes and levers the stones were coaxed onto boats or rafts. They were then floated across the river to the end of the causeway leading to the pyramid site. They were hauled in the same way to the open-air workshops where the masons were waiting for them.

Sand or fragments of hard rock were used to polish the stones so that they fitted closely. The joints between them were accurate to one-fiftieth of an inch, not just on the edge but over an area of 35sq ft (3.25sq m). The joints between the fine white limestone casing blocks were even closer: a piece of paper cannot be slid between them.

The blocks were dragged on sleds up temporary ramps to their place on the pyramid. A fine mortar run in between them was probably used as a lubricant to make the upper blocks slide in place over the lower ones.

Herodotus was told that the pyramids were completed from the top downwards. Once the ramp reached the top, the capstone would have been put in place and masons would begin smoothing the fine white limestone casing. As the work was completed, the ramp would have been gradually removed.

Building the tomb chamber

As the pyramid rose, a second tomb chamber was constructed a little way above ground level. This was also a precaution against Khufu's untimely death, for it was not the final burial chamber. That was constructed in the heart of the pyramid, 137ft (42m) above ground level.

The entrance to the Great Pyramid, which was so well concealed that it defied explorers and archaeologists for a long time, is on the north side, about 55ft (16.75m) up.

It begins with a passage sloping down at an angle of about 26 degrees, which goes underground to the first, unused burial chamber. Back at ground level a passage once concealed by a stone door leads steeply upwards. It is so low that people must bend double to walk up it. A horizontal passage off it leads to Burial Chamber No 2, now misnamed the Queen's Chamber. No queen was ever buried there.

The rising passage continues upwards into what is called the Grand Gallery, 150ft (46m) long and 28ft (8.5m) high,

HOW THE PHARAOH WAS ENTOMBED

When Khufu died in 2567 BC, his body was embalmed and swathed in bandages to form a mummy. After many rituals, which continued for several weeks, the pharaoh's body was at last brought to the Great Pyramid.

The wooden coffin was taken by the priests up the low, narrow passageway (1), through the Grand Gallery (2), to the burial chamber (3), where it was lowered into the sarcophagus – a stone outer coffin (4).

When the final ceremonies were completed the priests, or workers under their supervision, began closing the tomb to prevent grave robbers from getting at the sleeping pharaoh and his possessions.

First they knocked away props holding up three large stone portcullises (5) at the entrance to the Burial Chamber, sealing it. Then scaffolding in the Grand Gallery was knocked away, and three more huge blocks of granite slid down the ascending passageway until they came to a point where it narrowed. There they rested, blocking the entrance (6).

The priests and workers may have escaped down a narrow vertical shaft (7) which goes from the Grand Gallery to the descending gallery leading to the first burial chamber. After blocking the shaft entrance with a stone slab they walked up the descending gallery (8) past the entrance to the ascending passage-
way, now blocked by the granite plugs. Once the priests and workers emerged from the ascending passageway – the only entrance to the pyramid – it was closed by a stone door which swung into place (9). It was such a good fit that it was almost impossible to find. As a final barrier against grave robbers they covered the entrance with casing stone.

But as long as there have been royal tombs and treasures in Egypt there have been highly efficient grave robbers. At some time, possibly not long after Khufu's funeral, these robbers found their way into the pyramid. When European explorers entered it in the 16th century, all they found was the empty sarcophagus. Everything else had been removed, including the mummy of the king and the lid of the sarcophagus. Arab accounts tell of some remains being found in the Queen's Chamber, but these were almost certainly later burials.

The other two pyramids were also robbed in antiquity. Nineteenth-century explorers found a sarcophagus in the tomb of Men-kau-Re, Khufu's grandson, together with a few bones. Nearby was part of a coffin lid bearing an inscription identifying it as that of Men-kau-Re. The sarcophagus was later lost at sea on its way to England. The lid and the bones are now in the British Museum.

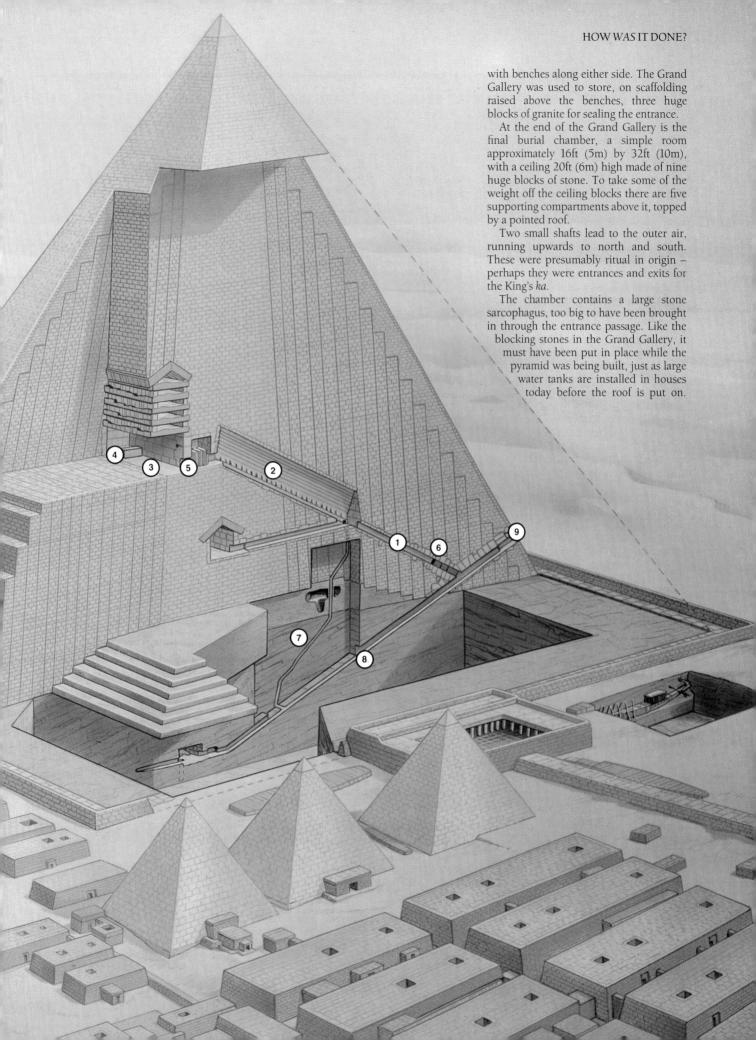

with benches along either side. The Grand Gallery was used to store, on scaffolding raised above the benches, three huge blocks of granite for sealing the entrance.

At the end of the Grand Gallery is the final burial chamber, a simple room approximately 16ft (5m) by 32ft (10m), with a ceiling 20ft (6m) high made of nine huge blocks of stone. To take some of the weight off the ceiling blocks there are five supporting compartments above it, topped by a pointed roof.

Two small shafts lead to the outer air, running upwards to north and south. These were presumably ritual in origin – perhaps they were entrances and exits for the King's *ka*.

The chamber contains a large stone sarcophagus, too big to have been brought in through the entrance passage. Like the blocking stones in the Grand Gallery, it must have been put in place while the pyramid was being built, just as large water tanks are installed in houses today before the roof is put on.

How X-rays reveal the diseases of ancient Egyptians

Mummies derive their name from an Arabic word *mumiya*, meaning 'bitumen'. This was because Arabic-speaking Egyptians of later times believed that the bodies were soaked in bitumen to preserve them. Although this is not true, X-rays show that some of the linen bandages used were soaked in a mixture containing bitumen.

The mummified remains of ancient Egyptian kings and nobles were buried in tombs – sometimes pyramids (page 319) – filled with household goods and food. The Egyptians believed that the body must be preserved for the spirit to re-enter it in the after-life. The mummies have been useful to scientists studying human development. X-ray studies have added to knowledge of mummification methods, and also supplied information about physical and dental health in ancient Egypt.

American scientists with portable equipment X-rayed the royal mummies in the Egyptian Museum at Cairo between 1967 and 1978. Because the mummies could not be moved, they had to be X-rayed through their wooden caskets.

Better conditions were available for the X-ray of 17 mummies from Manchester Museum, England, in 1975. They were moved to Manchester Royal Infirmary, where the X-ray equipment could move all round the subject, concentrating on particular sections and displaying the X-ray picture on a fluorescent screen. One of the mummies was also unwrapped.

The X-rays of the pharaohs of the New Kingdom (about 1600-1000 BC) in the Egyptian Museum produced results that questioned some of the previously accepted ages and relationships of the royal

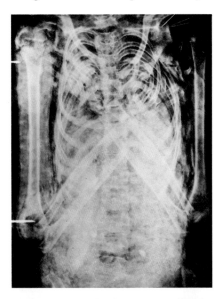

dynasties. The age of death estimated from skeletal changes showed that most pharaohs died younger than had been believed. Computer analysis of skull measurements showed marked differences between pharaohs who were believed to be related. This suggests that they were not, in fact, from the same family. The X-rays also showed that many pharaohs and their wives suffered from arthritis.

Egyptian toothache

Although the ancient Egyptians were generally free from tooth decay, they suffered excessively from tooth and jaw problems. The X-rays showed that the mummies' teeth were heavily worn down, which must have caused discomfort as well as inflammation or chronic disease of the gum. There was also evidence of abscesses. Many mummies also had abnormalities of the jaw.

The Egyptians ate a lot of bread (the Greeks called them 'eaters of bread'), but it was not just the coarseness of the grain that caused their tooth problems. It was the amount of sand they ate with their bread, blown in at all stages of harvesting and flour preparation, and added to hand-mills to aid grinding. Sand caused other health problems, too. Lung tissue from a Manchester mummy was examined under an electron microscope, which showed up lung disease from sand inhalation.

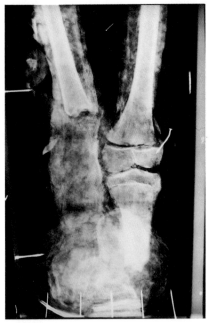

Beneath the wrappings *A mummy unwrapped at Manchester in 1975 was first X-rayed and revealed as a girl about 14 years old. Both lower legs were missing and replaced with artificial limbs (bottom picture). The bones show that the legs were amputated just before or after death. The reason remains a mystery. One theory, now discounted, was that they might have been bitten off by a crocodile.*

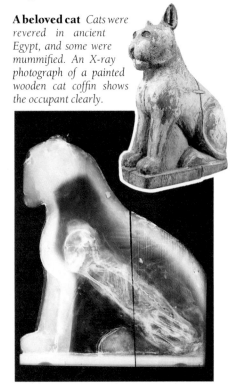

A beloved cat *Cats were revered in ancient Egypt, and some were mummified. An X-ray photograph of a painted wooden cat coffin shows the occupant clearly.*

On the table *With the special equipment available at Manchester Royal Infirmary, the mummies could be X-rayed from all angles, and the X-rays viewed on a screen.*

HOW A MUMMY WAS PREPARED

Investigation of mummies over the years has shown that techniques and the level of skill changed during the period mummification was practised – from about 2800 BC until the Arab invasion of about AD 640. The technique was at its most successful around 1000-950 BC, when the High Priests of Amon (king of the gods) were all-powerful – at the time Solomon and David were on the throne of Israel.

The process took 70 days, as described by Herodotus, the Greek historian, writing about 450 BC. There were, he says, three qualities and three prices. In the most expensive, the brain was extracted through the nostrils, and the contents of the trunk, usually with the exception of the heart, were removed through an incision made in the side with a flint knife. Then the body was dried out. In the less expensive method, the internal organs were not removed, instead cedar oil was injected into the body before drying. In the cheapest method the body was just dried.

Herodotus was writing at a time when the skill was on the decline. In earlier periods, in general, the internal organs and brain were removed and the body was packed with material that included sawdust, linen and mud. At the peak of the technique, packing was also inserted under the skin through small incisions.

Drying out took about 40 days, the body being covered with dry natron – a naturally occurring salt compound similar to washing soda. The remaining time was used for anointing with oil, adornment, bandaging and religious rites. The outer bandages were impregnated with beeswax and glued with gelatine.

The internal organs were also dried out in natron before being stored in four sealed vases, the canopic jars, near the body. But at one period, the organs were parcelled up and used as part of the body packing.

The wrapped mummy was given a face and chest mask made of cartonnage which consisted of linen and plaster. This might be gilded and have inlaid eyes and eyebrows. It was sometimes placed in a wooden case shaped to the body, then in a rectangular wooden coffin, and finally in an outer coffin, or sarcophagus, frequently made of stone. Decoration on the coffins included ritual verses to guard the spirit on its journey.

How scientists can re-create the faces of people from the past

With only a skull to work on, scientists can use their knowledge of anatomy to re-create the head and face of someone who died centuries ago. When the same technique is used to help the police identify bodies, the results can be startlingly true-to-life.

In 1977, at the Greek village of Vergina near Salonika, archaeologists uncovered a tomb they had long been searching for. Close by were the ruins of a palace thought

RE-CREATING THE FACE OF A MUMMY

After the mummy of a teenage girl was X-rayed and unwrapped in 1975 (see facing page), her face was brought to life from the reconstructed skull. Who she was will never be known, but both her legs had been amputated around the time of death. She was in poor health – her teeth showed she had been on a soft, mainly liquid diet.

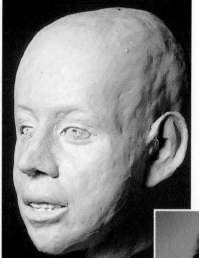

The starting point *The girl's skull was in pieces, with only the facial bones intact. These pieces were cast in plastic and then fitted together. Any missing parts were filled in with wax.*

An Egyptian teenager *The girl's face was built up with clay (above) on a plaster cast of the reconstructed skull. She was given the short upper lip that often goes with nasal congestion, because she had obviously breathed mainly through her mouth. Her nasal bones were seriously deflected, which would have caused swollen and congested nasal passages. Also, pitting on the bone round the upper front teeth was probably due to inflamed gums, caused by continuous mouth breathing. The finished clay model was cast in wax and the head was painted and fitted with eyes and hair to reveal (right) a face of some 2000 years ago.*

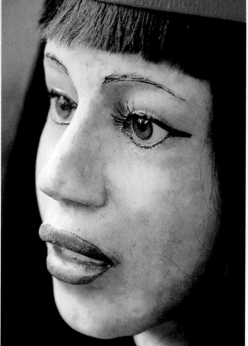

REMAKING THE FACE OF PHILIP OF MACEDON

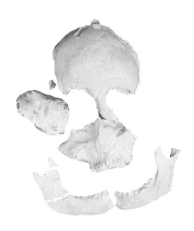

Plaster casts of the pieces of a skull found in a Grecian tomb in 1977 were reassembled by British scientists. They sought to prove the skull was that of Philip II, King of Macedon in 350 BC and father of Alexander the Great.

The darker areas of the rebuilt skull are missing parts filled in with clay. The right eye socket showed evidence of injury.

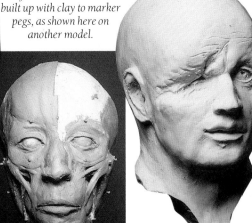

The flesh and muscles were built up with clay to marker pegs, as shown here on another model.

The finished clay head shows the scarred right eye.

to be the long-lost seat of the Macedonian kings, of whom the most famous was Alexander the Great. Professor Manolis Andronicos, who led the archaeological team, was convinced from the rich contents of the tomb that its occupant was Alexander's father, Philip II of Macedon. Philip – a formidable warrior and statesman – was assassinated at his daughter's wedding in 336 BC, at the age of 46. During his 23 year reign, he not only ended internal strife in his native Macedonia, but gained control of all Greece. Philip also laid the groundwork for his son's conquests.

The problem was to prove that the poorly cremated remains in the solid gold casket were Philip's. They included the skull, which was in pieces, and from this skull in the early 1980s, a team of English scientists proved conclusively that the remains were Philip of Macedon.

The team anatomist, Dr Jonathan Musgrave of Bristol University, thought that fire damage from the cremation had not seriously affected the skull's contours, and Richard Neave, Assistant Director of the Department of Medical Illustration at Manchester University, set about reconstructing the face. First, he took plaster casts of the skull pieces.

A serious distortion around the right eye socket puzzled him, but plastic surgeons confirmed that he had put the skull together correctly. The distortion was due to a terrible wound that had caused the loss of the eye. The team archaeologist, Dr John Prag of Manchester Museum, confirmed that Philip had lost his right eye from an arrow wound in 354 BC.

Once the skull was re-created, Neave began to build up a model of the flesh. First

he embedded wooden pegs of different lengths into the model skull at 23 points for which the average thickness of flesh on present-day skulls is known. The measurements were compiled by scientists at New Mexico University in 1982.

Next, Neave modelled in clay the muscles of the head, the glands of the neck and face and the other soft tissues. He inserted a blank glass eye into the left eye socket and modelled the injured eye on the appearance of a scar from a similar wound – an axe wound sustained by a lumberjack.

The finished model was copied in wax

and then coloured. There was little or no evidence to indicate Philip's colouring. Ancient writers merely described him as bearded, so he was given typical colouring of a southern European man of middle age. The finished model, however, closely resembles portraits on medals and coins, and an ivory miniature that was found in the tomb.

Richard Neave and his colleagues also reconstructed the face of Lindow Man – an Iron Age man whose preserved but distorted body was found in a peat bog in Cheshire, near Manchester. Here the technique was rather different, as the whole

REMAKING THE FACE OF LINDOW MAN

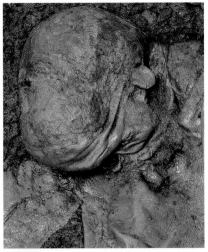

In 1984, a distorted body was recovered from Lindow Moss, a peat bog in Cheshire, in the north of England. It was that of a man aged about 25 years. He had apparently been strangled in Celtic times, 2000 years earlier.

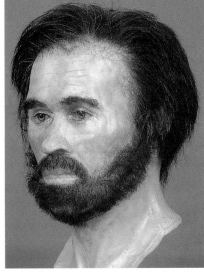

A model was made of the man's skull from X-rays and photographs of his remains. His rebuilt face was given Celtic colouring.

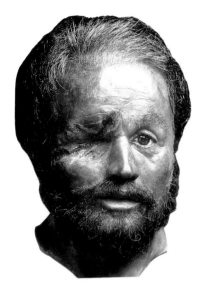

A coloured wax cast reveals the face of King Philip, assassinated in 336 BC.

body, including the soft tissues, had survived. But because the head and face had been squashed by the long burial, the features were almost unrecognisable.

A model of the skull was made with the aid of radiographs – photographs taken using X-rays – and ordinary photographs. The right side of the skull was severely distorted, and had to be calculated from the shape of the left side.

The eyes were formed to a size and colour considered suitable for a Celt of the period – similar to those of a modern person with blue-grey irises. The result depicted the man looking, according to Neave, 'very much as he would have done shortly before his death'. He was about 5ft 7in (1.7m) tall and very strong, and is thought to have been strangled, probably as a ritual execution.

The secrets of the skull

From the skull, an expert can estimate a person's age – an adult has worn teeth and fully merged, solid bones. The sex is generally distinguishable because a woman has a smaller skull and a more delicate jawbone than a man. The shape of the skull indicates race.

A pioneer in the techniques used by Richard Neave was the Russian scientist Mikhail Gerasimov, who died in 1970. He began the work in the 1930s, and the heads he reconstructed include those of Tamerlane and Ivan the Terrible.

Forensic scientists are now experimenting with a technique of reconstructing faces by measuring the skull with laser beams. They need a whole skull to work from, but can then produce a three-dimensional image on a computer screen within days.

How Stone Age craftsmen made tools and weapons

People had been relying on stone tools for about 2½ million years before metal first came into use about 8000 years ago in the Middle East. They made stones into knives, scrapers, axes, saws, sickles, hammers and weapon heads. With these tools they could kill and skin animals, scrape hides, cut up meat, cut down trees, shape wood and reap their crops.

Even down to the present day, stone has been either the only or the most suitable material available for tool-making in many parts of the world. The survival of stone-working, or knapping, skills among Australian Aborigines, for example, and in gun-flint making in Europe, provides archaeologists with useful insights into the techniques used thousands of years ago.

Making a stone spear *An English flint worker, John Lord from Suffolk, made this stone spearhead in the old way (see right).*

Flaking a stone *A stone hammer was used to strike off a large flake for a spearhead.*

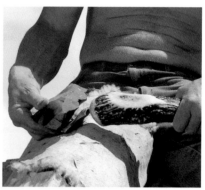

Shaping the head *Smaller flakes were struck off with a bone or antler baton.*

Final shaping *Pressure flaking with a wood or bone point gave a thin, well-shaped tip.*

A finished spearhead *The sharp-edged flint point was lashed, or glued with resin, to a long wooden haft.*

From earliest times, raw materials for making stone tools were collected from exposed rocks or river beds. In many areas the only stone available was coarse-grained or crystalline rocks such as basalt or quartz, which are very difficult to work. But even 2 million years ago, skilled tool-makers could fashion useful tools from them. Fine-grained rocks such as flint, chert and obsidian are ideal for tool-making because they fracture evenly. The Egyptians mined chert for tool-making 30,000 years ago, and in Europe about 4000-6000 years ago, early farmers cut pits into the chalk to mine along the seams of flint.

The earliest tools
Early people discovered how to flake a block of stone by striking it near one edge, using another stone as a hammer. This is known as knapping. The main part of the stone could be shaped to form a heavy tool such as a chopper, and the flakes struck from it could be made into light tools such as scrapers.

To flake a stone, it was held in one hand or against the thigh, or sometimes it was held on an anvil stone. Then it was struck with a hammer stone to detach a flake. Then the core was turned to strike off a flake from another surface. The edges were sharpened by striking off small flakes with a soft hammer of bone, antler or wood, or sometimes by pressure flaking – pressing the flakes with a wood or bone point, a technique used to make thin, well-shaped spearheads and arrow tips.

By careful flaking, tool-makers could detach flakes of the size and shape they required. Long, narrow flakes, or blades, suitable for setting into handles, have been efficiently made in this way for about 30,000-90,000 years.

Sometimes a tool-maker would discard dozens of flakes before getting one that was suitable. Discarded flakes have been found by archaeologists on the sites of ancient flint workshops. Tool-makers had also learned to reject flawed stones – those with hairline cracks that would not flake evenly.

For more than 2 million years, stone tools were hand held. Not until about 200,000 years ago did tools start to be fitted with handles, and stone-tipped spears did not become common in Europe until about 35,000 years ago. Stones inserted into handles were fixed with plant fibres or resins. Sometimes the resins were mixed with beeswax or bitumen.

Small, sharp, finely worked stone barbs were used in making arrows, spears and harpoons. These tiny flakes, or microliths, were used as knives or saws, mounted like saw teeth in a length of wood. This method of making tools first appeared in Europe about 14,000 years ago, but finds in Sri Lanka in 1988 confirm that hunters there were using them around 30,000 years ago, at about the same time as hunters in southern Africa.

About 8000 years ago, early farmers began to use new grinding and polishing techniques to give tools a sharper cutting edge. The grindstone was a hard, wet rock, and sand grains were used as an abrasive.

How did the Easter Island sculptors create their statues?

Hundreds of gigantic statues – some standing on stone platforms, others buried up to their necks in the soil or lying broken on the ground – dominate a remote Pacific island, only 62sq miles (160sq km) in area. The island has been known to the outside world as Easter Island since it was discovered by Europeans on Easter Day in the year 1722.

Although the statues, called *moai* by the Polynesians, are sometimes found along ancient roads, they were carved to adorn coastal shrines, known as *ahu*. To date, 239

ahu have been recorded. They are platforms built of huge blocks of stone up to 196ft (60m) long. Burials have been found in some platforms. Bodies were exposed on the *ahu* until only the skeletons remained, and the bones were then interred in vaults beneath.

There are about 1000 of the giant Easter Island statues. They range from 3ft (1m) to 70ft (21m) high and probably represent famous chiefs or long-dead ancestors of the islanders who erected them.

The largest statue ever erected on an *ahu*

was 32ft (9.8m) high. It now lies broken on the ground – intentionally pushed off the *ahu*, although no one knows why. It has been estimated that a team of up to 90 men would have taken about 18 months to carve this and get it in position.

Ever since Easter Island became known to the Western world its population has never exceeded 4000, but in former times the numbers were much higher. The statues show no scars that might have been caused while moving them, which suggests that protective timber cradles were employed. The island today has virtually no trees although there is now evidence that it was once heavily forested. So there would have been plenty of timber available for constructing sledges for transport.

Easter Island is the most easterly point of the scattered islands of Polynesia, and it has a present-day population of about 1600. Like other Pacific islands, it is volcanic in origin.

The statues were carved from tuff, a stone composed of compressed volcanic ash from Rano Raraku, a low volcanic peak in the east of the island. Some of the statues wear huge red 'topknots' carved of stone called red scoria. The largest topknot is 8ft (2.4m) across, 6ft (1.8m) high, and weighs 11.5 tons, but most are considerably smaller. They were quarried at Punapau, a low volcanic peak in the south-west.

Birth of a statue *Partly carved statues, channelled out from the volcanic rock, still lie in the outer quarries.*

have been 70ft (21m) long, weighing around 200 tons. The statues were apparently created over a period of several hundred years, ending about 200 years before the first Europeans arrived in the 18th century.

Near the top of the quarry are pairs of holes about 3ft (1m) deep bored into the rock. They are linked at the bottom by a channel, and appear to have been used for ropes. Beside these holes are marks which were obviously made by ropes that were up to 4in (100mm) thick. The ropes were probably plaited from the fibres of plants such as hibiscus. Horizontal wooden beams set in stone channels were also used to hold ropes, as were bollards carved from projecting rock.

Controlled by the ropes, the statues were slowly manipulated down the stone and rubble slopes of Rano Raraku. There are 103 statues standing on the lower slopes of Rano Raraku, mostly buried almost up to the neck. Excavations indicate that they were slid into pits to bring them upright, so that the shaping of their backs could be finished off.

Transporting the statues

The late Professor William Mulloy of the University of Wyoming suggested in the 1970s that the statues travelled to their final destination face down, lashed into a kind of curved timber cradle or sledge. He thought that the pot-bellied design of the *moai* fitted in with this notion and such cradles could have been moved forwards between two large poles. Dr Van Tilburg's work, however, shows that the design of most of the statues would have made such a method impossible.

Any transport method depended on two things: a large labour force and plenty of timber. New evidence has recently come to light which suggests that both factors were present when the statues were transported. Archaeologists have found the stone foundations of many houses and villages, with evidence that timber structures were built on them. It is estimated that between AD 1000-1500, at the time the statues and *ahu* were made, the population may have been as high as 10,000.

The first clue to the timber mystery came from the crater lake of Rano Raraku itself. A British scientist, John Flenley of Hull University, took samples from the bed of the lake that yielded large quantities of fossil pollen, which had settled there over many centuries. The pollen showed that Easter Island once had a rich plant life. There had been a palm forest on the island for about 30,000 years until about 1000 years ago.

The island's trees were probably destroyed to provide agricultural land for the growing population. And the competition for living space might have led to wars

Unfinished journey *Buried chest deep on the south-west slope of Rano Raraku, this* moai, *like many others, never reached a coastal shrine. Carved from one of the quarries, it was slid down the slope into a pit for its back to be finished, and stayed forever.*

Abandoned tools can still be found in the quarries of Rano Raraku. Called *toki* in the Rapa Nui language of Easter Island, they are adzes, axe-like tools made of basalt, a dark volcanic rock found in lumps in the softer volcanic tuff.

There are 394 statues at the quarry in various stages of completion. Some are no more than sketched out on the face of the rock; a few are almost completely finished, needing only a few more adze blows to detach them from the cliff. Some statues lie on their backs, others on their sides in recesses in the cliff, like bodies in a catacomb. A few are nearly ready to be moved, their weight supported on rounded stones.

Dr Jo Anne Van Tilburg, an American archaeologist, has recorded and described 823 of the Easter Island statues. Her studies have confirmed that, all over the island, the more recent the statue the bigger it tends to be. The largest – still at the quarry and only partly finished – would which killed large numbers of islanders.

Another theory about the moving of the statues was put forward by Professor Charles Love of Western Wyoming College, who believes they were moved while standing upright. To see if the method would work he cast a concrete replica of a statue and tried moving it on a wooden sledge, travelling on timber rollers.

Volunteers hauled on ropes to drag the statue along, or kept tension on other ropes to prevent the statue from toppling over.

The method worked on the replica, though only a few of the real statues have big enough bases for this mode of travel.

Dr Van Tilburg, who has studied 47 statues lying along prepared roads between Rano Raraku and coastal *ahu*, suggests that the basic mode of transport was horizontal. A statue may have been partially wrapped for protection before being placed on a wooden sledge, which was drawn over rollers using levers and strong ropes. This method would have been sufficient to

move the average 13-16ft (4-5m) long statue. Larger statues of about 33ft (10m) were not successfully moved more than about a mile (1.6km) from the quarry.

To stand one of the huge statues upright on its pedestal was a major task. In the 1960s, Professor Mulloy and a team of islanders re-erected seven 16 ton statues at Ahu Akivi in the west of the island. This led him to suggest how the island's largest statue could have been erected on the north coast (see below).

A GIANT STATUE MOVES FROM QUARRY TO COAST

The largest Easter Island statue, known as Paro, now lies broken in front of its *ahu*. It is 32ft (9.8m) tall and probably weighs 82 tons. The late Professor William Mulloy of Wyoming University estimated it would have taken 30 men about a year to carve Paro, 90 men two months to transport it nearly 4 miles (6km) from the quarry to the coast, and 90 men three months to raise it upright.

The 'topknot', 6ft (1.8m) high and weighing 11 tons, would have had to be rolled 8 miles (13km) from the Punapau quarry. In 1970, Professor Mulloy suggested that Paro was balanced face down on a forked wooden sledge weighing about 5 tons and 'walked' forwards using two angled poles. But experts now suggest that most of the statues were probably moved on sledges drawn over rollers.

In the quarry *Carved on its back, the statue was left attached by a keel.*

With the keel cut away, it was held by ropes and slid down the slope.

The statue slid into a pit. It was raised up with ropes and levers.

Carvers could now reach the back of the statue to remove the keel.

The upright statue was then ready to be put on a sledge for transport.

Possible transport *A curved, Y-shaped sledge was lashed on.*

Earth was dug out so the statue could be tipped forward.

The statue was slung by its neck between two angled poles.

A rope was pulled forwards from the back-tilted posts.

When the posts were pulled, the statue moved as well.

At the end of the movement, the poles were reset.

Raising the statue *The topknot was secured by beams lashed to the head.*

The statue was levered up on each side and a stone support gradually built up beneath it.

Ledges on each side of the mound were built to support men using eight levers 20ft (6m) or more long.

The levers fitted into notches in the head beams and sledge. Stones were slid under the statue as it lifted.

When the statue was nearly upright, the levers were used from the head end, against a long crossbeam lashed under the chin.

Ropes were also used to pull the statue upright. The sledge, unlashed and buried in the stones, kept the statue in place.

With the statue on its pedestal, the beams were unlashed from the head and the mound of stones then removed.

Guardians of the shrine A row of 25 ton statues look inland from their ahu on the north coast of Easter Island. The giant statues travelled 'blind' to the site. After they had been raised, workers may have used scaffolding to stand on while they carved the eye sockets. Then they fitted eyes made from white coral and red scoria. The 'topknots' may have represented hair tied in a knot at the top of the head.

The Great Wall: monument to a million labourers

In the mountains north of Beijing, the Great Wall of China winds snake-like from mountain crest to mountain crest for mile upon mile. This is the most spectacular part of the world's longest man-made wall, which starts in the arid west at the Jiayuguan fortress at the foot of the Qilian Shan mountains.

Crossing deserts, pastureland, river valleys and forested ridges, the wall reaches to the Yalu River on the Korean border in the east – a stretch of some 2000 miles (3200km) across northern China. But when branches from the main wall are included, its total length is around 4000 miles (6500km).

How the wall began

About 3000 years ago, the many warring states of northern China built defensive walls round their territories. In 221 BC, the Prince of Qin, one of the states, annexed six other states and called himself China's First Emperor, Qin Shi Huang. He destroyed all but the northern walls, and linked them to protect his territory from the Huns and other nomadic northern tribes.

In the following centuries, other rulers rebuilt and extended the wall, particularly those of the Han Dynasty (206 BC-AD 220) and the Ming Dynasty (AD 1368-1644).

Hard labour and skilful engineering

General Meng Tian, in charge of constructing the wall for Qin Shi Huang, had 300,000 troops for the job. Sub-commanders were responsible for different sections, and all had to build with local materials. It took nine years to complete the task.

Nearly 1 million labourers were conscripted, many torn from their wives and families. There were also convicts with shaven heads and iron collars, sentenced to years of hard labour on the wall. Some of the convicts were scholars who had disobeyed an imperial edict forbidding the use of books considered 'unsettling', and some were negligent civil servants. They had to work in difficult terrain in extremes of weather – temperatures plummeted from 95°F (35°C) in summer to −5°F (−21°C) in winter. They were pushed to exhaustion, and often left without food.

Although Meng Tian built a road as a

Mountain wall *The Great Wall of China snakes over the peaks of the Taihang Shan mountains north-west of Beijing. A defence tower guards the wall every 200yds (180m).*

333

supply route for garrisons and workers, food often did not reach the outlying places – it was sold or eaten by the carriers on the way. Thousands of men died, and were buried in the wall foundations. Traditional poems and folk songs tell of their anguish, and name the wall as the longest graveyard in the world.

Although oxcarts or handcarts could be used on flat ground or gentle slopes, in mountain areas where the wall was built along the top of steep cliffs the building stones had to be carried on men's backs, or on baskets slung from a pole – loads of about 1cwt (50kg) per man. On narrow paths, loads were passed from hand to hand along a human chain. Large stones were manhandled by gangs, who rolled them on logs and pushed with levers to inch them up slopes.

In areas where there were no stones, the wall was made of layers of hammered earth, built up between boards supported by wooden posts. In the sandy areas of the Gobi Desert, it consisted of 8in (200mm) layers of sand and pebbles alternating with 2in (50mm) layers of desert grass and tamarisk twigs tied in long bundles.

Because of the difficulty of transporting food, Qin Shi Huang began a policy of growing crops on wasteland beside the wall, a policy continued by successive dynasties who repaired or rebuilt the wall. Peasant farmers who resettled in the area doubled as farmers and militia, standing guard or fighting as required. The garrison soldiers were also allotted small plots.

Among the water conservancy schemes organised to irrigate the crops was the Han Qu Canal, fed from the Yellow River near Yinchuan in the central area of the wall.

Farmer-soldiers were obliged to grow not only grain but fruit trees as well, so there were other crops to fall back on if one harvest failed.

The Ming Wall

Much of the Great Wall standing today was built 300-600 years ago during the Ming Dynasty – mainly as a defence against the scattered armies of the Mongol Yuan Dynasty, who had fled beyond the wall after being overthrown by the Ming. Much of it is a massive wall of stone and brick, at its most magnificent between

Juyongguan Pass north of Beijing and Shanhaiguan Pass near the east coast.

The construction of each section was organised from one of 11 fortress towns, from Liaodong in the east to Zhangye in Gansu province in the west. The total garrison numbered nearly 1 million men and even more conscripted labourers. Soldiers guarding the wall wore identity tags, and orders were inscribed on discs, or tallies, for runners to carry between sub-commanders.

Where possible, bricks and lime for building were produced in kilns alongside the site. But they still had to be carried to the high ground – mostly by men, although some donkeys were used.

Huge slabs of stone were also used, some weighing about a ton. How they were

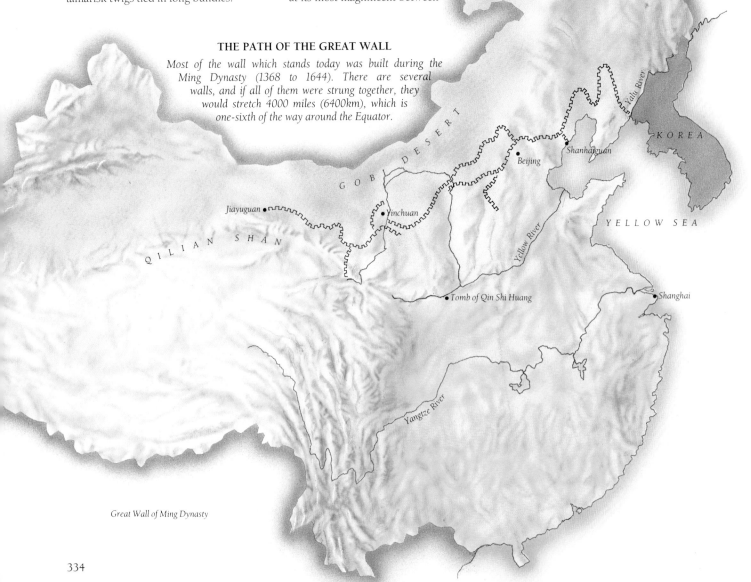

THE PATH OF THE GREAT WALL

Most of the wall which stands today was built during the Ming Dynasty (1368 to 1644). There are several walls, and if all of them were strung together, they would stretch 4000 miles (6400km), which is one-sixth of the way around the Equator.

Great Wall of Ming Dynasty

hauled to the heights no one knows. Some may have been hoisted with windlasses – rope wound round a drum with a cranked handle. Cornerstones were sometimes fixed in place with iron tenons, the molten iron being poured into cut-outs in the stones.

Almost every section of the wall has an inscribed tablet naming the engineers and construction chiefs. But for the many men who died on the job, the wall itself is the only monument.

Eastern gateway and western fortress

The Shanhaiguan Pass is the gateway from north-east China to the central plains. The three-storey gate tower of the Great Wall is over 30ft (9m) high, and a tablet over the gateway reads 'First Pass Under Heaven'. The sign is a replica of the original, kept inside, which was inscribed in 1472 by Xiao Xian, the most successful scholar in the year's imperial examination.

The Jiayuguan Pass controls the corridor through Gansu province in the north-west, much of it arid loess (clayey yellow soil) and desert. The fortress, built in 1372 to guard the pass, is made of rammed earth and has walls about 30ft (9m) high, 22ft (6.7m) thick at the base, and just over 6ft (1.8m) wide at the top.

The wall's height and width varies. In the Badaling section north of Beijing, it is about 26ft (8m) high, 22ft (6.7m) thick at the base, and about 20ft (6m) thick at the top – wide enough for five horsemen or ten marching men abreast. At the Jiaoshanguan Pass in the Yan Shan mountains, from where you can see the sea, the wall is only about 16in (400mm) wide in places.

In the wider parts, battlements about 6ft (1.8m) high line both sides of the wall, and there are towers at roughly 200yds (180m) – two bow-shot – intervals. Some towers are just weather shelters, others have sleeping quarters or storerooms. Beacon platforms for signal fires, some away from the wall, were sited at about 9 mile (15km) intervals, and a signal could be sent across country within 24 hours.

Smoke signals

Beacon signals were sent as smoke during the day or fire at night. According to folklore, smoke signals were often made with wolf dung, because the smoke hung in the sky for a long time.

The number of smoke columns, or fires, lighted at each beacon depended on the message. One column meant the area was being attacked by a small force (under about 500 men). For a large force, such as over 10,000, four separate signals were lit.

A clay army to protect the 'Tiger of Qin'

For over 2000 years a secret army of clay soldiers has protected the hidden tomb of China's First Emperor, Qin Shi Huang. Until 1974 no one knew of its existence; now Chinese archaeologists are gradually unfolding the mystery.

In 247 BC, the 'Tiger of Qin' came to the throne in north-west China when he was only 13. By 221 BC he had conquered the whole of China and founded the Qin Dynasty. He tried to unify China and he also ordered the construction of the Great Wall to protect his new country.

The days had passed when slaves and courtiers were buried alive with their dead king. But to guard him in his afterlife the emperor ordered an army of over 7000 life-size clay soldiers to be made.

When he died his burial place was as

Horse and rider *A clay cavalryman standing 5ft 10in (180cm) tall holds his saddled horse. The bit and bridle, crafted in bronze, will fit a real horse.*

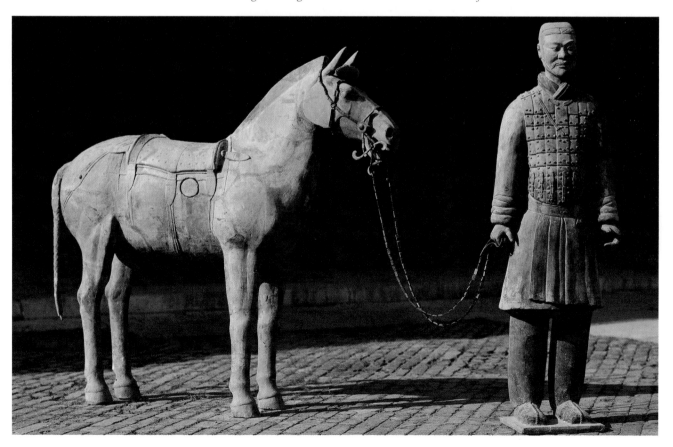

magnificent and bizarre as even the treasure-laden tombs of the Egyptian pharaohs. The site of the tomb measures some 3 miles (5km) across and it took 700,000 conscripts to construct it. The finest craftsmen were gathered from every part of China. They carved out a great palace for the emperor under Mount Li, in the Black Horse Hills of Shaanxi Province, in central China.

Many of the wonders of the tomb were described by a Chinese historian, Sima Qian, writing less than a century after the First Emperor's death. He wrote of rare jewels and a panorama of China's rivers with their waters represented by mercury. But Sima Qian never mentioned the terracotta army, which was discovered by a team of well diggers in 1974.

It is the detail of the terracotta army that makes it so valuable. The soldiers were not stamped from moulds, but each one was individually modelled from local clay. The sculptures represent a standard of art that experts had believed was far beyond the craftsmen of the Qin dynasty.

Each man was built with solid legs and a hollow torso. The heads and hands were fired separately in the local kilns and then attached to the body with thin strips of clay. After the finishing touches had been added by skilled artists, using a finer clay, the soldiers were painted. One colour scheme consisted of dark blue trousers, black shoes with red laces, and green tunics with gold buttons and purple cord. Even rivets, belt buckles and the tread on the shoes of kneeling soldiers were painstakingly copied.

Weapons stolen

The soldiers were originally armed with bronze swords, spears, and bows and arrows. But soon after the burial there was a revolution in China and rebels broke into the vault to steal the weapons.

All the standing warriors were attached to clay plinths that rested on the tiled floor, which still resembles a modern pavement. The soldiers were arranged in battle formation, with 600 clay horses and 100 life-sized working wooden chariots.

Chinese archaeologists have been meticulous and patient in their work. The main tomb containing the emperor has yet to be opened and there is hope that it is still intact. It is said that molten copper was used to line the tomb, poured in as the vault was being sealed.

The tomb may hold some grim secrets: contemporary accounts say that those of the First Emperor's concubines who had borne no children were put to death and entombed with him. It is also said that the craftsmen who had decorated the tombs were walled up alive inside it, so they could not betray its secrets.

Archaeologists who eventually enter the tomb will have to do so with care. Qin Shi Huang left instructions that mechanical crossbows should be fitted, set to shoot any would-be robbers who approached the sacred person of the emperor.

Infantry officer *Each terracotta figure is unique, possibly a portrait of a member of the emperor's army. They are all strikingly lifelike, with natural-looking features, hair and beard, and folds in the clothes which make them drape like cloth.*

How did the Incas shape massive stone blocks to a perfect fit?

When an earthquake shook the city of Cuzco in southern Peru on May 21, 1950, the ancient town in the heart of the Andes mountains was devastated. But the mortarless stone foundations on which the town stood remained in place. These were the lower walls of ancient temples and palaces built by the Incas – the rulers of Peru before the Spanish conquest.

So cleverly had the Inca masons constructed the walls – the massive blocks fitted together in precise mortarless joints – that their structures were heavy enough to stand firm but flexible enough to yield to the shock, and were undamaged. Only a few joints had moved slightly apart. The stones, some weighing 100 tons, were shaped without the aid of iron tools, yet were so close-fitting that a knife blade could not be forced between the joints.

Shaping and fitting the stones

In 1609, the Peruvian-born Spanish historian Garcilaso de la Vega, whose mother was an Inca princess, wrote that the Incas dressed their stone by pounding it with 'some black stones', rather than by cutting.

These statements were borne out by the experiments of Jean-Pierre Protzen, a lecturer in architecture at the University of California, who began to investigate the stonemasonry in 1982. Working at an ancient Inca quarry near Cuzco, he was able to dress some abandoned stones using stone hammers found on the site – stones,

Ramparts of the devil *The Spanish conquistadores thought the walls of Sacsahuaman fortress near Cuzco to be the work of the devil. Some of the stones weighed around 100 tons (100,000kg), and had dimensions such as 15 × 8 × 5ft (4.5 × 2.5 × 1.5m).*

such as quartzite, not natural to the quarry but obviously picked up from the river banks near by.

He discovered that the Incas used three different sizes of hammer to dress and fit the stones. They roughly shaped the blocks with large hammers weighing 17-20lb (8-9kg). Medium-sized hammers weighing 4-11lb (2-5kg) were used to smooth the faces, and small hammers weighing less than 2lb (1kg) were used to chip away the margins at an angle.

Protzen took about 1½ hours to dress three faces and five margins of a block 10 × 10 × 12in (250 × 250 × 300mm).

The medium-sized smoothing hammer was held lightly in both hands at an angle of 15-20 degrees from vertical to chip off tiny flakes. By twisting the wrists just before impact, the angle was more or less doubled, giving a better cut. After each stroke, the hammer rebounded some 6-10in (150-250mm), so the work did not need great effort.

The smallest hammer, too small to rebound, had to be held tightly and struck with force to chip the margins of each edge at an outward angle. This was necessary before smoothing the adjoining face with

the larger hammer, to prevent the stone flaking at the edges.

The knife-tight joints were achieved by patient shaping and testing until the fit was perfect. Most of the dressed stones had an outward curving surface on each face. Once a course of stones was laid, the top of each stone was cut to an inward curve to match the shape of the bottom of the stone to be fitted above.

The upper block would have to be put into place several times to get a matching fit. Dust from the hammering on the lower stone probably served as a guide to cutting. The pattern left in it by the uneven surface of the upper stone showed where deeper cutting was needed – in the places where the dust was compressed.

The sides of each stone were cut in the same way, by constant comparing and cutting.

What the stones cannot tell

How the Incas managed to move the huge stone blocks to the building sites, often over many miles, is still a mystery. Some blocks show evidence of being dragged, but an enormous number of men would have been needed to drag them up the

Shaped to fit *The stone blocks used by the Incas were rarely square or of uniform size. Yet each edge was fitted precisely against the adjacent stone. Projections and indentations at the base were probably used in handling the stones during building. They had two main shapes, one for tying ropes to, and one for supporting a lever.*

narrow access ramps still remaining at some sites.

Jean-Pierre Protzen calculated that it would have taken 2400 men to drag the largest block at Ollantaytambo up the slope of the access ramp. This block weighs about 138 tons. How the men could have been harnessed to the block and have had enough room to pull may never be known.

Stones at the Rumiqolqa quarry southwest of Cuzco were dressed at the quarry – unmoved stones can still be seen at one ancient pit. There is no evidence that the stones from this quarry were dragged to their building site. If wooden rollers and sledges were used, few traces of them now remain. Blocks were probably allowed to slide freely on downhill slopes.

Stonehenge: building a massive and mysterious monument

For more than 800 years, prehistoric people in southern Britain had used the exposed site on Salisbury Plain, Wiltshire – today known as Stonehenge – as a place for their rituals. Over those eight centuries two circular banks of earth had been built and two incomplete circles of stones had been erected.

But in about 2000 BC, the most challenging task was still ahead. It was then that workers began the job of erecting the largest structures of Stonehenge – the five trilithons forming a horseshoe at the centre of the circle. Each consists of two 50 ton upright stones around 20ft (6m) high with a 7 ton stone resting across the top.

To set the first upright in the ground, the men dug a pit 8ft (2.4m) deep with one sloping side. They shifted the soil using deer antlers as picks and ox shoulder blades as shovels. Then they hauled the first 50 ton stone into position on wooden rollers, so that one end hung over the sloping wall of the pit. Dozens of men struggled to raise the other end of the stone. They levered it up with long wooden poles, and pushed logs underneath to support it and provide a fulcrum for the poles.

As more and more logs were jammed under the stone, it began to tilt, until at last it slid off the logs and down the sloping side of the pit. The huge stone must have thudded with tremendous force into the opposite side of the hole, which had been lined with wooden stakes to prevent it collapsing.

Ropes made from strips of animal hide and plant fibre were used to haul the stone upright. These ropes were not of uniform strength and probably broke quite often, so to prevent the stone crashing back down, it was supported with wooden props fitted into rope 'collars' lashed round its top. As soon as the stone was upright, workers packed soil, logs and stones round the base.

On the flat tops of the uprights, the stonemasons had left small protruding knobs. These were for fitting into a hollow ground out of the lintel (the crosspiece), to create a mortise-and-tenon joint.

Raising a 7 ton lintel some 20ft (6m) onto its pair of uprights was probably the most dangerous and demanding job in building Stonehenge. Most likely, each lintel was raised on a bed of logs, each end of the lintel being levered up alternately while logs were pushed under it.

In this way, a wooden tower was built up under a lintel until it was level with the top of the upright stones and could be levered

Bird's eye view *Seen from the air under snow, the pattern of Stonehenge clearly emerges. Ringing the stones are the banks and ditch. Beyond are the Heel Stone and the outlines of the Avenue, split by the road.*

Fallen giant *A huge fallen lintel lies in front of the tallest sarsen stone – 22ft (6.5m) high and weighing over 45 tons. The mortise-and-tenon joints, which held the two stones together, can be clearly seen.*

into position. At least 250 logs, each 20ft long, would have been needed for the tower's construction.

The three phases of Stonehenge

Stonehenge was built in three distinct phases over a period of about 1700 years. Professor Gerald Hawkins, formerly of the Smithsonian Astrophysical Observatory in Cambridge, Massachusetts, USA, has estimated that the entire monument would have taken a total of about 1,500,000 working days to construct, and involved about 1000 workers at a time.

Phase I was begun about 2750 BC, nearly 200 years before the Egyptians started work on the Great Pyramid. It is a circle some 380ft (115m) across consisting of a low outer bank surrounding a ditch, with another bank about 6ft (1.8m) high inside the ditch. Inside the inner bank, the Stone Age Britons dug 56 equally spaced pits, called the Aubrey Holes after the 17th-century antiquary John Aubrey, who first noticed them as slight dips in the turf. What they were for is not known.

There is an entrance on the north-east side of the circle. Outside it stands a huge block of rough sandstone about 16ft (5m) high, known today as the Heel Stone. From the centre of the circle, you can see the sun rise over it on Midsummer's Day.

Phase II of the construction began around 2100 BC, and was carried out by the Beaker Folk, who were so called because of the shape of their pottery. They erected 80 large bluish stones – known today as the bluestones – in two incomplete rings in the centre of the monument. They also built a wide roadway, now called the Avenue, leading north-east towards the River Avon about 2 miles (3km) away.

The bluestones came from the Preseli Mountains in south-west Wales, 130 miles (209km) distant, and were probably brought most of the way by water – loaded on rafts at Milford Haven and shipped up the estuary of the River Severn. By using a network of rivers, only a short overland journey was left, from Amesbury to Stonehenge along the Avenue.

Support for this theory was provided in 1988 when a bluestone block was discovered on the bed of the River Daugleddau at Llangwm in Dyfed. It is of similar size to those used at Stonehenge, and its position

suggests that it could have sunk while being floated down the river to the sea.

The pale green, broken Altar Stone, once standing but now lying flat among the central trilithons, came from the shores of Milford Haven, probably also by water.

Phase III, lasting from about 2000 to 1100 BC, was carried out by early Bronze Age people. They removed the bluestone circle and erected a ring of about 30 sandstone uprights (averaging 30 tons in weight), linked by stone lintels. The ring is 16ft (5m) high overall, and inside it they put up the five even taller trilithons. Finally they re-erected the bluestones in two groups.

The sandstones, or sarsens, came from the Marlborough Downs, 20 miles (32km) away. They must have been manhandled on sledges, with oak logs used as rollers.

Professor Hawkins has calculated that 800 men would have been needed to haul one of the giant 50 ton sarsens. Another 200 would have had to clear the route and continually move the heavy oak rollers from the back of the stone to the front.

The upright sarsens were shaped with a slight bulge in the middle so that when viewed from below they would appear straight. The workmanship of the sarsen circle, which is about 100ft (30m) across, is such that the top is level all round. The lintels were cut in a curve so that when fitted together they made a circle.

The stones were shaped by chipping away at the surface with other stones. Larger lumps may have been split off by heating the stones along carefully marked lines, throwing cold water on them and then hitting them.

Upright giant *Stonehenge's biggest structures, the trilithons (below), stand in the centre of the circle. Originally there were five, the tallest standing about 21ft (6m) high. Now only three remain standing. Each trilithon consists of two huge upright stones supporting a horizontal stone lintel.*

Handling the huge stones *To erect the giant trilithons, deep holes were dug in the chalk soil. A row of stakes was then driven in to stop the chalk being crushed by the stones. Next, the stones were raised with levers and ropes a few inches at a time, until they slid down into the holes. Gangs of men using ropes hauled the stones upright. The stone lintels were raised with levers on decks of logs, a new deck being added each time the stone was levered up. Finally, the lintels were levered sideways into position.*

Ancient remains: how scientists discover their age

Only in the past 50 years have archaeologists had any definite means of dating the finds that they use to study the history of ancient peoples. During the 19th and early 20th centuries, they relied mainly on soil stratification as a guide, estimating the age of their finds, such as bones, pottery and timber, from their position in the soil layers. For example, anything found beneath a datable layer – such as a Roman floor – ought to be older than the floor.

Dating by carbon atoms

Since 1955, the chief means of dating organic remains, such as bone, shells and plants, has been radiocarbon dating. It was developed by an American physicist, Willard F. Libby, while working at the University of Chicago. He was awarded the Nobel prize for Chemistry in 1960.

Radiocarbon is another name for a radioactive isotope of the element carbon, which is present in all living things. An isotope is an atom with a different atomic mass from the commonest form of atom in the element. Carbon generally has an atomic mass of 12, but radiocarbon has a mass of 14, so it is also called carbon-14 or C-14 for short.

Plants and animals absorb carbon dioxide from the air as long as they live, taking in one C-14 atom to every million million C-12 atoms. When they die, their C-14 atoms begin to disintegrate although their C-12 atoms do not. As the rate of decay of C-14 is known, and is not affected by external factors, the age of the remains can be calculated by counting the total number of carbon atoms and comparing the ratio of C-14 to C-12 atoms.

To count the atoms, a small sample of the remains is heated in a furnace to convert it to carbon dioxide gas. The gas is passed through a machine called a mass spectrometer, where an electron beam ionises the atoms – that is, converts them to ions (electrically charged atoms). The ions are drawn through a series of magnetic

HISTORY UNDER THE STREETS OF LONDON

This imaginary section shows the levels of building which have been found in London. It is an example of the soil stratification method of dating things found below ground. The section represents an excavation about 33ft (10m) deep – from the natural gravel (1) and brick-earth (2) at the bottom to the 19th-century floor (26). The oldest man-made remains are 1st-century pits (3 and 4) dug to extract brick-earth for building. First-century Roman remains are a drain (5), a wall (6), and a tile floor (7), covered by a 2nd-century gravel surface (8), and burnt debris (9), indicating a destructive *fire. The next evidence of building is a medieval surface (10), but a post hole (11) means a timber building may have been here. A 13th-century cesspit (12) is covered by a 15th-century house with a chalk wall (13) and floor (14). A 16th-century surface (15) is cut by a chalk-lined cesspit (16), with a 17th-century floor (17) and debris from the Great Fire of 1666 (18) above. Remains from the 17th to 18th centuries are cobbles (19), a brick-lined cesspit (20), and well (21). Builders in the 19th century added a surface (22), drain (23), foundation (24), and wall (25).*

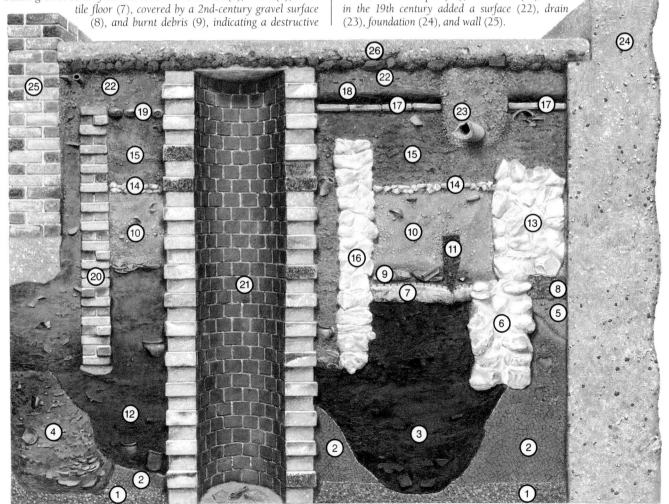

HOW TIMBER CAN BE DATED BY READING TREE-RING PATTERNS

Two floorboards taken from the same house are shown edge-on.

Dates of the rings were established as 1444,1445 and 1475 by comparing the boards with a master pattern of trees in the region.

1444-5

1475

Narrow ring of poor growing season

Wide ring of good growing season

Floorboards laid together show matching growth rings.

fields. This separates them according to the ratio of their charge to their atomic mass, and the C-14 isotopes are fed to a detector plate, where they are counted.

The radiocarbon calendar

As radioactive substances decay, they give off particles, and the time by which they lose half their particles is known as their half-life.

Carbon-14 has a half-life of about 5700 years. After two half-lives (about 11,400 years) only a quarter of the C-14 remains, after three half-lives (about 17,100 years), only one-eighth. Detection of progressively smaller amounts gets difficult, so radiocarbon dating cannot be used for remains much more than about 35,000 years old.

LIFE IN ANCIENT TIMES

A hearth found in a cliff rock shelter in a remote area of north-east Brazil by French archaeologists in June 1986 provided charcoal that was radiocarbon tested. It revealed that there were people living there about 32,000 years ago – 21,000 years before the previously accepted date for the first people in the New World.

Radiocarbon tests on a 6ft (1.8m) long boat found off Korshavn, Denmark, in April 1987, showed it to be 7000 years old – the oldest Stone Age boat ever discovered in Denmark.

Peat from the base of a prehistoric footprint found in the Severn estuary in Britain in December 1986 was radiocarbon tested. The footprint was found to have been made 7000 years ago. Scientists think it may have been made by someone hunting wildfowl in a reed swamp.

A recent development is the Accelerated Mass Spectrometer, which separates and detects atomic particles of different mass. It can establish dates with greater accuracy, using a much smaller sample than older carbon-dating methods.

Accelerated mass spectrometry was used in 1988 to date the Turin Shroud, a relic kept in Turin Cathedral, Italy, and believed to be the shroud in which Christ was wrapped after his crucifixion. It has a faint imprint on both the front and the back – almost like a photo negative – of a bearded, long-haired man with injuries similar to those suffered by Christ.

Three fragments of the shroud were radiocarbon tested independently by laboratories in England, the USA and Switzerland. All produced a date between AD 1260 and AD 1390, proving that the shroud was of medieval origin, and could not have been Christ's.

Dating by tree rings

The age of a felled tree can be calculated by counting its growth rings – one for every year of its life – which vary in width according to the weather and climate for the year. For example, narrow rings indicate restricted growth in very dry or cold conditions. The growth patterns are similar for individual tree species over a fairly wide area, and master patterns for various areas, which include trees felled at a known date, have been compiled for comparison. This method is known as dendrochronology, and it can be used for dating old timber, as long as a large enough sample of the timber is available. The growth rings are compared against a master pattern to establish the felling year.

When archaeologists unearthed remains of dozens of wooden stakes buried 18ft (5.5m) below London's Victoria Embank-

ment in 1988, they were able to compare the growth rings to give a felling date of AD 665-710. This showed the stakes were probably part of the quayside of the Anglo-Saxon port of London.

Until 1989, the only way of counting the number of tree rings and matching the patterns was to do it manually. Now Danish scientists have invented a scanner, similar to the electric eye which reads supermarket bar codes, to count the rings. The information is stored in a computer and analysed automatically. Whereas a researcher could study three sections a day, the scanner can read 30 samples.

Dating by gas formation

The formation of some rocks that are more than 100,000 years old can be dated by measuring the amount of rare radioactive Argon gas they contain (in younger rocks there is too little to measure). This method, known as Potassium-Argon dating, was used to date the world's oldest-known humanoid relic, a jawbone around 5½ million years old found near Lake Baringo in Kenya in 1984.

Potassium is the seventh most abundant element in the Earth's crust, and its radioactive isotope (K40) emits the rare gas, Argon 40 (Ar40), as it decays. In rocks formed from molten lava, the gas produced before the lava solidified would have escaped. Any gas trapped in the rock structure has accumulated since formation. K40 has a half-life of about 1300 million years, so comparing the amount of K40 with trapped Ar40 dates the rock formation, and also any embedded fossils.

Dating by light emission

Rocks which have been exposed to naturally occurring radiation accumulate electrons within their minerals. The number of

Reading the past from pollen grains

Microscopic grains of pollen are helping scientists to reconstruct the world's past. The tiny grains can explain how the environment has been changed by man, and how the climate fluctuated thousands of years ago.

One oak tree releases more than 100 million pollen grains into the air every year. Some smaller plants are even more prolific – the common sorrel of waysides and woodlands emits an incredible 400 million grains annually.

Most windborne pollen ends up on the ground and decays in the soil in the presence of oxygen. But some falls into lakes or bogs, where it is preserved because peat deposits and the sediment at the bottom of lakes contain no oxygen. Some of the grains last for many thousands of years and fossilise. As new layers of sediment are formed, they trap pollen from plants growing at the time.

This fossil pollen provides a 'book' that enables palaeobotanists – scientists who study ancient plant life – to build up a picture of the vegetation, and hence the climate, of the past few thousand years.

Pollen grains vary in size from 15 to 50 thousandths of a millimetre across, and have individual structures varying from plant to plant that can be identified under the microscope. The grains' tough outer walls are preserved because they contain a decay-resistant protein. Fossil pollen is counted by taking a core sample (with a hollow cylindrical drill) from an organic deposit such as a peat bog. Then specimens are taken at regular intervals throughout the depth of the deposit and dated by radiocarbon dating.

The amount of pollen recovered in this way is very large. Samples taken have ranged from 20,000 grains per cubic centimetre from deposits made 11,000 years ago, to 650,000 grains per cubic centimetre a few thousand years later.

From this huge quantity a representative sample of about 1000 grains is analysed, and the proportions of the various plants are calculated.

Scientists can see, for example, in what way plants colonised the northern lands after the last Ice Age about 12,000 years ago. One of the first trees found was juniper, which thrives in cold climates. As the weather became warmer it was replaced by birch, then oak and elm. A change to a moister climate brought alder.

It is also possible to see how people have influenced the vegetation by cutting down forests and growing crops. Pollen analysis carried out in 1987 on sediments from the Sea of Galilee (Lake Kinnereth), in northern Israel, showed that oak forests were cleared about 5000 years ago to make way for olive trees, grown for their fruit and oil. In the 3rd century AD the number of olive trees declined when the Jews left Palestine.

These 15th-century floorboards from a house in Yorkshire have been dated by matching the growth patterns indicated by the tree rings visible at the edges of the timber, to the known patterns of growth rings of British trees. Modern computerised techniques using a scanner to count the growth rings mean that tests can be carried out quickly to date the timber found in ancient buildings or sites.

trapped electrons is a measure of the radiation dose. Heating frees the electrons, which makes the radiation dose zero.

Clay is made of rock sediments, and when it has been fired in a pottery kiln, it can be dated by a process known as thermoluminescence. When the pot is reheated at temperatures of 300-600°C (about 570-1110°F), radioactive energy is released in the form of light.

Scientists can calculate the age of the pot with a margin of error of about 10 per cent.

Thermoluminescence can be used to detect fake antiques – ceramics or bronzes (which have a clay core). What was thought to be a Roman pottery lamp in the British Museum collection was discovered, after testing by thermoluminescence in the 1970s, to have been made about 1920.

Dating by magnetic field

A compass needle points to magnetic north rather than the true north marked on a map. But the Earth's magnetic field shifts from time to time, and the changes do not have a constant pattern. For example, 1500 years ago the deviation from true north was 50 per cent greater than at present. Some 5500 years ago it was only about 40 per cent.

Iron-oxide particles in molten rocks and in clays align with the Earth's magnetic field, and when the rock sets or the clay is fired in a kiln, the particles are fixed in the position they were pointing at the time of heating. Scientists can measure the directions with a magnetometer. This has led to a dating technique known as thermo-remanent magnetism. The magnetic field of a rock can be compared with a date chart of the changes in the Earth's magnetic field. The chart has been compiled from comparison with sites of known dates and the Potassium-Argon dating of rocks.

LIVING AND FOSSILISED POLLEN

Each plant produces pollen grains of a distinctive size and shape. These minute particles can fossilise, providing clues to the vegetation and climate of an area in ancient times.

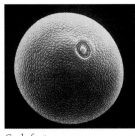
Cocksfoot grass

Pine tree

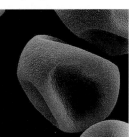
Timothy or cat's tail grass

Common oak

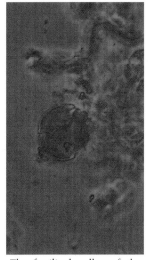
The fossilised pollen of the common oak has been used to help study life in the Middle East. These grains (above) are from before 3000 BC, when the vast oak forests were cleared for olive trees.

343

How Hannibal crossed the Alps with his elephant army

When Hannibal led an army with 37 elephants across the Alps to invade Rome 2200 years ago, he created a reputation for daring that lives on today. As well as the elephants, Hannibal's army consisted of some 50,000 men and 8000 horses.

They took 15 days to battle their way about 132 miles (212km) through difficult terrain and over snowy heights – it was October and winter was approaching – while being harried by hostile tribesmen. Their average speed of about 9 miles (14km) a day on a climb to over 9000ft (2750m) was a remarkable feat.

But the Alpine crossing was only a part

of the army's five-month, 1500 mile (2400km) march to invade Rome by the back door – the most brilliant campaign of the second Punic War, which was part of the long struggle for supremacy between Rome and Carthage. Rome had already wiped out the Carthaginian navy, so a seaborne invasion was out of the question. Nor could Hannibal take the easier land route along the French Riviera, for it was inhabited by a Greek colony, in what is now Marseilles, which was an ally of Rome.

It was in May of 218 BC that the 29-year-old Hannibal left his base at Cartagena on the south-east coast of Spain.

He began his march with nearly 60,000 men, but part of the army rebelled when they reached the Pyrenees mountains and realised what lay in store. About 7000 men were left behind.

The first real obstacle in Hannibal's path was the River Rhône. Historians disagree about where Hannibal crossed, but the Greek historian Polybius, writing about 150 BC, suggests that Hannibal chose the lowest practicable point, between Four-ques on the west bank and Arles on the east bank. This is just above the place where the Rhône splits into two for its final journey to the sea, and where it is shallow and

The route over the Alps *Hannibal led his army through one of the highest passes in the Alps, Col de la Traversette, to attack the Romans in the Po valley, the end of a five-month march from Cartagena in Spain. This last*

part of the route was the most hazardous. Up to 20,000 men died from cold, landslides and attacks by tribesmen, but the elephants survived.

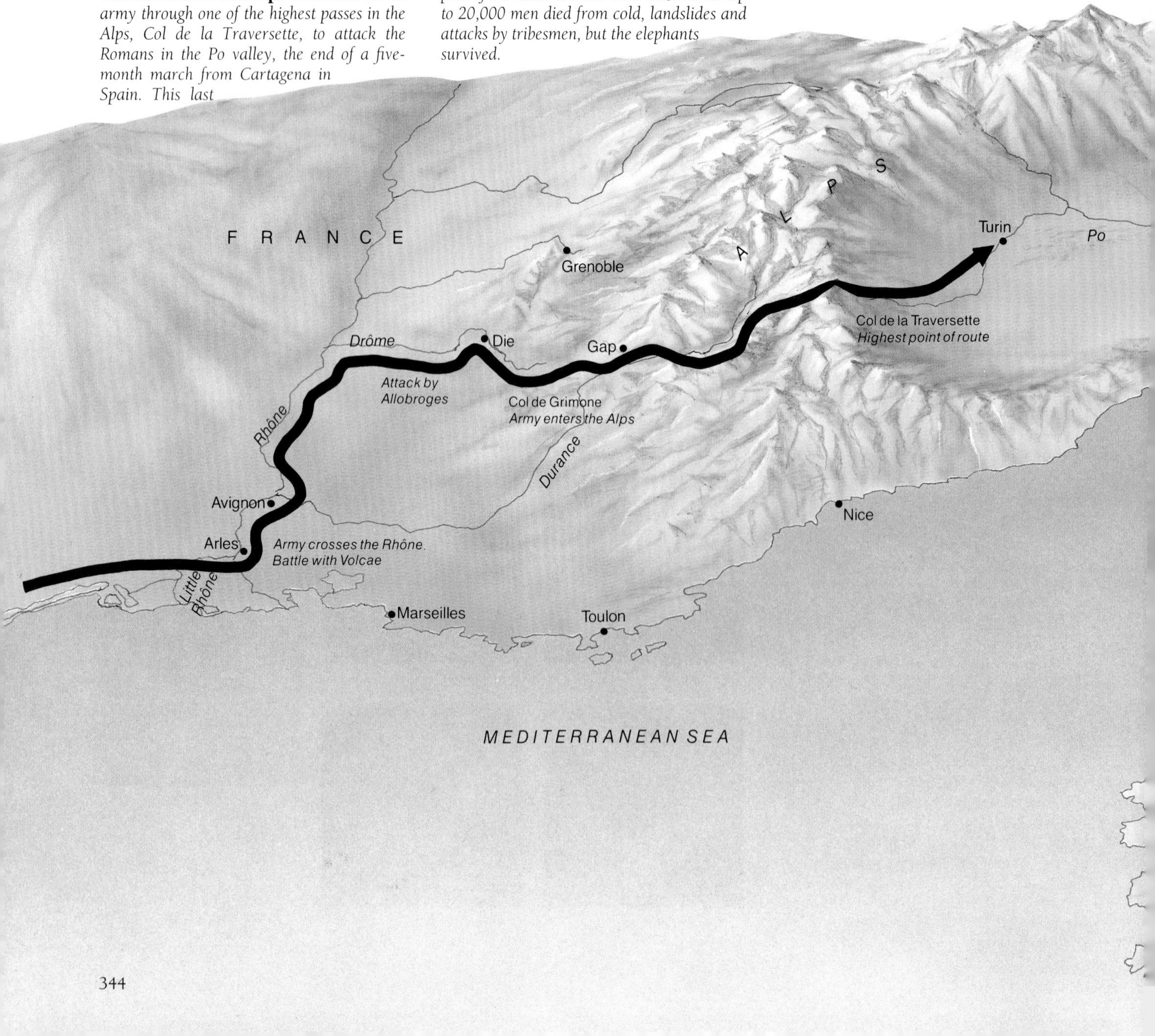

FRANCE

A L P S

Turin

Po

Grenoble

Col de la Traversette
Highest point of route

Drôme

Die

Gap

*Attack by
Allobroges*

Col de Grimone
Army enters the Alps

Rhône

Durance

Nice

Avignon

Arles

*Army crosses the Rhône.
Battle with Volcae*

Little Rhône

Marseilles

Toulon

MEDITERRANEAN SEA

slow-running, although wide – about half a mile (800m).

A Gallic tribe, the Volcae, massed on the east bank to dispute his crossing, so Hannibal sent a small force of infantry under his brother, Hanno, to cross farther upstream on improvised rafts, and outflank them. Hannibal then commandeered boats and built rafts, and when the first wave of his men stormed across, the Volcae found themselves caught between two forces. They broke and fled.

Hannibal now turned to getting the bulk of his army across. For the elephants, the Carthaginians built piers about 200ft (60m) long out into the river, and covered them with soil. Large rafts, also covered with soil to deceive the elephants, were moored at the ends of the piers. First

WHY DID HANNIBAL TAKE THE ELEPHANTS?

Elephants were used in warfare mainly as a shock force – not only to scare the enemy but also, like tanks, to push them aside. And they could carry small towers on their backs, from which marksmen could launch arrows or spears – although there is no evidence that Hannibal's elephants carried them. On marches, elephants proved useful pack animals, being able to carry up to ten times more than a horse. A disadvantage, though, was the amount of food needed – an elephant eats up to 300lb (140kg) of vegetation a day. As the army climbed even higher and snow made grazing impossible, the elephants suffered severely from hunger.

Hannibal's elephants were not very large, standing probably about 8ft (2.4m) at the shoulder. Hannibal captured them from the foothills of the Atlas Mountains of northern Africa, where elephants have become extinct since his day. Hannibal also had a few Indian elephants, which Carthage had obtained from Egypt.

That elephants were held in high esteem by the Carthaginians is evident from some of their silver coins, which feature them on the reverse. The fronts of the coins showed gods and important people, including Hannibal (above left).

ITALY

Venice

ADRIATIC SEA

Genoa

• ROME

the cow elephants were led on to the rafts, and the bulls followed. A few beasts panicked and fell into the water, but the river was shallow enough for them to wade across underwater, with only their trunks showing – held high like snorkels.

The army marched north along the east bank of the Rhône as far as the Drôme, then east into the Alpine foothills. Their exact route across the Alps is not known, but evidence from ancient writers suggests it began east of Die, probably at the Col de Grimone, and went through the Col de la Traversette into the Po valley in Italy.

Right at the beginning of the crossing, the army had to beat off an attack by a Gallic tribe, the Allobroges, and lost many men and horses. The same day Hannibal captured a town where he replaced some of the horses and obtained supplies. To supplement their food the army had to live off the land, and as they climbed higher and snow prevented grazing or browsing, fodder for the animals became a problem.

Often they had to travel along narrow cliff tracks with a steep drop on one side. On the way, there were skirmishes with hostile tribesmen. In one place the attackers rolled down heavy stones from above (probably in the Combe de Queyras), and on the seventh day Hannibal had to station part of his army on a bare rock overlooking the gorge to protect the pack animals as they slipped through in the night (this may be near Château Queyras). Cold and landslides, however, caused more casualties than did attacks, and many soldiers and pack animals slipped over the edge. The army reached the summit on the ninth day, after losing their way several times, then rested for two days before descending.

Even on the descent they ran into trouble. On the twelfth day a landslide completely blocked the way, and the trail had to be cleared before the elephants and horses could continue. One huge rock was cleared by lighting a fire to heat it, then dousing it with sour wine until it cracked and could be broken up with pickaxes.

On the fifteenth day the Carthaginian army reached the plain of the River Po. Hannibal had lost at least 20,000 men, but still had all of his 37 elephants (although all but one died later during the severe winter). And he defeated a Roman army under Scipio that had gathered on the plains by the Ticino River.

Hannibal continued to fight the Romans in Italy for 15 years, winning three major battles and many minor ones, but although he had many allies among the Italian tribes he never had enough troops to shatter the might of Rome. In 203 BC he was called back to Carthage, which was under attack from Scipio. Carthage was destroyed by Rome some 50 years later. By then Hannibal was dead – he took his own life in 183 BC to avoid capture.

Bread and beer from the Stone Age

Bread and beer both come from grain. Bread was made from wild wheat and barley in the Stone Age. Beer-making may have started as a byproduct of early bread-making, and no one knows whether the first grain was cultivated because of a need for bread or a taste for beer.

Stone mortars, pestles and grinding stones found on ancient sites indicate that people in the Middle East were making some form of unleavened bread or mash with wild grain even before they knew how to make pottery.

With wild grain, it is difficult to separate the edible seed from the chaff – the outer sheath. Archaeologists believe that early people learned to split the chaff by parching the grain on hot stones while they were threshing it. Mixing the parched grain with water would have produced an edible mash. Unparched seeds may have been moistened and left to sprout, like bean shoots. Natural yeasts could have fermented the liquor left from such sprouting, making it into beer.

The first people known to have grown their own grain were the Natufians, who lived around Mount Carmel in what is now northern Israel. Research by a British archaeologist, Dr Romana Unger-Hamilton, in 1988, showed that they were using flint sickles to cut wheat and barley they had grown themselves as long as 13,000 years

Bake and brew *Egyptian tomb figures show baking and brewing 3000 years ago.*

ago. She found sickles with scratch marks caused by dust, showing that the plants were reaped in cleared ground, not among natural vegetation where ground cover from other plants keeps the dust down.

The Sumerians, who lived in southern Mesopotamia (now mainly modern Iraq) around 5000 years ago, used about 40 per cent of their grain harvest to make beer of eight different flavours. About 1750 BC, King Hammurabi of Babylon, in southern Mesopotamia, issued laws regulating the quality of beer to be sold in taverns.

The ancient Egyptians were the first people known to have made leavened bread, in about 2600 BC. They used wheat flour to keep a store of sour, fermented dough (sourdough) that was added to each mix to make the bread rise. Sourdough may have been discovered by accident, when airborne yeast entered dough that had been mixed and put aside before baking. Later civilisations, such as the Celts, used barm – the yeasty foam from fermenting beer – to leaven bread.

Ancient skill *These models of Egyptian bakers date from about 1900 BC. By then, leavened bread had been made for 700 years.*

Patterns in stones

Only from the air is it possible to recognise this drawing of a monkey in the stony desert on the Pacific coast of Peru. It covers an area of nearly 5 acres (2 hectares); one of its hands is over 40ft (12m) across.

The monkey is just one of the many mysterious stylised drawings and ruler-straight lines set out in the desert around 1000-2500 years ago by the Nazca people. The Nazca Lines, as they are called, were not discovered until 1926, and their full array – covering 200sq miles (500sq km) – was not evident until 1941, when the Peruvian air force photographed the desert.

To make the lines and drawings, the ancient Nazcans simply moved the desert's brownish-black stones to expose the yellow soil underneath, and piled them to one side in mounds. Why they did so, or how they achieved such results, no one knows.

How Stone Age artists created masterpieces by lamplight

Even with modern electric lighting, the painted caves of southern France and Spain are still gloomy. When the Stone Age artists of around 12,000 to 30,000 years ago drew their vivid animals on the walls, they had to work in near darkness, even by day. Some of the paintings are a long way from daylight; the great chamber of the cave at Niaux in Ariège, France, is just over half a mile (800m) from the entrance.

The cave artists had only the dim light of

Tools and paints *An engraving tool, with hardened ochre still on its working edge, lies beside two sculptor's picks and some bits of ochre and manganese. Stone Age artists once used these artefacts to paint caves in France.*

flickering lamp flames to paint by. A number of these lamps have been found, and the walls and paintings show smoke traces from many more.

The lamps are stone slabs or cobbles with saucer-like hollows to hold the fuel of animal grease, and a wick of dried moss or

lichen. Juniper twigs were also used as wicks at the Lascaux cave near Montignac in south-west France.

The artists were particularly inspired to paint the animals on which they depended for their food and raw materials. Many of the paintings are outlines drawn in a single colour; others are filled in with colour. Sometimes the outlines were engraved with sharp flints or painted in black. On occasions, the artists painted with their fingers.

Colours were mixed from natural pigments such as iron oxide and red and yellow ochre

Colour range *These 12 pigments, ranging from pale yellow to black, are similar to those used in the Lascaux cave. They consist of powdered minerals.*

Early light *Hollow stone lamps such as this lit the scene for the Stone Age cave painters. The fuel was animal tallow.*

(reds and yellows), manganese oxide (black), haematite (reddish-brown), and porcelain clay (white). At Lascaux evidence shows that the painters ground the minerals using pestles and mortars, and they then blended the colours on stone palettes to produce various shades. Substances such as charcoal and quartz were used in the blending process.

Waterproof paint

The colours were probably mixed with fat to make the paint waterproof; those at Lascaux were mixed with cave water high in calcium carbonate, which made them durable. Paints were applied with brushes made of feathers, animal hair, or twigs, and with pads of moss or fur.

As well as working in poor light in the inner chambers and the deep recesses of the caves, many of the cave artists must have endured considerable discomfort. Some paintings are in narrow recesses less than 3ft (1m) high, and to paint them the artist would have had to crouch uncomfortably. Others are at heights that could have been reached only from ladders of scaffolding, which were made of wood.

Working lunches

In part of the Lascaux cave, archaeologists have found evidence of scaffolding – some of which must have reached as high as about 16ft (5m). Holes 4in (100mm) deep are cut into the rock on both sides of a passage. They are at a height of about 7ft (2m), and were most likely supports for a platform, cemented into the holes with clay. This would have allowed artists to reach the ceiling. There is also evidence of 'working lunches' – reindeer bones scattered on the floor.

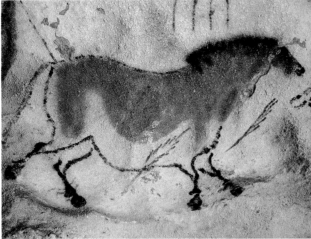

Hall of the Bulls *The Lascaux artists in south-west France used the walls and ceiling of the Hall of the Bulls for their paintings and engravings of animals. These included a brown horse (above); a yellow bull (top right); and three stags (bottom right).*

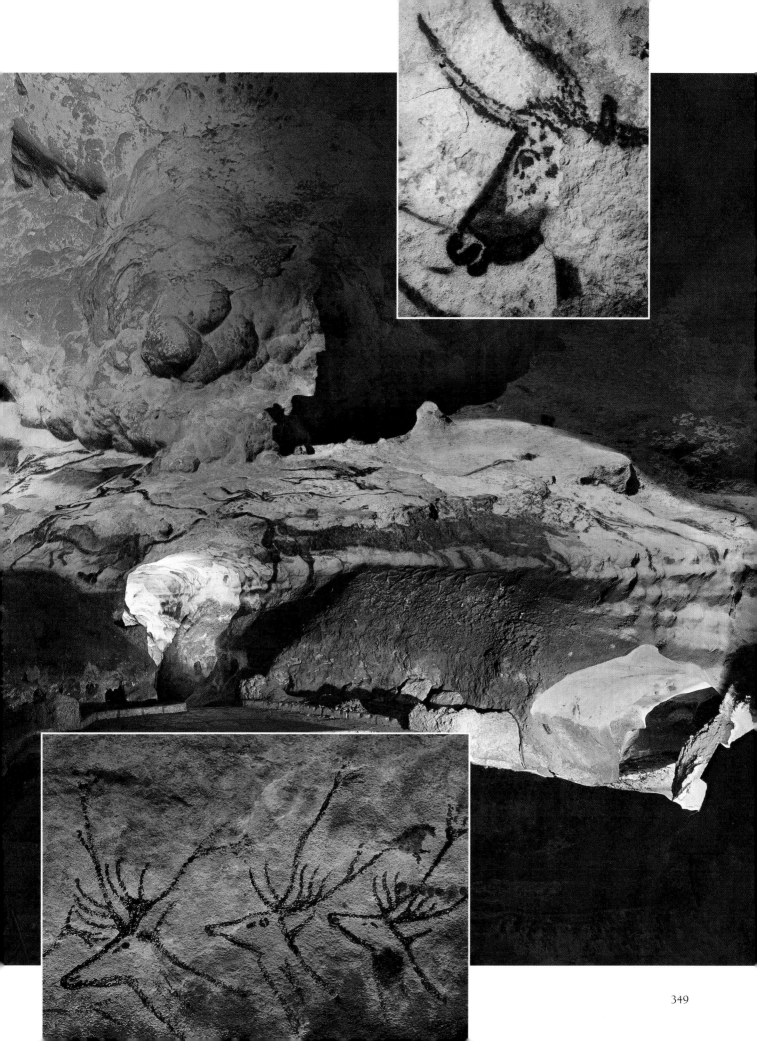

Roman Games: staging the savage shows at the Colosseum

From dawn to dusk, the Roman Colosseum resounded to the roar of the crowd enjoying the Games – a spectacle of butchery and bloodshed that could last for months. The peak of the entertainment was reached in the *munera*, the gladiatorial combats in which armed men fought each other – often to the death. More than 2000 men might fight during the course of a single day's games.

The Games originated as small spectacles organised by Roman noblemen, usually to mark a funeral – the first was in 264 BC. It was believed that the souls of the dead could be propitiated by human bloodshed. The official games, organised by the Roman consuls for the year, were first held in 105 BC.

Grim monument

The Colosseum, completed in AD 80, is one of the finest buildings of ancient Rome still in existence. The great four-storeyed stone amphitheatre could hold 50,000 spectators. The most privileged – officials, priests, vestal virgins – sat on the lowest level (the *podium*) of the steeply tiered seats, the poorest on the top row. The sand-filled arena was about the size of a football pitch.

Animals in the arena

Lions, tigers, bulls, bears, elephants and buffaloes were all used in animal combats or hunts in the arena. Sometimes they were pitted against men, sometimes against each other. At the dedication celebrations for the Colosseum in AD 80, 5000 animals were killed in one day.

The beasts were kept below the amphitheatre, and cages were hauled up to the entry tunnel using ramps and hoists. The spectators were protected by a 13ft (4m) high metal grating around the arena.

Hunts were sometimes organised, with the hunters using bows or spears from the safety of the seating area. At other times they entered the arena with hounds.

The men who fought the animals in the arena with bow, spear or dagger were called *bestiarii*. Condemned criminals or lowly prisoners were sometimes thrown to the animals defenceless.

There was a vast industry in capturing animals from all parts of the empire, and some species, such as the North African elephant, disappeared.

The fighting men

The gladiators were recruited from among slaves, condemned criminals and prisoners of war. A few desperate men or bankrupts joined the ranks of their own free will for an agreed term, for a hiring fee and in the hope of prize money. But even the free men had to swear an oath of submission for the duration of their contracts, agreeing to be 'burnt with fire, shackled with chains, whipped with rods and killed with steel'.

There were well-organised training schools for gladiators. A novice learned how to use his weapons, and was well fed on a special diet to strengthen the muscles – barley, considered health-giving, was a staple food.

Each gladiator was trained to fight with particular weapons. One group of gladiators, called Samnites, used the weapons and armour of the ancient Samnite tribe conquered by the Romans. They each had a short sword, a large, oblong shield, a visored helmet, a shin guard on the left leg, and a metal or leather sleeve on the right arm. By contrast, the *retiarii* ('net men') wore only a short tunic or apron and each carried a net, trident and dagger. A *retiarius* was usually pitted against a *secutor* ('pursuer'). The *secutor* had a helmet and shield and was armed with a sword and also a stick weighted with lead, used to ward off the net the *retiarius* was trying to entangle him in.

Sometimes a *mirmillo* – armed like a *secutor* but with a fish crest on his helmet – was pitted against a *retiarius*. Or a *mirmillo* fought a Thracian, who had a small round shield and a curved sword. The *bestiarii* who fought animals in the arena were not classed as gladiators.

Death in the stadium *Gratifying the blood-lust of tens of thousands of Romans, armed men fought wild animals (below) or each other. Gladiators like the Samnites, protected by shields and helmets, pitted their strength and their skill in swordsmanship against the nets and three-pronged spears of the* retiarii *(below right).*

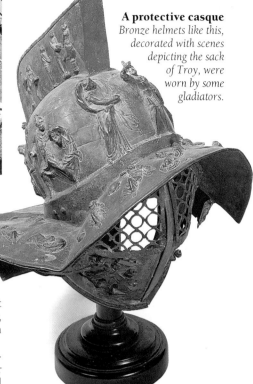

A protective casque
Bronze helmets like this, decorated with scenes depicting the sack of Troy, were worn by some gladiators.

The Colosseum's crumbled ruin *Completed in AD 80 by the Roman Emperor Titus, the Colosseum echoed for four centuries with the roars of 50,000 spectators. The floor of the oval arena – 287ft × 180ft (87.5m × 54.8m) – has since fallen away. All that can be seen now are the underground passages where beasts and prisoners were kept before being hoisted up in cages to the entry tunnel – and almost certain death.*

The night before a combat, gladiators on the list to fight next day were entertained to a generous banquet laid on by the organiser of the show. Many spent the night – most likely their last – in feasting and drinking.

Gladiators rode from barracks to amphitheatre in chariots, then marched through one of the 80 archways into the arena. Some wore ornate helmets and purple cloaks, and had slaves to carry their weapons. Halting at the *pulvinar*, where the emperor and his party sat, they extended their right arms and chanted: 'Hail, Caesar and emperor, those who are about to die salute you.'

Animal combats or hunts usually began the programme. Before the gladiatorial combats began, officials checked the weapons and equipment. After a few warm-up fights with wooden weapons, the comba-

tants for each fight were chosen by lot. Then to the clamour of bugles, pipes, horns and water organs the first combat began – perhaps Samnite against Thracian or *mirmillo* against *retiarius*, mostly in single combat but sometimes in squads.

While the crowd howled encouragement or derision and placed bets on their favourites, the training instructors incited their men to action with both words and whips, laid on by the *lorarii* ('floggers'). Sometimes reluctant combatants were prodded with red-hot irons.

When a gladiator was wounded the crowd shouted '*Hoc habet!*' ('He's had it'). A disarmed, wounded or defeated gladiator raised a finger of his left hand – or his left arm if he was on the ground – in appeal to the crowd. They meted out mercy with

thumbs up or a waving handkerchief – death with thumbs down. But it was the emperor who decided the man's fate, generally following the mood of the crowd.

Some fights were billed from the start as being to the death, and went on until one man was finally killed. The loser was then dragged away to the *spoliarium* ('death chamber'). If he was found to be still alive,

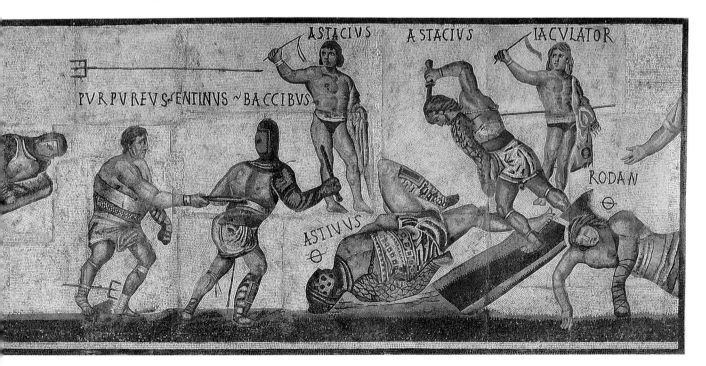

attendants finished him off. At the end of the day, the list of gladiators was marked with P, V or M, indicating who had perished, who were the victors and who were *missi* ('losers') allowed to live to fight another day.

Brief days of gold and glory

Gladiators were the pop stars of ancient Rome. The darlings of the crowd were the combat veterans whose names ensured a high attendance, and who were lauded in the graffiti. A contest winner was rewarded with gifts and gold pieces to enjoy until his next combat. But not many survived long enough to win the *rudis* ('wooden sword') given to an outstanding gladiator along with his liberty.

A few noblemen took part in gladiatorial contests, attracted by the glamour and thrills. The eccentric Emperor Commodus, who was assassinated in AD 192 (he was strangled by his wrestling partner), took part in a number of gladiatorial bouts, slaying opponents who were either un-armed or had only blunt weapons.

Some women – often noblewomen – entered the profession, but they were banned by the Emperor Septimius Severus in AD 200.

Christianity eventually brought the age of the gladiator to an end. The Emperor Constantine the Great forbade the con-demning of criminals to the arena in AD 326, and gladiatorial combats were finally outlawed in AD 404 – after the monk Almachius, who tried to separate two gladiators, was stoned to death by the spectators.

Besieging a medieval castle: breaching the defences by force or cunning

The massive walls of medieval castles were formidable defensive barriers. Before gunpowder came into use in the Western world in the 14th century, laying siege to a castle was a difficult and lengthy task. If time was no object, the simplest way to capture a castle was to surround it and starve the garrison into submission.

But garrisons were often small – 20 men could defend a fair-sized castle – so provisions might last a long time. As long as the water supply held out, a siege could last for months and prove expensive – the besieging army, composed largely of mercenaries, had to be fed and paid. The alternatives were assault or subterfuge.

Launching an assault

A typical medieval castle had an outer bailey (a large courtyard) surrounded by a defensive wall. Another wall enclosed the inner bailey – a smaller courtyard. Up to the 13th century, the main strongpoint was the tower, or keep, inside the inner bailey. Changes in the castle plan from that date gradually lessened the importance of the keep as a strongpoint. The castle was often built on a hill or cliff to give a commanding view of the landscape and to make assault difficult. If possible it had the protection of a river or a moat. Some castles were set on an island.

Because the vulnerable points of a castle were its entrances, they were well defended. The main entrance was protected by a barbican – an outwork often consisting of a narrow, roofless passage where intruders could be attacked from above. The door was usually shielded by a portcullis – a heavy, spiked grating that could be lowered in front.

If the castle had a moat, there was a drawbridge that could be raised, forming not only an extra barrier but a gap between attackers and defenders. Often there was also a postern – a small emergency exit. It was also used as a sally port from which counterattacks could be made.

Attackers usually relied on bombardment to weaken the defences before making a direct assault. Defenders appearing on the walls were a target for archers with longbows or crossbows, although crenellated battlements gave them some cover. The crossbow fired bolts (also called quarrels), had a longer range – over 300yds (274m) – and was easier to use, but slow because it had to be mechanically redrawn. Longbowmen needed to be very skilled, but were faster – a good archer could send 12 arrows a minute to a range of at least 220yds (200m), sometimes nearly twice that distance.

To weaken or breach the walls, the attackers used engines of war. These long-range weapons went under many different names, but most were effectively giant catapults. Any convenient rock could be used as ammunition, but it was usual to shape the stones so that they were roughly spherical and consequently would fly better. They were typically 17-20in (430-510mm) in diameter.

Engines of war were also used to hurl

burning projectiles, in the hope of setting fire to the castle buildings. Sulphur and pitch were used, but the most effective flammable material was Greek Fire, used by Greeks defending Constantinople (modern Istanbul) against Muslim attackers in AD 673. Its exact composition is still unknown, but as it would burn on water and could not be put out with water, it was probably based on petroleum.

Getting to grips

For close assault the attackers had to move up under the walls. If there was a moat,

Bombarding the battlements *A late-15th-century illustration records the English siege of the château at Mortagne-sur-Gironde, on the south-west coast of France. Among the arms used were longbows, crossbows, hand cannon and cannon.*

they had to build a pontoon bridge across it, or fill it with stones to make a causeway. Close assault was hazardous work. Stones and boiling water could be rained down on them by the defenders through holes, known as machicolations, in the overhanging part of the battlements. They could also be picked off by the defending archers.

So the attackers worked under a mobile shed or mantlet mounted on wheels and made of heavy timbers. This was known as a 'tortoise' or, in Latin, *testudo*, because of its covering and slow movement. Alternatively it was called a 'cat' because of its stealth. With this protection they could hammer at the walls or the gate with a battering-ram – a huge log of wood swung

Crusader stronghold *Crac des Chevaliers, in Syria, was built by Crusaders before 1142, on a spur with steep slopes on three sides. The base of the walls was fortified by a talus – a sloping mass of soil and debris – to guard it against mining.*

MURDEROUS WEAPONS USED IN A MEDIEVAL SIEGE

To weaken or breach castle walls, attackers used long-range artillery as well as close-range weapons. The long-range engines of war were effectively giant catapults. Any convenient rock could be used as ammunition, but it was usual to shape the stones so that they were roughly spherical and would fly better. These machines were also used to hurl burning projectiles. For close attack, rams or bores and belfries were used, and occasionally the attackers would tunnel under the walls.

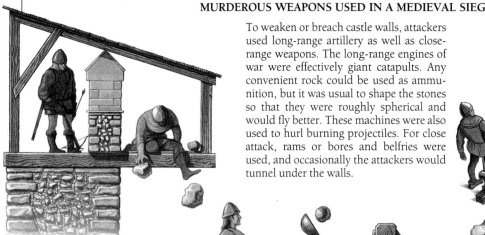

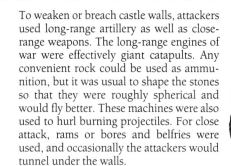

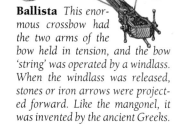

Hoardings *These wooden extensions to the castle walls were covered and had slatted floors through which boiling liquids or missiles could be dropped onto the attackers beneath. Their main disadvantage was that they could be set on fire or damaged by missiles.*

Trebuchet *A heavy box fixed at one end of a long arm caused the arm to flip up when it was released from the windlass, and hurl the projectile.*

Mangonel *A tightly wound skein of horsehair, rope or sinew held a long arm under tension, and a stone was loaded into a cup or sling. When the skein was released, the arm jerked up, hurling the stone.*

Ballista *This enormous crossbow had the two arms of the bow held in tension, and the bow 'string' was operated by a windlass. When the windlass was released, stones or iron arrows were projected forward. Like the mangonel, it was invented by the ancient Greeks.*

Belfry *A high wooden tower was wheeled up to the castle walls, and the attackers shot at the defenders from inside. They might then storm the castle along a drawbridge at the top of the tower.*

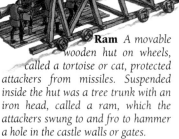

Ram *A movable wooden hut on wheels, called a tortoise or cat, protected attackers from missiles. Suspended inside the hut was a tree trunk with an iron head, called a ram, which the attackers swung to and fro to hammer a hole in the castle walls or gates.*

Bore *Before a ram was used against the castle walls, the stonework was weakened by a large pole with a metal spike, which was rammed repeatedly into the mortar.*

Mining *If a castle was not surrounded by a moat or built on rock, its attackers might dig a tunnel, supported by wooden props, up to a wall or corner tower of the castle. They could then weaken the foundations and build a fire at the base of the wall. The heat would crack the stones, the props would burn, and the wall would collapse.*

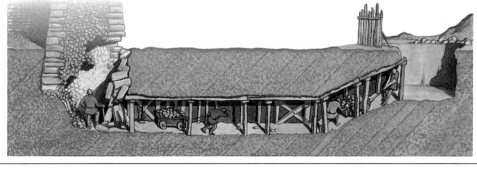

to and fro by soldiers, sometimes with the aid of slings mounted under the tortoise. The ram's head had an iron cap, often with a point. Early versions had metal in the shape of a ram's head at the battering end, hence the name.

Another method of attack under cover of the tortoise was with a tree trunk that had a spike at one end. The spike was jabbed into the mortar to loosen stones. Men with picks or crowbars also chipped away at the mortar to remove stones.

Scaling ladders were used to get men over the walls. Attacking soldiers climbed up under the covering fire of archers, who harried the defenders with a storm of arrows to stop them pushing the ladders away. The archers were often sheltered by large mobile shields.

Often the besiegers built a mobile wooden siege tower, or belfry, so that their archers could shoot at defenders from the same level as the battlements or even from above. The siege tower had several platforms, and a drawbridge at the top. If the attackers could manage to wheel it close to the walls, its drawbridge could be used for men to cross onto the walls.

Tunnelling and explosives

If the castle had no moat and was not built on solid rock, the attackers often tunnelled their way under the walls. When they had a big enough section of wall undermined and supported with wooden props, they built a fire around the props. As the props burned through, the wall would collapse.

The coming of gunpowder and cannon (in the 15th century) made the task of besiegers easier, although for many years the primitive explosives and guns were barely more effective than the old engines of war, and were certainly more dangerous to the people using them.

One of the earliest uses of gunpowder was in the petard, a small iron pot filled with explosives that was either ignited then hurled by hand at the enemy, or first attached to a gate or other weak point to blow a hole in it. But the engineer igniting the petard might not reach safety before the explosion – hence the remark of Shakespeare's Hamlet: ''Tis sport, to have the engineer hoist with his own petard.'

The fall of a mighty fortress

When it was built by Richard the Lionheart, King of England and Duke of Normandy, in 1196-8, Château Gaillard at Les Andelys, near Rouen in France, was considered one of the strongest fortresses in Europe. It was set on steep 300ft (90m) cliffs overlooking the River Seine, and could be approached only from the south-east. When Richard died, it became the property of England's King John. In 1203, King Philip Augustus of France attacked the stronghold.

After capturing the opposite bank and destroying the river bridge, Philip's army dug in and surrounded the château. King John sent an army and a naval force to lift the siege, but they were routed.

Roger de Lacy, the English commander of Château Gaillard, calculated that he had enough food to feed a strong core of soldiers for a year. The rest, along with those local inhabitants who had taken shelter in the castle, were turned out. With the gates shut behind them and French troops in front turning them back with spears, hundreds were left in misery to starve between the two armies. Philip did, however, finally allow them food and passage through the attacking army when he went to inspect his troops.

Philip decided to attack in the following spring, and his army eventually managed to bring down part of a wall of the outer bailey by tunnelling and fire. The defenders then set fire to the rest of the outer defences and withdrew, leaving the attackers to try to find a way into the impregnable inner area, with two more moats and baileys.

They achieved it when a party of six soldiers swarmed up a latrine drain and gained entry to a window in the crypt of a chapel (an addition by King John) in the middle bailey. They managed to lower the drawbridge. Tough fighting followed, but the last bastion, the inner bailey, fell when the attackers succeeded in weakening the walls under the shelter of a projecting rock that had been left as a partial bridge over the moat. The castle finally fell to the French army in March 1204, after a siege lasting around five months.

Medieval germ warfare

Engines of war were not only used for hurling missiles – another practice was to catapult rotting carcasses over the walls. Dead animals, even horses, were slung into a besieged castle to spread discomfort and disease among the defenders.

One such incident had far-reaching and disastrous consequences. In the winter of 1346-7, bubonic plague broke out among a Tatar army that was besieging the fortified port of Caffa (modern Feodosia, in the Crimea). The Tatars had probably caught the plague from new arrivals from central Asia, where the disease was endemic.

The besiegers thought to speed up the siege by hurling the corpses of some of the plague victims over the ramparts. But the disease spread rapidly among both attackers and defenders and the Tatars had to abandon the siege.

Among the defenders was a group of Italian merchants, who had taken refuge there from the Tatars. Those who survived took ship to Genoa in Italy, carrying the plague with them. The disease spread throughout Europe, killing at least a quarter of the population. Known at the time as the Great Pestilence, it was renamed the Black Death in the 19th century.

How ancient sailors explored the seas

Long before the magnetic compass needle came to be used by European sailors in the 12th century, ancient sailors were finding their way across the open seas.

By the 5th century BC the Phoenicians, who lived in what is now Lebanon, were taking their curved, broad-beamed galleys beyond the Pillars of Hercules (the Straits of Gibraltar) and crossing the often stormy Bay of Biscay to trade for tin in Britain and the Scilly Isles.

In the Pacific Ocean, the ancient Poly-nesians crossed thousands of miles of sea in outrigger canoes during the 1st millennium AD. They settled in islands within the triangle of ocean between Hawaii, Easter Island and New Zealand.

Sounding coastal waters

Sailors have used sounding lines to pick their course through coastal waters since earliest times, when they generally kept in

Early traders *The ancient Phoenicians ventured beyond the Straits of Gibraltar and traded for tin in Britain as long ago as five centuries before Christ. This stone relief shows one of their vessels.*

sight of land and hove to or went ashore at night. A sounding line was a weighted rope. The weight was often lead, with tallow stuck in its hollowed base.

The rope measured the depth to the sea bottom and the tallow revealed what lay there – by the sand, shingle or mud that it picked up. If the tallow was clear, the ship was above rock. The rope was marked with tags to measure the depth, and they were commonly a man's arm-span apart. The traditional measure of a fathom – 6ft (1.8m) – owes its name to the Vikings. It is derived from an old Norse word for 'embrace'.

Steering by the stars

In the open seas, sailors could find their general direction from the sun's position by day in fair weather. At night they used the stars. The ancient Phoenicians were guided by the Little Bear constellation. They knew it was always in the north.

The ancient Polynesians also steered by stars. They sometimes provisioned their 60ft (18m) canoes for journeys of around 2000 miles (3200km) lasting several weeks. They knew the latitude of various islands by the stars that rose to their zenith above them, and could set their course by a star rising or setting low down on the horizon. They picked another star at the same point when the first had either risen too high or sunk out of sight.

The way of the wind

The Greeks and Phoenicians knew which way the prevailing winds blew in the Mediterranean, and used them as direction guides. These winds were drawn out on a compass-like diagram known as a windrose. The navigators could estimate the direction of the wind by its relationship to the sun, and relate it to the windrose. They could also distinguish a wind such as a north wind or south wind by its strength, temperature, and how wet or dry it was.

The windrose continued to be used by later seafarers, and was inscribed on medieval charts. The Italians named the winds marked on it after the areas they blew from, such as Greco (north-east), Levante (east) and Sirocco (south-east).

Reading the water signs

Ancient Polynesian navigators not only used the stars, they could read the ocean as skilfully as North American Indian trackers could read signs on land. The lore of the sea and sky was handed down from father to son over the centuries.

Skilled seamen could steer by their senses – feeling ocean swells and the slightest currents through the deck boards, and using them as direction guides. They knew if a current was likely to carry them off course, and altered their direction. By the pattern of the swell they could tell whether they were heading into a sea broken by islands or towards open sea. They could also tell if clouds were over an island, by the way they massed and by the colours reflected in them from below.

One way in which they recognised the direction of land on overcast nights was by 'underwater lightning' – streaks of bluish-green light emitted from many kinds of sea creatures, such as shrimps. The streaks stretch out from an island in all directions for up to about 100 miles (160km).

Early map makers

A Greek astronomer named Pytheas, who lived in the 4th century BC, was the first man known to have used the sun to fix the latitude – the distance north or south of the Equator – of the places he visited. He sailed round the European coast from Cadiz in Spain to Britain in 310 BC.

Pytheas fixed the latitude of his native Massilia (modern Marseille, then a Greek colony), and this was used by the Greco-Egyptian astronomer and geographer Ptolemy when drawing a map of the world in the 2nd century AD. Ptolemy also used the work of a 1st-century Phoenician, Marinus of Tyre. He originated the idea of a grid of parallel lines on seamen's charts.

How Columbus discovered the 'New World'

Before 1492, no European knew exactly what lay beyond the Canary Islands and the Azores. When Christopher Columbus set sail westwards, he was looking for a sea route to eastern Asia – the Indies. What he discovered was a new continent, one that the greatest explorers and geographers in Europe did not know existed. Later they called it the *Mundus Novus*, or 'New World'. Today it is North and South America.

Columbus reached the Caribbean islands, not North America. His momentous discovery was the result of a major error, but he never realised this. To the end of his days he insisted that he had reached the 'Indies'. That is why the West Indies have their name, and why the inhabitants of North America became known as the American Indians.

Columbus was born in Genoa, Italy, in 1451, and went to sea at the age of 14. By the time he was 30 he was an experienced seaman and navigator.

In the 15th century the Portuguese were trying to find a sea route to the Indies, from where there was a rich overland trade in spices, gems and silks. Their navigators were probing the eastward route, round the southern tip of Africa.

From his studies of the Bible, ancient literature and the few scientific books he could get hold of, Columbus formed the opinion that it would be quicker to sail west to the Indies. His annotated copies of Marco Polo's *Description of the World* and Cardinal Pierre d'Ailly's *Imago Mundi* are still in existence.

Greek warship *The ancient Greeks used the prevailing winds as direction guides. This decoration on a 6th-century BC drinking cup from Athens shows a bireme – a warship with double banks of oars. Its spiked prow was used to ram enemy ships.*

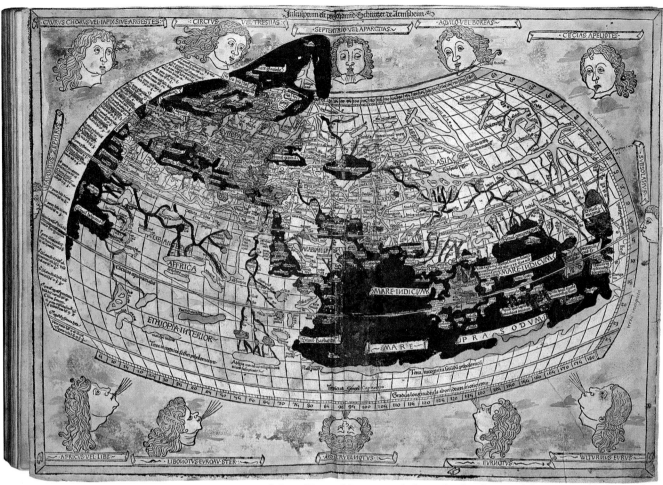

Map of the Old World *Six years before Columbus discovered the New World, this woodcut map of the Old World was published in Ulm, Germany. It comes from a map-enhanced edition of the* Geography *of the Greco-Egyptian geographer and astronomer Ptolemy (about AD 90-168). His work helped to inspire Columbus in his bids to find a western route to Asia.*

Westward ho! *Columbus set out westwards to find the Far East and never realised he had discovered the new continent of America.*

In the *Imago Mundi*, written in about 1410, one passage reads 'Aristotle says that the sea is little between the farthest bound of Spain from the East and the nearest of India from the West'. Marco Polo claimed that Japan lay 1500 miles (2400km) east of Cathay (China), making it appear to be much nearer to Spain than it actually is.

Columbus was misled by the writings of d'Ailly and Polo, and by a statement in the Apocryphal Second Book of Esdras, which said that the Earth consisted of 6 parts land and 1 part sea, instead of the real figure – 1 part land to nearly 3 parts sea.

To make matters worse, he made all his calculations in Italian miles, unaware that they were shorter than the Arabic miles used in many contemporary maps. So he concluded that the Indies were only about 3900 miles (6300km) west of the Canary Islands. Had he used the Arabic measurement, his calculation would not have been far out – about 5200 miles (8320km).

Columbus tried to sell the idea of a westward venture to the King of Portugal, João III, but the king rejected the plan in 1482. Columbus was eventually backed by the joint rulers of Spain, Ferdinand of Aragon and his wife Isabella

Pointing north *This Italian mariners' compass – complete with box and lid – is typical of those used in Columbus's time. It has a fleur-de-lis to mark the North.*

of Castille, exactly ten years later – 1492.

Columbus was given three ships for the voyage: the decked ship *Mariegalante*, which he renamed *Santa Maria*, and two smaller caravels, the *Niña* and the *Pinta*. The *Niña* was about 50 tons and only 67ft (20m) long, with three or four masts. The *Pinta* was about 60 tons.

The crews were small – 40 men aboard the *Santa Maria*, 26 on the *Pinta* and 24 on the *Niña*. Some were friends of Columbus, but most were men from towns and villages in Andalusia. A few were convicts who had been pardoned in return for undertaking the voyage. Columbus captained the *Santa Maria* and Martin Alonzo Pinzón the *Pinta*, with his brother, Francisco Pinzón acting as navigator. Another brother, Vicente, skippered the *Niña*.

The ships sailed from the little port (now silted up) of Palos de la Frontera in southern Spain on August 3, 1492, and made for the Canary Islands. The voyage took nine days, during which the *Pinta* lost her rudder. Repairs took more than three weeks. Columbus tempered his impatience by taking the opportunity to alter the *Niña*'s sails. At last on Thursday, September 6, with its supplies replenished, the little fleet again sailed, westwards, into the unknown.

With the aid of a quadrant (for measuring altitude) and compass, Columbus was able to steer a more or less straight westward course by dead reckoning. Speed was measured by throwing a chip of wood over the side near the bow and counting how long it took for the ship's stern to pass it. Columbus may have carried hourglasses for measuring time, as they were widely used in medieval Europe.

When three weeks had passed and there was no sign of land, many of the men grew restless, and began to murmur amongst themselves. They believed that the wind – now behind them – always came from the east, and if they failed to find land the return trip into the wind would take so long they would run out of food and water. Several times mutiny threatened.

Finally, more than five weeks after leaving the Canaries, the welcome cry that land was in sight came at 2 o'clock in the morning of October 12. By the light of the moon the look-out on board the *Pinta* had seen the shadowy coast about 6 miles (10km) ahead. They did not know it, but they had reached the Bahamas.

Soon after dawn Columbus landed and claimed the land for Spain, calling it San Salvador. It turned out to be an island, which he described in his log as 'quite large and very flat and with very green trees and many waters, and a very large lake in the centre, without any mountain'. On the beach their arrival was watched by a group of young people, naked except for some body paint.

Columbus and his crew were enchanted by the people and the island they visited. But after the *Santa Maria* ran aground on a reef and had to be abandoned, Columbus took command of the *Niña* and set a course for Spain, landing at Palos on March 15, 1493. The triumphant discoverer was made Admiral of the Ocean Sea and Viceroy of the Indies.

Columbus made three more voyages to the New World. He landed on the South American mainland on his third voyage, but in 1500 he returned to Spain in chains, accused of mismanaging the lands he had discovered. He was pardoned, but fell from royal favour.

Where did Columbus actually land?

The island where Columbus landed in 1492 was called Guanahani by the Indians who lived there. Exactly which island it was has puzzled experts for many years.

Until the 1980s, Watling Island in the Bahamas, renamed San Salvador in 1926, had long been the favourite – with three monuments marking the event. Then a group of experts began to re-examine the evidence. They plotted the route across the Atlantic, using computers to take account of wind speed, currents and magnetic variations.

Their conclusion was that Guanahani could only have been one of two places – Watling Island or Samana Cay, 60 miles (100km) to the south-west. They claim that Samana Cay's landscape and surroundings fit Columbus's description better than San Salvador, but the controversy continues.

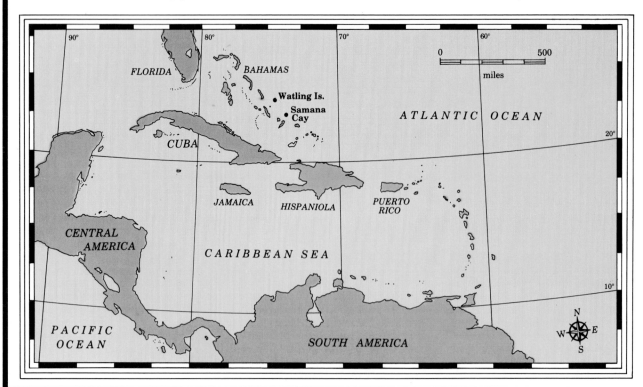

The raising of Lady Liberty

The lady in Paris *The Statue of Liberty was built and erected in Paris before being shipped to her new home in America in 1886.*

The Statue of Liberty towers more than 305ft (93m) above the waters of New York Harbour, where, in the words of her creator, 'people get their first view of the New World'. It is the largest metal statue in the world, and took more than 15 years to build at a Paris workshop before being transported across the Atlantic to America.

The graceful folds of Lady Liberty's robes give no clue to the huge, pylon-like supporting structure beneath. You can climb the 171 steps that spiral through her body to an observation platform concealed in the rim of her crown, for a spectacular, statue's-eye view of the vast sweep of city and sea.

Each of Liberty's eyes is the length of a man's arm, her nose is 4½ft (1.4m) long, and her index finger 8ft (2.4m). She stands an imposing 151ft (46m) tall, on a pedestal and base of about the same height again, and has a 35ft (10.5m) waist.

To create a statue on such a massive scale more than 100 years ago, took the artistic vision of an inspired young sculptor and the innovative engineering skills of the man who later built the Eiffel Tower.

The sculptor Frédéric Auguste Bartholdi was dining at the home of a distinguished French historian in the summer of 1865 when the idea of a gift from the people of France to the Americans was born. A statue of 'Liberty Enlightening the World' (her

The lady in New York *The twin towers of New York's World Trade Center provide a striking background for Lady Liberty.*

Copper sculpture *The copper plates or sections which form the giant hand and tablet can clearly be seen in the close-up below. Altogether some 300 hand-hammered plates were fashioned for the completed statue. Temporary braces prevented the plates from buckling – and holes were then punched for the rivets which connected all the plates into one great figure.*

Plaster model *Section by giant section, Liberty was created in her Paris workshop (above). Dwarfed by a full-size model of Liberty's left hand, craftsmen put plaster on the wooden framework. Sculptor Bartholdi (lower right, bare-headed) supervised the entire operation.*

official title) would mark the centenary of American Independence which the men and arms of France had helped to win, and would be a lasting symbol of friendship and shared ideals between the two great nations.

Inspired by the legendary Colossus of Rhodes – a gigantic bronze statue of the Greek sun god Helios, one of the Seven Wonders of the Ancient World, that stood at the harbour entrance at Rhodes in the 3rd century BC – Bartholdi designed and built a 36ft (11m) high plaster model. His finished statue would be more than four times taller and need to be strong enough to withstand the ravages of time and weather, yet light enough to ship to America.

The solution was to make Liberty hollow, with an outer shell on an inner framework – the same technique that was used for the Colossus of Rhodes. But whereas the Colossus had an outer shell of cast bronze,

Simplicity
Liberty's creator Frédéric Bartholdi spoke of the simplicity of her appearance. 'The details of the lines ought not to arrest the eye.'

Bartholdi decided to use thin sheets of copper, a light and relatively flexible metal. Instead of casting the copper, he proposed to use a method of shaping called *repoussé*, meaning 'pushed back', beating the metal into shape over sculpted wooden moulds. This copper outer skin would 'hang' on an inner, tower-like framework of iron.

Bartholdi cut his master model into

Internal damage *Renovation work on the statue's interior in the 1980s showed that the iron armature connecting the copper plates to the framework was severely corroded. The whole network, including the rivets, had to be renewed with modern materials.*

THE $69 MILLION FACELIFT

In the early 1980s, Liberty was given a thorough examination, and it was found to be disintegrating.

Over a century of high-level exposure to the elements – and condensation from the breath of millions of sightseers climbing up the inside – had caused severe corrosion. The statue had always leaked; in later years, some of the rivets that held the copper skin together gave way, allowing more moisture to seep into the vulnerable iron framework. Much of Eiffel's original asbestos insulation, the buffer between the copper skin and iron skeleton, had worn away and nearly half of the armature had become badly rusted; 1800 bars had to be completely replaced. Liberty's torch was in danger of falling off, and the torch-bearing shoulder needed reinforcing.

Fund-raising

It took a pooling of technological expertise and funds from both sides of the Atlantic for the 3½ year, $69 million restoration. The French initiated the fund-raising campaign and lent leading architects and craftsmen.

Liberty was encased in what was probably the largest freestanding scaffolding structure ever, and her vital statistics fed into a computer to create detailed new structural plans. French craftsmen rebuilt the torch, replicating Bartholdi's original design using the *repoussé* technique, and master gilders from Paris gold-leafed the flame with 24 carat gold, so that it would gleam when floodlit.

The skin itself was in good condition once the rivets were replaced. Over the years the copper had lost its original 'new penny' colour and acquired a naturally weathered, pale-green patina. When the statue was cleaned, this patina had to be carefully preserved as it forms a protective coating against corrosion. On the inner surface, seven layers of old paint

that were trapping moisture in the seams had to be frozen and cracked off with sprays of liquid nitrogen cooled to $-325°F$ ($-163°C$). The layers of tar beneath them were blasted off with jets of a bicarbonate of soda solution.

Exact copies of each of the rusted bars from the armature were made in stainless steel (which does not react corrosively with copper as iron does). This job had to be done section by section – no more than 12 bars could be removed at any 24 hour period without jeopardising Liberty's stability. To prevent contact between the two metals, protective, waxy layers of Teflon tape were placed between the bars and the copper skin.

Two technologies

To guard against the build-up of condensation inside, the renovated stairwell has wider railings, and a glass-enclosed hydraulic elevator has been installed. And, for those who cannot face the whole climb, closed-circuit televisions relay images of the statue's interior, showing just how it has been constructed and improved – the remarkable, combined achievement of two technologies a century apart.

High rise *Scaffolding erected during the restoration work rose to just over the height of the statue itself – 305ft (93m).*

Old flame *In 1916 the flame was resculpted into a lantern with amber glass in a copper grid. But it was poorly sealed and water leaked in.*

New flame *In 1985 a new copper flame was made, gilded with thin but durable sheets of gold leaf. As well as being rain-resistant, the leafing has a warm, rich, golden glow.*

sections, and made thousands of meticulous measurements before scaling up each section into a full-sized plaster replica. Wooden moulds were then carved to exactly match each of the enlarged sections. The finished 'skin' was made by hammering 300 thin copper sheets into the moulds from the inside.

Meanwhile, Alexandre Gustave Eiffel, an engineer renowned for his brilliant bridge-building, was working on the interior framework, which was to be the tallest iron support structure attempted up to that time. His design anticipated that of modern skyscrapers; like them, Liberty's outer shell is non-loadbearing, and 'floats' on its frame.

A framework of iron ribs radiates horizontally from a central backbone of four vertical girders that reach from Liberty's base to the nape of her neck. Attached to this is the armature, made of spring-like iron bars that curve and twist to follow the shape of the statue, like the framework of a dressmaker's dummy. To minimise the direct and potentially corrosive contact of copper and iron, the sections of copper skin are hung on this interior skeleton with copper brackets covered with an insulating material to keep the two metals apart.

The statue cost the people of France $400,000; but the flow of funds was

sporadic, and work progressed fitfully. The mighty arm that bears the torch of liberty was finished in time for America's 100th birthday in 1876, but it was not until June 1884 – nearly 20 years after she had first been thought of – that Liberty was finally completed. She towered triumphantly above the streets of Paris, and was formally presented to the American minister to France on Independence Day, July 4.

Six months later, the statue was completely dismantled, and packed, numbered section by numbered section into more than 200 enormous crates, to be carried to America in the French naval transport ship *Isère*.

How they carved the Mount Rushmore memorial

Four giant faces gaze out from a mountain side in the Black Hills of South Dakota in the USA, shaped into the granite mountain top. If the bodies were carved into the mountain as well, each figure would be about 460ft (140m) tall.

The faces are those of four US presidents, hewn and blasted from the top of Mount Rushmore with pneumatic drills and dynamite by men dangling over the cliff edge. The work was directed by an American sculptor of Danish descent, John

Gutzon Borglum. The mammoth operation took 14 years to complete.

The mountain carving is a national memorial, and the four presidents – chosen to represent the nation's birth and ideals – are George Washington, the first president, Thomas Jefferson, the third, Abraham Lincoln, the 16th, and Theodore Roosevelt, the 26th.

The idea for the memorial developed from suggestions put forward by the South Dakota state historian Doane Robinson in

1923. He proposed the Needles, a group of tall granite spires in the Black Hills, to be carved into statues of western heroes such as Kit Carson and Buffalo Bill Cody. Borglum, the sculptor engaged for the project, did not consider the Needles or the subject suitable. He felt that such a grand undertaking should be of national importance.

The Mount Rushmore National Memorial was carved between 1927 and 1941 at a cost of $990,000, raised mostly from

MEASURING IN THE STUDIO AND ON THE MOUNTAIN

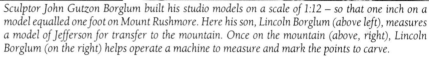

Sculptor John Gutzon Borglum built his studio models on a scale of 1:12 – so that one inch on a model equalled one foot on Mount Rushmore. Here his son, Lincoln Borglum (above left), measures a model of Jefferson for transfer to the mountain. Once on the mountain (above, right), Lincoln Borglum (on the right) helps operate a machine to measure and mark the points to carve.

federal funds but partly from private donations. The actual carving took about six and a half years, but work was slow because of money difficulties in the early years, and because of periods of unsuitable weather. Most of the men who worked on the carving were local miners or quarry-men. For 14 years around 360 were employed, working in teams of about 30.

Planning and 'pointing' the heads

Borglum chose the 5725ft (1745m) Mount Rushmore for the memorial because of its fine-grained granite. Even so, tons of weathered and cracked surface stone had to be removed to expose suitable rock – for Washington's head they had to cut back about 30ft (9m), and for Roosevelt's, the rearmost of the group, some 120ft (37m). Some 450,000 tons of rock were cut away in the course of the carving, and still lie at the foot of the mountain.

Borglum decided to carve one head at a time so that he could make it blend with its neighbour and its surroundings. Washing-ton's was the first. He made a plaster model of it, one-twelfth life size.

The model was 5ft (1.5m) high, and on the top of the head, Borglum fixed a flat plate marked in degrees. Pivoted from its centre was a horizontal steel bar 30in (760mm) long, marked off in inches. A

Heads of state *The heads of four US presidents – (left to right) George Washington, Thomas Jefferson, Theodore Roosevelt and Abraham Lincoln – are cut out of Mount Rushmore in South Dakota.*

sliding plumb line, also marked in inches, was suspended from the bar. By swinging the bar and sliding out the plumb line to any point on the face, such as a nostril, the necessary measurements could be made.

To transfer measurements from the model to the mountain, a similar device 12 times larger was set up on the cliff top at the spot chosen for the top of Washington's head. Borglum called the device a pointing machine, and the men whose job it was to measure and mark out the shaping points on the rock were known as pointers.

Shaping the rock

After the points had been chosen, the rock was drilled to the depth indicated by the pointer, to make holes for dynamite charges that would blast away the outer rock to within about 6in (150mm) of the final surface. Drilling had to be very precise, because cutting too deep would remove too much stone, and it could not be replaced.

Each driller was strapped in a leather-lined seat hung by cable from a winch, with his 85lb (39kg) drill slung from the same cable. The winchman was too far back from the cliff top to see the driller, whom he had to haul from point to point. So a call boy in a safety harness sat on the cliff edge and relayed messages between them.

Using a pneumatic drill while dangling perhaps 250ft (76m) from the cliff top was difficult. To exert enough pressure for deep horizontal holes, drillers had first to set up a length of chain so they could brace the back of the seat against it. They slung the

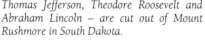

363

chain on steel pins fitted into vertical holes drilled in the rock face.

Drill bits were blunt after about 15 minutes, and hundreds had to be sharpened every day by a full-time blacksmith. Workers moved up and down among the drillers carrying the bits in potato sacks.

As the drillers moved from point to point, the powdermen began inserting dynamite in the drilled holes ready for blasting. They set 60 or 70 very small charges at a time. Blasting took place twice a day – at lunchtime when the men left the face, and at the end of the day.

To cut the roughly shaped surface down to the finished dimensions, drillers honeycombed the rock with rows of short, closely spaced holes, so that the final layer could be prised off with steel wedges and hammers. Then the surface was 'bumped' smooth with special drills.

The problems with Jefferson's head

Washington's head was dedicated in 1930, and work then began on Jefferson's. It was started on Washington's left (from the viewer's standpoint). But in 1934, poor quality rock resulted in the head having to be blasted away and repositioned on the other side of Washington.

The new rock was badly fissured, and 60ft (18m) had to be removed to reach a suitable surface, leaving just enough thickness between the cliff face and the canyon behind it. Even then, a long crack where the nose was to be carved caused Borglum to adjust the head to a different angle. Other smaller cracks were filled with a mixture of linseed oil, white lead and powdered granite.

Jefferson's head also has the only patch needed in the whole work. A small pocket of feldspar, which could not be carved, was revealed during work on the upper lip. So it was cut away to leave a hole about 2ft (600mm) long and 10in (250mm) wide and deep. Two steel pins were set in the base of the cavity to hold a granite plug that was cemented with molten sulphur.

The master touch

The four heads are each 60ft (18m) high. On average, each head has a nose 20ft (6m) long, a mouth 18ft (5.5m) wide, and eyes 11ft (3.4m) across. On this scale, to give character and expression to the carved heads needed a master touch.

Borglum gave the eyes a lifelike sparkle by leaving a granite column about 22in (560mm) long in each hollowed out pupil as a highlight. The sunlight picks out the column against the shadow of the hollow.

Borglum died on March 6, 1941, at the age of 73, shortly before the memorial was completed. The finishing touches were supervised by his son, Lincoln, who, as a boy of 15, had worked as a pointer at the beginning of the project.

THREE STAGES IN THE MAKING OF LINCOLN'S HEAD
A driller prepares the site for Lincoln's head (above, left). Later another driller 'honeycombs' the site (above, right) to allow the last layers of rock above the 'skin' to be prised off. Lincoln's beard was formed of irregular vertical markings (below).

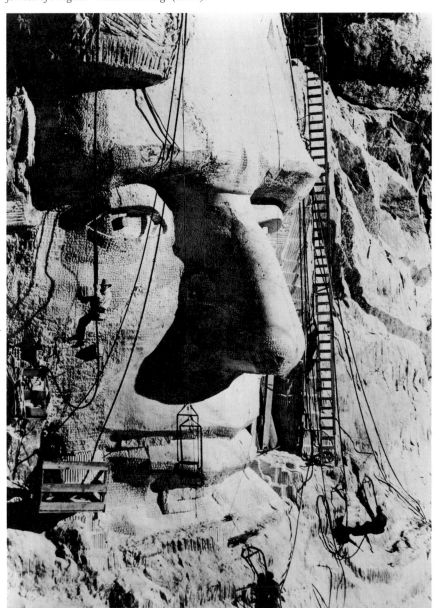

Roman waterworks: supplying public fountains and baths

Around 40 million gallons of fresh water a day were supplied to ancient Rome, mostly to public fountains, basins, baths and latrines.

Some of the water was supplied direct to the homes of the rich, who lived in villas or ground-floor apartments in blocks of flats. But people living on the upper floors had to collect their water from fountains or ground-floor basins. There were also professional water carriers, called àquarii.

At least 40 cities of the Roman Empire had similar water supplies, and the remains of some 200 aqueducts are still to be seen. They include the breathtaking, three-tiered Pont du Gard that helped to supply Nîmes in France, and the two-tiered, 119ft (36m) high Segovia aqueduct in Spain.

Channelling the water

All Rome's water was carried by a network of 260 miles (420km) of channels or pipelines from springs, lakes or rivers in the hills around.

Most of the water supply could not be turned off and constantly flowed away into the drains. A few villas had taps consisting of a cylinder pipe inserted crossways into the supply pipe. The cylinder had a hole through it, and could be turned to close or open the supply. The standard supply pipe, about ¾in (20mm) across, was called a quinaria.

Water flowed by gravity through the supply system, so its course had to follow the lie of the land to keep the flow steadily downwards. The channels (aqueducts) were made of brick or stone with a watertight cement coating on the inside, and were on average, 3ft (910mm) wide and 6ft (1.8m) deep. Some ran underground and had air shafts about every 240ft (73m), to prevent airlocks.

The channel top was covered with stone slabs to keep out dirt. The first channel to serve Rome was the Aqua Appia, built about 312 BC, during the Republic. It was about 10 miles (16km) long and ran mostly underground from a spring on a private estate.

If a channel could not be routed round the head of a valley, it was usually carried across by a series of arches high enough to allow the road or river in the valley to pass underneath.

The Aqua Marcia, built in 144 BC, took 57 miles (91km) to carry drinking water into Rome from springs in the Anio valley 23 miles (37km) away. It was mostly a covered channel, but for the last 7 miles (11km) into Rome it was mounted on arches.

The Emperor Trajan built the Aqua Trajana in AD 109 to supply the commercial and industrial area on the east bank of the River Tiber. This aqueduct was over 100ft (30m) high in places, and even supplied market fishponds on the fifth storey of the Forum – a market square.

By AD 350 there were 11 major aqueducts supplying Rome.

When the supply reached the city, it was collected in reservoirs or tanks. Rome had nearly 250 at various points in the network.

Siphoning through lead pipes

Water was usually carried across valleys on aqueducts, but lead or earthenware pipes were used in some parts of the empire.

Well and water tank *Water from mountains 50 miles (80km) away was carried by aqueduct to the ancient African port of Carthage. The water was kept in a well – complete with earthenware pipes (top, left of picture) – and then piped into the adjacent cistern, or water tank. Each day people visited the cistern, lowered pitchers through the hole in the roof (above) and drew up the water.*

Running water *Built in the reign of Emperor Trajan (AD 98-117), this Roman aqueduct at Segovia in Spain is still in use. It brings water to the city over a distance of 12 miles (19km). Its double-tiered granite arches are rough-hewn and laid without lime or cement.*

Pipes were directed down one slope of the valley and up the next to a slightly lower level. The pressure from the fall on the higher side forced the water across the flat and up the other side. The supply to Lyon in France was taken this way across the river valleys of the Garonne, Beaunant and Brevenne. Some 12,000 tons of lead were used to make the pipes.

The Roman sewers
An elaborate system of drains took the waste water from the city to discharge into the River Tiber, and so into the sea. The smaller sewers fed into one massive one, the Cloaca Maxima, which stretched from the Forum to enter the river under a 16ft (5m) archway by the Ponte Rotto. It is still in use, 2500 years after its construction.

Rome's sewers were built long before the water-supply system. Building began in the 6th century BC to drain the marshlands. The sewers were also connected to ground-floor public and private latrines, but there were no pipes to them from latrines on upper floors.

Although the water was not treated, the engineers took care in assessing good sources. One test was to note whether the water would leave any spots when sprinkled on a good bronze vase. Another was whether it could be boiled and poured off without leaving any mud behind, and yet another was whether green vegetables could be cooked in it quickly.

Some water was not considered good enough for drinking. The Aqua Anio Vetus, for example, built in 272 BC, carried water 43 miles (69km) from the upper reaches of the River Anio. But it was used only for watering gardens or washing clothes.

The water system was administered by a commissioner and two assistants, who had a staff of secretaries, clerks, gangs of masons, lineworkers, and reservoir keepers. The channels needed constant inspection and repair, because leaks damaged the structure and also wasted water.

Rome's public baths were some of the finest ever built. The first dated from the 2nd century BC, built by public benefac-

tors or as business concerns. Later, various emperors had them built. Ruins of two of the finest still remain, the baths of Caracalla (AD 217), which covered 27 acres (11 hectares), and the baths of Diocletian (AD 306), which covered 32 acres (13 hectares).

The baths were heated by underfloor furnaces (*hypocausts*), which circulated steam and hot air. There were usually three main baths, the cold *frigidarium*, the gently warmed *tepidarium*, and the hot *caldarium*.

It was usual for bathers to be massaged with oil and then to join in sports or physical exercises before entering the hot bath. Then they went to the steam room where the oil and sweat was removed with a metal scraper (*strigil*). After that they visited the *tepidarium* before plunging into the cold pool.

Men and women bathed separately, although mixed bathing became common in the 1st century AD. But it was frowned upon by many. The Emperor Hadrian forbade it in AD 138, and as there were not always separate bath houses for women, separate bathing hours were allotted.

Early medicine: performing brain surgery in the Stone Age

Brain surgery is not a modern skill – it was carried out by Stone Age man around 12,000 years ago. Ancient skulls with holes cut in them have been discovered in Europe (especially France), Africa and South America – by far the most in Peru.

Many of the ancient skulls that have been discovered have new bone growth round the edges of the hole, showing that the patients lived for some time after their operations. An ancient skull found at Cuzco, in Peru, had three separate holes, each one showing new growth during a long period of healing.

Skull fractures
Primitive brain surgery was still being practised by Pacific islanders in the 19th century. Trepanning (or trephining) operations – to relieve depressed skull fractures received in combat from being hit on the head by a stone – were graphically described to *The Medical Times* by two British missionaries – the Rev J.A. Crumb and the Rev Samuel Ella – in 1874.

They told how, while the patient was unconscious, bone was scraped and cut with a hard sea shell or a flake of glass-like obsidian to make a hole about 1in (25mm) across, leaving the brain exposed. After the scalp had been replaced, the wound was bandaged with strips of banana palm fibre. Eight out of ten patients recovered.

Studies of ancient holed skulls, and experiments by scientists, reveal that Stone Age surgeons must have worked in much

the same way. They used sharp flakes of flint or obsidian to gouge away the bone. Some Peruvian skulls have rectangular openings, which seem to have been made by a flint saw.

Another method sometimes used was drilling a circle of small holes. This is evident from the small, circular dents round the edge of the large hole that was created. A sharp-pointed flint set into a stick was probably rotated with a bow. Primitive bow-drills were made by looping the bow string once round a stick or arrow, which turned as the bow was sawed to and fro.

But brain surgery was not limited to warriors with head wounds from battle. Stone Age patients from Europe (Poland and Portugal), South America (Peru) and North America (Alaska) included men, women and children aged from six to 60 who had suffered serious accidents to the head in the course of their daily lives.

As the Stone Age gave way to the Bronze and Iron Ages, superstition took over from healing as the motive for skull surgery. And skulls were trepanned – usually after death – so that discs of bone from them could be worn as amulets to ward off evil spirits.

Modern scientists who have used simple stone tools to make trepanning experiments on skulls have generally been able to make a neat hole in about half an hour.

Skull and tools *Found in the north-west of South America, this 2000-year-old skull (left) has the scars of two trepanning operations. In the 1930s, an English doctor, Wilson Parry, performed operations using stone tools. The two tools without wooden handles (below) are Neolithic knife blades. The three wooden-handled blades were made by Parry himself for his experimental work.*

Paints, powders and poisons as early cosmetics

Eye shadow was used by the ancient Egyptians more than 5000 years ago, for practical reasons as well as adornment. Paint on the eyelids and round the eyes helped to protect them from the glare of the sun. The eye paint used was a thick paste of malachite – bright green copper salts.

Like other Egyptian women of the 1st century BC, Queen Cleopatra used blue eye shadow made from ground lapis lazuli stones for her upper eyelids, and malachite for her lower ones. She darkened her eyebrows and eyelashes with kohl – fine powdered lead sulphide mixed with sheep's fat. Red ochre (iron-stained clay) provided her with lipstick and cheek rouge, and her palms were painted with henna to give them a youthful pink glow.

Henna, a reddish-brown dye made from Egyptian privet, was also used by Egyptian women as a nail varnish. It was thickened with catechu – a tannin-containing substance from the wood, bark or fruit of various trees, such as acacia. Egyptian men hennaed their hair and beards.

In ancient Greece over 2000 years ago, a pale face was considered more attractive than rouged cheeks, so women used ceruse – white lead mixed with wax, fat, oil or egg white – as face powder paint. It certainly gave them a becoming pallor, but its long-term effect was to poison them. The lead, absorbed through the skin, caused poor appetite, stomach upsets, dizziness, shortness of breath, paralysis of the limbs, headaches, and sometimes blindness and death.

Affluent Romans – both men and women – also used white lead, and a rouge made of red lead. The Emperor Nero and his second wife, Poppaea, both used lead face paint in the 1st century AD. But they also used a face pack of dough and asses milk at night, to counteract the effect of the paint on their skin. Accordingly, they took a herd of she-asses with them whenever they set out on a journey.

Returning Crusaders introduced white and red leads to Western Europe in the late Middle Ages, and despite its damaging effect, white lead was used as face paint until well into the 18th century.

Another form of poison came into use for adornment in Renaissance Europe in the 15th or 16th centuries. This was belladonna, the juice of the deadly nightshade plant, applied as eye drops. Its name means 'beautiful woman' in Italy, where it was first used, because it dilated the pupils

Sweet smelling *Women with perfume cones on their heads attend a banquet in Thebes in ancient Egypt. The wax cones – perfumed with herbal extracts – melted over the women's wigs, giving off a sweet smell. The scene is part of a tomb wall-painting of about 1400 BC.*

and gave a sparkle to the eye. But belladonna contains the drug atropine, which if used to excess, strains the eyeball and causes blindness.

Women in Renaissance Europe wore scarlet lipstick of cochineal, made from dried female scale insects found on cacti in Mexico and the Indies. The dye was bound with egg white and alum, and formed into a lip pencil with plaster of Paris or ground alabaster. A common 17th-century rouge ingredient and freckle remover was mercuric chloride, a poison so deadly that 0.04 oz (1 gram) can cause death. Absorbed into the skin, it kills tissues and eventually destroys the nervous system.

How the Greeks measured the Earth

Ancient Greece's wisest scientists did not go along with the generally accepted thinking of their ancestors – that the Earth was a circular plate supported by four elephants standing on a huge sea turtle. They had already concluded that it was a sphere. The idea was mooted about 500 BC by followers of Pythagoras, who considered the sphere to be the perfect shape.

The first man to be credited with measuring the Earth's circumference was the Greek astronomer Eratosthenes in 230 BC. He reasoned that if the Earth was a sphere, then the line joining two places was an arc of a great circle. If he could measure the distance as both a length and as a proportion of 360 degrees (a complete circle), he would have an arc from which he could calculate the total circumference.

It had been recorded that at noon at the summer solstice (about June 21), the Sun was directly overhead at Syene (modern Aswan) because it shone vertically down a deep well. So at the same time of year at Alexandria, many miles to the north-west of Syene, Eratosthenes measured the angle of the Sun from the vertical and found it was one-fiftieth of a complete circle – exactly 7.2 degrees in today's measure.

He then needed to know the crow's-flight distance between Syene and Alexandria. One of the ways in which he may have calculated this was by the journey time of camels. A laden camel keeps up a steady pace, and could travel at around 100 stadia a day – today 1 stade is usually regarded as about 605ft (185m). Since a camel caravan took 50 days to travel between Alexandria and Syene, Eratosthenes made the distance 5000 stadia – about 575 miles (925km). This produced the figure of 250,000 stadia, or roughly 28,740 miles (46,250km), as the circumference of the Earth.

Bearing in mind his lack of equipment and his rule-of-thumb measurements, it is remarkable that he arrived at a figure that is less than 15 per cent too long compared with modern measurements. Had he known the exact distance between Syene and Alexandria – 526 miles (847km) as the crow flies – his answer would have been just under 230,000 stadia, about 26,440 miles (42,550km), and only 6 per cent out.

Today, we know that the Earth is flattened at the North and South Poles, and the circumference at the Equator is about 24,900 miles (40,075km).

Unlocking the secrets of forgotten languages

When scholars have set out to decipher the script of an ancient language – one no longer spoken or understood by anyone living – they have generally looked for two main aids. One is a bilingual example, where the unknown language is written alongside the same text in a known one. The other is proper names – those of kings and gods, for example, which are sometimes known in other languages and are often the first step to comprehension.

The hieroglyphics of the pharaohs

For hundreds of years, scholars were fascinated by the hieroglyphics – picture writing – inscribed in, or painted on, the interior walls of ancient Egyptian monuments. But knowledge of the meaning of the script, used by the Egyptians for over 3000 years, died out in Roman times.

The discovery of the Rosetta Stone in 1799 was the key to deciphering the hieroglyphics. The stone had inscriptions carved in three different scripts: hieroglyphics, another unknown Egyptian script called demotic, and Greek. The Greek section, which could be read, stated that all three texts contained the same message. They were a decree in honour of Ptolemy V dated to 196 BC.

The first scholars who tried to decipher the Egyptian texts concentrated on the demotic section, and started by locating proper names in it in relation to the Greek text. But they made little headway in transliterating them. The first step towards success came in 1816, when an English physicist, Thomas Young, was the first person to realise that the demotic script had developed from the hieroglyphics, and that in the writing of names, at least, hieroglyphics had a sound value and were not merely symbols.

A French scholar, Jean-François Champollion, was finally successful in showing that hieroglyphics had a sound value in 1822. He was familiar with both Greek and Coptic – the final phase of the ancient Egyptian language, dating from the 2nd century AD and written in Greek with a few demotic characters.

When comparing the 1419 hieroglyphics on the stone with the Greek text of just under 500 words, Champollion noticed that there were only 66 different hieroglyphics, and that some of these were frequently repeated. He concluded that the

Stone of secrets *The Rosetta Stone, found in Egypt in 1799, bears inscriptions in hieroglyphics, a cursive script called demotic, and ancient Greek.*

Code-breaker *A French scholar, Jean-François Champollion, deciphered the Rosetta Stone, the key to understanding Egyptian hieroglyphics.*

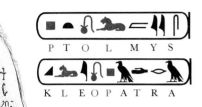

Royal names *Scholars assumed that the oval or 'cartouche' in the hieroglyphics contained a royal name – Ptolemy. Champollion then compared the signs with other signs in a cartouche of Cleopatra found on an obelisk from Philae and identified P, O and L. After that he deduced the sound value of the remaining signs.*

hieroglyphics were phonetic, representing spoken alphabetic signs and syllables and that there were several alternatives for the same sound, as in the English k and q. He worked for 14 years and compiled an Egyptian grammar and dictionary.

The discovery of the Rosetta Stone

When General Napoleon Bonaparte led a French Republican army to occupy Egypt in 1798, they were accompanied by a party of scholars and scientists whose task was to study and recover archaeological remains.

But it was by accident that, during the course of the two-year campaign, an engineer lieutenant named Bouchard discovered the Rosetta Stone. He was supervising fortifications at Rashid (Rosetta) on the west bank of the Nile Delta and, so the story goes, noticed the black basalt stone built into a fairly modern wall and half buried in the mud. When the importance of the inscriptions was realised, the stone – which is 3ft 9in (1140mm) high and 2ft 4½in (720mm) wide – was removed to Cairo and then Alexandria.

The French force surrendered to the British army in 1801, and the stone is now in the British Museum.

The writing of ancient Persia

Cuneiform writing consists of wedge-shaped symbols sometimes engraved in stone but mostly impressed on clay tablets with a sharp tool known as a stylus. It was used in ancient Persia (now Iran) more than 2000 years ago. A 17th-century Spanish ambassador to Persia, Garcia Silva Figueroa, first described it to the modern world in 1618. He recognised the ruins near Shiraz, where he saw the script, as 6th-century BC Persepolis (the ancient capital of Darius the Great).

But it was more than 200 years before Persian cuneiform script was deciphered, largely by two men working independently. They were Professor Christian Lassen of Bonn, Germany, and Major Henry Creswicke Rawlinson, an English officer who was military adviser to the Governor of Kurdistan. Both were helped by the earlier work of a Dutch teacher, Georg Friedrich Grotefend of Göttingen, who had deciphered the names and titles of the kings Darius and Xerxes.

Professor Lassen, a student of languages, worked on the small number of texts available by comparing them with other languages, including Sanskrit and the hieroglyphics of Egypt.

Major Rawlinson studied the huge inscription carved on a rock face 200ft (60m) above ground level in the Zagros

Court writing *This example of cuneiform writing is part of a wall relief from the court of Ashurnasirpal II of Assyria. It dates from about 860 BC and was found in the ancient Assyrian capital of Kalhu (today Nimrud in Iraq). The ram's head is a boss on a chair.*

Mountains near Behistun in western Iran. His translation of the first two paragraphs, completed in 1837 after several years' work, agreed with those of Lassen, published in 1836.

The decipherment of Persian cuneiform opened the way to the understanding of at least six ancient languages, including Babylonian.

The script of ancient Greece

When the British archaeologist Sir Arthur Evans uncovered some inscribed clay tablets at Knossos, in Crete, at the beginning of the 20th century, no one knew for certain what language they represented. It was thought to be that of the Minoan people of ancient Crete, dating from the 14th to the 12th centuries BC.

After other tablets bearing a different but related script were uncovered at the same and other sites, the script was given the name Linear B. The second and earlier script was called Linear A.

Not until 1952 was Linear B deciphered, by a 30-year-old British architect, Michael Ventris. He had the benefit of earlier work by an American, Alice Kober, in the 1940s. She developed a rudimentary method of establishing the relationships of signs by attempting to compare word endings and prefixes.

Ventris set out to analyse the script like a code, fitting it into a table showing the frequency of related signs, and apparent changes in word endings. The breakthrough came when he realised the script was using the Greek language, and he was able to identify town names. Ventris was killed in a car crash in 1956. His work on the decipherment of Linear B forms the basis for most further researches on the script. Linear A, however, remains largely undeciphered.

How the first nonstop flight was made across the Atlantic

The first nonstop flight in an aeroplane across the Atlantic Ocean took place only 16 years after the Wright Brothers made their first 120ft (37m) hop across the sands at Kitty Hawk, North Carolina.

It was accomplished by two British aviators, 27-year-old Captain John Alcock, a pilot who had served in the Royal Naval Air Service during the First World War, and 33-year-old Lieutenant Arthur Whitten Brown, born in Glasgow of American parents. Brown was the navigator and had given up his American citizenship to join Britain's Royal Flying Corps during the First World War.

In 1919 five British teams competed for a £10,000 prize offered for the flight by the *Daily Mail*. The first attempt was east-west, but the aircraft finished up in the sea off Ireland. The other teams decided to fly from Newfoundland to Ireland with the prevailing west-east winds. One plane

crashed on takeoff; a second suffered engine failure 600 miles (960km) out to sea, and its crew had to be rescued by a passing steamship. The third was a Vickers Vimy bomber, a biplane fitted with two Rolls-Royce 'Eagle' engines. This was the aircraft flown by Alcock and Brown.

Despite poor weather conditions, Alcock decided to take off on June 14. He was spurred on by the knowledge that an American flying boat had just made the first Atlantic crossing, though not nonstop. It had broken its journey by landing in the Azores, and spent 57 hours 16 minutes in the air. Alcock and Brown reckoned they could do the trip in 16 hours.

For several hours the two men waited for crosswinds to drop sufficiently, then took off into the teeth of a 40mph (64km/h) wind. The heavily laden plane only just struggled into the air from a very bumpy 'runway', created from five rough fields at a place called Monday's Pool, near St John's.

Alcock and Brown sat side by side in an open cockpit, protected only by a windscreen. Brown described it as an 'isolated but by no means cheerless room'. They wore battery-heated clothing.

As they headed out over the ocean, Brown quickly made as many observations as possible of the sea, the horizon and the sun. But soon a huge fog bank hid the sea, while a layer of cloud hid the sun. The first problem arose an hour after takeoff: a small propeller on the wing which powered a generator for the wireless transmitter fell off. From then on Brown could hear messages, but could not send any.

The second crisis came an hour later, when the starboard engine began to make a machine-gun-like noise. This was due to a

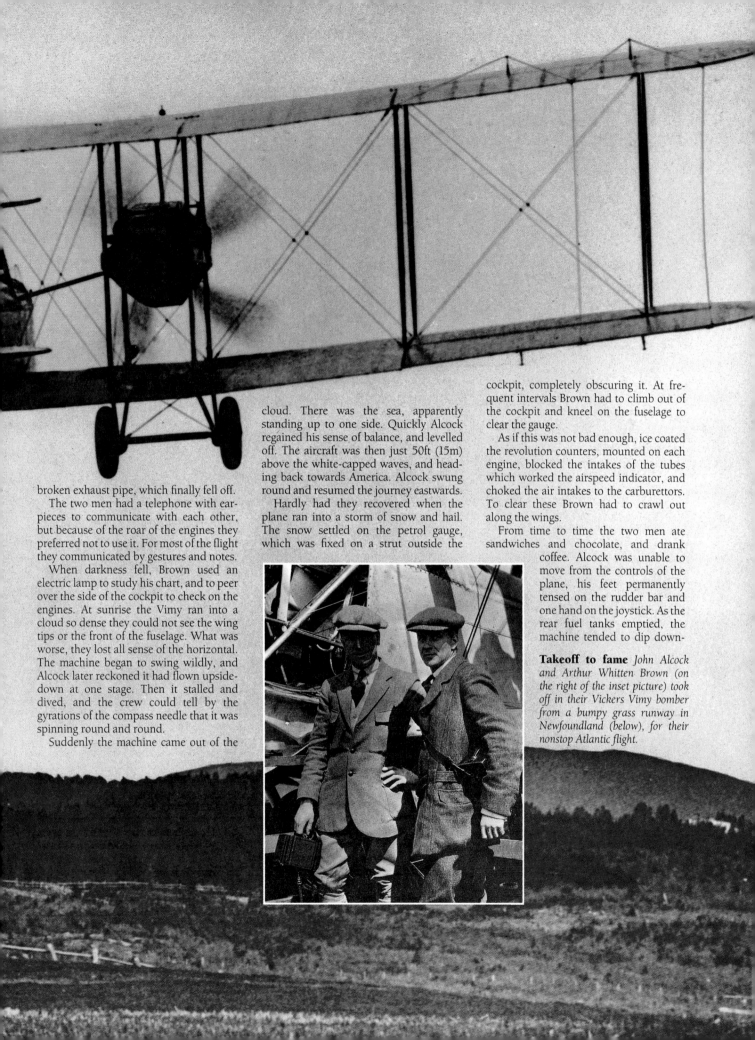

broken exhaust pipe, which finally fell off.

The two men had a telephone with earpieces to communicate with each other, but because of the roar of the engines they preferred not to use it. For most of the flight they communicated by gestures and notes.

When darkness fell, Brown used an electric lamp to study his chart, and to peer over the side of the cockpit to check on the engines. At sunrise the Vimy ran into a cloud so dense they could not see the wing tips or the front of the fuselage. What was worse, they lost all sense of the horizontal. The machine began to swing wildly, and Alcock later reckoned it had flown upside-down at one stage. Then it stalled and dived, and the crew could tell by the gyrations of the compass needle that it was spinning round and round.

Suddenly the machine came out of the cloud. There was the sea, apparently standing up to one side. Quickly Alcock regained his sense of balance, and levelled off. The aircraft was then just 50ft (15m) above the white-capped waves, and heading back towards America. Alcock swung round and resumed the journey eastwards.

Hardly had they recovered when the plane ran into a storm of snow and hail. The snow settled on the petrol gauge, which was fixed on a strut outside the cockpit, completely obscuring it. At frequent intervals Brown had to climb out of the cockpit and kneel on the fuselage to clear the gauge.

As if this was not bad enough, ice coated the revolution counters, mounted on each engine, blocked the intakes of the tubes which worked the airspeed indicator, and choked the air intakes to the carburettors. To clear these Brown had to crawl out along the wings.

From time to time the two men ate sandwiches and chocolate, and drank coffee. Alcock was unable to move from the controls of the plane, his feet permanently tensed on the rudder bar and one hand on the joystick. As the rear fuel tanks emptied, the machine tended to dip down-

Takeoff to fame *John Alcock and Arthur Whitten Brown (on the right of the inset picture) took off in their Vickers Vimy bomber from a bumpy grass runway in Newfoundland (below), for their nonstop Atlantic flight.*

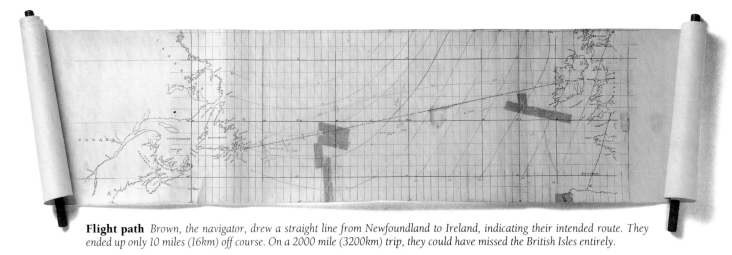

Flight path *Brown, the navigator, drew a straight line from Newfoundland to Ireland, indicating their intended route. They ended up only 10 miles (16km) off course. On a 2000 mile (3200km) trip, they could have missed the British Isles entirely.*

HOW THEY FLEW A STRAIGHT LINE ACROSS THE OCEAN

The navigator of a small aircraft, with its constantly vibrating compass, has only to make an error of one degree in his reading to be a mile off course after 60 miles (96km).

Alcock and Brown's flight covered nearly 2000 miles (3200km) over a featureless ocean, and any compass error would have been compounded by crosswinds. Without skilled navigation they could have missed the British Isles completely. Reaching Ireland only 10 miles (16km) off course was a remarkable achievement.

To fly along the line they had marked between Newfoundland and Ireland, Brown used both dead reckoning and astronomical observation, and checked one against the other.

For dead reckoning he constantly used his compass to ensure they were flying in the right direction. His air-speed indicator told him their apparent speed, but he had to calculate the effect of the wind, which might speed up or slow down the aircraft. A device called a drift indicator also told him how far they were off course. From his clock he could work out how far and in what precise direction they had flown since the last calculation. He could then tell Alcock of any need to alter course, and mark their position on the map.

As there were no landmarks to confirm the dead reckoning, he checked by taking a 'fix' with a sextant. The sextant gives the angle above the horizon of a star or any other heavenly body. By taking readings on three known stars and noting the exact time of each reading, he could consult navigation tables and draw three lines on the map. The point where the lines crossed indicated the position of the aircraft.

wards, and Alcock was constantly hauling on the control wheel.

Then through the mist two tiny specks appeared in the sea. They were the islands of Eashal and Turbot, off the coast of Ireland. Ten minutes later, at 8.25am, the Vimy crossed the Irish coast. Soon the wireless masts at the village of Clifden in County Galway, loomed ahead through the mist.

A likely looking field lay near the wireless station. Alcock brought his plane in for a perfect landing – but the field turned out to be a bog. With a squelch the plane tipped up and buried its nose in the soft ground. Petrol from a burst pipe flooded into the cockpit, but Alcock had already turned off the electric current so there was no fire.

The plane was just 10 miles (16km) off the course Brown had planned in Newfoundland. 'What do you think of that for fancy navigating?' he said.

Engine noise *Because of the roar of the engines, Brown communicated with Alcock by notes scribbled on a pad (right).*

'Very good', said Alcock, and the two solemnly shook hands. Men from the wireless station came racing over. 'Anybody hurt?' they asked, and then: 'Where are you from?' Polite laughter greeted the answer: 'America.' It changed to cheers when they realised that Alcock and Brown had indeed crossed the Atlantic.

The two men were stiff and weary, and altogether they had been 40 hours without sleep. Their coast-to-coast time was 15 hours 57 minutes for a straight course of 1890 miles (3024km), and they had been in the air for 16 hours 28 minutes. Their record stood until Charles Lindbergh made his historic solo crossing in 1927.

Five days after they landed Alcock and Brown were knighted. Sir John Alcock was killed in an air crash in December, 1919. Sir Arthur Whitten Brown died in 1948.

Nose dive *Alcock thought he would make a perfect landing, but did not count on an Irish bog. Soldiers guard the plane.*

Curiosities of food and drink

*Bubbles in champagne, the hole in macaroni, seaweed in ice cream –
the food and drink we consume abound with oddities that make them
fascinating as well as nutritious.*

How milk is preserved
indefinitely, page 381.

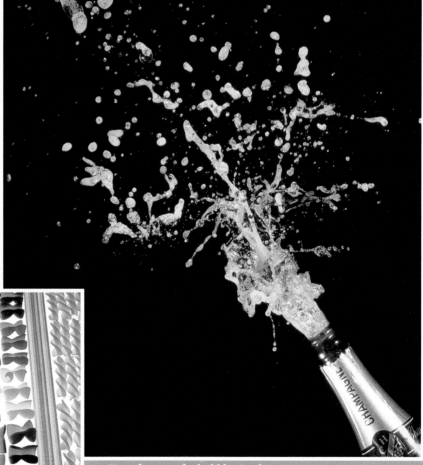

How they put the bubbles in champagne, page 393.

How pasta is made –
with holes and without, page 375.

How does a fully grown pear get inside a liqueur bottle?

You are in a high-quality wine merchant's, looking for something just a little bit different. The shelves contain spirits, liqueurs and wines of every colour and strength. You scan label after label. But when you see it, it's not the label that attracts you – it's the contents. A pear, complete with stalk, resting in a bath of clear liquid.

How did it get there? Was the bottle cast round the pear? Hardly: the heat of the furnace would have shrivelled it. Perhaps the bottle was made in two pieces. But there is no sign of a seam. Was the pear

shrunk and then re-expanded by some piece of modern technology?

No – this is a traditional drink, and the bottle comes from a small pear orchard in southern France. The pear actually grew inside the bottle.

Your pear probably started to develop in May when it would be a miniature fruit less than ¾in (20mm) across. The grower, making sure he had a perfect specimen, carefully cleaned it, and then inserted it through the neck of an upended bottle.

He then suspended the bottle in a net, which was tied to a branch above. Thus

protected from birds and rain, the pear matured well in its miniature greenhouse. In September, the grower carefully untied the bottle and eased the ripe fruit away from its branch, stalk and all.

It only remained to give the bottle with the pear a wash and add the locally distilled, fermented pear juice, and voila! – *Eau de Vie de Poire*, with a real pear.

Bottle harvest *These French pears grown in bottles are ready to be picked by hand. The bottles were placed over the miniature fruits just after they formed.*

Eau de Vie de Poire *This traditional French liqueur containing a whole pear has been made since the 17th century.*

How they make pineapple rings all the same size

Cut up a fresh pineapple on a kitchen chopping board and the slices will vary in diameter, because of the tapering shape of the fruit. But buy a can of sliced pineapple and the rings are all the same diameter. This is because the pineapples are put through an almost entirely mechanical process to make them fit into the cans.

A machine called a Ginaca processes up to 120 pineapples a minute. It cuts out a cylinder of the pineapple's juicy flesh, removes the horny outer shell, cuts off the shell at top and bottom and punches out the core. A device called an eradicator scrapes off surplus flesh adhering to the shell to make crushed pineapple or juice.

The cylinders of pineapple flesh are inspected on a conveyor belt by teams of trimmers, who remove remaining fragments of shell and any blemishes. The cylinders are then carried to a slicing machine, which produces the precision-chopped rings.

Packers inspect the rings and put them in the cans. Broken pieces are used as crushed pineapple.

Each can of rings is topped up with either syrup or pineapple juice, mechanically lidded and sealed under vacuum. They are then cooked in pressure cookers known as retorts. Finally, the sterilised cans of fruit are cooled in water or by air, labelled and packed.

Most of the world's pineapples are grown in Hawaii, the Philippines, Thailand, Malaysia, Taiwan, Kenya and the Ivory Coast. Over a three-year period, a pineapple plant produces two fruits, each weighing about 4.8lb (2.2kg). To simplify harvesting, the plants are made to flower at the same time by being sprayed with a growth regulator such as ethephon. This means that the fruits all ripen at about the same time – between June and September.

How they get the hole in macaroni

Round strings of spaghetti, macaroni with holes, flat ribbons of tagliatelli – all these are *pasta*, which is Italian for 'paste'. They are made from coarsely ground wheat flour, called 'semolina', mixed into a stiff paste with water.

You can make the dough in your own kitchen, but usually it is done with large mechanical mixers in pasta factories. The paste is then formed into whatever shape is required. In the kitchen, you can simply roll it out and cut it with a knife into strips of tagliatelli, or you can extrude it through a simple press (like a mincer with holes that do not rotate) to make spaghetti.

In industrial pasta presses, the dough is squeezed by a screw, like the one in the middle of a mincer, and forced under high pressure through a perforated die.

Outside the die, a knife cuts off the strings of pasta as they emerge. When the knife moves slowly you get long strings, when it goes more quickly you get short pieces, and at top speed it gives thin slices.

The shape of the holes in the die governs the shape of the pasta – round holes for spaghetti, star-shaped holes for little stars, and so on.

For macaroni, however, the hole has to be more complicated. It has a solid centre connected to the edges by fine spokes. The sticky paste comes through under high pressure, leaving the large hole in the middle, but the gaps left by the spokes join up again afterwards.

How do they stuff an olive?

Stuffed olives – those popular cocktail-hour appetisers – are usually stoned and stuffed by machines. The pimiento (red pepper) filling is a kind of paste, made by mixing the pimiento with a gelling agent.

The olives are aligned in rows on a perforated conveyor belt, and the stones are removed by an automatic machine head, rather like a dentist's drill. A nozzle then pumps the pimiento paste into the drilled hole in the olives.

The stones are later ground and used for animal feed – or to produce a low-grade oil.

Some high-quality stuffed olives, containing anchovy, smoked salmon, chopped almond or other nut fillings, are stoned with

Double stuffings *Green olives have been stoned by a machine, then stuffed with half a sliced almond and a piece of pimiento by another machine. Packing in the jars is also done by a machine.*

a hand-held scoop and then filled by hand.

Olive-stuffing machines can process 1800 olives a minute. Manual olive stuffers – mostly in Portugal – can average only around 18 a minute, and are poorly paid.

Olives are grown around the Mediterranean, and in Peru, Chile, California and British Columbia. The green variety, preferable for stuffing because of their firmer texture, are the unripe fruit.

Before the stuffing process, olives are soaked in a solution of sodium hydroxide (caustic soda), which reduces their bitter flavour. Then, after washing in water, they are immersed in brine with added lactic acid to neutralise any remaining alkali. While soaking they are allowed to ferment, which encourages harmless bacteria and yeasts to grow to achieve the characteristic flavour and texture.

Putting the soft centre in a chocolate

Filled chocolates *In the upside-down world of the chocolate factory, hard fillings are covered with runny chocolate. The chocolate is left to harden, and the fillings are then made soft and creamy by enzymes which break down the sugar.*

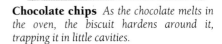

Chocolate chips *As the chocolate melts in the oven, the biscuit hardens around it, trapping it in little cavities.*

The secret of putting creamy centres into chocolates is that the centres are made into solid shapes first, covered with liquid chocolate, then made creamy inside the chocolate coating.

Soft-centred chocolates contain fondant, which is made by mixing sugar with a quarter of its own weight of water. The solution is heated slowly until the sugar dissolves, and then the syrup is boiled until it reaches 240°F (115°C). The hot, sticky, clear solution is then poured out – traditionally onto a marble slab – and left to cool to 100°F (38°C), when it becomes a mass of tiny sugar crystals.

The fondant is reheated to 110°F (43°C), when it is pliable enough for natural or artificial colours and flavours to be kneaded in. At the same time, another ingredient is added – invertase. This is an enzyme (a substance which assists chemical changes) extracted from yeasts.

The next step is to mould the kneaded fondant into fancy shapes, by reheating it until it is just liquid, and pouring it into cornflour moulds. A shallow flat bed of cornflour passes under a machine which stamps indentations for the shapes, which are then filled with the liquid fondant. As it cools and hardens, the fondant centres pull away from the cornflour slightly, and are then turned out onto another conveyor.

This carries the fondants through a bath of melted chocolate, which covers the base, while a curtain of melted chocolate covers the rest of the shape. When the chocolate has hardened the covered sweets are heated to 86°F (30°C), which is not hot enough to melt the chocolate, but activates the invertase. Invertase breaks down the sugar in the fondant into its two main components – glucose and fructose. These are both more soluble than sugar, and they

combine with the water in the fondant to liquefy the centres and make them creamy. The process takes several days.

The process for liqueur chocolates is a little different. Alcoholic spirits are mixed into the fondant syrup, which is then poured directly into the cornflour moulds. As the liqueur-syrup cools, the sugar forms crystals which sink to the bottom of the mould, making a hard crust. The moulds are inverted onto a flat cornflour bed, and another crust forms on the other side. The liquid centre has now become enclosed in a hard sugar shell, which is covered with chocolate in the same way as for fondants.

Putting the chocolate chips in biscuits

Although chocolate-chip biscuits are baked at temperatures of 350-400°F (175-200°C) – well beyond the melting point of chocolate – the chips themselves do not spread throughout the biscuits. Why?

The biscuits are made by mixing fat and sugar together, beating in eggs and binding the mixture with flour. The chocolate – consisting of cocoa, sugar and milk powder set in cocoa butter – is added as chips.

As the biscuits are baked in the oven, the chocolate melts, but at the same time the flour and eggs harden. The biscuit mixture is too solid for the melted chips to ooze away from their positions. When the biscuits cool the liquid chips re-harden to the same shapes, occupying the same small spaces as in the uncooked mixture.

Fish fingers: coated cod fillets ready for frying

Although fish fingers originated in America, Britons eat the most, at 50 per head each year. This accounts for 10 per cent of Britain's yearly fish catch. The Americans are the only others who eat fish fingers in significant amounts – 30 per head a year.

Fish fingers came into being as a result of Clarence Birdseye's invention in 1929, in America, of the plate froster, the first quick freezer. This started a whole new food industry, because quick-frozen food maintains its texture much better than slow-frozen food.

The plate froster sandwiched food between hollow plates containing a refrigerant. To ensure good contact – and thus rapid freezing – the food needed to be in slim rectangular slabs. In the USA, a very suitable candidate for plate-froster freezing proved to be a product called fish sticks – these were slivers cut from large fish and dipped in breadcrumbs for deep-frying.

In Britain during the 1950s, the large herring catch was mostly pickled and exported to other North European countries. It was felt that such a cheap and highly nourishing food might find greater appeal on the home market if it could be presented in a new way. So herring fish sticks were made, to be known as 'herring savouries', and were tested on the market against a bland control product of cod sticks, sold as 'fish fingers'. Shoppers in Southampton and South Wales, where the

The most complex part of producing fish fingers proved to be forming the fillets into blocks for freezing and sawing. How do you get the fish to stick together without any air gaps in between? Air spaces in sausages gained them the nickname of 'bangers' because of their explosive behaviour in the frying pan. An explosion in a deep-fat fryer caused by an air space in a frozen fish finger could be dangerous.

Merely pressing the fillets together in frozen blocks was not successful – they broke up when the blocks were sawn. The problem was overcome by using the V-shaped wedges cut from the fillets as a mince. The mince is mixed with the fillets in a giant stainless-steel machine resembling a concrete mixer, and the mixture is pressed into blocks without the risk of leaving any air gaps.

Originally, a phosphate solution was mixed into the mince. It acted as a plasticiser and formed the mince into a thick fluid ideal for sticking the fillets together. But phosphates have been used to excess by some unscrupulous manufacturers merely to retain excess water added to their products. And phosphates – along with many food additives – are now regarded with suspicion. Manufacturers of higher-quality fingers therefore leave them out, but this means that more fingers break up during processing, resulting in an increase in the price.

be sawn into fingers, they have to be tempered back to 18°F (−8°C). Anything colder would blunt the saw blades too quickly. The sawn fingers, called blanks, are typically 3in long, ¾in wide and ⅜in deep (80 × 20 × 10mm). Each block yields more than 500 blanks. Some break up during processing, and the wastage is used for products such as fish cakes.

A conveyor propels the blanks through a curtain of sticky batter and an avalanche of breadcrumbs, and this coating doubles the thickness of the finger. Each is then passed through a hot vegetable-oil bath for about one minute. This seals the coating, and the soaked-in oil ensures that the finger can be satisfactorily grilled or fried. Lastly, each

finger is sent on a spiral path through a blast of cold air at a temperature of −22°F (−30°C). This lowers the temperature at the centre to −4°F (−20°C) in less than 20 minutes, and after packaging it is stored at −18°F (−28°C), ready for distribution.

Once in the shops, fish fingers stored at a temperature below 5°F (−15°C), should keep their quality for three months.

Although often lampooned as the epitome of processed 'junk' food, the humble fish finger offers as many essential minerals and vitamins as fresh eggs and has more than three times as much protein as milk. Its fat content and calorie count are less than half of what you would get in the same weight of caviar.

How fast-food chains make millions of 'French fries'– all identical

In 1987, just one fast-food chain – McDonalds Hamburgers – sold upwards of 200,000 million French fries, or chips, throughout the world. And they were all nearly identical in length and thickness.

To ensure that their chips have a consistent taste and that they are ready at the same time as the hamburgers, a fast-food chain puts all its potatoes through the same preparation process.

Before the potatoes are even planted, the company agrees to buy a farmer's entire crop. It also specifies the type of potatoes and their growing conditions, such as soil treatment and fertilisers. Varieties of potatoes are chosen – such as Majestic, Maris Piper or the Pentland series – for their keeping quality, because they will be needed all year round. Large, round ones are preferable because they are easy to peel and clean and there is little waste.

Once harvested, the potatoes are loaded into silos or large boxes and kept in the dark at a constant temperature of 48-50°F (9-10°C), which slows down organic changes that would make them deteriorate. They are regularly inspected and batches

that show any signs of rotting are removed.

At the processing plant the potatoes are again inspected and weighed to check their density, which reveals if they have become soft and 'floury'. They are passed over sieves to remove small stones or dirt, and magnets and electronic detectors remove any metal particles. After the potatoes have been washed, the skins are softened with alkali and removed with steam.

Next, they are sliced into square-sectioned strips. Thin strips will cook faster but will become hard if they are overcooked. An ideal size for fast-food chips is a cross-section of about ¼in (6mm).

The cut strips are blanched on a wire-mesh conveyor belt which passes them through a tank of hot water or a dilute solution of phosphate or citrate salt. This helps to prevent them discolouring.

The cut potatoes are then frozen, bagged in polythene, packed into cartons and kept at −4°F (−20°C) until collected for delivery to the fast-food outlets in refrigerated vans.

Within only minutes of being removed from freezers in the restaurants, a bagful can be fried and served up.

test was carried out, confounded expectations by showing an overwhelming preference for the cod rather than the herring.

So cod fish fingers were introduced in Britain in September 1955, and became immensely popular after television advertising began in 1958. So great was the demand that new factories had to be built and a new fleet of fishing vessels commissioned to bring in the cod.

From fillet to finger
On modern production lines, headless fish are processed through a machine with twin circular saws that remove a fillet from each side of the backbone. The fillets then pass over a wheel and a blade that separates the skin from the flesh. Machine filleting, however, leaves a few pin-like bones in the fillet, so the flesh containing the bones – a V-shaped wedge at the thickest end – is cut out by hand.

Fillets are formed into frozen blocks and stored at very low temperatures −4°F to −13°F (−20°C to −25°C). Before they can

How machines peel prawns

Every year 1 million tons of prawns and shrimps are caught around the world and sold through restaurants and supermarkets. Until the late 1950s, when peeling machines were developed, shrimps and prawns had to be shelled by hand, making them a luxury food. Now they are almost all shelled by machines and have become a more reasonably priced item in supermarket freezers. Whereas an expert hand-

peeler can peel 56lb (25kg) of prawns an hour, a machine can peel 880lb (400kg) an hour.

The great bulk of a prawn fisherman's catch, however, is wasted. Only about a sixth consists of shrimps and prawns – the rest is called 'trash fish' or 'by-catch' which is thrown back into the sea.

The 'head' of the prawns, which is in fact the stomach, thorax and head, is usually removed by hand at sea immediately after the catch has been sorted. It has to be removed as quickly as possible because enzymes and bacteria can cause unsightly dark patches on the prawns called 'black spot'. The fishermen are experts at snapping the heads off two prawns at a time, one in each hand.

After the heads have been removed the catch can be stored in ice for up to four days. Once it has been landed it is quickly transferred to a processing factory.

The prawns are inspected for quality and graded in size on a machine with angled rollers. As the gap between the rollers gradually widens, successively larger prawns fall through onto different conveyor belts.

The prawns are carried to machines which have been adjusted to peel a specific size range. The prawns slide into slots where they are pressed down onto a blade that splits the shell and flesh down to the 'vein' along the length of the tail.

The prawns then pass onto a bed of narrowly spaced rollers. Adjacent rollers turn in opposite directions, pulling the shells through the gaps and leaving the flesh which is too large to pass between.

Finally the 'vein' has to be removed. The vein is really the prawn's intestine, which is full of food and sand. Removing it increases the value of the prawns and improves their keeping quality. The vein should have already been dislodged by the cutting process and as the prawn passes through a revolving cylinder with a rough surface, the vein catches on the indentations and is washed away by water.

The prawns are cooked in boiling water, immersed in iced brine and individually quick-frozen, packaged and distributed.

The race to keep frozen peas fresh

Frozen peas are fresher than the peas you can buy at the greengrocer's in season. Why? Because they are frozen within two to three hours of harvesting. Traditional peas in the pod are delivered overnight to markets, then distributed to shops, deteriorating all the time, becoming less tender, bruised and losing flavour before they are bought and cooked, hours or even days after being picked.

Garden peas belong to the legume family which also includes pulses – soya beans and lentils. While pulses are usually left on the plant until they are fully mature, garden peas are picked when they are young.

As they mature, their natural sugars change to starch, giving a harder texture and a less sweet taste. The time of harvesting is critical. The peas should be in the factory and blanched within two to three hours of harvesting.

The entire operation, from planting, through harvesting, processing and packing is carefully integrated. A packer usually contracts with farmers near the factory to plant an agreed area of land with peas. The planting time is overseen by a field adviser, who inspects all the farms.

Day and night harvesting
Depending on planting time, soil, temperature and weather, the peas are ready for harvesting at different times. Mobile field harvesting machines work throughout the day and night. The pods are stripped from the vines and burst open in a rotating drum. The shelled peas are deposited in a truck or trailer which follows the harvester. At this stage of maturity, the peas 'breathe' rapidly, generating heat, which changes their natural sugars into starch, making them tougher.

To obtain good-quality frozen peas, they must be delivered to the processing factory as rapidly as possible – within two to three hours of harvesting. On arrival, a sample is taken and tested for tenderness in a machine called a 'tenderometer' or 'maturometer'. Only tender peas are selected – tougher ones are sifted out for canning. If samples prove tough, an entire truckload may be canned.

The peas are cleaned by fans and washed, usually in a mild oil-detergent-water mixture. The better-quality ones sink, while any skins or foreign material, such as thistle buds, float and are removed. The peas are washed again with clean-water sprays and blanched to inactivate any enzymes which would cause colour and flavour to deteriorate, even at freezer temperatures.

Blanching involves passing the peas on a wire mesh through a tunnel of boiling water for a minute, or through steam for two to three minutes. They are then quickly cooled to less than 68°F (20°C) and passed through a brine solution in which over-mature ones sink and are removed for canning.

Good-quality peas are washed again in clean water and carried by conveyor to an inspection point. They are then frozen rapidly – it takes about half an hour to freeze half a ton.

The peas are packed into bulk bags or bins and transferred to cold storage at 0°F (−18°C). They may be stored for weeks or months before being removed, inspected again, size-graded and bagged for distribution in refrigerated vehicles to retail outlets.

How radiation is used to preserve foods

Meals that have been bombarded with radiation are served to transplant patients – and patients in intensive-care units – in many hospitals. Some countries irradiate supermarket foods. Similar food is also eaten by American and Russian astronauts during their missions in space.

Food irradiation is designed to kill bacteria that cause food poisoning – a particularly grave threat to weak hospital patients, or astronauts who are cut off from medical help. Irradiation also helps to prevent food from going bad while it is being stored. Although at the low recommended doses it does not give indefinite preservation.

The process has been known since 1921 when an American scientist discovered that X-rays could kill a parasite, *Trichinella spiralis*, which can contaminate pork.

Irradiation now is done by exposing food on a conveyor belt to the radioactive isotopes caesium-137 or cobalt-60 in a lead-shielded chamber with walls 5ft (1.5m) thick. The isotopes give off electromagnetic ionising radiation in the form of gamma rays. Alternative methods use X-rays or beta rays, both forms of radiation (page 216).

Doses of radiation
The effect of radiation is measured in units known as Grays (Gy). Doses less than 1kGy are used to kill parasites in meat. Low doses are also used to kill or sterilise insects in cereals, cocoa beans and other crops. They prevent stored crops such as potatoes and onions from sprouting, and slow down the ripening of some fruits.

Medium doses – from 1-10kGy – can extend the shelf-life of food by reducing spoiling organisms in meat, fish, fruit, vegetables and spices. They also kill food-poisoning bacteria, such as salmonella, in raw poultry and shellfish. About half the poultry sold contains live salmonella, which are usually killed by cooking. However, some of the bacteria can survive if the poultry is not cooked right through.

For complete sterilisation of foods, high doses of above 10kGy are used. Animals on sterile diets regularly eat food irradiated up to 25kGy with no observed ill effects. Sterile diets are used when scientists are seeking side effects in various trials – and want to eliminate food poisoning.

Food irradiation is governed by international agreement through United Nations agencies.

Preserving food by freeze-drying

Any hiker who has ever bivouacked up a mountain will appreciate the advantages of freeze-dried 'ready meals'. They are a quarter of the weight of fresh foods, remain tasty for years in sealed packages and can be eaten hot by adding boiling water.

The process was first used in the 1950s when the American government sponsored a scheme to provide lightweight ration packs for astronauts, explorers and the armed services.

The freeze-drying process preserves food by rapid freezing, followed by complete dehydration to remove all the moisture. The food is placed in a tightly sealed chamber between hollow plates containing refrigerant liquid, which freezes the food while a high-powered pump creates a vacuum.

When the food is frozen hard and the pump has removed nearly all the air, the cold refrigerant liquid in the hollow plates is replaced by warm gas. The ice in the food is then converted directly into vapour without first turning into water.

To keep its nutrients, flavour and appearance, the food must be frozen as quickly as possible, but the drying process is quite slow. The 'steam' is immediately removed by the vacuum pump, but the food takes about 20 hours to dehydrate completely. It must then be packaged to protect the contents during handling, and to seal out all oxygen and moisture.

The freeze-drying process gives the food an open texture, and if oxygen enters, any fat becomes rancid. If moisture gets in, microbes in the food grow, causing it to decay like fresh food.

Because the food must be frozen rapidly, the best results are obtained with food which is sliced or ground. Fish, meat, vegetables and fruit can all be freeze-dried, but coffee and made-up meals with chopped ingredients are particularly successful.

Today, improvements in technology have shortened the process and 'accelerated freeze-dried' products are becoming more common. They are still expensive, but are extremely convenient when weight and lack of refrigeration have to be considered. They are reconstituted by adding boiling water, and retain their nutrients, appearance and flavour very well for several years.

Frozen and dried *Over 600 different foods can be freeze-dried, and can then be used to make up a variety of meals. The best results are small foods, like berries and prawns, or chopped or ground ingredients.*

CHICKEN

PRAWNS

BLACKBERRIES

INSTANT COFFEE

BLACKCURRANTS

PEAS

SWEETCORN

Making instant coffee in a giant pot

The French author Honoré de Balzac drank his coffee black, cold and thick as soup to keep him awake while writing through the night. He is said to have consumed 50,000 cups in his lifetime. The French philosopher Voltaire drank an estimated 72 cups a day, and Beethoven is said to have used 60 beans for every cup.

Today, coffee drinkers in many countries use the instant variety, which is what remains after ground coffee beans have been 'brewed' and the water evaporated. In Japan and Britain, about 90 per cent of coffee drunk is instant. In the USA, however, it accounts for only a quarter of the coffee drunk, while almost all Scandinavians and Italians prefer their coffee freshly ground.

Attempts to make instant coffee in the late 1800s failed because of poor flavour. Then, in 1906, George Washington, a Belgian-born engineer of English parentage, was visiting a mountainous region of Guatemala when he noticed a brown deposit on the outside of a coffee pot that had boiled over. Tasting it, he thought its flavour was pleasant – and deduced that this was due to lower atmospheric pressure at high altitude. The lower boiling point of water at the high altitude, he decided, allowed the water to evaporate with less heat damage to the dissolved coffee.

Three years later, he opened the G. Washington Coffee Refining Company in Brooklyn, New York. His instant coffee's immediate success was boosted during the First World War, when the US Army included it in infantry rations.

Making instant coffee involves 'brewing up' on a giant scale. Coffee is delivered to the manufacturer ready roasted, blended and ground. It is then percolated – the process of filtering hot water through the grounds – in batches of up to 2000lb (900kg) at a time. Some of the water is evaporated from the coffee to leave a highly concentrated liquid.

To produce powdered instant coffee, the liquid passes through a large cylinder in which it is subjected to hot air, which evaporates the remaining water. This leaves the powdered coffee ready for sealing into jars or packets.

Granular instant coffee is made by freeze-drying. The concentrate is first frozen, and broken up into granules. The granules are then heated gently inside a vacuum chamber. Because water boils at a low temperature in a vacuum, the remaining moisture can be evaporated off without subjecting the coffee to great heat and impairing the flavour.

How artificial flavours are put in food

When a young Welsh couple hit on the idea of selling hedgehog-flavour potato crisps, they were faced with the problem of what a hedgehog tasted like. Unwilling to catch and cook one themselves, they approached a group of local gypsies, for whom hedgehog roasted in clay is a traditional dish. The gypsies' description of a 'smoky, beefy' flavour was passed on to a flavourist – a chemist specialising in creating artificial flavours.

The flavourist was able to produce a flavour compound – pronounced realistic by the gypsies – which was dusted onto the hot crisps just after cooking. The crisps went on the market, and proved a successful forerunner of other unusual flavours, including pickle, cider, and yoghurt and cucumber.

What, exactly, is in the hedgehog-flavour powder is a trade secret. However, an approximation to almost any flavour on Earth can be reproduced chemically.

The flavour of any substance is determined by a complex combination of chemicals – scientists have identified at least 4300 different ones, and believe that there are many more. Hundreds, or even thousands, of these basic chemicals can be present in a single natural food. For example, 800 different compounds have been identified in coffee, combining to produce the distinctive taste.

When you drink the hot liquid, the flavour compounds stimulate nerves on your tongue and in your nose, enabling you to identify it as coffee. The tongue can only sense four basic tastes – sour, salty, bitter and sweet. The nerves in the nose are far more sensitive, and can discriminate between an infinite variety of flavours.

In theory, scientists can discover the chemical components which produce the flavour of any food by vaporising or liquefying a sample, and then analysing it in a machine called a chromatograph.

Further analysis is then done to determine the way in which the molecules are assembled, because different configurations may produce different flavours.

Using this information, the flavourist can create a synthetic substance that should be virtually identical to the natural flavour. In practice, however, it is well nigh impossible to duplicate a natural flavour exactly. This is because the mechanisms controlling taste are too subtle for a machine to predict.

The basic way of making flavouring compounds is to concentrate extracts, such as boiling down maple sap to make maple syrup and sugar. Or by isolating naturally occurring chemicals from plants – to create menthol from mint, for example. Flavours made in these ways can be described as 'natural', although not in a form that appears in nature. Totally synthetic flavours are made by imitating the chemical structure of naturally occurring molecules. The chemicals isolated in food can also be used to create new flavours, such as hedgehog, which started with the flavour components of smoked beef. Over 800 synthetic flavours are available to food manufacturers.

Flavours are taste-tested for acceptability, first by specially trained people and then by potential consumers. Not everyone can qualify to become a flavour expert, and candidates are screened to find those with highly perceptive senses of taste and smell. The taste for exotic flavours is also growing, and flavour scientists have the potential to create hundreds of new tastes.

Fish into crab
Cheap fish is ground, artificially flavoured and pressed into crab sticks (above). Crab-flavoured paste can also be moulded to resemble expensive crab claws (left).

Lightning speed of a baked-bean sorter

Shiny white beans, all destined to become canned baked beans, race in single file between two narrow beams of light. The light is reflected back from each bean to 'magic eyes' on each side, which check that it is white enough. If a bean is mouldy, dirty or discoloured (even on one side only) or if a stone or seed is on the track, the magic eye registers a dull reflection. A computer then triggers a small puff of air, precisely timed to remove the faulty bean farther down the track, while leaving all the perfect beans to pass on undisturbed.

Each machine sorts up to 3 tons an hour on 12 parallel tracks – more than 200 a second on each track – at lightning speed. A large cannery may have 20 machines, inspecting 60,000 beans every second.

The beans are small haricots grown in large amounts in Michigan, USA, and in Chile. Romania, several East African countries and China are also important haricot producers.

The selected beans are blanched in steam to soften the skin, reduce the 'beany' flavour and lessen the chance of any unpleasant flavours developing in the can. They then pass on a conveyor through a long oven for baking.

Some canning companies feel that the difference in taste caused by baking is not worth the extra process. Their product must be called 'beans in tomato sauce' or something similar.

The sauce for the beans is usually made of diluted tomato purée, plus sugar, salt, spices, thickeners, onion and garlic. It meets the beans on the canning line, where the cans also arrive without tops. The exact number of beans is discharged into each can, which is then filled with sauce and carried to another machine which fits the tops. The metal top is placed onto the open end of the can and a series of rollers squeezes the edges of the top and the can together. A fine rubber gasket ensures that the join is completely airtight. In the biggest canneries, the cans are filled and sealed at the rate of 13 a second.

Finally the sealed cans are sterilised in pressurised steam, labelled and packed for distribution.

How beans are turned into 'meat'

Whether they know it or not, most people have eaten artificial meat. It frequently replaces up to 25 per cent of the meat served up in various forms – pies, sausage rolls, stews, casseroles – in school dining rooms, office and factory canteens and other large-scale catering operations.

The main ingredient of artificial meat is the highly nutritious and versatile soya bean, which has been cultivated in China for centuries. It is now a major crop in the USA, where it is grown mainly for its edible oil which is used as cooking oil and also in margarine.

As more people became increasingly health-food conscious in the 1960s, a number of US companies began producing meat substitutes. And they used the high-protein residue of soya, left over after the oil had been extracted.

The first step in the process was to convert the residue into fibres – and experience in the production of man-made fibres, such as nylon and rayon, helped. First, the soya residue was treated with alkali (caustic soda), which extracted the concentrated protein from it in a viscous, syrupy form.

In the manufacture of man-made fibres, molten nylon or rayon is pumped at high pressure through thousands of tiny holes in an apparatus called a spinneret. The fine filaments which emerge solidify on contact with the air.

In the same way, the soya protein syrup was forced through a spinneret's holes into a solution of phosphoric acid and salt, which caused it to coagulate into long, thin fibres. When bunched together, the fibres formed a bundle about ¼in (6mm) thick. This was then stretched to one-fifth of the original thickness, washed in water to remove the acid and salt, and coated in egg white to bind the fibres together. The fibres were cut into uniform lengths, air-dried, packaged and stored.

Later, by blending with water, vegetable oil, colouring and flavouring agents, the fibres were used to simulate different meats, or even poultry. Substitute bacon has been made by binding alternate layers of red and colourless soya fibres to imitate the lean and fat portions.

American manufacturers have actually produced whole 'ready cooked chickens' – complete with plastic wishbones – but they were not a commercial success. They were obvious copies and were little cheaper than the real thing.

Recently, another method of producing a 'meat' alternative has become popular among manufacturers. This type of soya is dry and aerated, like a sponge. But it turns soft and chewy when wet and resembles cooked meat. It is used in instant savoury snack products – noodles and curries – which require only the addition of boiling water to produce a meal in a plastic carton. It is also available in different flavours and shapes for use in home recipes.

It, too, is produced in a machine adapted from the plastics industry – an extruder. The soya residue is forced down a barrel under increasing pressure and temperature. The residue becomes a hot, plastic mass which, when forced through a hole at the end of the barrel, expands because of the sudden release of pressure. This causes the water content to evaporate, leaving the dry, aerated product.

Preserving milk in many forms

Man has been using animal's milk for thousands of years. Cattle were probably first domesticated about 7000 years ago.

But because milk curdles rapidly, particularly in hot climates, cheese and yoghurt-making must have developed quickly as ways of keeping the milk longer. Butter was probably accidentally discovered by transporting milk in containers. The agitation would have caused its cream to congeal.

Both the ancient Hindu scriptures, the Vedas – the oldest written records of mankind – and the Old Testament refer to milk and cheese. The ancient Sumerians of Mesopotamia had a well-organised dairy industry more than 5000 years ago. And a frieze at the ancient site of Ur, dating from about 2900 BC, depicts milking.

Cows and goats were probably the most common animals milked by early farmers, although the inhabitants of ancient Persia also milked camels. Mare's milk was favoured by the Tatars and Mongols, who also produced a fermented, alcoholic beverage – Kumiss – from it. Early Africans used buffalo milk, while nomads of the Eurasian tundra milked reindeer.

The early Vikings carried supplies of cheese on their voyages and Genghis Khan's armies had rations of dried milk.

The beneficial effects of boiling milk have been known for a long time – in 1824 William Dewes of the University of Pennsylvania recommended heating milk to near boiling, then cooling it for infant feeding. The French scientist Louis Pasteur (page 386) discovered the use of milder heating to control the fermentation of wine in the 1860s. This was later applied by others to the treatment of milk to kill the bacteria which cause tuberculosis, a once

Making butter in an old-fashioned churn *A farmer's wife in Normandy, France, uses an old-fashioned wooden churn to make butter (below). Cream is poured into the barrel, which is then rocked with the wheels, like a cradle, to churn the butter. Normandy butter (left) is rich because it is made from the milk of cows grazed only on the local grass. It is usually unsalted, so quickly goes rancid.*

sterilisation. The most popular method is UHT (ultra high temperature). The cream is heated rapidly to more than 285°F (140°C) for at least two seconds, then cooled down.

Butter production

When cream is agitated in containers, its fat globules collide and lump together, forming butter. The process happens most rapidly at 50-57°F (10-14°C).

On farms, cream is agitated in churns. The watery buttermilk, left over once the fat has lumped together, is drained off and fed to pigs. The remaining butter grains are washed, salt is usually added to give taste and as a preservative, and the butter is compressed into blocks. Butter should contain at least 80 per cent fat and not more than 16 per cent water.

In large-scale dairies cold cream is fed through a heater to warm it to about 54°F (12°C). It then passes into a butter-making machine which beats it vigorously. This causes the cream to break down into small granules which pass into a second chamber where they are gently tumbled to form grains about the size of rice. The liquid buttermilk is drained and the grains are pressed into blocks. Salt may be added. A single butter-making machine can produce more than 5 tons an hour.

Powdered milk

Most powdered milk is made from the skimmed milk left over after the cream has been removed. It is pasteurised, then concentrated by evaporating off most of the water. The concentrated milk is then sprayed into a steel cylinder 32ft (10m) high. Air, heated to 392°F (200°C), is blown into the spray dryer and evaporates the remaining water, leaving a fine milk powder.

Producing yoghurt

Yoghurt is milk curdled by bacteria. The early type eaten in the Middle East was simply curdled goats' milk. Today, a wide range is available, from skim milk low-fat yoghurt to whole milk high-fat types. Cows' milk has too little protein to give a good texture so it is concentrated by evaporation or by adding skim milk powder.

A culture containing the yoghurt bacteria is added to the milk which is kept at 108°F (42°C) while it curdles and sets. Flavours or fruit may also be added.

Cheese – more than 2000 varieties

There are three main categories of cheese: soft, hard and mould ripened. Yet variations in the process of making it have resulted in more than 2000 different types.

The process of making the common hard cheese, Cheddar, is fairly typical of hard cheese making.

widespread killer disease. Modern processes involve heating the milk to at least 161°F (72°C) for 15 seconds, then cooling it to less than 42°F (5°C). This process is also used to delay the souring of milk.

Milk is the most nutritious natural food. It consists of minute fat globules mixed with water and also contains proteins, sugar and mineral salts.

Separating cream

As the fat globules of milk are less dense and lighter than the rest of the liquid, they float to the surface to form a creamy layer.

To separate the cream, early farmers simply skimmed it off the top. Today, milk is put in large centrifuges which whirl at high speed and force out the heavier skimmed milk.

Skimmed milk may then be put back into the cream to produce different grades. Double cream contains 48 per cent milk fat, whipping cream 35-40 per cent, single cream 18 per cent, and half cream (for coffee) 12 per cent.

Cream can be given a longer shelf life by

Pasteurised milk is cooled to 86°F (30°C) and poured into a vat. Selected bacteria (*lactococci*) grown in milk or whey are added to ferment the milk, converting its lactose (sugar) into lactic acid, which is both a preservative and a flavouring. The milk is left for 30-60 minutes to allow the bacteria to multiply. Rennet – a mixture of enzymes taken from the stomachs of cows or produced synthetically – is stirred into the milk. One of the enzymes breaks down part of the milk protein, causing the milk to

clot. The solid material is cut up into a mixture of curds (solid) and whey (liquid), and gently heated. After about an hour the curds are allowed to settle and the whey is drained off.

The curds clump together and are cut into blocks, stacked, turned and restacked to compress them more solidly. The curd is then cut into small pieces and salt is added to prevent harmful bacteria from developing, and the curd is pressed in moulds to form the cheese. The cheese is stored at

42-50°F (6-10°C) for at least two months to produce a mild flavour, and up to 12 months to produce a mature variety of Cheddar cheese.

During storage the enzymes from the rennet and from bacteria bring about a slow breakdown of the milk protein and, to a lesser extent, the milk fat. These changes cause the development of the characteristic flavours in the cheese.

In making soft cheeses there is little or no heating of the curd after cutting and

HOW BLUE CHEESE IS MADE – WITH MOULD SPORES AND NEEDLES

Wheels of Roquefort cheese mature on oak racks deep in limestone caves in southern France.

Blue cheeses are the result of moulds that produce blue pigments. Originally cheeses must have been accidentally contaminated by natural moulds floating in the air as spores. Once the mould had grown, it would colonise cheese cellars or storage caves and subsequent cheeses stored there would also be contaminated.

Modern blue cheese production minimises the chances of the mould failing to grow. A suspension of the mould spores is either added to milk at the same time as starter bacteria or is sprayed over or injected into curd pieces which have been drained of the liquid component of milk, whey.

The mould used to make blue cheese is called *Penicillium roquefortii*, named after Roquefort in France.

The cheese has to be porous since the mould needs oxygen and space to grow, so pressing – the compression of curd in the mould, used for some other types of cheese – is avoided.

The cheeses drain slowly and are relatively soft. They have to be turned each day or they lose shape.

The temperature and humidity vary according to the type of cheese and its age. Typical conditions are between 41-59°F (5-15°C) with humidity of 90-95 per cent. Too high humidity encourages excessive growths of yeasts and bacteria; too low causes the cheese to crack.

As the cheese matures, the supply of oxygen to the mould growing in the pores can be increased by piercing the cheese with stainless-steel needles. For Stilton cheese, 40-48 holes may be made at each piercing. The former use of copper needles led to the popular misconception that the blue colouring was caused by copper wires oxidising in the cheese. As the mould grows it not only produces the blue colour, but also enzymes. These break down the fats and proteins, producing the characteristic flavour, and making the cheese softer.

MAKING A HARD CHEESE THE TRADITIONAL WAY

Single Gloucester cheese, a full-fat hard type, is shown here being made on a British farm. Milk is heated in the tub, then rennet is added. An hour later the curds and whey are separated with a long curd knife.

The curd is cut into square blocks. They are turned frequently to increase acidity, which will improve the flavour of the cheese. The turning process lasts for at least half an hour. The whey has been drained off and will be fed to pigs.

The blocks of curd are crumbled and spread in the tub. Salt is spread over the levelled curd. Salting helps to bring out the flavour of the cheese. It also acts as a preservative and slows down the development of acidity.

The curd is packed into a mould or vat lined with muslin cheesecloth. The mould, which contains and shapes the cheese, may be made of steel or wood, so long as it is strong enough to withstand the considerable force put on it by the press.

The cheeses are subjected to pressure in the press, which squeezes out the liquid and compresses the cheese. Single Gloucester is pressed for five days – the times for other hard cheeses vary.

During pressing, the cheeses are turned every day, and the cheesecloth is changed. When the pressing is finished, the last cloth should be dry because all of the water has been squeezed out.

Each cheese is wrapped in a bandage of cheesecloth sealed with a flour-and-water paste. This prevents the cheese from spreading, drying out or cracking while it is ageing, and protects it in transit.

Single Gloucesters mature for about eight weeks, and must be turned every day. The ageing process is necessary for all hard cheeses, and the time can be up to two years for sharp Cheddars.

---

little or no pressure is applied to the curd in the moulds. Less moisture is lost so the cheese is softer.

Ice cream – a luxury food

Originally a luxurious delicacy, ice cream was made popular all over Europe and in the United States during the late 17th and early 18th centuries by Italian ice-cream sellers who went about major towns with brightly painted barrows. During the mid-17th century, they had mixed ice from mountains with sweetened milk to produce an early form of ice cream.

In modern times, manufacturing and content standards vary from country to country. A 10 per cent milk fat content is acceptable in most. Sweetness varies according to consumer tastes – from 13 per cent sugar in Scandinavia to 15 per cent in the USA.

Skim milk powder is added to milk or water. The mixture is heated and sugar, emulsifier and stabiliser – traditionally gelatine and egg yolk – are added, followed by cream or butter. The mixture is heated to pasteurise it and maintained at 150°F (66°C) for 30 minutes.

Vigorous stirring is followed by rapid cooling, preferably to below 41°F (5°C) for at least two hours. This allows the milk fat to crystallise and the proteins and stabilisers to absorb water.

After flavour and colouring are added, the mix is whipped and frozen. Fruit and nuts may be blended after freezing. For storage or 'hardening', the ice cream must be cooled to below −0°F (−18°C).

For long-term storage, below −13°F (−25°C) is necessary. The lower the storage temperature the longer the ice cream will keep.

Why they put seaweed in ice cream

As long as 5000 years ago, seaweed was used as a food and medicine in China. And today it is still eaten around the world. It is found in the Japanese fish-and-rice dish *sushi*, in Welsh laver bread (seaweed fried with oatmeal) – and in ice cream.

Seaweeds provide ingredients called alginates and carrageenans, which are used in ice cream as stabilisers, so the ice cream does not become 'grainy' in the freezer.

When ice cream is made, most of the water content freezes into very small ice crystals about 50 microns in size. (A micron is one-thousandth of a millimetre.) As the thermostat of a deep freezer switches the refrigeration off and on, the temperature in the freezer fluctuates. Water melts off the crystals as the temperature rises, causing smaller ones to disappear. Then as the temperature drops again, the water freezes onto the remaining crystals, which grow in size. This causes the texture to coarsen.

Stabilisers slow the growth of the ice crystals, by forming a protective layer around them, so the ice cream retains its smooth texture longer.

Carrageenan is obtained from red seaweeds found around rocky shores in northern Europe and North America. The seaweed is harvested, then dried to preserve it. Carrageenan can be extracted by immersing the dried seaweed in hot water. The extract is purified and then ground to a fine, cream-coloured powder. Alginates are extracted in a similar way from brown seaweed in several parts of the world.

Before being used in ice cream, the alginate or carrageenan is usually blended with other compounds such as guar gum (extracted from the seed of the guar plant of India and Pakistan) and locust-bean gum (from the seeds of the locust bean or carob tree, which grows in the Mediterranean area) to provide mixtures which are more effective than a single stabiliser.

Stabilisers are used in ice cream at about 0.2 per cent of weight, so that a litre of ice cream contains less than a gram of the seaweed extract.

Mayonnaise: how a cook can make oil mix with water

To make mayonnaise, six egg yolks and 4fl oz (115ml) of vinegar are mixed in a bowl. Then, whilst beating vigorously, 1¾ pints (1 litre) of olive oil is added drop by drop. A pinch of salt and the juice of a lemon improve the flavour, and 3 tablespoons of boiling water stop the mayonnaise curdling.

Most cooks are unaware what is happening when they make mayonnaise. How are egg yolks, vinegar and oil transformed into a thick, creamy sauce? What stops the oil separating from the vinegar, as it does in salad dressing, and how is so much oil absorbed by the mixture? The answers lie in the curious properties of egg yolks.

Like many foods, mayonnaise is an emulsion consisting of fat and water which will not dissolve in one another. Sometimes water droplets are suspended in oil or fat, as in margarine or butter, and sometimes fat droplets are suspended in water, as in milk or cream soups. Usually the droplets take up only a small proportion of the emulsion. Mayonnaise is unusual in that the oil droplets account for 80 per cent of the product's weight.

The vinegar can only hold so much oil with the help of the emulsifying properties of egg yolks. An emulsifier is a substance that is made up of molecules that have one end which prefers to dissolve in water whilst the other prefers to dissolve in oil. In fact, egg yolks contain several natural emulsifiers; lecithin is the best known.

By having each of its molecules in oil one end, and water the other, the egg yolks form a protective skin around the oil droplet. As the oil is broken up into droplets by continual beating they are prevented from coalescing – even when they collide the droplets bounce apart.

If lemon juice is added to give extra flavour, its acidity prevents bacteria breeding quickly and makes the mayonnaise keep longer. It also causes changes in the egg proteins which thicken the mixture.

In cheaper mayonnaises and salad creams, which contain less egg yolks and oil, the mixture is thickened with gelatined starch or with natural gums obtained from the locust bean or seaweed.

Many food emulsions are homogenised. This process makes the droplets smaller

Oil droplets *A microscope picture of mayonnaise shows the oil droplets of different sizes closely packed together.*

and more uniform by smashing them at high pressure against a metal surface. Smaller droplets take longer to coalesce and rise to the surface than large droplets. For this reason milk is homogenised to try to stop all the cream from rising to the top of the bottle. Good mayonnaise with a high oil content should not be homogenised, because the only way that all the oil can be accommodated in the mixture is by having it in droplets of different sizes, so they can pack together in a smaller space.

The origin of mayonnaise is uncertain. One theory is that the Duc de Richelieu was so impressed with a delicious new sauce during a visit to Menorca in 1756, that he sent his head chef to learn how to make it. He named it 'Mahonnaise' after the island's main town, Mahon. A more probable explanation argues that mayonnaise comes from the old French word for egg, 'moyeu' – hence 'moyeunaise'.

Separating machine *An egg separator in a French mayonnaise factory carefully cracks the eggs to keep the yolks whole.*

Louis Pasteur: waging war on germs

In the autumn of 1860 the French chemist Louis Pasteur went on a climbing trip to the Alps near Chamonix. He took with him more than 30 sealed flasks containing liquid yeast extract and sugar which, he had shown, became contaminated when exposed to dust-filled air. Once in the pure, germ-free air some 5000ft (1500m) up the mountains he opened the flasks, filled them with air and re-sealed them. Later, back in his laboratory, he showed that the liquid had not fermented or decayed.

His findings led to the elimination of germs in milk, wine and beer – making them safe and pleasant to drink. It was the result of years of study into the 'diseases' of different liquids, caused, Pasteur asserted, by bacteria in the lower atmosphere which harmed the health of living matter. 'In the field of experimentation,' he wrote later, 'chance favours only the prepared mind.'

His mind had been prepared since the late 1840s, when he was appointed Professor of Chemistry at the Academy of Sciences at Strasbourg, in eastern France. In 1851 he wrote to a friend saying, 'I am on the verge of mysteries, and that veil which covers them is getting thinner and thinner!' Six years later he analysed the fermentation process in alcohol, and stated that microscopic organisms which he later called 'microbes' caused some liquids, such as vinegar and wine, to turn bad.

The Emperor Napo-leon III later commissioned Pasteur to deal with the germs which were ruining the quality of one of the country's major products – wine. Pasteur visited dozens of vineyards. He questioned the workers there, sampled their products, and took away specimens of immature, ripe and decayed wine.

Tests revealed that the disease-causing microbes could be destroyed at a temperature of 131°F (55°C) without affecting the wine. The process, later called 'pasteurisation', was extended by Pasteur to make milk disease-free.

Bacteria, in fact, had first been observed under the microscope some 200 years before. But then the microorganisms were mistakenly thought to be the *effects* of putrefaction and not its *cause*. Pasteur was the first person to correct this view.

Before long he was seeking a cure for various human and animal diseases – and putting forward the revolutionary concept that germs did not 'mysteriously appear from out of nowhere', but had a definite and traceable source: dirt and dust.

Louis Pasteur was born the son of a tannery owner in the small town of Dole, near Dijon, on December 27, 1822. Refusing to follow in his father's footsteps, he had progressed from student chemistry teacher to – at the time of his historic climb – Director of Scientific Studies at the *École Normale Supérieure*, the renowned teachers' college, in Paris.

Four years later, in 1864, he gave a lecture on his work at the Sorbonne – the seat of faculties of science and letters at the University of Paris. Pointing to some organic liquid in a sealed container, he said: 'It is pure since the experiments I began several years ago. It is pure because I have kept it from the germs which float in the air.'

He spent much of the next 17 years working on a preventive medicine (a vaccine) for chicken cholera and anthrax – the malignant and deadly boils most common in sheep and cattle, but which can be communicated to man. He observed that once farm animals suffering from the diseases had recovered, they did not have any further attacks. So, by injecting them with a weakened form of the germ, he gave them protection for life. 'Simply stated,' he said, 'my method is to set the microbes at war with each other so that they eventually kill themselves off.'

He next became interested in the possible cure and prevention of rabies – and in December 1880 a friend and veterinary surgeon gave him two rabid dogs to work with. People who were bitten by such animals usually showed no symptoms for about three to 12 weeks. Then convulsions, delirium and a terror of swallowing liquids set in. Within a few days after that the victims were dead.

Life's work *Louis Pasteur spent years discovering how to eliminate bacteria from wine, beer and milk – making them safe to drink. 'Pasteurisation' was first devised to protect wine at the request of Napoleon III.*

Studies in fermentation

Much of Pasteur's early work as a chemist involved the analysis of fermentation. In his book Studies on Beer, *published in Paris in 1876, he illustrated various cases of fermented substances – those which have slowly decomposed. They consisted of: 1 red wine; 2 sour milk; 3 rancid butter; 4 ropy (coagulated) wine; 5 vinegar; 6 non-crystalline deposit; and 7 microscopic vegetable matter.*

Air attack *Pasteur's experiments showed that fermentation is caused by airborne organisms. Here, fluid is sterilised by boiling in a flask. The neck is then sealed, and it is only when its tip is broken off, and air allowed in, that fermentation occurs. The illustration appeared in a German textbook on bacteria published in Wiesbaden in 1889.*

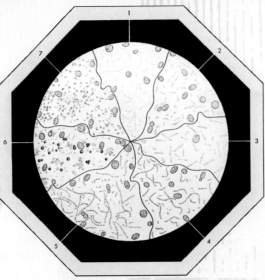

What treatment there was consisted of cauterising the bites with carbolic acid or red-hot pokers. Often the 'cure' itself succeeded in killing the patients, and Pasteur – intent on producing a more humane method – retired to the Forest of Meudon near Paris, where he kept 50 rabid dogs in cages. Tests showed him that the rabies germs were contained in the animals' saliva and within their nervous systems. In the spring of 1884 – after scores of experiments on dogs and rabbits – he cultivated a vaccine containing an attenuated (weakened) form of the rabies virus.

As well as providing a means of combating rabies, Pasteur's work on vaccination opened the way to the branch of medicine called 'immunology'. And today some 30 potentially crippling or lethal diseases – including measles, poliomyelitis and diphtheria – can be forestalled by immunisation.

In 1888 the Pasteur Institute was opened in Paris, partly to undertake further research into the prevention and treatment of rabies. Despite a stroke which left him semi-paralysed, the now world-famous chemist headed the institute until his death on September 28, 1895. He was buried in a magnificent marble tomb in the institute, and he had provided his own epitaph when he wrote:

'The law of which we are the instruments – the law of peace, work and health – seeks ever to evolve new means of delivering man from the scourges which beset him.'

THE SAVING OF JOSEPH MEISTER

In July 1885 the case of nine-year-old Joseph Meister was presented to Pasteur. The youngster had been savaged by a mad dog in his village home in Alsace in north-east France. The local doctor despaired for his life and sent him to Paris to see the great chemist. Pasteur was appalled by the dozen or so deep bites on the shepherd boy's hands, legs and thighs. Later the same day, a colleague of Pasteur's, Dr Jacques Grancher, inoculated Joseph with a fluid taken from the spinal cord of a rabbit which had died of rabies two weeks before.

Joseph – who was accompanied by his mother – then went to lodgings which Pasteur had arranged for, and so began a long and anxious wait – while each day the wounded boy was given a stronger injection.

'In the closing days of the treatment,' wrote Pasteur afterwards, 'I inoculated Joseph Meister with the most virulent rabic virus obtainable, that of a dog reinforced by being passed through a long succession of rabbits ... My justification for doing this was my experience with my fifty rabid dogs ... Once immunity has been attained, the most virulent virus, in any quantity, can be injected without ill effects.'

Towards the end of a fortnight – with Joseph's fate still undecided – Pasteur could no longer stand the strain of waiting in Paris. He went on a short holiday to the wine-growing province of Burgundy.

'Every day,' he said later, 'I lived in dread of receiving a telegram saying that the worst had happened – and that little Joseph was dead!'

But the telegram did not come – and Pasteur returned to Paris to find that the youngster had made a complete recovery. During the next 18 months some 2500 people – men, women and children from all over Europe – were similarly treated by him after being bitten by rabid animals. All but ten survived.

Rabies cure *Young Joseph Meister appeared to be doomed after he was mauled by a rabid dog. He went to Paris, where Pasteur saved his life with a course of inoculations.*

Devotion *In middle age, Joseph Meister takes his daughter to see Pasteur's bust in Paris. As concierge of the Pasteur Institute, Meister committed suicide in 1940 rather than open Pasteur's tomb for the Nazis.*

Cooking roast beef for 1000 people

How do you cook a piece of meat that is 125 times the weight of the average family roast – and enough to feed more than a thousand people?

Spit-roasting a whole ox in the open air is now mostly done by professionals with specialised, heavy-duty barbecue equipment – and confined to major celebrations and festivals. A carcass that weighs around a quarter of a ton (250kg) can take up to 24 hours to cook. Success depends on expert judgment and a great deal of careful preparation.

The butcher needs two weeks' warning to save a whole beast (beef carcasses are usually halved or quartered for easier handling), and to allow for ten days' hanging. The ideal combination of taste, tenderness and manageable size – about 500lb (227kg) – comes from a 14 to 18-month-old animal.

Head, skin, hooves and tail are removed, and the front legs are tied back and together so they do not splay out awkwardly while rotating on the spit. Most importantly, the H-bone, or pelvic girdle, which is split during normal butchering, must be left intact. It plays a vital part in anchoring the carcass to the spit.

Such a massive weight takes two or three strong adults at each end to lift, and a spit made of scaffolding poles to support it during cooking. The crossbar, of galvanised iron or steel, needs to be at least 2½in (65mm) thick and secured to heavy iron tripods at each end. The bar is pushed through the ox's bony pelvic girdle and out through the neck, following the backbone as closely as possible.

Heavy-duty metal clamps hold the spine to the spit. For extra security, the carcass is impaled on metal skewers up to 3ft (900mm) long that are bolted into the spit.

Ideally, the spit is made so that the meat can be moved away from or closer to the fire to control the level of heat getting to it. Maintaining the fire at around 375-400°F (190-200°C), and the meat at sizzling point, is crucial. Too high a temperature, and the outside gets completely charred; too low, and the centre of the meat may spoil.

To keep the fire going throughout the cooking will take about 10cwt (500kg) of charcoal. The fire is laid in a trench about 2ft (600mm) deep, and started a couple of hours before cooking begins so that the heat can build up. A windbreak, made from turf saved from the trench and fire-resistant bricks, reflects heat back into the carcass.

The spit is often set to the side of the fire rather than directly over it. This means that the fat can drip directly into trays placed on the ground beneath rather than spit dangerously into the fire itself.

The ox needs to rotate slowly on the spit – at a maximum rate of about ten revolutions an hour, with the meat being constantly basted.

When the meat juices run clear, carving can begin. The cooked outside is sliced first, while cooking continues.

Ox-roast *An 18th-century German print shows the cook tending a roasting ox.*

Making meals for millions of pets

Cats and dogs may be fussy about the food they eat, but their owners – who have to buy it – are even more so. And the market created by their preferences is enormous. In the USA there were 58 million pet cats and 49 million dogs in 1987, and their owners spent more than $5600 million feeding them.

People living in the European Community own 28 million dogs and 25 million cats, which eat more than 4500 million tins of pet food a year. That's 13 million cans a day, not including dried pet foods.

One of the largest canning factories in Europe is in fact a pet-food factory – Pedigree Petfoods at Melton Mowbray in Leicestershire, which produces several million cans a day. One of its production lines has an output of more than a thousand cans a minute.

Since a pet can live well on a single type of food for its whole life, brand loyalty is crucial for the manufacturers. They fight for their share of the market by producing an extraordinary range of foods from an equally extraordinary range of raw materials, all designed to appeal to pets and marketed to appeal to owners.

Most pet foods are made of meat that is not normally used for human consumption, mixed with soya, milk proteins and cereals. Vitamins and minerals are added to ensure a good nutritional balance.

Almost all pet foods are one of three types: canned, dried or semi-moist. The popularity of each varies from country to country. In Europe, owners prefer canned foods, whereas in the United States dried foods are slightly more popular.

In most canned products the meat is held in a gel. Pet-food gel is made from one of two seaweed extracts, carrageenan or alginate. When heated and cooled, solutions of the seaweed extracts solidify, trapping all the ingredients. Ordinary gelatine degrades when heated, but seaweed gels are stable at the high temperatures needed to cook the food and kill bacteria.

Another type of canned food consists of powdered meat, either in the form of a thick mixture held together by a cereal binder, or in the form of meat chunks in gravy (a type particularly popular in the United States). The chunks are often formed by making use of protein's ability to gel when heated (as egg white does).

Pet-food canneries are massive and sophisticated factories. The meat arrives in frozen blocks which are crushed and mixed automatically with the other ingredients. After the cans are filled and sealed, the contents are cooked and sterilised in pressurised steam.

To make dried pet foods, wheat flour, soya, ground bone, vitamins, minerals and fat are mixed and forced – under great heat and pressure – through a large machine like a household mincer. As the mixture is squeezed out of the far end, most of the water in it evaporates off rapidly as steam, giving it a porous texture. It is then cut into chunks and dried.

In semi-moist pet foods, spoilage is prevented firstly by partial drying, and then by the use of humectants – small molecules that act as preservatives by partially turning the water into a jelly.

The mysterious ingredients of Coca-Cola

In a safe-deposit vault at the Trust Company of Georgia, USA, lies the secret of one of the world's most popular soft drinks – Coca-Cola. And, it is said, only the company directors can authorise the opening of the vault.

Although numerous outlets around the world have a franchise to bottle or can and distribute Coke, none knows the precise ingredients. They are simply supplied with syrups and other ingredients from the Coca-Cola Company – and mix them with carbonated water. Many competitors – and even the US government – have tried to discover the secret formula of Coca-Cola's distinctive flavour. But none has yet succeeded.

However, the American author William Poundstone did some painstaking research which he published in his 1983 book *Big Secrets*. He suggests that Coke's basic ingredients – numbered one to nine and known as 'merchandises' by the company – are as follows: 1. Sugar; 2. Caramel; 3. Caffeine (although a caffeine-free version is available); 4. Phosphoric acid; 5. Coca-leaf extract (with its cocaine content removed) and a small amount of cola-nut extract; 6. Citric acid and sodium citrate; 7X. Lemon, orange, lime, cassia (a type of cinnamon), nutmeg oils and probably others; 8. Glycerine; 9. Vanilla.

Although the proportions of some of these ingredients – all mixed with carbonated water – can be discovered by chemical analysis, the most important and most elusive is the mixture of essential oils in 'Merchandise No 7X'. (The use of the X has never been explained.)

The flavour of this mixture is not simply the sum total of the oils, because other flavours are created by the interaction of the oils. Anyone trying to reproduce the mixture would need to know the exact ingredients – which are difficult to analyse with certainty – and their precise proportions, which have hitherto defied analysis. The question of the coca content has even been before the courts (see below).

Coke bottle *The world-famous Coca-Cola bottle was designed in 1916, and the logo in the 1880s.*

THE DRINK THAT BECAME A HOUSEHOLD NAME

Coca-Cola was originally formulated by Dr John S. Pemberton, a pharmacist from Atlanta, Georgia, more than a century ago. In 1885 he concocted his own version of a popular contemporary drink called Vin Mariani. Pemberton's formula simply involved adding leaves of the coca plant, which grows in South America and contains the stimulant cocaine, to red wine.

Discouraged by poor sales, the following year he revised the formula, leaving out the wine and adding the African cola nut, which contains the stimulant caffeine. To dull the bitter taste, Pemberton added sugar and flavourings. His partner, Frank M. Robinson, designed the now-famous Coca-Cola logo, writing the name in the flowing script still in use. The drink then went on sale at local pharmacies as 'an esteemed brain tonic', which could either be taken neat or diluted with water. To begin with, it sold steadily at the rate of about 13 glasses a day.

In 1887, Pemberton sold the formula to Willis E. Venable and George S. Lowndes. Five months later they too sold the rights to Woolfolk Walker and Mrs M.C. Dozier who, a year later, sold out to Asa G. Candler. That year, Pemberton died – and Candler mixed the syrup with carbonated water. He was the first to recognise Coca-Cola's potential as a popular soft drink – plus the need to build up a mystique by keeping the formula secret. Although by this time at least seven people knew the ingredients, Candler revised the formula, took on Frank Robinson as his partner, and in 1892 the Coca-Cola Company was incorporated.

Until 1903, only Candler and Robinson were allowed to mix the syrup – behind locked laboratory doors. They removed the labels from the ingredients delivered by various chemical supply companies. Only Candler dealt with company mail, paid the bills so the firm's accountants could not learn the ingredients, and kept the sole key to the file where invoices were kept.

As the company expanded, Candler and Robinson could not prepare all the syrup themselves, so the ingredients were simply numbered one to nine. And the managers at the branch factories were told only the proportions required and the mixing procedure.

In 1909 the US federal government impounded 40 barrels and 20 kegs of Coca-Cola – and charged the company with violation of the Pure Food Act, because the 'Coca' ingredient implied the presence of the illegal drug cocaine.

But during the trial – various counter-appeals continued for nearly ten years – none of the analysts who gave evidence could find traces of cocaine in the form of coca extract, nor cola. Yet a witness for the company which supplied Coca-Cola's ingredient No 5 described how it was made from coca leaf, with its cocaine content removed, and extract of cola nut.

So, does Coca-Cola contain either ingredient? As author William Poundstone says in his book *Big Secrets*: 'Indeed, there is precious little coca or cola in Coca-Cola . . . neither coca nor cola has much, if anything, to do with the taste.'

Certainly it was the taste that appealed to General Eisenhower during the Second World War. As chief of the Allied Forces in North Africa, he asked for 3 million bottles of Coca-Cola and machinery for ten bottling plants, capable of 6 million bottles a month. It was not until after the war – in 1955 – that Coca-Cola was packed in cans.

How grapes are turned into wine

Fermentation is one of the oldest known natural methods of preserving food. Every year, more than 70 million tons of grapes are grown worldwide. But grapes cannot be kept fresh for long. Some are preserved by drying – producing sultanas, raisins and currants. Most, however, are fermented to make wine. And every year they produce 6500 million gallons (300 million hecto-litres) of wine.

After the grapes, which acquire natural yeasts during growth, are harvested the juice is extracted in presses. Solid matter, such as the seeds and the stems, is taken out in a high-speed, rotating centrifuge.

Sometimes the juice, or 'must', is heated gently to kill unwanted microorganisms. Alternatively, sulphite – derived from sulphurous acid – is added to control the microorganisms.

The must ferments naturally, due to the biological activity of the natural yeast of the grapes. They convert the natural sugar in the grape juice into alcohol.

Red wine, made from black grapes, is fermented at 70-85°F (21-29°C) for about two weeks. Its colour derives from the skin pigment, anthocyanin. White wine is fermented at 50-60°F (10-15°C) for three to six weeks. Cooler temperatures need longer periods for adequate fermentation. Red wine, being more complex, requires higher temperature fermentation.

Rosé wine can be made in three different ways, depending on the particular region of production and the type of product wanted. The most common method is by fermenting black grapes and their skins for one or two days, after which the skins are extracted. Alternatively, pinkish-red grapes are fermented with their skins. The third method is simply to blend white and red wines to produce the pink colour.

After fermentation, the wine is filtered to remove sediment, then stored and later bottled. Most wine is now stored initially in large steel tanks. It may be matured for one or many years, during which important flavour changes occur.

Wine press *For the best white wines, the grapes must be pressed on the day of picking. After the stalks have been removed by machine the grapes are put into a horizontal press. As they are crushed, the juice runs into a trough and is then pumped into a vat where the yeasts that grow on the skins cause fermentation.*

Filled baskets *White grapes have been hand-picked and piled in baskets, waiting to be transported to the winery in France. It takes about 6lb (3kg) of grapes to make just one bottle of white wine.*

FERMENTATION: THE PROCESS THAT MAKES WINE AND BEER

Grape juice becomes wine through fermentation, a natural and spontaneous process. Yeasts – microscopic fungi which grow naturally on the grape skins – convert the sugar content of the juice into alcohol and carbon dioxide gas, which is given off as bubbles. Other yeasts may be added to encourage the process.

It was the 19th-century French scientist Louis Pasteur who discovered that yeast was active in using the fruit's sugar. Both sugar and alcohol are made up of the same three elements – carbon, hydrogen and oxygen – but in different combinations of molecules. The action of the yeast converts sugar into alcohol through a complex series of reactions.

To make beer, yeast is added to a mixture of water and malted barley, which provides the sugar that gets converted into alcohol.

For champagne, the wine is fermented twice, and the carbon dioxide produced by the second fermentation is retained in the liquid to make the bubbles.

Testing the wine *While the wine is fermenting, a sample is drawn from each barrel and tasted to see if it is ready to be put into bottles.*

Maturing the vintages *Racks of bottled red wine are stored in a controlled-temperature cellar in Portugal and left to mature for several years.*

Fermenting in oak *Californian Chardonnay – a white wine – is fermented for weeks in oak barrels. The S-shaped glass fermentation lock, attached to each barrel, allows carbon dioxide produced in the fermenting process to escape without letting in more air.*

The mysterious changes that give a fine wine its flavour

The secret of the flavour in a good wine lies in mysterious changes that occur while the wine ages in casks and bottles.

To achieve a fine wine in the first place, the right varieties of grapes must be grown in the right type of soil on sunny slopes. And the yeasts that live on the skins of the grapes help to create subtle flavours as they cause the grape juice to ferment and create alcohol.

But most of the flavour is produced in the years that follow. The alcohol reacts with acids in the wine to form flavour compounds called esters.

White wine is usually matured for one or two years (nowadays in bulk tanks of stainless steel). Fine red wine is matured in wooden casks for three or four years, and a good wine will continue to improve in bottle after that, the length of time depending on the wine. Full-bodied Bordeaux wines, for example, improve over several years, while others take less time. The formation of esters, with their distinctive flavours, is helped by oxygen which passes slowly through the wood of the casks.

A wine contains several different acids, but the dominant one is acetic acid, which is also found in vinegar. In combination

Fine grapes *Good wines must begin with high-quality grapes. These red Sangiovese grapes, bearing the 'bloom' of the yeast, are one of the most widely planted varieties in Italy, used for Chianti and other red wines.*

with alcohol it creates the esters which turn into vapour, helping to give the wine its bouquet.

As your nose is much more sensitive than the taste buds in your mouth, the bouquet of a wine is even more important than its taste. Professional wine tasters judge a wine by the smell, as they warm it in their hands to release the volatile esters.

Good wines are matured in cellars at a fairly consistent temperature of 52-60°F (11-15°C). At warmer temperatures, the wine will mature more quickly, but the changes in flavour will be different. With some wine this may be desirable. Sherry, for example, is often heat-treated (or 'baked') at 122-140°F (50-60°C) for 10 to 20 weeks to develop its characteristic flavour.

Ageing in caves *The Rioja region of Spain has produced fine red wines for over 200 years. Thousands of bottles are stored in caves for up to a decade (above).*

Wine tasting *As it matures, wine is tasted frequently to check its progress. The wine taster (left) uses a cup on a rod to draw a sample from the bottom of the cask.*

Putting the sparkle into champagne

The sparkle and fizz in beer, champagne and soft drinks is caused by carbon dioxide gas – a by-product of the brewing and wine-making process.

The important property of carbon dioxide in drinks is that it is 50 times more soluble in water than air is. At room temperature a bottle of water can absorb its own volume of carbon dioxide.

The solubility of carbon dioxide decreases as temperature increases. So when a cold drink warms up in a glass, carbon dioxide bubbles rise up through the liquid and escape from the bubbly surface. Its solubility decreases, too, as the pressure falls – so when you remove the cork from a bottle of champagne or the stopper from a bottle of soft drink, a rush of bubbles surges to the top. For the same reason, drinks still give off bubbles at low temperatures – the result of being bottled under pressure.

Sparkling wines such as champagne are made in the normal way like still wines, and are then chilled, filtered and clarified to remove any solid material.

The wine then goes through a second fermentation. From 1 to 3 per cent yeast is added, along with about 2 per cent sugar. The wine is left for one or two months while the yeast converts the sugar into more alcohol and carbon dioxide. Fermentation occurs at room temperature.

During the first fermentation, the carbon dioxide escapes into the air. The second fermentation takes place in the bottle. The carbon dioxide is not allowed to escape, so the pressure inside the bottle increases and the wine becomes sparkling.

True champagne comes only from the Champagne region of northern France. For this process, wine bottles which have been filled a year earlier are tilted downwards at 45 degrees, and the yeast cells settle onto the cork. The bottle necks are then frozen, the cork is removed and the high pressure of carbon dioxide produced by fermentation expels the plug of solid yeast. The bottle is topped up with wine, sugar solution or brandy, before being recorked. Still further fermentation may take place inside the bottle.

The fizz in soft drinks

Soft drinks are made fizzy by direct carbonation in which carbon dioxide under pressure is pumped into the liquid as it is bottled.

For all fizzy drinks, the bottles must be strong enough not to explode under the pressure of the gas. The glass is thick and heavy and the bottom of a wine bottle is usually indented to redistribute the pressure. Aluminium cans and plastic bottles with reinforced bases are used for carbonated soft drinks.

In beer brewing, the yeast which is added ferments the barley 'wort' to alcohol and carbon dioxide. Surplus carbon dioxide is often collected in cylinders or tanks and can be used by companies that make and bottle soft drinks.

THE CHAMPAGNE PROCESS – PUTTING IN THE BUBBLES

When the yeast sediment has settled on the corks, the bottle necks are frozen and the corks are removed, sometimes by hand. The gas pressure expels the yeast.

For less expensive types of champagne, large machines remove the tops. All bottles of champagne then have a new cork wired in before they are stored.

Champagne is made from grapes grown in the northernmost vineyards of France, and the wine must be bottled in that region to qualify as champagne. After bottling, the wine is stored with the bottle necks pointing down. The bottles are turned and shaken, so that the yeast sediment settles on the corks as it converts the sugar in the wine into alcohol and carbon dioxide gas.

The best vintage champagne is aged for up to 15 years, undisturbed in its racks (right). Because the wine is under pressure, bottles sometimes blow their corks, or even explode, like the one in the centre of this rack. When ready for distribution, the bottles are removed, washed and labelled.

How barley is turned into beer

Grain fields *Barley ready for harvesting. Of the 220 million tons grown annually, 96 per cent is turned into beer.*

Barley is the world's sixth largest food crop – but almost none of it is eaten. Only sugar, wheat, rice, maize (corn) and potatoes are produced in greater quantities. All these other crops are recognised as solid foods eaten regularly. But what happens to the 220 million tons – with Europe leading production – of barley grown every year?

The answer lies in drink. Barley is the major raw material for beer, of which 15.5 thousand million gallons (700 million hectolitres) are drunk every year. West Germany tops the world consumption league, drinking an average per head of population of 33 gallons (150 litres) a year.

To turn barley into beer, harvested barley grains are moistened with water and allowed to germinate until they sprout. Sprouted barley is called malt, and it is dried for use later.

Most modern breweries buy prepared malt. They soak it in warm water, in what is called the 'mashing' process, and then extract the liquid, which is called wort.

The liquid wort is boiled with hops which give the characteristic flavour to beer. It is then cooled and selected strains of yeast are added. Like most plants, yeast grows faster at warm temperatures. For ale, the brew is fermented at 68-80°F (20-27°C) for two to six days. Lower temperatures of 50-60°F (10-15°C) are used for lager, with a fermentation time of eight to ten days. Lager yeast requires a cooler temperature in order to grow.

At the end of the fermentation, the beer is filtered or spun in a cylinder called a centrifuge which removes the yeast cells. It may then be pasteurised by heating to give it a longer life, and is often casked, bottled or canned and aged before being drunk.

Barley to malt *Top to bottom, barley is steeped, dried, germinated for five days, then roasted to produce malt.*

The word lager comes from the German word meaning stored or aged beer.

Beer contains 85 to 93 per cent water. It may also contain a small percentage of sugar, between two and ten per cent alcohol, and some minerals and B vitamins.

Cloudy, unfiltered beers, like those made from other cereals, such as maize and sorghum grass in Africa, contain higher levels of B vitamins. They can save people on poor diets from contracting nutrient-deficiency diseases such as pellagra.

Milled malt *After the barley has been processed and baked in huge ovens to produce malt, it is milled. The ground malt is then mixed with water to produce wort, the liquid that is used for beer-making.*

Hop cones *Hop is a perennial climbing plant. The green cones, ready for picking here, are used in some beers.*

Fermentation tank *Prepared malt, hops, yeast, sugar and water are mixed in an open tank. Copper pipes contain cooling water.*

Frothy yeast *After about five days the yeast has foamed to the top of the tank. The beer is ready to be filtered.*

Beer kegs *Apart from bottles and cans, beer is also distributed from the brewery in metal kegs for sale on draught, or tap.*

Just for fun

Ski-jumpers and skydivers fly through the air. Roller coasters whirl their passengers in corkscrew circles. A magician saws a woman in half. Life is full of wondrous moments.

How ski-jumpers really float through the air, page 434.

How roller coasters keep you in your seat, page 405.

How skydivers learn their spectacular skills, page 435.

How to saw a woman in half – and 'mend' her again

The buzz-saw trick *American magician Harry Blackstone Jr, using a circular buzz-saw, appears to cut his elegantly dressed assistant neatly in two. In fact, the girl has arched her back into a hollow in the table, while her dress is held in shape by a strip-metal framework 'body'.*

One of the most renowned and spectacular tricks in modern magic – sawing a woman in half – was created in 1920 by the British stage magician P.T. Selbit. He caused a sensation in London with his dramatic new illusion – in which his glamorous girl assistant was placed in an oblong wooden box and then apparently sawn in two. A few moments later she was made 'whole' again.

During the trick only the girl's head could be seen, protruding from a hole at one end of the box. All she had to do was draw her knees under her chin while the sawing took place. An American magician, Horace Goldin, introduced an improved version of the trick in New York in 1921. The girl's head, hands and feet were clearly

visible, poking through holes in the ends and sides of the box. However, he used not one girl but two.

To begin with, Goldin 'hypnotised' the first girl and told her to lie down inside the box, which rested on a deep wooden table. Once the lid was closed and padlocked, Goldin spun the box and table on a turntable so that the girl's feet were briefly out of the audience's sight. Immediately, she pulled up her legs and placed her feet against a footrest inside the lid. Simultaneously, the second girl – concealed inside the hollow table-top – thrust her legs through two trapdoors: one in the table-top and the other in the box. She then pushed her feet through the holes at the

end of the box. When the turntable stopped, the audience was looking at the head and hands of girl No 1 and the feet of girl No 2.

Goldin – with the help of an assistant – then cut through the centre of the box with a large saw. As soon as the saw was withdrawn, two metal plates were inserted into grooves, one on either side of the cut. The magician pulled the halves of the box apart – and the metal plates kept the audience from seeing inside. The 'victim', apparently cut in two, smiled and wiggled her hands and feet. Next, Goldin pushed the box together again, removed the metal plates and undid the padlocks. He awakened the original girl from her 'trance' and she emerged from the box unharmed.

Ever the showman, Goldin kept an ambulance waiting outside the theatre, and had a uniformed nurse and stretcher bearers standing at the back of the stalls. He later introduced a giant buzz-saw (circular saw) to 'saw the woman in half'.

The American magician Harry Blackstone developed the buzz-saw trick, using only one girl.

The girl is 'hypnotised' and told to lie face down on a flat table containing a torso-shaped hollow 30in (760mm) long, 15in (380mm) wide and 8in (200mm) deep. Under her stretchable dress she has on a strip-metal framework 'body', which includes a strip of flesh-coloured, cardboard 'back'. As the magician talks to the audience, she undoes the snap-fasteners on the framework and sinks into the hollow, leaving her head, shoulders, arms, lower legs and feet in view.

The magician then slides a hefty piece of wood 'under' the girl (in fact, it passes over her back) to prove that the saw is real.

The 24in (600mm) buzz-saw is switched on and – by using a crank – the table is moved below and past the whirling blade.

It seems that the girl's body is still flat on the table and is being cut in half by the saw, together with the wood. When the saw has finished cutting through the dress, framework and wood, the magician shows the sawn wood to the audience. With a snap of his fingers he brings the girl out of her 'trance' and she gets down from the table, all in one piece, and takes her bow.

Television spectacular

The latest variation of the trick is the 'Thin Model Sawing'. It was performed by the American magician Doug Henning in a television spectacular in 1982. It uses one girl in a box only about 12in (300mm) deep, as opposed to some 20in (500mm) in the original model. The end of the box contains a hinged door to which is attached a pair of remotely controlled rubber feet.

The box – which is in two parts hinged together – is placed on a table. The girl gets in with her head and feet protruding. The box is then turned so that her head faces the audience while she is being 'hypnotised'. At the same time, she pulls her feet into the box, kicks the false-feet door into place – so that the rubber feet protrude through the holes – and turns onto her side with her knees up to her chest. The table is turned sideways, and the sawing begins.

To add to the 'authenticity', the magician opens a small trapdoor in the side of the first box, revealing the girl's arm; while a similar door in the second box opens to show a fake rubber leg. Pulling on a concealed cord, the girl wiggles the false feet, which are on hinges. The process can be reversed in a matter of seconds – and the 'sawn in half' girl is back on her feet.

How a magician produces a rabbit out of a hat

The master illusionist Houdini thought that producing a rabbit from a hat was the most impressive of all conjuring tricks. 'It looks so impossible,' he declared, 'and yet *there* is the rabbit!'

In one of the most popular versions, the magician stands behind a table which is draped by a large felt cloth and invites a member of the audience up on stage. He asks him to inspect a top hat placed open-end up on the table between them – and make sure that it is empty. Then, as the volunteer holds up the hat by the brim, the magician thrusts both his hands into the hat and pulls out a live white rabbit.

The trick is done by sleight-of-hand, and calls for quick timing and a keen eye for angles of sight. As the volunteer steps onto the stage, the conjurer grasps the brim of the hat with his right hand. With his left hand he feels through a gap in the tablecloth and takes hold of a black felt bag hanging by a drawstring from a headless nail in the rear of the table.

He brings the bag (containing the rabbit) up behind the hat, making sure it is not in the sight-lines of the volunteer or the audience. When the volunteer has examined the hat, the magician turns it with his right hand so that the crown faces the audience. At the same time, he rapidly swings the bag in his left hand into the mouth of the hat.

As soon as the bag is inside the hat, he grasps the brim and the top of the bag with his left hand and lets go with his right. With the crown still facing the audience, he waves at the hat with his right hand, pointing out that there is nothing concealed around the sides or the brim.

'Heavier and heavier'

During all this, the magician looks directly at the volunteer and chats animatedly to him – keeping his attention away from the hat. Raising the hat above eye-level with both hands, the magician asks the volunteer to take hold of the brim on opposite sides. Slowly he lets go of the hat, saying: 'Now the empty hat is growing heavier and heavier!'

When the volunteer has full charge of the hat, the magician suddenly reaches into it with both hands, opens the bag by pulling the drawstring through its rings, and takes out the rabbit with his right hand. Meanwhile, with his left hand, he makes sure the bag stays safely out of sight in the gleaming top hat.

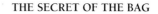

The magician closes the bag containing the rabbit by pulling a drawstring that is threaded through metal rings.

The bag is hung from the edge of the table behind and below the top hat, out of sight of the audience.

The empty top hat is shown to the audience, with the bag hidden behind it.

The magician turns the crown of the hat to the audience. With the other hand, he quickly swings the bag into the hat.

A volunteer holds the hat while the magician secretly opens the bag and lets out the rabbit. The magician then takes the hat and shows the rabbit to the astonished audience.

Fatal finale Chung Ling Soo (right) thought he had perfected his bullet-catching feat – his act's finale. Then one night it went wrong.

Death of a bullet-catcher

On the night of Saturday, March 23, 1918, the packed audience at the Wood Green Empire, in north London, awaited the climax of Chung Ling Soo's magic act – in which he 'caught' two speeding bullets between his teeth and then spat them onto a china plate.

A hush fell as two assistants – one of them Soo's Oriental-looking wife – loaded their rifles with circular lead bullets marked by two members of the audience. They took aim, fired – and, instead of the sound of bullets pinging onto the plate, a bullet struck Chung Ling Soo in the chest. It passed through his body and lodged in the scenery. Clutching his chest, the magician staggered backwards into the wings. He was taken to a nearby hospital, where he died the next day, aged 58.

Soo – who was actually a New Yorker named William Ellsworth Robinson and was married to an Englishwoman – had successfully performed his 'Catching the Bullets' illusion hundreds of times in theatres on both sides of the Atlantic. Each of his muzzle-loading rifles had a steel tube fitted under the barrel to hold the ramrod when it was not being used. It was the ramrod tube – filled with a blank charge – that was actually fired, not the barrel itself.

The trick with the marked bullets was even more ingenious. Carrying two unmarked bullets in a cup, a girl assistant went down into the audience and asked two people to scratch marks on them. The cup had a false bottom containing another pair of bullets already marked by Chung Ling Soo. It was these that were loaded into the rifles by two more members of the audience on stage. The other two marked bullets remained in the cup.

The magician had a third pair of bullets, which he had also marked, hidden in his mouth. When the rifles were fired, he spat his two bullets onto the plate – and showed them to the members of the audience on stage. They confirmed that the bullets had

the marks on them – although, of course, they did not know whose. The girl put the bullets into the cup and went back down into the stalls. Operating the trick bottom for a second time, she showed the first two volunteers the bullets they had marked and which had never left the cup.

The stunt seemed foolproof. But on the fatal night the exploding percussion cap in one of the rifles accidentally ignited both the blank charge in the ramrod tube and the live charge in the barrel. Constant use had damaged the insides of the weapon so that the fine gunpowder worked its way from the ramrod tube into the barrel.

The fault lay with Chung Ling Soo, who – afraid of sharing his secrets with a gunsmith – had insisted on servicing the rifles himself.

Levitation: how a magician makes the girl float in thin air

Making mystical passes, and speaking in a low soothing voice, the magician puts his girl assistant into a deep trance.

Obediently, she lies down on a raised, cloth-draped board resting on two pedestals. Immediately behind the board is a plywood imitation candle, electrically lit, which shines down on the motionless girl as if to show that there is nothing 'funny' going on.

Walking briskly across the stage, the magician removes first one and then the other pedestal. Once this is done, the girl is seen floating in midair on top of the apparently unsupported board.

The magician then moves behind the girl, and with a flourish he passes a large, solid hoop around the girl's sleeping body. The pedestals are replaced, the girl is awakened with a snap of the magician's fingers – and she joins him to acknowledge the audience's applause.

The hoop trick

The act – one of several similar 'suspensions' or 'levitations' – is a clever illusion. The board is supported in the centre by a vertical iron bar which is hidden from the audience by the wooden candle.

The magician revolves the hoop around the girl as shown in the diagram below. With careful manipulation, it seems as though he has passed the hoop completely around the girl.

A clever, but risky, method of performing the trick eliminates the candle or similar device. The magician hides the vertical bar by standing in front of it.

This modern suspension act which is performed in a nightclub or private house started life in 19th-century theatres as the art of levitation – in which someone or something apparently floats and rises in the air. It was introduced by a French magician, 'Professor' Alexander Herrmann, with his act 'the illusion of Trilby'. In it, he pretended to hypnotise a beautiful young girl and make her obey his will – as does Svengali, the sinister hypnotist in George du Maurier's novel *Trilby* (1894).

Herrmann set his theatrical scene by placing a long board between the backs of two chairs. His Trilby then entered carrying a bouquet of roses. Stepping onto a footstool, she lay down on the board and rested the bouquet on her stomach. Herrmann, as Svengali, walked around her and fussed with the curtains behind the set-up – as though making sure that they met in the middle. He then made some hypnotic passes over the girl and took away the chairs, one by one. When the second chair had been removed, she appeared to be completely unsupported.

In response to some more passes, Trilby, still lying on the board, rose in the air. Then, when bidden, she sank back to her original position. Herrmann replaced the chairs and waved his hands over Trilby, bringing her out of her trance. Clutching her bouquet, she stepped down, the chairs were removed and – to show there was nothing peculiar about the board – Herrmann threw it down onto the stage.

The stagehand's job

The levitation trick was worked mechanically by means of a strong frame set just behind the curtains. The frame was fitted with a slide which could be moved up and down by a stagehand using tackle. A steel bar, with a forked socket at one end and a handle at the other, was attached horizontally to the slide. Once the girl was lying on the board, the socket end of the bar was thrust through the gap in the curtains.

While adjusting the curtains, the magician guided the socket – which was masked by the girl's bouquet – so that it gripped the board. When the chairs were removed, the girl and the board appeared to be floating in the air. By turning the handle, the stagehand raised and lowered the board – and the 'hypnotised' girl with it.

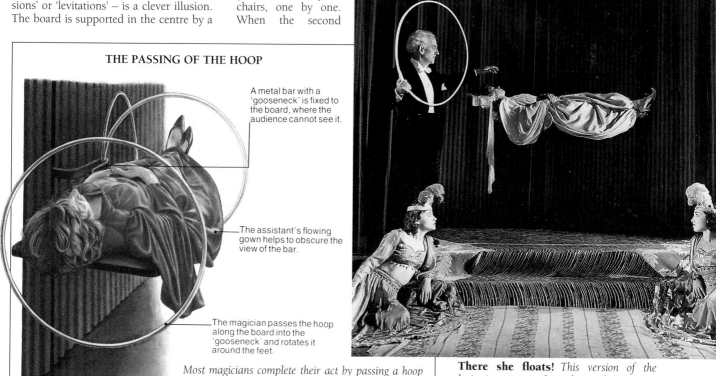

THE PASSING OF THE HOOP

A metal bar with a 'gooseneck' is fixed to the board, where the audience cannot see it.

The assistant's flowing gown helps to obscure the view of the bar.

The magician passes the hoop along the board into the 'gooseneck' and rotates it around the feet.

Most magicians complete their act by passing a hoop around the floating girl. But this is a clever illusion achieved with a 'gooseneck' in the support bar.

There she floats! *This version of the levitation act is performed on a theatre stage and makes use of the curtains. The board that the girl is lying on is supported by a bar sticking through the gap between them.*

Rise and fall of the Indian rope trick

As dusk descends on a narrow valley in India, a fakir (a Hindu miracle-worker) prepares to perform the rope trick to an audience of natives and, perhaps, a curious traveller from abroad. Grouped beneath a ring of lanterns, the audience watches as the fakir takes a length of hemp from a wicker basket and throws it in the air. He does this several times to show there is nothing unusual about the rope.

Then, as he again throws the rope up, it miraculously rises until the top is lost to sight in the growing darkness. Next, the fakir's partner – a slimly built boy of about eight – swarms up the rope and apparently disappears into thin air.

The fakir calls to the boy to come down and receives a rude answer.

Cursing with rage, the fakir produces a lethal-looking knife, puts it between his teeth, and climbs up the rope after the boy. He too vanishes from view, then comes a series of blood-curdling screams – and the boy's dismembered limbs are thrown to the ground, quickly followed by his blood-stained torso and severed head.

The fakir hurriedly climbs down the rope and joins his assistants in a grief-stricken circle around the boy's remains – which are then put into the basket. As the lamentations reach a climax, the boy suddenly springs from the basket – alive and in one piece. According to tradition, this is how the Indian rope trick appears to its audiences.

An explanation of the trick is given by an American journalist and travel writer, John A. Keel, in *Jadoo* (1958) – an account of his occult experiences in India and the Far East. In the mid-1950s – when he was aged 25 – Keel met an old fakir near the city of Hyderabad who claimed to have performed the rope trick. Sketching in the sand with his stick, the fakir showed Keel how it was done.

A thin cable made of black hair plaited together is stretched across a valley, some 50 ft (15m) from the ground. The cable is virtually invisible against the background of darkening sky and hills. Slung over the cable is an even thinner cord – one end of which is held by an assistant, who is placed well back, out of sight of the audience. The other end – on which is a small hook – dangles by the side of the fakir.

Distracting the audience's attention with his chatter, the fakir makes a set number of 'test throws' of the rope. He then surreptitiously slips the hook into a hole in a small but heavy wooden ball attached to the end of the rope. He next throws the rope as high as he can towards the horizontal cable. At the same time, the hidden assistant pulls on the cord until the rope is erect – with the wooden ball jammed against the cable.

Next, the boy climbs up the rope. Once at the top, he takes a hook from his pocket and secures the ball to the horizontal cable. He is followed up by the fakir, and both stay there, hanging onto the cable.

Straining to see in the gloom, and dazzled by the lanterns, the audience is completely taken in. The cut-off limbs and torso that are taken from the fakir's

STAGING THE ROPE TRICK AS EVENING FALLS

A thin but strong cable of plaited hair, stretched high over the dimly lit valley, acts as the support for the magician's rope. Hiding some distance away behind a convenient bush, an assistant pulls a cord which helps to hold the rope erect so that the boy can climb up it.
Meanwhile, dazzled by the hand-held lanterns, the spectators do not notice the cable or the hidden assistant.

Aloft *The English conjurer 'Karachi' and his 11-year-old son 'Kyder' performing the rope trick in 1935.*

clothing and thrown down are those of a dead monkey in similar clothes to the boy's. The 'blood' is red paint; and the severed head is a wooden model in a turban.

The boy then slips his arms and legs into a harness inside the fakir's loose-fitting robe, and is carried down the rope. Back on the ground, while the fakir and his assistants are lamenting, the youngster sneaks out of the harness and – masked by the tricksters – creeps into the basket.

A short while later in Delhi, Keel saw a crude version of the rope trick performed in broad daylight on a spacious clearing in front of a mosque.

The magician, named Babu, erected a platform some 6ft (1.8m) square, behind which was a low canvas backdrop. He then passed a rope about 10ft (3m) long among the spectators. After they had examined it, he dropped it into a wicker basket and began to play on a native flute.

As the weird music wafted over the spectators, the rope rose rigidly from the basket and loomed above the backdrop. A small boy came onto the platform, pulled on a long red hood that completely covered him, and shinned to the top of the rope. Babu clapped his hands three times. The hood fell to the stage, empty. And a few seconds later the boy reappeared from behind the crowd.

Keel saw through the trick immediately; and Babu later confirmed that he was right. There was a small hole in the bottom of the basket, directly over a matching hole in the platform. In a pit beneath the platform crouched an assistant holding a long bamboo pole wrapped in hemp. After the genuine rope was dropped in the basket, the assistant pushed the pole up through the holes for the boy to ascend.

The boy's hood was also 'rigged'. Inside it was a collapsible wire frame shaped like his body. On reaching the top of the pole, he hung the hood on a hook attached to the bamboo. While Babu distracted the audience with some 'mystical' talk, the boy unbuttoned the hood, slipped out of it and jumped down behind the backdrop.

From the spectators' viewpoint, it seemed as though the boy was still inside the hood. Babu then clapped his hands, stealthily pulling a thread which collapsed the frame – and the hood fell limply down.

'Crude though it was,' wrote Keel of the demonstration, 'it fooled the native spectators, and they went away thinking they had witnessed the genuine rope trick. Their tales of the experience probably added to the native legends about the trick.'

The explanation of the rope trick most commonly given is that of mass hypnotism – in which a fakir is said to put his audience into a trance, and make them see things that are not there. More frequently, however, the trick is dismissed as a traveller's tale or a total myth.

Memory and the mind-reader

Blindfolded and with his hands pressed to his forehead, the mind-reader prepares to give a demonstration of his power of 'second sight'. His smiling girl assistant interviews a subject in the audience – for instance, a prosperous-looking woman – and the magician proceeds to reveal all sorts of personal things about her.

In response to his assistant's clearly voiced questions, he states that the subject's first name is 'Betty'. She is married and her nationality is American. The article which his assistant is holding up – and which, of course, he cannot see – is the woman's diamond wristwatch, a Rolex, and on the back of it are engraved the words: 'From Robert, with all my love.'

Two-part code

The secret of the mind-reader's act is a two-part code, transmitted in the seemingly innocent questions put to him by his assistant. One part of the code transposes the letters of the alphabet, then uses them to spell out words. In the case of the woman called Betty B is I; E is C; T is P; and Y is N. The term 'Hurry up', means 'repeat the last letter'. So to transmit the name 'Betty' to the mind-reader, the assistant starts each of her questions to him with the appropriate initial letter.

'I have a name here,' she calls out. 'Can you tell what it is?' 'Please try.' 'Hurry up!' 'Now have you got it?' In other words, the name is B-e-t-t-y.

The second part of the code consists of tables which cover everything from the contents of people's pockets to their favourite foods. The number of tables is limited only by the memories of the magician and his assistant. Each table contains about a dozen alternatives, and the magician is told which table is coming up by the assistant's opening question. Betty's marital status, nationality and the description of her wristwatch are conveyed by means of the tables.

Personal possessions

For instance, when the assistant asks 'What kind of article is this?', the mind-reader knows that by using this particular sentence she is referring to the table covering expensive personal possessions.

Her next question, 'Can you say what I'm holding?' begins with the third letter of the alphabet – and the third article in the table is a lady's watch. The fact that it is a diamond Rolex is similarly conveyed by means of one or more of the tables. Even the inscription on the back can be passed on, using one table for the message and another for the name.

If, however, her husband's first name is an unusual one – and is not in the relevant table – the assistant simply ignores it.

Mind-reading by code was devised in the mid-19th century by the French magician Robert-Houdin, whose skills inspired the American illusionist Houdini.

How a ventriloquist throws his voice

Smiling broadly – and chatting with a dummy seated on his knee – a ventriloquist exercises his art with breath control and the movement of his tongue.

In order to throw his voice, and make it appear that the dummy is talking, he breathes in deeply and forms his words in the usual way. However, he retracts his tongue, moving only its tip. This lifts and shrinks the larynx (the organ in the windpipe containing the vocal cords), narrows the glottis (the opening between the vocal cords), and puts pressure on the cords. In turn, this muffles and diffuses the sound – making it seem to come from another direction.

He distracts the audience by activating the dummy's eyes and head with hidden strings and levers, and by moving its mouth in time with the words. His broad smile – which appears to be in response to the dummy's 'chatter' – allows him to talk easily without noticeably moving his lips.

Vowel sounds can easily be pronounced without moving the lips. But consonants – particularly b, p and m – are much more difficult to say. That is why ventriloquists use animal or schoolchild dummies, whose 'voices' can be distorted or unformed.

To suggest a voice coming from a distance, a ventriloquist presses his tongue against the roof of his mouth, allowing very little of the voice to emerge. With his tongue in the same position, he uses a deep, harsh voice to suggest that it is coming from, say, the inside of a box – and a sharp, shrill voice to suggest it is coming from a ceiling or rooftop.

The word 'ventriloquist' comes from two Latin words: *venter* meaning 'belly', and *loqui*, meaning 'to speak'. The Romans thought that vocal sounds came from the belly; and their sorcerers threw their voices when prophesying the future.

Houdini: the great escaper

Snow was driving across the frozen Detroit River as the world's leading escapologist, Harry Houdini, prepared to make a 'Dive of Death' wearing handcuffs, leg-irons and body chains.

Shortly after midday on November 27, 1906, he leaped from Belle Isle bridge near the city centre and vanished through a specially cut hole in the ice, some 25ft (7.5m) below. As the minutes ticked by, and he did not reappear, the onlookers – including reporters, photographers and policemen – began to fear the worse.

In fact, the short and sturdily built escapologist had experienced no trouble in getting out of his shackles. He carried master keys in his mouth with which he unlocked the police handcuffs and leg-irons – and he was used to wriggling his way out of chains. However, he said afterwards, a fast-flowing current swept him downstream – and he found himself pressed up against a seemingly endless roof of ice.

He then noticed that some

Body secrets *Skeleton keys hidden about his body allowed Houdini to escape from the manacles and irons that bound him.*

THE MILK-CHURN ESCAPE

The trick involved a bottomless inner lining which fitted inside the outer churn. Houdini could simply lift it up.

Labels: Padlocks, Sham half rivets, Lining lifts up, Water

Houdini first performed his milk-churn escape in St Louis, Missouri, in 1908. It was billed as a 'death-defying mystery', and audiences were warned that Houdini faced a watery grave.

HOUDINI'S DEATH-DEFYING MYSTERY
ESCAPE FROM A GALVANIZED IRON CAN FILLED WITH WATER AND SECURED BY MASSIVE LOCKS
FAILURE MEANS A DROWNING DEATH!

'silvery bubbles of air' were trapped between the ice and the water. Turning his head sideways, he managed to inhale these and remain conscious. He swam in ever-increasing circles until he found the hole and was hauled out of the freezing water, eight minutes after entering it.

From then on, underwater escapes featured among Houdini's most spectacular stunts. In rivers from the Hudson in New York to the Mersey in Liverpool, he was handcuffed and shackled with irons, placed in sealed wooden packing cases, taken out in a tugboat, and lowered by crane into the water.

Houdini – who was born Ehrich Weiss, the son of a Budapest rabbi, in 1874 – took his stage name from that of the renowned 19th-century French magician, Robert-Houdin. His family moved from Hungary to the USA when he was a child. He was doing conjuring and card tricks at the age of six, and by the time he was 11 he was expert at picking locks and untying ropes. He spent his young manhood touring America with carnivals and circuses – when he devised and perfected some of the feats that were to make him famous.

THE UNDERWATER PACKING-CASE ESCAPE

He quickly tired of stage handcuffs, which came apart by pressing a secret spring, and made his first jump into a river wearing police handcuffs at Dresden, now in East Germany, in 1901.

Five years later he was topping variety bills throughout Europe and America. He accepted challenges from banks, police and locksmiths; and he beat them by using high-speed trickery and by concealing his actions behind curtained-over cabinets and screens.

One of his most effective acts was escaping from a 'burglar-proof' steel bank safe – which was searched by a team of officials to make sure there was no key hidden inside it. Dressed in a bathing costume, Houdini was examined on stage by a doctor, who confirmed that the magician did not have a key concealed anywhere on him. Houdini then shook hands with the doctor and the umpire – who happened to be one of his closest associates. The umpire slipped a key into his hand and the audience watched in anticipation as Houdini entered the safe and curtains were drawn across it.

Thirty . . . forty . . . forty-five minutes went by. Meanwhile, the theatre orchestra played lively music; but there was still no sign of the escapologist. People in the audience began calling out to the management to release the 'dying man'. However, Houdini's distress signal – a series of knocks – had not been given. Then, as women started screaming, the curtains opened and there stood Houdini in front of the closed safe.

In fact, he got out of the safe within a few minutes of entering it – and spent the rest of the time sitting on a chair reading a book. The secret was that the safe was delivered to Houdini some hours before the curtains went up. His team of mechanics changed the lock with one which could be opened by the hidden key from

inside the safe. By the time the safe was returned to its owners, the original locks had been replaced and the safe appeared not to have been tampered with.

A similar atmosphere of suspense surrounded his escape from a milk churn brimming with water. Houdini got volunteers to fit four padlocks to the lid of the churn. Crouched inside it, there seemed to be no way he could possibly reach the locks on the outside. Again, the curtains were drawn around the cabinet and the orchestra played breezily away. And again Houdini performed the 'impossible' and appeared, dripping with water, to the astounded audience.

The answer was that the churn had a separate inner section, without a bottom, which fitted snugly inside it – and into which the magician stepped. The lid and padlocks were fitted only to the top of the inner section; and sham half rivets – which

THE CHINESE WATER-TORTURE-CELL ESCAPE

Houdini introduced his Chinese Water Torture Cell in Germany in 1912. It was a large, metal-lined wooden trunk with a plate-glass front, filled with water. With his feet in stocks, Houdini was hauled aloft and then lowered head-first into the cell. The stocks were padlocked to the top of the cell, which was then curtained over. Twisting himself round, Houdini worked his head and shoulders to the top of the cell. He then pressed a secret spring which slid the rear part of the stocks from its frame. This released his feet and there was enough space for him to wriggle free. He escaped in 3½ minutes. Houdini built up the tension by delaying his appearance through the curtain even longer.

appeared to keep the lid firmly in place – were secured only to the inner section. Houdini twisted this around until the catch holding it in place was released. He then pushed it up and was free.

Houdini's reputation rested largely on two other stage stunts: 'Walking Through a Brick Wall' and 'Escaping from the Chinese Water Torture Cell'.

The brick wall was built onto a steel frame about 12ft (3.5m) long and 10ft (3m) high, which was mounted on wheels and pushed onto a fully carpeted stage. The wall was placed at right angles to the audience, so that they faced one end of it. Two screens, 6ft (1.8m) high, were then placed one on each side of the wall. After the set-up had been inspected by a group of volunteers, Houdini stepped behind one of the screens, waved his hands above the top of it, and shouted, 'I am going!' A few moments later he emerged from behind the screen on the other side of the wall crying, 'I am back!'

Far from walking through the wall, he had *crawled under it* by means of a trap door set immediately below the wall. As he opened the trap door, the one-piece carpet sagged beneath the wall – just enough to let him wriggle under.

In October 1926, while on a tour of North America, Houdini's confidence in his strength and resilience proved his undoing. One day in his dressing room he allowed a student from Montreal's McGill University to punch him several times in the stomach. The heavy blows were delivered before Houdini was ready, and he collapsed in agony. A gangrenous appendix and peritonitis (inflammation of the stomach lining) developed and he died two days later in the next place on his tour. It was Detroit, the scene of his sensational river jump 20 years earlier.

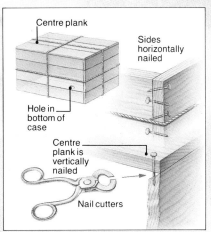

Centre plank

Sides horizontally nailed

Hole in bottom of case

Centre plank is vertically nailed

Nail cutters

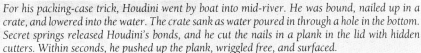

For his packing-case trick, Houdini went by boat into mid-river. He was bound, nailed up in a crate, and lowered into the water. The crate sank as water poured in through a hole in the bottom. Secret springs released Houdini's bonds, and he cut the nails in a plank in the lid with hidden cutters. Within seconds, he pushed up the plank, wriggled free, and surfaced.

How they hide 'the lady' in the three-card trick

'Come on, folks', cries the operator as he sets up his folding card-table in a busy city street. 'Find the lady and make your fortune!' Soon he is surrounded by a throng of curious onlookers, some of whom cannot wait to try their luck.

Talking all the while, the operator takes three cards – usually two aces and a queen – and lays them face down on the table, with the queen (or 'lady') in the middle. The cards are slightly bent in the centre, making them easier for the operator to pick up. He does so several times, showing the faces of the cards to the onlookers and then rearranging them but keeping the queen in the middle – always keeping to the same routine.

Quick shuffle

He picks up the left-hand ace in his left hand and the right-hand ace and the queen in his right – with the queen underneath the ace. He throws the queen face down in front of him, then the ace from his right hand to the left of the queen and the ace from his left hand to the right of the queen.

Next, he shuffles the cards about and builds up the prospective gamblers' confidence by showing the queen where they expect it to be.

After a final 'deal', he invites people to bet on which card is the lady. The winner will collect the kitty. The queen again seems to be in the middle – and a number of onlookers bet on that. Smiling broadly, the operator turns over the cards to reveal that the queen has changed places and is now on either the left or right of the middle card.

No matter how often the trick is performed, the public will always lose and the operator will always win. The trick is nearly always done by a team – the operator and a couple of stooges. The stooges make bets and are allowed to win, to encourage the punters to follow. Sometimes the punters are allowed to win a few small bets. But when it comes to the 'big one', they invariably lose.

The secret of the three-card men's success lies in the final deal, known as the 'fake throw'.

The operator picks up the cards as before – with an ace in his left hand and the queen and an ace in his right hand, with the queen

underneath. But instead of throwing the bottom card from his right hand in front of him he actually throws the top one.

As he is about to make the throw he closes his ring finger on the front of the queen and releases the middle finger from the ace. This allows the top card (the ace) to fall on the table in front of him. He then throws the remaining card from his right hand to the left and the ace from his left hand to the right. So the queen is no longer in the centre; it is on the left of the operator.

Gullible gamblers

He does this so quickly and deftly that it is never spotted by the gullible gamblers, who believe that the queen is still in the middle. Variations of the trick – which is also known as the Three Card Trick, or Three Card Monte – are performed on shopping streets and racecourses throughout the world. It breaks up when the 'suckers' have lost enough money – or a policeman appears on the scene intent on arresting the tricksters.

MAKING THE QUEEN SWAP PLACES

Normal throw *In the normal routine, the operator first throws down the bottom card (the queen) from the right hand.*

Fake throw *To cheat the punters, he releases the top card (the ace) by holding onto the bottom card with the ring finger.*

The ancient trick of switching the pea

The thimbles and peas trick – in which a pea vanishes and then reappears under one of three thimbles – was performed in Egypt about 5000 years ago, using cups and balls. Travelling conjurers later introduced it to the fairs and markets of Asia and Europe when people were urged to bet on which particular cup a ball was under.

The routine is still performed in much the same way. The conjurer places three thimbles – say one red, one blue and one yellow – mouth-down on a table. He puts a pea under the red thimble and, using both hands, swiftly

moves the thimbles around in small circles. He then asks the spectators which thimble the pea is under. 'The red one!' comes the response. Smiling, he prepares to pick up the thimble. He places his second and third fingertips, nails down, on the table, to the right of the thimble. Grasping the thimble between the tips of his thumb and forefinger of the same hand, he moves it in an anticlockwise semicircle.

About halfway through the semicircle he lifts the thimble just enough for the pea to roll out. Instantly, he catches it between his second and third fingertips, concealing it from the audience. Next, he lifts the thimble in the air, showing that the pea is not there.

Unknown to the onlookers, he has already jammed a pea in the narrow bottom end of each of the other thimbles. He then frees one of the peas by squeezing the bottom of, say, the blue thimble. The pea drops onto the table as he lifts up the thimble.

The trick – and its variations – is still sometimes perpetrated in shopping streets and markets as a way of cheating naive gamblers. But it is mainly now a mystifying trick performed by entertainers at children's parties.

Place your bets *This early 15th-century drawing shows a German cups-and-balls conjurer at work.*

Why you don't fall out when a roller coaster loops the loop

The phenomenon that keeps people in their seats on a fairground roller coaster is the same that keeps water in a bucket when you swing it round. But what exactly is it, and how does it work?

On fairground rides the inertia created can be stronger than gravity, so even when people are upside down there is no chance of anyone falling out. For those brave enough to keep their eyes open, it seems as though the world has been turned upside down, rather than them. The safety harnesses which are provided would only come into action if the cars were going too slowly.

Speed and inertia also enable fairground motorbike riders to cling to the Wall of Death as they roar around the circular pit. It is a law of physics that once an object has been set in motion by the application of a force, it will continue moving in a straight line until it is halted or diverted by another force. The object's reluctance to change its motion is called inertia.

Topsy-turvy *Passengers take a round trip on the high-speed, corkscrew roller coaster at Seaworld, Queensland.*

If a train stops suddenly, the passengers are thrown forward because inertia maintains their forward motion.

Similarly, passengers in a car get thrown to one side when it takes a tight corner. The car's direction has changed, but the inertia of their bodies pushes them out in the original direction. In the same way a child stepping off a fast-moving roundabout will be flung off in a straight line.

Although the motion of the roundabout is circular, a circle can be regarded as an infinite number of overlapping straight lines, each one of which realigns the child's direction of travel.

Altered image *The bumps, hollows and curves in the glass reflect light rays back to the observer's eyes at odd angles.*

How a distorting mirror tricks you

The illusion created by distorting mirrors can range from amusing to horrific. In reality it is the mirrors that are distorted, with bumps, hollows and curves. Because each part of a person is reflected in different sections of the mirror, the legs may be long and thin, the stomach short and wide, while other bits may be upside down.

Mirrors work by reflecting light rays from our bodies back to our eyes. A flat mirror reflects them evenly, but a dis-torting mirror sends them back at various strange angles.

A bulging – or convex – surface makes things look smaller. A car's rear-view mirror is often slightly convex to give a wider view. A concave surface – curving inwards – gives a magnified image. An example is a shaving mirror.

When you see an image of yourself in a mirror, your brain assumes that the rays have come direct to your eyes without being reflected. It is as though a person identical to you were standing behind the mirror. In a normal mirror, your other self seems to be the same distance behind as you are in front.

A convex mirror makes the rays diverge and your image appears to be smaller. A concave mirror makes the rays converge. Your image appears to be larger.

Making 'fog' for stage and screen

Three ancient crones gather on a heath. Thunder rolls, lightning flashes. Wispy, white mist swirls. But it is an illusion for a theatre performance of *Macbeth*.

One of the simplest ways to create 'fog' or mist is with dry ice – solid carbon dioxide (CO_2). Carbon dioxide is a gas which turns liquid when cooled under pressure. If the pressure is removed and the low temperature maintained, CO_2 solid-ifies into snowlike crystals which can be compressed into dry ice cakes.

Then, if a lump of the substance is removed from its refrigerated container and immersed in hot water, it rapidly turns to mist. The fog-making process can be better controlled by a dry-ice machine. This consists of a closed tank with an opening from which the vapour billows. A hose attached to the opening is used to direct the 'fog'.

For a lighter fog, which will hover, non-toxic oil is vaporised by a heating element in a fog machine. Fog produced from oil tends to linger longer than dry-ice mist which vanishes quickly.

Stage lightning
The traditional method of creating stage lightning is with a flash pot. A small charge of flash powder, containing the flammable metal magnesium, is ignited in a container by an electric spark.

Alternatively, photographic flash bulbs or carbon arc lamps may be used.

Forked lightning can be simulated by projecting a photographic slide of a lightning flash onto 'sky' scenery.

Most flash effects on stage are controlled by the fire regulations.

How film makers create their effects

Stop motion, back projection, travelling matte, motion control – these are simply some of the tricks of the film-maker's trade. Some are strikingly simple, others highly technical and innovative.

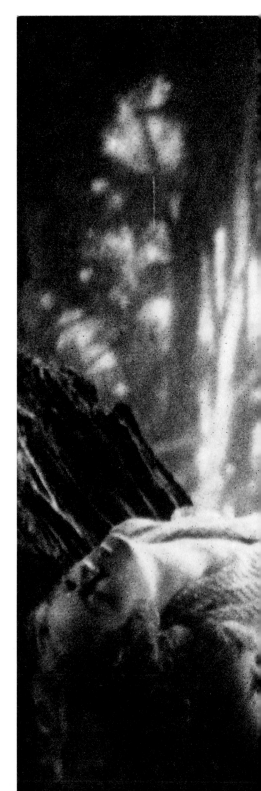

Back projection: combining beauty and the beast

The giant ape King Kong crashes into the jungle clearing to find his female sacrificial victim tied between twin pillars. With one finger he unwinds her bonds, then picks her up and lumbers off, clutching her in his gigantic paw. In fact, for most of this scene in the film *King Kong* (1933), the 'monster' was a model, 18in (460mm) high.

The effect was achieved through a technique called back or rear projection, by beaming film of the ape and background scenery onto the back of a translucent screen, while the actress Fay Wray played her role in front.

The main snag with the system is that the back-projected image tends to look flatter and dimmer than the foreground action. This is because the amount of light penetrating the screen is less than the light illuminating the foreground action.

The system was improved in the 1940s with the development of the triple-head process. It involved one projector shining directly on the rear of the screen and two others on either side bouncing identical images from mirrors so that they were precisely superimposed. This technique produced a brighter picture.

Kong looms *The giant ape was merely a model – back-projected onto a screen behind the real Fay Wray, and filmed from the front.*

Front projection: making Superman fly

When mild-mannered reporter Clark Kent became the Man of Steel in *Superman* (1978), he was made to fly through the sky over Metropolis – through a technique called front projection.

It is the reverse of back projection. The background scene is projected onto a screen behind the actor. But it is beamed from the front. So how do they avoid the background scene showing on the actor?

A projector bounces a low-intensity background image, too dull to show on the actor, off a mirror, angled between projector and camera. The image is reflected back at the camera from a screen, the surface of which is composed of glass beads, which intensify the image. Because the light from the screen travels in straight lines, the actor's shadow is masked by his body.

In the *Superman* flying sequences, the actor Christopher Reeve was supported by a hydraulic arm protruding from the screen. Like his shadow, the arm was concealed from the camera by his body.

Zoom lenses on both camera and projector provided the illusion of movement and perspective.

One of the first film makers to use front projection effectively was Stanley Kubrick in *2001: A Space Odyssey* (1968). It provided the background scenery in the opening sequence of ape men.

Simulating flight *The hydraulic arm that supports Superman is masked by his body. The city scene behind is front-projected.*

A FLYING FANTASY MADE REAL

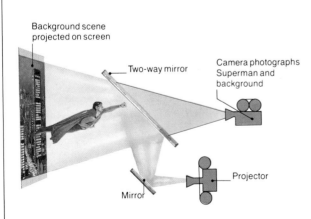

Background scene projected on screen

Two-way mirror

Camera photographs Superman and background

Projector

Mirror

Mirror magic *Filmed background scenes bounce off two mirrors, one of them two-way, onto a screen behind Superman. A camera films through the two-way mirror, blending both of the images.*

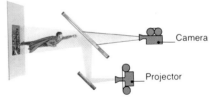

Camera

Projector

In flight *Camera and projector are synchronised. Superman does not move but the background does.*

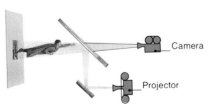

Camera

Projector

Close-up *The camera zooms in on the actor. The scene behind also zooms, providing perspective.*

On the finished film it looks like this: Superman is flying high over Metropolis.

City buildings seem to recede as he flies closer. Both are zoom lens effects.

Motion control: the camera creates the movement

The action sequences in *Star Wars* (1977), with speeding spaceships in dramatic dogfights, were achieved with models that never moved. In a technique called motion control, the camera does all the 'flying'.

The effects supervisor John Dykstra wanted to avoid the time-consuming and costly method used in *2001: A Space Odyssey*. For that film, the camera remained fixed while models were moved past it. For a scene in which the spaceship *Discovery* travels through space, it was necessary to film the model many times.

This was so that other elements, such as crew members visible in portholes, and star backgrounds, could be incorporated. The model was 54ft (16.4m) long and each camera pass on its 150ft (45.7m) long track took four and a half hours.

Dykstra's solution was to mount his model spaceships on rigid pylons coloured blue so that they would not show up against a blue screen background. The camera, mounted on a crane, travelled along a track. The crane arm moved up and down and rotated, and the camera could tilt, take sweeping panoramic shots (a pan), and track (follow any object) in all directions. It was computer-controlled so that each movement could be duplicated precisely to film different images on each pass, using the same film each time. So laser flashes, exhaust glow, explosions and starry backgrounds all ended up on the film in their right positions.

Stop motion: giving models life-like movement

In 1922, the author Sir Arthur Conan Doyle – creator of Sherlock Holmes – showed a film of model dinosaur animation to the Society of American Magicians. It made headlines in *The New York Times*: DINOSAURS CAVORT IN FILM FOR DOYLE.

Conan Doyle did not explain to his astounded audience that the film had been shot using a technique which had already been used somewhat unconvincingly in other silent pictures – but greatly improved upon by the American effects technician Willis O'Brien. It was a sequence from the movie of Conan Doyle's novel *The Lost World*, which was released in 1925.

Models are made to move by exposing a single frame of film at a time and adjusting the model to a new position between each shot. When the film is projected at the normal speed, the model – a brontosaurus, giant ape or some other creature – seems to move naturally.

'Flying' cameras *Like the model spaceships in* Star Wars, *the supersonic Soviet fighter in* Firefox *(1982) did not fly. The model, about 5ft (1.5m) long, was mounted on a computer-controlled support arm which was invisible on film. And the cameras ran on tracks to provide the illusion of movement – a technique called motion control. Clint Eastwood, who directed the film, played an American sent to Moscow to steal the plane.*

Model monsters *Ever since its full potential was exploited in* King Kong, *the stop-motion technique has been used to make models interact realistically with human actors. To make this scene from* Clash of the Titans *(1981), Harry Hamlin, as the hero Perseus, wielded his sword against imaginary adversaries. The model scorpions were photographed frame by frame. Their moves were adjusted to match those of Hamlin's, who was back-projected onto a screen, along with the background scenery.*

Matte painting: adding scenery to action

Any scenery, from the skyline of ancient Rome to an alien landscape, can be added to a film background by a matte painting – a technique used to mask part of a scene which will be added later. The technique evolved from glass painting, invented in the 1930s.

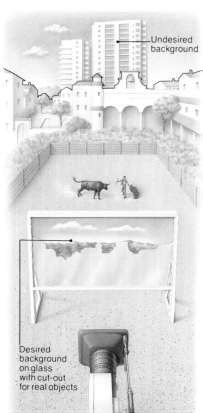

Masked *The camera shoots through painted glass to eliminate unwanted background.*

Undesired background

Desired background on glass with cut-out for real objects

Art work *A realistic warehouse interior in* Raiders of the Lost Ark *was a painting by a studio artist. The live action was added in the small area left blank in the middle of the painting. It saved building a costly set.*

A scene was painted on a sheet of glass, placed in front of the camera so that it merged with the action being filmed. Later silent-film makers developed 'in-the-camera' matte. It involved shooting live action with part of the scene 'matted out' by black paint on a glass sheet in front of the camera.

The partially exposed film was rewound and transferred to another camera.

A frame of the film was projected onto an easel and an artist added what was required to the matted-out area, leaving the live action area black.

The two segments – painted scenery and live action – were then combined, using a special 'optical printer', invented by a Hollywood technician, Linwood Dunn, around 1930. A type of film copying machine capable of superimposing and blending different portions of film, it can create a variety of effects. They include dissolves (in which one scene seems to 'melt' or fade into another), wipes (a shot which sweeps off the screen to be simul-taneously replaced by another), freeze frames (a pause in the action on one shot) and the combining of several, separately shot sequences.

Travelling matte: fantasy made feasible

In the 1957 science-fiction film *The Incredible Shrinking Man*, the actor Grant Williams had to appear to shrink in size daily. Parts of the film were made by building giant-sized sets, complete with outsized armchairs and tables. But in some scenes, as when Williams is chased by his cat – gigantic in comparison to him – a process called travelling matte was used.

In a similar way to a stationary matte painting, travelling matte involves creating a 'hole' in a film background, so that separately filmed action can be superimposed. But the travelling matte 'hole' has to shift position or change in size from frame to frame, to match the area wherever the actors or vehicles are required to move.

The system was used extensively in the

Blue screen process *Actors can be filmed – and then the background added later. First the subject is shot against a blue screen. This helps to create a travelling matte 'hole' which shifts position wherever the actors are, when blended with the background. Stages of the process during filming of* Raiders of the Lost Ark *show the studio filming, using a blue background screen (left), and (below) the actors after an outdoor scene is added.*

Superman films, especially when Superman was required to fly long distances or to recede to a very small size.

The most commonly used method is the 'blue screen' process. Actors, miniatures or other objects are filmed before a blue screen and the colour negative is then printed onto a black-and-white master, which captures only the blue area. The result is a film in which the background is clear, while the foreground action appears in silhouette.

This is the travelling matte. It is then run through an optical camera to mask the unwanted foreground, while the background film is exposed.

Thin blue line

The process is next reversed to mask the background when the foreground action is added to the negative. The film then contains both foreground and background footage combined on each frame.

Sometimes, a thin blue line or fringe is visible around the outline of the actor or model. But modern optical-effects technicians can now eliminate the line, which was caused by reflected light from the blue background screen.

Another – yet more laborious – method of creating a travelling matte was used by Stanley Kubrick for his spectacular film *2001: A Space Odyssey*.

To superimpose film of space vehicles on that of backgrounds of stars would have resulted in the stars also showing up the images of the spaceships. To solve the problem, Kubrick needed to have spaceship-shaped holes made in the starry backgrounds – holes that would move around to match the movements of the various craft.

The oldest, most time-consuming and costly method of creating travelling mattes was resorted to: painting spaceship silhouettes onto hundreds upon hundreds of frames of film.

Puppetry: secrets of *Alien* and *ET*

In the science-fiction thriller *Alien* (1979), the actor John Hurt has a sudden fit of violent coughing – and a hideous 'baby' alien bursts bloodily from his chest.

The illusion was created by the special-effects man Roger Dicken thrusting a puppet through a hole in a dummy torso.

Puppets have become popular with film makers to create terrifying creatures. Many are sophisticated pieces of engineering.

For *Jaws* (1975), three 25ft (7.6m) long sharks were built. One was pulled through the water on a type of sled, with scuba divers guiding it and working the fins and tail. The other two models were merely the left and right sides of a shark, to be filmed from only one side. They ran on an underwater rail and a hidden pivot arm enabled them to dive and surface.

The most endearing alien of all, *ET* (1982), was in fact several different ETs – three full-scale working models, a separate head and torso for close-ups and a midget actor in a costume.

Miniatures and models: small is effective

Miniatures – often easier to build, manipulate and film than the real thing – can be anything from model cars and aircraft to entire cities and landscapes. Many are not particularly small. The model battleships used so effectively in *Tora! Tora! Tora!* (1970) were 40ft (12m) long.

Moving miniatures are usually filmed with high-speed cameras, so that when the film is played back at normal speed, the movement looks more realistic. The motion of model ships in tanks of water, for example, is difficult to capture realistically. The same applies to ships' wakes and ocean wave patterns. Slowing down the projected film helps to make models look more cumbersome, ponderous and realistic.

'Hanging miniatures' are models suspended close to the camera to create the illusion that they are full-sized and being photographed from a distance. In the James Bond film *The Man With The Golden Gun* (1974), the villain's jet-powered, flying car was, in long shots, a model about 5ft (1.5m) long, with a wingspan of around 10ft (3m).

Many of the 'outdoor' scenes in *Close Encounters of the Third Kind* (1977), such as an Indiana landscape over which superimposed UFOs appeared, were meticulously constructed miniatures, with houses less than 1in (25mm) high.

Realism reduced *'Miniatures' used in films are not necessarily tiny. This large-scale model boat was used in* The Private Life of Sherlock Holmes *(1970).*

Explosion on ice *For this scene from* The Living Daylights *(1987), the French stuntman Joe Cott drove James Bond's car into a boathouse, pushing it onto a frozen lake. Then he smashed his way out of the wooden building. Seconds later it was blown up by special-effects men.*

Explosions: safety first

Explosions on screen come in many sizes – from the blowing-up of models to the destruction of full-sized buildings. The most common in war films are simulated bombs and shells. Since actors and stunt men are usually involved, it is crucial that the explosions are safely carried out.

According to the British special-effects expert Cliff Richardson: 'It's surprising how close you can stand to a hole in the ground with several pounds of gelignite in it, which will blow a ton of earth into the air.'

One of Richardson's biggest explosive jobs was during the making of *The Battle of Britain* (1969), when he and his team had to blow up a huge, sturdy aircraft hangar.

'Inside the hangar we had the partition walls knocked down to weaken the structure and this virtually left the roof of the hangar supported on 30 brick piers,' Richardson said. 'One hundred and fifty shot holes were drilled into the piers to receive the cartridges of explosives which were all linked together with Cordtex detonating fuse.

'It was necessary to add a number of extra effects to make the shot spectacular. These included two "fougasse charges", which are a type of mortar made, in this case, with 50 gallon drums of petrol which can be fired horizontally or vertically. I used one vertically to create a fireball effect through the roof of the hangar.

'The hangar doors were taped with Cordtex and a mock-up Spitfire was suspended just inside. A horizontal fougasse was then positioned to produce the

wall of fire which carried the Spitfire and the shattered doors across the roadway outside.'

In science-fiction movies, effects men are often called upon to blow up entire planets – as in *Star Wars* and *Superman*. A model of the planet is hung from the ceiling of a shooting stage and the camera shoots from below. When the charge goes off, the pieces fall towards the camera, creating the illusion of an explosion in space.

Storms at sea

Whether they involve ancient galleys hurling balls of Greek Fire or Second World War battleships with blazing guns, naval scenes are usually filmed in a studio tank. The tank at 20th Century Fox studios in Hollywood, for example, is 360ft (110m) square. It was used for the Pearl Harbor sequences in *Tora! Tora! Tora!* The effects supervisor, L.B. Abbott, won an Oscar for his work.

He explained: 'To create the sequences where the Japanese fleet is seen battling a violent storm on its way to Pearl Harbor, we used just about every fan we could get our hands on.

'To create foam for the storm-driven waves, it was necessary to add detergent to the water.

'The conventional way of propelling models through a tank is to attach them to underwater cables. In the case of *Tora!* the models were fitted with engines from golf-carts. These worked satisfactorily in some scenes but were not suitable in the more violent storm sequences because the engines lacked sufficient power to drive the

models through the rough water and we had to resort once again to cables.'

The giant ocean liner capsized by a huge wave in *The Poseidon Adventure* (1972) was a model. But for the chaotic scenes that ensued in the ship's dining salon, a huge set was built. It could tilt 30 degrees, while tilting cameras completed the illusion of the capsize. For the scenes in which the room appeared upside down, the same set was reversed from floor to ceiling.

Bullets and blood

Violence has been a feature of movies almost from the beginning – starting with the first silent film to tell a story, *The Great Train Robbery* (1903), a Western.

In the early days, bullets hitting walls, bottles or fences were actually fired by a marksman using live ammunition. But it was potentially dangerous and other techniques had to be developed.

For bullets splintering a wooden wall, detonator caps of gunpowder were inserted and exploded to synchronise with the gunshot. For bullet hits on people, a similar cap was attached to a metal plate that the actor wore under his clothing. The cap was electrically detonated by wires leading to a technician's 'keyboard'. But it could result in burns or lacerations from fragments.

So effects men developed the 'squib' – a small, smokeless, non-metallic, explosive charge. It can be detonated by small batteries strapped to the actor, by wires from a control board, or by radio control.

For her 'death' in *Bonnie and Clyde* (1967), Faye Dunaway had scores of squibs concealed beneath her clothing. The effects man Danny Lee arranged them in sequences, and they were wired to an off-camera battery which detonated them in sequences. The car in which Bonnie was machine-gunned was first punched with holes into which squibs were inserted and then painted over. Faye Dunaway's body shook with convulsions as the bullets peppered her. The scene was shot at high speed

Western shootout *As Yul Brynner is 'shot' in a barroom fight, an explosive squib is detonated under his shirt, bursting a 'blood bag'. The scene is from* Westworld (1973).

which, played back normally, gave the killing a slow, dreamlike quality.

The Wild Bunch (1969) made use of lots of fake blood. The effects man Bud Hulburd attached latex 'blood bags' to the squibs. The bags were filled with bright red, gelatine-based fluid. When the squibs burst the bags, the 'blood' spurted.

To create the effect of a spear, arrow or knife striking someone, the most common technique is to fire the projectile, which is hollow, along a wire from a compressed air device. The wire is attached to a metal plate strapped under the actor's clothing. The spear speeds along the wire and thuds into a cork pad fixed to the plate.

Topsy Turvy *To create the scenes of mayhem when the giant ocean liner in* The Poseidon Adventure *capsized, the entire dining salon set (left) – 118ft (36m) long, 60ft (18m) wide and 20ft (6m) high – was turned upside down. The outdoor scenes for the film were shot in a studio tank using a quarter-scale model of the ocean liner.*

Wind and wave *The storm sequence in the 1962 remake of* Mutiny on the Bounty *was produced in a 300ft (90m) square tank at MGM studios, using a replica of the ship (right). It was mounted on rails which rocked it back and forth. Wind and wave machines lashed the sea, and gallons of water were released from huge 'dump' tanks mounted above the sides of the main tank. Several stuntmen were injured when they were washed overboard during the filming, according to the special-effects man in charge, Arnold Gillespie.*

London Blitz *A disused Thames-side warehouse was fitted with 50 liquid propane gas burners to recapture wartime bombing of London in* The Battle of Britain. *Special-effects expert Cliff Richardson and his son John later devised the 'Dante' fire machine.*

Creating film fires: the 'Dante' machine

Because ordinary flames tend to appear transparent on film, chemicals are added to enhance movie blazes.

In the early 1970s, the British special-effects expert Cliff Richardson and his son John developed the 'Dante' fire machine – a device which enabled him to produce spectacular fires that remain perfectly under control. A car engine mounted on a two-wheel carriage drives a pump through which two 50 gallon drums of fuel mixtures can be squirted. Jet primers ignite the fuel and the machine can create a 60ft (18m) wide wall of fire.

City Hall 'blaze'

Dante machines were used in the James Bond movie *A View To A Kill* (1985) when John Richardson was required to set fire to San Francisco City Hall – without causing any damage. He fireproofed the roof with insulation boards, corrugated iron and sand. He also fireproofed window frames through which the Dante units would spout flames to give the impression that a fire was raging inside. Powerful flares created a large aerial glow overhead.

Richardson 'set fire' to the City Hall 25 times during three nights of shooting, with city fire-fighters standing by.

Los Angeles Fire Department was also on standby during the blaze sequences of *The Towering Inferno* (1974). Officials insisted that each blaze – created by propane pumped from valve-controlled hoses – lasted only 20 to 30 seconds.

Some 57 sets were built, including a five-storey, full-scale section of the tower, and a 110ft (33m) tall model of the whole building. Four camera crews shot the movie in only 70 days, and no one was hurt except a studio fire chief who cut his hand on broken glass.

London firemen stood by when Cliff Richardson rigged a Thames-side warehouse with 50 liquid propane gas burners to re-create a Blitz scene for *The Battle of Britain*. Richardson described it as 'one of the most difficult jobs I've ever been called upon to do'. The disused warehouse, already damaged by a real fire, was flanked by others still in use.

The illusion of an entire city ablaze was created for the 1936 Clark Gable movie *San Francisco*. It also featured a spectacular and realistic earthquake, for which an entire set was built on a rocking platform. It shook up and down and shifted to and fro up to 3ft (1m). Houses and walls collapsed, roads cracked open and furniture smashed around in a 20 minute quake.

Of 400 extras who were required to stand on balconies which crashed down at the touch of a button, none was injured.

Stuntmen: the screen's fall guys

Behind almost every spectacular fall from a horse, plunge from a cliff, hair-raising car crash or furious fist fight is a breed of specialists – the stuntmen.

Despite their dangerous work, many remain obscure and unsung. A few achieve fame and become stars.

Riding to fame, and danger, on horseback

A world rodeo champion, 'Yakima' Canutt became one of Hollywood's most famous stuntmen – specialising in working with horses. He began his career in the silent era. At that time, studios liked audiences to believe the stars did their own stunts.

Canutt's most celebrated feat was in John Ford's *Stagecoach* (1939), when he leapt from his war pony onto one of six horses pulling the coach. Shot by the hero John Wayne, Canutt fell between the horses and was dragged, before finally losing his grip. The stagecoach thundered over him, its wheels passing on either side, and Canutt struggled to his feet, proving it

Filming fights – with fists, glass and furniture

Fights, whether with weapons or fists, are carefully choreographed – especially if a star is involved. Punches are pulled in a technique first perfected for cinema by Yakima Canutt (left) – and the sound of fist connecting with jaw or body is added later. Protective pads for shins, shoulders, back and elbows are sometimes needed.

However, accidents happen. Christopher Lee, who began his film career as a stuntman, described a slip-up during a fencing sequence with Errol Flynn during the 1954 making of *The Dark Avenger*: 'The director, Henry Levin, hired me as an expert to ensure that none of his stars, particularly Flynn, got hurt. In one scene, I doubled first for Flynn and when he stepped in for close-ups I switched over to take the place of his opponent. I fought for hours. During the final take I could hardly raise my arm. When I did, Flynn ran his sword into it. Just above the elbow.'

In scenes in which people are hit over the head with bottles or flung through windows, the 'glass' is a special resin which looks and shatters like the real thing. But it is perfectly safe. It is expensive to produce so in stunts involving large amounts – such as entire shop windows – one take is preferable. Previously, fake glass was made from sugar.

Furniture and other props – known as 'breakaways' – play an important role in fight scenes. Chairs, tables, doors, or banister rails – often made of balsa wood – are sawn almost through so that they will shatter on impact. The cuts are painted over to conceal them.

was no dummy in a trick shot. The stunt has been imitated many times since. Canutt won an Oscar in 1966 for his lifetime stunt achievements and developing protective safety devices for stuntmen.

Even the best-planned horse stunts carry an element of danger. Former doyen of British stuntmen Bob Simmons described how his friend Jack Keely was killed during the desert adventure film *Zarak* (1956): 'All appeared to be going well. Both our horses fell beautifully. The call came, "Cut!" And then the familiar, "Everybody all right?" I looked around for Jack. I saw that he had gone down just short of the camera pit. He didn't get up. He was lying there motionless. Tragically, his horse had fallen on top of him and broken his neck.'

Training a horse to fall is done by strapping up one of its forelegs so that it stands on only three legs, then tugging the reins to the opposite side.

The animal, off-balance, will fall. After constant repetition, the horse will fall to order while galloping or cantering when it feels the bit being jerked sharply to one side. The technique is called falling 'on the bit'. So that the animal is not injured, the spot where it will fall is dug up and filled with sand or peat moss.

In the early days of the cinema, trip wires were used, rigged to the horse's foreleg, with the other end firmly tethered. But the cruel technique was banned because it could injure a horse's back or neck and the animal would have to be shot.

Falling horse *In* Stagecoach *(1939), a horse is brought down by tethering its forelegs with wire. It was ridden by Yakima Canutt (also shown in inset). The stunt was banned in the mid-1940s as being too cruel.*

Hit and miss *Pat Roche reacts to a feigned right hook from Harrison Ford in* Raiders of the Lost Ark *(1981). But the camera angle makes it look like a real piledriver.*

Breaking a fall from an exploding ski lift

Falls can range from a tumble down a flight of stairs to a plunge from the top of a high building.

For high falls, giant nylon air bags, which inflate to the area of a living room, are used to cushion the impact, as in Jerry Hewitt's plummet (right) from an exploding ski lift in *The Soldier* (1982).

Before air bags were introduced in 1971, stacks of cardboard cartons covered with mattresses served the purpose. These were then covered by tarpaulin and roped together to prevent them from bursting outwards. One layer of boxes for every 10ft (3m) of fall was the standard procedure.

When the Olympic swimming gold medallist Johnny Weissmuller – the cinema's popular portrayer of Tarzan in the 1940s – appeared to dive off Brooklyn Bridge in *Tarzan's New York Adventure* (1942), there were rumours that the actor actually did the 110ft (33m) plunge. But it was a trick. Weissmuller dived into a tank of water – then the film cut to a shot of a dummy plummeting off the bridge.

In *Butch Cassidy and the Sundance Kid* (1969), a leap to freedom from a cliff into a raging torrent was also faked. The actors Paul Newman and Robert Redford simply jumped onto a small platform a few feet below the cliff edge. Then two stuntmen were filmed jumping 72ft (22m) into a California lake.

Until about 1960, 60ft (18m) was the maximum unaided high fall. But modern stuntmen now fall more than 1000ft (300m) – using low-level parachute rigs and 'descender wires'.

The American stuntman Dar Robinson specialised in spectacular falls. He developed a technique of doing head-first falls from high buildings on a thin wire – a 'deceleration cable' – attached to a harness under his clothes. A winch slowed the fall as he neared the ground, bringing him to a halt, hanging upside down, a few feet up.

In *Highpoint* (1984), Robinson, doubling for Christopher Plummer, fell from the CN Tower in Toronto – at 1815ft (553m), the world's highest free-standing building. He plunged the equivalent of 120 storeys before making a delayed parachute descent. Robinson was killed seven years later, at the age of 39, while riding home on a motorcycle.

Soft landing *The hero of* The Soldier *(1982), played by Ken Wahl, was required to fall 75ft (23m) from an exploding alpine ski lift, blown up by terrorists. The American stuntman Jerry Hewitt actually took the plunge. His headlong fall was broken by a giant inflatable air bag made of nylon.*

Landing safely after a blast

A scene of someone being blown through the air by an explosion is usually achieved by the stuntman launching himself from an off-screen trampoline. Protective clothing shields him from flash burns. Sometimes, powerful springboards, activated by compressed air, are used. The stuntmen usually land in pits of sand or peat moss.

Normally, insurance companies do not like the stars risking injury. But in Douglas Fairbanks' *The Black Pirate* (1926) he slid down a ship's sail, apparently supported only by a dagger which sliced the sail. The 'dagger' was a handle attached to a counterweight behind the sail, which gave him stability, while the sail had a seam which tore evenly.

On fire – but unharmed

Great precautions are taken for stunts involving fire – they are among the most dangerous of all. Fire gel, usually alcohol based, is rubbed onto the stuntman's outer clothing. It produces a vapour barrier between material and flames – the alcohol burns *above* the clothing, much like brandy on a Christmas pudding, scarcely singeing the fabric. The stuntman wears a fireproof suit beneath the outer clothing, and beneath that, woollen underwear, which does not burn easily.

For head-to-foot engulfment, more sophisticated suits, with helmets and built-in air supplies, are worn. Film-unit members with fire extinguishers stand by.

Man on fire *Smeared with flammable gel, this stuntman wore protective clothing and mask for* To the Devil a Daughter *(1975).*

Crashing a car the safe way

Cars required to crash or roll over for a spectacular movie or TV scene are strengthened inside. The stuntman also wears a safety harness, padding and a crash helmet, provided he will not be seen.

When a car has to be rolled, it is either driven up a ramp out of camera shot, or it has a hydraulic arm which shoots out beneath and forces it over. Some of the more spectacular crashes are so dangerous that a dummy replaces the stunt driver. In these scenes, the cars can be catapulted by an air cannon, a device like a giant air gun welded to the rear of the car.

The device was used in *Grand Prix* (1966) in a scene in which a car plummeted into the sea. A camera was mounted behind the driving wheel and dummy hands fixed to the wheel completed the illusion.

Computer car stunt *The James Bond film The Man With The Golden Gun (1974) was the first picture to incorporate a car stunt worked out in advance by a computer – at Cornell University, New York State. It allowed stuntman Bumps Willard to do a corkscrew flip as his car soared over the gap in a carefully built 'broken' canal bridge and land safely on the other side. From the viewpoint of the audience, Bond himself (Roger Moore) was at the wheel.*

Christo: why he wraps landscapes

At dusk on September 17, 1985, Christo the Wrap-Around Artist prepared to give a long-awaited present to the citizens of Paris: his gift-wrapped 're-creation' of one of the city's best-loved bridges, the Pont-Neuf. Crowds had gathered expectantly on either side of the historic bridge, and a great cheer arose as giant pleated sheets of rich, honey-yellow fabric were pulled by ropes from a small fleet of barges up over the bridge by a team of alpine mountain-climbing guides.

The timing was well chosen as the fabric – which matched the colour of many of the surrounding buildings – was highlighted by the rays of the setting sun. For the next 12 hours the guides – assisted by tree pruners, who were also accustomed to working at heights – hauled the rest of the wrapping over the balustrades of the early 17th-century bridge.

The following morning, as workers streamed across the bridge, Christo's gift was seen in all its glory. Except for the roadway in the middle, and the bronze statue of its builder, Henry IV, the Pont-Neuf's span was covered in golden-hued nylon. The bright autumn sunlight made the fabric glitter and gleam. And at night, when the ornamental lamps were lit,

they shone through their wrappings like golden beacons against the purple sky.

The new-look bridge was the latest brainchild of the New York-based artist Christo Javacheff, born in Bulgaria, in June 1935. It typified his desire to bring art out of the galleries and into the streets where it can be enjoyed – free of charge – by everyone as part of their daily lives.

The Pont-Neuf, he asserted, had been taken for granted for too long. Each day hundreds of thousands of Parisians crossed it or passed by it. But how many of them actually *saw* the bridge and took the time to appreciate it? Not many, he claimed.

He planned to change all this with his colourful nylon wrapping, which would add a new dimension to the bridge. So much so that, long after the fabric was removed, people would have a fond and lasting affection for the noble stonework.

Christo made his first impact on Paris in 1962, when he illegally blocked a narrow street in the Latin Quarter with his *Iron Curtain* – a 13ft (4m) high wall of empty oil drums which mocked the Berlin Wall set up by the Russians in August 1961 to block road and rail traffic between East and West Berlin. In Paris, the *Iron Curtain* brought traffic to a standstill for several hours.

Two years afterwards he moved to the USA, where he launched a series of startling 'art events' including *Store Fronts* in New York City (1964), and *Packed Museum of Contemporary Art* in Chicago (1969). The first of these consisted of life-size replicas of store fronts with wrapped-up windows; the second in-

In the pink *In 1983 Christo created his* Surrounded Islands *in Biscayne Bay, Miami. First, he used a map of the area (far right); then he made a picture of it (right). Finally, he skirted the islands with 6½ million square feet (60,400sq m) of pink fabric (above).*

Running fence *In 1976 Christo's Running Fence – made of woven nylon fabric – snaked its way for almost 25 miles (40km) through northern California to the Pacific Ocean. The 18ft (5.5m) high fence was supported by more than 2000 steel poles.*

volved covering the museum with 62 sections of brown tarpaulin, tied with 2 miles (3.2km) of brown rope.

In 1972 he created *Valley Curtain*, at Grand Hogback, Rifle, Colorado, when he bridged a gap of some 1300ft (396m) between two mountain peaks with a gleaming, orange nylon curtain.

His most ambitious project came in 1980-3. Eleven islands in Biscayne Bay, Miami, Florida, were fringed with 6½ million square feet (60,400sq m) of pink fabric. Seen from the air, the islands resembled vast tropical flowers floating in a green-blue sea.

Christo's detractors claim that his work is too large and too short-lived to have any true artistic or aesthetic value. They also cite the cost of his creations – which, in most cases, amount to hundreds of thousands of dollars. His reply is that he pays for everything himself. He raises money from the sale of his multitude of drawings, sketches, scale models and lithographs to museums and private collectors.

In 1985 came *The Pont-Neuf Wrapped*. But the idea originally occurred to him ten years earlier when he began a detailed study of the site. Since it was opened in 1606, the Pont-Neuf – or New Bridge – had become a favourite haunt at night for lovers; a 'must' for sightseers and tourists; and a much-used artery over the Seine.

Christo had photographs taken of the bridge – with its 12 graceful arches – from

Image-maker *By wrapping natural and man-made features in contrasting fabrics and colours, Christo aims to make people more aware of the beauty around them.*

dozens of different angles. He then drew over the photographs in ink and paint, and pasted them together in collages to see how various colours and wrappings would look. He pored over blueprints and histories of the bridge – paying special attention to the boats and barges that passed beneath it and the thousands of motorists, cyclists and pedestrians who crossed it every day.

Permission to wrap the bridge had to be obtained from half-a-dozen authorities. It took Christo six years to get the approval of the Mayor of Paris, Jacques Chirac. And

Bridge of gold *All Paris came to view the Pont-Neuf in the autumn of 1985, after Christo had wrapped it in 50,000 square yards (41,800sq m) of golden fabric tied with 43,000ft (13,100m) of rope.*

President François Mitterrand did not give his assent until July 1985 – two months before the bridge was due to be shown to the public in its new garb.

Technically, the wrapping of the Pont-Neuf was a triumph.

The bottom of the fabric was anchored by professional scuba divers to cables just over 3ft (1m) beneath the surface of the Seine. More workmen secured the sheets with heavy ballast in the gutters of the roadway. In addition, the wrapping was tied to concrete blocks, special frames and hidden ramparts. And the entire creation was fastened with rope and supported by steel cables.

Nowhere did the cocoon-like nylon touch the stonework itself. The tensions and stresses balanced each other like a huge cat's cradle.

People came in their millions to stare and gape, to enjoy and admire, and – in some cases – to mock and belittle. The bridge remained 'under wraps' for two weeks. The nylon fabric was then removed – but not before some 750,000 free samples of it had been given to those who wanted to remember the Pont-Neuf in its brief, golden splendour.

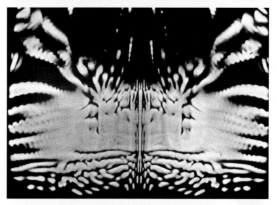

How do TV shows achieve their graphic effects?

Unearthly, abstract shapes that transform into solid-looking lettering; pictures that turn, tumble or appear to fly away; actors in fantastic alien landscapes. These are just some of the visual effects created by television's graphic designers.

More than 130 countries throughout the world have television networks – and all use the work of graphic designers. Since TV broadcasting began more than 50 years ago, increasingly sophisticated techniques have been devised to make programme presentation more spectacular. Now, computers help designers to achieve the seemingly impossible – and literally to 'paint' with light.

Electronic 'mist'

An eerie, other-worldly mist began to swirl across British television screens in 1963. Its symmetrical patterns were like a moving ink blot in negative. Pulsing electronic music accompanied the shifting shapes. Then they began to form blurred lettering which gradually resolved into two words: *DOCTOR WHO*.

BBC Television was launching its new children's science-fiction series about the adventures of a mysterious time traveller.

The unusual title sequence was created by the graphic designer Bernard Lodge. He and a team of technicians used an electronics phenomenon which became

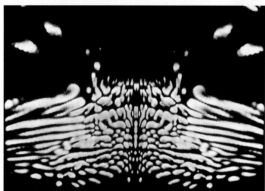

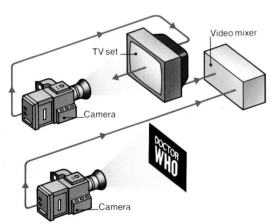

Eerie effect *To create the titles for the BBC children's serial* Doctor Who *(right), a video camera was aimed at its own monitor (above). This creates a 'loop' effect. A second camera fed in the title and the signal went round and round the loop, creating the unusual 'mist', which eventually resolved into the name of the show's eccentric hero.*

known as 'video howl-round'.

It involves pointing a video camera at a monitor screen to which it is transmitting a picture – of the screen. If both camera and monitor are stable, that is, squarely facing each other, nothing happens. But any signal that is introduced, such as the reflection of a torch on the monitor screen, will set up an electronic feedback between the monitor and the camera and back again. Any alterations to the monitor's controls – brightness or contrast, for example – or to the camera position, will pass round and round the feedback 'loop', creating abstract patterns.

It is visually analogous to the feedback effect caused when a microphone is pointed at, or gets too close to, an amplifier.

For the *DOCTOR WHO* sequence, a second camera transmitted the programme's title logo to the monitor to trigger the effect. An electronic mixer was used to mirror the image and to combine the lettering from the second camera.

'Exploding' the face of the Statue of Liberty

The climax of the opening title sequence of the 1984 documentary series *Crime Inc* was an image of the face of the Statue of Liberty exploding. The graphic designer Lester Halhead wanted to symbolise 'the complete break-up of American society'.

To create the effect, a picture of the statue's face was printed on sheets of sugar glass. As its name implies, it is made of sugar, breaks easily and does not cause injury. It is frequently used for film and TV effects. The glass, with small explosive charges attached to the back, was put in a wooden frame and hung horizontally from a studio ceiling. The image on it was reflected in a mirror beneath, angled at 45 degrees. A high-speed camera filmed the reflection. When the charges were detonated the sugar glass broke up and fell towards the mirror. When the film was played back at normal speed, the image appeared to explode slowly towards and past the camera.

To complete the sequence, a similar process was repeated with the programme's title logo

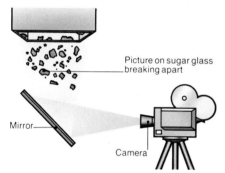

Break-up *Graphic designer Lester Halhead's title sequence was meant to symbolise the collapse of US society during the gangster era of the 1920s.*

For example, any two pixels can be joined up to create a line. Other points can be joined to make geometric shapes, or lettering. Once created, a shape can be reduced, enlarged, or repeated any number of times. Each pixel is then stored in the computer's memory in the form of numbers.

The manipulation of the images is done with a keyboard, through which the operator can call up any picture to be projected on a monitor screen. Then, using an electronic device called a Paintbox, the operator moves a stylus, wired into the system, over a panel. The stylus makes no actual marks on the panel, or drawing tablet, but its every move is electronically translated into artwork on the monitor

Blow-up *The 1984 documentary series* Crime Inc *opened dramatically with the face of the Statue of Liberty 'exploding', then 'imploding' to form the opening title. It was done by hanging the images, painted on fragile sugar glass, over a mirror. The camera filmed the reflection as the sugar glass was shattered by five explosive charges. The second half of the sequence was run in reverse.*

printed on sugar glass. When the film was edited and spliced the title sequence was played in reverse so that the statue appeared to explode and then re-form into the title. A final dramatic touch was a patch of fake blood superimposed on the lower left of the title.

Computer-aided animation

Computers can be used either to create pictures from scratch – or to add or subtract images from film or stills which are fed into them by a video camera. They do it by manipulating the tiny picture elements (pixels) – the points of coloured light which form the image shown on the TV screen.

Mixed media *The opening sequence of the pop music show* Wired *combined filmed sky and model buildings with moving artwork figures. Representing street musicians, like this stylised drummer, the figures were animated by a computer system.*

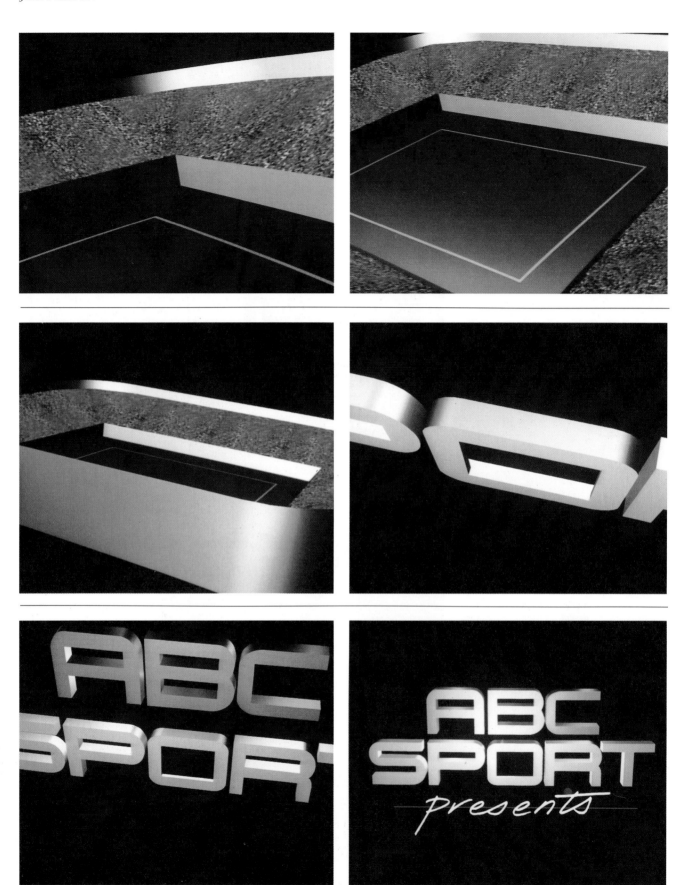

Mobile title *Australia's ABC SPORT lettering was first drawn by the graphic artist Julian Eddy, then turned into solid-looking, metallic form, complete with light and shade, on a computer. The seven-second sequence of 750 frames took some 15 to 20 minutes' work for each frame. The letter 'O' of the word 'SPORT' was made to resemble a stadium, with its terraces full of spectators.*

screen. In this way, the picture on the screen can be altered and modified.

The range of effects that can be achieved is remarkable. Any colour picture can be reduced, enlarged, reversed in mirror-image fashion, repeated any number of times, or turned into a stencil which can be moved anywhere, in any size on the screen. Different types of media used by conventional artists – watercolours, pastels, oils, airbrush texturing – can be emulated. Perspective, light and shade, tone and movement can all be applied to an existing picture, or added and subtracted from a prefilmed sequence.

The designer Matt Forrest's opening sequence for a TV pop music programme, *Wired*, featured computer-animated musicians, made up of segmented geometric shapes. They appeared, along with model buildings, on a cracked desert landscape against a stormy sky. The 40 second sequence, which took three months to generate on a computer system, won 16 television design awards.

Towards the end of the sequence, a number of artwork drumsticks fly up into the air, whirl around and form the lettering of the programme title.

The images were first hand-drawn, then fed into a computer, coloured, textured and animated.

The Australian Broadcasting Corporation's sports promotion sequence, *ABC SPORT*, features three-dimensional lettering which looks solid and metallic. The lettering was designed by the artist Julian Eddy – then 'drawn' on a digital paint system. It was shaped, coloured and textured by computer.

Then the lettering was computer-manipulated. In the finished sequence, the 'O' of the word 'SPORT' is seen in close-up, lying on its side. Its inner rim represents the inside of an oval sports stadium thronged with spectators. This effect was created on a device called a Mirage, by generating thousands upon thousands of coloured points of light. When viewed on a television screen, they give the impression of a crowd of people. As the camera appeared to pull back, the lettering was made to turn into an upright position – again, an animation effect generated on a computer – spelling out the title, *ABC SPORT*. The word 'presents' was added afterwards in handwritten script on the digital paint system.

For its 1986 World Cup introductory graphics, the Italian TV network RAI commissioned a complex animation sequence. It took three months' work with a powerful computer and a Paintbox to produce a 90 second videotape. It featured

Flying figure *The whirling components of Britain's Channel 4 sign were artwork that was coloured and animated by computer.*

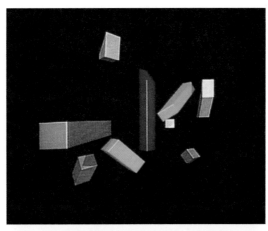
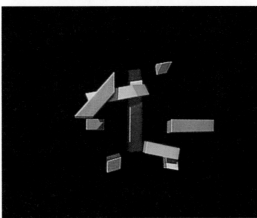

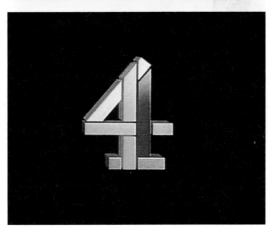

footballs apparently floating in space, like planets. One of them loomed into close-up and, as it retreated, was seen to carry the words 'The World Cup' on its surface in English, printed in gold lettering.

One of the first television networks to use computer-aided animation on a large scale was the Brazilian station TV Globo, launched in 1975. An Austrian designer, Hans Jurgen Donner, living in Rio de Janeiro, persuaded the station to use facilities in the USA to create a logo, or 'trademark'.

The station also has a late-night news programme with distinctive graphics titles. It depicts a purplish, metallic-looking globe, segmented rather like a tangerine, which eventually transforms into the first letter 'O' in the third of the words *JORNAL DA GLOBO* ('World Journal'). When the elaborate animated logo for Britain's fourth TV network, Channel 4, was designed by a London company in 1982, no computer firm in Britain had equipment that was sufficiently sophisticated to create the effect. So the job of generating its components, making them look three-dimensional and colour-textured, was given to a company in Los Angeles. Then the graphics were returned to London and animated there.

The finished image consisted of a number of multicoloured, solid-looking segments which appeared to fly into view. They whirled around, orbiting each other – then fell into place as the figure 4.

Combining TV images

A news presenter sits at a desk before the TV camera. As he or she reads a news item, a video-taped picture in the background helps to illustrate the story. Yet in reality, there is nothing behind the newsreader except a blank, blue wall.

The filmed background is actually being run through a second camera, while a device known as Chromakey, Ulti-matte or Colour Separation Overlay (CSO) automatically integrates both pictures – newsreader and background images. It works by 'ignoring' the blue colour of the wall – and superimposing another picture in its place.

The same computer systems can be used to combine actors, filmed against a similar blue background, with fantastic painted landscapes, model sets or photographic scenes. In this way, the British graphic designers Barry O'Riordan and Peter le Page mixed live actors, animals and props with Biblical backgrounds based on Renaissance-style paintings for a production of the oratorio *L'Enfance du Christ* by the French composer Hector Berlioz, for Thames Television.

'Instant' photo files

Digital video equipment allows TV stations to store thousands of still photographs on computer discs. The system, known as Electronic Stills Stores (ESS), requires very little storage space. And a producer can 'key in' a still picture almost instantly – anything from a building bombed by terrorists to a hi-jacked airliner.

In this way, a newsreader may be reading an item about, say, an incident in New Orleans or Moscow, and a background shot of the place can be added to the screen alongside the newscaster.

Miracles – by Mirage

Still photographs can also be used to create seemingly magical effects. The computer system Mirage, designed in the United States and produced in 1982, can make pictures appear to 'fold', turn over or transform into a variety of geometrical shapes – pyramids, spheres, cones, tubes and cylinders.

The computer is programmed with the information of how a piece of paper would look if it were folded into the various shapes. Using this mathematical information, it can then superimpose any picture that is fed into it over a moving image that has all the 'in-depth'

appearance of being three-dimensional.

The system has been frequently used to switch from one section of a programme to another. The final image of the preceding section might, for instance, be framed in a pyramid shape, spin around and then recede into the distance like an object falling from a height.

Brief link sequences between programmes or pauses for commercial breaks can be created in this way.

Holy Land settings *Instead of using costly sets, live action was blended, by a device called Ultimatte, with painted backgrounds for a production of* L'Enfance du Christ. *The blending was done so 'naturally' that it totally deceived the eye.*

Geometric magic *The Quantel Mirage device can turn flat images into three-dimensional shapes and make them 'fly' around the TV screen.*

BLACK-AND-WHITE MAGIC

Stark white lines edge jerkily over a totally black cinema screen. The soundtrack is a raucous, menacing jazz theme by the composer Elmer Bernstein. The lines eventually merge to form a stylised, jagged outline of a forearm and hand. The film is *The Man With The Golden Arm*, a drama about drug addiction starring Frank Sinatra, released in 1956.

Saul Bass, who designed the sequence, said: 'Until then titles had tended to be lists of dull credits, mostly ignored.' Many consisted merely of lettering, superimposed on a background of draped satin. Bass's artwork not only changed the film-maker's approach to titles, but also went on to influence generations of television graphic designers.

His titles were made simply by photographing, frame by frame, a series of painted images. They were placed, one at a time, in a frame. A stationary camera, mounted on a rostrum, took the pictures. When the finished reel of film was projected at the normal speed of 24 frames a second, the artwork appeared to move – in the same way as animated cartoon images.

Bass was working with the film's director, Otto Preminger, when he created his titles. At one stage, said Bass later, they looked at each other and said. 'Why not make them move?' For some time, added Bass, he had felt that 'the audiences' involvement with the film should really begin with the very first frame . . . To create a climate for the story about to unfold.'

Secrets of the animal and bird TV stars

It took a month to teach the longhorn bull named Merrill how to behave in a china shop. Each day the three-year-old beast was hand-fed to encourage gentleness – and then led patiently through a clutter of crates and bales representing the showcases found in a high-class boutique.

At last he was ready to face the cameras and star in his first television commercial – in which he wandered around a china shop containing some $40,000 worth of Wedgwood china and Baccarat glass. The actual shooting sessions took 16 hours, at the end of which Merrill had not so much as chipped a saucer or cracked a vase.

He was advertising the prestigious international investment company, Merrill Lynch – whose advertising theme in 1980 was described as: 'Merrill Lynch is agile and clever in addition to being large.'

A native of Southern California, Merrill was put through his paces by two of America's top animal trainers: Joan Edwards and Stevie Myers. At their ranch in the San Fernando Valley the two women have taught all kinds of animals – including geese, chickens, sheep, dogs, rabbits and horses – how to act on film. Their secret – especially with large, potentially dangerous animals like Merrill – is endless patience and kindness. They charge advertising agencies high fees, and ensure that the animal stars receive their share in food and comfort. 'Every bull and horse is treated like a member of the family,' says Joan Edwards.

Similar animal training establishments are found throughout the world – there are more than 20 in England alone – and some of the dogs, cats, bears and birds used in the commercials have become just as well known as the products they advertise.

Public appearances

The Old English sheepdog in the Dulux paint ads on British television is constantly in demand to open supermarkets and paint stores. But it is usually a look-alike that makes the public appearances, while the Dulux dog himself works mainly in the TV studios.

In 1986 it was decided to teach the dog a new trick – and have him roll on his back in the commercial. Eight sheepdogs were auditioned for the part – and the winner worked with a trainer eight hours a day for three weeks until he perfected his roll. Philip Rowley, a Surrey dog breeder and

Fireside friends *Matthew the bulldog, Sylvester the cat and Mickey the mouse 'starred' in a 1989 television advertising campaign for household coal. The film was shot in London over a period of four days. Once the animals got used to the studio atmosphere, they soon settled into their acting roles. Only Sylvester showed stage fright – and seemed terrified of Mickey. He had to be lured to the fire by a trail of prawns. Once there, however, he settled happily with Mickey and Matthew in front of the blazing coals. The animals cuddled up to each other and even exchanged 'kisses'.*

the owner of Duke, the original Dulux dog, put his training success down to persistence and sweets. 'Duke'll do almost anything for a couple of Polo mints,' he said.

The much-loved golden labrador puppy who frolics with a seemingly endless roll of lavatory paper in the Andrex commercial on British television is actually not one dog, but 20. The look-alikes – aged about six weeks – are filmed separately and the various pieces of film are later joined together. Very successfully, too. By 1987 some 900 million miles (1450 million km) of the paper had been sold in Britain.

Trick photography and deception are staples of many TV commercials – which look none the less realistic for it. One of the most successful and striking of these was made in France in 1985 for a car-hire company. In it a clutch of vultures was called on to 'devour' a car – the message being that, when you went to a good rental firm, that sort of thing did not happen.

The birds' trainer, Pierre Cadeac, began by putting large pieces of meat on top of a car and getting the vultures to eat them. Gradually, he made the pieces smaller and smaller – and hid them around the car. The vultures tenaciously dug out the meat and demolished it. Finally, he replaced the rubber of the windscreen wipers – and the rubber around the windscreen itself – with scraps of meat.

After three months' training, the birds swooped down on the car and were filmed as they 'feasted' on it.

The tiger which bounds across the snow in one of the international Esso ads is not out in the cold at all. The 'snow' is, in fact, gypsum – a soft, sand-like mineral from which plaster of Paris is made.

The commercial was shot in the heat of White Sands National Monument in New Mexico, USA, using three tigers. When one animal became bored – and therefore unpredictable – another one took its place. Three animal handlers were also employed. The first handler released one of the tigers; the second handler got the big cat to rush forward by offering it a shovelful of meat; and the third handler stayed protectively with the camera crew.

In Britain, one of the most publicised television cats has been the white and handsome Arthur of Kattomeat fame.

Arthur achieved stardom through his habit of eating a tin of cat food with his paw, something which came naturally to him. The only element of pretence involved his sex and name. For Arthur was really a female named Samantha, who was re-christened because the cat in the original Kattomeat commercial was called Arthur.

As well as earning a generous daily salary and expenses for studio work and personal appearances, the animals receive star treatment. They are ferried to and from work in chauffeur-driven limousines; they are given all their favourite food; strict rules govern their care and safety; and a veterinary surgeon is on the set.

What it takes to be a game-show contestant

Each week throughout the world thousands of people apply to take part in television shows such as *Wheel of Fortune* and *Sale of the Century*. On average, out of every 150 applicants only one is chosen to appear on a particular show.

'When it comes to choosing contestants, game shows are very picky,' states American author Maxene Fabe in her book *TV Game Shows*. 'They are looking for people with whom their viewers will feel comfortable; they are looking for people who will play the game with verve . . .

'They are not looking for contestants who are merely nice, or deserving or even needy. They are looking for contestants who will boost their ratings.'

Anyone aged 18 or over can apply to take part in the game show of their choice. Normally they write or telephone to the programme asking for an application form. This contains questions about the applicant's occupation, marital status, ambitions (serious and fantasy), interests and hobbies, nicknames (if any), pets, and favourite and least favourite people, places and things. It may also ask for a recent cheerful photograph and want to know which national newspaper he or she reads. Sometimes the shows' producers advertise for contestants in the media.

Most TV companies employ researchers to sift through the applications and compile a shortlist. Next come the interviews and studio auditions, when the programme makers are on the lookout for competitors with happy smiles and peppy personalities, who can laugh at themselves as well as others, and who are not afraid to show their zeal – especially in urging on their fellow contestants.

Applicants for some shows – such as the popular Australian programme *Press Your Luck* – have to sit a lengthy general knowledge test. Those who pass it are then asked to stand up and tell a funny or embarrassing story about themselves. The applicants who are still left in the race then compete in a practice game. Finally, the most suitable players are chosen.

On some programmes – notably the intellectually inclined *Mastermind* in Britain – contestants can choose their own specialist subjects. These have ranged from 'The art and archaeology of Minoan Crete from 2000-1450 BC' to 'the spy novels of John le Carré'. And the contestants have included a lorry driver, a Benedictine monk and a retired ambassador.

A family doctor who applied unsuccessfully to the programme later described the interview with the producer. First, the doctor explained his specialist subjects, without being asked questions, then he was given a trial run through some general knowledge questions.

'He was terribly kind and assured me that the questions would be harder than the ones on the show. I was grateful for that crumb of comfort as I mumbled "Pass . . . Pass . . . I've no idea . . . Sorry . . . I don't know". What does esurient mean? That was the first question; I had never heard the word. (The answer: greedy.)

'After five negative replies I contemplated making a run for it. In the end I did achieve a few correct answers – I recognised a line from Keats' *Ode to a Nightingale*. But I was not in the least surprised to receive a polite letter two weeks later turning me down.'

In some countries tax officials keep a close eye on game-show contestants and their winnings. This was so with Ginny Swinson, a housewife and former schoolteacher from Charlotte, North Carolina, when she appeared on *Wheel of Fortune* in Los Angeles in 1985. She won $27,000 worth of merchandise – including a replica of a 1952 MG-TD roadster and a trip for two to Mexico. Her husband and some relatives were in the audience, and they dashed up on stage to congratulate her.

'Everyone was jumping up and down and screaming and crying,' wrote Ginny afterwards. 'As we left the stage, we were led to a table right out front, where a smiling woman handed us a California State tax bill for $1300. She told us that three months after the tax was paid I'd get my prizes.' With federal tax, Ginny had to pay more than $6000 on her winnings.

The unusual and the unexpected can also play a part in the shows. None more so, perhaps, than *The New Newlywed Game* in the USA – in which newly married couples answer questions about their respective spouses. One particular bridegroom could not remember his bride's 'vital statistics' and gave the combination of his work locker instead. On another notorious occasion, a female viewer spotted her missing husband on the show – together with his new 'wife'.

Roulette: how they prevent you breaking the bank

In 1891, an English roulette player named Charles de Ville Wells 'broke the bank' at Monaco's casino not once but six times in three days. By doubling his stake every time he lost, and then winning, he turned an initial 10,000 francs into a million. He died penniless in 1926, but he inspired a popular song, *The Man who Broke the Bank at Monte Carlo*, and a potent myth: that it is possible to devise a system that can beat the roulette wheel.

There is certainly a seductive magic about roulette. It is easy to play. It has an aura of sophistication and drama. And, occasionally, there are astonishing runs of winning numbers – Number 10 came up six times in a row at the El San Juan Hotel, Puerto Rico, on July 9, 1959.

Roulette can give the gambler the strong impression that character and intelligence ought to pay off, so long as he can devise a suitable system. Usually, any system involves spotting a pattern. The theory, in its simplest form, goes like this: in 100 tosses a coin is likely to come up heads about 50 times. If it comes up tails 20 times in the first 20 tosses – so the theory goes – then there is a higher chance of it 'correcting' itself by coming up heads the next time. Any roulette table has its avid watchers trying to spot a 'trend' – such as the black numbers coming up several times in succession – in order to bet against it. Sometimes, gamblers call this 'The Law of Equilibrium', or the 'doctrine of the maturity of the chances'.

In fact, there is no such law. A more accurate name is the 'Monte Carlo fallacy'. The odds remain the same for every throw, whatever the previous run. The truth is that it simply is not possible to beat the house legally, for several reasons.

First, the wheel itself gives a built-in advantage to the house. All bets are placed on one or more of the 36 numbers, or a variety of combinations of them – odd or even, black or red, high or low. The payouts are calculated as if the ball had a 35:1 chance of landing on each of the numbers.

But there are, in fact, one or two additional 'boxes' – 0 on a European wheel and 0 and 00 on an American wheel. This gives the bank an advantage of from 1.76 per cent up to 7.89 per cent, depending on which wheel is used and which bets have been placed.

Even the 'Martingale' system – doubling up your bets every time you lose – adopted by Mr Wells will eventually fall victim to this built-in advantage.

There are other advantages possessed by the house. In a betting match between two otherwise equal rivals, the one with more money almost always wipes out the other, simply because he can go on betting longer. The house can always send for more money, while most gamblers at some point decide to call it quits, and walk away losers. Then there are house rules by which the croupier pays out fractionally less than the odds dictate – for example, by rounding down figures in favour of the house.

The gambler himself often makes mistakes, no matter how well he knows the odds or his system. Since there are 12 different ways to place bets, combining black or red, odd or even, individual numbers and any number of numbers up to 12, all governed by their own odds, it is easy to become confused.

In theory, it should be possible to devise a computer system that predicted the position of the ball on landing. The technology has existed for some years to sense the movement of the ball, its spin and velocity, and apply complex mathematical principles to predict its final position.

Gamblers in the USA have tried to better the odds by using computers to analyse play statistically, strapping computers to their bodies, or even hiding them in their shoes.

However, the casino security guards are easily made suspicious of anyone communicating by radio, or suspected of concealing computer equipment. Although this kind of system is not illegal in the USA, the participants would be encouraged to leave the casino and not return.

To prevent the return of unwanted gamblers, some European casinos employ men called physiognomists, who have photographic memories for faces and names. People known to be big winners, whatever their system, may be refused entry to the casino.

The art of the crossword compiler

The first stage in compiling a crossword puzzle is to design some blank grids. Most newspapers, or feature agencies which supply crosswords, work on a set of stock grids which are used in rotation.

To fill in the grid, the compiler begins with the longest words. As a rule the aim is to have vowels or common consonants on squares where words cross. A 'z' on such a square, for example, might make the solving of the puzzle too easy. The compiler must stick as far as possible to familiar words, which can include proper names, and to accepted spellings. In choosing words it must be borne in mind that some words tend to come up all too frequently, and others are difficult to write clues for.

Once the grid is compiled, the clues have to be written. There are two kinds of clues, straight and cryptic. Straight clues are little more than dictionary definitions, and are mainly a test of knowledge. In cryptic clues the meaning is cunningly concealed, though in the best crosswords it is usually there in 'straight' form too.

Almost anything goes in cryptic clues – anagrams, quotations, puns, deliberate misuse of words with two or more meanings, and even some abstruse items of learning. Even the location of the word, across or down, may be used to baffle the solver. Here are some examples:

Anagrams Formerly these were done straight, as: *Neat stag* (anag) (8) – STAGNATE. But modern practice is to conceal the anagram: *Make no move to get Satan exorcised*. 'Make no move' is the straight definition of stagnate. 'Get Satan' is the anagram. And 'exorcised' is typical of words used to hint at an anagram.

Read-throughs The clue is concealed in a sentence: *Employer discovered in hideous error* (4) – USER. A user is an employer and the word is made of the last two letters of 'hideous' and the first two of 'error'.

Double meanings The words are used in both their meanings: *Lines of West Country flowers for the chop?* (4) – AXES. Axes are coordinate lines, and there are two West of England rivers 'flow-ers' called Axe. A simpler example: *Wizard bird* (6) – MERLIN.

Puns The play upon words may be obvious, or devious, as: *Heggs!* (11) – EXASPERATED (eggs aspirated).

Dividing word The separate elements are given, as well as the whole word: *Country of tin girl* (6) – CANADA (can plus Ada).

Positional clue An example of a clue for a down word: *Overconfident bird?* (8) – COCKSURE. 'Cocksure' means overconfident and the bird 'cock' appears over 'sure' (confident). The clue can only be solved if the position on the grid is recognised as being important.

And one for an across clue: *Floating second-rate worker following you around* (7) – BUOYANT (B-UOY-ANT). 'b' is second-rate, 'ouy' is 'you' turned around, followed by 'ant' – notoriously a worker. The clue would not work in a down position.

There are a few words that linger on in crosswords long after they have passed out of regular use. Al Capone (d. 1947) is often invoked for the letters AL in words – as in instrument-al.

How computers can outplay chess champions

The world of chess was rocked by a game that took place in a hotel at Long Beach, California, in November 1988. A computer program beat an International Grand Master for the first time in a tournament.

The program, called 'Deep Thought', was created by five graduate students at Carnegie Mellon University, in Pittsburgh. The Grand Master was Bent Larsen of Denmark, one of the world's top players and a former candidate for the world championship.

After its triumph over Larsen, Deep Thought went on to tie for first place in the tournament with the former British Grand Master Tony Miles. As computers are not eligible to win the prize-money under the tournament rules, all the $10,000 prize went to Miles.

But Deep Thought was compensated by receiving the $10,000 Fredkin Prize for becoming the first computer to reach the level of Grand Master. It was also ranked as one of the 30 best players in the United States.

'It brings the spectre of a computer world chess champion by the end of the century closer to reality,' according to Vince McCambridge of the US Chess Federation.

McCambridge had played Deep Thought to a draw during the tournament and for a time actually held an advantage. But, he said, 'I relaxed when I was winning. It never gets tired and it never gives up.'

Deep Thought's success lay in its two microprocessors with their massive memory. A human chess champion plays mainly by instinct; even top players can only think a few moves ahead. They rely mainly on their knowledge of how games develop to plan their strategy.

Computers have no instinct, but they can check all the possible moves from a particular position, then all their opponent's possible countermoves, and then all their own responses, as far as 15 or 20 moves ahead in some variations. When it beat Bent Larsen, Deep Thought was examining 700,000 positions a second.

Deep Thought's memory contained the details of 900 games played by human Grand Masters which had been programmed into it by its creators.

Despite its awesome ability, it was still much too slow in 1988 to take on the world champion Gary Kasparov who, according to one study, is the greatest chess player of all time. The leader of the computer team,

Feng-Hsiung Hsu, said the program would have to be 100 to 1000 times faster to beat Kasparov, which was 'not out of the question' in a few years.

In the chess world Kasparov has a rating of 2775 points (points are awarded on the basis of performance in tournaments). A beginner rates about 1200 points and an expert 2000. After the Long Beach tournament, Deep Thought had an impressively high rating of 2550.

The programmers who designed Deep Thought are quite unable to beat their creation. None of the five is a top-class chess player. The best, Murray Campbell, is rated 'expert' which is not high in competition terms.

Having won their Fredkin Prize of $10,000, the team can look ahead to one of $100,000 for the first machine to prove itself better than the world champion. An earlier prize of $5000 – offered by Professor Edward Fredkin of the Massachusetts Institute of Technology – was won in 1983 by two scientists from the Bell Laboratories who designed the first computer program to be rated as a chess master.

Capturing a dandelion 'clock'

The seed head of a dandelion, so delicate that the puff of a child's breath will explode it into scores of tiny 'parachutes', can be imprisoned in a ball of solid plastic.

Craftsmen, working with polyester 'embedding' resin, are able to capture the freshness of newly picked flowers, seed heads or autumn leaves as paperweights. One medical laboratory gives away paperweights containing artificial heart valves.

The secret of embedding a delicate object lies in extreme care.

First, a thin layer of resin is poured into a mould. Protected from dust by a covering, it is allowed to set, but not solidly, for three to four hours. Then the flower is gently laid on it. Further resin, a layer at a time, which helps to prevent bubbles, is added until the mould is full. When fully set, the casting is removed from the mould and mounted.

Dandelion clock *A perfect seed head is preserved forever in plastic (top). The technique for embedding an object involves building up many thin layers of resin in a mould (bottom), allowing each one to set slightly before adding the next, then unmoulding and mounting on a base.*

How to put a model ship inside a bottle

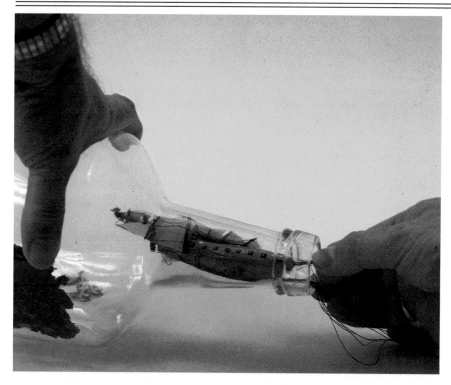

Sailing in glass *The miniature sailing ship is modelled first, and the masts and sails are attached to the hull on hinges. The model should just fit through the neck of the bottle (left). The sails are unrolled when the model is in place on its Plasticine 'sea', and all the finishing touches are added. The bottle is then corked to keep out dust (below).*

The secret of putting a ship into a bottle is simple: the masts are on hinges and are pressed flat against the deck when the ship is passed through the neck of the bottle. Once inside, they are pulled upright by threads that are snipped off at the neck of the bottle and glued to the Plasticine 'sea'.

The first step in this craft, which developed on 19th-century clipper ships, is to carve the hull from hardwood.

The ship is assembled outside the bottle. Then the masts are folded down and deck fittings such as the wheel and the ship's boats are removed so that the masts lie flat. Once the model is inside the bottle and its masts upright, the fittings, each dotted with glue, are put back in place on the end of a long wire.

The sails – made of cloth or paper – are only partly attached before the ship goes into the bottle, so they can be rolled up. With square-riggers the yards which support the sails have to be swivelled parallel to the hull to go in the bottle.

But before the ship is inserted into the bottle, model-makers use blue Plasticine, pressed into place with long steel rods, to represent the sea.

The model is slid stern first into the bottle, because one of the controlling threads passes through the bowsprit which must face outwards. When the model is almost in position, the threads controlling the masts are gently pulled to bring the masts upright. Sails are carefully unrolled

and fastened with tiny drops of glue on the tip of a thin rod. The thread at the bowsprit is also anchored with a dab of glue. Those coming out under the hull are kept taut and pressed into the Plasticine after the hull is secured. Surplus thread can be cut off with a thin-handled modelling knife.

Splitting seconds to time Olympic runners and swimmers

In the Seoul Olympics of 1988, the British swimmer Adrian Moorhouse won the 100 metres breaststroke from Karoly Guttler of Hungary by just one-hundredth of a second, or 16mm (⅝in). The computerised timers, however, could have coped with a separation down to one-tenth of that, just 1.6mm (1⁄16in).

For centuries, no one cared much about the time taken over short races. Only the winner mattered, and the human eye was good enough to decide. In the mid-19th century, however, the invention of the stopwatch changed all that. Athletes now had times to run against.

But even the best stopwatches were dependent on a number of variables: the reaction and judgment of the timekeepers at the start and finish, the distance of the athlete from the starting pistol (those

farther away would hear the report a fraction later), and the tendency for athletes to 'jump the gun'. Only in the 1980s did it become possible to exclude human error, with timers that can record thousandths of a second with totally objective methods of measurement.

Modern systems are thoroughly computerised. The starting pistol is attached to a sensor that automatically starts a computerised timer, and also sends a signal along cables to loudspeakers immediately behind each athlete, thus eradicating the difference in the distance over which the sound travels.

Sensors on the starting blocks allow a computer to measure the delay between the sound of the starting pistol and the athlete's reaction against the blocks. The fastest an athlete can react is reckoned to be

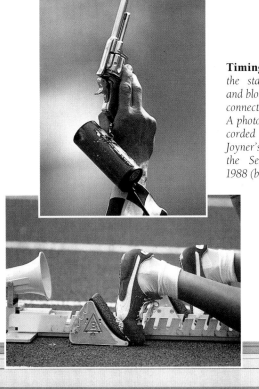

Timing winners *Both the starting pistol (left) and blocks (below left) are connected to a computer. A photo-finish camera recorded Florence Griffith-Joyner's 100 metre win at the Seoul Olympics in 1988 (below).*

about one-tenth of a second. If the computer records a reaction time faster than that, or a reaction that precedes the pistol, the computer registers a false start, and sounds an alarm to the starter, who calls the athletes back and also records who the offender was.

At the finish, systems are different for swimmers and sprinters. In swimming, touch-pads on the ends of the pool, just above and below the water line, feed directly to the timing computer. At the end of a sprint, runners pass in front of a photo finish camera aligned along the finishing line. As the athletes cross the line, the camera records an image of them set

against a computerised timer accurate to one-thousandth of a second. When developed, the film reveals in pictures and numbers who won and in what time.

The picture is not, however, a normal photograph. It is a record, not of a large area at a split second of time, but of a tiny area – the finishing line – over an extended period of time, the time it takes all the competitors to finish.

The picture is taken on a strip of film which is not divided into frames like normal film. The film moves past a slit a mere four-thousandths of an inch across. As a runner passes the slit, the moving film photographs each segment in sequence.

In one-thousandth of a second, a world-record sprinter covers 10mm (⅜in) – enough of a lead to show up on the photo-finish picture.

How an electronic line judge calls the shots in tennis

Professional tennis players serve balls at more than 120mph (200km/h) – faster than the eye can clearly see. When a ball is in flight, the eye sees just a long blur – an optical illusion. After it strikes the ground and slows down, the blur suddenly becomes denser and so more easily seen. How then can the umpire and his linesmen tell with certainty just when a disputed serve is 'in' or 'out'?

The answer is that they don't any more – at least not with the eye alone. They rely on a small electronic device called Cyclops, which was invented in Malta in 1978 by a local woman, Margaret Parnis-England, and a British engineer, Bill Carlton. It is now used on courts around the world, including the Centre Court at Wimbledon and the main courts at Flushing Meadow in New York.

Cyclops emits a number of invisible infrared rays, which span the court very

close to the ground. If a ball passes through one of the rays it sets off a signal. The service line itself is monitored by a master ray. If a ball hits the ground anywhere on the service line, including its outer edge, a yellow light flashes, indicating to the umpire that the ball is in.

Other rays, called fault rays, monitor the area just outside the service line. If a ball strikes this area, a red light is accompanied by a bleeping sound – announcing that the ball is out.

The master ray is normally positioned about ⅝in (16mm) above the line and between 2½in and 3½in (65mm to 90mm) from the outer edge of the line. A speeding ball will pass through it before hitting the line. The nearest fault ray is placed about 4¾in (120mm) from the service line and parallel to it.

Cyclops has been used widely since 1980, but it has been criticised – by the

former world No 1 player John McEnroe, among others. A different system called Accu-Call has been developed by an American inventor, John Van Auken, a pioneer in the development of photocopier technology.

Accu-Call promises to dispense altogether with linesmen. In their place, a mesh of electronic circuitry, embedded in the tennis court and the net, 'reads' the position of the ball whenever it hits the court or net. The 'readings' are triggered by wires woven into the ball's covering which complete electric circuits when the ball touches four or five wires in the mesh.

A compact control console in front of the umpire displays each disputed shot as varying audible calls or coloured lights, showing whether it is in or out of court.

Accu-Call is not suitable for grass courts, as the moisture in the grass might interfere with the electronics.

How do sportsmen get a ball to curve in the air?

Sportsmen who play ball games know all about spin, using it not only to make the ball change direction when it hits the ground but also to make it curve in flight. In baseball, football, golf, indeed in all except one case – a fast bowler in cricket – this is done with spin.

Why spinning balls curve in flight was a question answered a century ago by the British physicist Lord Rayleigh, who named it the Magnus Effect, after an earlier German researcher, Heinrich Gustav Magnus.

As a spinning ball passes through the air, it drags air around itself in the direction of the spin. The air moving past the ball is also speeded up on one side and slowed down on the other. Since air moving faster also exerts less pressure, the air on the opposite side of the ball is at a relatively greater pressure. It is this difference in pressure that produces the force which causes the ball to curve.

The effect is obvious in many sports. Many good tennis players can manage a top-spin lob, which appears to be going 'out' but drops sharply before the baseline.

A golfer automatically imparts a spin when driving, so that the ball hisses away from the tee at over 100mph (160km/h) with a back spin of about 50 revolutions per second (rps). The spin initially counteracts the effect of gravity so the ball flies in a straight line rather than in a curved trajectory. With the higher-number irons which produce greater spin, the ball can even be seen to climb. If the shot is miss-hit with the club's head at an angle – as every aspiring golfer soon discovers – the same force can take the ball away sideways into the rough.

In baseball, a pitcher uses various hand grips to impart different spins, and thus different curves, to the ball. The most common, known as a 'curve-ball', is a curve that breaks downwards and away from the batter. Some pitchers throw a so-called 'fade-away' or 'screw-ball', curving the ball towards the batter. A 'slider' breaks sharply at the last moment. Such curves involve spins of up to 38rps, which can induce a swerve of some 2ft (600mm) in the 60ft (18m) between the pitcher's mound and home plate.

In rugby and American football, the same effect can be used with great subtlety. An elongated ball kicked to spin around its long axis will go straight while travelling along the line of that axis. Only when it begins to drop, and the spin axis is different to the line of travel, does it start to swerve. A skilful player can therefore kick a ball parallel to the touchline, knowing that it will curve out of play as it falls back to the ground.

In cricket, curve – or swing – can be created without spin by a medium to fast bowler making judicious use of the single raised seam. The seam induces a slight air turbulence, causing the air to flow more quickly over one side of the ball. As before, a different speed of airflow on the two sides will produce a difference in pressure causing the force that swings the ball.

Many bowlers increase the difference in roughness between the two sides of the ball by polishing one side on their trousers.

Curve-balls *New York Mets baseball pitcher Bob Ojeda throws one of the curve-balls which helped his team to win the 1986 World Series (above). Tennis players, such as 1988 Wimbledon Champion Stefan Edberg (inset), curve the ball by putting on a top spin as it leaves the racket (below).*

How the dimples created modern golf

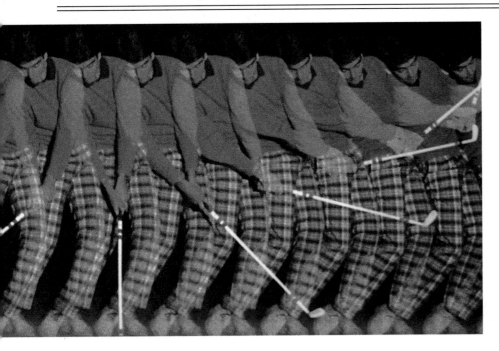

Dimple patterns *Dimples can be as much as .01in (.25mm) deep. Each ball has between 300 and 500 dimples, grouped in one of six designs. In one design, 480 dimples form 20 equilateral triangles. The patterns make little difference to the distance the ball will travel.*

Limiting drag *After the ball flies off the club, air clings to the surface until it is near the rear. To minimise drag, the air should stay attached as far back as possible, reducing the size of the wake.*

The dimples that cover the surface of golf balls revolutionised the game when they were introduced this century. A well-driven modern golf ball can travel up to 300yds (275m). If it were smooth, it would only travel about 70yds (65m).

When golf was first played in Holland and Scotland in the 15th century, smooth leather balls stuffed with feathers were used. In the 19th century, balls made of a rubbery substance called gutta-percha were introduced. They were found to fly farther after being marked by club blows.

Makers began patterning balls with crisscrossed grooves. Then, in 1906, when rubber-cored balls had arrived, the first dimpled ball was produced.

Why do dimples help the ball to go so far? When a ball is in flight, a thin layer of air clings to its surface at the front. As the air passes over the ball, it breaks away from the surface, setting up turbulent eddies behind. The eddying air draws its energy from the ball, slowing it down. Dimples cause the air to cling to the surface until it is well towards the rear of the ball. When it finally breaks away, a narrower stream of turbulence is created, causing less drag than for a smooth ball.

The dimples have another purpose as well. Since the golf ball always spins backwards when it is struck, the dimples carry air upwards over the top. The air going over the top has to travel faster than the air going underneath because of this rotation. This creates a lower pressure above than below, so the ball experiences lift which keeps it in the air longer.

What makes a boomerang return to the thrower?

Australian Aborigines have used boomerangs for the past 10,000 years to kill animals and birds for food. Their heavy hunting boomerangs are designed to fly straight at the quarry and deliver a killing or stunning blow. The boomerang then drops to the ground. Only smaller, lighter boomerangs, used by the Aborigines for sport, are intended to come back to the thrower.

The longest officially measured throw of a boomerang was made in November 1981 at Albury, New South Wales. In the Australian boomerang championship, Bob Burwell – a Brisbane radio telecommunications engineer – threw a boomerang 364ft

Weapons like 'wooden swords'

The first white man to describe an Aboriginal boomerang was Sir Joseph Banks, the English naturalist who was a member of Captain Cook's landing party in south-east Australia on April 29, 1770. Among the 'reception party' at Botany Bay were two natives who eyed the explorers with suspicion.

'Each of these held in his hand a wooden weapon about 2½ feet long, in shape much resembling a scymeter (scimitar),' wrote Sir Joseph. 'The blades of these lookd . . . smeard over with the same white pigment with which they painted their bodies.'

The explorers regarded the weapons as no more than what Captain Cook called 'wooden swords'. Then, in the early 1830s, another naval officer – Lieut

W.H. Breton – became the first person to record an Aborigine throwing one of the banana-shaped objects. It moved in 'a very considerable curve,' he stated, to 'finally, fall at his feet.'

Boomerangs are made from hardwoods such as black wattle and sandalwood. They are sometimes coated in red ochre – and, for ritual use, are decorated with red, yellow and white.

As well as for killing game, Aborigines used them for cutting open the bellies of dead animals, for clearing fire sites, digging cooking pits, and unearthing honey ants. Sometimes they were used for lighting fires, by rubbing them against logs. And they were banged together to beat out the rhythm of a dance.

(111m) before it began its return flight.

The traditional banana-like shape of the boomerang is not essential for it to return. Boomerangs shaped like the letters 'T', 'V', 'X', and 'Y' can be made to come back to the thrower. Two wooden rulers fixed at right angles with an elastic band make an effective boomerang.

The essential element in the design is that each arm, in cross-section, is shaped like an aeroplane wing, curved on the top and flatter on the bottom. When thrown, the boomerang travels at about 60mph (100km/h) and spins at a rate of about ten times a second. As it does so, each arm provides lift and it makes a low whirring sound.

When held almost upright and thrown hard forward by a right-hander (for left-handers the flight pattern is reversed), the boomerang zooms naturally upwards. It curves to the left, then swoops down to the right, and up again into a wide, circular loop that ends with a steady drop back to the thrower – who, with practice, can catch it. The path can even extend into a double loop like a figure-of-eight.

Why returning boomerangs fly in this way is a complex problem of aerodynamics and physics. In essence, the spinning boomerang is two objects in one: an aerofoil and a gyroscope.

As an aerofoil, the spinning boomerang is unstable. As the arms spin, the right-hand arm moving in the direction of flight becomes in turn the left-hand arm moving in the opposite direction. Since the boomerang is travelling forward, the right-hand arm travels much faster relative to the air than the left-hand one, and has more lift. Aerodynamic forces therefore constantly attempt to tilt the boomerang to the left.

This instability is counteracted by a gyroscopic effect that forces the boomerang back towards the horizontal, much as a spinning top remains stable. Once pushed off its 'true' course by aerodynamic forces, the boomerang reacts by first flattening

Night flight *A boomerang, with a light attached, makes a typical curved flight at night.*

out, then tipping slowly over to the right, forming a typical wide loop. If the flight is long enough, it will then veer back the other way, to begin the more elaborate figure-of-eight pattern.

Hunting boomerangs have only a slight bend and not much curve on their upper surface to provide lift. They retain a flat flight path, travelling up to 100yds (90m) before falling to the ground.

Variety of shapes

Boomerangs can be many shapes, depending on the wood they are made from. Those that return to the thrower's hand can be up to 30in (760mm) long and weigh up to 8½oz (240g). Hunting boomerangs are usually longer and much heavier. Both types are sometimes decorated with pigments in colours such as red, white and yellow.

Walking barefoot over red-hot stones

Silently, the file of barefoot men and boys – the oldest nearly 60, the youngest eight – emerged from the hut. Still in silence they walked to a pit full of stones, where a log fire had been burning for many hours. The embers had been raked away, but heat haze still shimmered over the pit. Without a pause they walked unhurriedly across the stones and out the other side. The temperature in the pit was about 1200°F (650°C). Yet their feet were unharmed.

It is a feat often performed on the Fijian island of Mbengga, whose firewalkers are world famous. Similar rituals are practised in India and Sri Lanka and by the Greek sect of Anastenaria. They have been reported in South America and Surinam, and the tiny Pacific island of Rarotonga. In Hawaii, hot lava has been used instead of stones or hot coals. Firewalking has also taken place in the USA and Europe.

In Fiji, India, Sri Lanka and Greece the ritual is associated with religious ceremonial. Firewalkers of the Western world usually prepare by psychological training. All maintain that a particular state of mind

is the key to remaining unharmed. Unlucky aspirants who suffer burns are often deemed to be mentally unprepared.

In Fiji, preparation includes avoiding the company of women during the days beforehand, and no firewalker should try it if his wife is pregnant.

Scientists tend to discount the 'mind over matter' theory. They suggest that walking over damp grass beforehand, which some firewalkers do, provides temporary protection through a phenomenon that accounts for the surprising amount of time that a drop of water bounces over a hot griddle before evaporating. The bottom of the drop vaporises, providing a brief insulation of vapour between the drop and the griddle. The dampness of the firewalkers' feet could have a similar effect.

Scientists also think the stones used in Fiji and elsewhere – and the coals used in the West – give off heat relatively slowly.

But most are convinced that, whatever the reason for the firewalkers' apparent immunity, it can be dangerous.

The tower divers of Pentecost Island

High above the hillside in a jungle clearing, the man balances precariously on two planks projecting from the top of a 100ft (30m) rickety-looking wooden tower. Spectators hold their breath.

Suddenly the man tosses a spray of leaves in the air. As it spirals down, he leans slowly forward and falls head first after it in a spectacular dive. But just as it seems his head is about to strike the ground, he is jerked up again in an arc which swings him to a safe landing on the hillside.

For both the man's ankles are tied with lianas – tough jungle vines – tethered to the top of the tower. The death-defying dive is the climax to an annual ceremony called the Naghol or Gol. It is held on Pentecost, one of 80 islands of the Pacific republic of Vanuatu – until 1980 the New Hebrides.

The ritual features many divers leaping from progressively higher platforms, the lowest around 40ft (12m).

Why do the Pentecost islanders risk their lives in such a bizarre and dangerous way?

The true origin of the Gol is unknown, but the participants see it as a test of courage – the closer they swoop to the ground, the greater their bravery.

The ceremony has a relatively high safety record, but sometimes it goes wrong. In 1974, one diver's lianas snapped as they were jerked taut and he was killed. The ceremony was witnessed by the Queen and other members of the British royal family.

The tower is a flexible structure of palm trunks and bamboo, constructed around a living tree, stripped of most of its branches. The lianas that tether the divers are the real key to safety, however. They must be the right age and diameter and are cut two days before the ceremony. If they were cut earlier, they could dry out, become brittle and lose the elasticity. They are also carefully cut to suit the height from which each diver plans to fall. The cutting is done by an experienced man who can calculate the elasticity of the vines.

Although the Gol's origin is lost, a legend tells that the first diver was a woman. Her husband, discovering she was being un-faithful, chased her, intending to beat her. She climbed a tall palm, but he scrambled up after her. At the top, he demanded to know why she had been unfaithful. She replied that he was a coward – and dared him to jump with her from the treetop. The husband agreed. They jumped. The man was killed, but his wife had surreptitiously tied a vine to her ankle to break her fall.

Defying death *A Pentecost islander jumps 100ft (30m), held by jungle vines.*

How a ski-jumper learns to 'fly'

When the 18-year-old Austrian Sepp Bradl became the first person to ski-jump more than 100m (328ft) in 1936, the engineer who had designed the jump – in Planica, Yugoslavia – shouted: 'That wasn't ski-jumping. That was ski-flying!'

It was true. A new sport had been born, in which skiers had to develop a totally new skill, turning themselves into aerofoils. Their ability to win now depends less on jumping than on flying. As he glides through the air, the skier leans forward with his body slightly curved. The same aerodynamic forces that keep an aeroplane flying help the ski-jumper to remain in the air longer and travel farther. The air passes over his curved back faster than under his front, creating a partial vacuum which causes lift.

Since Bradl's 100m jump, the world record has been almost doubled, to 180m (590ft) in 1989.

Ski-jumpers start learning at practically any age. First, the jumper learns how to build up speed. This is done on a normal ski slope. The skier crouches down in a position that minimises air resistance, with the arms swept back. World-class jumpers take off at up to 60mph (100km/h).

Before making his first real jump, the skier must know how to land. He learns to touch down with one foot slightly in front of the other, and the knees bent.

Fledgling skiers build up experience by making small jumps from low banks or platforms. This teaches them to cope with the takeoff. If balance is wrong on takeoff – in particular, if the weight is too far back – wind will flip the jumper over.

The true glory of ski-jumping is the flight itself. The beginner's first real jump will probably carry him about 10m (30ft). Only when they become teenagers are most children able to make jumps of 40m (130ft), for which they must adopt the true aerofoil position.

The flight itself is a complex operation. As he loses horizontal motion, the jumper contracts his body a little, ready to meet the slope beneath him. As he falls, he loses speed but bends forward, and with skill can thus extend his glide.

In flight, perhaps the greatest danger of all comes from wind. However, although injuries happen, fatalities are rare.

Ski-flying *A ski-jumper takes off at the 1984 Sarajevo Olympics (below). By bending into an aerofoil shape, a jumper can make his flight last longer (above).*

Skydiving: the sport of floating through space

Free-fall *A team of half a dozen skydivers jump head first from an aircraft (left). The record for the number of stacked parachutists is 24 men, set by the Royal Marines team in 1985 (right). The jumpers joined the stack from the bottom, while in free-fall, then opened their parachutes when in the line. The first man to leave the plane was the last one to join the stack, but still the first to land.*

As the skydiver stands at the door of the aeroplane nearly 12,000ft (3700m) up, the earth below is a patchwork of colour seen through patches of cloud, with houses almost too small to be picked out.

The aeroplane arrives at the jump point and the skydiver launches himself into space – arms and legs outstretched, body arched slightly backwards, head pulled up. His speed increases for about eight seconds when he reaches the highest speed a body will fall – about 120mph (190km/h), known as 'terminal velocity'.

His altimeter tells him his height second by second as he plunges earthwards, and he knows that, to make a safe landing, he must open his parachute before he reaches 2000ft (610m).

So the free-fall will last less than one minute – a brief, floating interlude during which the parachutist carries out the acrobatics which are the real purpose of skydiving. As he completes his skydive he opens his parachute and directs his approach to his landing spot by controlling the two steering lines.

Skydivers use many different types of parachute, but the principles are much the same. The type of parachute used by beginners is the familiar circular canopy with two L-shaped gaps cut at the back.

As air rushes through these gaps, it produces a forward thrust which enables the parachutist to steer to the landing place, otherwise he would drift with the wind. In still air, he travels forward at what on land would be a brisk walking speed.

Whatever type of canopy is used – round or square – the jumper is suspended in a

nylon harness. Four nylon strips called 'risers' connect the harness to the rigging lines of the canopy. Two steering lines from the canopy allow the jumper to steer left or right by pulling on them.

The jumper also has an emergency parachute, in case the first should malfunction. Jumpers always pack their own parachutes, at first under detailed supervision.

For most jumps, a small, high-winged aircraft, such as the three-passenger Cessna 172, is used. If several skydivers are jumping together, a larger aircraft, such as a Short's SkyVan, which carries up to 16, is needed.

When the plane arrives above the chosen spot, an experienced parachutist dives

through the open door. The free-fall time depends on the altitude at the time of exit, and can be as short as eight seconds or as long as one minute.

The first aerial gymnastics performed by beginners are usually simple somersaults and turns in the air. As skydivers become more experienced they advance to formation falls, joining up with other skydivers to complete a series of rapidly changing patterns. This is called relative work.

These displays require great skill, as the divers are travelling at speed and may have to 'track' across the sky to join up with the other divers. To achieve this, they must be almost vertical, with the body forming a slight curve. Arms must be held to the side and the legs together and extended.

The 'lift' created by air passing over his curved body causes the parachutist to travel forward as well as down. The forward movement can be fast enough to cause injury if two skydivers collide. So to break the speed a parachutist brings his arms up, presenting a greater area to the airflow and slowing down his body. This skill must be mastered before he can join in formation jumps.

Controlled docking – joining up – with other divers is carefully planned. After free-falling in formation, the jumpers separate for a few seconds before opening their parachutes. This prevents the risk of entanglement. Despite this risk, some jumpers perform 'canopy relative work' – linking up while under parachutes, creating the spectacle of a bouquet of parachutes floating together in the sky.

Diving in formation *A large team can form spectacular patterns. This jump by 126 people was made over Belgium in 1987.*

How do surfers ride a wall of water?

The sport of surfing – which has been practised for centuries in Polynesia – is now enjoyed by millions of people around the world, all seeking the 'perfect wave'.

Some of the finest surfing is still in Hawaii, where ocean swells travel for thousands of miles from Pacific storms before roaring into the beaches up to 30ft (9m) high.

The aim of every surfer is to skim along the face of this wall of water, parallel to the beach, while the crest of the wave breaks above his head. For up to ten seconds he may ride his board inside a tunnel of water. The ride is a race against the breaking wave, and if the surfer loses he can be 'wiped out' (smashed onto the sea floor) by the weight of the collapsing water.

To begin, the surfer paddles his board – lying flat or kneeling – out to the seaward side of the breaker zone. He then watches and waits for the right wave to approach. When he sees one, he starts paddling towards the shore, his speed nearly that of the wave. As the wave reaches him, the board lifts up and accelerates rapidly until it is travelling as fast as the wave. The surfer then pushes himself up, first kneeling and then standing on his board on the very crest of the wave. Using gravity as his power source he then rides down the wall of water, travelling faster than the wave, at a speed of 9½ miles (15km) per hour.

As he rides down the face, the surfer watches for the place where the wave is beginning to break. Then he turns his board to ride along the wave, staying just ahead of the breaking crest.

The ride ends when the surfer leans backwards to slow the board down and then 'kicks out' over the unbroken wave into the calm waters behind. Or, of course, he may lose control of the board or be overtaken by the breaking 'curl'.

Experienced surfers perform stunts as they ride the 'wall'. By shifting their weight to the rear of the board they can ride back up to the top of the wave and then get a second, and third, ride down.

Most modern surfboards are less than 6ft 6in (2m) long, and weigh about 7lb (3.2kg). In Hawaii, the original longer and heavier boards are still used.

The 'perfect wave' *Surfers travel the world in search of waves that are tall and long. If a surfer can catch the right wave, he can ride it for several minutes. These waves are in Hawaii, Australia and Bali.*

INDEX

Page numbers in **bold** type indicate a reference to an illustration.

Acknowledgments

The publishers wish to thank the following individuals and organisations who gave their help in compiling and checking the information contained in this book.

Access, Carol Andrews, Audi Volkswagen, Austin Rover, Automatic Vending Association of Britain.

Tony Bacon, Bank of England, Berol Ltd, Bic Biro Ltd, BMT Fluid Mechanics Ltd, The Boots Company plc, Bostik Ltd, Dr Brian Bowers, Nicholas Branch, Professor Keith Branigan, Dr Warwick Bray, British Aerospace, British Airports Authority, British Airways, British Computer Society, British Gas, British Nuclear Fuels, British Parachute Association, British Petroleum, British Plastics Federation, British Ski Federation, British Sub-Aqua Club, British Telecom, P.R.B. Brooks, Sarah Brown, Bryant and May, Mrs Hilda Butler.

Cable and Wireless (Marine) Ltd, Canada-Post, Canon UK Ltd, Clothing and Allied Products Industry Training Board, Bill Carlton, John Carter, Central Electricity Generating Board, Christopher Chippindale, Civil Aviation Authority, Henry Clother, Dr Noel Coley, Mrs L.H. Collins, Comite International Olympique, Dr Jill Cook, Courtauld Institute of Art, Susan Cowles, Dr James Cox, Cunard Line Ltd.

Dr Rosalie David, Dr John Davies, Department of Transport, DHL International (UK) Ltd, D.S. Colour International, Du Pont (UK) Ltd, Duracell UK.

Fiat UK Ltd, Dr David Fisher, Fisons Horticulture, John Flewitt.

G.E. Superabrasives, Elida Gibbs, Val Gilbert, Glasgow Art Gallery & Museum, Goodyear (GB) Ltd, Stan Greenberg.

Peter Harrison, Andrew Healey, HM Customs and Excise, Bruce Hogg, Hong Kong Hilton, Hovercraft Consultants Ltd, Tom Hutchinson.

ICI Garden Products, Institute of Food Science & Technology (UK), Institute of Physics, International Stock Exchange, Laura Jacobus, JCA Marketing Services Ltd, Dr Peter Jonas, Martin Jones.

Nigel Kent-Lemon, Gillian Kermode.

Michael Langford, La Poste, Lever Brothers Ltd, Dr Archibald Levey, David Levy, Lion Laboratories Ltd, Lloyd's Register of Shipping, Loctite UK, London Waste Regulation Authority, Luton & Dunstable Hospital Intensive Therapy Unit.

Dr John McCann, Alan McKenzie, Gordon Mackerron, Murdoch MacLennan, Marconi Radar Systems Ltd, Meteorological Office, Brian Miller, Ministry of Defence, A. Monnickendam Ltd, Mountain Rescue Committee, Mount Rushmore National Memorial, The Moving Picture Company, Jane Murray.

Andrew Nahum, National Association of Waste Disposal Contractors, National Maritime Museum, NCR.

Omega Electronics Ltd, Optilon Ltd, Otis Elevator plc.

Pan Britannica Industries Ltd, Fred Pearce, Nicholas Phillips, Pilkington plc, Dr John Pimlott, Jane Portal, Premier Brands UK Ltd, Fay Presto, Magician (Who Does Not Use Animals In Her Act), Harry Puckering.

Racal Guardall, The Really Useful Company Ltd, Francis Reid, Dr Frank Rosillo-Calle, I.W. Rowlands, RAF Museum, Royal Society For The Prevention of Accidents, Royce Thompson Electric Ltd, John Russell.

Sasol Ltd, Selectus Ltd, Skidmore, Owings and Merrill, James Smith, Society of Motor Manufacturers & Traders, Stainless Steel Advisory Centre, Standard Telephones and Cables plc, Simon Stephens, E.A. Stokoe, Patrick Stone, John Stott, Tony Stuart-Jones.

Thames Water Authority, Thomas Bolton & Johnson Ltd, 3M (UK) Ltd, Transport and Road Research Laboratory.

Frank Underdown, John A. Van Auken, Dr Jo Anne Van Tilburg, Vauxhall Motors.

Bill Waddell, C.A. Walker, Dr Helen Wallis OBE, Derek Ware, Warren Springs Laboratories, Lieutenant Commander D.W. Waters, Western Riverside Waste Authority, Tom Westgate, West London Waste Authority, Charles Wight, Wilkinson Sword Ltd, Dr Trevor Williams, Dr L.H. Wise, John Wood, Wreckers (Pty) Ltd.

The publishers acknowledge their indebtedness to the following books:

One Life by Christiaan Barnard (© 1970 Christiaan Barnard; reprinted by permission of Curtis Brown Ltd, NY).
The Discovery of the Titanic by Dr Robert Ballard (Peter Elek).
The Shell Book of Firsts by Patrick Robertson (Michael Joseph, London).
Passenger Ship by Hannah Jacobs (Hamish Hamilton, London).
Yeager by General Chuck Yeager and Leo Janos (© 1985 by Brig. Gen. Chuck Yeager; reprinted by permission of International Creative Management Inc, NY).
TV Game Shows by Maxine Fabe (Dolphin/Bantam US).
A Tremor in the Blood by David Thoreson Lykken (McGraw Hill).
Big Secrets by William Poundstone (by permission of Quill Books, a division of William Morrow & Co, Inc).

Picture credits

The pictures in *How Is It Done?* were supplied by the people listed below. Names given in italics refer to illustrations that are Reader's Digest copyright.

T=top; *C*=centre; *B*=bottom; *L*=left; *R*=right.

4 CL Science Photo Library/Dr Jeremy Burgess, C Frank Spooner/E. Sander/Liaison/GAMMA, CR Noel Chanan/Private Collection. 5 CL Science Photo Library/Dr Tony Brain & David Parker, C Science Photo Library/NASA, CR Katia & Maurice Krafft. 6 TR Science Photo Library/Lowell Georgia, C Science Photo Library/Petit Format/CSI, BR ZEFA/A. Wetzel. 7 TL Martin Marietta Energy Systems Inc, C The Image Bank/Robert Phillips, BL Science Photo Library/Jonathan Watts. 9 C Science Photo Library/Dr Jeremy Burgess, BL Science Photo Library, BR Science Photo Library/John Hestletine. 10 L Colorific/Alan Clifton, BL ZEFA, BR The Image Bank/Harald Sund. 11 (all) Mark Edwards. 12 Artist Pavel Kostal, *photos Martin Cameron*. 13 *Artist Kuo Kang Chen*, *TR Martin Cameron*, CR Science Photo Library/Dr Tony Brain. 14 (all) Science Photo Library/Dr Tony Brain, with thanks to Berol for their help. 15 *T Martin Cameron*, with thanks to Berol for their help, BC Ciba-Geigy Plastics. 16 *Artist Malcolm McGregor*, CR Science Photo Library. 17 TL Science Photo Library, TR 3M, BC,BR Colorsport. 18 *Artist Precision Illustration*, TR *Reader's Digest*. 19 TR Science Photo Library/Dr Anthony Burgess, BR Science Photo Library. 20 *TL Martin Cameron*, B Susan Griggs/Dimitri Ilic. 21 BC Science Photo Library/R.E. Litchfield, *BR Martin Cameron*. 22 TL,TC,BL Hackney Archives Department/Courtesy of Bryant and May. 22,23 *Martin Cameron*. 24 TL Du Pont, TC Science Photo Library, TR Science Photo Library/NASA. 25 Quesada/Burke, New York, *Artist Pavel Kostal*. 26 TR Oxford Scientific Films/T. Middleton, BR Science Photo Library/Dr Jeremy Burgess. 27 *Artist Precision Illustration*, TC Bruce Coleman/Kim Taylor, CL,CR Science Photo Library, BR Science Photo Library/Dr Jeremy Burgess. 28 TR Richardson-Vicks Ltd, *BL Martin Cameron*, *BR Artist Mick Gillah*. 29 C,CR Gillette UK Ltd, BR,BL Science Photo Library/Dr Jeremy Burgess. 30 Picturepoint Ltd. 31 T Frank Spooner/E. Sander/Liaison/GAMMA, BL Frank Spooner/Taroy/Perrin/GAMMA, BR John Hillelson/Georg Gerster. 32,33 The Image Bank. 34 Enrico Ferorelli. 35 T Robert Rathe/Folio Inc, BC,BR The Press Association Ltd, BL Rex Features Ltd. 36 British Telecom Overseas Division. 37 British Airways. 38 (all) Popperfoto/Reuter. 39 TL Art Directors Photo Library, TC Frank Spooner/Morimoto, BR The Photo Source/G. Freston. 40 TL Frank Spooner, CL Rex Features Ltd, BR Phillips & Drew. 41 The Associated Press. 43 T Ford Motor Company, B Courtesy of Fiat SpA. 44 Telegraph Colour Library/Athtar Hussein. 45 T Science Photo Library/Dan Farber, BR NOAA. 46 Science Photo Library/Nigel Press Associates. 47 John Hillelson/Georg Gerster. 48 TL Black Star, New York/© Jim Pickerell 1986, BC Frank Spooner. 49 TL,BR Canadair Inc. 50 TL Photri, BC Jeffery Cutting. 51 TL The Mansell Collection, TR Art Directors Photo Library, BR ZEFA/Photo Researchers. 52 T (all) © SNV, BL Jerrican/Weiss. 53 Susan Griggs/Ian Bradshaw. 55 Photography and Survey by Clyde Surveys Ltd, Maidenhead. 57 TR Network, BL Rex Features Ltd. 58 TL,TC Telegraph Colour Library. 60 TL Colorific/Picture Group/Jack McKigney, CR Photri, BC Military Archive & Research Services/Lockheed/Georgia Company. 62,63 Tony Stone Photo Library, London. 63 (all) Chris Fairclough. 64 Colorific/Peter Jansson/Lehtikuva. 65 Colorsport. 67 The Ronald Grant Archive/courtesy of Columbia Pictures Industries Inc. 69 David Crossthwaite. 70 TL,TR,BC Clive Barda, London. 71 TR,BC John Cleare/Mountain Camera. 72 TL Frank Spooner/Figaro/GAMMA, BR John Cleare/Mountain Camera. 73 CL Permission of the Board of the British Library, CR Noel Chanan/Private Collection, BR Rex Features Ltd. 74,75 Aviation Week/William G. Hartenstein/Renphot. 75 Courtesy Lockheed Aeronautical Systems Company. 76 TR Imperial War Museum, CR Photo Researchers Inc/Stan Wayman © 1972, BL Military Archive & Research Services. 77 TC,CL Brian R. Wolff. 78 The Hulton Picture Company. 79 (*Walker*) Wide World Photos, C Popperfoto, BR The Hulton Picture Company. 80 Ullstein. 81 Permission of the Board of the British Library, Add. 8056.184. 82,83 (all) Chris Morris. 84 TR Chris Morris, BL The Hulton Picture Company. 85 TC Melvin Harris, TR Noel Chanan/Private Collection, BR Janet & Colin Bord. 86 B *Neil Holmes*, TL,TC Melvin Harris. 88 Wide World Photos. 89 TR,CR,BC Health & Safety Executive, BR Harwell. 90,91 (all) The National Gallery, London. 92,93 (all) Metropolitan Police. 94 Cellmark Diagnostics. 95 TC The New Scientist, London, BC Electronic Graphics Ltd. 96 TL Federal Bureau of Investigations. 97 British Telecom Overseas Division. 98 TL Colorific/Picture Group/Steve Starr, CR Rex Features Ltd, BR Impact/Alain le Garsmeur. 99 Rex Features Ltd/SIPA/Claude Vest. 100 TC Rainbow/Hank Morgan, TR Woodfin Camp/Sepp Seitz. 101 TR Science Photo Library/Dr Gary S. Settles and Stephen S. McIntyre, BL Science Photo Library/David Parker, BR Science Photo Library. 102 TL Dorling Kindersley, BC ZEFA. 102,103 ZEFA. 103 TC Dorling Kindersley, TR,BR Johnson Matthey. 104 CR Frank Spooner/GAMMA/J. Sloan, BL,BC,BR Pilkington plc. 104,105 *Artist Precision Illustration*. 105 TR,BL,BR Pilkington plc. 106

Sonia Halliday. **107** *T (photos) Martin Cameron, (micrographs)* Science Photo Library, *BR* Ann Ronan Picture Library. **108** *TL* The Bodleian Library Arch.Bb.10 Folio 292v-293r vol 1, *TC Martin Cameron.* **109** Bruce Coleman/Eric Crichton. **110** *TR* Science Photo Library. **111** *TC* Science Photo Library, *(micrographs)* British Textile Technology Group. **112** *BL,BR* ZEFA. **112,113** ZEFA. **113** *TC* British Textile Technology Group, *TR* Science Photo Library, *BL,BR* ZEFA. **114** *BR* Du Pont, *(inset)* Science Photo Library. **115** *TC* ICI Fibres, *BR (both) Martin Cameron.* **116** *(both) Martin Cameron.* **117** *(all)* Lectra Systems Ltd. **118** *Artist Pavel Kostal/Weir Westgarth Ltd.* **119** *TC,TR,CR* Aspect/Mike Wells, *BL* North London Waste Authority. **120** *(all)* Aspect/Geoff Tompkinson. **120,121** Colorific/John Moss. **121** *TR* Science Photo Library/US Department of Energy, *BC* ZEFA/H. Adam. **122** *Artist Mick Gillah.* **123** *TL* United Kingdom Atomic Energy Authority, *TR* Science Photo Library/US Dept of Energy. **124** *TR* Planet Earth Pictures/Ken Lucas, *B* ZEFA. **125** *TL* Central Electricity Generating Board, *TR* Science Photo Library/Simon Fraser. **126** *CR* Science Photo Library/Adam Hart-Davis, *BL* NHPA/Silvestris, *BR* Science Photo Library/Andrew McClenaghan. **127** *TL* Visum/Wolfgang Steche, *TR* Ford Motor Company of Australia, *BR* Sandia National Laboratories. **128** *TL* ZEFA, *TR* Science Photo Library/Lowell Georgia, *BR* NHPA/Stephen Dalton. **129** *L (all)* Science Photo Library/Martin Dohrn, *TR* Oxford Scientific Films/Peter Parks, *CR (and inset)* NHPA/Stephen Dalton. **130** *TL* Oxford Scientific Films/David Shale, *TC* Oxford Scientific Films/Peter Parks. **131** *Martin Cameron*, with thanks to the following for their help: Lillywhites (sports goods), Lin Pac Plastics (helmet and chairs), Amber Plastics (guitar case), Hepworth Building Products (rainwater goods). **132** ZEFA/B. Bingel. **133** *TR,C* Susan Griggs/Anthony Howarth, *BL* Science Photo Library/Precision Visuals/Teleco Drilling Tech Inc. **134,135** Susan Griggs/Martin Rogers. **136** Popperfoto. **137** *TR* The Associated Press, *CL,BR* Frank Spooner. **138** *Artist Precision Illustration, TR,BR* Susan Griggs/Adam Woolfitt, *CR Adam Woolfitt.* **139** *TR,BC,BR Adam Woolfitt, CR* Susan Griggs/Adam Woolfitt. **140** *TL* Planet Earth Pictures/Flip Schulke, *BL,BR* Science Photo Library/Klein Associates Inc. **141** *Artist Malcolm McGregor, TR* Planet Earth Pictures/Carol Roessler. **142** *TL* GE Corporate Research and Development, *BC* De Beers Consolidated Mines. **143** *TC* De Beers Consolidated Mines, *(others) Martin Cameron.* **144,145** All except Crown Jewels taken from the Joseph Asscher family album, kindly lent by A. Monnickendam Ltd. **145** *BL,BR* Crown Copyright, by permission of the Controller of Her Majesty's Stationery Office. **147** *TR,CL* Photri. **148** *TR,BL* Quadrant, *CR* Photri. **149** Frank Spooner. **150** Richard Cooke. **151** *TR* Richard Cooke, *BL* GEC Avionics Limited. **152** Richard Cooke. **153** *Artist Malcolm McGregor, BL* Richard Cooke, *BR* Jeremy Flack/Aviation Photographs International. **154** Science Photo Library/David Parker. **155** *TR,CL,BR* Photri, *CR* TRH Pictures. **156** *TL,TR* Aspect, *C* Military Archive & Research Services, *BL* Aerospatiale/CEV. **157** *TR,C* Pilkington P.E. Ltd. **158** *TL* Science Photo Library/Professor Harold Edgerton, *CR* TRH Pictures/DOD/US Air Force, *BR* Photri. **159** *TL,TR* Science Photo Library/US Department of Defense, *BC* Science Photo Library/Alexander Tsiaras. **160** *TR,CR* TASS, *BR* Frank Spooner. **161** *Artist Mick Gillah, TR* Beken of Cowes Ltd. **162,163** *(all)* Scala. **164** *TC* Superintendent, Radiographic Laboratory of Monuments & Fine Arts, Milan, *BR* Aramco World/Tor Eigeland. **165** Science Photo Library/NASA. **166,167** Aspect/Ken Novak. **168,169** Science Photo Library/NASA. **170** NASA. **171** *TL* Aspect/NASA, *TR,BL* Science Photo Library/NASA. **172** *TR* Science Photo Library/Julian Balm, *BL* Planet Earth Pictures/Flip Schulke/NASA, *BC* Aspect/NASA. **173** *TC,BR* Science Photo Library/NASA, *BL (and inset)* Aspect/NASA. **174** *CL* Aspect/NASA, *BR* Science Photo Library/NASA. **175** The Associated Press. **176** *TL* The Hulton Picture Company, *TR* Topham Picture Library. **176,177** *(background)* Museum of the History of Science, Oxford. **177** Museum of the History of Science, Oxford. **178** Science Photo Library/NASA. **180,181** Aspect/Geoff Tompkinson. **184** Science Photo Library/Dr Jean Lorre. **185** *TL* Max Planck Institute/Courtesy H.U. Keller, *TR Artist Pavel Kostal, C* Telegraph Colour Library/Space Frontiers. **187** *C* Katia & Maurice Krafft, *BL* Science Photo Library/Lawrence Berkley Laboratory, *BR* John S. Shelton. **188** *TC* Science Photo Library/Philippe Plailly, *CR,BL,BR* Aspect/Geoff Tompkinson. **189** *Artist Malcolm McGregor, TR* Science Photo Library/Dr Jeremy Burgess, *C,BL,BC,BR* Science Photo Library/Eric Grave. **190** Science Photo Library/Dr Jeremy Burgess. **192** *(all)* Colorific/Nina Leen/Life © Time Inc 1972. **194** *BL Artist Patrick Oxenham, BR* Michael Freeman. **195** *(all)* Trustees of the British Museum (Natural History). **197** *T* Science Photo Library/Hank Morgan, *B* Science Photo Library/Dick Luria. **198** *Artist Malcolm McGregor, C* The Cavendish Museum, Cambridge. **199** *TR* Science Photo Library/C.T.R. Wilson, *C,CR* Science Photo Library/Lawrence Berkley Laboratory. **200** *TR* IBM, *CR,BL,BR* Jack Harris/Steve Berger, Dennis McMullen and John Macaulay. **201** *TL* Jean-Loup Charmet, *TR Artist Malcolm McGregor.* **202** *TC* John Frost Historical Newspaper Service/Times Newspaper, *C,CR* ICM/Permission of Chuck and Glennis Yeager. **202,203** *Artist Ivan Lapper.* **203** *TL,C* Bell Aircraft Corporation. **204** *BR* Susan Griggs/George Hall. **204,205** Colorific/Black Star/Jim Balog. **205** *CR* John S. Shelton. **206** *TC* Colorific/Black Star/Jim Balog, *BL* Art Directors Photo Library, *BC* John S. Shelton. **207** *TL,BL,BC* Science Photo Library/Dr Steve Gull/Dr John Fielden/Dr Alan Smith, *TR* Trustees of the British Museum (Natural History). **208** *Artist Precision Illustration.* **208,209** Katia & Maurice Krafft. **209** Science Photo Library/NASA. **210** *Artist Gary Hincks.* **211** *CL* Martin Marietta Energy Systems Inc, *CR* Science Photo Library/Hank Morgan, *BL* Science Photo Library/Dr Jeremy Burgess, *BR* Science Photo Library/Dr Brad Amos. **212,213** Spectrum Colour Library. **214** *Artist Precision Illustration.* **215** *CR* The Science Museum, London, *BR* The Hulton Picture Company. **216** (car) *Martin Cameron*, (Orson Welles) Popperfoto, (Moon walk) Aspect/NASA, (radar) Science Photo Library/David Parker, (thermogram) Science Photo Library/Geoff Williams & Howard Metcalf. **217** (beach) Susan Griggs/Robert Frerock, (X-ray) Science Photo Library, (H-bomb) Aspect, (nebula) Spectrum Colour Library. **218** *Artist Precision Illustration, CR* Science Photo Library/Vaughan Fleming, *BR* Science Photo Library/Robin Scagell. **219** *TL* © Woods Hole Oceanographic Institution, *BR* Mary Evans Picture Library. **220** *Artist Precision Illustration*, with thanks to JVC for their assistance, (TV/video machine) Amstrad. **221** *Artist Precision Illustration*, Science Photo Library. **222** *CR* Michael Holford/Science Museum, London, *BL* Roger-Viollet/Boyer. **223** *Artist Precision Illustration, TR* Science Photo Library/Jeremy Burgess. **224** *BL* Ann Ronan Picture Library, *BR* Michael Holford. **224,225** *(background)* Mary Evans Picture Library. **225** *TL,CL and filmstrip* US Department of the Interior, National Park Service, *BR* The Science Museum, London. **226** *Artist Kuo Kang Chen, TC* Science Photo Library/David Parker, *C* Science Photo Library/Dr Jeremy Burgess. **227** Paul Brierley. **228** *Artist Kuo Kang Chen.* **228,229** Schott-UK. **229** *BC* Science Photo Library/Philippe Plailly. **230** *BL,BC,BR* Popperfoto/UPI. **231** *Artist Mick Gillah.* **232** *T* The Anthony Blake Photo Library/Lee Boltin, *BR Martin Cameron.* **233** *Artist Precision Illustration, BR Martin Cameron.* **234** *(film) Martin Cameron, BL* Art Directors Photo Library, *BR* Science Photo Library/Prof Harold Edgerton. **235** *BR Martin Cameron.* **236** *(all)* Michael Freeman. **238** Martin Marietta Energy Systems Inc. **239** *TL* Science Photo Library/Hank Morgan, *TC* Science Photo Library/Paul Shambroom, *TR* Science Photo Library/David Scharf, *BL* Science Photo Library/Ray Ellis. **240** *TR* NASA, *C* Science Photo Library/Dale Boyer, *BR* Science Photo Library/Jerry Mason. **242** *TR* John Tann Ltd, *BL* The Ancient Art & Architecture Collection. **244** *BR* Michael Holford/Science Museum, London. **245** *BC* Science Photo Library/CNRI, *BR* Science Photo Library/Biophoto Associates. **246** *BL* Science Photo Library/Tadanori Salto, *R* The Kobal Collection. **247** *TC* Science Photo Library/Sheila Terry, *BR* Hank Morgan. **248** *TR* Colorsport, *CL* Shell Research Limited, *BR Artist Inkwell Design.* **250** BMW. **251** *Artist Precision Illustration, TC* Goodyear Great Britain Ltd, *C* Dunlop/SP Tyres UK Limited. **252** *TC* Science Photo Library/NASA, *BC* Holt Studios Ltd/D. Smith. **253** Science Photo Library/Dr Jeremy Burgess. **255** Crafts Council/J. Poulton, *Artist Precision Illustration, BR Artist Precision Illustration.* **256** *Artist Precision Illustration, BL* Fotoflite. **257** Photri, *(inset)* The Science Museum, London. **260** *TR* The Mansell Collection, *CR* Chris Kapolka/C.F.D. Whetmath. **260,261** *Eileen Tweedy, (background)* The Mansell Collection. **261** *CR* The Mansell Collection, *BR* The Science Museum, London. **262,263** Quadrant. **264,265** *Artist Precision Illustration.* **265** Tony Stone Photo Library, London/Jean Pragen. **266** *Artist Precision Illustration, C* The Image Bank/Aram Gesar. **267** (portrait) The Mansell Collection, *Artist Mick Gillah, CL* The Hayward Gallery, *BL* The Science Museum, London. **268** *Artist Precision Illustration.* **269** *TL* Photri, *CL,BR* M.J. Hooks. **270** *TC* Magnum/Harmon, *BL* Frank Spooner/Sander-Liaison/GAMMA. **271** *C* Smithsonian Institute, *BR* Frank Spooner/Laurant Maous/GAMMA. **272** *TC* Dick Kenny Relations/Boeing, *BC* ZEFA. **272,273** Colorsport/E. Zurini. **273** *Artist Mick Gillah.* **274** *TR* Sunday Times, *C,BL* Photri. **275** *CL* Science Photo Library/Dr R. Clarke & M.R. Goff, *CR* Science Photo Library/CNRI, *BR* Science Photo Library/Petit Format/CSI. **276** *TC* Science Photo Library/Martin Dorhn/IVF Unit, Cromwell Hospital, London, *C* Science Photo Library/Hank Morgan. **276,277** Science Photo Library/Petit Format/CSI. **277** *TC* Science Photo Library/Petit Format/CSI, *C* Rex Features Ltd. **278** *TL Martin Cameron*, ophthalmoscope lent by Carleton Optical Equipment Co Ltd, *CL* Science Photo Library/Don Wong, *BL* Science Photo Library/Argentum. **279** *(all) Jonathan Green.* **280** *CL* Ullstein, *C* Royal National Institute for the Blind/*photo Martin Cameron.* **281** *T* Numerical and word puzzles reproduced courtesy of Mensa, *B* Max Menikoff, based on designs from *Introduction to Psychology*, Seventh Edition by Ernest R. Hilgard, Richard C. Atkinson, and Rita L. Atkinson, © 1979 by Harcourt Brace Jovanovich, Inc by permission of the publisher. **282,283** Science Photo Library/CNRI. **284** *TL,TR* All-Sport (UK), *C* All-Sport (UK)/Tony Duffy. **285** *(all)* John Hillelson/D Kirkland/SYGMA. **286** Science Photo Library/CNRI. **287** *C* Science Photo Library/James Stevenson, *CR* Science Photo Library/Philippe Plailly. **288** Science Photo Library/CNRI. **289** *TR* Frank Spooner/GAMMA, *BL* Science Photo Library/Ethicon Ltd. **290** *TL* Topham Picture Library, *BL* Ullstein, *BR* Private collection. **290,291** Science Photo Library/*(background)* C. Powell, P. Fowler & D. Perkins. **291** *TL* Topham Picture Library, *CR* Science Photo Library/C. Powell, P. Fowler & D. Perkins, *BL* Ann Ronan Picture Library. **292** *TL,TR* Science Photo Library/Alexander Tsiaras. **293** *BC* Colorific/Yoav Levy, *BR* National Medical Slide Bank. **295** *(both)* John Timbers. **296** *TR* Popperfoto, *BL* John Frost Historical Newspaper Service/The Daily Mirror, *BR* Topham Picture Library. **296,297** *(background)* Topham Picture Library. **297** *BL* Topham Picture Library, *BR* Popperfoto. **299** *TL* David Lee, *CR* Science Photo Library/Lowell, Georgia, *BC* Rex Features Ltd. **300** Susan Griggs/Robin Laurance. **301** *TR* The Image Bank/Romilly Lockyer, *BL* Robert Harding Picture Library, *BC* Aspect/Geoff Tompkinson, *BR* Rex Features Ltd. **302** *L* Bruce Coleman/Norman Tomalin, *TR,CR,BR* CN Tower. **303** Aspect/Alex Langley. **304,305** *(all)* The Image Bank/Lawrence Hughes. **306** Donald Innes/Ivor Innes. **306,307** Arcaid/Richard Bryant. **307** *TL,TC* David Lee. **308** High Rise Services Ltd. **308,309** Susan Griggs/George Hall. **309** *TL* South America Pictures, *TR* The Image

ACKNOWLEDGMENTS

Bank/Joseph P. Brignolo. **310** *Artist Malcolm McGregor*, with thanks to Morrison-Knudson Inc, San Francisco, for their help. **310,311** South America Pictures. **311** UPI/Bettmann Newsphotos. **312** *Artist Malcolm McGregor*. **313** Susan Griggs/Adam Woolfitt. **314** Planet Earth Pictures/Peter Scoones. **315** Planet Earth Pictures/Ken Vaughan. **317** *TR* ZEFA/A. Wetzel, *CL* Robert Harding Picture Library/John Ross, *BR* ZEFA. **318,319** Susan Griggs/John G. Ross. **319** William MacQuitty. **320** *Artist Malcolm McGregor*, *TL* Permission of the Trustees of the British Museum, *TR* William MacQuitty, *C* Gwil Owen. **321** *Artist Malcolm McGregor*. **322,323** *Illustration by Gerald Eveno*. **324** *TC,BC,BR* Prof I. Isherwood, Dept of Diagnostic Radiology, University of Manchester, *CR,BL* The Manchester Mummy Project/Manchester Museum. **325** *TL* Manchester University, Dept of Medical Illustration, *TR* The Manchester Mummy Project/Manchester Museum, *BR* The Manchester Mummy Project/Sean Edwards. **326** *BC* Permission of the Trustees of the British Museum, *(others)* Manchester University, Dept of Medical Illustration. **327** *R (all) Martin Burke*, flint knapping demonstrated by John Lord, *TL* Manchester University, Dept of Medical Illustration. **328** South America Pictures/David T. Horwell. **329** Isabella Tree. **330** *Artist Malcolm McGregor* After: William Mulloy 'Techniques of erecting Easter Island statues' *Archaeology etc of Oceania*, vol V, No 1, April 1970. **331** South America Pictures/David T. Horwell. **332,333** John Hillelson/Georg Gerster. **334** *Artist Malcolm Porter*. **335,336** Metropolitan Museum of Art. **337** *TC* South America Pictures/Marrion Morrison, *CR* South America Pictures/Hilary Bradt. **338,339** *(both)* English Heritage. **340** Michael Holford, *Artist Ivan Lapper*. **341** *Artist Malcolm McGregor* after an original in The Museum of London. **342,343** Dr Ruth Morgan. **343** *TL* Science Photo Library/Dr Jeremy Burgess, *TC* Science Photo Library/R.E. Litchfield, *TR* Biophoto Associates, *BL,BC* Science Photo Library/Dr Jeremy Burgess. **344,345** *Artist Malcolm Porter*. **345** *TL* Michael Holford. **346** *TR,BR* Michael Holford/British Museum. **347** *TR* South America Pictures, *C* Photographed by José Oster/Collection Arlette Leroi-Gourhan, *BL* Sisse Brimberg/National Geographical Society, *BR* The Science Museum, London. **348,349** *(all except BL)* Colorphoto Hans Hinz. **349** *BL* Rapho/De Sazo. **350,351** *(all except TL)* Scala. **351** *TL* Sonia Halliday. **352,353** Aspect/Larry Burrows. **353** Permission of the Board of the British Library, Roy.14 E.IV 23. **354** *Artist Stanley Paine*. **355** Michael Holford/British Museum. **356** Michael Holford. **357** *TL* Michael Holford, *BL* Metropolitan Museum of Art, Gift of J. Pierpont Morgan, 1900 (00.182), *BR* Michael Holford/National Maritime Museum. **359** *TL* Susan Griggs/Adam Woolfitt, *TR* Edimedia. **360** *C* Ullstein. **360,361** *(all except C)* Dan Cornish/ESTO. **362,363** Susan Griggs/A.J. Hartman. **363** *TL,TR* National Park Service. **364** *(all)* National Park Service. **365** *BL* John Hillelson/Brian Brake, *CR,BR* Michael Holford. **366** *TL* Angelo Hornak, *BR* Werner Forman Archive/Centennial Museum, Vancouver, Canada. **367** Michael Holford. **368** *BC* Musée du Louvre, Paris. **368,369** Michael Holford. **369** *TR* Michael Holford. **370,371** *(all)* Vickers plc. **372** *TC,C Martin Cameron*/Royal Air Force Museum, London, *BR* Vickers plc. **373** *R* Science Photo Library/Jonathan Watts, *CL* Jacqui Hurst, *BL* Aspect/Michelle Garrett. **374** Malcolm Cowen Ltd/J. Bertrand. **375** *Martin Cameron*. **376** *(all) Martin Cameron*. **379** *Photo Martin Cameron*, freeze dried products kindly supplied by The Commercial Freeze Drying Co Ltd, Preston. **380** *TR*

Time Magazine/Doug Wilson. **382** *TL* Jacqui Hurst, *C* Ann Hughes-Gilbey. **383** Jerrican/Berenguier. **384** *(all) Colin Molyneux*. **385** *CR* Science Photo Library/Dr Jeremy Burgess, *BL* Jerrican/Labat. **386** *TL,CL* The Hulton Picture Company, *CR,BR* Ann Ronan Picture Library. **386,387** *(background)* Ann Ronan Picture Library. **387** *BL,BR* Archives Photographiques Musée Pasteur. **388** Mary Evans Picture Library. **389** *C Martin Cameron*, *TR,CR* The Mansell Collection. **390** *BL* Jerrican/Berenguier, *BR* Cephas Picture Library/Mick Rock. **391** *TR* Ann Hughes-Gilbey, *BL,BR* Cephas Picture Library/Mick Rock. **392** *TC* John Sims, *BL* ZEFA/Stock Market/J. Miller, *BR* Cephas Picture Library/Mick Rock. **393** *CL* Jerrican/Ivaldi, *C,CR,BR* Ann Hughes-Gilbey. **394** *TL,TR* ZEFA, *TC* The Brewers' Society, London, *(others)* The Anthony Blake Photo Library/Gerrit Buntrock. **395** *CL* The Image Bank/John Kelly, *BL* Tony Stone Photo Library, London/Peter Lamberti, *BR* The Image Bank/Robert Phillips. **396** Ken Howard. **397** *Artist Malcolm McGregor*, from a demonstration by Fay Presto, who does not condone the use of live animals in tricks. **398** *Artist Ivan Lapper*, *CR* Topham Picture Library/Edwin A. Dawes Collection. **399** *Artist Malcolm McGregor*, *BR* George Johnstone. **400** Mary Evans Picture Library/Harry Price Collection, University of London, *Artist Ivan Lapper*. **402** *TC* Mary Evans Picture Library/Harry Price Collection, University of London, *CL* Library of Congress, *CR,BC,BR* Private Collection, *BL* Culver Pictures. **402,403** *(background)* Brown Brothers. **403** *TR* The Raymond Mander & Joe Mitchenson Theatre Collection, *BC* Brown Brothers. **404** Tubingen University Library, *Artist Malcolm McGregor*. **405** The Photo Library of Australia. **406** *TC* Colorific/Carl Purcell. **406,407** The Kobal Collection/RKO. **408** *Artist Malcolm McGregor*, The Kobal Collection/Superman II © 1980 Film Export A.G. **409** *TL* Alan McKenzie/Firefox © 1982 Warner Bros Inc, *BR* Alan McKenzie/United Artists. **410** *TL,CR* Lucasfilm Ltd. **411** *TL,C* Lucasfilm Ltd, *BR* John Brosnan. **412** *TC* The Ronald Grant Archive/UIP, *BR* The Kobal Collection/20th Century Fox. **413** *TR* John Brosnan/United Artists, *BR* The Kobal Collection/United Artists. **414** The Kobal Collection/United Artists. **415** *TL* The Kobal Collection, *(inset)* The Museum of Modern Art/Stills Archive, *BR* The Kobal Collection/Lucasfilm Ltd. **416** *L* Frank Spooner/GAMMA, *BR* The Ronald Grant Archive. **417** Alan McKenzie/UIP. **418** *BL* © Christo 1980-3/CVJ Corp/Wolfgang Volz, *BR* © Christo 1983/Wolfgang Volz. **418,419** © Christo 1972-6/Gianfranco Gorgoni. **419** *TL* © Christo 1976, *TR* © Christo 1985/CVJ Corp/Wolfgang Volz, *C* © Wolfgang Volz. **420** *(all)* Bernard Lodge. **421** *T (all)* Thames Television plc, *BR* Digital Pictures. **422** *(all)* Australian Broadcasting Authority. **423** *(all)* Channel Four Television. **424** *TR,C,CR* Thames Television plc/Richard Waiting, *BL* Quantel. **425** Saatchi & Saatchi/Solid Fuel Advisory Service. **428** *Martin Cameron*. **429** *TL* © United Nautical Publishers SA, Basel, Switzerland/Joop van Schouten, *TR* ZEFA. **430** *TL,CL* All-Sport (UK), *BL* Omega Sports Timing. **431** *TR (and inset)* Colorsport, *BL* Split Second. **432** *TL* Split Second/Iundt/Ruszniewski, *Artist Malcolm McGregor*. **433** *TR* Frank Spooner, *BL* Axel Poignant Archive, *BC* Spectrum Colour Library. **434** *TC* Camera Press/Mark Woolley, *CR* Split Second/Leo Mason, *BR* Colorsport. **435** *TL* All-Sport (UK)/Vandystadt, *TC* Simon Ward, *BR* Frank Spooner/S. Ward/GAMMA. **436** The Image Bank/Don King. **436,437** All-Sport. **437** The Image Bank/Don King.

Typesetting: Apex Computersetting, London.
Separations: Scantrans PTE Ltd, Singapore
C&S Studios, Luton.
Paper: Hannover Papier, Alfeld, West Germany.
Printing and binding: Mohndruck, Gütersloh, West Germany.

40-220-1